# Management
# Footsteps and
# Foundations

# Management Footsteps and Foundations:

## *History, Education Management, and Management Education*

By

Ian Waitt

*To Andrew*
*With thanks & appreciation for*
*your contribution to this book &*
*all best wishes,*

*Ian*

**Cambridge**
**Scholars**
Publishing

13/5/2023

Management Footsteps and Foundations:
History, Education Management, and Management Education

By Ian Waitt

This book first published 2023

Cambridge Scholars Publishing

Lady Stephenson Library, Newcastle upon Tyne, NE6 2PA, UK

British Library Cataloguing in Publication Data
A catalogue record for this book is available from the British Library

ISBN (10): 1-5275-9287-1
ISBN (13): 978-1-5275-9287-2

To Ari, Kris and Susan

For your support, encouragement and patience in enabling
the production of this work, belief in its value and purpose,
and sustaining its management, my eternal gratitude …

# CONTENTS

# LIST OF ILLUSTRATIONS

Cover and footprint designs by Susan Diamond with Nick Lewis

Note: Unless otherwise fully credited, images are drawn from Wikimedia.

It is unusual in Management Studies for a text to be extensively illustrated, even more extraordinary for there to be extensive use of colour. Management is a human activity, carried out in the human construct of society. Appreciation of significant persons contributing by thought, word or deed to the performance of management is enhanced by sight of their images, and even more so when illuminated by the colour spectrum. Presentation of many such portraits, photographs and depictions is offered to the reader to enrich the experience of learning from and reflecting upon this work, and to emphasise the essential human element in the managerial process.

# LIST OF FOOTPRINTS

# TIMELINES

# ACKNOWLEDGMENTS

This book is the opening work of a management project. Not all contributions made by the persons listed below have yet been evidenced in print, although their advice, insights and contributions have been reflected in material presented here and currently in draft. Their direct registration time will come. Further project works will expand the acknowledgements listed as writing, drafting and editing continues.

The Surtees Society and its Honorary Secretary Richard Higgins have been most helpful and generous in allowing the reprinting of extracts from *The Law Book of The Crowley Ironworks.* It is hoped that their dedication to the promotion of scholarship will be rewarded by renewed interest and research in this unique record of the commencement of the management of an industrial revolution. The endeavour is greatly enhanced by the generous action of the Trustees of the Land of Oak and Iron Trust in making available their collection of Crowley material photographs as published in their ed. Val Scully, 2021, *Crowley's: Industrial and Social History 1691–1966.* The *Law Book* Appendix 2 and Case Study 1 are supported by a selection of the images from the *Crowley's* publication, kindly compiled by Trustee Geoff Marshall.

A very special thanks is extended to Kris Millegan in Eugene, Oregon, USA, who first saw the value and potential of this work. He believed in it, backing the composition and development with his own investment of a financial advance, production advice, compilation, typesetting, cover and publication preparations. His generous hospitality during development visits as the project grew was matched by his tolerance as publication dates and deadlines receded and as the project grew inexorably. When its depth and scope produced market potential greater than his resources could service, he supportively made way for the greater reach and physical proximity of Cambridge Scholars Publishing of Newcastle upon Tyne, UK. It has been a pleasure to contribute to his podcast series, and to work with him once again in the application of his familiarity with the contents in the compilation of the index. I look forward to future collaboration.

Professor Morgen Witzel of the University of Exeter gave his time generously at the conception of this work to comment, encourage and point the way to further improvement. His contribution of the Foreword is deeply appreciated.

Professor John F. Wilson of Northumbria University provided significant advice and support when the work was at its early, difficult stage of inception.

Emeritus Professor Dr Bruce Lloyd of South Bank University provided wise comment and important source advice.

Double Emeritus Professor Dilwyn Porter, friend since undergraduate days, made a significant presentation suggestion, and in his unfailing support has maintained a watchful historian's eye.

Dr Anita Rupprecht of Brighton University and Professor Bridget Bennett of Leeds University gave helpful references on slavery.

Emeritus Professor Roger Austin of Ulster University not only supplied detail of the research and experience leading to a Case Study currently in draft and the first planned **Improvement**, to be included in the *Managing Mass Education, and the Rise of Modern and Financial Management: Footsteps and Foundations* sequel to this work, but has contributed insightful textual comment with added vital social education management input. Former NATFHE Assistant Secretary Salaries and Employment Law, Keith Scribbins, also contributed to this work, confirming the closing colleges' selection account recorded.  Prime mover in the preservation of the Hitchin Museum Robert Dimsdale, 9th Baron Dimsdale, High Sheriff of Hertfordshire 1996 and Deputy Lord Lieutenant, gave generous research assistance regarding Lancasterian method adoption in France. In addition to supplying important subsequent historical information for that next work, Dr John Huitson, Darlington College's last principal, also provided first hand detail of the Darlington College closure process, and has been a valued friend and supporter throughout.

Lynton Gray, collaborator in many an education management endeavour, gave his habitual, generous encouragement. Leon Gore supplied an educationalist's perspective with his typical enthusiasm, and Emile Mardacany former Soviet Union management insights.

David Konyot provided invaluable insight into the worlds of clowning and circus, generously providing written material upon which a later case study bearing his name depends, deserving of a co-authorship credit. High-tech professional Andrew Dixon gave invaluable advice on linguistic expression in his esoteric world, down-to-earth observation on current information technology development prospects, and exploration assistance.

Dr John Atkin's incisive comment, the benefits of his long experience of senior multinational corporate management and engagement with the Management Studies industry have provided invaluable direction. Reverend Louise Magowan provided expert insight into Christian ethics. Brian Murphy's practical management expertise and experience, acute observation and exemplary patience in commenting, have greatly informed and improved content.

Sergejs Ovsiannikovs drew attention to the work of Anton Makarenko and, as Director at IBD Grain, kept that business functioning whilst its chairman wrote, sustained from time to time by Sergejs's incomparable "proper soup" of smoked ribs and chick pea broth, ambrosia and nectar fit for Olympus.

John Bagshaw provided vital assistance in the comprehension of quantum matter and other scientific and technical issues, as well as excellent photography. Cliff Winlow contributed steady support and provided the Northumbria photo portfolio. Thanks also to the British Schools Museum, Hitchin, for the *Mass Education* photographs of the Lancaster system school rooms, and museum manager Sam Mason and curator Mark Copley for their guidance concerning the Museum; and to the London Brunel University Archive Centre for permission to reproduce the Lancaster monitor medals images.

Susan Diamond marked the end of a long endeavour by contributing an exuberant picture of the author in his study, designed by her, with which to conclude the current book.

Rebecca Gladders, Sophie Edminson, the team and board at Cambridge Scholars Publishing are thanked for their impeccable professional performance and for backing a book and an author from outside the standard Management Studies and business biographies' establishment.

I express gratitude to Professor Henry Mintzberg for permission to quote his list of Management Competencies, from page 68 in his *Simply*

*Managing*; to Scott Peters, author of *Mystery of the Egyptian Scroll*, for helpfully permitting the reproduction of his guide to the basic translation management of Egyptian hieroglyphics; to Robert Locke for permission to reproduce in a later volume his New Paradigm from page 3 of his *Management and Higher Education since 1940.*

Manuscript Room staff at the British Library kindly allowed my photographing of pages from the Crowley *Law Book.*

Nick Lewis of the Department of Illustration and Design, Faculty of Arts and Creative Industries at the University of Sunderland contributed all line drawings except the common domain Taylor "watch book", provided the Cuthbert map, and co-ordinated the artwork produced by his student Trevyn Bell, whose Apollo image adorns the *sub rosa* entry.

The National Portrait Gallery (NPG) granted an academic licence regarding the reproduction of its copyright images. NPG license team member Lisa Olrichs was especially helpful in the making of arrangements. A donation after publication is made to Wikimedia Commons in respect of its provision of public domain images included in the listed Illustrations.

Acknowledgment of fair quotation for critique and review purposes is extended to all authors and publishers whose quoted works are credited in the text, footnotes, endnotes, and Bibliography.

The production computer assistance of Irin Kashtanov and Dmitry Baranoshnik in Montreal, and Susan Diamond's proofreading, computer skills, creative artistic design and editorial advice at home in Gateshead, were invaluable, as was their eternal, heartening, cheerful encouragement.

Any and all errors are my responsibility alone.

Ian Waitt, Gateshead and Montreal, 27 March 2023.

# FOREWORD

The purpose of this book, the author tells us in the very first sentence of the preface, is to set the study of management within its real and true context. That is a service which is badly needed. Ever since the formal study of management began in the nineteenth century attempts have been made to de-contextualise management and treat it as something mechanical with little or no human influence. This was particularly true after the publication of the Carnegie Report in 1959 which, while it did good service in urging management studies to become more research-based, also began to drive the discipline towards a pure science paradigm to which it most definitely is not suited. The term 'management science' came into use, and while thankfully it is starting to fall out of fashion, the influence of a purely scientific approach to management remains strong.

But management, as Ian Waitt tells us, is fundamentally a human activity. Managers are human beings and they exist within human systems: organisations, firms, markets, all of which are social constructs. The scientisation of management had another depressing effect, too; it all but eliminated any sort of role for ethics, because as a science, management was presumably beyond the reach of ethics. When I first became involved in business studies in the early 1990s, only a few business schools taught ethics at all and even then only as an elective course, with the result that the only people who studied ethics in a business context were the people who already understood the value of and need for ethics. It was the others, the ones who dismissed ethics or saw no role for it, that we really needed to be dragging into our classrooms.

I was originally a historian, before I went over to the dark side and started teaching in business schools, and when I read articles and books that treated management as if it was a set of scientific principles, I knew instinctively that this was wrong. The diaries of Marino Sanudo, the letters of Francesco Datini, the records of business stretching back into the mists of time, showed it to be a distinctly human activity. That is why behavioural economics is so powerful a tool for explaining managerial behaviour and business performance; it admits and incorporates the human element into the heart of the business model. And also, if you accept that businesses, firms and markets are human institutions, then as Ian Waitt points out, we must also look at their historical roots.

The past helps to explain the present, and as George Santayana pointed out, those who forget the past are doomed to repeat it. (Unfortunately, those of us who do remember the past usually get dragged down into the whirlpool with them.) So we have cycles of boom and bust, regulation and deregulation, irrational optimism and equally irrational pessimism. Today, economists laugh at Herbert Stanley Jevons who thought that economic cycles were caused by fluctuations in solar activity and solar flares. The reality is even more absurd; economic cycles are caused by us.

Culture matters, too. Ian Waitt shows us how cultural similarities and differences pervade our thinking, including our approaches to management. The scientisation of management stopped us from learning from different cultures, and that too has been a great loss. The *Tao The Ching* and the *Bhagavad Gita* have powerful lessons to teach about management and leadership, but rarely are those lessons learned. The vast majority of business case studies in common use around the world still tend to come from North American or Western European organisations, meaning the worldview of management studies is dangerously narrow. Western politicians speak blithely of competing economically with East Asia and South Asia, but that will never happen until we learn to understand and embrace other cultures.

Other books have looked at management methods in different cultures and earlier times, but rarely in as much detail as Ian Waitt provides here. There are exceptions: Moore and Lewis's *Foundations of Corporate Empire* concentrates on the ancient world, and Raoul McLaughlin's *Rome and the Distant East* focuses on links between the Roman and Chinese empires, but both do so more or less in isolation. Waitt, on the other hand, gives us continuity, showing us how management thinking and practice evolved over time, with time itself becoming an influencing factor. He shows us how the distant past and the present remain intimately connected. Over and over, he takes us out of the box of 'pure' management and shows us both the impact of social forces and trends on management, and the impact of management on wider society. Chapter 16, 'Exploring Applications to Children', ought to be required reading.

So what? Does this detailed and meticulous historical narrative matter, or is just a fascinating story? The answer is yes, it does matter, because the past doesn't just explain the present, it also conditions and shapes it. Path dependency theory tells us that decisions made in the past influence and constrain our ability to make decisions freely in the future, just as the decision to accept the Carnegie Report shaped and – arguably – constrained the future of business schools. Waitt shows us how past thinking conditioned the present and future. The chapters on the Enlightenment and the so-called Age of Reason, for example, are particularly fascinating in this respect. The Enlightenment gave us direct influences through Adam Smith, but its influence has also been more pernicious; from the Enlightenment came the philosophical doctrine of positivism, whose direct descendant is Taylor's scientific management and, from it, the modern notion of management science.

In economics, utility theory tells us that we have unrestricted free will. We enjoy this notion, and we are sometimes reluctant to admit the power that the past exerts over us. We are the children of our ancestors; even in our greatest achievements, we stand upon the shoulders of the giants who came before us, and our failures are conditioned by the mistakes others have made.

Paradoxically, the best way to escape the influence of the past is to study it and learn from it. Ian Waitt argues for a thorough reform of management education, and I agree with him. We need a more human-centred paradigm, one where ethics and values lie at the core of every business model, where we recognise that the purpose of business is to create value, not to earn a profit. Evidence supporting this model can be found in the past; all we need to do is look for it. And of course, there is also plenty of evidence of what not to do, of pitfalls and errors that we can avoid. If we can educate a new generation of business leaders to see themselves as servants of the world around them, rather than its masters, and to learn from the lessons of what has gone before, then we will give them a chance to break out of the path-dependent trap and create a new vision of how firms and markets should work.

Can we actually do this? Ian Waitt's book shows us that a new way of thinking is possible. It is up to us now to read this book, take in its lessons, and think about how we can apply them in management education to make it fit for purpose, in the present and in the future.

Morgen Witzel
University of Exeter Business School

# PREFACE

The aim of this book is to set firmly the study of management within it's real and true contexts. If the proper study of mankind is man within the whole human experience, the consideration of management must be equally comprehensive. It is not that those staples of Management Studies as proclaimed through academia via such vehicles as the MBA, quantitative method, and functional components, are lacking in themselves. The issue is one of tunnel vision, lacking wider context; the danger, the elevation into elite status of notions, and approaches of lessening touch with reality; and the promotion of inappropriate, dangerous, misguided theory accompanied by complacency. Evidence is, here, as obvious as it is generally overlooked, such as the excesses of the economics of neoliberalism, the increase of inequality, and the financial crises of 2007-08. Here, the Management Studies mainstream followed conventional thought and unthinking greed, failing to recognise the crash before it broke. Even the most cursory assessment of the world accommodating such approaches to the consideration of management must conclude that the gap between aspiration and reality is widening.

Long in gestation, this work reflects and replicates parts of the author's learning and both personal and professional experience, garnered through a long, varied, sometimes challenging, career in education, business and management. It crosses and interlinks three areas of study, if not disciplines, essential for the proper comprehension of management. These are: modern Management Studies, education, and history, within and across differing cultural and academic contexts.

The synthesis is rooted in personal experience. Working life has embraced 35 years in business, and 20 years' prior experience of education in: historical research, school teaching, teacher training; higher education lecturing in history, education management, and management; freelance writing; business, educational and management consultancy, with various publications at each stage; and as a company director and chairman.

Business experience includes events design and management; commodities and general commerce; trade shows and publications; with political, economic and educational consultancy. Writing in books, learned articles and the press has extended from a text book for children to ghosting an entrepreneur's autobiography; technical education; and being the main author and editor of what the *Guardian* described as the "college bible", *College Administration*[1]. The author claims to know something of which he writes.

I have taught at every stage of education, except the infant, the observation of which showed me how valuable good teachers at that level are, and the difficult and demanding nature of their jobs. At the postgraduate and post experience levels, the first factor to appreciate is that invariably, in every class, someone will know more than you do, have more insight and experience, and often be better at presentation and public speaking as well. Moreover, the breadth of the study as well as its length over time, where the nature of the subjects does not allow comprehensive cover of all the available evidence and, therefore, the selections made, may not be seen by all to meet the challenges of the attempted task. Many readers will know more than the author on many topics, have greater experience, and better ideas. Their tolerance and understanding are sought in what is proposed in the utilitarian manner to be the greater good.

That greater good is to seek to bring some new order to the worlds of management and management education. One result of the current failings is that there is no clear base from which effective reform might be made. Because of the very disparate character of management education across and within the constituent subject areas, few usually know entirely what they are talking about; and in doing, with some honourable exceptions, even less.. The component studies don't always communicate effectively or, where they do, only partially, and without understanding or appreciation of the others' competences, relevance and wisdom.

There might be, for example, competition in memoir compilation or to gain the most lucrative consultancies, the highest government advisory sinecures, or the fame of the latest guru accolade, but these are tunnel vision pursuits; in the current jargon, silo operations whereby business divisions operate independently to avoid sharing information. A stable, realistic, broad, balanced base for management education is what is required, towards the construction of which this work seeks to contribute. Through the understanding of the further subdivision of a history of management, education management, and management education, a new core for the

---

[1] Waitt, Ian. ed. 1980. *College Administration.* London: NATFHE, and 1987 Longman.

development of Management Studies might be found. Here, at my estimable publisher's indirect guidance, we enter the historian's refuge of choice: detection; and the detective story.

I had decided in mid-2017 that the time had come to renew my efforts in the world of writing, to retreat from business other than to maintain a presence with one company and be available for occasional projects with two others. The bulk of my time would be spent in writing about the topic upon which I had lectured for approaching a decade in higher education, some 30 years ago: management, seen through the perspectives of education management and management education, within the context of a history of management. I was confronted by seemingly exclusive, opposing realities. Management Studies appeared to have become an academic closed shop; an economics and finance emphasis had become dominant, and management disconnected from the entities it was supposedly managing. Whatever was new was upheld and applauded. The voices of experience went unheeded if not unheard.

It was, therefore, with great appreciation that I had come across the verdict of the distinguished Canadian commentator Morgen Witzel (1960-) of Exeter University, who had opined sadly in his definitive study of the history of management thought:

> …management thinking is increasingly becoming a closed world, and I do not think it is too strong to say that it exists for selfish ends. I have already remarked that it is rare for non-academics to be invited to write for management publications save for a few exceptions such as the *Harvard Business Review*. Unless non-academics choose to write their own books – and can find a publisher – management thinking is now the province of academe.[2]

As that province was the body which had assisted the financial disaster of 2007-2009, comfortable with the amorality of the economism supportive of rising inequality, and now seeks to close the door on its secret garden, it cannot be held that Management Studies is in safe hands.

Witzel has observed the "slow but steady disengagement" of academia from "real world" publishing. He reported having heard academics refusing publication in popular journals lest their reputations might be damaged; of universities discouraging young academics from writing books or even

---

[2] Witzel, Morgen. *A History of Management Thought,* pp. 237-8.

chapters in books, or anything other than for peer-reviewed journals (which are read only by very few). The game is tawdry. It shows research is being done and makes reputations, enabling the employing institution to bolster its ranking record, so to enable its acquisition of more funding agency income. The result is to deny access to practising managers, employers, potential students and the tax paying public, cheating fee-paying pupils as well.

Such suppression of access, denial of contribution, and creation of a self-serving, closed elite, hoarding its oligarchic fruits and privilege is a woefully under-reported scandal. That outrage is magnified as management and business studies have become the most popular university courses, at ever-escalating cost, to students beginning their adult life burdened by considerable, consequential, possibly life-long debt. Morgen Witzel went so far as to write of the struggle to reform Management Studies as being a battle between good and evil. He defined management thinkers' tasks as being to work out what management is for, what its principles are, and teaching those to new generations of leaders and managers so that they may tackle future problems confidently and skilfully. To this *quondam* academic making a living in business and as a manager, such brave denunciation with its constructive remedy formed a decisive inspiration to expand this work into the form adumbrated in these introductory pages.

Meanwhile, the weight of evidence of inequality, climate change and pandemic made major reappraisals and world altering changes imperative. Without them, it is difficult to comprehend their challenges and associated pressures on people and resources being successfully managed. The infrastructure of management plainly requires urgent strengthening.

There is a human tendency, a bias in the language of the behavioural economists, to take what we might term a *sapiocentric* view of the world. Everything revolves around humans, as if they were the sun, an inversion of the helio-centralism which marked the turning point of the Renaissance. We don't know the causes of the viral transmutation of Covid-19, or the earlier eruption of *Yersinia pestis,* bringer of plague. Maybe such mutations are prompted by climate change; maybe not. We can't foresee the unforeseeable; but we can expect it. History is full of it. People may cause it, suffer from it, or both.

It is people who have made the varieties of civilisation which are now confronted by the greatest management tasks and issues ever known to humanity. How did we get here? Where do we go from here? How do we manage it? Our detective tale includes all that can be construed as Management Foundations. These may be as obvious as those itemized in **Case Study 3**, of such major indirect consequence as the siege of Kaffa, or as obscure to western culture as Taoist method. Exposed through literary archaeology perhaps, overt reference to the foundations is sparse. The evidence being all around us, the title *Management Footsteps and Foundations* on the front cover of this book may safely be left to speak for itself. With so much historic evidence and contingency advice arising in abundant supply, it might have been thought that management of the latest misfortune to befall humanity might have been better tackled from inception.

In the case of the pandemic, the damage done to the economies of the US and UK was attributable to their acting too late. Each saw themselves as so well prepared that neither need concern themselves - so they did not, even initially selling protective equipment elsewhere.[3] The resurgence of competence shown in their successful vaccine programmes highlights the initial failure. The medical science management paradox is that the better you are at solving problems, the less likely it is that your serious warnings will be heeded. Capitalism (and Apollo, to anticipate the following classical theme) shows that prevention doesn't pay; but disease does.

Hindsight is a valuable attribute of history. The historical mind is accustomed to expect and accept it, which is why it is an essential presence in Management Studies. The concept of the *pre-mortem* is another valuable insight of behavioural economics: whenever a new policy is presented to a company board or government ministry, consider where fault and blame would be laid should the initiative fail. The historical approach can be its own validation. The *Footsteps* in the title mark a journey through history, a stroll through the civilised side with occasional monstrous gallery shows, a trek from myth through many managerial milestones and foundations.

The antecedents of the dominant Anglo-American modern management model result from historical inheritance: from Roman models, the Enlightenment inspired creation of the revolutionary United States of America, and the nature and consequences of the Industrial Revolutions. While Hegel lamented that a lesson of history was that we did not learn from history, it is those very historical foundations which are vital to managing

---

[3] Lewis, Michael. *The Premonition: A Pandemic Story*, Introduction.

the present and informing future management. The crucial importance of bringing main facets of the history of human management to attention now can be illustrated with one simple but devastating circumstance.

As water power was overtaken by steam power, $CO_2$ emissions began to rise. In 1776, the first year that James Watt (1736-1819) marketed his steam engine, people caused the emission of some 15 million tons of $CO_2$. By 1800, the figure had doubled. In 1850, it reached 200 million tons a year. At century's end, the amount was almost two billion. Now, the figure is close to 40 billion tons, with the atmosphere so altered by humanity through its industrial and agricultural processes that one out of every three $CO_2$ molecules in the air was the result of human action.[4] Never can the change management rule of the occurrence of unintended consequences have been better illustrated.

I have been fortunate in having experience of working in South Korea, China, India and much of South East Asia, as well as parts of Africa and the Arab world. Oriental management inheritance has influenced heavily the growth of modern East Asian managerial technique. Cross fertilisation through the Islamic world, competing religious influences, warfare and resultant advances in technology have all spurred the development process. Perhaps the least known and noticed is the fusion of Taoist thought and rational economics as set forward by Adam Smith. A further number of countries, east and west, may make justifiable claims to current and future primacy but the Anglo-American phenomenon, for all its inevitable flaws, remains core to an understanding of how we got to where we are, and how we might go forward.

It is my experience and consideration that those processes require an understanding of the history of management, its primary forms and purposes. Approaches differ according to times and context. To the individual manager, an understanding of company, institution, public service or charity history can be vital to an organisation's health. The standard management forms of autocracy, oligarchy, bureaucratic hierarchy and representative democracy all have long antecedents. Divinity, and therefore legitimacy, by ancestry, association, acclaim, appointment and anointment were attached to autocracy.

Cooperative, mutual and representational forms emerged over time. From

---

[4] Kolbert, Elizabeth. *Under a White Sky,* pp. 147-8.

state management to that of private and public enterprise, with many hybrid functions, organisational forms, from family, to partnerships and associations, have been created and deployed to serve perceived needs. Within those, common themes arise: the preference of reliability to talent; the accommodation of entrepreneurialism; the means and nature of controls; the degrees to which leadership and management can be taught (if at all), mentored, or learned through experience.

People in the construction business have long learned that it is unwise to build on sand or swamp, or raise the roof beams before the support joists can bear the load. The problem with the management business is that foundations may be variable according to conditions. What, managers may ask, may be safely relied on? What is to be avoided? Valid though such questions are, they may apply only to long held assumptions, outdated method, or be dependent on circumstances. Search for foundations may be as variable as reliance thereon. It is as reasonable to ask if the manager knows what she or he is doing, as it is to inquire after the methods or means of assessment. For guidance, there is always the perspective of history, provided careful appraisal is applied.

For the present and future, the wealth of the formative information of the past forms a central column of validated experience which stands as a permanent recourse - not for prediction, but as an assistance to thought, guidance towards wisdom. Such has been humanity's progress that it has now reached the god-like status of being able to create and artificially adapt life, and so its responsibility for sustainability has heightened. In that process, what we do has been superseded as a responsibility by how we do it.

Management, at all levels and in all contexts, has become glaringly apparent in requiring ethical conduct. Human behaviour varies according to times, context and opportunity; human nature appears to have been predictable, if not knowable, since inception. Given that, if management is about doing things right, and leadership doing the right thing, then management education is concerned with developing the understanding of those principles within a known, if infinitely variable, context – until the next unforeseeable interruption.

Law and regulation are always out of step with developing need, requiring an understanding of emergent issues before making interventions. Such has been the rate of technological change in the current century, and so great the necessity for increased managerial responsibility, that it has become necessary to lay out a programme of reform which I have categorised as **Improvements** in management. These are for subsequent release in a successive volume but are cited here to indicate the sequence of composition. This current book provides a history of management, education management and management education, with important digests of what has already been found to work in management, managerial competencies, and includes extracts from the first manual in industrial management. More is to follow, for the foundations may be built upon. The purposes of the whole work when completed is, as expressed by Marx:

> Philosophers have hitherto only interpreted the world in various ways;
> the point is to change it.[5]

At the time of writing, the Great Moderation (that period of decreased macroeconomic volatility experienced in the United States from the mid-1980s) had been summarily ended by the financial crises of 2007-2009, and the financial system weakened by the failure to fully institute reform. The COVID-19 pandemic of 2019-2021 had wreaked medical, social, and economic havoc. While climate change and inequality strove for agenda-heading resolutions, Russia's 2022 invasion of Ukraine overturned the resource allocation decisions which arose from the international settlement resultant from the 1989-1992 collapse of the Soviet Union. That toxic mix was exacerbated by such aberrations as the chaotic populism of Donald Trump (1946-), Brexit, and the growing repressive authoritarianism of China. Although decisive response came in the re-energising of NATO, the developed world otherwise faced and still faces conditions described by some as radical indecision. Faced suddenly with inflationary pressures, dramatic escalation in the cost of living and ever-increasing natural disasters provoked by climate change, the crucial question becomes ever more acute - how best to manage such changes in today's world?

Although the applications and advances of technology were, and still are, increasing at astonishing rates, with wealth expanding and currency being exchanged hourly at the barely imaginable sizes of trillions, the great majority of people gained less and only the few increased their capital. Agricultural skills, technology, and efficiency had created a reliable food supply, until the disruption caused by the assault, blockade and plundering of Ukraine caused reception issues. The less developed world suffered

---

[5] Final line of the 11th *Theses on Feuerbach*, posthumously published by Engels in 1888.

increased shortages and many of the more fortunate an unhealthy diet. Greedy, careless bankers who had devastated the world's financial system in 2007-2009 went largely unpunished, and the ordinary citizenry had to, and still do, pay for their misdeeds. In international relations, unreasoning warfare elsewhere continued to wreak devastating destruction and suffering upon ordinary citizens. The institutions of western civilisation, the supposed leader of global progress and inheritor of the fruits of five millennia of human experience, appeared powerless to exercise reasonable authority to enable all their citizens to live freely in an equitable society.

These were management failures of magnitude. That they should arise in a society in which management and business studies have become the most frequently undertaken university courses is an anomaly, at best; confusing and without clear forward direction, a source of great perplexity, at worst. The modern labels of analysis paralysis (and its sub-divisions of process, decision precision, and risk uncertainty) do not quite reach the nub of the issue. The ancient Greeks called the condition *aporia:* intense puzzlement, an impasse, a state of such indecision as to be incapable of decision, thus undermining existence itself.

Socrates (c.470-399 BCE) described the purgative effect arising. By questioning, it was possible to reduce someone to *aporia*. That condition shows people who thought they knew something that they do not, in fact, know it. This instils a desire to investigate. Such investigation is part of the overall purpose of this work, requiring the consideration of a history of management. A start is made here with the questions posed at the end of case studies. The reader is requested to enquire further. The **Improvements** in management will subsequently conclude the process. Such an accumulation will produce what is known in Management Studies as a new paradigm.

Aristotle (384-322 BCE) offered two significant principles for such a model. More, he defined a continuing human goal. The purpose of human life, and hence its organisation, was the achievement of excellence. This was to be in accord with virtue, through *eudaimonia*, which may be translated as the "good life." This has more meaning than having a good time. A general interpretation is fulfilling potential, ethically rather than selfishly, and so performing to the best of what a person is good at - for self-expression, improvement, and the benefit of society. Thus, education was to encourage and facilitate such attainment.

However, *eudaimonia* goes further. The word is a combination of *eu* (good) and *daimon* (god, spirit, or demon), thus carrying implications of divinity, spirituality and good fortune, or favour. *Eudaimonia* serves at least as a lasting companion to management education curriculum but Aristotle went further, approaching the practical. He defined knowing what should be done as *phronesis,* which translates as *"prudence."* Thus *phronesis,* or *prudence,* enables managers to determine what is good in specific times and situations and to undertake the best actions at those times to serve the common good.

Faced with need for change, then, a summary of Aristotelian thought was that, through education, those responsible for management should behave ethically, do the right thing, and so promote the well-being of the managed. Education being a whole life process, the relevance to management is that of its history, too. It is impossible to divide the manager from his or her education. What preceded specific vocational and managerial study remains integral and relevant. Therefore, any historical approach must recognize both.

Realism requires the further recognition of informal education – that is, education which is acquired through the processes of living, in working, interacting and surviving. The informal custom and practice may conflict with, or indeed deny, Aristotelian high-mindedness. There are those who claim to have gained their qualifications in the university of life, to which the rejoinder has ever been that there are third class degrees, even in that.

Humanity - at its best, worst, and most mediocre - has to be managed. This book and its subsequent fellows are written from a realistic but egalitarian perspective. The managerial heights might have become part of the preserve of the elite but the ways into that, via front or back door, arise from knowledge and appreciation of management history, education management, and management education.

This comprehensive introductory work to management's past, present and future offers a readable, grounding insight into an increasingly essential subject, as relevant to young people beginning their business studies as it is to MBA participants and those teaching and consulting at post-experience levels. It culminates in Case Study (3): Management Matters, a digest of what is proven from management theory to be workable in practice and of what management is all about on a daily basis.

# PROLOGUE

## MANAGEMENT *SUB ROSA*

I had always been fortunate in never having to find a publisher. They had always, one way or another, found me; one further benefit of which was being able to write my own headlines in press articles; and to write without restraint, or guidance even, in books; where editing was required, to be able to provide that function myself. It was no different when work on this compilation began. Speculatively, composition commenced in the August of 2017. A friend and business colleague became aware of my diversion, recommending me to his new publisher, then reissuing a reprint of his international best seller. Sufficient initial content had been produced by December of that first year for a contract to be offered, accepted, and an advance paid.

A happy relationship ensued, albeit punctuated by several false starts as the concept grew in scope and application. The business crunch arrived in 2022. My Oregon publisher ran a small but energetic business, with distribution to the trade undertaken by the Independent Publishers Group, operating out of Chicago. His reach was to the USA and Canada only. We agreed the project had outgrown its incubator. The advance was repaid. While we might collaborate on other business, it was time to find a new publisher, with worldwide access and a well-known, widely respected reputation. Here was a new personal management experience: could an outsider, although a former academic now with extensive business and management experience, find a publisher in an environment a distinguished commentator had feared was becoming an academe closed shop?

The first attempts were token steps to test the market, a mix of former publishers who might recall me and some of the major names. With various response times, the answers were identical: all "very interesting"; "we wish you well"; but "in the Management Studies field we have other plans and initiatives in process". If that was the case, then reason suggested it was best to revert to the early inspiration of the Witzel diagnosis. The letter to his former editor at Routledge was written in the presumption that, at best, since fears had been expressed under that imprint of Management Studies becoming an academe closed shop, then here was a submission worthy of response, at least. The positive answer, while repeating the message that the company had plans of its own, produced a short list of quality recommendations. One of these being located near my current UK residence, target choice was obvious.

Happily, Cambridge Scholars Publishing was prepared to proceed to contract. As a prudent company knowing its markets and sales prospects, there were conditions. Although a series of several books was acceptable, each work, in turn, must stand on its own merits. Moreover, CSP could "not accept series entitled 'volume 1', 'volume 2' etc.", in its previous format as they had been advised by aggregators that such is "bad for sales". Any sensible commercial company must necessarily manage accordingly, but there was a more serious knock-on effect. Each of the planned volumes had a further subtitle: the name of a deity, usually classical, with a modern exception. As the tripartite title with its *Footsteps and Foundations* summation demanded sufficient prospective purchaser and reader attention, further subtitling was felt to be too much, likely to confuse rather than attract. All sensible, commercially valid decisions perhaps; but compromising an essential ingredient of a central concept. How then to manage the preservation of an invaluable component?

Readily came the answer, drawn from the history of practical management. There had to be a section of each book presented *sub rosa*: confidentially, in secret. The reader gets to know only through purchase, bookshop browsing, or library access. Secrecy and management have a long history, from the contents of the Trojan horse to the Manhattan Project. Inspirer of the practice of espionage, industrially and militarily on the grander scale, it has served also the morale of the oppressed. "Comrade Stalin is a pig", ran the old Soviet-era joke, "but we must not say so. It is a crime to reveal state secrets".

The gaining awareness of agricultural secrets has perhaps caused the greatest human exploitation: from indigenous Indian sugar via Madeira and the Canaries to the plantations of the New World, and the reverse journey of the potato and tomato from Peru and Bolivia to the rest of habitation. In language management perhaps the most evocative word derived from and applied to other species is the Roman word for secret: clam. If a mollusc able to close decisively was able only figuratively to describe the maintenance of silence, it was through the disguise of an elegant flower that indication of the need for confidentiality was covertly proclaimed.

In Greek and Roman mythology, possibly from an Egyptian root, roses were symbolic of secrecy. The Greek god of silence, Harpocrates, was given a rose by Eros (Cupid) so that he would not reveal the secrets of Aphrodite (Venus). Fashion among the Roman elite grew to the decoration of banqueting rooms with rose carvings, suspension of the cut flower above dining areas, and at such places of refuge where secrecy was at a premium. The symbolism made a late transfer into the Christianity of Roman origin whereby roses were carved into confessionals to emphasise the secrecy of revelations.

Later still, the burgeoning secrecy industry of 16th century England was reflected in the ubiquity of the Tudor rose as a ceiling carving in the greater houses of the land. In 20th century London, the tradition took a further turn with the 1927, refined in 1992, invention at the Royal Institute of International Affairs of the Chatham House Rule. Sometimes also adopted by the European Central Bank and other organisations, this provides the condition that anyone attending a meeting is free to use information from the discussion, but not allowed to reveal speaker or other participant identities.

For our purposes, in the front pages with their Arabic numerals, this and each successive book will display a deity portrait. This will carry a note on his or her attributes and archetypal function. Each deity represents a spiritual dimension, reflecting the themes, issues, characteristics and challenges of the book(s) themselves. Titled in Latin to emphasise origins, the beginning classical manager is Apollo, here characterised as governor and custodian.

This classical theme is not to deny or denigrate any of the great monotheistic religions - it is to observe that monotheism is a difficult concept to characterise when manifold aspects are subsumed in a single entity. Indeed, the Islamic expression became one of abstract geometry. Moreover, to understand the human development of management, it is essential to comprehend the position and power of myth in its creation. Contemporary with Aristotle's prudent advice on managing work, life, and its affairs on and through the spirit of *eudaimonia,* was the reality of his own, personal induction into the Mysteries of Eleusis and the fate of his philosopher predecessor, Socrates.

Found guilty of impiety because of his relentless questioning, so that the gods be not offended and take vengeance on Athens at a difficult political period, Socrates was obliged to commit suicide. By self-sacrifice, he endorsed official religion. Zeus, CEO of the Greek gods of Olympus, had a different approach to *aporia.* When humanity misbehaved or needed significant correction, he sent thunderbolts. When it became intolerable, he dispatched a great flood. Thereafter he kept a close watch on the species for, after his rogue Titan friend Prometheus had given it fire - meaning energy, light, drive and destruction as well as physical fuel - he and his colleagues were fearful of being supplanted by their creation. The Zeus management problem was renewal and the succession, the perpetual issue of the autocrat-led family business.

The Greek myths were the human relations side of that enterprise. They explored human nature through the creation of divine images, exemplars of heroic, transformative and cautionary tales; with the continuing, essential issue being how humans might best manage their freedom. The gods made interventions, too, marking fates - as Apollo's deadly arrows of disease might remind us. As a body of management thought and guidance, the myths represented a colourful construct of problems, opportunities, inspirational heroic deeds, dark interventions, transformations, ingenuity and imagination, all of which rested upon the power exerted over people by and through a good story. Myth may be seen in regular action today in play via video games; in business, through company cultures and their interpretations of their corporate histories; in national identities and international assumptions.

Yuval Noah Harari (1976-) has argued that human ability to co-operate in large numbers arises from its unique capacity to believe in myth - such imaginary constructs as gods, money, freedom – and therefore even management.[6] Harari claims that all large-scale human co-operation systems – including religions, institutions, trading and political structures – owe their emergence to *homo sapiens*' distinctive creative cognitive capacity for fiction: explanatory, justifying, myth. Thus, Harari sees money as a mutual trust system and political and economic systems as essentially

---

[6] Harari, Yuval Noah. 2015. *Sapiens A Brief History of Humankind*. London: Vintage.

ideological, like religions. His argument runs further in that direction; through its advances in biology and information technology, humans have become what Zeus feared: gods who might replace him. They may control their environment; and, through genetic engineering, control creation; with artificial intelligence surpassing even themselves, rendering humanity compromised in a new hybrid form.

Even then, the argument is partial; in 1987 the phrase "masters of the universe" made its coincidental appearance in a Hollywood fantasy film and a Tom Wolfe (1930-2018) novel, *Bonfire of the Vanities,* applied to investment bankers. Those false gods were exposed, but their successors reign on. As with the ancient Greeks, we still inhabit a dual universe of rationality and values, ethics and *realpolitik;* of gods and monsters, aspirations and realities.

That duality is also susceptible to what has been termed *narrative fallacy*, whereby flawed stories of the past influence our view of the world, our identities, and our expectations. We are prone to fooling ourselves by constructing congenial but flimsy stories of the past while accrediting them with truth. It being easier to construct a story where little is known, with consequently few pieces to fit a myth or pattern, the reverse of our story-telling ability is the construction of apparently secure foundations based upon ignorance, superstition or aspiration. Such a danger and tendency are permanent, as applicable to ancient assumptions of knowledge as to the ideologies and supposedly rational models applied to management today. As reminders of origins and continuing symbols of management, each series book has a classical *sub rosa* presence. The secret to be revealed concerns a new model for Management Studies: of foundations with a core of sustainable ethical development through appreciation of history, beginning here from our first knowledge of human organisation.

Classically chosen and derived deities are presented as they are most evidently referenced in the Anglo-American tradition, which has dominated in the creation of Management Studies. This is not to detract further from the influences of the Eastern, Christian and Islamic worlds, so important in their belief and behavioural systems. The progress to Enlightenment, the industrial ages, and the post-modern may be marked successively through aspects of Apollo, Mercury, Columbia, Athena, Zeus, Demeter and Persephone. Essentially, we're all potential gods and goddesses now, with management issues to face, needing all the assistance we can get. As the Demeter and Persephone symbols will mark the summation and renewals of experience to come, so the **Improvements** will be put forward as instruments to assist the bringing forth of a new dawn. Eos awaits.

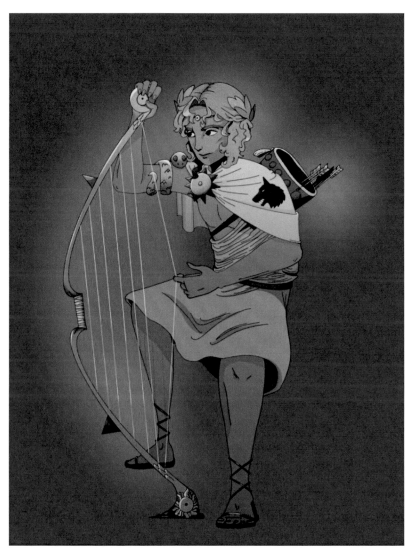

**Procuratio Sub Rosa: Apollo, Gubernator et Curator**
Management Sub Rosa: Apollo, Governor and Custodian

# APOLLO

Although the chief Syrian deity Astarte might have been invoked to represent the ancient Middle East, or the Buddhist goddess Mazu to personify China, synthesis with the East may best be reached by a path whereby human behaviour and its management from earliest times were, and are, considered in the Taoist construct, as a way of life. That is explored in Chapter 5. The most appropriate ancient deity here in the West, to begin the journey through management, is the leader of the Muses, the bringer of light and enlightenment, the Greek sun god Apollo.[7]

Often portrayed as driving his horses and chariot across the heavens, holding the reins of power, this is a grand-master on display, dazzling with his multiple capabilities.

One of the twelve Olympian deities and son of Zeus, golden Apollo is a complex bisexual figure presiding over both health and disease, also dedicated to music, truth and enlightenment; commemorated significantly in Athens as Apollo Lyceus, the wolf god, whose image adorned the Lycaeum, the gymnasium and public meeting place at which Aristotle subsequently taught. Appropriate for students, as well as being an image of youthful beauty, Apollo served juveniles by bringing them out of adolescence. His protective embrace extended to fugitives, refugees, and foreigners. For the spread of civilisation, his deity encouraged the foundation of settlements, the establishment of the constitutions by which they could be governed, and protection of the crops they might grow. That could involve pest control, at which he was adept, at all levels. Patron of herdsmen and shepherds, prevention of harm from disease and predators was a primary duty. As an archer whose golden arrows never missed, he could cause sudden death or deadly disease. Attributed the invention of

---

[7] To Charles Handy in *Gods of Management,* the figures of Apollo, Zeus, Athena and Dionysus represent contrasting but stereotypical leadership styles, to each of which he attaches consultancy and anecdotal evidence to produce diagnostic situations for attribution and resolution. His depiction of Apollo as "a kind god" of bureaucratic style is illustrative of the limitations of such an approach.

string music through the instrument of the lyre, he brought accompanying lyric poetry.

His wide jurisdiction included the giving and interpretation of legislation. Apollo's oracles were consulted before newly established cities set their laws. Mathematics, logic and reason were under his aegis, their expression and uses powered by rhetoric. Such earthly practicality was leavened by the playful joy of his spirituality. He founded his temple at Delphi, heart of the ancient western world's risk and insurance hedge prediction business, by riding there on a flying dolphin.

Apollo's powers included prophecy, medicine and healing, assisted by a son, the demi-god Asclepius, who presided over the healing aspects of medicine. Perhaps the most attractive deity of the pantheon, Apollo - as the leader of truth, reason and enlightenment, armed with pest control and germ warfare - retains an almost ideal image: a figure of guidance in emergence from darkness but with a hint still of danger when roused, and the predatory nature of the wolf. The Romans had their own names for many of the Greek originals but in both mythologies Apollo, who was subsequently also appropriated by the Romans, was unchanging, always Apollo.

Contrary to some statuary, the gods, being immortal, were eternally youthful and physically perfect, except when marked by their occupation, like Hephaestus (Vulcan) the blacksmith. Athena, like huntress Artemis, was a perpetual virgin. In their relationships with gods, humans were expected to approve of, even chat up demigod heroes such as Heracles, and the Athenian favourite Theseus. The human task was to discover the will of the gods, so that they were not angered or upset. Here, truth became a difficult commodity, for whatever happened would be capable of more than one interpretation.

Apollo's disease and healing functions, with concern for hygiene, made purification a primary concern. Yet, his greatest skill was associated with his gift of oratory - an accomplishment in which he outshone even Zeus. An expression of this talent was displayed at Delphi where the Pythia, the ordinary woman giving pronouncement to Apollo's voice, was believed to breathe through her vagina, with words coming out of her mouth. She channelled his advice by consultation in his temple. Simple questions only were required, preferably in a single sentence: was it better to do, or not do, whatever was at issue.

The obscurantist early Greek philosopher, Heraclitus of Ephesus (c.535 BCE-c.475 BCE), held that a Delphic Oracle neither tells the truth nor conceals it, merely heeding it. He observed, "The lord whose is the oracle at Delphi neither speaks nor hides his meaning but gives a sign." Delphi was special in the ancient world, for it was the god Apollo himself who spoke. Practiced at such manipulation of words and meaning, the Greeks knew oracles were constrained in their responses, therefore constructing their questions in the way they thought the gods wanted them to be. A popular formula in framing the question was to ask, "Is it best to.......?" Such inquiry has characterised the human condition since inception.

Priests were prone to bribery, a capital offence in oracular matters; but not the Pythia. If a prophesy was ambiguous, it was assumed that Zeus, being in charge overall, would know what any prophesy meant: it was humans who got such matters wrong - the gods were not wicked, but humans were. Delphic ambiguity preserved the prophesy currency. Offerings to the god were central to the temple economy. Supplicants might offer gifts in expectation, gratitude, invocation or placation.

The Athenian treasury of dedications and votive offerings dominated the pilgrim pathway to the temple on the next page, emphasising the power both of Apollo and Athens. The space program of 1961-72 in his name came in ways a mythologist might have predicted. All crew were killed in a fire before the first mission left the ground. The 11th propelled men into the first human landing on the moon. Number 13 suffered an explosion in flight but the crew escaped in their lunar module to make a safe return, an adventure celebrated in a subsequent Hollywood film.

**The Temple of Apollo at Delphi**

# INTRODUCTION

*Ideas are ruthless. In the right time, context and place they are unstoppable.*
*Wise, just, sustainable application is thus essential to their management.*

[Ian Waitt]

To know where we might be going, cope with what that future might bring, and to manage it as best we may, it is necessary to know where we've been. Recent evidence of the disastrous disregard of history can be seen from the Iraq Wars, the 2007-2009 financial debacle, the current plight of Palestine, and the disastrous miscalculations of both Putin and the NATO countries in managing the aftermath of the fall of the Soviet Union. The consequent war in Ukraine, rising inflation, demise of many companies, inequality, the decline of well-being, and the degradation of the planet all require attention and management beyond that currently extended.

There is nothing new about management. It has been part of the human story since inception, implicit throughout. Organisational performance and corporate culture are constant, rooted in society and history. Issues such as control, leadership, initiative, and investment are perpetual, varying according to time, fashion and need. Types, forms, and structures rise, fall, and may revive according to societal and historical circumstances. The only sure way to understand the present and attempt to prepare for the future is to evaluate and adapt, considering the evolution over time.

One way of attempting this is by the exemplar method of the case study. A critique of such an approach is made subsequently but it can be a useful means to illustrate and identify processes, problems and achievement. Ambrose Crowley III, James Cook, and a cornucopia digest of theorist-practitioners (respectively entrepreneur, farm boy, and management icons) were all high achieving, brilliant managers and leaders. One ended prematurely, another badly, and the third achieved prominence individually as proponents of workable aspects of management. Such positions confer power, and issues arise over how that power is used. Genghis Khan and Julius Caesar were superb managers of towering genius with utterly ruthless, disciplined efficiency and effectiveness, supremely rational in their actions. The Management Matters Case Study (3) digest offers many different styles and types of operation.

Throughout history, the same management debate has recurred: is it better to be feared than loved? Do managers essentially replicate human frailties in successively different guises, knowing what's right but doing the opposite? The responsible exercise of power, that characteristic of good leadership, was expressed daily in his unfortunately short reign by the Roman Emperor Titus (39-81 CE) who, Suetonius (69-122) reported, would lament, "Friends, I have lost a day," when one twenty-four hours passed in which he had not brought someone benefit. To Thomas Hobbes (1588-1679) in *Leviathan*, fear of another's power provided a counterbalance to the appetite for power, so preventing people from struggling constantly for its attainment. Humans sought peace only because of fear of death and bodily harm. To Hobbes, mediation between fear and power was termed "manners," the forms and expression of management.

The wider context of management is that it affects us all. As education is managed, so is society - its institutions, organisations, and businesses. We all manage, and we're all subject to management. The subject has relevance to everyone. The broad purpose of its presentation is to suggest, provoke and stimulate thought – particularly in the instance of freedom. Somewhere within these pages are information and perspectives of direct relevance to every reader. These philosophies, practices, and illustrations are drawn from millennia of human experience: all concern how we manage and are managed, how we control and are controlled. Freedoms held or aspired to exist only within their contexts, other than by and in anarchy. Learning may be formal, or informal and intuitive. Most of the former is expressed through recognisable processes.

Those processes are familiar enough. Schools, guilds, religious organisations, the armed forces, businesses, and governments provided education according to their perceived needs. Management of the activity was emphasised by the requirements of the provider, in quantity and quality sufficient only to the perceived needs of that provider. If you were surplus to provider requirements, you either didn't get any, or got a smattering at best. This was quite natural. Recourse was only to the informal, or media, where that existed. Vocational education came through some form of apprenticeship (learning on the job).

There was little apparent need for pupil-centred learning in a military academy. Similarly, the concept of management did not sit easily with many of the providers. For the religious providers, education was the means of the transference, perpetuation and glorification of the faith; for the irreligious, goals could be mirrored, opposite images. For the military academy, instruction, discipline, and performance were paramount. Onerous issues were decided hierarchically, albeit with the potential contributory difficulty of innovation often being crucial in warfare while hard to acquire or control, requiring delegation either to bureaucratic procurement or officer expertise. Armed forces management being crucial to national survival, it was integral to the services. The same principle applied throughout society: management happened within a context and, where that was of any scale, in a bureaucratic, contained form.

Deriving from tribal systems, which usually possessed delegated or elective elements among the sub-divisions' organisation, the state management model was predominantly autocratic, bureaucratically supported, operated as and through a family business at all levels. This is true of monarchies, religion, business, trade, industry and public affairs. These organisations were supported by hierarchical bureaucracies down to the level of the owner master, who had to do it all by himself, with family support and such outside agencies as were available. At the top, in east and west, the autocrats were supported by their oligarchs, or were in conflict with them as they became over-mighty, and ultimately had to increasingly share power until revolution, religion, and change grew progressively to restructure society.

The current management education curriculum can be criticised as unbalanced - a fault attributable to its historical development. The set, formal beginning is often with F.W. Taylor, ignoring three millennia of development and several prior decades of Victorian innovation. Neglect of history has greatly impoverished the study of management, a revisionist view of which these volumes seek to impart. History is not a static discipline. It evolves as greater evidence comes to light, as successive generations of historians reassess the perspectives of their predecessors. Contributions from other disciplines may challenge or enforce long held assumptions, such as biologists' findings of the links between increased nutrition and the growth of civilisation and Greenland ice core records proving the accompanying stability of climate amenable to such growth.

The case studies - passages of narrative history such as Marius's creation of the professional Roman army, the Enlightenment and its consequences - all address continuing societal management issues. The range is from the personal example of an individual to corporate and international affairs. The purpose is to address five millennia of human management experience through a series of examples bound by a coherent narrative, eventually leading to positive, practical proposals for change and development in a subsequent publication. In assembling the evidence for this pointillistic approach, it has been necessary to write at some length. The intermittent sketches of philosophers are necessary, for theirs is the stimuli to knowledge, to learning, its form and content – and the provocation to further thought that such knowledge or reflection might supply.

An imagined Socratic dialogue, for example, between Chuang Tzu and Descartes, would have high entertainment value, at least: the one asserting that he was, because he knew he was, and the other questioning whether he was Chuang Tzu, or a butterfly. How business and technology influenced and influences education is further addressed in the partial, gobbet style. That children do not feature greatly in much of the material is a mere reflection of historical fact: they did not figure in the great scheme of western human development very much after the fall of Rome. It is not until the 18th century that they re-emerge in the narrative - at least for the better off, it is not until the 19th century for the rest. Learning, for most, came through their occupations, family, and friends, not their schooling (where it existed). China's imperial bureaucracy entrance examinations began in the early 7th century, yet education, from the earliest years, remains a prime means to address and reduce inequality.

In a snapshot historical gallery, the Egyptians began the written management manual; the Sumerian invention of temple capitalism was made multinational by the Assyrians; the Phoenician control model overtaken by Greek entrepreneurialism; and the Romans consolidated the business and organisational systems into an autocratic framework and thereby allowed family-based free enterprise within the first European union, containing around a third of the world's population. To the east, there were variations on the same theme. Chinese family capitalism was expressed through a state underpinned by Confucian systems; India experienced centralised authority, through which local entrepreneurialism gained expression; and the rise of Islam brought respectability and encouragement to trade. Each of these developments featured the growth of ethical systems, and each experienced the excesses of human nature. By the later medieval period both Europe and Asia had developed business partnerships and alliances based on faiths, ethics, and myth, all of which spawned corporate forms of organisation.

Religion brought both control and strife, inspiration for the greatest and darkest of deeds. The pragmatism of early Islam stimulated a cultural and mathematically based flowering. Yet, its restrictive prescription of inheritance caused it to fall behind Christian entrepreneurial expansion. That faith broke apart to renew itself, as new won freedom and the technological advance of printing led to a spreading of the ideas of the Enlightenment. The managerial power of its revelations can be appreciated at two levels: the triumph of statecraft in the success of the American Revolution enabled the liberation of people to be able to think for themselves; and the reach of education to the middle classes, and to their children. That the popularity of grand intellectual processes bore such trivial pursuits as the jigsaw and heroines like Goody Two Shoes prefigures the social media and video gaming of our own day.

Creating and managing opportunity derived from diverse stimuli is an indication of human ingenuity. Yet, in many ways, the greater the management of cross-cultural models, the less its foundations are noted. It is only very recent research and illustration which have proved how much the building of Christian cathedrals from the 13th century onwards owed to the Arabic mastery of construction, first known through the militarised tourism of the Crusades.

Forms of management emerged through the cultural processes stemming from location. Landscape may not have been the ultimate determinant but it has always influenced heavily human settlement and development, from the remoteness of the Amazon rain-forest, the inaccessibility of the Afghan hinterland, and vast emptiness of deserts. Great movements have either emerged from them, like Islam; or vanished into them, as did those unsung explorers who never came home. James Cook's seagoing explorations began the management foundation known as globalisation, opening fully a world only partly known until then. Ambrose Crowley III began industrial factory management, the wonder of his times; but the lessons were largely lost or forgotten and, if re-learned, came to be imperfectly applied by and to managements thereafter. Sometimes, foundations fail - not because of inherent fault, but because successors ignored them and chose not to build upon them, or did so only partially.

It is impossible to write a complete history of either education or management. Both are individual and collective lifelong processes, across the entire span of human existence. Here, the management, education, and history items and topics are signposts only, markers in the marches of the human journey. Much will have been missed, emphases open to dispute, and selection inevitably bound by the limits to the author's knowledge, experience, and judgment. Those who managed had first to be educated, in some form, and that education formed and informed management.

No distinctions are made between leadership and management. All managers have to lead the organisation of whatever it is that they are required to manage. All leaders have to manage their followers, the environment in which they act, and the consequences of their actions and interactions. Because attitudes derive from their contexts, the conditions within which managers were, and are, educated becomes important to their understanding, and to our own comprehension of their actions and policies.

The accumulation of material in this and successive works is intended to create pictures and presentations of aspects of management. Some individual items might appear superfluous, of niche interest only, but the intent is to paint the big, small, and medium sized pictures of management through multiple aspects, across many times, with the constant reminders of the brevity of individual experience against the comparative longevity of the collective understanding.

This book provides an overview of management and education up to the advent of printing in the west, the retreat into isolation of China, and the spread of the ideas of the Enlightenment. From those times, it predominantly follows the progress of Anglo-American education, as the English language began its course to global prominence. It concludes with the growth of modern management reaching the stage of discrete study, the advent of the business schools and production of theory. The case study method introduced without comment here is subject to continuing analysis in subsequent publications.

More than a text book, this first (and thus far only) history of management, education management, and management education is also a reference work, leading to the further functions of allowing and seeking reader reaction, involvement and participation. Among the prime intended consumers are young people, ideally before business school orthodoxy has invaded their thinking capacities; managers seeking greater understanding of their functions; and all experiencing the processes of being managed. The subsequent **Improvements,** later Case Studies, and campaigning platform will enable readers themselves to take part. Real management is about doing – not modelling, theorising, or lecture receipt – and that is what the books will seek to inspire. The aim is to provoke thought, discussion and action. To lighten the process, the writing includes moments of humour, diversion and entertainment, for it is also a work to be enjoyed: after all, as the next book *Mass Education* subsequently illustrates, the modern manager did seemingly first appear in the theatre; the earliest mass management undertakings, the ancient religious rites with theatrical festivals of Greece and the circuses of Rome. The classical framework seeks to emphasise the context of growth over time within a broad, themed, conceptual framework. This is neither religious nor ideological. Ideas are indeed ruthless, requiring of careful handling. The historical analysis aspires to be neutral. The overall approach is pragmatic, seeking to make for better management. There is no ideological agenda beyond that of responsible freedom, doing the right thing, as equitably, ethically, effectively, efficiently and sustainably as possible.

In order to aid comprehension of an inevitably broad work of substantial scope, occasional **Footprints** mark the passage of major movements, themes, and events. They invite readers to reflect on the journey, increase awareness and consider their own arising perspectives from the narrative. Annotation is provided at the end of each chapter, and a case study where applicable. It departs from the current academic convention of the accumulation of citations. Fine for fact-checkers, academic calculation, and promotion points this mode may be, it results in a significant amount of usually-unread bulk at the end of a book. The purpose here is to inform and support the text. Reference may be sparse in passages, because the information is well known, here merely referred to in what is a novel form. Where extensive, the notes are written to be read. They may amplify the text and main themes, but they are also meant to be worthy of study and consideration in themselves. Annotation has ever been subject to improvisation.

To assist understanding of what may be unfamiliar or required aids to comprehension for some readers, three timelines are provided. The first timeline marks the passage of pre-history, the period which ended with the discovery of writing signifying the commencement of civilisation, and detailed immediately on the next page. This is followed later by timelines of the two main subsequent civilisations; that for the West being found after the end notes at the conclusion of Chapter 2; that for China preceding Chapter 5.

# TIMELINE:
## PRE-HISTORY AND HUMANITY

Approximately 4.5 billion years ago, it is suggested, a major impact from a collision between the proto-earth and a Mars-sized planet caused the ejection of material which became our moon. Formation of that moon and earth with their gravitational interdependence thus began.

Asteroids and comets brought water to the earth. Our planet then underwent various developmental experiences, as a result of which life began, the current climax of which commenced with the appearance of the first hominids.

In the geologic time scale, in the Miocene Epoch (around 11.6 million years ago), human and chimpanzee ancestors gradually separated. By around 3.6 million years ago, in the Pliocene Epoch and when the Greenland ice sheet developed, the Stone Age began. Around 0.77 million years ago, now in the Pleistocene Epoch, *homo sapiens* began to supplant the previous hominids. The last 11,700 years of the earth's history, as dated from 9700 BCE, saw the ending of the latest Ice Age (although a "Little Ice Age" affected earth between 1200 and 1700 CE). In geological terms, the Pleistocene and Holocene form the Quaternary Period.

By common scientific consensus we have now entered the Anthropocene Epoch, that period where the predominant planetary influence is human. Like it or not, in today's world, conscious of the seemingly unlimited potential of our own DNA and equipped with historical information from the past, humanity now has the knowledge to take management responsibility for the future of this planet on which it dwells.

Timescale dates, names and brief details of mankind's prehistory are listed on the next page .[1]

---

[1] Oxford Reference. 2012. *Timeline: Prehistory.* Oxford: History World.
https://www.oxfordreference.com/view/10.1093/acref/9780191735349.timeline.0001

| DATE | SIGNIFICANT PRE-HISTORIC EVENTS |
|---|---|
| c. 1.8 million years ago | *Homo erectus*, probably the first identifiable ancestor of modern humans, found to have lived in east Africa. |
| c.1.7 million years ago | Ice ages begin, interrupting and delaying human development. *Homo erectus* moves from Africa into Europe and Asia. |
| c. 1 million years ago | Speculation that human speech developed around this time. |
| c. 800,000 years ago | Stone tools made in Britain. Last common ancestor of humans and Neanderthals evolves in Africa. |
| c. 500,000 years ago | Evidence of Peking man having dwelt in caves and used fire (although this may be earlier in Africa). |
| c. 250,000 years ago | First evidence of humans hunting: a spear of hardened yew found in Saxony between elephant ribs. |
| c. 230,000 years ago | *Homo sapiens* evolve. |
| c.120,0000-35,000 years ago | Neanderthals and modern humans coexist in Europe and Asia. |
| c.90,000 years ago | Fossilised bones found in Israel are of anatomically correct modern humans. |
| c.60,000 years ago | First humans' crossing from south east Asia to Australia. |
| c. 45,500 years ago | First known cave paintings, Sulawesi, Indonesia. |
| c..35,000 years ago | After a decline in numbers over 15,000 years, Neanderthals go suddenly extinct, leaving *homo sapiens* as the only species survivor. Earliest Venus figures and hide covered tents supported by mammoth bones found. |
| c. 31,000 years ago | Lion, mammoth and rhinoceros figures featured on cave walls, south France. |

| | |
|---|---|
| c. 30,000 years ago | Renewed Ice Age reduces sea levels, allowing formation of a land bridge between Siberia and Alaska, allowing humans to enter America. |
| c.27,000 years ago | Burnt clay figures provide the earliest known examples of ceramics. |
| c. 25,000 years ago | First Venus figure to have facial features. |
| c. 23,000 years ago | Mammoth ivory carved figures. |
| c. 16,000 years ago | Large number of cave paintings at Lascaux, France. |
| c. 15,000 years ago | Earliest bows (from yew or elm) and arrows (flint). Ivory and bone needles capable to accommodate thread as thin as horse hair. North American plains shown by archaeology to have an extensive human population. |
| c. 15,000 to 10,000 years ago. | Humans advance into South America but while improving the fashioning and use of tools, remain nomadic hunter-gatherers. |
| c. 12,000 years ago | Mesopotamian evidence of earliest dog domestication. |
| c. From 8,000 BCE | Latest Ice Age melt causes large animal extinction and increased land fertility, encouraging and enabling permanent human settlements. Two types of wheat are grown in the Middle East; sheep are first domesticated in Iraq; the requirement of wool production stimulates the natural development of the spindle in process of hand powered twisting of fibres into thread. Often cited as the first town, sun-dried brick constructed Jericho grew to a settlement of ten acres, subsisting on wheat, its tower becoming the world's earliest surviving fortification. Migration out of Siberia continued with crossings into Japan but the rising sea levels submerged the Bering land bridge, isolating the former immigrants into north America, so becoming native aboriginals. As temperatures warmed, some moved back northwards. Known at outset as the Neolithic or New Stone Age period, describing any community still using stone tools, the Neolithic Revolution continued at differing times and places as communities changed to crop cultivation and animal breeding. |

| c. 7,000 BCE | The first hammered copper implements begin in eastern Anatolia, marking a move out of the Stone Age. Barley cultivation begins in the Middle East. |
| --- | --- |
| c. 6,500 BCE | An Anatolian town where cloth was later found has buildings with windows set in rectangular rooms, found to be containing pottery. A Cyprus town has a paved public street with lanes leading off to courtyards with round houses. |
| 5,000 BCE | Existing mainly as marine animal hunters, groups of humans adapt to the conditions of Greenland and Canada. The first plants cultivated in Mexico are chili and squash. In Africa, neolithic communities are able to live in a Sahara region still sufficiently damp enough to support hippopotami until it begins to dry out around two thousand years later. |
| 4,400 BCE | First evidence of a loom is found in Egypt but it is assumed that weaving began much earlier. Draught oxen are used in the Middle East and Europe although hand-held ploughing in Egypt and Mesopotamia pre-dates animal power by a century. Beer is brewed from barley in Mesopotamia. Grapes are cultivated in an area around the Caspian Sea, where they grow naturally |
| c. 3,800 BCE | In Iran in various places, copper is extracted from iron ore by smelting. |
| c. 3,500 BCE | Olives, soon to become a staple of Mediterranean trade, are cultivated in Crete. |
| c.3,250 BCE | Ötzi, aka "the Iceman", the natural mummy of a murdered herdsman, found in 1991 in everyday clothing with impedimenta of his neolithic time, on the alpine Austria-Italian border. |
| c. 3,100 BCE | Sumer develops as Mesopotamia's first civilisation. With the unification of Upper and Lower Egypt into a single kingdom, the first Egyptian dynasty begins. At Sumer writing develops as cuneiform script on clay tablets while Egyptian hieroglyphics begin around the same time. **Achievement of the ability to record in writing marks the transition from pre-history to history.** |

**The Earliest Known Art**

Dated at c.44,000 years old, Leang Tedongnge cave in Sulawesi, Indonesia, shows a supposed hunting scene with humans attempting the capture of three pigs (labelled 1,2, and 3 beneath). Image credit: Oktavianna

# CHAPTER ONE

# EARLY CIVILISATION

Physics in the forms of matter and energy came first, manifested in the creation of the earth about 14 billion years ago. We humans have not been around very long, only for nanoseconds of the universal time scale. From the beginning, however much we sought security and stability, we have had to manage our existence in conditions of uncertainty. Around three million years ago, humanoids began using rock tools.

*Homo sapiens* is first known to have appeared more than 315,000 years ago in what is now Africa. Its further development took a long time (in human terms), but management was present from the start. Upright Man, or *homo erectus*, spread from Africa to Asia, adapted to different habitats, ate varied food, lived in groups, had the stamina to outrun some of their prey, probably developed sailing and seafaring abilities, and may have advanced beyond rudimentary communications and creative skills. Hunting abilities extended to medium and large animals. The crafting of stone tools demonstrates considerable skill in the management of the material. Their lifespan on earth of some two million years demonstrates sustainable management of available resources.

Controlled fire management by earlier species, probably *homo erectus,* is dated from 1.4 to 1.5 million years ago, credited to early *homo sapiens* from 300,000 and 125,000 years ago to its present, modern variety. The oldest known art management came later than fire management in the form of cave paintings, interestingly differently located: in Sulawesi, Indonesia, some 45,500 years ago, from 35,000 in Spain and 32,000 in Colombia.

In the Lascaux Caves, almost 6,000 figures of large animals, humans, and abstract signs have been painted using predominantly mineral pigments, in a strikingly sophisticated style. Equines and stags are the most numerous of the identified animals, with cattle (bulls and aurochs) next; plus some felines, a bear, bird, rhinoceros and a human.

.

**Lascaux Cave Painting (replica)**

Their decoration painted some 20,000 years ago, located in the Dordogne region of south west France, the Lascaux caves were discovered in 1940 but closed to the public in 1963 because of the contamination resulting from 1,200 visitors per day. Replica images now serve for public reference

Speculation as to the images' purpose includes the recording of past hunting success; spiritual ritual to improve hunting endeavour; and as accompaniment to such spiritual adventures as trance-dancing, perhaps by flickering, animating torch or firelight. Speculative perhaps, but draught-propelled flickering firelight or the guttering of tallow candles, especially during the consumption of stimulants, may have caused the illusions of animation with consequent spiritual experience. In what is known as the cognitive revolution, perhaps attributable to brain mutation or evolution, fictive language appeared some 70,000 years previously. Fireside tales may have been told to accompany and expand visual awareness.

Only language can fully convey narratives, and so history began. Stories could be told.[1]

Narrative is of three types: belonging, obligation, and causality, all of which fit together to form webs of reciprocal obligation, combining to form belief systems. Explanatory myths, epics of heroism, and essential gossip helped humans to create analogies, test arguments, enlist others, and reach reasoned decisions and action. The invention of mythologies to explain forces beyond understanding helped create belief systems. Division of labour facilitated the accomplishment of tasks; group co-operative action provided self and mutual protection.

Between 50,000 and 30,000 years ago, palaeontologists speculate, there appeared clusters of people, mutually supportive but not necessarily related. These humans hunted, foraged and gathered, roaming a forested earth with untamed plants and animals in abundance. It is most likely they gathered together co-operatively in groups, in order to better exploit natural resources and defend against predators. The optimal size for a social group has been estimated at around 150. Only after this number do ranks, orders and formal organisations become necessary. Thus, informal group management through social co-operation is possible only up to that maximum number. Within the group, examples, role models, and ethical custom can form the management culture and tradition. Beyond that, binding myths become essential, together with and part of formal order. At that point instruction, law and records have to be made.

The administrative means to establish such institutions and the conduct of affairs required group organisation based upon meetings. Such gatherings required order, regulated by rules. A prime concern was prevention of violence when matters became contentious. The gavel is said to descend from the Norse double headed axe, ceremonially displayed. The British parliament forbids the presence of weapons in its debating chambers, providing cloakroom hooks for members' swords. Despite such precautions, the precedent for violence set by the Ides of March 44 BCE assassination of Julius Caesar (100-44 BCE) in the debating chamber by a group of senators has been followed since, by protective measures instituted by over 50 legislatures. Management of people about the people's business remains a significant concern.

The Agricultural Revolution saw plants and animals domesticated for human use around 12,000 to 10,000 BCE. It is thought that in earliest forms of society, anarchy gave way to civilisation through "roving bandits" realising that a "stationary bandit" could gain more. Whilst the rovers' incentives were probably theft and destruction, sedentary prospects were greater. Economic success gave expectation of longer lasting, and greater predictability of, power. Thus, settled leaders began to take on governmental and protective roles. The pattern is still replicated where warlords emerge from anarchic states. It may be argued that nomadic herding led to pastoral settlement, but the processes had dominant common factors.

The common story of an historical determinism, whereby humans have progressed inexorably from cave dwellers to high rise concrete inhabitants, seed scattering ploughers of fields to artificial meat manufacturers, was challenged in 2021. Previously, pre-history had been interpreted in two ways. The "neo-Hobbesians" argue that, particularly after the Enlightenment, modern civilisation is a progression away from nasty, brutish origins.[2] "Neo-Rousseauians", on the other hand, associate progress with the loss of freedom.[3]

A different perspective was offered by the anthropologist David Graeber and the archaeologist David Wengrow, who posited that the process of human choice made for a non-uniform prehistory. There could have been myriad social arrangements, some of which involved large cities of monarchical or egalitarian rule, some served by slave labour. Even after the growth of agriculture, the argument is that there was no fixed model of community organisation. Instead, a rich diversity of societies flourished, using agriculture but not dominated by hierarchical social demands.

In their international, much translated best seller, *The Dawn of Everything A New History of Humanity,* the authors plainly report their sources' evidence:[4] Hunter-gatherer bands were egalitarian because they were so small, a collection of many experimental social forms. Moreover, the first farming communities were relatively rank and hierarchy free.

> And far from setting class differences in stone, a surprising number of the world's earliest cities were organised on robust egalitarian lines, with no need for authoritarian rulers, ambitious warrior politicians, or even bossy administrators.[5]

Farming often began as an economy of desperation, only being invented from necessity, when there was nothing else to be done. Thus, it tended to happen first in areas where wild resources were thinnest on the ground. Despite its growth potential, especially when domestic livestock were added to cereal crops, and the primacy apparent to archaeologists of farmers' creation of more rubbish and their building with mud brick, larger communities concentrated around water, rivers, coastlands and deltas, and these had become the earliest sites of cities.[6] These show evidence of being "places of self-conscious social experimentation", [7] a developed example of which at Tlaxcala in pre-Columbian Mexico shows a flourishing republican city-state, Teotihuacan rejecting human sacrifice and monument construction in favour of a social housing project.[8] By contrast, the Aztec capital of Tenochtitlan - with its temple, palace, and site for royal ritual - presented an important opposite.

Defining the limits to power as the three principles of sovereignty, administration, and competitive politics in their search for whether humans and their consequent institutions were "good" or "bad" at origin, these authors conclude that our present understanding of human progress is, itself, myth. Humans, they contend, from rediscovered past capacity, through this new knowledge have the ability "to rediscover the meaning of our third basic freedom…to create new and different forms of social reality".[9] If so, then it is apposite in the extreme to indicate that this will become utterly vital if we are to adapt to the conditions, predicted by some, to become prevalent through unbridled climate change, finite growth, and advance of the Anthropocene.

Our foraging ancestors came out of the Pleistocene (Ice Age) into the phase of a warmer global climate known as the Holocene. This has been the most stable, generally agreeable climate known to our planet, the period most conducive to the growth of human civilisation. The Anthropocene refers to the present, where humanity is responsible for planetary change.

The evidence comes from the unlikely source, separately recorded, of the US Army's Project Iceworm.[10] Part of this involved drilling through the Greenland ice sheet. The drilling team pulled up long cylinders of ice, continuing until they encountered bedrock. The total of over a thousand cylinders constituted the first complete Greenland ice core.

The ice sheet is made of compacted snow, made denser and thinner over time, providing an evolutionary clock. At around a hundred and forty feet down there is snow dating from the US Civil War; twenty-five hundred feet, from the time of Plato (427-348 BCE); and five thousand three hundred and fifty feet from the cave paintings era. Each layer contains tiny bubbles of trapped air, enabling the tracing from atmospheric pollution by such sources as volcanoes, Roman smelting and Mongolian dust. From this comprehensive if unusual archive it was possible to discover that the last ice age was so climatically unstable that every time humans had built the beginning of a culture, they had to move.

Then came the present interglacial period (as shown by the ice core evidence): ten thousand years of climate stability, productive of perfect conditions for agriculture. The civilisations of Mesopotamia, India and China all began together, around six thousand years ago, with each developing writing, religion and urban life, all about the same time, because the climate was stable.

Now that we inhabit the Anthropocene, the period where humans have notional control, we, the people, are responsible for the welfare of our planet. The management task and duties now, have become very great indeed. We have become the guardians of our own creation of civilisation, and responsible for keeping its climate stable.

The rediscovery of human capacities and their management to cope with this responsibility, however, is material for a future publication. The task here is the understanding of those foundations of management which have brought us here. Civilisation began, we have noted, in settlements close to water. While rivers had long allowed ease of movement, truly serious transport began around 3,500 BCE with the Sumerian invention of the wheel. Now, there were whole businesses of substance involving logistics to be managed. Management has been central to the human condition from the very start. Fully to establish that management, essentials had to be recorded, probably beginning with trade tallies and accounts.

Our earliest records of writing begin around 3,100 BCE, when the order and process of society required written records. Writing may be described as a data recording and storage system. The Sumerian variety was the combination of two types of sign, known as cuneiform, pressed into clay tablets. One sign type represented numbers. This used a combination of base-10 and base-6 numerical systems, bequeathing such legacies as the division of days into 24 hours and the 360-degree circle. The other sign system was for objects, areas, and dates.

The sign combination allowed the recording and expression of more data than could readily be memorised. Used initially for trade, the first known sign record is that of an accountant. The rulers used the script for decrees, bureaucracy began with recording scribes, and personal letters followed as an initial social media. Thereafter, laws, records, and literature ensued.

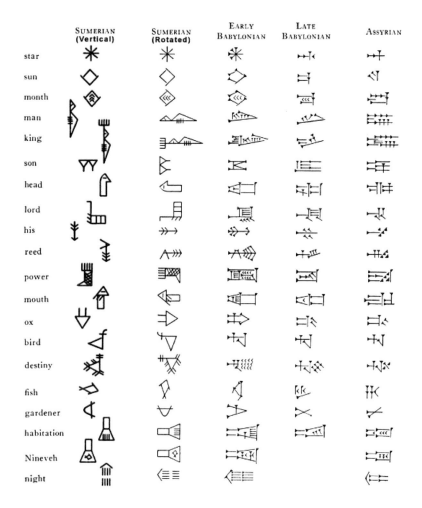

**Example of some of the first written languages, and evolution of cuneiform script** extracted from *Cuneiform evolution* by William Albert Mason (1855 -1923).

**A large cuneiform inscription found on the south side of the Van Castle hill, four kilometres west of modern-day Van, in eastern Turkey.**

The direct message is from King Xerxes, roughly translated by Bjorn Christian Tørrissen from the Old Persian, Babylonian and Elamite:

> Ahuramazda is the great god, the greatest god who created the sky and created the land and created humans Who gave prosperity to the humans Who made Xerxes king of many kings, being the only ruler of the totality of all lands. I am Xerxes, the great king, the king of kings, the king of the lands, king of all the languages, king of the great and large land, the son of king Darius the Achaemenian. The king Xerxes says: 'the king Darius, my father, praised be Ahuramazda, made a lot of good, and this mountain, he ordered to work its cliff and he wrote nothing on it so, me, I ordered to write here.' May Ahuramazda protect me, with all the gods and so my kingdom and what I have done.

The two important script systems of hieroglyphics and cuneiform were very similar. Each had essential core signs. For example, the sound of A, as pronounced "AY" (as in the word aid) is represented in the basic Egyptian alphabet as an arm; the A when pronounced "AH" (as in the word harmony) is pictorialized as a vulture, the sound resembling the squawk of that bird.

The sound of C was represented as a cup, but could also quite literally mean a cup. There were many different signs representing letters of the alphabet, syllables, whole words, or combinations of words and ideas. There were indicators which signalled which sort of word came next, such as a type of object or person. Complicated in that there were seven or eight hundred signs in the repertoire, the systems were restricted to professional writers. [A quick guide to Egyptian hieroglyphic basic alphabet script is included in Appendix 1.]

Late in the 4th millennium BCE, cuneiform writing appeared in southern Iraq, providing accounts for what temples needed to manage: goods, labour, land, and animals. Early Egyptian hieroglyphs found in the tombs of kings refer to the numbers and concrete objects of grave goods in the chamber. The first writing records ownership, then a display language for showing off the great feats of royalty. The writing technique had spread southwards to Egypt, first manifesting in hieroglyph pictorial temple designs and then developing into religious literature.

**Hieroglyphs from the tomb of Seti I**

The first great masterpiece of literature, the *Epic of Gilgamesh*, has origins in the third millennium BCE. Rediscovered in 1853 on cuneiform tablets found near Mosul, Iraq, they recorded the story of a king of Uruk, Gilgamesh. The gods create a companion, Enkidu, to stop Gilgamesh oppressing his people. Together, they fight a monstrous forest guardian and kill the Bull of Heaven, for which the gods make Enkidu mortally ill. Gilgamesh goes on a long journey trying to learn how to live forever, which ultimately proves unsuccessful. Learning about the Great Deluge on the way, and reconciled to the inevitability of death, his remarkable building works guarantee his fame will last long after his demise. He has managed a legacy.

By the time such literature appeared, the trading of raw materials for finished goods had also begun. Money, in the form of standardised measures of barley, had been invented by the Sumerians as a means of commercial exchange. Development took time. Standardised coins minted from gold, silver and bronze were known in Athens from the 7th century BCE, widespread throughout the Mediterranean world by 250 BCE. Measurement, mathematics and the use of materials facilitated construction. The Egyptian architect Imhotep designed the Saqqara pyramid complex, built between 2630 and 2611 BCE. The Great Pyramid (Pyramid of Khufu) was completed in 2560 BCE, the only one of the seven wonders of the ancient world to remain largely intact. These, together with irrigation, monumental sculpture, literacy, numeracy, manufacturing, trading and distribution, a stable government, and religion, distinguished a managed civilisation such as that of Egypt.

The most significant aspects of that management were domination and wishful thinking. The dominance of state power was emphasised through its monumental architecture. From the geometric grandeur of the pyramids to the height of obelisks and the colossal statuary, Egyptian craftsmen were masters of baked mud, brick, and stone. From the foreheads of pharaonic head-dresses, the cobra image typified the fear inspired by such a dangerous creature, reinforcing the intimidating and commanding authority of the ruler.

Such power would further be associated with the ruler's protective goddess. The ubiquitous wishful thinking was demonstrated by the utopianism of the after-life depicted in wall paintings found in the tombs of the elite and the complements of grave-goods. Tomb robbers were well acquainted with the uncomfortable fact that such items and food meant to accompany the deceased instead remained stationary and rotted in their places. Since tomb robbery penalties were execution by burning or impalement, disclosure of uncomfortable realities was inadvisable.

However, power was administered through theocracy-dominated and restrictive management by control, leading to progressive ossification and entropy. Rival states rose and fell, some distinguished by their contributions to the progress of managed civilisation, such as that of Babylon's Hammurabi (1810-1750 BCE), the first codifier of law to make its provisions openly visible to all by means of display on an engraved stone column. His (approximate) 300 state management laws of c. 1790 BCE are concerned with the preservation of order, around a fifth of which being concerned with trade. Citizens' rank, rights, and duties were specified, with clear regulation of slavery. These were all subject to bureaucratic administration. Slavery, it seems, has disfigured human progress from near the very start. We owe the development of astronomy to the Babylonians. Movements of the sun and moon were seen as normal, but eclipses were viewed as portentous. Temple priests made monthly observations, establishing the patterns and movements of heavenly bodies.

By the second millennium, there were fully developed mathematical texts. Construction improvement could be found in the increased numbers of timber expeditions. These, like everything else Babylonian, were recorded in lists. Accountancy's importance in the development of Babylonian society was measurable through the ubiquity of its lists. The unpopularity of the Babylonians in Herodotus and Israelite criticism has been attributed to their "other" status – they existed outside of the Greek and biblical worlds. Like much ancient history, this is conjecture based upon reasonable supposition, such as the assembly of evidence making possible the following assertion.

The first known job description, with governmental, administrative directions for managerial action, is Egyptian, drawn from manuscript fragments and tomb inscriptions from the reigns between Thutmose III (1479-1425 BCE) and Rameses II (1279-1213 BCE) They are known collectively as the *Duties of the Vizier*, and they describe and give instruction for the appearance, tasks, and behaviour of the pharaoh's chief minister.

> When conducting a hearing, he is to sit on a stool, skins on his back and at his feet, 30 scrolls on the floor, staff at his arm, overseer to his right, manager to his left, scribes at each hand, with the reporting officials, applicants or supplicants to be heard in order of their rank. Domestic and national comings and goings, treasury matters, the conditions of the land, country and its security are matters of daily report. The vizier is supreme in his office, under the pharaoh.

The vizier's messengers rank as him in the delivery or receipt of communications. Rolls of transgressors are to be maintained, the vizier's seal applied to "concealed" documents; councillors, mayors and governors are appointed, bade to come and go; reporting time limits set; applications for land and mining may be heard; fortress maintenance, military and shipping requirements and action required; the dispatch and reporting of the "multitude of bureaucrats" whose duties are to record every land holding; and from the opening of the gold house with the treasurer, to judicial matters, and the administration of all conceivable royal business, "it is he," the vizier, who has responsibility; and this is the recorded start of devolved authority.[11]

It is not surprising that many viziers came from pharaonic families. From the beginning, autocracy was a family business. Pharaoh, chairman of the family board, did policy. If the vizier was the CEO, then the overseer and the manager shared COO duties.

There could be a multiplicity of vizier titles. Under Amenhotep II (r. 1427 b.1401 or 1397 BCE) they included: Chief of the Entire Land; Overseer of Foremost Lands; Priest of Maat; One Who Hears in the Six Great Houses; Controller of All Kilts; and Master of Secrets of the West. The predecessor vizier, Rekhmire, was recorded as having over 30 titles, including Overseer of the Double Gold Treasuries and of the Double Silver Treasuries; Overseer of crafts; Overseer of Archives; Master of the Secrets of the palace; and "He of the Curtain".[12]

The Egyptians knew enough about surveying and measurement to have managed the construction of pyramids from c. 2630 BCE. It is further known that practices now ascribed to management were in use by the Egyptians by around 1500 BCE, as cited above. Strategic management, planning, organisation, control, information systems, record keeping and equitable dealing were, by then, as integral to the pharaonic administration system as was the commissioning of art to its religious and cultural base. Management has been as essential to human civilisation as it was when our life form evolved or arrived, both actively and conceptually. However, the determining thrust of the containing economic system (autocratic and hierarchical or democratic; entrepreneurial or bureaucratic; socialist or capitalist; hybrids and third or middle ways) forms the character of the managerial product. This is further formed, or informed, through its education.

All myths which form societal foundations feature a strong leader with a range of obstacles and troubles requiring attention, Virgil's *Aeneid* being a prime example. Such obstacles are overcome or coped with; provide focus and unifying purposes; and establish relationships between leaders and followers, environment and society, exemplifying how they might be managed. Duties and obligations arise, society expands and order must be maintained.

Business, however, had been in operation at the beginning of recorded time. Sumerian traders had developed property ownership contracts by 3,000 BCE, where temples had further functions as banks and state overseers. By Christ's time, Judaic temple banking had become a sufficiently sophisticated money exchange centre to detract from the building's supposed main purpose, causing bankers' ejection and eventual relocation to benches outside. Capital and organisational skill facilitated Mesopotamian long-distance trading, funded by public institutions and temple resources and managed by crown functionaries who, in time, were able to ascend to independent trading status: the self-employed merchant-princes. Partnership agreements were known during the Assyrian ascendancy of 2,000-1,800 BCE, with the establishment of time-limited trading funds. These became the trading methods of choice throughout the Mediterranean region. Enterprises could be executed by a professional manager – albeit under state regulation and bound by the partnership limitations. Assyrian military might and expansion created the circumstances for the first multinational concerns to arise.

Between the 14th and 12th centuries BCE, the new technology of bronze production had become understood by the powers of the eastern Mediterranean and both the Near and Middle East. This was the process of amalgamating copper and tin in a 10 to 1 ratio by smelting, a delicate scientific process which could have been achieved only by the uses of the senses of smell, sight (appearance), and perhaps taste in the creative process. The new material led to great increases in trade and military applications, which spawned more trade. This expanded interaction and interconnection throughout Europe and the other trading regions.

Kings were meant to be splendid in appearance, action, and construction. They began, or increased, the building of temples and fortifications, as well as the size and power of their armies. Bronze was necessary for the new weapons of swords and chariots, the cutting of stone, and as a replacement for stone and copper in such artefacts as arrow heads. Although beaten leather shields remained tougher than their metal counterparts, bronze symbolised more power. Its acquisition and use have been shown, through shipwreck evidence, to have spurred more trade in cloth, silver, gold, oil jars, ivory, and gift goods.

Around 1177 BCE, there was conflict, of which we know very little. In 1150 BCE, there was climate change (as suggested by tree ring evidence), of which we know even less. We do know, however, the results: the retrenchment of Egypt, the collapse of the Hittite Empire (of Turkey), depredations by "the Sea People" and waves of marauding destruction. Several centuries later, the successors of the Etruscan and Latin peoples, with the Greek city states and Phoenicia, began their rise. This Bronze Age Collapse has been further attributed to succession problems; rulers then forfeited approval if they became too powerful. The increasing deposit of items of value as grave goods also weakened monarchical authority. Conflict accelerated destruction. It was not possible to hold a monopoly on the plentiful copper supply.

States were further bound by trading relationships. The emergence of iron did not supplant copper trading, but it was now smaller entities which carried on the activity, driven by family groups. Bronze was also a transforming material. It afforded new opportunities for the artistic representation of the human body, consolidating its use as a central human commodity. This was now available for wide exploitation. Phoenician and Greek entrepreneurialism expanded commercial scope.

The Phoenician model of trading through membership of interrelated guilds, dominated by merchant-princes, followed that of Sumerian temple-capitalism in a similar blurring of the public and private. However, the sea-going Phoenicians expanded upon existing, and added further, regulation and control in business. Managed protection of trade product secrecy was exemplified by the imposition of the death penalty for revelation of the process of extracting from murex shellfish the ancient world's only colour-fast dye: Tyrian purple, which clothed the most opulent and was worth more than its weight in gold. Knowledge acquisition and management developed seafaring capacity. The rise of Athenian power was partly attributable to the maritime capacity underpinning the strength of its trading base, and its foundation on a rule of law, with open access to outsider participation. The emergence of the entrepreneurial private Greek trader came as the age of bronze was supplanted by that of iron. Such development was not welcomed by Homer, who recorded their huckster image, but the very need for security in trading impelled organisational development.

Ashurbanipal (r. 669-631; d. 631), last great king of Assyria, noted for his cruelty, was an avid literary collector. His library was spread across two locations, and amassed a collection of some 30,000 cuneiform tablets, comprising some 10,000 texts, together with further numerous writing boards and hieroglyph papyri. The Gilgamesh epic was discovered in the collection. Despite the monarch's acquisitive obsession, securing many texts through the fear his reputation inspired, the materials were finite, declining in number through time. A major fire resulted in mixture of loss, breakage, and preservation; although many artefacts were destroyed or broken, the heat of the fire baked many of the fragmented tablets, thereby ensuring a form of preservation.

As the story of Ashurbanipal's library indicates, scribes and scribal education had become conservative. Knowledge of some 600 signs was necessary to read hieroglyphics; knowledge of 300 was required in the case of cuneiform. There had been many more to begin with, but scribes had been able to reduce them as they became more familiar with the forms of sounds each sign produced. The signs then stayed the same for millennia, routinely taught at scribe training schools. Curriculum was static.

Using cuneiform wedges on clay to record syllables; names; lists of names; and parts of trees, for instance, provided working nouns. It was from such nouns that numbers, and by extension multiplication tables, might be learned. After a long elementary period, pupils began to learn how to write: whole sentences; model legal documents and contracts; proverbs; and pieces of literature through copying and listening, again and again. Pupil numbers were small, tuition groups minimal. Each city had only a few dozen literate citizens. Most pharaohs could read and write, but money was needed to pay teachers the fees necessary to produce scribes.

It had been long known that objects could be put together to make words and sounds. The most obviously quoted example is "thin" plus "king." Abstract and concrete ideas, concepts, riddles, and poetry could be accessed using this method. A brilliant, unsung genius in the port town of Byblos, Lebanon had the idea to take this further. It was possible to go from a picture of water, to the wavy lines of a wave (www), to syllables of water, and finally to a w. Some words have names which contain sounds, like Cleopatra, but the Egyptians had not realised they had a sound system inside their script: picture>syllable>sign. WWW was wavy water; d was a door. The end sign was that of the language of choice - in this case, that of the Semitic Canaanite inventors.

The Byblos invention occurred around 1,000 BCE, where it stayed in its small local area for many years. The alphabet spread via immigration, trade, and power structures, but the conservative Assyrians held on to their cuneiform because it was the long-established form of the communication of power and control; they left this upstart alphabet for less important matters. Trading Phoenicians, who were West Canaanites, took the alphabet across the Mediterranean, where they encountered Greeks moving east. As the Bronze Age Collapse broke down the old systems, tribal states like Israel did not use the old cuneiform and hieroglyph systems, rejecting the old scribal hand method.

From the Phoenicians, Greeks were learning the trade system of recording transactions in writing. They, too, wanted a method of common accounting to better inhibit cheating. The Phoenicians had worked on the innovation: content was standardised, letters of uniform size, written from left to right. However, the Canaanite alphabet of 22 letters was without vowels and the Greeks needed vowels. They, therefore, turned various sound signs they did not use into a sign for each sound, not a syllable. Language was broken down into the sounds of its speakers. By the first half of the $8^{th}$ century, the alphabet had appeared in an unofficial form: in scribbles, graffiti, and the Greek habit of annotating pieces of broken pot. We may deduce that Homer was writing very early in the alphabet's history.

Although most western historical attention is paid to the Graeco-Phoenician conjunction, the alphabet also travelled on to southern Iraq, then to India. A brief summary of the whole birth of writing might read:

> **Cuneiform:** the bureaucrat's implement of choice.
> **Hieroglyph:** a tool of display, for showing off.
> **Alphabet:** the merchant's essential.

Known to inhabit the area of Lebanon from around 3,200 BCE, settled in cities such as Tyre and Sidonia with which they identified rather than the general description derived from their dye export, "purple people" Phoenicians had expanded around the Mediterranean, establishing trade colonies. They had adapted and exported the invention through the north Syrian port city of Ugarit around 1,400 BCE, of the written version of the 30 letters corresponding to sounds inscribed on clay tablets - although oral method would have been earlier. Able to prove ownership and raise contracts, this invaluable trade management tool was communicated to Greece, as Herodotus records, here dated to around 750 BCE.

Endowed with a geography plentiful in trees but a rocky terrain inimical to agriculture (which assisted the development of sophisticated farming), the

Phoenicians naturally turned to the sea. Their crafting of the finest, fastest ships based on the "cut water" of a sharp prow assisted their domination of trade routes across the Mediterranean. Propellant deployment was usually by sail at sea, with oars used to negotiate harbour entry and exit. With eyes painted at the prows, they conceived of their ships as living creatures. To placate the gods and insure against bloodletting occurring at sea, vessels were ridden over the bodies of slaves and warfare captives at their launch. Such superstition descended to the sacrifice of children aged between one and two months in such colonies as Carthage, Sardinia and Sicily.

The temples of the Phoenician city of Tyre exemplified management through the conjunction of religion with trade as a means of control and regulation. Temples were the sites of deal making with priestly oversight; weights and measures were standardised, with priests as notaries, and their gods serving as fear symbols against fraud and breach of contract. International admission to Phoenician trading thus became entry to a form of religious common market, the further currency of which was knowledge access, assisting the expansion of the business network throughout the Mediterranean on a regulated basis.

Establishing trade colonies most famously at Carthage and in Spain, Tyre's god Melqart, equivalent to Hercules, was the export and symbol of the new trading management culture, and was absorbed into the local pantheons. With ships led by an image of the chief goddess Astarte (the original figurehead), wherever the presence of Melqart was established, technology transfer in shipbuilding, bronze and, eventually, iron working followed. Religion followed trade routes. Ironically, it was the trade route infrastructure of the Roman Empire which later allowed Paul of Tarsus to evangelise from such regional centres as Ephesus and Thessaly. Thus, he sowed the seeds of the monotheistic belief system which would eventually overwhelm and take over the very definition of what it meant to be Roman

Such definition, combined with religion, provided for confirmation through an oath. This "conditional self-curse" was of three parts. A declaration was an assertion that something was the case, or promising to do something in the future: an assertion or promissory oath. Specific superior powers were invoked to mete out punishment were the oath to be false, such forces usually being gods or emphasised through the swearing on sacred objects. The curse being called down upon oneself was either specified or left to be understood.

The earliest written record of an oath refers to a 1280 BCE treaty of vassalage wherein the Hittite monarch would recognise only a line of kings. Use of oaths was made by both sides in the *Iliad*. Oath swearing could be accompanied by, or made part of, the sacrifice of an animal, or pouring wine onto the earth as a libation. Observers of today's lawyers may see such pre-legal management practices perpetuated as ritual forms of contract and magic.

To ancient peoples, an oath was statement validated by a superhuman power. If the promise was not carried out, the power would exact punishment. The promise did not carry divine retribution in or of itself: that came with the force it was sworn by. In a largely illiterate society, the issue was belief in what you said - a condition also naturally pertinent to the literate. Similarly, the power of the oath depended on its strength and belief: "by almighty Melqart/Zeus/Jupiter..." Difficulty arose in foreign relations where the gods invoked were not necessarily believed in by all parties. Generally, however, the oath was a successful managerial instrument of control whereby society could be kept in order, as vividly illustrated in democratic Athenian and Roman self and state identity. In the administration of local government under the Empire, officials and persons of consequence swore an oath to uphold Emperor and Empire.

While false witness was punished in the ancient world, perjury was not. Such offence was left for punishment by the supreme power; oath breaking was a matter for the gods. As noted, as there was an immunity where parties could not be bound by others' gods. Therefore, in the swearing of oaths to treaties, terms had to be agreed with as little room for the inevitable reinterpretations as possible. Those known to break oaths without due cause could suffer public ostracism or other punishment. Such practice extended to sports; athletes for the Olympics were required to swear that they had been in training for the prescribed period, and judges were to swear that they would judge impartially. They would be penalised by having to erect a statue for Zeus if this were not so. The remains of the stadium at Olympia show the bases of many statues erected for Zeus.

Ultimately, these were practical matters. "There are no sure oaths between men and lions" said victorious Achilles as he refused the dying Hector's plea for him to swear provision of a decent burial. Lysander, (d.395), the Spartan admiral who wished to replace the Athenian Empire with a Spartan hegemony, as recorded by Plutarch cynically observed: "You cheat boys with dice, but men with oaths".[13] Notoriously untrustworthy, he knew that of which he spoke.

Maritime trading relied heavily on trust, for a captain could easily disappear. This entailed restricted partnership numbers and provision against risk. Trading partnerships were, thus, small businesses, with the land counterparts also restricted in size. The biggest business, as always, was the arms trade. However, even the largest of such, the shield factories, appear not to have employed more than 100 slaves.[14] Management was family-based and autocratic. Even so, the practice of management – what those possessing or charged with managerial authority actually did – mattered, for that was the direct element of production most likely to produce competitive edge.

Both recording through writing and comprehension through reading were not possible to communicate by informal means, and so a formal setting had become an early necessity. Thus, schools arose – but they were not for everyone. Their purpose was to inform, instruct, and perpetuate the elite. Due to the process being administered to children, whose natural behaviour was not always necessarily in conformity with adult requirements, violence became part of the package. An ancient Egyptian clay tablet records the process: "Thou didst beat me and knowledge entered my head".[15] Management by coercion began early. Scribal educators, however, knew that their job was the best their society could offer:

> I will make you love books more than your own mother…
> The scribal profession is greater than any other.
> There is nothing like it on earth.[16]

The beaten youth was probably of a successful family and attending scribe school. Craft apprenticeships within families served the social levels below, with the Prince's School above undertaking the education of the children of the royal family, nobility, and high-ranking officials.

Knowledge resided in the military, where in Persia children were trained in horsemanship, archery, and telling the truth. According to Herodotus, this began as early as the age of five.[17] Lying was deemed the worst of offenses; military prowess, the greatest of virtues. At court from the age of 16, noble youths were instructed in justice, obedience, self-restraint, government, temperance, courage, worship of the gods, riding, archery, spear-throwing, and hunting. In areas under Persian control such as Egypt and Babylonia, formal education in scribe schools contained grammar, mathematics, and astronomy. However, literacy reached the levels of crafts and tradesmen in societies more advanced than their conqueror's: business need created access. Restrictions remained however: education was only for boys and, an Egyptian dignitary reported, there were no children of "nobodies" in the medical school restored by Darius I (550-487 BCE).[18]

Outside the direct military, trade, and craft contexts, the process of education was first administered by those in charge of literacy: the scribes of the court or the temple, where these were distinguishable from each other. Such methodology in Europe persisted throughout medieval times until technology interfered. Only the advent of printing opened the way into the secret garden of literacy. In the meantime, the ancient Greeks had interposed the third process of learning: the discussion and discovery of meanings in life and ways in which to live and govern that life, known as philosophy: "love of wisdom." The cans of worms there opened sufficed to inform and bedevil civilised existence up to, and including, our own day.

What was then the pastime of the rich and the elite is now accessible to all. We might sadly reflect, chastened indeed, that the Internet ravings of the adherents of violent *jihadists*, fake news, and vindictive trolls fall far below the standards of debate set out by Socrates, Plato, and Aristotle. Once the genie was out of the educatory bottle, the issue was input and control as well as output.

The Jews were the first people to realise the dilemma, but not the first to devise a belief system of control. While the Jews had the words of God to go by, scripture to rely on, with a persuasive history to back up the story, it was a Persian king who had seen that obedience could best be ensured by belief. In as bold an example of leadership as the world had then seen, "die for me in battle and you will have everlasting life", promised Darius I the Great, King of Kings and Pharaoh of Egypt. The Jewish collective answer to create unity of nation, religion, and rules for living, with the aspiration of statehood, was the rabbinical system.

The synagogue was as much for education at it was for religion. Basic numeracy and literacy were taught from the ages of from six to thirteen, after which brighter youth had access to the rabbi in educational as well as religious contexts. The rabbi had to be known within the community as a person of superior intelligence, education, and knowledge to have attained such a position. One prime and very obvious reason for the greater success in business of Jewish people was the simple reality of their being better educated.

The exploitation of success was something which also characterised the Greeks. Not a nation state but an agglomeration of some two thousand city states scattered around the Black and Mediterranean seas, the Greeks had a very clear idea of their own identity, even though it underwent constant transformation. There were the Greeks, and the others, the rest, termed "barbarians". However, the root of the word *barbarous* is Mesopotamian; the Greeks used a barbarian word to describe barbarians, and therein lay the key to their genius. They used the entrepreneurial management techniques of research, copy, adapt, and improve better than any people had before. In learning from their neighbours, they amassed the basics for the establishment of the greatest cultural and commercial flowering of the ancient world.

They learned geometry from the Babylonians, art and architecture from the Egyptians, and metal working from the Scythians. The great military and transport advances of the chariot were derived from Scythian technology. Phonetics came from Phoenicia, their east Mediterranean neighbours in the Levant. Thus, the alphabet allowed the writing of sounds into words, replacing the cuneiform method of recording. Whereas stylus on wax tablet, stone inscriptions, and writing on papyrus served more formal needs, everyday accounting, notation, and messaging was effected through the economical recycling of broken pottery, typically the neck and shoulders of amphorae, executed in ink by reed pens.

Amphora, a ceramic container with a characteristic pointed bottom and shape, was the ancient world's bulk container of choice: from wine and olive oil to fish sauce (*garum*) and other liquids. They fit closely together in storage, or could be tied together with rope and easily transported by land or sea. The ancient Greek variety could provide for a cargo of 300 amphorae of grain, the equivalent of around 6,200 litres. Later Roman standard size (recorded with other essential weights and measures' standards at the

Temple of Jupiter) provided for an approximate yield of 8,350 litres from a 300 amphorae cargo. Discoveries of shipwreck remains provide for continuingly useful archaeological evidence. By the second century CE, a typical ship of 75 tonnes could carry 1,500 amphorae. Cheap and in plentiful supply, there being no reason to return to place of origin, amphorae were frequently broken up after contents discharge. Recycled in broken form, they provided the writing surface for annotation of all forms, including tax receipts.

Ink could be made simply from lampblack, vegetation such as hawthorn bark, and animal and mineral sources. Official Athenian notices were posted on wooden boards, displayed in the Agora, the market place. Known as *ostraca,* broken pottery shards were multifunctional, even used in official contexts as permits, tax receipts and voting materials, for instance. In 5th century Athens, persons deemed to be dangerous to democracy were voted upon by casting ostraca into a pot. When a certain number of ostracon was reached, the culprit was expelled for ten years and thus ostracised, a continuing form of social management (albeit now conducted informally).

In its development of societal policy and management, ancient Greek culture had new and different goals to present. Its pantheism, with deities formed in resemblance of human attributes, allowed for secular thought and escape from the dominance of religious control. Religious observance remained important, often of a sacrificial nature. As it was especially necessary not to annoy or provoke the gods, placation and pleading were as prevalent as worship, but the educative role was preparation to serve the state as a good citizen. What constituted good citizenship varied according to the nature of the city state, or later the kingdom or empire.

Such debate reflected the widespread intellectual development of the 6th and 5th centuries BCE. Progress emanated from accumulated expertise in food production. A burst of energy was provided to humanity between 500 and 300 BCE in the Eastern Mediterranean, Ganges, Yangtse and Yellow River valleys by a more-than 20,000 calories per person intake in food, fodder, fuel and raw materials.[19] Drastically improved agricultural, transport, and logistical management allowed civilisation to develop. Larger cities could be afforded, with scholarly and priestly classes. Short-term survival strategies with propitiatory and sacrificial emphasis could be balanced, if not replaced, by long-term goals of harmony, attainable through asceticism and self-control.

**FOOTPRINT:**
**Humanity Comes into Existence**

- **Humanity as we know it had come into existence with improved, if imperfect, management.**

- **How much of our instinctive managerial behaviour is inherited, subject to evolutionary and genetic influence, or part of our animal nature, and therefore itself manageable, let alone quantifiable, remain matters of academic speculation.**

- **Humanity's growth has been largely uncontrolled. At 10,000 BCE, there were around four million people. Now, there are approaching eight billion.**

## Endnotes

[1] Christopher Booker (1937-2019) took 34 years to write his 2004 *The Seven Basic Plots: Why We Tell Stories* (Continuum, 2006), in which he argued that however many characters appear in a story, each is an expression only of some aspects of the heroic central figure. That figure then leads the story, which may take the forms of: overcoming the monster; rags to riches; the quest; voyage and return; comedy; tragedy; and rebirth. Some critics have disputed Booker's categories but story telling management remains central to the fiction industries, from video gaming to Hollywood and the high literary.

[2] Pinker, Steven. 2011. *The Better Angels of Our Nature.* London: Penguin; Pinker, Steven. 2019. *Enlightenment Now.* London: Penguin.

[3] Harari, Yuval Noah. 2015. *Sapiens A Brief History of Humankind.* London: Vintage.

[4] Graeber, David and Wengrow, David. 2022. *The Dawn of Everything A New History of Humanity.* London: Penguin.

[5] *Ibid.* p. 4.

[6] *Ibid.* pp. 274 – 275.

[7] *Ibid.* p. 326.

[8] *Ibid.* p. 337.

[9] *Ibid.* p. 525.

[10] Colbert, Elizabeth, *Under a White Sky,* pp. 187 – 197.

[11] Boorn, GPF van den. 2013. *Duties of the Vizier*. London: Routledge.

[12] Ryan, Donald P, *24 hours in Ancient Egypt*, pp.136-140.

[13] Plutarch, *Lives*; "Lysander", 293.

[14] Harris, Edward M. et al. ed., *The Ancient Greek Economy: Markets, Households and City-States,* p.161.

[15] Guisepi, Robert ed. *The History of Education*, International World History Project, history-world.org/history_of_education.htm. A c. 2,000 BCE Mesopotamian writing exercise records a pupil being caned successively for an omission in writing; rising; speaking; speaking in another language; and leaving the premises, all without permission. Houston, Stephen D, ed. *The First Writing: Script Invention as History and Process*, p.222

[16] Ryan, Donald P, *op. cit.,* p.115: *Satire of the Trades.*

[17] Herodotus, *The Histories*, 1.136.

[18] *Education In the Achaemenid Period*, Encyclopedia Iranica, Vol. VIII, Fasc.2, pp. 178-179; quoting Posener, G. 1936. *La premiere domination Perse en Egypte,* Cairo.

[19] Baumard, Nicolas *et al.,* "Increased Affluence Explains the Emergence of Ascetic Wisdoms and Moralising Religions," *Current Biology,* Volume 25, p.11.

# CHAPTER TWO

# MANAGING GODS

Of all the ancient mythical figures, Zeus, god of order, is the most applicable to our present condition. The Hellenistic bardic tradition was concerned with exploring and explaining the world, the universe, and all therein and there under. That exploration culminated in a mixture of religion, superstition, and a broad rationale for the entire system.[1] The earliest written evidence appears in the works attributed to Homer, conventionally dated to the 8th century BCE, describing events 400 years earlier: an Iron Age commentary on Bronze Age events. The *Iliad* is concerned with the Trojan Wars, in which Achilles was an archetypal hero, Athena favoured the Greeks, Apollo the Trojans, and Zeus remained neutral. The system was that within which humans had to manage. The manager, CEO of the whole enterprise, was Zeus. His accession to managerial power had not been easy.

At the commencement of the concept of creation was Chaos. The Chaos which began everything is the same entity to which all will return. Out of Chaos came darkness and night, day and light. Gaia, the earth; Tartarus, the depths below the earth; and Ouranos, the sky, were formed simultaneously as principles, not gods. Gaia achieved the virgin birth of the sea, Pontus. Ouranos seeded mother Gaia but their progeny was of mixed appeal. Some were so revolting that Ouranos thrust them back inside Gaia's womb. Furious and in pain, Gaia sought revenge. Long denying Ouranos her favours, she sought the assistance of her Titan children, primordial gods. As she appeared to relent, Ouranos was about to cover her, when Kronos pounced, slicing off his father's genitals in one mighty sweep of his sickle. Life sprang forth from each drop of the spilt divine blood, the first shoots to appear being the Furies of remorseless, jealous rage and vengeance (Alecto, Megaera and Tisiphone), known thereafter in placatory fashion as the Eumenides, the "kindly ones."

Ouranos cursed all his offspring to suffer from straining ambition (hence the Titan name) as his youngest son led him deep into Tartarus, where his huge destructive power would be buried - and so it was, until uranium was mined and released, millennia later. Kronos's further act of dispatch was to hurl his father's severed genitals far into the sea, from which the very opposite of evil destruction emerged from the foam: Aphrodite, perfect love and beauty, known to the Romans as Venus, from whom Julius Caesar traced his ancestry.

Kronos, with his sister Rhea as his queen, reigned supreme over the Golden Age, where law was unnecessary as everyone did the right thing - except Kronos. Haunted by prophesy that he would be overthrown by his own child, he ate his offspring immediately after birth. The increasingly angered mother tricked him into unwittingly allowing one, Zeus, to survive. Shock at the discovery caused Kronos's indigestion to be cured, at the cost of all the regurgitated siblings pledging loyalty to Zeus: they would all be gods, ruled by him. The Titan Civil War began. Battle lines were drawn: Zeus and loyal Titans against Kronos, dissident Titans, and their Giant allies. Both sides bred and multiplied. Zeus was particularly profligate, fulfilling what he saw as his duty whilst also having fun. Thus, the Charities; the Three Graces; the Horai, responsible for law and justice; the Fates, spinning the threads of life; the Muses; and the spirits of air, earth, and water came into existence, their function being to inspire. Once the battle was won, the defeated Titans and victor couplings were put to work. Clio "the Proclaimer," daughter of Mnemosyne by Zeus, became the Muse of History.

Revenge on Kronos, who Zeus could not kill, was condemnation to pace the earth for eternity, sickle in hand, measuring out each second, his image forever as that atop the pavilion of Lord's cricket ground: Old Father Time, (pictured on the next page) giving his name to chronic, chronology, and chronicle for evermore.

Zeus and allies set up their god business. At their seat of power on Mount Olympus, they ruled as King, Queen, and ten oligarchs. Some of them were difficult. One was a headache, right at the start, being born out of Zeus's head by cranial excision; Athena's wisdom came at a cost. Each had a responsibility, like Poseidon's for the sea. Apollo was lord of mathematics, reason, logic, medicine, rhetoric, settlement, knowledge, the golden sun, and enlightenment – spiked by the arrows of disease, predatory as a wolf but guardian of justice. While Artemis, the chaste female huntress, was named Diana by Rome; and Ares, god of war, became Mars; Apollo remained Apollo.

**Old Father Time**

After the life size weathervane at Lord's cricket ground,
closing play for the day

This family business had its difficulties. Zeus didn't like Ares who, curiously, got on well with Aphrodite. His wife, Hera, did not get on at all well with Zeus's by-blows, of which there were many, due to his shape-shifting abilities, fathering heroes, immortals and others promiscuously.

So jealously vengeful did Hera become that she caused the deaths of various humans with whom Zeus had intimate relationships. He rescued the foetus of one these, Dionysus, nurturing him from his thigh. So attached was Zeus that he insisted that Dionysus be a god, resident on Olympus. The implacable Hera persecuted Dionysus.

To escape, Dionysus travelled, where he discovered vines, grapes, and the arts of viticulture, spreading the joys of wine among humanity. At one end of the spectrum was the free thought and expression it provoked, conviviality and companionship; at the other was inebriation, loss of control, and debauchery. Thus, leopard skinned Dionysus became known as

*Liber*, the liberator. He was also notorious in his Roman guise as Bacchus, where rites in his honour could lead to extremes and excess. His benefits and demerits to humanity continue – matters of management.

It was Zeus's Titan friend, Prometheus, who caused the greatest bother. To entertain the gods, he had made little figures out of clay, which he fashioned from the four elements. That was acceptable but there was a prohibition: on no account were these *Anthropos*, humans, to have fire. That said, Zeus approved and humanity rapidly spread itself throughout the world. The humans enjoyed participation in the Golden Age: free food for all, serial cereals, courtesy of the goddess Demeter (who the Romans knew as Ceres). There was no war, famine, disease, or poverty, only innocence and easy harvesting; a charming idyll of the earth and humanity at their best. Prometheus had a problem, however. He thought that, to truly appreciate life and progress, these creatures needed fire.

Surreptitiously slipping into Olympus, Prometheus took a fennel stalk, lit it in the fire of the gods, and scampered down to the villages below, bearing his gift and demonstrating its uses. Looking down, Zeus saw what was happening. He went into an almighty rage. Fire was not just physical heat, it was energy: mental force, physical action. With this theft, *Anthropos* could use and usurp the power of the gods, rendering them redundant. Worse, these unreliable, irresponsible, and unpredictable humans could play with fire. They might develop its power - the road to nuclear warfare, mass extinction and planetary destruction was open. Zeus, victor over Kronos, Giants, and Titans, had a very major management problem on his hands. And it had been begun not by enemies or a family squabble, but by a friend: a betrayal. What to do with the traitor? What to do with the *Anthropos?*

Hesiod, the first known ancient Greek written poet who lived between 750 and 650 BCE, also provided the first written versions of Greek myths. He related that Zeus caused the creation of a beautiful girl, upon whom the gods conferred multiple talents and attributes, thus naming her All-Gifted or All-Giving, Pandora in Greek. She was characterised by Hesiod more ambiguously as "a beautiful evil". To be married to Epimetheus ("Afterthought"), brother of Prometheus ("Fore-thought"), Zeus sent a parting gift in a container which she was forbidden to open. Pandora's curiosity drove her to disobey. Thus ended the Golden Age, for as part of Zeus' revenge, out flew the descendants of the goddesses of darkness and the night: old age, misery, deceit, blame, violent death, ruin, discord, hardship, pain, quarrels, disputes, fraud, lies, wars, battles, manslaughter, and murder. Realizing the horror, Pandora hurriedly closed the box, trapping inside one forlorn creature: hope.

Nonetheless, the human beings could now breed and use their gift of fire, learning to live life independently in what was now the Silver Age.

They sacrificed to Zeus, who monitored the progress of this new humanity. No paragon himself, Zeus nonetheless knew right from wrong. There were certain things which just weren't done. The king of Arcadia, Lycaon, killed and roasted his son, whom he served to Zeus, who had come as a guest to his palace, as a test of his omnipotence. So revolted was Zeus that he turned Lycaon into a wolf, bequeathing the word, if not the deed, to humans as lycanthropy, and determined to end the entire ghastly human experiment by summoning up a storm so great as to flood the entire Greek world. All were drowned, except for two: the son of Prometheus, and Epimetheus's daughter, the foreseeing fire-giver having provided another box, an equipped wooden survival chest. The survivors, however, had a further problem. They were old, with the woman well past child bearing age.

Rescue came from Apollo's oracle at Delphi, which advised them to find their mother's bones, and throw them over their shoulders. As their parents were immortal and thus in full, permanent possession of their skeletons, the oracle's instruction presented a further difficulty. Perhaps Athena or Apollo gave them a nudge but the survivors eventually cracked the problem. Gaia was their true, ultimate mother and her bones were all around them. So, they picked up the rocks and stones on the pathway from Delphi, throwing them over their shoulders. When they looked back, they saw the gathering swarms of busy, new humanity. These humans were born of the parental and family generosity, curiosity, loyalty, and impetuosity of tricky Prometheus, with the further ability of Epimetheus to reflect and consider what they did, plus all the gifts of the gods of Olympus, and made flesh from and by mother earth. Only one final task awaited Prometheus.

In order for his new humanity to survive, Zeus had to be appeased for the theft of fire, the great betrayal. To save his people from the further wrath of Zeus, there must be sacrifice. When Zeus, transformed into an eagle for the purpose, called for vengeance, Prometheus submitted to being chained to a rock whilst his doom was pronounced. His liver was to be pecked out and eaten, every day, by an eagle sent by Zeus. As Prometheus was immortal, he would not die. At day's end, he could sleep, reawaken the next with a renewed liver, sentenced for the process to be repeated for eternity.

As humanity multiplied, the gods did, too. Division of labour was necessary. The ultimate pantheon became its own expanding universe. One cause for expansion was the promiscuity of Zeus. Hera became increasingly angry with incessant infidelity, focusing her enmity on Zeus's products with humans. One of these, apparent heir to a throne, had his name changed to Heracles to appease her. Her behaviour merely worsened. She delayed his birth so that the throne went to another, who joined her in subsequent persecution. He survived, only for the usurper to conspire with Hera to set Heracles a number of tasks to which, on completion, two more were added. Each of these heroic tales of Heracles's strength and virtue were accomplished against immense odds. Upon conclusion, the hero – for Heracles was the leading member of that sub group below the Olympians, the heroes – sets about many further, spectacular adventures. One of his missions was to free Prometheus, which he achieved by shooting the eagle with an arrow and releasing the Titan from his chains. Prometheus, who knew rescue would come sometime, was now free to help humanity.

After many more heroics, valiant Heracles is treacherously poisoned, builds and mounts his own funeral pyre and, as his human part dies, Zeus raises him to Olympus as a god. Shape-shifting Zeus had that accomplishment practiced upon him when the Romans conquered the Greek world, transforming him into Jupiter, but the mythology continued, and multiplied further.

The Romans made Heracles into Hercules, Athena into Minerva. They practiced religious toleration in allowing conquered peoples to keep their own gods, while appropriating many as their own. Only monotheism was an issue, for that threatened the entire social fabric.

The Indo-Persian origin Mithra, Mithras in Greek, was a mystery god cult popular in the Roman army, meeting underground and with a recognition handshake. The Bona Dea (Good Goddess) cult was female only, the sole Roman religion to allow women to practice blood sacrifice and enjoy the consumption of strong wine. The advance of the functions of ancient society can be tracked through the acquisition and growth of gods. Myth is potent. They were also the change agents of multiple transformations: humans and other life forms, such as nymphs, might become plants, rivers, stones, and animals for reasons ranging from punishment to pity, enlivened many a tale of morality, humour or revenge.

The gods presented a form of social psychology, their characteristics being exposition of behaviour, examples, and warnings. Libertine drunks like the lower order mythical creature Silenus (companion and tutor to the wine god Dionysus), while not an Olympian himself, typified the type of behaviour which might still be witnessed in certain Mediterranean and Mexican resorts for the young today. Entertaining, moral, immoral, and amoral, but nonetheless overall about "doing the right thing," crime and punishment, the mythology provided an explanation of people and life, with advice for living – and reminders of the capriciousness of external forces. During Caesar's Gallic campaign, he practised psychological warfare. The Gauls followed Druidic religion which involved rituals conducted within groves in woods. To lower the opposition's morale, Caesar cut down the trees. Destruction of others' gods, so emerging as winner overall, further assisted the acceptance of conquest by the vanquished and the paying of obedience thereafter.

There is nothing new about such management concepts as "radical uncertainty." Gods and spirits were everywhere. Many were local. The deities of the river, dryads of the woods, and sylphs hovering over the traveller's pathway had all to be paid respect. The *lares* and *penates* served as gods of the hearth and home. Underpinning much ancient religion was the belief that gods could intervene in matters beyond human power, solving such matters as fertility, health, and the weather. In exchange for their mastery over plants and animals, humans offered devotion, sacrifice, and respect. The gods might be worshiped, placated, appealed to, glorified, or housed in temples but, most importantly, were not to be offended or annoyed, and the Fates certainly not tempted.

At the small picture level, among the defining characteristics of ancient religion was the choice available for individual adherence and the need for recognition through dedication and sacrifice (usually of animals). Today, the traveling salesperson might sport a St Christopher medallion dangling from a vehicle rear view mirror. The Roman traveling merchant would probably have carried a small image of a personal god of choice, the standard being Mercury, with a supplement of Neptune if goods were to travel by sea. The all-purpose insurance and thanksgiving policy of an altar dedicated to Jupiter Optimus Maximus as a permanent memorial, if affordable, would be wise. The identity of the mover of the invisible hand might not be certain, but acknowledgment of the best and greatest was sensible.

Moreover, there was a powerful presence of justice, social order, and communal assemblies. Law was among Apollo's many responsibilities but

Themis, another Titan and known as "the lady of good counsel," stood as the personification of divine order, fairness, natural law, and custom. This was symbolised by her holding the scales of justice. Pragmatic and balanced, Themis stood for a divine law rather than human construct, and for proper procedure and custom. Dike, her daughter by Zeus, represented moral justice and human law. She was put on earth by her father to keep humans just. Realising that this was impossible, Zeus relocated her to Olympus. As overlord, law, order, and justice remained the primary concerns of Zeus, his chosen methods of retribution being thunder and lightning.

Under continuing elemental threat, humans were thus responsible for local administration, in support of which they developed approaches to determine ethics, this being "character" or "custom": being, embracing, or doing "the right thing." Ethics, from this root, is communal. Morals are individual matters, but the discussion and investigation thereof as moral philosophy takes the form of ethics.

Humans might have taken on some of the gods' powers and responsibilities, but Zeus' retributive thunderbolt, real or perceived, could take as many forms as its shape-shifting master; Hera's vengeance was deadly; and Apollo's arrows mortal dangers. Fear was an important component of the system, compounded by the gods' capacity for capriciousness. There is a very clear message in the mythology, worth repeating: do not presume, anger, or, especially, insult the gods; they are not to be trusted, bargained with, or believed, for their blessings might turn out to be the reverse, and their promises merely lures to destruction; and as their power is absolute but their insecurity high, any form of impiety is highly dangerous.

That element was crucial to the bothersome philosopher Socrates. Although his advances in ethical thinking were great, founding the principles upon which his followers Plato and Aristotle built and providing a base from which debate continues today, his constant questioning of people was destabilising the state in the view of the rulers of Athens at a difficult time in the long Peloponnesian War. His attitude and the nature of his questioning gave rise to charges of offending the gods, so imperilling all citizens. He was put on trial for corrupting the minds of youth and impiety: "not believing in the gods of the state." Sentenced to death, he complied to show loyalty. Allowed to choose the means of dispatch, he chose hemlock tea. It first numbed his limbs, then his body, allowing him to manage his departure, conversing with friends to the end.

The works of his recorder and follower Plato show acceptance of the Golden Age ideal. While historical method and science had been established by the times of Socrates, Plato, and Aristotle, myth remained a most pervasive influence upon life and its management.

**Aristotle, with Plato in rear**

Roman copy of an original,
carved 325 – 300 BCE.
National Archaeological Museum
of Athens

When Aristotle's pupil Alexander the Great (356-323 BCE) was campaigning in Egypt, he made a diversion into the Libyan desert to Siwah. With supposedly divine assistance, he found the shrine of Ammon, a god of the Semitic peoples (Middle and Near Eastern, here particularly Phoenicians and Carthaginians) adopted as an equivalent of Amun, their leading god, by the Egyptians. He was following in the footsteps of a previous visitor, mythical Heracles.

The kings of Macedon claimed direct descent from Heracles, son of Zeus. Olympias, wife to Alexander's father, Philip II, claimed direct descent from Achilles, another of Alexander's personal heroes. It is assumed that Alexander also sought confirmation of descent from Ammon, so having another deity to confirm his ambition. He did not disclose what the oracle said but did progress to conquer Egypt. Contrary to high destiny, Aristotle's pupil and editor Eudemus (c.370-300 BCE) quoted the view of the half-animal Silenus: since it was man's destiny to die, he should achieve that as soon as possible. In that case, it followed that it was good to get drunk quickly, frequently, and excessively. This, Alexander seems to have done as, later, did Peter the Great of Russia. Binge culture is not new. However, the ancient Sumerian Gilgamesh myth had long taught that death was an inevitable human destiny, and that people must learn to live with it. Self-management well knew the context within which to function

Modern management writers and theorists, particularly of ethics, make considerable reference to Aristotle, especially his advocacy of the "good life." It is important, in considering his philosophy, for the context of his times to be recalled and realised. Platonic and Aristotelian thinking was based on logic and rational inquiry, the belief systems in which, and to which, that which was proposed to be applied had to be tacitly recognised - if only to avoid the fate of Socrates. Aristotle's was still a world of gods and monsters, realities which troubled subsequent Islamic and Christian philosophers considering his works. However, reflective of the Platonic republic and the ancient Greek model, from the my Thomas More's (1478-1535) *Utopia* of 1516 onward, the model city state has been a consistent constituent of western idealised, localised governmental management. Some ancient ideas enjoy longevity, as do the gods.

The Muse Urania never gave up, her work an everyday matter in the worlds of astronomy and astrophysics. Whenever and wherever a new celestial object or location is found, it is named often with an ancient myth or creation. Astronomers are forever close to their Muse. The power of myth also demands further recognition, for it is a formidable management tool. Described in a later volume, the Jensen-Meckling Fallacy is a main attributable cause, rooted in an erroneous myth of the distortion of capitalism of the later 20th century. Zeus might still be considering the dispatch of a thunderbolt, if Apollo's COVID-dipped arrows have not been heeded.

Considering the above, managers might reasonably wonder what, other than myth, mystique creation and insight into the management of a powerful group has to do with them or their tasks. One answer is context. This was the world inhabited by Aristotle, still the source for key concepts in management ethics, processes, and theory. They influence some of that taught and offered by business schools today. The relevance is that if any of those wondering or aspirant managers have to encounter academe in their acquisition of qualifications or training, then they will know where some of their teachers are coming from, thus the better to be able to learn from them, challenge them, and profit from the experience.

Another answer is that the ancients lived in an unpredictable, partially known and understood world of autocratic, idiosyncratic, capricious management, where all had to shift as best they might. Autocracy was usual by the time of written records, despite such episodes as Athenian democracy and the Spartacus revolt; management was done by state bureaucracy, family, or connection in business; and sacrifices made to the unpredictable gods. How management principles, practice, and behaviour have developed since is discussed in this and subsequent publications.

A further answer is that offered by *Sapiens*, in which Yuval Noah Harari claims that all large-scale human co-operation systems – including religions, institutions, trading and political structures, and hence their management – owe their emergence to *homo sapiens*' distinctive creative cognitive capacity for fiction: explanatory, justifying, myth.[2] Thus, Harari sees money as a mutual trust system, with political and economic systems as essentially ideological, like religions. His argument runs further: through its advances in biology and information technology, humans have become what Ouranos, Kronos, and Zeus feared: gods who may control their environment and, through genetic engineering, control creation.

This is the "big picture" of management. It posits that the present state of our planet is what it is because humans cooperated and interacted to produce what we have today, overcoming the gods of the ancients - this being based on our capacity for imagination and the creation of realities. We're all Zeus now. In all that follows therefore, we are considering how humans managed to get to where they are, how that management developed, and where it might take us next. That big picture is composed of as many miniatures as the Hellenic pantheon, significant representatives of which are illustrated below.

However, the problem with big pictures is that, as in physics, small things might behave and exhibit differently to the larger. There is also a human tendency to exaggerate, claiming powers beyond its abilities or influence. This exemplified by the *hubris* of Alfred D. Chandler Jr, who claimed that the visible hand of managerial capitalism could replace an invisible market influence cited by Adam Smith.[3]

The final answer for managers, then, is that the present and future are what you co-operate to construct. Thus, it is essential to be aware of the history of such construction to date. Without appreciation and understanding of the foundations, any architectural successor is overwhelmingly likely to be insecure. It is such insecurity which has brought western liberal democracy to its present crisis. The chaotic combinations of the processes of managerialism, economism, neo-liberalism, neo-conservatism, and the ultimate amoral "value-free values" advocated by the economist Michael Jensen (1939-) compounded by the existentialist challenges of Trumpism, are reminiscent of conditions which prompted Zeus to decisive intervention in human affairs

For the creation of this work, inspiration was necessary. In early Greek mythology, there were three Muses - inspirational goddesses of the arts, science and literature, tradition.  By the time of Hesiod in the 7th and 8th centuries BCE, they had become nine, designated as the daughters of Zeus and Mnemosyne, the Titan goddess of memory. The legislation of the Athenian statesman, law giver, and poet Solon (c.638-c.558 BCE) failed to correct the moral, economic and political decline of the ancient Athens of his day, but he did lay the foundations of Athenian democracy. As a poet, he saw the Muses as "the key to the good life." Their inspiration brought prosperity and friendship by helping people to do their best. By having all debt forgiven, no Athenian remained in serfdom under his chief magistracy, but Solon did not approve of equal shares for all. Rather, "the wise man of Athens" insisted that a balance was to be found between the forces of the poorer and the wealthy few.[4] Looking to justice and a good balance, he sought to prevent power grabbing, tyranny, and oligarchy through the rule of law. The Muses' inspiration to people was thus to be activated through balanced justice, the founding principle of democracy. Consideration of what is later described as the Athena Issue properly begins here.

Depicted as young and beautiful, usually recognizable with scrolls and books and sometimes accompanied by a laurel leaf, Clio served as the Muse of History. The meaning of her name is to recount, celebrate, or make famous: "the proclaimer." Neither management nor education having Muses of their own, we might assume that they are subsumed by Clio, the other Muses, and within the original trinity. It is the Muse of Clio which inspires these pages, in the search for the origins and new beginnings of the "good life" of management, education management, and management education. The purpose is to carry forward that "good life," with "good profit," inspiring friendship and bringing prosperity by helping people to do their best: the task of the management gods.

## Endnotes

[1] The most comprehensive guide to the mythology is to be found at www.theoi.com.; the longstanding comparative study of religion and mythology being Sir James George Fraser's *The Golden Bough* first published by Macmillan in 1890, now an Oxford World Classic and free in the Amazon Electronic version.
[2] Harari, Yuval Noah. 2015. *Sapiens: A Brief History of Humankind*, London: Vintage.
[3] Chandler A D Jr. 1977. *The Visible Hand: The Managerial Revolution in American Business*, Cambridge, Mass.: Harvard University Press.
[4] Solon divided the population into four classes, three of which were citizens: the "five-hundred-bushel-men" (aristocrats); knights (able to provide a horse); and hoplites (able to arm themselves). The lower class were the metics, (metoikos:

"changers of dwelling place") free non-citizens born elsewhere who might, nonetheless, function in such essential occupations as merchants, clerks, soldiers, sailors, priests, and tavern keepers. From ship building and rowing to maintenance, this group were drivers of the economy. Athenian democracy was for the male middle class and above. Foreigners, like the Macedonian Aristotle, might live and work in Athens but were barred from civic activity in government, at law, or residence in certain areas. Slaves, being property, had no rights. Their owners could take legal action if such property were damaged, abused or stolen by others.

# MINI-CASE STUDY (1):
# HOPE

**Hesiod's original telling of the myth describes Zeus' present transported by Pandora as carried in a *pithos*, a jar. This was mistranslated in the 16th century CE by the monk Desiderius Erasmus (1466–1536) as a box, by which Pandora's gift parcel has been popularly known ever since. Zeus had prepared the first part of his cunning revenge against Prometheus. If the beautiful, all-gifted Pandora and her kind could learn obedience, then they could continue to enjoy the idyllic benefits of the Golden Age. If not, then all the evils transported in the jar, as presented by his messenger Hermes, would be imposed upon humanity for eternity. As a curious human, Pandora followed her instincts, with calamitous results. The revenge of Zeus had begun... yet hope was still left in the jar.**

This myth has fascinated commentators, provoking many explanations. Perhaps humanity was to be plagued by all the ills of the world without hope of resolution; for death, anyway, was inevitable. Thus life, and all human endeavour, had to be managed without hope: the fate of Sisyphus. He had twice cheated death, for which his punishment was to push a heavy boulder up a steep slope in Tartarus, the depth of the underworld, only for it to roll down again for eternity. The poet Dante's interpretation was the instruction to all passing through the gates of hell to abandon hope, the implication being that hope had already abandoned them. Thus, even attempting management beyond the endurance of torment was futile: managers should expect only the worst, despite their aspirations. Here, reaching very deep, are the roots of what this work terms "economism."

Yet, even if the rest of the Zeus gift was poisonous, was hope a good, or an evil? Whereas the jar preserves hope for us, in a revenge story how can this be good? To Plato, hope was a passion, one of the drives of the uneducated, but it did have the capacity to allowSoc us to rise above our passions and therefore master ourselves. In Judaism, with time and experience being linear, so is hope, meaning that God will fulfil his promise and come to live with his people.

Building on this, Christianity teaches hope as a good. Christ gives hope to lives otherwise without meaning, whereby people can dwell with God, rising above mortal existence. Apostle Paul put hope firmly as one of the three virtues: faith, hope, and love (charity). To Aquinas, hope became a theological virtue, so called because it was for the next life. Hope for a future glory, a supernatural end which, it appears, we can't achieve by our own power becomes something we want but seems we cannot ourselves attain. Thus, it becomes a virtue given by grace, the means through which Christ completes creation.

Peter Lombard (1096-1160), Bishop of Paris, simplified the theology: if you have faith, you don't need hope. To Luther, faith was central and hope secondary, of itself only a block to faith, and relegated to being a vehicle regarding the second coming. By the time of the Enlightenment, philosophical emphasis had shifted to rationality, the cornerstone of Kant's philosophy. From a rational basis, Kant questioned: what could we hope for? His answer was that, within the limits of reason, hope lay in trying to establish moral ends, in which endeavour God's assistance was to be hoped for.

Perhaps this reached the troubled Nietzsche (1844-1900), for to the young incarnation, hope was a delusion, an evil, quite the worst of all Pandora's gifts. Here, hope was the worst of evils, for it prolonged the agonies of life. Although without hope humans were free to live and enjoy without delusions, the older version saw that hope could give illusions by which we can live, loving life, and so loving hope.

Such late uplift was applied by 20th century existentialists, such as Albert Camus (1913-1960) who held that ultimately Sisyphus, without hope, would have been happy. He would have embraced his fate, loved his rock, and got on with his task. Instead of hoping, the way to cope was through acceptance. To Martin Heidegger (1889-1976), hope became impossible, for assessment could occur only at death, its point of extinction anyway.

The philosophical argument not yet having been settled, unless one has faith, perhaps the most rational solution is to hope for the best whilst preparing for the worst. There are less appropriate ways of addressing, then managing, climate change – and any other managerial issue.

Perhaps a further answer reverts to the passion identified by Plato, and then the object identified as well demonstrated by the American historian, writer, and activist Rebecca Solnit (1961-): "Hope is an axe you break down doors with in an emergency… hope should shove you out the door, because it will take everything you have to steer the future away from endless war, from the annihilation of the earth's treasures and the grinding down of the poor and marginal... To hope is to give yourself to the future, and that commitment to the future makes the present inhabitable."

Another extension is that the last being to be trapped in the box was the most damning of all, for its captivity allowed humans the delusion of being able to achieve. They could be happy, for a while, before the inevitable. As the John Cleese (1939-) headmaster character exclaims in the Michael Frayn (1933-) film *Clockwise*: "It's not the despair … I can stand the despair. It's the hope."

## Case Study Reflections

Please consider the following:

1. What are the arguments for and against managers expressing hope in the success of an enterprise?

2. To what extent should hope be expressed in any activity planning?

3. "Hope for the best; prepare for the worst" is a standard management cliché. How would you express this in any development plan for your work place?

# TIMELINE:
## CLASSICAL ANTIQUITY

Classical antiquity is the title conventionally applied to the intertwined cultures of ancient Greece and Rome. Although Greek development pre-dated the Romans, the population influx to Greece following the Bronze Age Collapse gives sufficient evidence of change to make an equation of parity between the traditional date for the founding of Rome (753 BCE) and the historical recording of the First Olympiad of Greece (c. 776 BCE). Timescale dates, names and brief details are:

| Date | Significant Events |
|---|---|
| 745 BCE | Assyria begins its rise to empire. |
| 700 BCE | Marib dam built in Arabia Felix (modern Yemen and Saudi Arabia). |
| 653 BCE | Rise of Achaemenid Dynasty |
| 612 BCE | Nineveh destroyed by Babylonian, Mede and Scythian alliance, causing subsequent fall of Assyrian Empire. |
| 563–483 BCE | Life of the Buddha (Siddhartha Gautama). |
| 551–479 BCE | Life of Confucius. |
| 550 BCE | Cyrus the Great founds Achaemenid Empire. |
| 546 BCE | Croesus, King of Lydia, defeated by Cyrus the Great. |
| 539 BCE | Fall of the Neo-Babylonian Empire and liberation of the Jews by Cyrus the Great. |
| 529 BCE | Death of Cyrus the Great. |
| 525 BCE | Cambyses II of Persia conquers Egypt. |

| 512 BCE | Darius I (Darius the Great) of Persia - with the subjugation of eastern Thrace, voluntary Macedonian capitulation, and annexation of Libya - extends the empire to its greatest extent. |
| --- | --- |
| 509 BCE | With the expulsion of its last king, Lucius Tarquinius Superbus (the Proud), the Roman Republic (trad.) begins. |
| 508 BCE | Athenian democracy begins at the Republic of Athens. |
| 499 BCE | The Graeco-Persian wars begin when King Aristagoras of Miletus, place of the origin of the Greek traditions of philosophy and science with Thales and Anaximander, incites all his Asia Minor neighbours to rebel against Persia. |
| 490 BCE | At Marathon, Greek city-states defeat Persian invasion. |
| 480 BCE | Xerxes I of Persia defeated by the Athenian-led fleet at Salamis. |
| 470/469-399 BCE | Life of Socrates. |
| 465 BCE | Murder of Xerxes I. |
| 460-370 BCE | Life of Democritus. |
| 449 BCE | Graeco-Persian wars end. |
| 447-432 BCE | Parthenon built. |
| 431 BCE | Peloponnesian War between Greek city-states. |
| 427–348/347 BCE | Life of Plato. |
| 404 BCE | End of Peloponnesian War. |
| 384–322 BCE | Life of Aristotle. |
| 358–281 BCE | The League of Corinth, known also as the Hellenic League, was created by Philip II of Macedon, turned into a Confederation of Greek States under his control to gain revenge against Persia. His son Alexander effectively made Greece a Macedonian possession. |
| 331 BCE | Alexander the Great completes conquest of Persia by defeating Darius III in the Battle of Gaugamela. |

| 326 BCE | Alexander defeats Indian king Porus in the Battle of Hydaspes. |
|---|---|
| 323 BCE | Alexander dies at Babylon. |
| 323–304/5 BCE | Ptolemy I Soter (367–282 BCE), one of Alexander's generals, takes his body to Memphis rather than the intended Macedonia, thence to Alexandria. Winning a power struggle, Ptolemy takes control of Egypt, Cyrenaica and Cyprus, establishes a dynasty which lasts until Cleopatra, becoming Pharoah in 304/05 BCE. |
| 321 BCE | Chandragupta Maurya overthrows the Nanda Dynasty of Magadha. |
| 321 BCE | Seleucus I Nicator (c.358-281 BCE), another of Alexander's generals, manoeuvred after his death to take over the eastern part of Alexander's empire, renamed the Seleucid Empire, which endured until 63 BCE. |
| 305 BCE | Chandragupta Maurya seizes the satrapies of Paropamisadae (Kabul), Aria (Herat), Arachosia (Qandahar, or Kandahar - Alexandria), and Gedrosia (Baluchistan) - Alexander's Afghan territories by conquest, from Seleucus I Nicator, then holding possession as the Macedonian satrap, in return for 500 elephants. |
| 250 BCE | Rise of Parthia as the second ancient dynasty of Persia. |
| 232 BCE | Death of Emperor Ashoka and decline of the Mauryan Empire. |
| 221 BCE | Qin Shi Huang unifies China. |
| 216 BCE | Rome defeated at Cannae by Hannibal in the 2nd Punic War. |
| 202 BCE | Scipio Africanus defeats Hannibal at the battle of Zama. |
| 167–160 BCE | Maccabean Revolt. |
| 149–146 BCE | Carthage destroyed at the end of the 3rd Punic War with Rome taking Tunisia and Libya. |
| 146 BCE | Rome conquers Greece. |
| 121 BCE | First Roman expedition into Gaul. |

| 107 BCE | Gaius Marius, reformer of the Roman army, elected consul for the first of a record seven times. |
| 82–79 BCE | After a second march on Rome, Sulla defeats the forces of Marius to become Dictator. |
| 71 BCE | Death of Spartacus and end of the Third Servile War (slave revolt). |
| 63 BCE | Siege of Jerusalem leads to the Roman conquest of Judea. |
| 58–50 BCE | Julius Caesar wins total victory in the Gallic Wars, vying with Pompey for military dominance. |
| 49 BCE | Roman Civil War of Julius Caesar against the senatorial forces of Gnaeus Pompey in Greece, and Cato the Younger in Africa. |
| 44 BCE | The Roman Republic ends with the murder of Caesar by a senatorial group led by Marcus Brutus, a son of his former mistress. |
| 31–30 BCE | Roman fleet victory at the Battle of Actium precipitates the suicides of Cleopatra and Mark Antony as Ptolemaic Egypt is added to the Roman domains. |
| 27 BCE | Commencement of the Roman Empire as Caesar's nephew, adoptive son and heir Octavian receives the name of Augustus and title of Optimus Princeps (meaning "greatest first man") from the Senate. The Praetorian Guard is formed to provide security and the period known as the *Pax Romana* begins. |
| 27–22 BCE | Amanirenas, Queen (*kandake*) of the Kingdom of Kush, leads armies against the Romans. |
| 6 and 4 BCE | Earliest theorised dates for the birth date of Jesus Christ. |
| 9 CE | Catastrophic loss of the Battle of Teutoburg Forest causes Rome to abandon its aspiration to conquer the whole of Germania, fixing the frontier instead at the Rhine. Thus, the course of world history is decisively altered. There were an estimated 15,000 to 20,000 Romans dead from an army of three legions, six auxiliary cohorts, and three cavalry squadrons. Of the survivors, some are ransomed or committed suicide; others enslaved, and the most unfortunate cooked in pots as part of religious rites. |

| 14 CE | Death of Augustus; accession of his wife Livia's (59 BCE–9 CE) son by a previous marriage, Tiberius (42 BCE–37 CE). |
| --- | --- |
| c.26–c.34 | Crucifixion of Jesus Christ, exact age and date unknown. |
| 40 | Rome annexes client kingdom of Mauretania. |
| 41 | In a plot by senators and the Praetorian Guard to restore the republic, Emperor Caligula is assassinated - but the Praetorians pre-empt events by swiftly installing his uncle, Claudius, as Emperor. |
| 43 | After earlier skirmishing by Caesar and Caligula, Claudius's Rome begins a serious invasion of Britain. |
| 54 | By rumour a poison victim, Claudius dies, to be succeeded by his grand-nephew and legally adopted step-son, Nero. |
| 60/61 | Major British tribal alliance revolt led by Boudicca (d. 60/61), Queen of the Iceni, defeated by the Roman governor, Gaius Suetonius Paulinus (d. 69 CE). |
| 68 | Infamous Nero, murderer of his mother, implicated in the deaths of his wife and foster brother, whose Golden Palace and theatrical performances scandalised society, commits suicide after being charged as a public enemy by army leaders. This precipitates politicians and generals into scrabbling for power in the "Year of the Four Emperors", a struggle won by the practical, down-to-earth general, Vespasian, founder of the Flavian dynasty. |
| 70 | Jerusalem and the $2^{nd}$ temple destroyed by the armies of Vespasian's son, Titus. |
| 79 | Destruction of Pompeii and Herculaneum by the Vesuvius volcano |
| 96 | Domitian (51-96), last of the Flavians, who had mixed popular appeal with authoritarian, paranoid government, is assassinated in a palace coup featuring the Praetorian Guard. Succeeded by one of his officials, Nerva (30–98), whose principal achievement was peacefully to arrange his own succession. |
| 98 | Accession of Trajan (53–117) brings Rome the greatest extent of its territories, with conquests of Romania, Iraq and Armenia. |

| 117 | Trajan dies naturally and his adopted son Hadrian immediately begins the rationalisation and limitation of the Empire by leaving Assyria, Iraq and Armenia. |
| 122 | Hadrian's Wall construction begins. |
| 126 | Hadrian renovates and completes the Pantheon in Rome, an expression of his religious ideal and celebration of his regard for Greek culture. This second of the "Five Good Emperors", judged by Gibbon to have been a benevolent dictator, died of natural causes, bequeathing the Empire to his adopted son, Antoninus Pius. |
| 138 | Accession of Antoninus Pius (86-161), whose rule was the only one in which Rome did not fight a war, but with a successful campaign attempted again to extend Roman territory in Britain with another eponymous wall. |
| 161 – 169 | Co-rule of Marcus Aurelius with his adoptive brother Lucius Verus (130–169), who died of natural causes after a successful war against Parthia. |
| 169 – 180 | Marcus Aurelius, notably skilled in law and philosophy, ruled alone, dying on campaign near Vienna. He is to be succeed by his natural son, Commodus, whose behaviour after accession was described by the historian Cassius Dio (c.155–c.235) as turning a kingdom of gold into one of iron and dust. |
| 220 | Three Kingdoms period begins in China |
| 226 | Fall of the Parthian Empire; Rise of the Sasanian Empire. |
| 285 | Diocletian becomes Emperor of Rome, splitting the Empire into two parts: the Eastern and Western Roman Empires. Begins major campaign of persecution of Christians. |
| 292 | Capital of the Roman Empire moved officially to Mediolanum (Milan). |
| 301 | Diocletian attempts price control by edict on maximum prices. Armenia the first state to make Christianity its official religion. |
| 313 | Edict of Milan declares toleration of all forms of religious worship in the Roman Empire. Despite declaring himself a Christian, Constantine waits until he is on his death-bed to be |

| | |
|---|---|
| | baptised. |
| 325 | Constantine I organises the First Council of Nicaea. |
| 330 | City of Byzantium officially named Constantinople, to become the capital of the eastern Roman Empire. |
| 337 | Constantine I dies, leaving sons Constantius II (317-361), Constans I (320-350), and Emperor Constantine II (316–340) as Emperors of the Roman Empire. |
| 350 | Deaths of his brothers leave Constantius II as the sole Emperor. |
| 361 | Death of Constantius in 361 brings his cousin Julian (331–363) to the throne. Known to Christians as Julian the Apostate, a noted philosopher, author, general, and social reformer, he attempted a revival of Greek Platonic tradition, becoming the last pagan Roman Emperor and dying in battle on campaign invading the Sasanian Empire. |
| 378 | Roman army defeated by the Germanic tribes at the Battle of Adrianople |
| 395 | Theodosius I (347–395) (The Great) was the last Emperor to preside over the entire Empire, won an important victory against the Goths, two civil wars and was instrumental in securing the adoption of the Nicaean creed. His descendants ruled the Empire for the next six decades. A devout Christian, he outlawed all religions other than Catholic Christianity. |
| 406 | Romans expelled from Britain. |
| 407-409 | Visigoths and other Germanic tribes enter Roman Gaul for the first time. |
| 410 | For the first time since 390 BCE, Rome is sacked; this time by Visigoths. |
| 415 | Spain entered by Germanic tribes. |
| 429 | North Africa entered from Spain by Vandals. |
| 439 | Vandals conquer territory by this date from Morocco to Tunisia. |

| | |
|---|---|
| 455 | Rome sacked again, this time by Vandals, who also capture Sicily and Sardinia. |
| 455 | Barbarian Asia-invaders are widely on the move: Skandagupta, Gupta Emperor of India (r. c. 455-467) repels a Hunas attack on India. The Hunas were Central Asian tribes, part of the Hun extended families, linked to the Huns of Iran. |
| 476 | Romulus Augustulus (c. 465–c. 511?), the last Western Roman Emperor is forced to abdicate by Odoacer (433-493), a Germanic tribal leader and statesman who proceeded to rule as King of Italy from 476 until his death in 493. |

## Notes:

1. Western historians disagree on the end date of classical antiquity. This author's undergraduate history degree course began with the fall of Rome in 476. Other end dates are the death of Justinian I in 565 CE and the rise of Islam from 632 CE.
2. Full personal dates are given above only where the persons concerned have not been cited in the main text.

# CHAPTER THREE

# WAYS OF THE WEST: GREEKS

Western Hellenistic culture is dated roughly from the late 8th or early 7th centuries BCE with the Homeric poems of the *Iliad* and *Odyssey,* those of Hesiod, and the fables attributed to Aesop, but it is not until the 6th and 5th centuries that Greek civilisation and culture begin to flourish. The "Seven Sages" marked the beginning of written management practice and advice. Of these, Pittacus of Mytilene (640-568 BCE), a general who had won his kingdom through defeating the Athenians in single combat, favoured the people above the nobility, and made law in poetry. He gave up the monarchy after a decade, leaving a series of aphorisms eternally relevant to management and entrepreneurship, among which are:

> Know thyself;
> Know thine opportunity;
> Whatever you do, do it well and;
> Forgiveness is better than revenge.

Of the other most remembered of the Sages, Solon of Athens framed the laws shaping Athenian democracy whereas Chilon (active 620-520 BCE), remembered for insistence on brevity – "less is more" – conferred militarisation upon Sparta. Only Thales of Miletus (625-546 BCE) of the septet may be ranked as a philosopher, one moreover of great scope.

Geometrician, engineer, astronomer, and natural philosopher Thales was the first known thinker to break with mythology to explain the world and the universe. Precursor to modern scientific method, he sought to explain natural phenomena through theories and hypotheses. Credited by Aristotle as the first philosopher in the Greek tradition, the first to whom mathematical discovery has been attributed, Thales also applied his scientific and philosophical expertise directly to business. The further explorations of his pupil Anaximander (c.610-c.546 BCE) in astronomy, physics, geometry, and geography led to his attaining the title of "the first scientist." He followed Thales as the Master of the Milesian school of Ionia, expanding scientific study.

There are three versions of the "birth of science" story, two referring to Thales's expertise in weather forecasting. Predicting a good harvest, he is said to have bought all the olive presses in Miletus, an Asia Minor coastal town. Aristotle's version has him reserving the presses in advance at a discount, renting them out at high prices when the harvest came in. Under the first version, Thales has executed the first recorded futures exercise; at the second, the first options venture; at the third, supplied an answer to the question often directed at philosophers, economists and some consultants: "if you're so clever, why aren't you rich?"

Although rudimentary examples of futures and options contracts have been found on Mesopotamian clay tablets dating from 1750 BCE, we have no detail. The sharp approach to business acquired by gaining such competitive edge was apparently introduced by the Greeks. Expanding from small, independent enterprises, entrepreneurial Greek maritime traders introduced the world's first free market economy, precursor to the Anglo-American capitalist consumer and shareholder model of the 19th and 20th centuries. Whilst the Phoenician trading base was one of large corporate hierarchies, the Greeks sailed forth into the Mediterranean and Black Seas as independents, initially acquiring iron ore and prestige goods for resale in local markets. This was complemented by Greek settlers throughout the region establishing their own colonies, growing their own wheat, so forcing homeland competitors to diversify into vines, olives, and oranges, then to seek and acquire export markets.

A further consequence was the replacement in many Greek settlements ruled by oligarchies of wealthy farmers by the rule of an individual, usually a successful entrepreneur and often an outcast aristocrat, known as a tyrant. The word did not carry its negative modern applications of oppression until Athens, in the 4th century BCE, rejected the evolution of repression. Before such time, the term represented the autocratic rule of a strong leader. By contrast, the consolidation of the commencement of democracy was achieved by Pericles (c 495-429 BCE), the ultimate class traitor. This wealthy member of the elite led the flowering of rule by the people, "the mob" to its opponents. Pericles's genius was to theorise the greatness of Athenian democracy through an artistic building programme expressed through construction, sculpture, poetry, oratory, philosophy, intellectual glory, drama, and festivals. Financed through cultural norms whereby the wealthy contributed to the public purse, efficient extraction of funds from allies, victory in warfare, and the application of slavery, Athens, under the control of its citizenry - the ordinary middle-class people - brought an enormous expansion in the scope and expression of civilisation.

While skill in the developing arts of oratory and rhetoric might sway the all-male citizens' assembly, Pericles exploited the one public gathering at which the attendance of women was permitted: funerals. We have no direct record of what he said, only the later account of Thucydides (c.460-400 BCE) – who was, however, known for his scrupulous accuracy and commencement of "scientific history." In commemorating the war dead from the ongoing war with Sparta, Pericles defined the management of the state and civilisation. He described the institutions and ideal of democratic Athens, defining the city as precious to the meaning of existence: this was what free citizens fought and died for. Democracy was Athenian. It was not imported, not from elsewhere; it was the regime of the many, not the few. Himself one of those few, Pericles sought to instil a discipline into the mothers, widows, and orphans who had lost their men - to bear the pain and continue to strive to support the ideal of Athens and its civilizing mission.

Darius the Great had promised everlasting life to his soldiers if they died for him in battle. Those forces had been resisted by an Athenian-led Greek coalition at Marathon in 490 BCE. This pivotal victory demonstrated to the Greeks that the previously all-conquering Persians could be beaten, that Sparta was not the only Greek military power, and the value of the Athenian mode of governance. A decade later, his son Xerxes I was defeated at sea at Salamis, off the Athenian coast. Further defeat on land at Plataea a year later so ended the Persian attempt to conquer Greece.

Athenian victory owed much to fruits of early industrialisation. Archaeological evidence shows primitive working since the Bronze Age (around 3200 BCE) of the Laurion mines near Athens, yielding lead, galena, and silver. Systematic workings began in the 6th century BCE, ore excavation achieved through underground shafts and galleries, as well as using slave labour. With work set at 15 hours per day; workers branded, collared, chained, naked; and with child participation, the mortality rate was high.[1] Ore could be washed on site to concentrate mineral content and release silver. This could be transported to small scale factories, the city workshops of private concessionaires, for treatment culminating in jewellery manufacture. Licenses were available for exploitation by private citizen "silver men" in exchange for fixed percentages of ore production.

The Athenian state retained mine ownership, production supplying much of the finance for the large naval fleet crucial in the Battle of Salamis and subsequent creation of the Athenian Empire (454-404 BCE). Discovery of a rich vein of silver prompted the early democrat leader Themistocles (524-459 BCE) to propose building a war chest from Laurion production rather than distributing the gains among the citizenry, meaning that when the Persian hostilities commenced, Athens had some 3 tonnes of silver at its disposal.

Coinage was hand-made by the block and punch method. An obverse design was carved into a block of iron or bronze, overlaid by a blank disc. This was then punched with a reverse image struck by a hammer. The high quality of the Laurion silver greatly increased the strength of Athenian trade. Student and friend of Socrates, military leader, philosopher, and historian Xenophon (430-354 BCE), famous commander of the "Ten Thousand" Greek mercenaries at the age of 30, devoted a chapter of his final work, the essay *Ways and Means,* to the further development of the industry. The context was the Athenian defeat in the Social War (357-355 BCE), continuing economic crisis and urgent need to raise revenue.

Xenophon's proposal was for economic development rather than more warfare and repression. To increase revenue from silver, Xenophon argued, an increase in the industrial work force would produce more wealth than its being deployed in agriculture, which could attain a plateau of efficiency only. Therefore, the business should be opened to foreigners as well as citizens. As demand for silver was endless, consumers would buy more - as much as they could afford - thereby increasing revenue. Even more could also be raised by public ownership in the slave business, gaining revenue by hiring out. The economic management logic was clear: possession of a high value commodity in public ownership allowed licensing of production, the labour for which could be acquired as a free by-product of warfare, hired out at profit to licensees. Their economic activity would allow production and acquisition of further goods.

This was pure public-private capitalism with minimum management costs, albeit as part of a slave labour economy. Earlier, when forced by the Spartans marauding into further conflict, Pericles had offered his people a freedom in the form of means to rule themselves in a civilised manner (albeit underpinned by slave labour from fruits of war).

The evidence of that, here and now, was all about them, from the patron Athena-dedicated Parthenon temple (and city treasury) atop the Acropolis, to the Agora ("gathering place") below. Designed and constructed under the supervision of the celebrated sculptor Pheidias (490-425 BCE), the Athena 'Parthenos' stood 11.50 metres in height (37.7 feet); the core, probably wooden, being panelled with ivory and gold. In times of emergency, gold from the clothing of the goddess could be removed to pay for ships and fighters, provided it was subsequently replaced. Athena was appropriately revered as the daughter of wisdom, the goddess of the battleline.

**The Parthenon**

Named after the Greek for "unmarried woman", the temple was built in thanksgiving for the Hellenic victory over the Persians. Converted to a Christian church in the late 6th century, after the Ottoman conquest in the mid-15th century it became a mosque, until badly damaged by a Venetian shell in 1687 landing on an Ottoman munitions dump. At the start of the 19th century, the 7th Earl of Elgin removed some of the frieze sculptures, considered the high point of ancient Greek art, which are now housed in the British Museum, London.

Finance, art, and debt management being combined reflected the entire tone of Athenian culture. A population estimated at 416 BCE to be of around 30,000 produced cultural achievement of astonishing beauty and value, a triumph of civic management. Its contemporary pottery was prized for the quality of its portraiture, its currency for value. Half a millennium later, Cicero was to pronounce an eternal, immortal verdict in *De Oratore* (2.9):

"The statues of Pheidias are the most perfect of their kind that has ever been seen." Calculation of the "golden ratio" determinant of beauty pursued by mathematicians, architects, and artists since Euclid and Pythagoras in Greece, as with Pheidias' supervision of the Parthenon frieze, are all aspects of the ancient Greek striving for human perfection.

Freedom required the application of justice, and Pericles increased citizens' powers by introducing pay-for jurors. No distinctions were made in law: civil, criminal and political prosecutions might be brought. Even Pericles was successfully prosecuted, but re-elected by the citizenry. The Spartan strategy of invading Athenian territory twice yearly by ravaging, hoping to force Athens to yield, was resisted by the dispatch of livestock to the island of Euboea - the citizenry retreated with their goods inside the city walls. This effective defence was breached by two concurrent epidemics, one of plague, the other of typhoid fever, beginning in the summer of 430 BC. The first wave caused the death of a fifth of the population, including that of Pericles, and an estimated third of those huddled inside Athens's walls overall. The successors of Pericles were inadequate, pursuing populist policies which ended in disaster. It was one matter to initiate and manage great change; another to secure its sustainability.

Greek expansion had brought its currency - particularly the Athenian drachma, made of high-quality silver and bearing the image of Athena's owl - into wide use. Pericles' policy of inviting the brightest and the best of the Greek world to contribute to Athenian life had expanded and enriched its culture, reputation, and influence. Exposure to many other gods had the indirect effect of lessening the hold of those deities upon trade, where such practical necessities as study of astronomy and the tides had direct relevance to business. If the gods did not intervene in the laws of nature, then reason dictated that the state, the Greek *polis*, should regulate trade and ensure market fairness. The logical further extension was to governance: even the replacement of oligarchy and tyranny by democracy, although limited by the exclusion of women and dependence on slavery. The management of trade had entailed rebalancing of the economy which then produced wider management of government.

However, increasing expense arising from the Peloponnesian War undermined the Athenian public finance system. Until the end of the 4th BCE, the accepted financial concept of civilisation was that wealth was derived by delegation from the city, the source of wealth creation. Tax was a public good, the payment of which an honour, for this was the mark of a good citizen. Therefore, the cost of state function and preservation fell to those who benefited most: the rich. Athens' greatest strength, need, and cost were all in its dual-purpose fleet (commercial and naval).

Trierarchs, those commanders or persons obliged to furnish ships to the state, who could build, fit, and provision a trireme – a galley with three banks of oars – were increasingly hard pressed.[2] The trireme represented a peak of Athenian technology. Skilled oarsmen functioned at three levels, exercising different strokes to achieve a unity of swift movement and manoeuvrability. The rowers were dedicated to their craft. Slave use was impractical, for they could not be relied on reliably to execute complex techniques. Comradeship in coordination was encouraged by such dietary management as the upper levels of rowers being discouraged from the consumption of beans. Wooden construction meant that even if a trireme was holed below the waterline, it would not necessarily sink. Athenian sea power became dominant through superior design and skilled ship management.

Trireme duty, however, became a burden to its financiers. At first this happened discreetly, even covertly and deviously, such as skimping on or delaying the duty. Soon enough, the rich began to try to avoid it completely. For the first time, without open admittance, the elite's opinion became that personal wealth was not meant to serve the city, but was instead for the holder's benefit. By 405 BCE, Aristophanes (427-386 BCE) could joke in *The Frogs* that putative trierarchs were disguising themselves as needy to avoid their obligations. Thereafter, the wealthy continued to fund civic costs, but with recognition of the right to private wealth; the honour of public office continued in recognition of fiduciary duty.

Athenian sea power, through its triple purpose fleet of fishing, commerce, and defence, increased its access to a dominant cultural commodity: fish. Described by a distinguished historian as popular a social consumption as sex, sprats and anchovies were considered as food fit only for beggars.[3] Delicacies were considered to be tuna (belly, shoulder and neck especially), sea-perch, grey and red mullet, gilt-head, sea-bass and types of langoustine. Above all was the undisputed master of the fishmonger's stall, praised as the ruler of everything else at the feast, despite having no backbone - the "prince of fish" was the eel. Culinary management, from acquisition to consumption and appreciation, was a further management skill enhanced by the Athenians.

Such conspicuous consumption as the obsession with fish-eating gained official disapproval and discouragement: scales of expenditure were indeed an issue. Most taxation in the ancient world was at around one to three per cent, levied on land, homes, real estate, slaves, wine, animals, hay, and monetary wealth. In all instances, a great stimulant to warfare continued to be the revenues resulting from conquest, pillage, and plunder - even if literature tended to express the heroic rather than financial achievements.

Aristotle developed the heroic theme. His "magnificent man" gave great amounts to the community. The poor, since they did not have the financial means, could never be "magnificent"; but they could be good. The pursuit of the good life also meant doing good. Patronage, in the distribution of money and gifts, and helping others to survive was a social responsibility. The teaching of the Hippocratic medical tradition echoed the point for doctors. Sometimes it was good to give service for free, particularly to help a stranger in financial difficulty.

The emergence of formal higher education accompanied attention to government and societal management. However, while the pursuit of knowledge led naturally from the foundation of Plato's Academy in c. 387 BCE to the provision of teaching, of methods of inquiry, and activity organisation followed tradition and perceived need. As a resister of what he perceived as mob rule (democracy), Plato sought a republic ruled by the elite. He can be seen as an early authoritarian thinker, whereby primacy in governance was given to strict direction. Management, as such, was an adjunct to a process, a part of a profession or activity. Even though state management was central to educational thinking, it was not recognised as a function in itself (despite the fact that any progression entailed action changes which we would now clearly acknowledge as managerial).

Since it came to figure so prominently in the development of Management Studies, the definition provided by biologist Sir Peter Medawar (1915-1987) is pertinent here: "science is the art of the solvable." From knowledge, the ancients required continuing solutions if they were to survive, maintain, and manage progress. The tragedy of Athenian democracy was its failure to achieve sustainability.

Where there was political control, the ancient world was administered rather than managed, but management remained essential for production and trade (even if rudimentary). Yet, exceptional managerial skill and application can be discerned in some of the ancient world's foremost leaders, and a case made for the foundation of management education to be discovered there. Other than in isolated democratic experiments, the mode of ancient management was invariably that of control. The manager controlled the activity for which, and under which, there were strict administrative processes.

The extreme example is Sparta, which held trade to be of low repute but elevated militarism to heights of unrivalled accomplishment. It began as it meant to continue.Lycurgus (c.700-630 BCE), the legendary founder, decreed that baby boys too weak to become soldiers should be abandoned and left to die on the desolate slopes of Mount Tygetos. The remainder were to be trained as fearless warriors. These hoplite citizen-soldiers were required to put the welfare of their state above that of their family which, through eugenics (the breeding of the best with the best), would perpetuate state power.

Greek hoplites served as heavy infantry and were responsible for their own weaponry and armour, the expensive equipment being passed down as family heirlooms. Their individual shield designs told much about the bearer and his family. All hoplites were trained in the discipline of the battle formation eight deep phalanx, but Spartans were exposed to harsher conditions and granted extra benefits. Going barefoot in winter and sleeping without blankets, young soldiers were rewarded with the opportunity to couple with as many as twenty women. Battles were decided when the lines of a phalanx broke. Spartan failure on the battle field was not tolerated. The hoplite who returned home alive but without his shield was disowned by his family and sentenced to death.

Such was the fearsome nature of Spartan achievement that it inspired Plato's indulgence in eugenics, and provided fodder for the ideologies of 20th century military dictatorships.[4] Echoes of the Spartan ethic in warrior, sporting, and related educative endeavours still remain. In management history, the eventual victory of totalitarian Sparta over mighty Athens and her Empire in the elongated war of 431 to 404 BCE is a prime example of how humankind was starting to organise and manage itself in new and experimental ways. The unfortunate reverse of the coin was that democratic, civilised Athens, with its aims of citizens versed in the ways of peace as well as war, lost because of the devastation caused by a plague pandemic, followed by arrogance, misinformation, poor leadership, and poor judgment

The 430-427 BCE Plague of Athens originated in Ethiopia, swept through the trade routes of north Africa, the Levant, and the eastern Mediterranean, entering Europe through the port of Piraeus. It killed a third of the Athenian population, including its greatest and most capable leader, Pericles. It was the democratic, overreaching decision, with inadequate preparation and investigation, which led to a disastrous 415-413 BCE invasion of Syracuse. The loss of treasure, men, *matériel*, and ships weakened the Athenians so much that they eventually had to succumb. The result, arguably, determined the political pattern of the following two millennia. The conflict stands as a misfortune and mismanagement monument: a Spartan triumph; an Athenian disaster; a catastrophe for humanity. Ill-advised referenda may continue to pose terminal problems for democracy.

The most obvious contrasting developments were between Athens and Sparta. The Athenian goal was the production of citizens versed in the arts of peace and war; Sparta sought disciplined soldier-citizens, produced through eugenics. Spartan boys had to leave home at seven, initiated into the camp only after enduring passage through ranks of older boys. These would flog them with whips, sometimes causing immediate death, justified by the philosophy adapted from Plato of furthering the selective breeding principle: if man could control nature by the selective breeding of plants and animals, then the same techniques could be applied to humans. The best was to breed with the best. Instead of the boys being fed, they were encouraged to steal food, being punished if they were caught. The rebuke was having been too clumsy to evade capture, not for theft.

The survivors then further endured a rigorous regime of increasing physical toughening until cadet training from eighteen to twenty, after which they served in the national militia until sixty. They may or may not have acquired literacy but, of the arts, only music and dancing were included in the training because of their military applications. Because Lycurgus the Spartan lawgiver recognised status for women, Spartan women enjoyed a remarkable degree of freedom; wholly unusual for Greece, they could engage in such sports as horse racing. All domestic tasks fell to the helot servant class, who were effectively slaves to the Spartan citizens.

Girls were not compelled to leave home but were subjected to a similar regime of running, jumping, wrestling, throwing the discus and javelin, in addition to the acquisition of domestic skills. They even participated in whipping contests, *diamastigosis*, to see who had most endurance. If men returned defeated from battle, women extended ostracism to shaming such failures into suicide.

Curriculum for the young in a wholly militaristic culture also provided further advanced life skills of killing, stealing, and lying. The first concerned the arts of warfare in hand-to-hand and associated combat; foraging prowess was essential to troop mobility; and practice as a liar was a perceived necessity in case of capture. The opposite of the greatest Persian virtue became a prime Spartan accomplishment, a skill necessary to achieve elite status.

The epitome of that elite were enrolled into the *krypteia*, the "secret ones", who were sent into the subjugated neighbouring territory of Messania to scout, spy, and kill. Messania, south west of Sparta, had been defeated and made subject in 720 BCE, revolted in 685-688 BCE, and was possessed again until 464BCE. The *krypteia* task was to identify the Messanian leaders most respected in their localities, and murder them. Whether those victims were pro- or anti-Spartan was irrelevant. The objective, achieved over centuries, was to keep the Messanians leaderless and terrified. As proven successful assassins, *krypteia* members gained automatic promotion to the *hippeis*, the elite of the elite, who functioned at large on missions of reconnaissance, espionage, and whatever of the black arts were required to accomplish Spartan policy objectives. Although intelligence service management is as old as human history, the Spartan variant serves as an exemplar of its type.

Athenian girls remained at home, with more formal education reserved for intended courtesans so that they had the ability to converse with and intellectually entertain their male clientele. In families of substance, women remained veiled, occupied at home in spinning, weaving, and household maintenance, and were assisted by slaves. Less well-off women would go out for shopping and business. Their society might be discrete but it was not prudish. Aristophanes deployed his satiric talents in 411 BCE, two years after the Sicilian disaster, in his play *Lysistrata*. In the play, the women of Greece band together, denying their men sex in an effort to end the long-running Peloponnesian War. To provoke the males, they would "wear saffron silks, with lots of make-up" but deny the pleasures of the "lioness and cheese-grater" position.[5]  Reconciliation, personified by a highly desirable young woman, brokers peace. The war is ended but, alas, this was an illusion no more attainable than an unrealistic sexual fantasy.

The boys of Athens had to undergo two years of military training from eighteen, but were otherwise under parental control regarding their formal education, which was available from the age of six at elementary schools.

The curriculum was a mixture of physical education with literacy, literature being at the centre of Greek culture. While the cost of elementary education was within the ability of most citizens, a choice had to be made between trade and craft apprenticeship or further education at a cost once the boys reached at thirteen- or fourteen-years-old.

There were no schools until the 4th century BCE, but teachers provided services, and continued to do so. Thus, pupils followed teachers such as Socrates, Plato, and Aristotle. More formal schools naturally followed, but private and individual tuition remained an important characteristic. There were two branches of this further learning: oratory and rhetoric for those seeking public office; geometry, arithmetic, harmonics (a mathematical approach to music), astronomy, and philosophy for those with practical civil or cultural aspirations. Focus upon this curriculum by the later Roman writer Varro during the early years of Empire brought its content to form the "liberal arts" of medieval times.

Plato's dialogues and dialectic approach brought a coherent framework of thought and action which has illuminated education ever since. For the purposes of management education, however, the role model of the philosopher king is suitable only in an idealised leadership context. Moreover, as modern commentary on Plato's *Republic* observes: "The trouble is that Plato's communities strike readers as potentially most unjust."[6] Those to rule are to acquire the best of education, so as to rule for "good," whereas the remainder are there to be ruled, and moreover according to his repressively stringent and dubiously dictatorial *Laws*. The reality was that when Plato was invited to have his philosophy of governance system tested in Syracuse, a probable political ploy by its tyrant of the day, results were such that he was lucky to escape with his life. Plato's principal legacy was not in the character of rulers, more in the establishment of philosophy as a specialist profession.

His pupil, Aristotle, author of the first comprehensive system of western philosophy, was held in much higher regard than Plato in medieval times, in both the European and the Muslim worlds, and in the making of the modern. Thomas Jefferson was an Aristotelian scholar. His famous contribution of the inalienable right to "the preservation of life, and liberty, and the pursuit of happiness" to the American constitution was derived from Aristotle via John Locke's *Second Treatise*. It should be noted here that the American republic was rooted in the radical Protestantism of New England and the book of Genesis but, to avoid sectarian issues, it was a Founding

Fathers' stroke of genius in the promotion of Christian values to cite them as originating from honoured but pre-Christian sources.

Politically astute, Aristotle still speaks of prime issues relevant to our own times. His enormous contributions to knowledge and philosophy remain such that even libertarian thinkers like Ayn Rand (1905-1982), whose individualistic world of struggle did not accommodate the common good, acclaim the extent of his influence. In Book V of his *Politics*, Aristotle identified inequality as a main cause of revolutions. As justice and equality were the fundamental basis of any state, inequality, as a type of injustice, gave potent grounds for challenging the state:

> The lesser rebel in order to be equal, the equal in order to be greater.
> These then are conditions predisposing to revolution.

COVID-19 has sharpened inequalities; subject to grumbling before, now in danger of being perceived as oppressive. It is such a situation which may again challenge the world of the West. Management education professionals like Nonaka and Takeuchi still develop positive theory from Aristotle's concepts of knowledge, discussed below.[7] He remains a subject of university studies of philosophy and natural sciences to the present day. Aristotle set a lasting curriculum core.

More, he defined a continuing human goal. The purpose of human life, and hence its organisation and management, was the achievement of excellence. This was to be managed in accord with virtue, through *eudaimonia*, the "good life"; more than having a good time, benefiting from good spirit. A general interpretation is fulfilling potential ethically rather than selfishly, and so performing to the best of what a person is good at for the benefit of society. Thus, education was to encourage and facilitate such attainment. Criticism has since been made that Aristotle and his pupils were men of privilege, served by women and slaves, an elite seeking reinforced, exclusive perpetuation. They were people of their times and cannot be judged outside of them.

Early pedagogic method was established by Socrates, based upon dialectic whereby the purpose was to investigate a concept in adversarial dialogue so that contradictions might be exposed and true knowledge revealed. Technique and dialogue contents were relayed by Plato's recreational writings. Aristotle had furthered the development of investigative techniques by his employment of the empirical method. Critical analysis employing data collection and categorisation was applied to a wide variety of subjects. While Plato concentrated on the abstract, such as the ideal republic, Aristotle's focus was upon the real. Their differences might be summarised as: Socrates asked questions; Plato wrote dialogues; Aristotle wrote as much down as he could; and we've all got on with the business of writing ever since. The trio all concurred that the purposes of education and inquiry were the acquisition of knowledge, but Aristotle took the concept further: logical reasoning could lead to knowledge and its application.

This was to be accompanied by virtue, which lay within the attainment of happiness or goodness. Virtue was divided into character and intellect. Teaching was able to increase intellect, and that was seen as the product of experience and training, or guided empiricism. Character was viewed as arising from habit, therefore good character could be created and enforced by good habits. Further, the aim of education was the greater welfare of the individual, thus to produce happiness and goodness in life.

The Aristotelian scheme of education followed Plato in declaring responsibility for education of infants to parents, with subsequent education being a matter for the state - although moral education remained a parental responsibility throughout a child's schooling. Curriculum stressed the importance of the physical; gymnasia were essential for maintaining physical fitness and the development of prowess in warrior cultures, where combat was never far away. Gymnastic training was not a matter only of athletic prowess but a means to develop sportsmanlike attitudes and self-control, especially regarding passions and appetites. It is perhaps unsurprising that the first person known to compile a list of Olympic Games winners was Aristotle. Literature and music were early accompaniments in education because of their suitability for intellectual and moral growth.

Reserved for higher education, mathematics, physics, and astronomy were seen as subjects suitable for developing the power of deductive reasoning. Teaching itself was to combine deductive and inductive methodology, thus establishing the basis and expression of what became known as scientific inquiry. For this, Aristotle has been awarded one of those ubiquitous paternity titles: "father of modern sciences." (It should be noted, however, that "science" as a word derived from the Latin *scientia,* "to know". It came into use meaning the systematic study of the natural world, using observation, experiment, measurement, and verification, only in the 14th century).

Aristotle's acceptance and approval of slavery; perception of women as having only enfeebled reason and thus being unfitted for freedom; and while advocating justice as a virtue did not grant its applicability to barbarians and females all make him a difficult hero of enlightenment. Similarly unfortunately, he accepted myth such as Atlantis, credulousness regarding ancient folk tales, and belief that the edge of the world was visible from the tops of the mountains of Afghanistan. His pupil Alexander, slogging back through the wastes at the edge of the Gedrosian desert, might have had cause to resent his teacher's aberrant sense of geography.

However, his observations on biology and natural history, famously including the sexual equipment of the octopus, have received continuous acclaim. The emphasis on philosopher-king leadership and emphasis on the educated "good" having sway over the remaining citizenry was naturally resisted by Athenian democrats, who detested the concept. Reviewing the flattery by Aristotle's academy successor, Speusippus (408-339 BCE), of the Macedonian conquests of much of Greece, a contemporary ancient historian has commented:

> It is a major warning against allowing a philosopher
> near foreign affairs.[8]

Nonetheless, building upon the revival of his thought by the moral philosopher Alasdair MacIntyre (1929-), Aristotle's concept of the trinity of forms of knowledge has been identified by contemporary Harvard management educationists as the "big idea" of practical wisdom, available to rescue the failures of modern leadership.

The origin of practical wisdom lies in the concept of phronesis, and is one of the three forms of wisdom Aristotle identified. In *Nichomachean Ethics VI.6*, he wrote that phronesis is "a true and reasoned state and capacity to act with regard to the things that are good or bad for man." He identified two other types of wisdom: esoteric or metaphysical wisdom, and practical wisdom, which Samuel Coleridge later wryly interpreted as "common sense in an uncommon degree."

Commentators Nonaka and Takeuchi have stated: "Practical wisdom, according to our studies, is experiential knowledge that enables people to make ethically sound judgments". Aristotle also identified episteme, or universally valid scientific knowledge, and techne, or skill based technical know-how. If episteme is know-why and techne is know-how, phronesis is know-what-should-be-done. Phronesis enables managers to determine what is good in specific times and situations, and to undertake the best actions at those times to serve the common good.[9]

The success and intellectual strength of Aristotle was such that, for over 1500 years, his scientific thought and writings became conventional, unchallengeable wisdom, the roots of much human progress and understanding. Empirical method informed the advances made from the 15<sup>th</sup> century. The failures were that, such was the height of his authority, it became a punishable sin in the hands of the Church to dispute him, even when he was found to be in provable error; that the heart of his scientific and pedagogical method lay largely ignored and unused after the period of antiquity, and during that time also. One reason for this lay in the rise of Rome.

By the 5<sup>th</sup> century BCE, free trade Athens had reached heights of power and prosperity, in contrast to Sparta opening the city to thousands of immigrants who often fulfilled the business functions disdained by the citizen-farmers, those hoplites, who provided military service. Many of the traders and managers were often neither Athenian nor Greek. Defeat in the Peloponnesian War and the loss of Empire, through limiting markets and straining the tax base, provoked ridicule of tyrants, merchants, and democracy. Plato and Aristotle envisaged governmental replacement by a utopian, managed society, run by prudent philosophers who would not engage in business or own property. Economic decline, however, did produce growth in the banking industry; trade had still to be financed. Merchants sought and received what came to be a routine banking function of protecting their assets from acquisitive governmental taxation, making secret loans, and guarding the confidentiality of deposits.

The Athenian political management question was solved by Macedonian and subsequently Roman conquest, but not before financial experts had assumed leadership roles. The Athenian free market revolution, with its creation of a cash-based society, had supported the Greek accomplishments in the arts, much as the Medici subsequently financed the Renaissance. The great change was that wealth and gain could be achieved by more interesting and exciting means than agriculture: banking, trading, mining and manufacture - all of which required management and, in some form, managers. The resultant social mobility allowed the growth of a rising, or immigrant, merchant class.

This was not uniform however. Other Greek cities and regions, such as Sparta, Crete, and Thessaly remained militaristically oligarchic, in what was to become the feudal model of manorial based serfdom, as also practiced in Persia, the Levant, and Carthage. Although Alexander's conquests spread

Hellenism, autocracy prevailed, as did the economic models of the regions into which it was transplanted. Nonetheless, forms of capitalism and the classical roots of management may be clearly discerned.

Development of the management of communication became a dominant feature of Greek culture, uniting myth, religion, politics, and the nature of life through the conventions of tragedy and comedy. From around 700 BCE, theatrical culture became an increasingly important part of Greek life. It was institutionalised as a central feature of Athenian life in the festival of the Dionysia, held in honour of the god Dionysius, and exported to its many colonies. The strength of the tradition is evident in modern western theatre, which has inherited many of its features. Formal presentation in a theatre elevated further the art of the storyteller and value of the spoken word. Setting information in writing, Socrates believed, denied it the opportunity to change and grow.

The quality of such opportunity as afforded by theatre was determined by competition, the first of which was held in Athens around 532 BCE. Some hold that the earlier Seven Sages and law-giver Solon who spoke in verse have prior originating claims, but it was Thespis who won the first competition as an actor. He further began touring theatre, speaking the words of characters, bringing masks and stage properties with him, and bequeathing his name to the ensuing occupational description of "thespian." Audience identification with presentations was high. An early play concerned with the fall of Miletus to the Persians brought obloquy upon its early tragedian author, Phrynichus:

> For when this poet brought out upon the stage his drama of the Capture of Miletus, the whole theatre burst into tears; and the people sentenced him to pay a fine of a thousand drachms, for recalling to them their own misfortunes. They likewise made a law, that no one should ever again exhibit that piece.[10]

Theatre developed its forms: first, tragedy; then comedy; and a burlesque named satyr, being comic treatment of myth. Tragedies were unique pieces written in honour of Dionysus, and so played only once - until after the Athenian loss in the Peloponnesian War, when repetition of old tragedies became fashionable. The devices of women being played either by slave girls or males, use of the chorus as plot movers, and deployment of costume and masks were honed as sophistication increased. A voiced, staged, fully theatrical public entertainment had been created - an enduring management matter in both content and presentation.

**"Mighty walled Tiryns" (left).**

As described by Homer, its main fortifications were raised between 1400 and 1200 BCE. They became associated with Heracles, who was said to have resided at Tiryns, possibly his birth place, during his labours. Tiryns is a Mycenaean site in the eastern Peloponnese region of Argolis.
[Photograph by the author.]

The labours of Heracles were storyteller staples. The potence of the Greek myths was emphasised by the continuing presence of supposed archaeological remains.

**Mycenae Palace Entrance (right).**
[Photograph by the author.]

Myth and Theatre:

Aeschylus (c. 525 – 456 BCE) won first prize at the 458 BCE festival, where his *Agamemnon* was first performed. It is tempting to imagine that this was the gate from which King Agamemnon, the mythical commander of the Greek forces, set out to fight the Trojan War and to which, ten years later, he returned. There, once inside, he introduced his mistress, Cassandra, in demeaning terms to his wife, the vengeful adulterous Clytemnestra who has ruled the kingdom of Argos in his

absence. Irrevocably bitter at Agamemnon having sacrificed their daughter Iphigenia to appease goddess Artemis, who was preventing his forces from reaching Troy, Clytemnestra murders her husband in his bath.

**Ancient Greek Theatre of Epidaurus**
[Photograph by the author.]

Built in the late 4th century BCE, the ancient theatre of Epidaurus, by the sanctuary devoted to Asclepius, god of medicine, is thought to be the finest example of acoustics and aesthetics from the ancient world. The sound of a dropped pebble hitting the ground can be heard clearly, magnified, at the uppermost tier of the auditorium.

# Endnotes

[1] A 4th century CE iron slave collar displayed in a Roman museum at the Baths of Diocletian bears a tag reading: *FUGI. TENE ME. CUM REVOCAVERIS ME D. M. ZONINO, ACCIPIS SOLIDUM: I have run away. Catch me. If you return me to my master Zoninus, you will receive a solidus*. A solidus being a gold coin, this must have been a valuable slave. Those consigned to mining especially were expendable. 30% of the population of ancient Greece and Rome is estimated to have been enslaved.
[2] Morrison, J S, Coates, JF, Rankov, N B. 2000. *The Athenian Trireme*. Cambridge: Cambridge University Press.

[3] Davidson, James. 2016. *Courtesans and Fishcakes: The Consuming Passions of Classical Athens,* London: Fontana.

[4] It would seem, probably in his youth, that the celebrated philosopher also had an indulgence for food. Plato was a nick-name, meaning "Fatso".

[5] Aristophanes, *Lysistrata*, line 231.

[6] Fox, Robin Lane. 2006. *The Classical World*, p.205.

[7] Nonaka, Ikujiro and Takeuchi, Hirotaka, "The Big Idea: The Wise Leader," *Harvard Business Review,* May 2011 Issue.

[8] Fox, *op.cit.*, p.210.

[9] Nonaka and Takeuchi, *op. cit.,* p.5. In his Northumbria University public lecture of 11/9/2017, *Insight Into the Evolution of British Business,* Professor John F. Wilson quoted this work, modified by his further insights, discussed later. See also: ed. Amann, Wolfgang and Goh, Jenson. 2017. *Phronesis in Business Schools: Reflections on Teaching and Learning,* Information Age Publishing.

[10] Herodotus, *The Histories*, 6.21, p.444.

**The Roman Colosseum (interior, and exterior).**
[Photographs by John Bagshaw]

# CHAPTER FOUR

# WAYS OF THE WEST: ROMANS

Roman conquest of Greece was largely reciprocated culturally. Literature was in Greek, which remained the language of the elite. Greek novels maintained the culture and attitudes of the 4th and 5th centuries BCE. The manner and expression of the guiding force of human conduct and management remained that of Greek philosophy. The dying Caesar, at his assassination, spoke not in Shakespeare's famous rendition into Latin but reproved Brutus with "you too, my child," in Greek. However, Roman state interest still predominated basic education - parentally guided instruction in Roman law, history, and customs, with physical training, added a powerful dimension to book learning. The course of honour for the elite entailed a mastery of public speaking, thus producing the curricular essential of oratory.

For most of society, child labour was the norm. Only the offspring of the rich could be indulged in a pursuit of learning deemed suitable to their social status and aspirations. The young elite was being instructed in how to rule, govern, and, within social constraints, manage. Between the ages of seven and twelve, boys and, sometimes, girls, studied reading, writing, and basic arithmetic at public elementary schools. From twelve or thirteen, upper class youth could attend "grammar" schools, so known because of the primacy in instruction of the declension of nouns and conjugation of verbs. Rote learning and memorising formed a basis for speech making: expertise in oratory was the ultimate goal, with the rhetoric tutorials or classes functioning as the finishing school.

It must be emphasised that culture in the ancient world was linguistic. Books were few, and much serious literature was in Greek. Therefore, speech and memory were dominant. Silent reading was not contemplated until much later: one read aloud to oneself. The thoughts of others were absorbed through listening, memorising, and repetition. The excellence of memory bequeathed us those ancient texts which we now possess – however, it was not always entirely accurate and, like the mistakes of scribes, has also brought us some unreliable evidence.

Practical in their perceived needs, the Romans relegated the Greek indulgences of science, philosophy, theatre, music and dance to secondary status except, in the case of the former, when put to practical military use. Although the cultures shared the same value of the production of good citizens, the narrow Roman perspective emphasised oratory. This had a clear function until the fall of the Republic and its replacement by Empire, effectively a military dictatorship. Under the Republic, free speech was essential to the office-gaining electoral process - although it could be dangerous, as the murders of the populist, reforming tribunes of the people Tiberius (c.169-133 BCE) and Gaius Gracchus (154-121 BCE) showed. It became suicidal under such emperors as Domitian (51-96 CE). Rhetoric was superseded by the study of grammar, emphasised by memorising. This had a progressively stultifying effect, resulting in the need for discipline to enforce the attention of generations of disaffected youth.

The literary art form which the Romans were able to claim as their own was satire. Only fragments survive of the *Saturae* poems counselling practical wisdom which "Father of Roman poetry" Ennius (c.239-c.169 BCE) often linked to fable to enforce the lesson. Lucilius (180,168 or 148-103 BCE), an equestrian of means, invented the political satire. Aggressive, censorious, criticism of people, morals, manners, and policies became an accepted literary style. Republican tracts of "in your face" banter were aimed at politicians as part of the hard-nosed nature of democratic exchange. Bringing a heightened linguistic awareness, the satiric approach sharpened the cut and thrust nature of Roman democracy.

The advent of Empire brought change, with satire becoming more introspective. Backer of the wrong side in the Octavian-Antony power struggle, Horace (Quintus Horatius Flaccus, 65 BCE-8 CE), was picked up, along with Virgil, by the quasi-culture minister of the renamed Augustus, Gaius Maecenas (70 BC-8 CE). Now effectively a court poet, Horace affected a sanitized form of satire, broadening targets to social observation. His was the popularisation of the "New Man" characterisation which the aristocracy had attached to the like of Marius and Cicero. Persius (34-62 CE) combined Stoicism with strong criticism of his poetic contemporaries. Nero's tutor Seneca (4 BCE-65 CE) satirised the deification of emperors by having the recently deceased and deified Claudius (10 BCE-54 CE) appeal for admission to an assembly of gods who, further addressed by the late Augustus, rejected him, condemning him thereafter to serve as Caligula's legal clerk.

The most subsequently celebrated of all Roman satirists, Juvenal (c.55-c.127), targeted the urban form of society, revelling in exposure of female wickedness (to later medieval monkish approval.) He brought attention to the minutiae of Roman life, with satire as self-critical as it was of society. While laughing at, rather than with, satirists might have become its classical conclusion, this addition to the Roman verbal armoury became another timeless management foundation threat: the means and ability to transform anger into laughter at the errors of power.

However, core Greek philosophical quests continued. As a young man, Marcus Aurelius (121-180 CE) had been warned off philosophy as being unlikely to help him or his career. This last of the "Five Good Emperors" was deeply influenced by the 3$^{rd}$ century self-control in harmony with nature theories of Zeno of Citium (336-265 BCE), founder of the theory of Stoicism. As both a Roman Emperor and philosopher, Marcus Aurelius practiced Stoicism and recorded his intellectual journey. Never intended for publication, his *Meditations* continue to provide a fine illustration of Stoic thought. He combined this exposition of happiness being found in virtue alone in the present moment, rejecting emotion as a basis for action with, a nonetheless very practical, Roman attitude:

> Make it not any longer a matter of dispute or discourse, what are the signs and proprieties of a good man, but really and actually to be such.[1]

In other words, stop talking about it; just get on with doing it.

His writings can be seen as training for rule, effectively management guidance, which to be fully understood and appreciated have to be set beside his practical achievements in delivering the governance expected of a second century Roman Emperor. He provided the stability of a long reign, campaigned effectively against the troublesome north Germanic tribes, slaughtering large numbers of barbarians; persecuted Christians, forcing them to become gladiators; provided circus entertainment with the killing of wild animals; while insisting on the registering of births to safeguard citizenship and encouraging the freeing of slaves. Such practical duality unsurprisingly won him Machiavelli's accolade of being a "good emperor," a fine manager for his time.

Marcus Aurelius retains a posthumous reputation as a highly competent ruler and philosopher, despite his deficiency in parenting skills. Although he gave great attention to his son's education, the product, Commodus (161-192 CE), anti-hero of the Ridley Scott (1937-) movie *Gladiator,* was held by Edward Gibbon (1737-1794) to mark the onset of the decline and fall of the Roman Empire.

The bardic tradition of poet-priest-philosopher was common to many ancient cultures. No more was this known as a means of state control than Rome under Augustus (63 BCE-14 CE; Emperor from 27 BCE), who approved the commissioning of the poet Virgil (70-19 BCE) to produce the epic *Aeneid,* modelled on Homer's *Iliad* and *Odyssey.*

Julius Caesar's nephew and adopted son, Octavian, took the name of Augustus on becoming Princeps (First Man), effectively Emperor of Rome, from 27 BCE.

**Bronze statue of Augustus**
**12-10 BCE**
National Archaeological Museum, Athens.

*Aeneid* told the story of the supposed journey of the hero Aeneas, from the destruction of Troy to the establishment of Rome. A foundation myth more congenial and heroic than the fratricide of Remus by Romulus, which also connected to the claim of Caesar's family of direct descent from Venus (Aphrodite), the *Aeneid* is accepted as one of the world's greatest literary achievements.

This was nonetheless parodied by the brilliantly mischievous yet fashionable poet Ovid (43 BCE-17/18 CE) in the first book of his masterpiece, *Metamorphoses* (Transformations). Ovid removed the Heroic Age from the listing of Hesiod to set forward his amended view of the progress of human civilisation:

> The Golden Age, with spontaneous nurture of the good and the true where people were entirely free, provisioned accordingly;

> The Silver Age, where civilisation began, with order and structure beginning;

The Bronze Age, which brought advances in technology accompanied by discord, divisions and conflict; and

The Iron Age, Ovid's present, where conflict intensified and each person pursued their own interests.

Myth had progressed into history. As those latter images have long been part of historical periodisation, so a contemporary commentator has applied the full Ovidian list to the state of Management Studies in 2012, later cited in **Case Study 3**. Such was the power of Rome for it to continue to add definition to western management education. Its language, Latin, remained the primary language of learning; its grammatical practice, intended originally for oratory, remained a constant for all access to education above the basic levels.

Roman pedagogical approaches dominated the expression of instruction. Until the 13$^{th}$ century, books of the West continued to be written in Latin. The language remained that of commerce, public service and education, the latter heavily dominated by the Roman Catholic Church. Up to very recent times, a classical education remained the badge of a gentleman, signal of membership of a civilised class - a cultural, social, and political passport to privilege. The management education inheritance was well established by the advent of Rome, of direct application thereafter.

Management has been defined as an art, a science, or both, in the achievement of goals, generally through and by the means of people; subdivided into supervision, where the overseer ensures that those persons do what they are supposed to do. How those functions are carried out depends upon time, place, and societal system. There were no specific management education guides or dedicated education in antiquity as such, but there were certainly administrative models, managerial practices, and management advice. Yet, management must be seen within the entire societal context; as Xenophon showed, the ancients knew of economic necessities, development, and planning. The first known work of Latin prose is a business plan.

Land ownership, always a particular mark of wealth and status, was the keystone of the Roman state, security of the food supply being fundamental to state control. Those working the land being, like the Greek hoplites, the part-time soldiers essential to ancient armies, and fully conscious of the value of farming, it was not surprising that a leading Roman politician should produce an agricultural management manual. Marcus Porcius Cato, the Elder (234-149 BCE) supplied educational, practical management and investment advice to a vital economic sector. His career spanned the period of emergent Roman power. At its beginning, Latin was but one of the many languages of the Italian peninsula and the Mediterranean world. By the time his great-grandson, the Younger Cato, left the Senate to fight Julius Caesar in North Africa, Latin and Greek had become the main languages of the region. Within a further century they had wholly replaced their competitors.

After the Persians defeated Tyre in 539 BCE, their model of economic management had continued to thrive under the leadership of Carthage. Its aristocratic managers concentrated their organisation of business under the protection of their fleet. Initiators of the convoy system, the (Carthaginian) Punic fleet protected merchant vessels from piracy, forming maritime capitalism as a type of military campaign. Militarised commerce, however, was not a viable long-term trade system. Moreover, as Bismarck was to observe, great power always raises up great forces against it.

The growing city of Rome, expanding through military conquest, encountered the Punic behemoth in a series of particularly savage wars from 264 to 146 BCE. These resulted in Rome becoming the dominant military and commercial Mediterranean power, impelled by the relentless cry of Cato the Elder at the conclusion of his every Senate speech: *delenda est Carthago:* Carthage must be destroyed. It fought using mercenaries, citizen-soldiers backed by a commercial arms industry which constructed fleets from a standing start - "legionary capitalism." A military-industrial complex had begun in an entrepreneurial state and private partnership, pitted against aristocratic state management backed by familial loyalties.

Carthage, in dominating the Mediterranean, had a forward base in Spain with control of much of the strategic islands: Corsica, Sardinia, and Ibiza. Principal trade goods included high quality cooking ware from Italy; exotic animals such as elephants for exploitation in games; the famous purple dye; and *garum*, a sauce made from rotting fish heads, eaten everywhere (the ketchup of its day). The city was extraordinarily opulent, comprised of spectacular buildings and six storied houses - a contrast to then provincial Rome, with a reputation for luxury and decadence offensive to conservative Romans. With each Senate denunciation, Cato brandished a fig, a fruit which could be consumed for much of the year, and a symbol of female pudenda. His was a campaign of overt moral cleansing.

The commercial reality was that Sicily, with its Carthaginian presence, became strategically crucial as Rome increasingly controlled Italy. It took twenty-two years of Sicilian conflict and three wars for the Romans to triumph. The destruction of Carthage, like that of Corinth previously, was a way of enforcing empire. They razed the city to the ground, ploughing its fields with salt; sold off its library; and, in destroying the habitation, sought further to destroy the civilisation based upon it. Wholly ruthless management marked this pivotal moment in world history, leaving Rome as the supreme Mediterranean power.

The Elder Cato had served with distinction in the Second Punic War, returning to his farm in breaks from the fighting where he earned the plaudits of his neighbours for his rigid conservatism, sharing the hard labour of farming with his workers, and upholding of the traditional Roman virtues of thrift, honour, and both physical and mental strength. His career in public office concluded, Cato continued to exert leadership in public affairs for the next thirty-five years through his senatorial speeches and prolific writings. Denouncing Greek culture, doctors, and Carthage, he called for the elimination of all, especially Carthage.

To Cato, individual life had to be as disciplined as public life. The individual seeded the family, which seeded the state. All had to be ruled by strict economy, all applied to hard, efficient work. A rigorous disciplinarian, he treated his family, slaves, and workers strictly, conduct which contemporaries and subsequent admirers upheld as Roman virtues to be viewed with respect, however harsh they may appear today. The further activity of this inexhaustible pillar of Roman rectitude was to continue to influence his fellow citizens through his writings.

As successful a writer as in all the other public areas of his life, Cato is credited as having been the first known author of consequence of Latin prose, the first historian of Italy in Latin, and the first to compile via literature a guide to Roman society through that canon: origins, aspirations, and management. Only the comic playwright Plautus (c.254-184 BCE) preceded him as a writer in Latin, although there may have been others whose works are lost.

His seven-book history, *Origines,* from the founding of the city, myths and all, was intended to instruct Romans in what it was to be Roman, emphasising his view of Stoic virtue. Typically, this was the text Cato used to teach his son to read. *On The Law Relating To Priests And Augurs* concerned how religion should be managed and conducted; *On Soldiery* dealt with military training and management; *To His Son* was a book of general advice; *Carmen De Moribus* concerned morals. The self-explanatory *Sayings* and *On Farming (De Agri Cultura),* together with his books of political speeches, completed his view of how Roman society should live, be governed and managed. This was a comprehensive view of the management and administration of the whole of Roman society of his day.

A further view is that Cato wrote to educate his son, and so his descendants. His modesty stood as his own memorial: "After I am dead I'd rather have people ask why I have no monument than why I have one". His advice to all to manage the condition known as "writers' block," was succinct and remains wholly applicable: "Grasp the subject, the words will follow". The only teachers then available were Greek, slave professionals; and Cato distrusted Greeks.

For Cato himself, as for all agricultural societies throughout most of history, life began early:

> I spent all my boyhood in frugality, privation and hard work,
> reclaiming the Sabine rocks,
> digging and planting those flinty fields. [2]

There was a Carthaginian farming manual and Greek compositions on farming, but Cato was unlikely to have been aware of these. His work was unique and original, without any form model, derived directly from his own practical experience. The economics were simple. Successful warfare had produced a surplus of cheap slave labour; land purchase was relatively inexpensive. New investors needed guidance in how best to gain returns. There is a tension in Cato's book between farming as an investment and as a way of life. Nonetheless, *De Agri Cultura* ("On the Cultivation of Fields") can be seen as the world's first known business plan, a plain precursor to the IPO, and a model still applicable in its example that any entrepreneur, or would-be start-up business person, must first fully understand and provide for the business in which he or she is aspiring to engage and manage.

Of all Cato's works, only *De Agri Cultura* has survived completely, probably because it has remained in use in some form up to and including the present day.[3] The work is a collection of rules of management and husbandry on the assumption of a farm being run and operated by slaves, with gangs of workers hired for specific seasonal tasks such as harvesting. His attitude to slaves may be held by some to have parallels with Stalin's implementation of "scientific management", but it is important here not to be judgmental: slavery was a normal aspect of the times in which Cato lived, a determinant of the economy. The acquisition of slaves was a benefit of successful warfare, common to humanity at the time, to which ethical practice could also apply.

Athenian law allowed pirate captured slaves to be released on liberation. Slavery could be a penalty for debt as well as a consequence of inherited status. Manumission, the granting of freedom to slaves, could follow an owner's death. Albeit to a minority, it could be given for faithful service or to better exploit ability. There was a hope of freedom, for a few. Freedmen were an important presence in Roman life, having learned business in service. The past is ever another country, where the inhabitants shift as best they might. Cato, however, very probably accommodated and maintained his slaves in no worse conditions, and indeed likely much better, than the 18th century Caribbean shippers and plantation owners, and those of the many of the victims of the world-wide, illegal but continuing practice today.

The *De Agri Cultura* sequence is: buying and developing a farm; selecting the property; directing the business; farm buildings; the farm manager; locations for planting; crops; supplies; harvesting; recipes; rituals and forms of contract: the type of dissection of activity well known to Management Studies. To Cato, trade was unsafe, members of the Senate barred by law from engaging in it, and money-lending immoral. To evade these restrictions and still make money meant investment, particularly in land as ownership brought other citizenship benefits, and the use of clients and intermediaries to manage the actual businesses.

The labour problems of running that business are wearyingly familiar over two thousand years later:

> As soon as you are clear how the business stands, what tasks are done and still to do, next day you should send for the manager and ask him how much of the work is finished, how much remains, whether what is done was done in time and there will be time to do the rest, and how it is with the wine, the grain and everything else singly.

> When you have this straight, you can get down to calculating people and days' work. If the work seems wanting the manager will say that he has done his best, slaves were sick, the weather was bad, slaves ran away or were requisitioned for public works: when he has put these and all his other

arguments, bring him back to the calculation of workers and their work! If there was rainy weather, what work could have been done while it rained? – washing and pitching vats, cleaning farm buildings, shifting grain, shovelling dung, making a dung-heap, threshing grain, mending ropes and making new ones; the slaves could have been patching their own cloaks and hoods. On holidays[4] they should have cleaned out blocked ditches, mended the public road, cut back hedges, dug the vegetable garden, cleared the meadow, cut sticks, pulled out brambles, husked the emmer,[5] tidied up. While slaves were ill, they ought not to have been given as much food.

When it is clear without dispute what work lies ahead, you must arrange for it to be done. You must check the figures for money and grain, check what is to be set aside for fodder, check the wine and oil figures – what is already sold, and the income from this, what is still to be produced, and what it will fetch – agree the difference and take charge of the agreed sum.

You must take stock; order to be bought whatever will be needed during the year; order to be sold whatever will be surplus; order to be contracted whatever needs contracting. You must give verbal orders on work that you want done and work that you want contracted, and also put the latter in writing. You must inspect the animals, and you must sell at auction: sell oil when it will pay; sell surplus oil and grain; sell aging oxen, runty calves, runty sheep; sell wool, hides, an old cart, old iron tools, an old slave, a sickly slave, and anything else surplus. The master has to be a selling man, not a buying man.[6]

Labour had to be kept busy, for "it will then be easier to prevent mischief and theft […] He must reward good behaviour, so that others will want to do well […] He must be the first up and the last to bed, having seen that the buildings are shut up, that everyone is in bed in his proper place, and that the animals have fodder."[7] The manager was forbidden to lend, must make regular accounts, and "must not engage the same tradesman or jobber for more than one day", nor make appointments with any "diviner, soothsayer, fortune-teller, or magician" and refrain from any business or contacts unknown to the owner. Instruction then extended to specific animal and crop husbandry, and to the details of many particular crops and their installation care, from vine planting to the types of manure best put to the roots of pomegranates, the whole summarised as "So much for the planning of a farm in various locations".[8] A current interpretation might include certain management gurus in the magician, soothsaying, and divination roles.

Extensive detail was supplied for crop instructions, buildings, and equipment. The latter included complete detail, from capital equipment such as olive and grape presses to the amounts and types of farm implement required according to the area cultivation size. In his section on "Provisions for the household", Cato's labour advice was similarly economically detailed but comprehensive: "For the chain gang, 4 lb. bread in winter; when they begin to dig the vineyard, 5 lb., until there begin to be figs; then revert to 4 lb." *De Agri Cultura* is management by empirical method and an instruction manual perhaps, but certainly efficient.

Economy is all: "If you cannot sell firewood and sticks and have no stone to make lime, make charcoal with your wood. Sticks and canes that are of no use to you should be burnt in the field. Sow poppy where you had the bonfire [...]".[9] "In rain, look for work to be done indoors. Rather than do nothing, do cleaning. Remember that the establishment will cost just as much if nothing is done".[10] Contractor prices were to be fair, arbitration the recourse in dispute. Cato died a wealthy man.

Maximum economic benefit was efficiently to be gained and maintained; costs minimised; and inefficiencies eliminated, meaning slaves were to be kept continually at their labour. Crops were viewed equally dispassionately. Vines were judged of highest importance, this because the wine trade at a time of rising consumer expansion, affluence and discrimination was of increasing profitability; olives were a continuing staple but grain was of a lower rank.[11] Trade stability did not arrive in Rome itself until towards the end of the Republic with the establishment of the grain dole. Even then, foreign competition, and the increasing need to import a commodity subject to price and availability fluctuation, made it an unreliable staple for the Italian domestic agricultural economy.

A strong case can be made for regarding Cato as the founder of written management theory and practice, but we have neither the full collection of his writings nor the practical, quantifiable results of widespread slavery. There is exhortation, example and instruction but the same might be said of Moses. The Cato approach was to know the business in intimate detail, supervise it, operate it fairly, maximise profit, eliminate waste, prepare for all foreseeable eventualities, think and act swiftly and decisively, all whilst behaving properly and ethically. He did not write conceptually, he wrote practically. Within the confines of his times and experience, he was an outstanding role model whose example still has much to teach.

Indeed, applications of the principles underlying *De Agri Cultura* provide a wholly adequate model for the foundation and operation of any start-up: know the business; cover all foreseeable eventualities; gain customers and be a seller; ensure that the management and workforce are fully occupied and productive; and deal fairly. Cato deserves the paternity title of "father of business planning." In noting later the stultifying effect of the Latin university curriculum on the bored offspring of the landed classes, it was always possible to receive a business education through the classics if, like any thorough historian, they knew where to look.

The Macedonian adventurers, Philip II and his son Alexander, expanded their domain through intrepid vision with military and leadership innovation. Aristotle's pupil was obsessed with Greek history and the battle for Troy. He saw himself emulating Homeric heroes, keeping a copy of the *Iliad* under his pillow. Herodotus had traced back the enmity between "Asia" (Persia) and the Greek world to the Trojan war. The retributive campaign against the Persian Empire had been begun by Philip and was taken over by his son.

The ultimate ruler, general, and military manager, Alexander was peerless. Perhaps only Genghis Khan and Napoleon come close, but Alexander had no defeats. Outnumbered four to one, he defeated the Persian army under Darius III in open warfare at the 331 BCE Battle of Gaugamela, or "Arbela," west of Erbil, Iraq. Using superior equipment, strategy, tactics, and morale, he precipitated the removal of the Persian king by one of his own generals. He had defeated the Persians at sea by the successful siege of its harbour on the island of Tyre, to which he built a still extant causeway. The Tyrians were punished with mass crucifixions, to send the message that Alexander was not to be disobeyed. In the depths of the Afghan winter, he took snowbound mountain fortresses. By the end, he was showboating by crushing small Asian settlements, then attempting in his retreat to link with his navy, commanded by a friend - perhaps he began to lose touch with reality. Yet, he remains history's most famous figures of the past two millennia; a statesman, man, and military manager beyond compare.

Alexander became the role model to Roman imperial rulers. His successes have obscured his father's achievements. They were co-inventors and exploiters of the improved Macedonian phalanx, an advanced battle formation built on a larger, further armoured version of the Spartan original. This became the norm until the creation of the Roman legions, the next great Western military advance. The shield wall had been a core infantry feature since the 7th century BCE. This rectangular military formation was composed of troops in ranks at least four lines deep who tightly linked arms, allowing their shields and spears to be locked closely together. They were trained to march towards the enemy to the beat of drums and pipes, breaking into a run just before battle commenced. A phalanx required total loyalty and depended upon every man in the fighting force. Just one drooping shield could expose the whole grouping to failure. The battle winners were invariably those with the strongest, most fearless soldiers, pushed hardest from the rear.

The significant further Roman addition was that of the *testudo*, the tortoise. Here, the first rank troops locked their long shields; the second ranks held their shields at head height, followed progressively by the further ranks. Tightly packed and with the outer soldiers locking shields at the side, a fully armoured unit was created, whereby arrows, stones, and other missiles bounced off the overhead canopy. The *testudo* was not invincible, however, for there were always lessons to learn.

When Gaius Marius (157-86 BCE) was elected junior consul in 107 BCE, charged with the military duty of concluding the North African war against King Jugurtha of Numidia (c.160-104 BCE), he had a most significant problem: there was no available army. Rome was, at that time, a republic, headed by two short-term elected consuls. The senior consul had another war to fight elsewhere and, being senior, had control of all the available troops. There was a shortage of fighting men because of the restrictions on recruitment, the nature of the composition of the army, manpower depletion due to a succession of conflicts, and the decline in small farms which produced the citizen-soldiers because of the expansion of large estates.

Soldiers had to be tax payers, own land, and able to supply their own armour. The poorest citizens (and usually the youngest) were known as the *proletarii (*fifth class citizens*)*. Unable to afford armour, they were placed in the front line with the job of hurling objects, usually but not necessarily javelins, at the enemy's opposing front with the general objective of causing confusion and diversion rather than damage. Thereafter, progressive lines of infantry, class and experience based, were flanked by those who could afford a horse, armed with a spear. These were members of the equestrian order, the knights.

An effective fighting force for its time, requiring close management and firm leadership, the Roman army before Marius's reforms was based on governmental rather than military needs: class, social stability, and economics were determinants. It was the latter factor, because of agricultural change which now made reform inevitable. Said reform was to change Rome, and the world, forever. In a revolutionary step, Marius gained the admission of the "head count" (the *capite censi*) - those who had no property were to be assessed in the census to determine their eligibility for army service. Equipping them with weapons and armour, providing pay and the opportunity to share in the spoils of successful campaigning, he had created the world's first fully professional army. The poor, land-less "head count", with no other way of acquiring status, flocked to join.

If they survived, Marius also secured the soldiers' futures. Retirement with a pension paid by their general, and a land entitlement supplied by the state was granted after 16 years' service, later extended to 20 with a five-year re-enlistment option. Commander and officer retirement benefits were much greater. An effective politician, Marius solved a further problem by granting Roman citizenship and benefits to members of the Italian allied states if they completed service in fighting for Rome. He provided immediate and continuing training, all year round. Standard drill, armour and equipment were successively followed by a standardisation of all military requirements. Fort design, for example, became commonly identical throughout the subsequent Roman world.

Each legion was formed of 6,000 men, 4,800 of whom were soldiers and the remainder non-combatants. Division of labour produced 10 cohorts of six centuries each, the century comprising 80 soldiers and 20 service providers, led by a centurion. Sub-division again produced 10 *contubernium* of eight soldiers and two servants, commanded by a *decanus.* The units marched, fought, and camped together. Each soldier carried his own armour and 15 days' provisions, packs weighing 22.5 to 27 kg. They were further served by approximately one mule per unit.

A truly rapid reaction force, kept fit by constant drill and exercise (including involuntary weight training), produced a military management system which effectively continues today. Moreover, the inbuilt reciprocity of information communication, from *decanus* to centurion, onwards to officers and *vice versa,* provided commanders with the close control and flexibility which were as evident on campaign as when the soldiers had occasion to proclaim their general *imperator*: originally, acclamation of excellence in the field (latterly as ruler: emperor).

The long-term effects of the reforms for Rome were far-reaching. A citizen militia was replaced by a professional standing army capable of the conquest and retention of much of the known world for half a millennium.

The settlement of veterans on conquered land had the further effects of Romanizing the area while adding to its retention and defence. The reverse of the coin was the transference of soldiers' loyalty from the state to their general, the font for their rewards, thus fuelling subsequent civil wars and the replacement of the Republic by Empire. The Roman military machine was not invincible, but nonetheless highly effective.

The great exception was the 9 CE Battle of the Teutoburg Forest under the early empire, when three legions, six auxiliary cohorts, and three squadrons of cavalry were ambushed and destroyed by Germanic tribes, the scale of the loss causing the Romans to abandon their dream of conquering the whole of Germania, instead making the Rhine the perman,ent frontier. This has been judged to have been Rome's greatest loss and a turning point in world history. It was organised and managed by Arminius (18/17 BCE–21 CE), a Germanic tribal chieftain who had lived in Rome, learnt Latin, served in the military, and attained equestrian rank. A knight of the empire who had served with distinction, he was sent as an aide to Publius Quinctilius Varus (46 BCE–9 CE) on an expedition to complete a Germanic conquest.

Instead, Arminius lured Varus into a trap from which escape was impossible, then orchestrated the ensuing massacre. So great was the distress of Augustus that Suetonius records him repeatedly banging his head against the palace walls, screaming "Varus! Give me back my legions!" Varus had taken the Roman way out, by falling on his sword. Arminius rose in power among the German tribes, but was assassinated by them, like Julius Caesar, for having become too powerful. The management lessons to all parties became starkly clear.

The Republic had become highly corrupt, dysfunctional, and increasingly incapable of the stable administration of the territories won by its Marius-empowered, competitive generals. Ornaments to traditional Roman virtues such as Cicero (106-43 BCE) and Marcus Porcius Cato the Younger (95-46 BCE) gave expression to ideals of freedom inspirational to many future generations, but were nonetheless deeply conservative. They held that the optimates (best people) or *boni* (good men), those who subscribed to their values, knew best and that they and their descendants were therefore the correct people to run the Republic. They were reinforced by traditional values, known as the *mos maiorum.* This was the unwritten code from which the Romans derived their social norms, such as the complete authority of the head of the household. This core management concept embodied the tradition of what it was to be Roman. Complementary to written law, the "way of the ancestors" (commemorated through household collections of generations of death masks) upheld conservative, traditional stability. This applied to all aspects of management of Roman life.

Young Cato was particularly proud of his great grandfather, frequently invoking his name in public debate: an impeccable symbol of the *mos maiorem*. Scrupulous and determined, pillar of stoic rectitude, famously incorrupt, constant Senate attendee, and acerbic critic of those who missed sessions, he could be a deeply annoying person, eating only when necessary and drinking the cheapest wine. Nonetheless, Cicero attributed to him, in a play and in letters, encomia of liberty:

> Whoever would overthrow the liberty of a nation, must begin by subduing freedom of speech.… Without freedom of thought, there could be no such thing as wisdom; and no such thing as public liberty, without freedom of speech…

> By liberty I understand the power which every man has over his own actions, and his right to enjoy the fruits of his labour, art and industry, as far as by it he hurts not the society, or any members of it, by taking from any member, or by hindering him from enjoying what he himself enjoys. The fruits of a man's honest industry are the just rewards of it, ascertained to him by natural and eternal equity, as is his title to use them in the manner which he thinks fit. And thus, with the above limitations, every man is the sole lord and arbiter of his own private actions and property.

Plutarch (46-119) further records Young Cato displaying his precocious republican principles as a youth. Asking his Greek tutor, Sarpedon, why no one had killed the Dictator Sulla (138-78 BCE), he provoked a recollection of Thucydides' report of the *Melian Dialogues* of failed peace negotiations, "They fear him, my child, more than they love him".[12] This central issue of leadership, in any context, reverberates throughout management history. Thucydides' account of the 416 BCE response of the Athenian delegation to the Council of the Melians epitomises the diplomatic attitudes of the ancient world:

> …we recommend that you should try to get what it is possible for you to get, taking into consideration what we both really do think; since you know as well as we do that, when these matters are discussed by practical people, the standard of justice depends on the equality of power to compel and that in fact the strong do have the power to do and the weak accept what they have to accept.[13]

One of those counted as weak in his power struggle with Mark Antony died for free speech republicanism. Marcus Tullius Cicero, lawyer, politician, and author, is commonly held as having the greatest influence on European language and expression, certainly up to the 20th century, with his prose style either forming that of literature or being that from which diversion occurred. Cicero is credited with having turned Latin prose from the utilitarian form as first expressed by the Elder Cato into a versatile literary version allowing of easy conceptual expression, elegance, and wit. He introduced Romans to Greek philosophy, expanded the Latin vocabulary, and became the most effective of lawyers, dominating with the brilliance of his oratory. His faithful client and recorder Tiro's (103-4 BCE) shorthand was probably a management device of necessity, given the volume of the Ciceronian output.

Although he rated his political career as his most important, - a claim with seeming merit as he achieved the consulship and (clumsily) foiled a plot against the state, which ultimately rebounded against him - it ended badly. His judgment and action in times of crisis was suspect. Caesar, with whom his relationship was uneven, observed of him that it was preferable to have greatly extended the frontiers of the human spirit, as he did, than to have expanded its borders, as did Caesar. This was management, by both, on a grand scale.

Although dominant in the late Roman Republic, his greatest fame arose through the admiration of the early and medieval Church, as well as the influence of his humanism upon and through the European Renaissance and, later, the Enlightenment. Early Greek philosophers (such as Thales, Anaximander, and others of the Milesian school) had sought to explain the world in terms of human reason and natural law without relying on myth, tradition, or religion. Socrates echoed Pittacus's injunction to "know thyself." Aristotle taught ethics and rationalism based on human nature - a stance which, to him and Epicurus (341-270 BCE), was a means to achievement of *eudaimonia*, the good life. Cicero's informal academy, the Studia Humanitas, taught "the art of living well and blessedly through learning and instruction in the fine arts," with his version of *humanitas* putting man and God at the centre of the world. *Humanitas* corresponded to Greek concepts of what makes us human, education, and the unwritten Roman code of conduct, the *mos maiorum*.

Cicero's academy called for a complete system of education, focusing heavily on personal development. He opposed what he considered to be outmoded or inappropriate Roman values, such as philistinism, pragmatism, and the superstitious tradition of popular religion. Olympian deities had to be replaced by something more rigorous. Reacting against macho Roman attitudes, he sought their replacement by Greek curriculum: poetry and physical training, all bound by and with philosophy. Learning to train oneself meant to care for oneself by looking inwards through that self; by philosophy, one might learn how to be a better person, so becoming happy with oneself.

The young Cicero had, first, to go to Athens to learn philosophy, then seek to turn it into something which the pragmatic Romans could use. That his approach became successful was remarkable. Traditional Rome saw its culture as being undermined by Greeks: *cf.* old Cato's attitudes, and the early opposition to the study choice of Marcus Aurelius. With Cicero, the new Rome was being civilised by Greek values. The salient point of entry was education. Every elite Roman was expected to get some form of it. Here, the tiny elite of the elite were being given a Greek-based education. As part of its leadership training and mental development, the intelligentsia was being taught poetry in a philosophy school.

Subversively, Cicero was changing the way Roman power thought about itself. This was achieved through the many philosophical tracts which Cicero issued; also, through his many letters, published soon after they were written, helping his readers to think and feel that they were part of some magic inner circle. Most importantly, the strategy made people realize that by reading, they could become part of this power centre. For his ideas to change things, Cicero had to reinvent "*humanitas*," turning its study into the key term for this curricular enterprise, taking philosophical transcendentalism and making it an ethical philosophy. The text of greatest influence was that which tested the responsibilities of a human being. Stoicism was a public duty, but also concerned the responsibilities of a citizen as a human being. In order to deal with power in the world of public duty, it was also essential to learn how to cope with supreme power.

Centuries later, depictions of Cicero's teachings had been changed into "classical humanism," a faith in the soft arts of the Greek world. The early church father, St Augustine of Hippo (354-430), was educated in the Ciceronian humanist tradition and, while rejecting it in favour of his Christianity, brought its non-religious values into Christian thought. Revived by Petrarch (1304-1374), rediscoverer of Cicero's letters, the aim in the Renaissance was to produce thoughtful secretaries and administrators, obedient and capable of working together.

His expression of republicanism was greatly influential in the French Revolution and to the Founding Fathers of the USA. While he has been applauded as the provider of the bedrock of the principles of liberty, Cicero has also been decried for his support of the Roman oligarchy and opposition to Caesar's popular reforms. Roman representation of "the People" (as in SPQR: the Senate and People of Rome, *Senatus Populusque Romanus*), even under the Republic, was a very unbalanced affair. The patricians had control with a prescribed wealth qualification necessary to reach the Senate or to achieve equestrian (knightly) status, with the ordinary citizens voting within and by their tribes in electoral matters. Nonetheless, it is certainly the case that Cicero's writings, and their form, have influenced thought, culture, politics, and therefore management ever since.

It is necessary to stress that when the Founding Fathers of the United States of America looked for a model from antiquity, it was not Greek democracy that they turned to, despite Tom Paine's advocacy of Pericles and the Athenian model. Instead, they turned to a republic, and the inspiration for that was Rome. What appears, in the early 21st century, to be an arcane representative electoral system has a design to avoid the fear of democracy or "mob rule" as its very clear origin. It could be argued that the Electoral College is a means for an elite retention of control.

The Roman Republic died with the Younger Cato and Cicero; it had outlived its time. At its worst, it was a corrupt, squabbling aristocracy of optimates, the "best" people settled wealth and power between them. Formally, the power figure would have swarms of clients, waiting in ante-rooms for an audience or awaiting the response to a request, soliciting a favour while doing the required favour in return. The stage above was that of political friendships, the essence of patronage where the motto *manus manum lavat* applied: one hand washes the other.

Caesar's reforms enabled a coherent, civilised, albeit militant rule over much of Europe, North Africa, and the Near East which endured for half a millennium. The successor Empire, disguised a little at first by the longevity, public relations expertise, and managerial skill of Augustus, became a family firm with an army. That is, until those increasingly wayward Caesar family descendants, the Julio-Claudians, ruined themselves. It effectively then became a well-managed military dictatorship up to the time of Commodus.

Yet both the Catos left indelible marks of what it meant to be a leader - not just of Roman society, but of enterprises as mundane as a farm and as all-encompassing as the management of a state. Of those Roman writers who ventured further than biography when writing their histories, Tacitus (54-120) makes reference to the direct, "hands on" style of Agricola (40-93), governor of Britain; while Arrian (86/89-146/160) considered Alexander's charismatic style as a means to win followers. Frontinus (40-103), an aqueduct engineer and the ultimate armchair general, set situations and how past generals had reacted to them, inviting the reader to choose options: good game but not much more than that. Vegetius (late 4th/early 5th centuries) wrote admiringly of the early Roman legions, but probably mainly to advocate reform in his own times. His writing on siege craft remained in use through the medieval period, all the way up to the Renaissance. Discussing such items as training, equipment, logistics, and organisation, he argues that the well trained, equipped, and prepared force will prevail. Interestingly, he also proclaims himself a Christian.

The strength of expanding Rome had mightily extended business. The legions' successes brought plunder aplenty, greatly increasing available capital. New wealth and territory introduced increased opportunities and revenues for the tax farming *publicani*. Rights were originally granted to members of the equestrian order, who were on the rung below the senatorial class. The levies grew to such sizes that no individual could guarantee returns. Thus, partnerships became necessary. These were termed *societates*, in which each partner had a share, the businesses expanding at once into the arms trade through making swords and shields for the legions. The groupings were informal, for tax farming was a short-term contract matter and arms requirements depended upon campaigning quantities and locations.

At all levels, business systems worked through family and client networks. Land was the stable basis of wealth; the detailed method and management of which Cato the Elder had illustrated. Great earnings, however, came from public contracting: arms supply to the legions, building contracts, collection of port duties, and other taxes. The tax farming of provinces was major international business. State security required the farming of contracts to those of capacity to ensure stable provision. The tax farming method, until its replacement under Augustus by a provincial land and poll tax, was prime *publicani* business. Effectively a prototype of public-private partnerships (large contracts grouped together), *publicani* introduced a form of limited liability partnership - first competitively, latterly as a cartel. There was then no concept of limiting liability in business, but personal liability applied and for which property confiscation and slavery stood as penalties.

The *societas publicanorum* thus invented the practice of common slave ownership, whereby a jointly owned slave served as the CEO of the enterprise. Slaves being objects, responsible only for their own costs, their owners were freed from responsibility for the business they conducted. From the establishment of custom, the practice continued whereby the corporations arising were considered to have a legal existence of their own, even if the agent or contractor, the *manceps*, were to die. The enterprises were of limited duration, for specific purposes, in various sectors, with *societas* membership while family based, flexible according to network and need variations.

However, the *societates* expanded the idea that an association of people could have a collective, and hence corporate, identity. That identity was distinct from the individuals concerned. The partners, the *socii* – associates – left management to a *magister* to operate the business. This allowed the aristocracy and the senators, who were not allowed to engage in trade, the opportunity of investing instead. The *magister's* duties included supervision and operation of agents, and the keeping of accounts, as demonstrated by the Elder Cato's instructions.

Intriguingly, *magister* – an all-purpose term for "master" – was also used as a synonym for *praeceptor*, teacher or professor, a further evolution of the managerial concept. Old Cato had written of himself as the master. Now the *opera* or *vilicus,* the overseers of *De Agri Cultura*, have ascended to the *magister* rank. Managerialism had begun, with upward drift. Agents were employed to supervise and operate their affairs outside the *societas* base. In a large tax farming operation, an agent might supervise tens of thousands of employees. Revenues could be enormous, as could business crashes.

The junior upper-class body, the equestrian order, could freely engage in trade. Knights usually led the *societas publicanorum* but operated on a lean management, case-by-case basis, with few, if any, central staff. Organised groups of skilled professionals in all the major trades, from tax farming to shipbuilding, did have their service employees and would operate on fixed contract bases. Plebians or freedmen undertook such enterprises as shop, tavern or stall holding; artisan trade; or as businessmen, of which there were two main types: *negotiatores* and *mercatores.* The system relied upon cheap labour, which itself provided a tradable commodity: slaves. Indeed, it was probably the availability of such plentiful cheap labour which inhibited industrialisation.

Steam power was known in the Greek world from the 3$^{rd}$ century BCE, and the steam engine in the 1$^{st}$ century CE. However, man and horse power, roads, canals, and the sea provided for then-current needs. Moreover, industrially generated produce requires mass demand, which was restricted to a small number of commodities. Most of the Empire's inhabitants were too poor to generate mass demand beyond a few basic needs, but service of those marked a beginning of industrial method.

The business classes within the system of "legionary capitalism," allowing for individual and group entrepreneurialism as part of a mixed economy, were clearly demarcated. *Negotiatores* bought and sold staples in bulk, or traded wholesale; operating as a mixture of brokerage and logistics management, bringing together buyers and sellers, fixing prices and organising transport. They also had a banking function as they lent money on interest. Here, the trader was further known as an *argentarius,* a dealer in silver, or a banker.

The *argentarius* money-changers kept deposits for clients, and cashed what amounted to cheques (*prescriptiones*: "written before"). Their *tabulae,* tables, or accounts were acceptable in court as legal proof. Their business coincided sometimes with the *mensarii,* the state-appointed public bankers. The *mercatores* hawked food and goods from open air stalls, markets, by the roadside, or, particularly to army camps, on an itinerant basis. Trade in booty, clothing and supplementary food could be brisk during conflicts. The peddling trade brought benefits of empire, such as perfumes and spices, to its communities. Auction houses provided an early type of department store, stocked in the manner of a modern charity shop, aiding the circulation of household goods in addition to the lucrative trade in *objets d'art.*

The later Republic had commenced the creation, consolidated by the Empire, in which a single monetary system applied in much of Europe, North Africa, and the Near East. It has been argued that, with taxation in the later Empire of around ten per cent per capita, the silver *denarius* approximating to a day's wages, and a mainly free internal market, Rome formed an early version of the European Union. From trading bases established in India, where trade with China was facilitated, this progressed to being the first world (but not global) economy. To service that dominion, industrial mass production began. Pottery, glassware, tiles, bricks, lamps, and stone work were produced in such volume that agents and wholesalers were required to service the market. There were a number of management models: co-operative potter partnerships; brick works on land owner premises supervised by a master-workman (*officinatore*); and the more sophisticated lamp production, confined to fewer locations.

"I found Rome a city of bricks but left it a city of marble," so boasted Emperor Augustus as recorded by Suetonius. It was actually mainly of wooden construction, a constant fire hazard. Augustus had instituted a fire-fighting force, managed on military lines in district cohorts, the *vigilis*. They also doubled as a rudimentary police force in an effort to combat rising crime, especially street violence. The *vigiles* paralleled private fire forces, such as that previously operated by the late Marcus Licinius Crassus (115-53 BCE). He had achieved plutocrat status through property dealing. His favourite acquisition method had been to order his men to the scene and neighbourhood of a fire among the tinder-dry apartment buildings, ready to create fire breaks with their artillery equipment, operate their rocking lever and force pump mobile fire engines. All the while, bucket chains and "mattress men" with blankets stood by, inactive, until householders gave in to sell and get what they still could as the flames advanced at ever decreasing property fire sale prices.

The first Emperor had been making the point of the splendour of the public buildings for which he was responsible. He was a main market in himself, and made many more. Marble from the major quarries was mined in bulk. It was stored in yards over long periods of up to 200 years. Marble columns were fashioned in standard heights. Different models of caskets were made for different markets, some of which had their own fashioning workshops. A nationalised, multinational industry involving mass production, standardisation, prefabrication, overseas agents, skilful operation of technical equipment, storage, local variation, marketing and sales: if limited, this was still early industrialisation, requiring managerial skill at several levels.

As the management of the Empire developed, its staples' provision was rationalised: grain came from Egypt, North Africa, and Sicily; olive oil locally from Greece, but in great bulk from Spain; and large markets in Rome specialised around such goods as fish, vegetables, animals and wine. With it being easier to transport goods by sea and the protection of the staples' supply essential, including that of Egyptian papyrus, the practice was the grouping of mercantile shipping under the protection of the state fleet. The *negotiatores* could thus have protection for the transport of high value items procured in or from India – such as spices, gems, ivory, bullion - and the produce exported through the Silk Road, the eponymous demand for which was high among the upper classes. Purchase appears, again, to have been through family networks.

Although senators and their sons were forbidden from owning a ship with a capacity greater than 300 *amphorae,* they used connections to circumvent. The amphora held under 50 kg, used principally for wine, and had to be in conformity with the demonstration model held in the main temple of Jupiter. Monetary exchange was expressed through the counting board and, using Roman numerals, the Roman abacus. There was a well-established business system with its own built-in management. Family, client, and network based at the top, working with and through selective intermediaries. This was replicated by skilled labour and service providers at the bottom through their "gatherings": *collegium.* Each section of Roman society was organised, from the patricians to the plebeians. Underpinning it all was the cheap labour provided by slavery, a currency deriving from successful military management.

Trade group organisation was mirrored in the lower societal ranks where merchants and craftsmen formed guilds, known as *collegia* or *corpora.* That the former gave its name to an educational grouping and the latter to public and private business formations is of significance also when origins are considered. The *collegia* and *corpora* elected their own managers and were required to be licensed. However, licensing could be refused or ignored according to circumstance. The proposal for a "licensed manager" has long antecedents.

Julius Caesar, in his rise to power in Rome, can be seen as a gang boss or manager in the human relations tradition, according to perspective, for he garnered much support from his patronage and use of working class *collegia.* The famous bequest reported by Mark Antony in Shakespeare's *Julius Caesar* was a payment of many kinds of dues:

> Moreover, he hath left you all his walks
> His private arbors and new planted orchards,
> On this side Tiber, he hath left them you,
> And to your heirs for ever, common pleasures,
> To walk abroad and recreate yourselves.[14]

Popular organisational management obligations had been publicly recognised. There is an economics debate on the extent to which the Roman Empire can be described as a market economy. Because economic actions in antiquity were socially based, driven by social concerns, it is argued that ancient humanity had no notion of the economy as a distinct sphere of activity. Against this is the evidence of technological change, the tax reforms of Augustus, and the interlinked nature of the Empire where many individual markets knitted together to form a market economy.

> There were enough market transactions to constitute a market economy, that is, an economy where many resources are allocated by prices that are free to move in response to changes in underlying conditions … typically equilibrated by means of prices. [15]

Forms of meritocracy characterised the early Empire. After the fall of the wayward Julio-Claudians, the frugal Emperor Vespasian (9-79 CE), whose family wealth derived from the mule trade, famously remarked: "money doesn't stink".[16] Roman pragmatism favoured business. To his son Titus' protest, Vespasian had taxed the urine-powered laundry business. This prime recycling concern provided teeth-cleaning for Celtiberians, a chemical combination of urea and nitrogen sufficiently powerful to clean and enhance the snow-white togas of politicians running for elective office, and all the general laundry services necessary for a crowded population largely engaged in sweat-producing occupations, often in aroma-high premises, such as a tannery.

Demand for the public baths was naturally high. The around 500 Roman *balneae,* smaller scale facilities which could be public or private, further proliferated throughout the empire. They also provided facilities for massage, reading, and socialising, often situated at the rear of a standard apartment building. Deterrents to theft, a frequent issue, slaves would be available to guard possessions. The aqueduct-supplied main *thermae,* imperial bath complexes, became construction status symbols in their own right. Early and late 3$^{rd}$ century, the baths of Caracalla and Diocletian were the largest established in Rome but the trend had begun with Nero's 22,000 square metres in the 1$^{st}$, overtaken by Trajan's 70,000 in the 2$^{nd}$. True to his motto of "excess in the best possible taste", Nero had set the template whereby between two and five thousand patrons per day could enjoy his epitome of relaxation:

> "What could be worse than Nero,"
> asked Martial (40 - 103),
> "or better than his baths?"[17]

The size of Rome alone, at a population of over a million, made it the largest European city before London in 1800. It had an agricultural supply chain and domestic capacity sufficiently efficient to feed the people, some of them well. *Pax Romana*, the Roman Peace, stimulated trade. Transport costs being lower than those by road promoted regional specialisations accessible by sea or river. In Rome itself, the restrictions of narrow streets and a burgeoning population inhibited goods' supply or export during the day, such traffic prohibition in daylight being forbidden by law. Noisy ox, mule, and donkey drawn, iron rimmed, solid wooden wheeled carts clattered through neighbourhoods whose inhabitants had either become inured to the noise or adjusted to disturbed sleep.

They may have awoken to the smell of baking bread and the sounds of production as the last of a sack of grain was ground by the mill stone endlessly rotated by the pulling of a plodding, blindfolded donkey. From the late days of the Republic, there was a grain dole for the poor. Bakeries for the poor's grain were meant to limit fire risk. Prices of grain and other staples, albeit limited, were uniform. Rome's market economy, irrespective of whether it was recognised as such by its denizens, was well illustrated by commerce outside its borders. High prices for silk and horses from the east contrasted with the stability of domestic production. Despite the difficulties cited above, living conditions were better than anything afterwards, up to the 18th century:

> The Roman Empire was a coherent political and economic system, operating on a scale that has seldom since been matched in Europe and the Mediterranean, and never for so long.[18]

Even so, health care, policing, and most social services were either rudimentary or non-existent. A high number of new-borns died before the age of 5. Rome's population kept falling, bolstered only by the ever-increasing immigration. Disease and injustice were endemic: hazards, perhaps sent by the gods, were to be endured and accepted. Grafitti found in the remains of temples and bars, such as those preserved at Pompeii, provides a record of the voices, opinions, and attitudes of the bulk of the population outside the elite. While illiteracy was high throughout most of the empire, this was not the case in urban areas inhabited by artisans, traders, and craftsmen who needed the ability to read and write to perform in their occupations. Apart from bawdy sexual frankness, such as boasts of having bedded the landlady, there seems to have been quotation from the best-known lines of great poets, occult curses to pursue enemies even after death, and reflections on life itself. A gaming board scratched record offers a succinct verdict:

> Hunting, bathing, gaming, laughing: that's living.[19]

The authorities were wholly duplicitous regarding gambling. They were as avid gamers as Emperor Claudius, senators bet on arena sports, but viewed their subjects as morally degenerate for indulging in the same pursuits. Whilst violent crime in the acquisition of goods was usual, and protests against inequality and injustice sparked by particular events, the have-nots were not revolutionary. Rather, they hoped to gain societal advance for themselves. The street corner bars selling take-away fast food from open counters with interior seating for gamers, diners, and drinkers might have provided sustenance mixed with conviviality, with brawling as occasion provided, but it was an aspirational, upwardly mobile society. It had sophisticated taste and an insistence on quality. Fish sellers kept their product alive and fresh where possible by delivering and hawking it in buckets of water. There was a continuing attempt to manage in a volatile world of changing and challenging uncertainties, still offering forms of personal freedom previously unknown. Slaves may gain their freedom; the lucky break might change a fortune; the gamble pay-off: and after all, you had to laugh.

Yet, ancient Rome retained an entrepreneurial attitude. It was the centre of the known world, where the action was - make it there and, as was said of another city in another civilisation, you could make it anywhere. This was partially attributable to the common attitudes born of communal living; apartment blocks housed communal lavatories, public baths and the habit of eating with friends and family (at home if monied, out if not) all made for a strong community spirit, especially as foreign conquests continued. Almost from the very beginning, Rome had religious protection stemming from the foresight of its second ruler after Romulus. This was the legendary, peaceable state management strategist Numa Pompilius (c.753–672 BCE), who was said to have devised much of Rome's calendar and most important religious institutions: the cults of Romulus, Mars, and Jupiter; the office of Pontifex Maximus (chief priest); and the Vestal Virgins.

Priestesses of Vesta, goddess of the hearth and home, and the six Vestals were held to be fundamental to the continuance and security of Rome. Their primary duty was to maintain the sacred fire, never allowed to go out. They were freed from their father's control, but were compelled to take a 30-year vow of chastity. The three decades of service were split equally into learning, doing, and teaching. Spare daughters of the aristocracy but able to enjoy their freedom after service, even to marry, Vestals also decorated state occasions and games while performing such useful social services as the storing of wills. The further obligation was the study and ensuring of the correct observation of state rituals forbidden to the college of male priests, and preservation of their sacred relics, emblems and talismans.

The latter duty was successfully accomplished during the 390 BCE raid of the Gauls upon Rome. Dereliction of duty however incurred severe penalty. Breaking of the vow of chastity, which occurred in 216 BCE and 113 BCE, was punished by burial alive. As the Vestals were sacred, the institution as old as Rome, although unchastity could cost fire, famine, earthquake, or loss in battle, they could not be killed. The management solution was to immure the victim within a cell cut into the city walls with a little sustenance, and so leave her to the fate of being buried alive.

Shocking such scandal was, the attendant gossip was the spice to many a tavern tale, part of the essence of Roman life. That communally managed system further required entertainment. Juvenal's celebrated phrase, *panem et circenses* – bread and circuses – was never more apt than at or near the end of his life when the Emperor Trajan (53-117) celebrated defeat of the Dacians in 107 CE. The revels occupied 123 festival days in Rome, featuring the slaughter of 11,000 wild animals, battles involving 10,000 gladiators, and paid for by the spoils of war quoted at ten million kilos of gold, twenty million kilos of silver and 500,000 slaves.

This outdid a predecessor, Titus, whose 80 CE opening of the 50,000-seater Colosseum had the same number of slaughtered wild beasts but only 100 days of drama and games. Colosseum construction was begun by Vespasian in 72 CE, completed by his elder son Titus in 80, and modified by the younger Domitian, d.96. Known also as the Flavian Amphitheatre after the imperial family name, it housed gladiatorial and public spectacles with a seating capacity of 50,000 to 80,000; average attendance of 65,000: the object of Juvenal's taunt on population control by *panem et circenses.* Below the arena floor were wild animal cages, cells and stalls for humans, and mechanics for battles spectacular.

Management skills in the ancient martial and leisure industries were well advanced: the games' masters knew their business. So too did the cooks, hired professionals, domestics, and those of the tavern and street, for the flesh of every creature slaughtered in the arena eventually ended its journey on a Roman dinner table, there in an exotic, highly spiced concoction; or for ordinary folk in a sausage, or pie-encased perhaps, fresh from a public bakery.

The circus can also be seen as a monitor of public taste and ethics through time, as the fount of practical civilian management. In addition to the ancient Greek temple origins of religious festivals, theatre, and street entertainers, organised public spectacle appears to have begun in Italy under the Etruscans, continued by their Roman successors from the 2nd century BCE. Arena-accommodated gladiatorial spectacle began as privately funded funerary games in honour of the dead. These then transmuted into a mix of private and public spectacles to commemorate victories in warfare, mark diplomatic visits, birthdays, public occasions and, by imperial times, to dignify such construction as the Flavian emperors' amphitheatre in their honour: the Colosseum.

**The Arch of Titus, overlooking the Roman Forum**.
[Photograph by John Bagshaw.]

At first events for single combat between slaves, captives, or rare professionals, they progressed to industrial scale wild animal slaughter, mass forced mortal combat, and to the widespread established creation of training camp gladiator schools as possibly the largest education conglomerate enterprise of the times. The shackled trainees were provided with combat and performance training, reasonably well fed with a barley-based diet, becoming unwilling pioneers of prison education. The schools and training camps became a big business.

The gladiator schools were operated by *lanistas*, managers, with teams of slaves equipped with leather whips and such persuaders to combat as red-hot metal bars. Public fights were usually to the death, with audience approval rating indicated by white cloth waving, raised thumbs, and (rare) cries of *Mitte!* (Let him go!). Gladiator production rate was high, but so was demand. As owners were protective of their investments, only an estimated one in five gladiator fights were fatal. Fighting around five times per year, performing for private households, gladiators could earn payment equivalent to the annual earnings of a skilled artisan. After-dinner exhibition bouts brought acceptable rewards, with the dangers being greatly increased in the public arena. Rock stars of their short day, high kill rate scorers won further fame as greatly prized lovers among society women. Juvenal's observation was sharp:

> He is a gladiator! It is this she prefers to children and family.
> What these women love is the sword![20]

The gladiator revolt of 73-71 BCE, led by Spartacus (111-71 BCE) and joined by many slaves, has been interpreted by some historians as a revolutionary attempt against slavery, but there is no corroborative contemporary record. A far more likely aim was freedom and land to settle. However, such a threat to the fabric of society had to be eradicated. With the main Roman armies busy elsewhere, command fell to the ambitious plutocrat Marcus Licinius Crassus, who eventually won the war. He marked the conquest with the crucifixion of some 70,000 combatants, displayed along the entire length of the main road between Rome and the prime gladiator training camps of Capua, the Appian Way. Making a spectacle was ever important.

Reform took a long time. Previously, the tags of Samnite or Gaul attached to combatants were dropped as politically incorrect when their territories became integrated parts of the Empire. However, in the early 5th century CE, German prisoners chose to strangle each other in their cells rather than provide spectacle for the awaiting, expectant tens of thousands in the arena. The *lanistae* must have had a difficult account to present. In 200 CE, women were barred from fighting as gladiators. After a monk had been stoned to death in 404 CE for stopping a gladiatorial contest in what was now a Christian state, Emperor Honorius prohibited such events. He had closed the gladiator schools five years earlier. In 476 CE, the Western Roman Empire fell, dispatching its insignia to the Eastern Empire of Byzantium. Those previous guardians of the insignia, the Vestal Virgins, once its saviour from marauding Gauls, had been disbanded soon after the confiscation of 382 CE. Almost a century later, the prophesised, threatened fate was realised; and none of the ancient gods were able to save Rome.

Rome's fall may be simply ascribed to a mixture of entropy and inability to cope with immigration, as a combination of population movements and invasions proved to be too great to manage. From 27 BCE to 180 CE (the accession of Augustus to the death of Marcus Aurelius), the *Pax Romana* brought relative peace and stability for a longer period than ever before experienced to some 70 million people, a third of the world's then population, according to United Nations data.[21]

At the time of its transition from Republic to Empire, with Caesar's assassination had come a change of strategic thought. Julius Caesar's next target had been Parthia. Indeed, had he spent less time with Cleopatra in Rome, he might have departed for his eastern campaign well before the fateful Ides of March. Given his brilliant military record, it is reasonable to presume that victory and further expansion of the Empire would have followed, although perhaps taking longer than anticipated. Caesar's successor Octavian, renamed Augustus on becoming Emperor, had other sights in mind; and two immediate allies for a reconstruction of Rome into the image he wished it to assume. Maecenas was there for the cultural angle, at which he excelled, with exemplars Virgil, Horace and Livy. Augustus's other great ally, Marcus Agrippa (63-12 BCE), the son-in-law general who won all his wars for him, and served as his deputy in the Senate, died young; but not before assisting Augustus in completing Caesar's plan for a thorough survey of Rome's territory. Agrippa commissioned an impressive building programme, renovating aqueducts, baths and gardens; and was instrumental in design of the Pantheon.

For Rome peaceably to govern its diverse Empire required complete religious toleration. Conquest and subjugation had to be consolidated by a broader, open-minded consideration. The Pantheon project, honouring all gods, became key to the imperial plan. The Pantheon is ancient Rome's oldest intact building, a lasting reminder and tribute to the glory of Roman civilisation. Commissioned by Agrippa under the reign of Augustus, later destroyed by fire, it was rebuilt by Trajan (53–117 CE), then Hadrian (76–138 CE) from Agrippa's original temple building. To save it from desuetude, from the 7th century, gifted by the Byzantine usurper Eastern Roman Emperor Phocas (r. 602-610) to Pope Boniface IV (550-615), it has since functioned as the Catholic church of St Mary and the Martyrs.

**The Pantheon:** Front view of the building (left);
View of the dome from a distance (right);
Interior of dome (below).

"Pantheon", with its generally understood meaning of "temple of all the gods", is most known for its outstanding dome-shaped roof resembling the heavens, with an opening at the top letting in the light of the sun and moon. A rectangular vestibule at the front entrance to the building is linked by a porch to the inner rotunda, topped by a dome made of the Roman invention of concrete, with a central opening (an oculus), a feature of Classical and Byzantine architecture. Measuring some 142 feet (43 metres) and with a height of 71 feet (22 metres), this remarkable unreinforced concrete dome construction remained, until modern times, the world's largest.

**Interior of the Pantheon** [Photograph by John Bagshaw.].

**FOOTPRINT:**
**The Coherent Social and Economic Management**
**System of Rome**

- **By the conditions and circumstances of the time Rome was well managed.**

- **Civilisation, after a fashion, had been established.**

- **Management skills, education and training had been greatly developed.**

- **It required another Empire, religion and civilisation to take them further forward.**

# Endnotes

[1] Aurelius, Marcus. *Meditations*, 10, XVIII, p.127.
[2] Cato, *Speeches* 128, quoted in trans Dalby, Andrew. 2010. *Cato On Farming De Agricultura*, p.8.
[3] See *ibid.* Totnes, Devon, UK: Prospect Books.
[4] Holidays were religious festivals with permitted activities prescribed. They were not "days off," except for the winter Saturnalia when, for a day, there was role reversal between master and servants.
[5] A species of wheat stored in the ear, later parched and pounded to extract the grain.
[6] Cato, *op. cit.* , 2, pp.57-9.
[7] *Ibid*, 3 pp. 65-6.
[8] *Ibid*, 7-9, pp. 69-81.
[9] *Ibid*, 38, p.125.
[10] *Ibid*, 39, p.127.
[11] As Rome expanded in prosperity, so did the demand for both quantity and quality increase. The Roman belief that wine was a daily necessity meant that viticulture expanded in accompaniment with the Empire, even to Britain, where devotional adjuncts of shrines to Bacchus have been discovered. This was a very lucrative

business.

[12] Plutarch, *The Life of Cato the Younger* 3(3).

[13] Thucydides, *History of the Peloponnesian War,* Book V, 89, pp. 401-402.

[14] Shakespeare, *Julius Caesar,* Act 3, Scene 2, 261-265.

[15]. Temin, Peter. *The Roman Market Economy*, p. 6.

[16] Fullers made such an extensive use of human urine in laundry procedures that c. 70 CE Vespasian taxed it, observing *pecunia non olet* (money doesn't stink). The most expensive dye was the Tyrian purple favoured by Emperors, the purple into which the most privileged were said to be born. Derived from decomposing sea snails, the stench was said to be hideous. The ancient world, where shepherds and goat herds would routinely bear their charges' aromas, and smoky urban streets smelt of dung, rancid cooking oils and sweat, provided ample stimulation for the bath house trade.

[17] Martial, *Epigrams,* 7.88.

[18] Wickham, Chris, *Farming the Early Middle Ages: Europe and the Mediterranean, 400-800*, p. 10.

[19] Beard, Mary, *SPQR, A History of Ancient Rome,* p. 460.

[20] Juvenal, *Satire* 6.347.

[21] United Nations, Department of Social and Economic Affairs, Population Division, *World Population Prospects*: 2017 Revision.

# MINI-CASE STUDY (2):
## MANAGING MYTH, PERCEPTIONS OF REALITY, AND THE BUSINESS OF ORACLES

**"As rich as Croesus", as a comparative synonym for a most wealthy person, began in Greek and Persian cultures.**

Lydian territory in modern-day Turkey included the river Pactolus, which then contained electrum, the alloy of gold and silver. According to Herodotus, such riparian deposits formed the basis of the enormous wealth generated by Lydia's king, Alyattes (r. 610-560 BCE), and his son, Croesus (620-547 BCE). Alyattes is credited with having minted the first electrum coin; Croesus, the first in gold. Pactolus was the river in which mythical King Midas supposedly expunged the ability to turn all he touched into gold.

The dramatic expansion to their realm was funded by taxation as well as by precious metals. Alyattes had expanded Lydian territory with the addition of several city-states, but his successor Croesus acquired not only a further clutch of such areas, but also islands allowing his participation in the lucrative Mediterranean trade. With combined wealth sources such as these, Croesus revelled in his well-being. Boasting of his happiness to Solon, sage, poet and law-giver, Croesus sought the assurance of being declared the happiest person on earth. Pragmatic Solon dourly replied that no one could be declared happy until they were dead, for any judgment of true happiness must be based upon a whole life. Reality had intruded.

Undeterred, Croesus continued to splash the cash whilst seeking the assurance of oracular support. He sent messengers bearing offerings and gifts, such as silver bowls, testing the oracles by asking them how he was feeling. Only two of the oracles made satisfactory replies. Therefore, to the oracle of Thebes he had presented a solid gold shield, spear and shaft; the shrine of Apollo at Delphi receiving a three-cubit high (5.5-foot) female statue with the necklace and girdles of his wife. After bestowing these additional gifts, the envoys of Croesus then relayed the key question, as reported by Herodotus:

Croesus, king of Lydia and other countries, believing that these are the only real oracles in all the world, has sent you such presents as your discoveries deserved, and now inquires of you whether he shall go to war with the Persians and, if so, whether he shall strengthen himself with the forces of a confederate". Both the oracles agreed in the tenor of their reply, which was in each case a prophesy that if Croesus attacked the Persians he would destroy a mighty empire, and a recommendation to him to look and see who were the most powerful of the Greeks, and to make alliance with them.[1]

An overjoyed Croesus rewarded both the Thebes and Delphi shrine managers with two gold coins each, in return for which Croesus and the Lydians gained precedence in consulting the oracles in the future, exemption from all charges, the best festival seats, and perpetual citizenship.

Croesus was now emboldened to ask a further question: "Whether his kingdom would be of long duration. Apollo's Pythoness responded:

Wait till the time shall come when a mule is monarch of Media;
Then, thou delicate Lydian, away to the pebbles of Hermus;
Haste, oh! Haste thee away, nor blush to behave like a coward.

Of all the answers received from all the oracles consulted, this pleased Croesus the best, for he could not conceive of how a mule should become king of the Medes. Alliance was made with the Spartans, who used the money Croesus provided, the availability of which had been as advised by Delphi, to gild their Apollo statue. The Spartans, however, took no part in the following conflict.

In 550 BCE, Cyrus the Great, grandson of Croesus's brother-in-law and the King of the Medes, defeated his grandfather to become King of the Medes and Persians. Croesus had attacked the Persian Empire in 547 BCE. Precise war dates are uncertain but by 539 BCE the defeat of Lydia, never to regain its independence, was complete. Croesus had failed either to note, or to make the connection, that being half Mede (by his mother) and half Persian (by his father), Cyrus could be categorised as a mule.[2]

Although Thucydides had long established the rules of the impartial writing of history, without the intervention of gods or myth and with the primacy of corroborated evidence, that is not to say that literate ancient society in general wholly embraced such a scholastic approach.Whereas Herodotus might record myth and the workings out of the supernatural through oracular interpretation, it became quite another matter when history was selected, embellished, or invented to create myth when required as part of societal manipulation.

While early Greek history pertaining to the fall of Troy represents a storytelling informed by beliefs in the nature, powers, and actions of gods, some seven centuries later it becomes a different matter when first Virgil through his *Aeneid* masterpiece, and then Livy (Titus Livius, 59 BCE-17 CE), set out to create what amounts largely to elegant (at least in Livy's early books) propaganda.

The actual history of the foundation of Rome is prosaic. It was a small settlement on an important trade route: the Salt Road. This essential, lucrative commodity was supplied from the salt marshes of the Tiber. It appears that the earlier Etruscan civilisation took a presence in Rome's growth, indeed supplying what became many of its founding families, and became merged with, then superseded by, the rising commercial power of the new entrepôt.

The Romulus and Remus foundation myth had its attractions in its originating 3rd century form, whereby the Vestal Virgin daughter of the usurped king of nearby Alba Longa is impregnated by the god Mars, giving birth to twin boys whom the usurper requires be abandoned to die on Tiber's banks. Instead, they are suckled by a wolf and raised by a shepherd. Ignorant of their birth, they are caught up in an Alba Longa dispute, learn their story, temporarily lose Remus to imprisonment, join forces when Romulus achieves his brother's liberation, have the usurper killed, and are able, with their grandfather, to have him restored as king. The brothers go off to found their own kingdom of Rome but in an estate management dispute concerning upon which hill to build, begin a quarrel. Appeal to the gods is decided to be determined by an augury contest, the result of which is a further dispute, terminated by combat. Either Romulus or one of his supporters kills Remus, Romulus ruling as King of Rome for many years thereafter.

Fratricide not being the most attractive of foundations for what Augustus intended to be the greatest power on earth, its ruler was fortunate indeed to have the services of Virgil. This poetic genius of such popular appeal, to have some of his best-known lines form part of the graffiti decorating the taverns and brothels of such towns as Pompeii, was able to eulogise an immigrant, one Aeneas, imported from the ruins of Troy. The grandfather of Aeneas had been joint founder of that city, the son of whom, Anchises, had a relationship with Aphrodite (the Roman Venus). This union brought forth heroic Aeneas. This paragon, ancestor of Romulus and Remus, becomes the first true, if borrowed, Roman hero.

Of independent means, a talented writer, and gainer of the friendship of Augustus and his Julio-Claudian family, Titus Livius (59 BCE–17CE) (known to us as Livy) set about the composition of a purported entire history of Rome, from foundation to the then-present day. Around three quarters of this monumental work have been lost, but there is more than enough to have produced many of what became well-known tales, as well as a mash of inventive interpretation of pre-existing sources. The entire work was imbued, in readable style, with Roman values and virtues. Livy's books became extremely popular, selling out on production, even inducing an admirer to travel from Spain just to see him. The closest modern comparison, although he did better research, was the English war correspondent and novelist G A Henty (1832-1902), whose encomiums in adventure tale form of the British Empire sold copies world-wide estimated at 25 million.

Livy used the annalist approach - the year-by-year but inevitably variable and incomplete listing of accounts of the deeds and incidents of consuls - but without researching all possible sources, and ensuring that "facts" fitted events. The period of the kings of Rome had to be made to fit the supposed period from the fall of Troy to the arbitrary date of 753 BCE for the founding of Rome. His method was to employ better style and arrangement. Poor transmission of records and a tendency to embellishment might exculpate Livy from invention beyond that of putting their own words into the mouths of protagonists with whom they were in sympathy – this was common to historians of the times. The interplay between myth, the requirements of good storytelling, and the plain historical record remained unresolved.

What is plain, however, is the value of sound analytical skills when invoking or interpreting the advice of ancient oracles.

## Case Study Reflections

1. Are there any redeeming managerial features to emerge from the conduct of Croesus in his direction of Lydia?

2. To what extent, and on what bases, are the Roman foundation myths believable?

3.  What foundation myth might you construct for your own family, city or business?

## Endnotes

[1] Herodotus, *op. cit.*, 1, 53, p.27.

[2] A mule is the offspring of a male donkey and a female horse. These domestic equines are different species, with different numbers of chromosomes. Easier to obtain than the hinny, the product of a female donkey and a male horse, the mule was the pack animal of choice of the ancient world. Rural and martial beast of burden, its strength, endurance and more docile nature made it a favoured means of transport for even such a prestigious commander as the Roman dictator, Sulla.

# TIMELINE:
## THE 13 DYNASTIES OF CHINA

China's history is usually presented by the dynasties of its rulers. From quasi-legendary, mythical beginnings, the 13 dynasties culminated in the abdication of 1912. Their dates, names and brief details are:[1]

| Date | Dynasty | Key Details |
|------|---------|-------------|
| c.2070–1600 BCE | **Xia** | Written records of this authority first occurred over 500 years. Its annals were apparently spoken, with its foundation attributed to the legendary Yu the Great (2123–2025 BCE). He is credited for the management triumph of the development of an effective, long-lasting flood control technique. |
| c.1600–1050 BCE | **Shang** | Archaeological evidence supports this earliest recorded ruling house whose territories included much of the Yellow River area. Known for a calendar system; an early form of modern Chinese language; and advances in art, mathematics, military technology and astronomy. |
| c. 1046-256 BCE | **Zhou** | Codified writing, coinage and chopsticks demonstrated cultural and civilisation expansion, dignified by the establishment of the philosophies of Taoism, Mohism and Confucianism, Legalism, and the practical strategy of Sun Tzu. The Mandate of Heaven concept, justifying the rule of kings, blessed by the gods, (but requiring just rule) was implemented. The Zhous did not survive the Warring States period of 476 -221 BCE, when city states fought for independence until subdued by Qin Shi Huangdi. |
| c. 221–206 BCE | **Qin** | China unified and expanded to include Hunan and Guangdong geographically and physically, through forced-labour construction of the Great Wall. Standardised currency, a legal code and uniform writing system accompanied speech suppression, book |

| | | |
|---|---|---|
| | | burning in 213 BCE, and the burial alive of 460 Confucian scholars. Megalomaniac Emperor Qin Shi Huangdi's city-sized mausoleum provided his corpse with a terracotta guard of over 8,000 life sized soldiers, 130 chariots with 520 horses and 150 cavalry horses. |
| 206 BCE–220 CE | **Han** | Central imperial civil service ran an organised government whose strength extended territorial control to most of China, produced peace and prosperity, opening the Silk Road. This increased trade, technical accomplishment in porcelain and paper making, cultural advance and exchange, including the introduction of Buddhism, expansion of Confucianism, medicine codification and the flourishing of literature. The dynasty's name became that of the nation's largest ethnic group. |
| 220-589 | **Six Dynasties Period** | Successive Han-ruled dynasties [Three Kingdoms (220–265); Jin (265-420); Northern and Southern (386–589)], all seated at Jianye (Nanjing), engaged in a prolonged power struggle. |
| 581–618 | **Sui** | Ruling from Xi'an (Daxing), Emperors Wen and Yang made their army into the world's largest. The Great Wall was extended, the Grand Canal completed and coinage standardised. Taoism and Buddhism superseded Confucianism. |
| 618–906 | **Tang** | As one of China's most peaceful and prosperous periods, when the country became the world's most populous, this has been viewed as a high point of Chinese civilisation, and its second Emperor, Taizon, (598–649) regarded as one of China's greatest, when there were major achievements in science, technology, art and literature. Empress Wu Zetian (624–705), sole female monarch, instituted a secret police force and national espionage network |
| 907 – 960 | **Five Dynasties Period, Ten Kingdoms** | Following the popular protest at the flood damage seen as violating the Tang Mandate of Heaven, there followed a half century of internal conflict and chaos, punctuated by such understandable reliefs as an increase in book block printing. Five intending dynasties attempted rule of north China while ten regimes controlled different regions of the country's south. |

| 960 – 1279 | Song | Reunified by Emperor Taizu (927–976), the dynasty's achievements included the inventions of gunpowder, paper money, the compass, and marine bulkhead sealants. Despite progressive policies, the Song first fell victim to territorial division by the Jin, then to full Mongol invasion. |
|---|---|---|
| 1279- 1368 | Yuan | The first non-Chinese to rule China, Kublai Khan, grandson of Genghis, moved the capital first to the Inner Mongolian location of Xanadu (Shangdu), then to Daidu (today's Beijing). The move signified China's importance in the vast Mongol Empire, then stretching from the Caspian Sea to Korea. Famine, flood, plagues and peasant uprisings brought an end to the unpopular Mongol rule. |
| 1368- 1644 | Ming | Although there was prosperity, great population growth, completion of the Great Wall, construction of the palace complex known as the Forbidden City, and perfection of the distinctive blue and white coloured porcelain, the dynasty was unable to resist another invasion, this time from the northern Chinese regime of Manchuria. |
| 1644–1912 | Qing | Even though it ruled world history's fifth largest Empire, retreat into isolation by the predecessor Ming had induced terminal entropy. Rural discontent, outdated military equipment and organisation, foreign power aggression, and vulnerability to the behaviour of armed industrial trade combined in compounding disasters. Humiliating defeats by foreign forces, imposition of opium import, and loss of territory were exacerbated by cascading political discontent and action. A culmination, and nadir, was reached with the deposition of Xuantong, the last Emperor, afterwards known otherwise by his personal name of Henry Pu Yi (1906-1967), in February 1912. |

**Note[1]:**
See also, Chao-Fong, Leonie 2021. *The 13 Dynasties That Ruled China in Order.*
*https://www.historyhit.com/the-dynasties-that-ruled-china-in-order*

**Emperor Qin Shi Huang
(259-210 BCE)**
Photograph by John Bagshaw

As first Emperor of a unified China, he ruled in a strictly Legalist manner - criticised for its brutality; but standardised many measures and practices. Using forced labour, he implemented a massive road building program, greatly expanded China's territory, and began construction of the Great Wall.

He also left the now famous Terracotta Army behind in his mausoleum, to guard him in the afterlife. Only discovered in 1974 by local farmers in Lintong County outside Xi'an Shaanxi, China, these life-sized figures are currently undergoing a process of restoration; a section of the Emperor's Army (from Pit 1) pictured below.

**Emperor Qin Shi Huang's Terracotta Army**

# CHAPTER FIVE

# WAYS OF THE EAST

The earliest known examples of written management education and instruction are to be found in the East. There, human society had benefited and grown through three aspects of the earth: agricultural geography, sericulture and metal working.

The enormous rivers - the Yellow to the north, and the Yangtse to the south - with their some 700 tributaries, prone to flooding, made China an ideal site for irrigated cultivation. Millet, for conversion into noodles, came from the drier Yellow River valley. Conditions were propitious for the cultivation of rice in Yangtse lands. This highly productive and nutritious food source, able to feed more humans per hectare than any other crop, makes it ideal for intensive cultivation and the support of large populations. Because its cultivation depends upon irrigation, which requires the construction and maintenance of canals, this required collective action. Communities working together, or under the direction of a landholder, were able to provide effective production, which individuals could not. Management of people, land, and resources were essentials in early rice-growing societies.

Sericulture, the natural process of making silk from the cocoons of mulberry tree-dwelling caterpillars, the *Bombyx mori*, began around the middle of the 3rd millennium BCE. It formed a highly lucrative product for trade, demand for which far exceeded the borders of the Chinese states. This lead to the instituting of the Silk Road to the Mediterranean region where, by the time of the late 1st century BCE accession of Augustus in Rome, demand was enormous. Chinese growers held a monopoly on silk production, the details of which they managed to preserve until later medieval times. It was not until the 14th century CE that Byzantine agents were able to smuggle out the secrets, allowing the further establishment of the industry in Italy and Arab held lands.

Efficient processing and casting of iron was more advanced than in Europe by some 2,300 years. The Chinese made the world's first blast furnace around 500 BCE. Advances in the smelting of iron had enormous agricultural impact. Harder iron ploughs meant that otherwise uncultivable hard, scrubby, heavy clay ground could be converted into high-yielding rice field. The iron also added to armed strength, the Chinese states warring with their neighbours and themselves until finally, in 221BCE, Qin Shi Huang 259-210 BCE), head of the terracotta soldier mausoleum guards, unified the country as Emperor.

Embracing the philosophy of Legalism, this Emperor attempted to govern in a strictly logical, although brutal, manner. He instituted what amounted to a reign of terror, characterised by the burning of all books which did not embrace loyalty to the state, and rigorously enforced through inspection local and regional government. Highly unpopular, his dynasty did not long survive his death, but the country remained unified for some time and possessed a model by which it might be managed.

Qin has been accused of megalomania. What had been essentially makeshift defences were transformed by his use of forced labour to commence construction - by joining sections with walls - of what we now know as the Great Wall. Described initially only in euphemisms because of the harsh building conditions, Chinese nomenclature of 'Long Wall' came only gradually into use.

While little of Qin's initiative survives, the barrier now of c. 13,000 miles existed to unite and expand the Empire's defences, fortifications, and towns, primarily to prevent invasions. In death, this Emperor equipped his mausoleum with an after-life guard: an unglazed earthenware ceramic life-sized army of 8,000 soldiers, 130 chariots with 520 horses and 150 cavalry horses; and a further company near-by of officials, acrobats, strongmen and musicians which endure to this day.

Concerning how states might be ruled, life lived, family and business managed, probably earlier than the first western historian, Herodotus, Lao Tzu (5th or 6th century BCE - 531 BCE) was a contemporary to the Greek Seven Sages, founders of Greek philosophy in its administrative and management senses. The first books of the Bible are said to have been written from oral tradition around 1,400 BCE, with the last book of the Old Testament written in 450 BCE and the New Testament in the first half of the 1st century CE. Thus, while the Bible was still in composition, Lao Tzu's eastern contribution to understanding (written on bamboo in the 4th century BCE) sits roughly in a later mid-point.

**The Great Wall**
[Photographs by John Bagshaw.]

Lao Tzu was reputedly the keeper of the Chinese imperial archives but the name by which he is known is honorific, meaning "Old Master." His real name has been quoted as Li Er, Li Dan or Er Dan. He has also been cited as the court astrologer who, while never opening a school, taught philosophy of administration, was said to have encountered Confucius, and was also said to have been consulted by many students.

**Lao Tzu Meets Confucius, Yuan Dynasty (1261 – 1368),**
an imaginary encounter but illustrative of the Mongol embrace of Chinese culture.

The story goes that he grew tired of corruption at court and travelled westwards, only to be apprehended by a border guard who recognised him. The guard then demanded that, in return for his freedom, Lao Tzu should write his philosophy. On reading the product, the guard is then said to have embraced its contents and to have accompanied Lao Tzu on his travels into India.

Another account has him meeting and teaching Buddha (c.563 or 480 BCE-483 or 400 BCE) en route. There is a further legend that he was the Buddha himself. There are many and various tales of how the guard-disciple Yinxi also became adept and carried the way of the Tao into the world where it became the basis of an eponymous religion. However, the form that Taoism took does not necessarily conform to the writing of the *Tao Te Ching,* the work traditionally attributed to Lao Tzu.

There was a western tradition that Book VI of Virgil's *Aeneid* had magical powers (because it dealt with travel in the underworld), and that if it was allowed to fall open, unhindered in one's hand, then the passage upon which the eye first fell was reputed to have a direct application. Charles I of England (1600-1649) is said so to have predicted his own demise by this method. Similar attribution of relevance has been made to the *Tao Te Ching.* There are three general applications: reading, browsing, or sampling the entire work; finding a supposedly relevant extract by an exercise with tetragrams; and allowing the book to fall open as it may. Asking the question, "which passages are most apt as an introduction for the readers of

this book," your author allowed a copy to fall open.[1] This produced
*RETURN TO SIMPLICITY* [*Passage 19*]:

> Discard the sacred, abandon strategies;
> The people will benefit a hundredfold
> Discard philanthropy, abandon morality;
> The people will return to natural love.
> Discard cleverness, abandon the acquisitive;
> The thieves will exist no longer.
> However, if these three passages are inadequate,
> Adhere to these principles:
> Perceive purity; Embrace simplicity;
> Reduce self-interest; Limit desires.

Here, Lao Tzu is advocating the abandonment by leaders of all learned
behaviour. Simple spontaneity, integrity, less self-interest, and the
limitation of desire leads to the recognition that the greatest happiness in life
arises from moments of pure simplicity. In *THE POWER IN
DESIRELESSNESS* [*Passage 37*]:

> The Tao never acts
> And yet is never inactive
> If leaders can hold on to it
> All things will be naturally influenced.
> Influenced and yet desiring to act,
> I would calm them with Nameless Simplicity.
> Nameless Simplicity is likewise without desire;
> And without desire there is harmony.
> The world then will be naturally stabilized.

Lao Tzu contends that the best leaders guide rather than rule. Because they
concentrate on leading the way whilst ensuring their own stability, they
don't interfere with others' lives and so do not provoke resistance,
resentment, or reaction. Keeping life simple, they resist misleading and
irrelevant desires, so promoting harmony and stability. Leaders have to
know when to stop and so practice non-interference. If management is open-
ended, then people have nothing to resent or resist, thus producing
spontaneous cooperation because attention has moved to the end rather than
the means.

In *THE GRAVITY OF POWER* [*Passage 26*]:

> Gravity is the foundation of levity.
> Stillness is the master of agitation.

Thus Evolved Individuals can travel the whole day
Without leaving behind their baggage.
However arresting the views,
They remain calm and unattached.
How can leaders with ten thousand chariots
Have a light-hearted position in the world?
If they are light-hearted, they lose their foundation.
If they are agitated, they lose their mastery.

The meaning of the above is that leaders in any context, from the home to
nation governing, have a duty to remain calm. To the ancient Chinese, ten
thousand chariots was a nuclear concept: unimaginably formidable power.
"Baggage" meant the retention of serious presence and purpose. Power
meant responsibility, which entailed being neither agitated nor light-
hearted.

The Tao has found its way into management education, the study of
leadership and personal growth, and even theoretical physics. Lao Tzu saw
in nature a unified field of forces which he named the Tao. Because this
could not be expressed in a logical or analytical manner, he conveyed
meaning through paradox emphasised by polarity, aimed at the promotion
of awareness. The polarity arises from the Taoist view of the origins of the
universe, which assumes that before existence, there was an idea: the
Absolute, the *T'ai Chi*, the Supreme Ultimate. In a sudden desire to know
itself, paralleling the Big Bang theory, the Absolute divided itself from non-
existence, causing cataclysm and the formation of the two states of being:
*yin* (negative) and *yang* (positive). The previously unseparated matter and
energy then separated and regrouped, becoming our universe. As everything
in existence came into reality through the *yin* and the *yang*, so these reflect
the purpose of the Absolute. Thus, if reality came about because the
Absolute wished to know itself, our evolutionary destiny must be to assist
its vision by investigating, observing and emulating nature. In the West, this
parallels empiricism and scientific method.

The concept of a universe where a polarity of ideas create intellect which
might cause reality, and that reality is shaped through the force of the
intellect, is fundamental to quantum mechanics (even though not readily
comprehensible to the rest of us). However, we can rationalise down to the
difference between logic and instinct in problem-solving; in the West we
cleave to logical analysis, whereas Lao Tzu's view stressed the insights of
intuition. East and West do meet at the libertarian edges. The *Tao Te Ching*
advises against too great state interference and limits the scope of

government, which appeals to the anarchist left as it does to the libertarian right.

Tao may be understood as the principle of how the universe actually is. To go with the flow of the natural way leads to fulfilment, but to ignore or resist it invites disaster. Thus, doing nothing becomes the most powerful action of all (sometimes you just have to step out of the way); and "effortless action" follows life in its natural flow. Meditation and Feng Shui are aspects of natural living, the one bringing calm contemplation to find the Tao way; the other the natural flow of life and surroundings. *Yin* and *yang* are natural energy balances in natural harmony; interactive, constantly moving cosmic forces, not moral forces. Together, these one and two give birth to the three of heaven, earth, and humanity, from which all things have their being.

The most skilful leader is the one unknown, whom no one knows is leading. As individuals, we have to strengthen our links to and with the Tao. One of the functions of Taoist priests was to bring rulers into harmony with the unseen world, the spirit world. For a dynasty, its leader was wished to be the one which the spirit world would have most wanted to sit on the throne.

By the 7th century CE, there was an established Taoist religion which had grown significantly by the 12th century, after which it became predominantly a folk religion. Yet, after 20th century persecution it recovered, to the extent of having some 26,000 temples today. Because of Taoism's spiritual dimension and contrast with the authoritarian supportive Confucian approach, there was always tension between the two belief systems. Management guidance, therefore, had differing, if from time to time complementary, sources.

Confucius (551-479 BCE), Kong Tze or Kong Qiu in modern Chinese, set forward (or is credited with) an amalgam of traditional Chinese belief based on family values, and an ethical system of secular morality with the golden rule, found later in Christianity, of "Do not do to others what you do not want done to yourself." More than an ethical precept, this is central to the concepts of equity and justice; it forms a corner stone of civilisation itself. Although the Confucius stance was secular, he makes reference to heaven and afterlife, and was treated as a divinity in Taoism, thus conferring a continuing religious status complete with temples in his name.[2] His works were not available in the West until translation into Latin became available in the 17th century. It is thought that his secular approach appealed to and informed the work of various Enlightenment period scholars. His core emphasis on interpersonal relationships, as opposed to the individualism of the West, is key to the different, and arguably more successful, 21st century management approaches of China, Japan, and South Korea.

His family, the Kongs of Liu, were common gentlemen without hereditary entitlements or privileges. They were, however, employable in the administration or army, being educated in the six arts: writing, numbers, ritual, music, archery, and charioteering. Confucius rose in the service of the dukedom of Liu in north-eastern China, before the unification which occurred between 230 and 221 BCE as Qin, the most westerly state, successfully successively subdued its easterly neighbours. His teachings assisted his rise from governorship of a small town to state Minister of Crime, and his success in the post lead to his participation in diplomacy, at which he further excelled. Discovered to be embroiled in political intrigue at home, he chose self-exile, setting off in search of rulers who he might influence to follow his advocated path of virtuous government.

As a common gentleman, he might rise as an administrator and serve as a consultant but he did not have the aristocratic power directly to intervene in events. In his wanderings he was accompanied by groups of young companions from all classes who followed him because they hoped that the acquisition of his wisdom would help launch their own administrative careers. Thus "Master" Confucius acquired a group calling itself apprentices or disciples. The mutual investment paid off. Some of the disciples appear to have subsequently gained positions and were able to influence the duke to invite Confucius to return with a retirement bequest.

During his wandering exile, he is reputed to have encountered Lao Tzu, chronicler of the ways of the Tao, but no proof of the encounter exists. He is credited with having written or edited most of the Chinese classics. Known particularly for his sayings which, compiled and edited after his death by disciples such as Mencius (372-289 BCE), are said to have been taught by Confucius's grandson. These form the book of sayings, the *Analects:* "Edited Conversations," the central text of Confucianism and key work of Chinese literature. In China, as in the West, the principal method of record was textual memorising. A written version did not appear until over 200 years after Confucius's death, the final edited version being dated between 206 BCE and 220 CE.

Administrative experience informed the heart of Confucius's ethical teaching. Established very plainly, at the very start of Chinese management education were the three central tenets of:

> Practice informing theory;
> The practical expression of ethical justice; and
> Study and appreciation of the past to gain from its wisdom,
> experience and reinterpretation.

Learning, moreover, was not merely utilitarian - like righteousness, it was to be loved for itself. He taught practical skills, but considered moral self-improvement the greater aim. He was said to have taught 3,000 students in his lifetime, but only some 70 are estimated to have thoroughly understood and absorbed his teaching.

The practical applied directly to personal exemplification, which held superiority over explicit rules of behaviour: knowledge of the rules was inferior to skilled judgment. Such capacity for judgment could be attained through self-improvement and the study of moral exemplars. He often employed indirect methods such as allusion or innuendo, and the use of the negative or omission rather than direct instruction. Thus the "silver rule" was a negative: "Do not impose on others what you yourself do not want others to impose on you." Confucius also presented the issue in a question: "Attaining a balance all the time in practical matters and in everyday life – is this virtue not the best?"[3] In contrast, however, he instructed his students always to make direct inquiry.

Virtue in and of itself was not enough, it required context. The test was reciprocity for while acting in self-interest was not incorrect, the impact upon others had to balance action. Fulfilling responsibility towards others was a culmination of the expression of generosity, kindness, diligence, seriousness, and sensibility. By following a path designed to benefit the greater good, the individual would become a better person. The need was to do the right thing for the right reason.[4]

The good leader led by example; people would accept and copy good rule, and behave badly if presented with the reverse. He had much to say concerning education. The various editions of the *Analects* carry modern and ancient commentary on the passages. Without such adornment, for the interested reader may explore further in the Confucian manner, here is a selection for consideration:

> To pursue strange theories or to get side tracked in your studies can only bring harm [2.16];

I was not born with knowledge, but I love antiquity, and I work hard in pursuing it [7.20]

When three of us are walking, I am bound to find my teachers there. I would single out the good points in others and try to follow them, and I would notice their bad points and try to correct them in myself [7.22];

If you know to correct yourself, what difficulty will you have should you decide to serve in government? If you do not know how to correct yourself, how can you hope to correct others? [13.13].[5]

For the attention of employers: If he himself is upright, he does not have to give orders and things will get done. If he himself is not upright, even though he gives orders, they will not be obeyed [13.6];

For the attention of employees: In serving your lord, carry out your duties with respect before giving thought to a salary [15.38];

To whom it may concern: ...With things he does not understand, a gentleman would know to keep quiet... [13.3].

Yet, perhaps the most penetrating and relevant observation to our own times was made when he was asked about what was important in government: "Sufficient food, a well-equipped army, and the trust of the common people." If he had to give up two of these, first would be the army, the second food, for death was part of the human condition, but a state cannot survive if it does not have the trust of the common people [12.7].[6]

His philosophy was grounded in tradition, and study was essential to its function as teacher as well as its preservation. This continuing central belief characterises modern Far Eastern societies - and can be seen especially in its student population, whose learning rates now outstrip those of its western counterparts. Confucius represented himself as a "transmitter who invented nothing." This emphasis of received and acquired wisdom over inventiveness is a further continuing characteristic. His collectivist ideals of enshrined duty, loyalty to family, self-restraint, and unselfish behaviour are not easy companions to entrepreneurial individualism, and can be seen as anti-capitalistic. As ever with philosophy, the extraction of the convenient according to perceived need influences the application of the thought.

Deep thought and thorough study were represented as the ways in which to address moral problems in particular, but the "study hard" concept remains inculcated in regional behaviour. After the communist interlude and Mao's deliberate assault upon traditional Confucian values in the Cultural

Revolution, it remains the case. It is also the case in neighbouring countries, such as South Korea, that education leaders are accorded the highest societal status. Moreover, Confucianism and moral values are now taught at all Chinese business schools. Confucian Institutes have been established throughout the world as vehicles of "soft power" akin to that of the British Council. The Confucian emphases on moral values and loyalty to the state, however nationalistic, have to be set aside revulsion at corruption and amorality.

The Confucian ideal was of a rule without laws. Han Feizi (279-233 BCE), also known as Han Fei Zi, had studied under a Confucian philosopher, but left him to pursue alternate studies more germane to the circumstances of the time, this being the "Warring States" period. He produced the body of work which bears his name, a synthesis of legal thought and principles comprising the "Chinese Legalist" school. This ended the Confucian aspiration, affirming instead the primacy of the rule of law. He held that institutions must change according to circumstances, particularly regarding human behaviour, which was determined not by morality but by economic and political conditions.

The emergence of the Legalist school cannot be attributed to any single individual. The ideas of Shen Buhai (400-337 BCE), the merit system favouring administrator of Han state, were incorporated in Han Feizi's thought. Leading reformer Shang Yang (390-338 BCE) transformed the small, western, previously peripheral Qin state into the militarily powerful, centralized entity wielding power through systems of punishments and rewards like those which first unified China. Administration through (ideally) impartial bureaucrats throughout the competing states brought a new dimension of control to government. Ordinary people could see that a legal system was preferable to aristocratic misrule, and here was an early example of a coherent state management system. Legal cases had to be investigated rather than decided in an arbitrary manner, and laws fixed the scale and nature of punishments: people knew where they were. That, however, was not readily comfortable - at its harshest, approximating to a reign of terror. Punishments could be collective. The transgressor and his entire unit of association could suffer penalty, which could be as extreme as execution. Criminals might be put to death in public. Offenders could receive facial tattoos, and disfigurements such as the cutting off of ears and noses. Ironically, because he had made a royal duke receive a legal punishment, when the duke became ruler he had Shang Yang himself executed by the *jūlié* method: dismemberment by being fastened to five chariots pulled by horses or cattle, and torn to pieces. His entire family was also executed.

A bedrock for states was established through the establishment of weights and measures, construction and monetary standards, and giving peasants rights to land, their persons available for military service and their land taxes funding government. However, it can be appreciated why commentators have described the system as one of *realpolitik* of which Machiavelli would have approved. Legalism again rose to prominence in the 20th century, when Mao instituted his anti-Confucianism campaign. Although advice to rulers as early as the 5$^{th}$ century BCE stressed the value of long-term planning against such phenomena as flooding or harvest failure, Han Feizi emphasised that while in former times of abundance people would host and feast casual visitors, during famine they struggled to feed themselves; people could be both generous and heartless, and in hardship, they would conflict and grab.

Rulers, therefore, should not attempt to make their subjects good, rather they should merely restrain them from wrongdoing. Nor should rulers seek popularity and consent, for people are not dependable, and are ignorant of their own best interests. To Confucians the monarch's right to rule is voided by misrule; to Han Feizi, meanwhile, possession of authority gave the right to require obedience. However, authority was not to be expressed unreasonably, but through law. That law could be reformed, but had to be obeyed. It was to be applied not arbitrarily, but through administrative competence or "statecraft" - by management, in other words. However interpreted, the convenience of Confucianism to state control ensured its longevity.

A stutterer, Han Feizi turned his disability into an advantage by writing everything down, thus producing a coherent management record. In this, he was insistent that there be respect for the ruler: absolute obedience. The ruler, however, should not show anything of himself or his plans to the bureaucrats, for that would open up weaknesses which those subordinates would exploit. The necessary evil of the officials, who were the link to the people, could be contained only through the achievement of their neutral, professional, but highly necessary performance. This was gained through their being salaried, elevated above economic fluctuations.

The peasantry had to be trained in the dual functions of military duties and agricultural performance. Just as maintenance of farming standards was essential to the economy, so farming and fighting have transferable skills. Hence, efficiency in training and performance meant the creation and maintenance of a strong state. This extended to the forced labour levies which built the massive road and canal systems, enabling the communications so important to the management of state administration. Intriguingly, in invoking the notions of Han Feizi and Legalism concerning strong administration and a strong state, President Xi's direct linkage to originating, ancient history and management is glaringly apparent, in his present Anti-Corruption Campaign and general policy.

After appointing officials, Han Feizi advised, the ruler was to demand satisfactory performance and punish failure, dereliction, or usurpation, as well as failing or exceeding targets. Thus secured, the ruler could employ military strength to expand his realm, in which the food supply was paramount. Therefore, all other occupations were to be subordinate, and the rich discouraged from giving to the poor, for that robbed the diligent and frugal in favour of the extravagant and lazy. Unsurprisingly, this recipe had great appeal to autocracy and was much admired in those circles.

Han Feizi was used as a diplomat by the ruler of Han in negotiations with the then King Zheng Shi Wang of Qin, who was attacking the Han state. Zheng admired Han Feizi. He probably intended to employ him after conquest. To forestall this, Li Si (280-208 BCE), Legalist and first minister of Qin, ordered Han Feizi to commit suicide, which he did by drinking poison. It might be argued that Han Feizi behaved ethically but, by obeying Li Si's order, proved his points that others did not - but obedience was all. Life at the top could be dangerous to philosophers, with poison the dispatch means of choice: Socrates took hemlock to support the state and appease the Athenians, who were scared and angered by his impiety; Seneca (4 BCE-65 CE) as an additive to the wrist-slitting ordered by his former pupil, Nero.

The philosophy of Mozi (c. 468-391 BCE), who had argued strongly against Taoism and Confucianism and instead stressed self-reflection, authenticity, and self-restraint, had been overwhelmed by the Legalist school. An eponymous book, the *Mozi*, had expressed its major ethical tenets of altruism, austerity, and utilitarianism with a respect and concern for all people. A further antidote to Confucianism was best expressed by one of the founding texts of Taoism, the *Chuang-tzu,* attributed to Chuang Tzu (369-286 BCE). Almost nothing is known of the author, and the contents of the later chapters of the work are held to have been added subsequently by writers following the original's distinct thought, style, and manner of expression. In classic Taoist manner, the *Chuang-tzu* seeks to stimulate learning and knowledge by paradox.

The material is presented, often whimsically, through anecdotes, allegories, and fables, all told in a satirical, witty, emotional manner. As with all well-constructed satire, refutation is difficult, all the more so as it emerges from a well-spring of anger, however urbanely expressed. Logical, rational approaches can be inverted by absurdity to illustrate the limitations to human knowledge and understanding of the natural world. The form of expression has been compared to the dialogues of Plato and Socrates.

The most often quoted story is that from the second chapter, "On the Equality of Things," the butterfly dream, a striking parallel to Kafka's 1915 novella, *The Metamorphosis*:

> Once upon a time, Chuang Tzu dreamed he was a butterfly, a butterfly flying about enjoying itself. It did not know it was Chuang Tzu. Suddenly, he awoke and veritably was Chuang Tzu again. We do not know whether it was Chuang Tzu dreaming he was a butterfly, or whether it was the butterfly dreaming that it was Chuang Tzu. Between Chuang Tzu and the butterfly there must be some distinction. This is a case of what is called the transformation of things.[7]

The Chinese historian and early Taoist economist Sima Qian (145 or 135-86 BCE) occupies a similar position to that of Herodotus in the West. In executing what began as his father's project, he took the exploration of the relationship between heaven and humans as his guiding principle, seeking to discern the pattern of ancient and modern changes from which a view of history may then be formulated. Punished by castration for disagreeing with his Emperor, Sima Qian's work has been praised subsequently by scholars for its liberal nature. His *Records of the Grand Historian* offer series of biographies covering some two thousand years. Among these were stories of Chuang Tzu, one of which concerned the offer of King Wei of Chu (r. 339-329 BCE), who sent messengers bearing lavish gifts to invite him to court to become chief minister. Chuang Tzu laughed, telling the messengers:

> A thousand ounces of silver are a great gain to me; and to be a high noble and minister is a most honourable position. But have you not seen the victim-ox for the border sacrifice? It is carefully fed for several years, and robed with rich embroidery that it may be fit to enter the Grand Temple. When the time comes for it to do so, it would prefer to be a little pig, but it cannot get to be so. Go away quickly, and do not soil me with your presence. I had

rather amuse and enjoy myself in the midst of a filthy ditch than be subject to the rules and restrictions in the court of a sovereign. I have determined never to take office, but prefer the enjoyment of my own free will.

The thought is apposite to anyone considering aspiration to management, power, and leadership in any organisation. The Taoist paradox here is that the type of person best suited to leadership is the one unwilling to do so. The compromise is the subsequent Roman examples of Cincinnatus, Cato, and Sulla: achieve the greatest offices but, after suitable service, step down and retire.[8] George Washington (1732-1799), father of his country, famously stepped down twice: on the securing of victory against the British and after the second term of his presidency (1789-97), earning him Byron's sobriquet of "the Cincinnatus of the West."

A further passage presents a meditative text relevant to all who would aspire to lead Management Studies, or any learning (in particular discussion of the European Enlightenment), and is a fine example of the Taoist approach:

Tao has no distinctions. Speech cannot be applied to the eternal. Because of speech, there are demarcations. Let me say something about demarcations. There are the right and the left, discussions and judgments, divisions and arguments, emulations and contentions. These are called the eight predicables. What is beyond this world, the sages do not discuss, although they do not deny its existence. What is within this world, the sages discuss, but do not pass judgments. About the chronicle history, and records of ancient kings, the sages pass judgment but do not argue. When there is division, there is something not divided. When there is argument, there is something that the argument does not reach. How is that? The sages embrace all things, while men in general argue about them in order to convince each other. The Great Tao does not admit of being spoken. Great argument does not require words. Great benevolence is not purposely charitable. Great purity is not purposely modest. Great courage is not purposely violent. Tao that is displayed is not Tao. Speech that argues falls short of its aim. Benevolence that is constantly exercised does not accomplish its object. Purity, if openly professed, meets incredulity. Courage that is purposely violent must itself fail. These five are, as it were, round, yet tend to become square. Therefore, he who knows to stop at what he does not know, is perfect. He who knows the argument that requires no words and the Tao that cannot be named, is called the store of nature. The store, when things are put in, is not full, when things are taken out, it is not empty; yet he himself does not know why it is so. This is called the preservation of enlightenment.[9]

In immediate, practical vein, when a warlord boasted of his staff of many Confucians, Chuang Tzu suggested he execute anyone wearing Confucian clothing failing to practice what he preached. Soon, none of the staff wore it. While not acquisitive, Taoist natural law thought supported the emergence of Chinese capitalism. Where the Confucian ideal was duty and integrity at the expense of personal gain, which had caused the sage to abandon and condemn a pupil who had become a rich merchant, Taoism taught that as the world could not be controlled, freedom harmonizing with it, and hence limited government with individual freedom was the way forward.

The French economic thinker Francois Quesnay (1694-1774), of the Physiocrat "power of nature" school, in his *Le Despotisme de Chine* of 1764 described Chinese politics and society. A supporter of constitutional Chinese autocracy, Quesnay's approval of the Taoist approach was given significant acknowledgment by Adam Smith in his *Wealth of Nations*. It had taken over a thousand years for the message to get through. In embracing free trade and the importance of the agricultural sector, with the *laissez-faire, laissez passer* tag, significant portions of Quesnay's work achieved Smith's approval. Smith was well aware of China's wealth, writing of it as being much richer than any part of Europe.

In a demonstration of the commencement and presence of capitalism in 3rd century BCE China, Sima Qian had posed the simple question that if everyone was a gentleman, who would mine, farm, manufacture or move goods to market? Although Chinese land-bound peasants were considered free persons in law, they were entirely dependent upon landowners for their living. For much of their history, a feudal system operated. Peasants could be traded, provide labour as tribute, and were subject to arbitrary justice. However, (prefiguring Smith) Sima Qian observed that, as economic activity had long occurred without a government, every person would do his best to acquire desired objects, seek profit, and produce without being asked. This accorded with Taoist principles, so requiring that such producers be given every incentive to make a profit rather than being made to conform to mandarin standards:

> Under the circumstances the best thing to do is to leave people the way they are, and the next best is to channel their materialistic desires through reason. Less desirable is to educate them so that they will reduce or lose such desires, and worse still, to use coercion to achieve the same purpose. Of all the possible courses to take, the worst the government can do is to join the people and compete with them for material gains. [10]

Sun Tzu, an honorific title meaning "Master Sun," - as Lao Tzu and Chuang
Tzu were "Master Chuang" and "Master Lao" - born Sun Wu (544-496
BCE), was a distinguished, highly successful Chinese general, whose
treatise *The Art of War* has inspired many leading military figures down to
the present day. Chairman Mao (1893-1976) quoted from it. Ho Chi Minh
(1890-1969) translated a copy for his army's use. His general, Vo Nguyen
Giap (1911-2013), was a vigorous proponent. So comprehensive was the
North Vietnamese victory over the French and the Americans that the
latter's generals Colin Powell (1937-2021) and Norman Schwarzkopf
(1934-2012) used some of Sun Tzu's precepts in the Gulf Wars of the 1990s,
and had the book included in the Marine Corps' reading programme.

From there, it reached western consciousness in this century through a variety
of media concerning management theory, business, culture, and sport -
although it is doubtful whether the West has fully understood the book's
influence and relevance to current Chinese growth and expansionist policy.
Understand Confucianism and Taoism, with Han Feizi, Chuang Tzu, Sun Tzu
and Lao Tzu, it can be argued, and the management of relations and business
with the Far East might be better conducted, particularly in how those are
managed. It might further be noted that the military appears to be more likely
to discover and learn from historical texts and cultural evidence than do their
civilian managerial counterparts. Perhaps predictably, the currently acclaimed
leading strategy expert of the Management Studies of the West, fails in a
recent book to mention Sun or his work.[11]

Sun Tzu's *The Art of War* is written within the Taoist context, although
opposed to its philosophy, and so to fully understand the work requires some
comprehension of Lao Tzu's *Tao Te Ching*. Like the *Tao*, the book is
presented aphoristically, in short passages. What appears at first sight to be
a list of aphorisms is actually a coherent body of strategic thought. The basis
of Taoism is the maintenance of balance between nature and humanity,
characterised by natural action with spontaneity, simplicity, humility and
frugality; *The Art of War*, meanwhile, is about winning battles and
managing conflict, seen as a masterpiece of strategy. Importantly, within
that is the vital message that the most successful battles are the ones which
you don't fight. The Taoist nature of the writing can lead to western
explanations of the thought being longer than the passages studied, with the
aphoristic pithiness inviting interminable quotations. It is easiest to advise
the reader here simply to consult the original text.[12] The samples below
serve only to exemplify style and method, although his echoing of Pittacus
in the matter of self-knowledge is particularly noteworthy:

All warfare is based on deception. [I.18]

There is no instance of a country having benefited from prolonged warfare. [II.6]

If you know the enemy and know yourself, you need not fear the result of a hundred battles. If you know yourself but not the enemy, for every victory gained, you will also suffer a defeat. If you know neither the enemy nor yourself, you will succumb in every battle. [III.18]

In battle, there are not more than two methods of attack – the direct and the indirect; yet these two in combination give rise to an endless series of manoeuvres. [V.9]

When you surround an army, leave an outlet free. Do not press a desperate foe too hard. [VII.36]

What enables the wise sovereign and the good general to strike and conquer, and achieve things beyond the reach of ordinary men is foreknowledge…Hence the use of spies. [XIII. 4-7]

Sun Tzu's times were those of the Warring States, which saw the emergence of a different kind of warfare. Bronze chariots bearing aristocratic hero warriors were being replaced by cavalry and infantry. This produced a need for new types of military managers and consultants: expert advisers such as Sun Tzu. He made his reputation in Wu, now the powerful modern Shanghai region but then merely an up-coming state on the southern edge of China, where he was hired as an adviser. There is only one story of his life. While it may be apocryphal, it is instructive. Asked by the ruler to demonstrate his expertise, Sun Tzu demanded, and was granted, complete control of an army. The ruler provided his concubines as the army.

Sun Tzu drilled them and required they then perform the instructed manoeuvre. They giggled. He repeated the exercise, this time with the warning that insubordination would be punished by execution. They giggled again. He had naturally placed the ruler's favourite as his immediate subordinate. He ordered her execution. The ruler protested that the loss of this concubine would be greatly damaging to him. Nonetheless, Sun Tzu had her executed. The concubines then performed the instructed manoeuvres perfectly. Sun Tzu had proved his point: in warfare, the general has to have complete command. The manager must be allowed to perform his management function.

The aphorisms are concerned with the highest level of management theory; they are about *how to think* according to the situation, rather than participation in the armchair sport of reviewing known particular situations - the level of cognitive application above the case study, in short. Conceptual thought is all very well; how to think precedes such construction, for that determines conceptual formation.

Where pacifist Taoism and Confucianism sought balance and harmony, Sun Tzu thought that warfare had a role to play in the creation of order. That being the case, because of the inevitable costs, it had to be over as quickly as possible. The previous aristocratic view of warfare, as seen contemporarily in Greece through Homer's *Iliad*, had been of a heroic fair fight – up to a point. Fairness and morality were of no concern to Sun Tzu. He was only interested in winning.

That meant out-thinking, out-witting, and out-manoeuvring the enemy, particularly by surprise attacks, trickery, deception, and espionage. In Homeric comparison Odysseus, rather than Ajax or Achilles, is the man for Sun Tzu. It was not until a French translation of 1772 that the *Art of War* was known in the West, a very long time indeed not to have known a key work of strategic management, all about winning. Stratagems such as alternatives to conflict - delay, alliances, intelligence acquisition, deceit, and the temporary submission to greater power - are timeless, applicable to many management situations and had been presented by "Master Sun" as early as the 6th century BCE.

The unifying, but short-lived, Qin dynasty (221-207 BCE) was succeeded by that of the Han, separated into two periods: the Western (202 BCE- 9CE) and, after a Xin usurpation, the Eastern (25-220 CE). This four centuries' continuity is considered the key formative period of Chinese history. It has influenced Chinese identity thereafter, with its dominant ethnic group (out of over 80) having given its name to people, language, and written language characters. The Emperor presided over government, but shared power with the nobility. Ministers were usually drawn from the scholarly gentry class, with a mix of direct government control and semi-autonomous kingdoms, which gradually lost independence. Official sponsorship of Confucianism in education and at court endured as policy from 141BC until the 20th century.

Coinage issued by the central mint in 119 BCE, a basis of the age of economic prosperity which was to characterise the dynasty, remained the

Chinese standard until the Tang dynasty of 618–907 CE. The Han period was marked by significant scientific and technological advance. This included the nautical steering ship rudder, the use of negative numbers in mathematics, hydraulic power-assisted astronomy, and earthquake detection at distance. Multiple clashes with the nomadic steppe peoples of central Asia eventually led to pacification and the establishment of the Silk Road. At the beginning of its rule, the Han followed the Taoist philosophy of "governance by doing nothing", however this new policy allowed recovery from warfare and Qin misgovernment.

Between 202–130 BCE, the Han population tripled from around 13 million to 36 million, and then to 59 million. The ship rudder invention greatly improved navigation throughout the water transport system. Hundreds and thousands of labourers worked on the empire's rivers and canals network. Invention and introduction of heavy ploughshares increased agricultural production and the consequent impetus to improved distribution, assisted by government advisory services to producers and users, with taxation revenues increasing as a further result. Postal stations provided accommodation and changes of horses for messengers charged with the transmission of official documents. 30,000 were established under Emperor Ping (9 BCE-6 CE, r.1 BCE-6CE).

Economic advance was accompanied by a growth in religion. Almost as a management index from material to spiritual expansion, the numbers of official temples rose throughout the Western Han period, reaching 1,700 by the interregnum period of Wang Mang (9-23CE). The gods worshipped were natural and personal: mountains, rivers, the sun, the moon, stars, wind, rain, and ancestors. Under Emperor Xin Liu (27BCE-1BCE), around 37,000 sacrifices were made annually, involving huge amounts of food and wine. At the imperial level, three types of ritual were held at Han mausoleums on daily and seasonal bases:

1. Four meals were offered to the dead ruler in the Resting Place and would resemble those he would have eaten when alive.

2. The prime minister would sometimes be sent by the court to make offerings in the deceased emperor's mausoleum.

3. Every month, the emperor's clothing and crown would be taken from the Resting Place, put on a cart, and processed around the mausoleum compound, presided over by the Master of Ceremonies.

Repeated ritual can induce entropy. Riven by Taoist religious dissent and disturbances, amid the machinations of the palace eunuchs, the Han dynasty eventually fell to a usurpation-campaigning family highly successful in the adaptation of Sun Tzu's instruction. Led by the warlord Cao Cao (155-220 CE) who, although failing to unite China through armed usurpation, achieved the posthumous title of Emperor Wu of Wei by courtesy of his achieving son, Cao Pi, who had proclaimed himself Emperor of the new state of Wei. Cao Pi had been frustrated, however, by the deceit and delaying tactics of opposing generals, the scholar-strategist Zhuge Liang (181-234) and Sun Quan (182-252). The result was the ending of the (Eastern) Han dynasty and commencement of the Three Kingdoms period (220–280 CE).[13]

Positive thought of many a persuasion throbs through management thinking. It is useful to note that inaction, negation, and delay may sometimes be the best possible strategies. Quintus Fabius Maximus Verrucosus Cunctator (280-203 BCE) achieved the agnomen of "the delayer" during the Second Punic War in frustrating Hannibal, elephants and all, by refusing pitched battle, attacking supply lines, and allowing small engagements only. Hannibal was worn down, delayed far from home, forced to waste time in failed sieges and fruitless pursuits, ultimately recalled to Carthage, with consequent final defeat. As Sun Tzu observed:

> To secure ourselves against defeat lies in our own hands,
> but the opportunity of defeating the enemy is provided by the enemy
> himself. [IV. 2]

Another ancient advocate of espionage was the Indian writer known as Kautilya (?350-?275 BCE), whose ideas are explored further in Case Study (3). Also known as Chanakya, or Vishnugupta, he is identified as the author or compiler of the *Arthashastra,* an encyclopaedic work of fifteen sections dealing with such governmental matters as coinage, weights and measures, fiscal policy, commerce, welfare, forests, agriculture, law, international relations, and military strategy. The purpose was the achievement of prosperity, resistance to Greek invasion, and victory over rival neighbouring states. Alexander had defeated the northern Indian states but moved on, leaving satraps behind. Kautilya, adviser and prime minister to Emperor Chandragupta (340-293 BCE), guided him in re-conquests and military expansion to achieve a state, the Mauryan Empire, covering much of India plus modern Pakistan, reaching into Afghanistan.

Kautilya referred to the *Arthashastra* as "the science of punishment," the economics of which have been quoted as the origins of that discipline. The theories were naturally reflective of his times but notable for his identification of the satisfaction of the needs required to produce state prosperity. Key were the qualities of the king, ministers, provinces, city, exchequer, army and allies. He has gained admiration for his political acuity and understanding of human nature but criticised for ruthlessness and the condoning of treachery – but these were commonplace factors of his times. His recommended espionage system extended throughout all levels of the state: an efficient management information system for his age. Maxims from the *Arthashastra* and two other works, particularly revealing for their political realism, the first known of their type, include important statements on education:

> Education is the best friend.
> An educated person is respected everywhere.
> Education beats the beauty and the youth.
>
> Learning is worshiped everywhere.... Rulership and scholarship are never equal. The ruler is respected in his country, the scholar everywhere.[14]

More than a millennium afterwards, the wars of the 19th century were fought essentially between the manufacturers Krupp of Essen and Newcastle's William Armstrong (1810-1900), the inventor of modern artillery. A Japanese exploratory delegation visited Armstrong's factories and the great inventor/manufacturer at his Cragside home in Northumberland, England, the first domestic residence in the world to be illuminated by hydro-electric lighting. The 1870 publication of Samuel Smiles' (1812-1904) *Self Help* in Japan acted as an enormous stimulus to that country's race to catch up with the West. Here, they did so with stealth. Their subsequent purchases were implemented quietly. However, it was no surprise to the late Lord Armstrong's management or the Japanese armed forces when they astonished Russia and the world with a comprehensive victory at the battle of Tsushima Strait in 1905, completed destruction of the Russian fleet at Port Arthur, and so suddenly emerged as a world power.

The Far Eastern business model of "research, copy, adapt, and improve" continues. This mirror of ancient Greek entrepreneurialism through to 18th century English behaviour in taking foreign innovations and adapting them to successful machine production in the industrial revolution, has characterised the later post-war 20th century manufacturing rise and market dominance of Japan, followed by South Korea, and now China. The *caveat* here, cited in a later volume, is that it may be China which takes the lead in "quantum Internet" research under the project banner of its ancient sage

Mozi, opponent of Confucianism and Taoism but whose works were displaced by the ascendancy of the Legalists.

The research component of "copy, adapt, and improve" was library and laboratory based, complemented by sending out scouts, recruiting foreign advice, and joint ventures. It was also developed from newly acquired knowledge foundations. This author gained first-hand experience of the business model when consulting as a national technical education adviser to the Republic of Korea government in the early 1980s. The business and management applications of the strategic advice of Sun Tzu flourish still.

If current dating is correct, it has been observed that a person in those days could have known Sun Tzu, Confucius, Buddha, Zoroaster and Socrates should they have lived to the age of 75. This is extremely unlikely, but it illustrates of the widespread intellectual development of the 6th and 5th centuries BCE. There are, however, intriguing parallels in the emergent thought of East and West concerning nature.[15] Such progress emanated from that burst of energy provided to humanity between 500 and 300 BCE in the Eastern Mediterranean, Ganges, Yangtse, and Yellow River valleys of more than 20,000 calories per person intake in food, fodder, fuel and raw materials.

It is important to note, however, that the East-West connection would have been barely conceivable before the late 3rd century BCE, when silk trading began upon the route to which it gave its name. In management education therefore, as in so much else, we might note that the Chinese were pioneers - even if this went unnoticed outside their hemisphere at the time. Although Kautilya knew of Aristotle, Plato and Socrates through Greek contact arising from Alexander's invasion and of Lao Tzu, Taoism, and Confucianism through trade with China, any further contact knowledge (particularly the reciprocal) is conjectural. Therefore, despite Kautilya's stark realism and Korean archaeological evidence of the ranking stone markers in palace assembly grounds indicative of where officials were to present themselves, study of management has to recommence fully in the West.

**FOOTPRINT: Increased Calorie Intake Produces Differently Inclined Civilisations But Recognisable Management Forms Emerge**

- **Stimulated by increased calorie intake, the ancient world produced autocratically led, warfare-prone civilisations showing recognisable management forms but with widely contrasting emphases.**

- **These were consolidated through myth, convenient fictions, and slow technological advance.**

- **A slave economy featured strongly in the West; forms of feudalism featured in the East. People were too poor to support mass production.**

- **Eastern philosophy inclined to natural duty and obligation, the West to freedom with responsibility.**

# Endnotes

[1] Ed.Wing, R L. 1986. *The Tao Of Power*. Wellingborough, Northamptonshire, UK: The Aquarian Press. A tetragram is a geometric formation of four lines with six points of intersection, the varying vertical and horizontal lengths and distances between make for different figures.

[2] For example, he invites retribution: *"If I have done anything wrong, may Heaven forsake me, may Heaven forsake me." Ibid,* p.15.24, p.259; 6.29, p.95. trans. Chin, Annping. *"Confucius The Analects,"* 6.28, p.95.

[3] *Ibid,* p.15.24, p.259; 6.29, p.95.

[4] *Cf.* Eliot, T S. 1935. *Murder in the Cathedral:* "The last act is the greatest treason/To do the right deed for the wrong reason."

[5] Chin, *op. cit.*, p.19; p.106; p.107; p.204.

[6] *Ibid.* p.200; p.266; p.197; p.182.

[7] Fung Yu-lan, *Chuang-Tzu A Taoist Classic*, pp.54-55. Referred to in Chapter 4

above and Case Study 16, the *Metamorphoses* of Ovid (43 BCE-17/18 AD), an epic poem chronicling the history of the world from creation to the Dictatorship of Julius Caesar through 250 intertwined narratives based on myth, is one of the most influential works of western culture. It provided inspiration and information for the works of Dante, Boccacio, Chaucer, and Shakespeare. Ovid's conclusion was that, apart from his poem, everything must give way to transformation and change: food for thought to all who aspire to management education.

[8] Ed. Horne, Charles F. *The Sacred Books and Early Literature of the East*, Volume XII: *Medieval China,* pp.397-398. Gore Vidal famously remarked, "Any American who is prepared to run for president should automatically by definition be disqualified from ever doing so," an observation complemented in the second volume of Douglas Adams's *Hitchhikers Guide to the Galaxy*, "anyone who is capable of getting themselves made president should be on no account be allowed to do the job;" and expanded by James Hoopes in *Hail to the CEO: The Failure of George W Bush and the Cult of Moral Leadership*: "Only those who recognize that they may be or become morally unfit to lead are morally worthy to do so."

Lucius Quinctius Cincinnatus (519-430 BCE), a highly respected Roman patrician, was famously summoned from ploughing his fields to rescue Rome from conflict arising over law codification, given the power of the Dictatorship, resolved the issue, and went home. Further difficulty arose; he was again given the state's supreme power, restored peace; and once more retired to his farm. Such self-effacement to the benefit of the greater good won Machiavelli's approval, has been compared to George Washington's restraint at the formation of the USA, and is commemorated in the naming of various places in his honour, in Italy, New York, and Ohio. However, accolades' bestowal here must be qualified by his consistent opposition to progressive reform. The Catos are cited above and below. The final example is even more difficult than Cincinnatus.

Lucius Cornelius Sulla Felix (138-78 BCE) after a prolonged power struggle and civil war was appointed to the Dictatorship by the Senate, the accession approved by the people's Assembly. After revising the constitution to eradicate earlier reforms giving more power to the people and proscribing his enemies, conforming to his conservative Roman beliefs, he voluntarily resigned the office and dismissed his legions, walking unarmed in public, available to answer any questions. Twice thereafter elected consul, he finally retired, according to some sources, to enjoy the debauchery which had characterised his youth. The lavishness of his funeral was not surpassed until that of Augustus. His resort to force to win the power which was his by right but denied by political opponents is held to have provided the model for the later civil wars which ended the Republic.

Lord George Byron (1788-1824)) wrote an *Ode to Napoleon* on the fall of the Emperor in 1814, the last verse of which referred to George Washington:

"Where may the wearied eye repose

When gazing of the Great;

Where neither guilty glory glows,

Nor despicable state?

Yes one the first the last the best

The Cincinnatus of the West

Whom envy dared not hate,
Bequeath'd the name of Washington,
To make man blush there was but one!"

[9] Fung, Yu-lan, *op. cit.*, pp.49-50. Although the title renders Chou as Tzu, which is the more usual westernized spelling, the text quotes Chou. For accuracy of quotation, this latter form has been retained. By "predicables" Chou refers in scholastic logic to that which may be stated or affirmed in the classification of possible relations.

[10] Chien, Ssu-ma "An Introduction to Economics" from "Biographies of Merchants and Industrialists," cited in Moore, Karl & Lewis, David, *Foundations of Corporate Empire*, note 20, p. 94.

[11] See later volume chapter, "Managing Strategy". However, a citation in Season 3, Episode 8 of the HBO gangster series *The Sopranos* and subsequent references as the book was circulated among Tony's family and "family" has caused a general increase in sales.

[12] Sun Tzu, *The Art of War,* trans. Lionel Giles, 1910, republished Pax Librorum Publishing House, 2009.

[13] Cao Wei, Shu Han and Eastern Wu.

[14] Subramanian, V K *Maxims of Chanakya,* 71 -72, p. 102.

[15] To Antisthenes (c.446-c.366 BCE), pupil of Socrates and founder Cynic, the purpose of life was to live virtuously in harmony with nature. Happiness could be attained through training and living in a manner natural to the individual, and the rejection of fame, wealth and power. The most prominent exponent, Diogenes (412-323 BCE), lived in a barrel (in the form of a ceramic jar) in the streets of Athens, expressing by example the philosophy of a simple life without possessions. Asked by an impressed Alexander the Great if there was anything he could do for him, the Cynic responded with a request to stand out of his light. Mendicant, begging Cynics survived into the Roman Empire, but the philosophy was refined into Stoicism while its austerity tradition later became absorbed into extreme forms of Christianity. By the 19th century, cynicism has declined into disbelief of the sincerity or good intent of any human action, aspiration or motivation. In *Lady Windermere's Fan*, Oscar Wilde (1854-1900) memorably categorised a cynic as "A man who knows the price of everything, and the value of nothing." This he contrasted with a sentimentalist, who saw an absurd value in everything and didn't know the market price of anything. Divergence between hemispherical traditions was thus complete.

# MINI-CASE STUDY (3):
# INSPIRED MANAGEMENT OF
# THE ARAB CONQUESTS

**During the 7$^{th}$ and 8$^{th}$ centuries, the tribes of the Arabian peninsula mounted an unprecedented campaign of sustained conquest. Instead of fighting among themselves, as was their habit, the tribes conquered the Middle East, Persia, North Africa and Southern Europe, spreading Islam as they advanced.**

In 632, the Prophet died, leaving behind the basis of a religion among a few tribes in the Arabian desert. They were small in number, divided, and surrounded by two rich, powerful empires. Within a century, Arab armies controlled territories from northern Spain to southern Iran, while Islam had refashioned those societies it touched. A profound and differing transformation of Greek and Persian societies into Islamic ones had commenced.

The Arabs were simply defined as those who spoke Arabic, geographically confined to a small, core area. Those closest to the late Muhammad, the Companions of the Prophet, made a series of bold, daring, inspired management decisions. They decided to use the ideas and principles of Islam to bring the tribes together, uniting them. They realised that if they weren't fighting outsiders, they would be fighting each other. They began with an audacious series of campaigns into Syria, Iraq and beyond. Most of the fighters and followers lived a Bedouin lifestyle, which conferred much military skill: wielding arms, traveling great distances, understanding terrain, living simply, and enduring great hardship.

At the heart of the leadership was the Caliph, the successor to Muhammad, God's representative on earth. The first holder of the office Abu Bakr al-Siddiq (573-634), father-in-law, oldest friend of the Prophet, noted freer of slaves, in a highly intense term, set out an aggressive, militant policy, determining that all the Arabs of the peninsular should follow its requirements. Their seemingly giant opponents of Byzantium and the Sasanian Empire of Persia had exhausted each other in prolonged warfare;

the Roman successors, weakened by plague, were attacked under the instruction of the new Caliph Omar in Syria and Iraq. Both were defeated in 636, at the battles of Firaz and Yarmouk, unavailingly attempting further resistance by allying against the Arabs. Large scale collapse of the existing systems followed, large swift raids completing the process.

Islam became the new ideology, now dating from 632, the Prophet's nativity. Fuelled by *jihad* enthusiasm, the poorly equipped but brilliantly organised Arab armies made effective use of their sharp swords. In forming relationships with their new subjects, they had the advantage of their continued presence not being expected to last. The Arabs demanded only acceptance of their sovereignty (or slavery and death), with the payment of taxes. Otherwise, the vanquished were left undisturbed, including in their religion. Anyone whose faith possessed a scripture was presumed to have the means to govern themselves. The Arabs did not try to convert.

Garrison towns outside of and adjacent to cities allowed both groups to retain their identities, leading to the gradual creation of a new civilisation. Only by the 740s were Muslims seen in the countryside, but they now enjoyed cultural self-confidence. In a multi-ethnic empire, God had spoken in Arabic, the language of the new elite; not Slav, or German, or Spanish.

Byzantine resistance was much weakened by the fall of Alexandria in 641 and the relocation of the Egyptian capital to Cairo. As the armies spread beyond Egypt and Baghdad, fighting became more bitter. This required more determined presence, encouraging troops' settlement with local women, producing second generation Arabs. As a result, the complexion of the armies changed. Most of the conquerors of Spain were Berbers. The impulse to continued conquest was spurred by the Arab Civil War, discussed below. Control of the wealth essential to maintain the state required both the division of booty and the imperative to keep fighting. The assassination of the 4th Caliph, the Prophet's cousin Ali, (601-661) by his successor Mu'awiyah I, (602-680), first Umayyad Caliph, owed a lot to the latter having much the greater resources as the Governor of Syria.

Abd al-Malik (644 or 647-705), 5th Umayyad Caliph, began the Arabisation project, making Arabic the official language of state. This began the eradication of Greek; if an official job was required in the administration, it was necessary to be able to speak and write Arabic. Spoken Greek had been the language of the Mediterranean and Near East for a millennium. Yet, in a generation, it disappeared, Aramaic and Syriac suffering the same fate.

Except for partial script adaptation, there was no linguistic change in Iran. Before al-Malik, there was nothing of religion in official documents. After him, on all documents, seals, and inscriptions, religious material became essential, a process accompanied by an enormous mosque building program. Islam had gone from being a conqueror's cult to a mass religion. Marauding brigands had been turned into a professional army; the conquest systematised. Conquest had been quick; its conversion into a state, slow.

At the start of the adventure, Muhammad had been a trader, preacher, prophet, politician, and military leader. Whoever succeeded him had to fulfil all those roles. He had not made it clear who was to succeed him. He may have nominated his first cousin, son-in-law, and husband of his granddaughter, Ali. Instead, his friend and ancient companion, Abu Bakr, was nominated by another friend to be the first Caliph. Engaged in funeral preparations with the family, Ali was disadvantaged in pressing his claim. Abu Bakr achieved the succession.

Caliphate power was entrenched in Abu Bakr's short but eventful reign. An oath of allegiance was required to a new caliph and, as further successors followed, a "Party of Ali" began to emerge. Omar (584-644), father of the Prophet's wife and whose model, traditional practice ("Sunnah") of Muhammad's principles brought use of the Sunni description to the dominant version of Islam, ruled as a respected leader until assassination by a Persian slave. 'Uthman, (574-656), the third caliph, was felt to favour his own tribe, the resultant tensions causing his assassination for not ruling in an Islamic way. Under Omar and by 'Uthman's time, the Empire had been created in some 30 years, extending from North Africa to the Hindu Kush.

The palace story then became complex. A combination of anti-Ali groups and the absence of revenge being taken for 'Uthman gave Ali caliphate problems, compounded when battle was suspended in favour of an arbitration, resulting in another blood revenge assassination when Ali himself was dispatched on grounds of not believing enough in himself and his rights. Christian divisions at this time were about the nature of God. This quarrel was about power in the Islamic community, stemming also from 'Uthman's attempts to impose a unified version of the Qur'an among the teachers, scholars, and jurists of Islam. Hovering significantly in the dispute with the effective new caliphate Umayyad dynasty was the fact that all Muhammad's successors had been members of his family, Ali the most prominent.

The Umayyads could claim relation only from a half-brother of one of the wives of Muhammad. The pivotal moments occurred when the late Ali's son Hassan (625-670) refused to swear allegiance and was poisoned, and his sibling Hussein (626-681) was killed in a hopelessly unequal battle by Umayyad forces. Ali, Hassan and Hussein became the first three (late) caliphs of the now breakaway Shiat: party of Ali. While a minority of some 10% against the Sunni 85% of Islam majority, the Shia remain dominant in Iran, Iraq, and parts of the Near East. The 7th century assassinations remain an immense setback for the Shia, but they can still interpret the Qur'an according to imams from the family of the Prophet or Shiite clerics.

In the matter of how they are ruled by their religion, Sunni and Shia agree on the divinity of the Qur'an but differ in interpretations of the Hadith and jurisprudence. Islamic law is rooted in the words and actions of the Prophet, but evolved as Islam spread. The legal code known as Sharia comes from the Arabic word meaning "the way," itself based on Muhammad's words and legal scholars' opinions. In the 7th century, Sharia started to replace the tribal laws of pre-Islamic Arabia. In an evolutionary process taking some 300 years, by the early 10th century there was a body of legal and religious scholarship recognising that a classical form of Sharia had emerged.

The Prophet had close personal experience of life as it was lived. He had been a merchant, then a religious leader, by the end of his life having established himself as a presence in Medina, a city which also contained both Christian and Jewish communities. Early Muslim groups had different legal systems: tribal law, honour codes, and compensation provisions. After 622, Muhammad had acted as an honest broker between the faiths, arbitrating with and between other local luminaries. The quality of his decisions, eminently just, won him followers - as did his standing up for the rights of the poor and oppressed. The message was important, for here lay the idea of a state which was moral, ruled by a just and moral man.

The early period of Sharia meant the uncovering of the law from what was meant by the core of the Qur'an. This referred to the revelations guided by God.

What the Prophet had said was in the complementary literature of the Hadith; what God said to Muhammad was in the Qur'an: the oneness (or unity) of God. The Qur'an is a continuation of the prophesies known to Judaism and Christianity. The sociolegal provisions deal with marriage, divorce and punishment of offence against God: alcohol, crime, theft, armed robbery, apostasy. The provisions concern the right way to be, and though not legal regarding offence and prescriptions, form the basis of Islamic law.

As the Muslim empire grew, it had to have rules. Muslims had to work out the law to be applied from prophetic inspiration to the solving of everyday problems. Two generations had to effectively wrestle with the problem of "Now what? What do we do now?" Sometimes, other, external law had to be imported, such as taxation law. In general, however, Islamic law took, or was given, precedence over all other law. To make complex decisions, scholars had to consider the Prophet's behaviour, the Hadith, the Qur'an, and recognise reasons for prohibition by God.

What, for example, of date wine? Prohibition of grape wine was clear enough: negative effects on behaviour and intoxication. As these negatives applied to liquor from dates, and indeed many drugs, these were all banned too. Traditional Islamic law has little to say about criminal law, for the emphasis is on local provision. Here, matters such as inheritance and property are to be decided by *quadi* (local judges), whose functions are academic rather than judicial.

There are four schools of Islamic law, the two most prevalent being the Shafi'i and Hanafi. Founded in the early 9th century, the Shafi'i scheme takes the Qur'an and Hadith as the sources of Islamic law, which itself becomes what scholars find in the traditions of that law, with all actions being traced back to the Prophet or inferred from those sources. The Hanafi school relies on legal analogy when the Qur'an and Hadith are silent or ambiguous. These form the major basis for all legal and religious judgments, the orthodoxy of the Muslim world.

Extreme punishments, such as amputations for theft or stoning for adultery, were not seen as important to Islamic law theorists and jurists, who are more concerned about correct action in everyday incidents, such as a neighbour known to be a drinker (with whom one may remonstrate in the street but not go into his house). In extreme eventualities, the evidential bar is high, four people having to witness the offence.

Despite official claims of judiciary reform and restriction in the use of the death penalty, on 12 March 2022 Saudi Arabia executed 81 imprisoned civilians, including a Syrian, 7 Yemenis and 37 Saudi nationals. Their convictions were for attempted terrorist attacks, arms smuggling, loyalty to foreign terrorist organisations, and holding deviant beliefs. These executions further damaged a Saudi image already tarnished by the murder of dissident journalist Jamal Khashoggi (1958–2018).

Despite its contemporary conflicts, Islamic oddities are more usually found in its copious, complex history. Abbasid and Umayyad civilisation is cited in Chapter 7. The Fatimid political and religious dynasty from 909 to 1171 controlled North Africa and much of the Middle East. Descendants of the Prophet's daughter and their first (late) Imam, Ali, this Shiite regime sought (unsuccessfully) to supersede the Abbasids (see below). Succeeded by Salah-ad Din (Saladin, 1137-1193), this "most famous Kurd in history" decisively defeated the Crusaders in 1187, realigned the territories of his Ayyubid Empire with the Abbasids, became Sultan of Egypt, and conquered: Syria, Yemen, the Kingdom of Jerusalem, Palestine, and parts of Mesopotamia. Noted supporter of culture, he gave his extreme wealth to the poor.

After an interregnum, Saladin's territories were taken over by the Mamluks, rulers of Egypt and Syria from c.1250-1517. Originally slave soldiers who deposed their masters, the Mamluks went on to repel Mongols and Crusaders and become the dominant force in the Islamic world. Although renowned as warriors, arts, crafts, and architecture flourished. Turkic slave soldiers, the Mamluks formed an elite. Because it was illegal under Sharia law to enslave Muslims, they were imported from the periphery of the Islamic world. Known for their martial qualities, Turks were the preferred group. They were trained in the most advanced military technology of the day, high quality exponents in the arts of archery and cavalry combat. Enslaved mercenaries made for a formidable force.

Eventually overthrown by the then all-conquering Ottomans, the latest Islamic force achieved a centuries' held ambition: the fall of Constantinople, ending Byzantium. Despite, or because of, the male heirs securing their thrones on accession by murdering their siblings, the rulers from the Sublime Porte were just as much a formidable fighting force as many of their predecessors. These new bearers of the crescent flag pursued conflicts in North Africa and deep into Europe, reaching their height in the 16th century, lingering as a great power on the world stage for a further three centuries subsequently. Whereas Kemal Atatürk (1881-1938) modernised Turkey into a secular, industrial nation, the current presidency incumbent, Recep Tayyip Erdoğan (1954-) has pursued a socially conservative, populist Islamic policy.

The success of the Abrahamic religions with the rise of monotheism brought change beyond themselves to the world, which became less tolerant as a result. While the more relaxed attitudes of Islam might be contrasted with the rigours of the beliefs of Christendom at the time of the Reformation and its Counter, it remains the case that the pagan approaches of polytheism allowed for a multiplicity of faiths for myriad purposes, with a tolerance of others' ways of being. None of those were necessarily better; but they were often certainly easier. The pagan world had been more comfortable for diversity.

## Case Study Reflections

1. What are the reasons, for and against, for designating a management successor?

2. What are the reasons, for and against, a family retaining control of its business?

3. What other management issues can be identified through this study?

**Constantine the Great**

Author of two momentous world management achievements, this first Roman Emperor to convert to Christianity, Constantine I the Great, renamed the city of Byzantium as Constantinople, the title by which it was known for over 1,000 years, bridging the period between later antiquity and early modern history.

# CHAPTER SIX

# TRANSITIONS AND RETREATS

Preserver of learning and culture during the emergence of new states, albeit sporadically and often dimly, the Roman Church provided a continuity of some access to classical knowledge, as well as structure, bureaucracy, and discipline derived from the traditions of the Roman imperial armies. Whether the formal conversion of the Emperor Constantine (272-337) to Christianity in 312 was genuine, or a *realpolitik* manoeuvre to consolidate his hold on power, or even a coincidental convenience, the strength and bureaucratic competence of the Roman state allowed for the creation of a viable institution with a clear belief system. The practical Emperor insisted upon a common version of the faith.

From this grew an ever more elaborate theology: the science of God. If myth and legend had informed knowledge and belief in the preceding phase of human development in the West, there was now a focus on a single story of many facets, a central message, guarded by clerics with monopolistic rights, rites, and ritual. Constantine had made two of the most important decisions of world history: moving the capital of the Roman Empire to Constantinople; and changing its religion.

The management of what became the twin pillars of the successor state had come together when Constantine made Christianity the official religion. The Church inherited the military traditions of discipline, order, and organisation. Although the state fractured into fragments ruled by barbarians in the west, Roman Byzantium survived in the east until 1453, and the occidental national successor regimes were united under the concept of Christendom. That was split in the 11th century when political and doctrinal differences resulted in the Roman Catholic and Eastern Orthodox churches functioning independently. Egypt-based, the Coptic Church had separated in 451.

The western Christendom concept applied in the medieval and early modern periods, where European states acknowledged the spiritual hegemony of

Rome, its' supposed moral authority, and the temporal possessions governed by its papacy. The Roman army management command model effectively transferred into the Roman Church, its hierarchic structure dominating religion, government and society until the Reformation. The Church was the pivot of Western society, owner of a third of the land of western Europe, the greatest single source of temporal power, and dominant management model.

Byzantium remained the continuing Empire of the Romans. After Justinian's failed attempt to revive that entity, the continuance of Greek culture within its natural habitat saw Byzantium become Greeker and Greeker. By the 7th century, Greek had replaced Latin as its general language. As befitted the culture, the highlights of the society over the succeeding near-millennium were in the arts and crafts: construction, religious art, mosaics, and the admittedly obscure referential literature.

Another practical ruler touched by religion was Charlemagne (742-814). His accession marked the decisive European power shift northwards from Rome. Becoming the new western Emperor when so crowned on Christmas Day 800 by Pope Leo III (d.816), he sought to encourage education and right action throughout his extensive European realm. Central to the mission were the production of Bibles on an industrial scale and a progressive group of clerics led by his favourite, Alcuin (735-804). This Northumbrian monk had an innovative approach to education, seeking to make it an enjoyable pursuit while also re-introducing classical authors, especially Aristotle. Preservation of the classics, although providing subsequently for stultified, deadening instruction, also greatly enhanced the progress of European civilisation.

Preservation of the questioning of Socratic method supported the philosophical tradition of speaking truth unto power, albeit usually with discretion. Expression and inspiration of liberty, moral behaviour, philosophy, scientific method, and artistic and literary excellence was available to all able to overcome the linguistic hurdles. The progressive Christianising of European society saw missionary pioneering into the emerging states, then amongst society by friars, and the development of canon law. Extremes of heretical priest burning, bodily chastisement, and denial contrasted with the increasingly ornate construction of places of worship. The monastic movement initially saw a retreat of ascetics and scholars, latterly a thriving religious business which also conferred rules for living, further to improve and so manage the people.

Church, cathedral, monastic, and palace schools provided the literate manpower necessary to staff bureaucracies and maintain organisational coherence. Universities spread the technology of administration. Franciscans and Dominican friars were particularly noted for their learning, forming a significant proportion of the teaching staff at Oxford. Monastic order and management had great influence on that of the universities (although the college concept is much older, of Latin root meaning *gathering,* dating back to Roman trade and workers' clubs, ranging from low status, such as the *collegium* of crossings-sweepers, to the upscale ivory carvers, and on occasion effectively to gangs which might become criminal, requiring of suppression by the authorities). The goal of education had changed, however. Now, its purpose was not only to produce good citizens but, apart from the subsidiary aim of creating lay administrators, to preserve, enrich, and enhance the faith.

Thus, the copying of Bibles and the writings of the Church fathers, the use of arithmetic to calculate religious festivals, singing to glorify the creator, and civil engineering devoted to church-building became the expressions of education, and therefore the fount of management. The preparation for life which characterised Greek and Roman education was supplanted by preparation for the assumed afterlife, a cultural reversion marking thousands of years in its echo of the ancient Egyptian focus on death. Compensatory advance was made in the development of Christian ethics and values but, extremely important as they were and are, their application was to an essentially stagnant society. There was progress, but it was not going anywhere quickly.

Medievalism died slowly. Although trial by ordeal had been abolished in England in the 12th century by Henry II (1133-1189) and in Christendom in the 13th by the Pope, it continued in some European countries until the 16th century. Until then, accused might be thrown into a pond to determine guilt (innocence being to sink); or set a time for a hand burn to heal, its cause being the forced grasping of molten metal; or required to undertake single combat to settle a land dispute. The managerial power of God was being held to determine guilt or innocence, with miraculous application, the logic of which was to weight the scales of justice to allow the Almighty to display His wondrous strength. Trial by battle (known also as wager by battle), the fighting by litigants themselves or their champions regarding land disputes, also continued in Europe until the 16th century. Effectively licensed duelling, this method of honour dispute management was not finally outlawed until the 19th century.

Meanwhile, the practicalities of life, other than governance, rested on the progress of commerce and crafts, complemented and inspired by the development of science. The rediscovery of the great scientists of antiquity such as the Alcuin-revived Aristotle, Euclid (d.285 BCE), Pliny the Elder (23-79 CE), and Archimedes (c.287-c.212 BCE) spurred a renewal of interest and scholarship. Naturally, military adoption was the commonest method of implementing the newly revived technologies, from concrete to siege engines, and significant advances in medicine and surgery.

The Romans' technology was so advanced because they were able, in the time-honoured manner, to copy and adapt from those they neighboured or conquered. The aeolipile, a primitive steam engine or turbine, is usually ascribed to Heron of Alexandria, in the 1st century CE. However, it had no perceived use other than as a toy or temple decoration. The industrial revolution was delayed. To mass market restriction, there was an additional fuel problem; the combination of Roman mining technology, charcoal, and vegetable matter could alleviate the wood shortage, but bulk transport requirements had been too great.

The Roman military expertise and accompanying civil engineering was, subsequently, largely neglected. This expertise had accomplished such feats as gravity-powered aqueduct water supply, a paved road network, sanitation systems, and fixed and movable bridge construction. The latter sufficiently advanced under Caesar to bridge the Rhine in a matter of weeks, and produce materials of projectile warfare whose power was unsurpassed for almost a thousand years.

After the fall of Rome, castle and church building reflected different priorities. Yet, in a way, the former represented progress even if the occupants used their strongholds as bases from which to subjugate and extort their local populations, and as the centres for both domestic and foreign expeditions of acquisition, plunder, and control. Direct slavery had been replaced by systems tying labourers to the land and servitude to the landlords, workers, to their trade masters. This was less an example of humane beneficence and more a means of reducing labour costs.

Outside the military, the Roman craft tradition had its own hierarchy and practice. Every trade, of itself or in sub-groups, had collections of artisans, skilled or semi-skilled. Naturally, those able to acquire the most expensive materials, from dye stuffs to precious metals, formed the wealthiest (if not necessarily the most prestigious) of groups. These *collegia,* or guilds (derived from the Saxon word *gildan*, to pay), had a master/apprentice structure, with knowledge communicated orally and a tradition of the preservation of trade secrecy. Thus, after the fall of the Roman Empire, few of these guilds survived in the West, with much technical skill and knowledge being lost.

However, high crafts such as jewellery and glass making survived. Guilds revived in the medieval period to become important and dominant determinants of much trade and business. Charlemagne had been reminded of how far behind the Arab world Europe was when exchanging gifts and letters with the 5th Abbasid Caliph of Baghdad, Haroun al-Rashid (763/766-809) - he of the *Thousand and One Arabian Nights* tales. Recipient of a chess set, brass candlesticks and a water clock which struck the hour, Europe's finest clearly lagged behind.

The earliest universities at Bologna (1068) and Oxford (1096) derived from guilds of students. Stone-cutting, glass making, and jewellery making were crafts which, with manuscript illustration, clearly continued. Eventually, the guilds became an important form of business organisation. In medieval times, they typically enjoyed a monopoly within a city in return for payments to the monarch. They set standards, trained members, appointed notaries and brokers, constructed meeting halls, and supported charities. Completion of an apprenticeship would allow a person freedom from conscription and permission to set up a business. Guilds served to protect their members' interests; essentially conservative, they were an inhibitor to change.

Example of post-Roman continuation of craft excellence is to be found in the "Northumbrian Renaissance" of the mid-7th to mid-8th century. This is celebrated in particular for the magnificence of its arts and crafts, as exemplified by the Lindisfarne Gospels, facilitation of missionary expeditions to Europe, intervention at the 664 Synod of Whitby in establishing the primacy of Roman Catholicism in England, and the romantic excellence of its King and Saint, Oswald (604-642), model for Tolkien's *Lord of the Rings* character of Aragorn and whose post-mortem career was as extraordinary as his life and death had been.

His severed arms and legs were displayed at Oswald's Tree, subsequently known as Oswestry. Many miracles were attributed to the place where he fell in battle, his skull bearing a cut sufficiently wide to accommodate three fingers, now in the custody of Durham Cathedral, was the leading exhibit of a plethora of relics venerated across Europe for their virtue and potency, his name becoming a common appellation. His British-Irish-Scot-Anglo-Saxon fusion gained expression in the artistic and cultural flowering exemplified by the Lindisfarne Gospels. A political legacy cited by his biographer as bearing partial responsibility for the Crusades, Henry VIII's break with Rome, and the idea of Britain as a Christian state has contributed to a view of his exceeding Tolkien's Aragorn as a monarchical romantic hero: "Oswald was the real thing".[1]

Pope Gregory the Great (c.540-604) in 597 ordered a band of monks to restore Christianity to Britain, his motives being by expanding to the extremes to hasten the Second Coming and to compete for ownership of the brand with other patriarchies. Among those were that of the Irish St Columba (521-597), whose establishment at Iona had sent St Aidan as bishop (d. 651), at the request of Oswald, to convert the peoples of Northumbria from his foundation of the new monastic base of Lindisfarne, a tidal island on the north-eastern coast.

**St. Aidan of Lindisfarne**
**(d. 651 CE),** the "Apostle of England", credited with having led the conversion of the country.
Photograph: Cliff Winlow.

Lindisfarne (also known as Holy Island), served by a causeway, was within sight to the south of the royal settlement of Bamburgh, an eminently defensible natural meeting ground with ports' services. The sect decision on location rested on the dating of Easter and preference for the Roman tonsure to the Celtic forehead crop, but the management issue was the reconciliation of the Celtic and Roman traditions.

That task fell to St Cuthbert (634-687), an ascetic who later became bishop. As a monk he was renowned for his abstemiousness and frugality, though also for charm and generosity to the poor; earning a reputation for insight on matters both mundane and mystical on which he was often consulted, and gifts of healing. Many attributed miraculous happenings were noted during his lifetime, passed on through oral monastic tradition, eventually recorded for posterity in various later manuscripts and hagiography.

**Cuthbert in charge of rescuing a piece of timber from the sea** for use as a roof beam (possibly for a house or church). Illustration from a 12th century manuscript, *Life of St Cuthbert,* commemorating his life and miracles; originally written in Latin, *Vita Sancti Cuthberti.*

Whilst ministering to the needs of the people, missionary work, and monastic duties, to also honour his need for a quiet contemplative life on becoming bishop Cuthbert retreated to a hermitage on the Inner Farne Island, close to the mainland and clearly visible from both Bamburgh and the Lindisfarne monastery (later a priory). A most individual version of hermitage, the canny Cuthbert had created a surveillance system allowing him to watch both centres of his responsibility whilst ensuring enough space to concentrate on personal prayer and meditation.

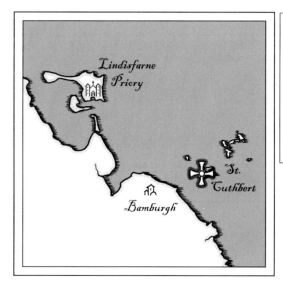

Active-passive supervision whilst fulfilling an individual's vocational and spiritual calling, remains a possibly unique management accomplishment.

**St. Cuthbert's remote management surveillance system**

**The Inner Farne island, site of St. Cuthbert's cell, seen from Bamburgh.**
Photograph: Cliff Winlow

**'Bamborough Castle (Bamburgh) from the Northeast, with Holy Island
(Lindisfarne) in the Distance'**
[by John Varley, 1827, Metropolitan Museum of Art, New York.]

[Royal Northumbrian fortifications at the site lasted from the 6th to the 10th century.
Destroyed by Vikings in 993, a replacement Norman castle was built on the site,
later falling into disrepair. After successive 19th century restorations, the castle was
rendered into his idea of what a castle should be by the industrial magnate, Lord
Armstrong. It remains a family home but offers residential accommodation,
restaurant and tourist services.].

Cuthbert's divine inspiration survived his death. The five-to-ten-year project to create the Lindisfarne Gospels was later dedicated to St Cuthbert; the principal author another Lindisfarne bishop, Eadfrith (d. 722).

**Page from the Lindisfarne Gospels, British Library**

The glossing of the gospels served further to increase the development of English. The materials procured were exceptional. The high-quality parchment was obtained from some 150 calf skins, donations from royalty, and gift exchanges from other monasteries; the Mediterranean palette recreated from local materials; and, specific to requirement, the lead pencil invented. The creation incorporated many Christian designs for multiple locations. Local Jarrow and Monkwearmouth styles were supplemented by Roman, Greek and Irish sources with German motifs.

The ecumenical reach and artistic display have been held as an equivalent to Bede's history. A gifted individual's gift to God, the book has been further described as an act of meditation glimpsing the divine. In a time when few could read, this was to be looked at. Immense example of the power of the visual, such artistic management served to bring many to the growing religious revival.

Yet, within three generations, all was despoiled as the kingdom fell prey to Viking raiders and invaders. The wealth of an otherwise well-managed state had gone into the glory of the Church, to the neglect of funds for basic coastal defence. The splendid, contemplative isolation of Lindisfarne was well suited to the monastic life and the exquisite illumination of biblical manuscript. However, due to its being wealthy, defenceless, and without strategic management, it was the softest of targets for the fury of pillaging Norsemen and uncontrolled immigration.

When the monks evacuated what had become their Monastic Cathedral on Lindisfarne, they undertook a peripatetic tour of northern Northumbria with their sacred baggage: relics of Oswald, Cuthbert's body, and the *Lindisfarne Gospels*. They eventually chose a resting place for Cuthbert, entombing their saint in what became Durham Cathedral. Such was the skill with which the body of this paragon was embalmed, it was found in the course of several removals and re-entombments to be inviolate.

Another significant indicator had shone from Northumbria in the form of the Venerable Bede (672/3-735), the monk of Jarrow. He was his country's first native historian, also a writer for children, and the last man, by popular anecdote, to have read every then-known book. Not to belittle Bede's remarkable achievement, it is nonetheless worth noting quite how much knowledge of the ancient world had been lost. The great library at Alexandria, established by the conqueror and the largest in the ancient world, at its height held some half a million scrolls. Books were the combination of a number of scrolls but, nonetheless, the amount of information was formidable for the times.[2] Bede's library at his Jarrow monastery contained some 200 books. It was viewed contemporaneously as being well stocked, and Bede's output marked history. He popularised the single universal chronology invented by Isidore of Seville (560-636), dating everything forward or backward from the entry of the divine into the womb of the Virgin Mary. A supreme and enduring management achievement, Bede had rendered the calibration of time itself as fully Christian. Father Time had been harnessed.

**Tomb of St Cuthbert, Durham Cathedral**
[Photograph: Cliff Winlow.]

Scholarship blended into the monastic tradition. Probably Buddhist in origin, the notion of enlightened dedication to God through groups in ascetic retreat had been the basis of the movement from the 4th century. This led to such extremes as the devotion to isolated discomfort displayed by the Syriac St. Simeon Stylites (390-459), who lived atop a pillar for 37 years, and unruly Roman monks in the next century accused of attempting to poison their reforming abbot, St. Benedict of Nursia (480-543/47). Benedict withdrew to found a new monastery which he hoped would serve as a model, this to be expressed through a Rule, probably derived from St. John Cassian (360-435).

Cassian is credited with having imported Palestinian/Egyptian monasticism into Europe, at Marseilles. The Rule expounded by Benedict was devotion to the glory of God, with instructions for its execution. The regulations specified the times of prayer, work, meals, and rest; required obedience; specified penalties; and named that direction to be done by the abbot, whose decisions were final but discussed beforehand with all the monks, known as the chapter.

Specific instructions were given to the abbot and his senior staff. The reasonable, balanced rules were widely adopted, the number of Benedictine monasteries eventually reaching over 1,000. The movement and its variants spread rapidly, all based on the Rule. A later Benedictine branch, the Cistercians, from the early 12$^{th}$ century developed the novel concept of acquiring tracts of waste, forested, or swampy ground for conversion to cultivable and productive use instead of relying upon the donation of land. Diversification into fishing, mining, viticulture, and the exploitation of water power followed. Their hydraulics and water uses through adaptive technology such as mills provided the base from which the industrial revolution later expanded. Commercially highly successful, they even made forays into banking and were adept in their futures dealings.

From the 12th and 13th centuries, English monasteries made future deals with foreign merchants to sell wool up to 20 years in advance. Other religious orders, all with derivative rules, abounded in medieval times. Orders of canons and friars – Augustinians, Premonstratensians, Dominicans, Franciscans – ministered and acted as controlling social workers in the community; military orders such as the Knights Templar existed to fight Muslims; and the Knights of St John and the Teutonic Knights mixed crusading with community welfare. The monks' numbers were never sufficient for the cultivation, exploitation and management of all their estates. Lay brothers, tenants, and hired labourers did the work, supervised by monks.

Buildings and facilities were also standardised, according to known patterns; just as with Roman forts, a Cistercian monastery was to the same design, wherever it might be. Administratively, a colonial cloning policy operated for expansion: "daughter" houses were established by, and accountable to, an existing foundation, and were required to follow its template. A pyramidal structure thus appeared. Monk management became the dominant model.

Women played a significant part in the development of early Christianity and the monastic life. Developed from ascetic withdrawal and hermit lifestyles into mixed communities gathered in convents as the base for mendicant ways of living, these institutions accommodated the rise of female organised communities. Led by an abbess or prioress, convents provided a practical, definitive base for female expression. Women of wealthy families could preserve their means and inheritance from loss and depredation through marriage, extending to personal independence within the regulations of their communities, allowing the development of career opportunities. Scion of the royal house of Northumbria, abbess St Hild of Whitby (614-680) there founded a monastery for men and women. The sexes lived separately in small groups but worshiped together in church and expressed their religion through contemplation and the active pursuit of virtue and charity.

Such overhangs and evocations of the female presence in paganism was not to the taste of the Roman Church, which began a campaign of limiting women's freedom within the religion from the 12th century. They were prevented from preaching, reading the gospels, taking precedence in processions, and hearing confessions. Administrative culmination of the Counter-Reformation, the 1545-1563 Council of Trent, ruled that women's orders must be overtaken by men. Formerly centres of higher education, convents were now prevented from teaching theology and doctrine. Even so, women gained more managerial experience through exercise of responsibilities for such operational functions as: finance, infirmary, kitchen, cellar, clothing, choir, almoner, supervision of stewards, lay officials, and the bailiff responsible for outlying property rents collection – all of this was additional to novice instruction, supervision, and discipline. Servants such as personal maids; brewers; bakers; maltsters; laundresses; dairy staff; herders of oxen, cows, pigs and sheep; carters; labourers; and casual workers at harvest time all had to be managed also. As well as providing management education for a section of religious society, female and male, standard business practice was exercised through the largest land-based sector

.

Such standardisation also affected business and the rest of society. The Benedictine Rules served as organisational models. The trade guilds followed the monastic pattern in their exclusivity, conditions of membership, guild master functions and consistency of aim. In a small community, the guild might represent all merchants; in a city, there were guilds where the trade was sufficient for their support. The most frequent adoption of administrative expertise, however, came from the use monarchs made of the sole source of public literate manpower: the Church and monasteries. The clerics and monks brought with them the administrative machinery inherited from Roman civil and military bureaucracy. The strength of the adaptation and improvement of these in reporting, recording, auditing, training, and the standardisation of practice has been held to be an indicator of how some emergent European countries, such as Britain, were able to perform above their apparent level internationally in matters of diplomacy and trade.

As Western society began to revive from the Dark Ages in the mid-7th century onwards, a reciprocal relationship between trade and religion had developed. In his introduction of Benedictine monasticism and the commissioning of ecclesiastical buildings to Britain, the well-travelled, Northumbrian advocate of papal supremacy St. Wilfrid (633-709) had imported skilled glass-makers, glaziers, and luxury items such as silk altar cloths, interwoven with gold thread. The 664 outcome of the Synod of Whitby further facilitated trade with the French and Germans, trading fair establishment being linked to religious sites and festivals. Almost from the outset, the new, infant western capitalism took different management forms. The reviving markets of Anglo-Saxon England encouraged merchants to locate on their own initiative, whereas the cities of the Rhine region began the tradition of state directed enterprise. Charlemagne concentrated craft industries in Bonn, Cologne, Frankfurt, Mainz, Strasbourg and Trier.

Europe's greater revival began around the second millennium. The population expanded, towns and universities were established, and a pre-industrial revolution utilised the natural powers of wind and water. The harnessing of the natural forces which drove the mills and transported goods was supplemented by agricultural improvements. Grinding grain or mechanising paper production, milling produced its own partner and family businesses as well as increasing the output of food and other supplies. The introduction of the three-field system and replacement of oxen by collared, harnessed, and shod horses pulling a deep, steel plough further enhanced agricultural production. Such innovation and technology management stimulated social change. As technical improvements in weaving increased textile production, the diligent application of the Cistercians by the mid-13th century brought such development in metal technology as the introduction of the blast furnace.

The growth of markets was enhanced through the abundant waterways of Flanders and Italy, leading the huge increase in textile manufacture. Until the devastation of the labour force in the 14th century by the Black Death, Europe began a boom period during which serfdom, whereby peasants were tied to the land, was progressively replaced in many areas in Western Europe by the emergence of yeomen: small-holding farmers. The city states of Italy, particularly Genoa, Venice and Pisa, were well placed to benefit from all these changes - especially through their shipbuilding capacity and proximity to Byzantium, the markets of the Arab world, and the lucrative trade of the east. The Crusades intensified trade and growth. The capture of Jerusalem in 1099 signalled the consolidation of the medieval war economy. Prospects of booty and plunder enticed all classes, with the further benefit of remission from sins where crusade was undertaken.

From the 13th to 14th centuries, Venice in particular had dominated international trade by using the Phoenician model. All the goods of its far-reaching trade empire passed through Venetian controlled waters, where its armed convoys escorted a state managed trade based on partnerships. Protection was a literal factor, extending as far as restricting foreign merchants within Venice itself to their own quarters. State management was that of trading and business process, rather than that of business itself.

The Italian cities performed the function of God's intermediaries, managing events to such an extent that Venice was able to divert the Fourth Crusade (1202-1204) from re-taking Jerusalem into the sack of Constantinople. Some of the spoils of this continue to decorate St Mark's Cathedral by the Grand Canal, a structure so enhanced that the longevity of its nickname, *Chiesa d'Oro* (Church of Gold), is sufficient explanation.

The crafts, architects, and building industries benefited from the competitive civic cathedral and other ecclesiastical construction industries of the 11th to 14th centuries, in the environs of whose buildings trade fairs flourished, set according to the Church calendar. Christian cathedral and church building owed much to Islamic construction technique, style, and design. Generally misattributed to the "gothic" form, spires, campaniles, pointed arches, ribbed vaults, rose windows, twin towered fronts, and types of stained glass and dome construction are all of Arabic origin in southern Spain and the Middle East.[3] Pilgrimages created and boosted tourist industries' trade and knowledge exchange. Sightseeing alone brought major consequences. The Crusades were a military disaster but an economic stimulant, bringing the reintroduction of spices, silk and perfume to European society.

**St Mark's Basilica, Venice: 'Chiesa d'Oro' (at night)**

Pilgrimage origins are traced to Christ's walk to the river Jordan to be baptised and to Calvary for crucifixion, creating the narrative which followed through martyrs' commemorations via hospital and church dedications, and the contact beliefs arising through the veneration and attribution of healing, restorative powers to relics. By the 11th century, the pilgrimage had become a mass movement, stimulated by the 1st Crusade, the papal remission of sins for participation, and the burgeoning cults of saints and holy sites. The Christianising of local wells into holy places, objectifying of faith through votive offerings, veneration of relics enforced by contact beliefs of healing and transforming power through grace all turned cult practice into big business. Pieces of the true cross, holy blood, and derived curative potions were prized acquisition for health and fortune management.

Venetian shipping developed the Holy Land business. Sickness (probably dysentery) attended the journeys. Will making and deaths were common; and everything, at each stage, had to be paid for; even escape from the undertaking, which could be imposed as a punishment. Those of deep pockets enjoyed comfort in tours of veneration and the diversions afforded. By the 15th century, for the affluent, the activity had evolved into an early version of the Grand Tour.

From around the start of the 13th century, built from an imaginary inspiration of Charlemagne's court, the notion of chivalry, originally meaning horse soldiery, brought aspirations to ethical behaviour to the knightly class. Drawn from French and British legend, such as Geoffrey of Monmouth's (1095-1155) tales of King Arthur, literary models appeared in the next century. The poem *Gawain and the Green Knight* and the "very parfait gentil knight" of Chaucer's *Canterbury Tales,* written between 1387 and 1400, illustrated the code of military training, bravery, service to others, and the honouring of (aristocratic) women. It marked an ethical ideal revival in secular social and moral virtues. Society management had now secular as well as spiritual ideals, with trade exhibiting its own *mores.* In the Ludovico Ariosto (1474-1533) satiric romance *Orlando Furioso*, Charlemagne's chivalric knights battle Saracens amid a dilemma of inter-faith love, still providing popular entertainment today in the street puppetry of Sicily, cultural melting pot of the Mediterranean.

The Genovese and Venetian trade institutions revived and modified the Roman and Arab models, both creating variants closely resembling the Muslim *muqarada.* Family, faith and trading expertise made for sound business partnerships among, and even between, Muslims, Jews, and Christians, particularly where government and public institutions remained weak. Whereas the Church had rather looked down on trade in the early medieval period, realism suggests that its proximity to money and the Church's income requirements meant more the preservation of haughty dignity than any refusal to engage.

Beginning in Flanders, the city-to-city network of trade fairs spread across western and northern Europe. Goods such as furs, leather and textiles were supplemented as the fairs grew by increasing sale of eastern produce. Merchants required protection and safe conduct along the dangerous surviving roads and tracks. State and civic guardianship secured some safety of passage. The fairs served local market purposes but also became conduits for regional and international trade. The Jewish communities had survived the fall of Rome and continued to be a source of family credit, a facility which could be extended to Christian merchants. The theological loophole of the allowing of trade credit assisted Church facilitation and partnership in trade fair organisation, maximising opportunity for all. The great fairs, necessarily of duration sufficient to allow credit arrangements and settlements, were supplemented by lesser but nonetheless significant events. Such was the case at Shrewsbury, where the occasion was held to coincide with saints' days, the display of relics, attendant devotions, and market opportunities.

The Cistercians' business acumen suggests an increasingly easy relationship between Church and commerce. By the 13th century, public and doctrinal attitudes had started to shift, the Islamic insistence on the benefaction and benefits of trade being an important fertiliser. Justification for attitudinal change was found in Aristotle's *Nicomachean Ethics*, where business was both moral and necessary. A breakthrough had come when Thomas Aquinas (1225-1274) entered the debate with a direct contribution: that value lay in exchange, and how much the other party was prepared to offer. He accepted that his idea of a "just price" would not always be seen as fair in times of scarcity.

Aquinas was seeking justification for trade within society, but in doing so inadvertently made a most significant contribution to the origins of modern economic theory: value can be added. Sellers could add value by undertaking risk, or improving goods' quality or availability. The "good" merchant, Aquinas surmised, was the one who served society. The eminent Aquinas having cleared the way, for writing on topics touching religion could endanger, others joined a burgeoning ethical debate. The increase in trade assisted by Aquinas was dramatically interrupted by the Black Death. The immense "creative destruction," a concept which was to become a feature seven centuries later of Joseph Schumpeter's (1883–1950) economic management and Charles Koch's (1935-) market-based management theory and practice, here operated on a vast scale. Producers faced a shortage of workers and lessened demand due to fewer customers; partnerships in trade and banking dependent on trusted agents suffered downsizing and bankruptcy.

Yet, heightened risk demanded new management techniques to control costs. The need for more accurate accounting included need for improved time measurement and reporting. In 1062, the Chinese polymath Su Sung (1020-1101) had designed and built a hydro-mechanical astronomical clock, news of which reached Europe. Al-Jazari (1136-1206) produced a weight-powered version, contained in a model howdah seated upon an elephant. The English abbot Richard of Wallingford (1292-1336) and Giovanni Dondi dell'Orologio of Padua (c.1330-1388) both produced clocks considered as masterpieces, stimulating the placement of clocks in most cathedrals - and by 1400 into most Catholic churches in Europe. Business could now be managed by the hourly bells of the clock, rather than the routines of sunrise, sunset, and the times of clerical services. Clocks standardised time, and with timekeeping came time saving, beginning the journey towards "scientific management" and the production line. The technology, like its modern equivalents, became smaller, soon leading to house and office time pieces, with portable clocks for travellers.

European curiosity towards Chinese matters had been stimulated by the Asian trade and travel stories of Marco Polo (1254-1324), his tales of Beijing and of his 17 years of captivity at the court of Kublai Khan (1215-1294), the 5th Great Khan of the Mongolian Empire, and from 1271, the 1st Yuan Emperor of China. Polo made little money himself from China, but the potential Sino-Italian trade bonanza resulting from his travel publicity was aborted by the successful revolt of 1368 which overthrew the hated Mongolian rule, and established the Ming dynasty (1368-1644). Although reactive to previous practice, during its early period, mercantile expansionism continued. From construction at the start of the 15th century, a vast fleet of some 1700 junks and support vessels, built to large scale and equipped with the latest technology under its eunuch merchant-admiral Zheng He (1371-1433), dominated the Indian Ocean, forcibly opening markets, and reaching as far as the Persian Gulf, Africa, Indonesia, Korea and Japan. Chinese domination of the Asian seaboard was complete.

World domination beckoned, but a succession of child emperors allowed Confucian bureaucratic traditionalists to reverse policy into introversion. When the Ming overthrew the Mongol Yuan, capitalism became the victim of the reaction against everything foreign. Expansionism was replaced by xenophobia, the unfettered market economy curbed, large estates broken up, and prosperous regions reduced by heavy taxation. The Treasure Fleet sailed no more, leaving a power vacuum for Europe to fill. A massive state management miscalculation delayed Chinese global presence by six centuries. The European retreat of monasticism had reversed outwards into trade. Self-sufficient and with its own large market, China had retreated inwards.

Surprisingly, it was the fairly obscure and quarrelsome English who were to make the most potent basic measure of human freedom, destined to spread throughout the Western world. Its clause 39 proclaimed:

> No free man shall be stripped of his possessions or outlawed or exiled or deprived of his standing in any other way, nor will be proceeded with force against him or send others to do so except by lawful judgment of his equals or the law of the land.

Thus, the *Magna Carta* of 1215, the foundational instrument of liberty, extracted by the English barony from one of the worst, nastiest, monarchs of all time, John I (1166-1216). Son of the able, highly successful Henry II, in 1204 John contrived to lose Normandy and most of his family's Angevin Empire French possessions. Strapped for cash to pay for his military losses and squatting in England after his defeat, he sought to squeeze his English possession by extortion and excessive taxation. The barons rebelled, aided by their negotiator Stephen Langton (1150-1228), Archbishop of Canterbury, took London, and forced John to capitulate into signing the charter. For the first time, a king was bound by and to law, the law of the land being expanded by Langton into God's law, too. For enforcement, 25 barons were enabled to seize the king's property. Tricky John immediately appealed to the Pope, who held oversight in such matters, and was duly relieved of his obligation.

John died the next year. The issue now became whether his under-aged son Henry III (1207-1272) would be allowed to inherit – if not, the son of the French king would take over. In the ensuing poker game, as French forces arrived in England, Henry's advisers had him accept the charter, now reissued in 1225, dropping the 25 barons' clause. As now constituted, the *Magna Carta* provided for the rights of free men, who must be free-standing, not engaged in menial tasks for their overlord; justice for all; establishment of the rights of widows and minors; reiteration and preservation of the right for trial by jury; and the freedom of the Church declared.

The *Magna Carta* has been central to English law throughout thereafter. It suffered stringent re-examination during the dissolution of the monasteries, and especially during the Civil War when clever lawyers used it to deny the monarchy the "ship money" it sought to evade financial responsibility to Parliament. Crucially, the Pilgrim Fathers took a copy with them to America, now a cornerstone of the legal system of the USA, its contents probably better known to US trainee lawyers than their UK counterparts -

not to mention the British Empire's transposition of it to multiple countries, and its terms finally being reflected in the United Nations' Declaration of Human Rights. Management foundation stones don't come much bigger than this.

**One of the four known surviving 1215 exemplars of Magna Carta** (British Library Cotton MS Augustus 11. 106).

**A Memorial Tribute**
Runnymede, England: location of the historic meeting between King John and the barons that led to the creation of Magna Carta in 1215.

Designed by English architect Sir Edward Maufe (1883-1974), and erected in 1957 by the American Bar Association on British soil, this neo-classical rotunda is filled with American stars and houses a pedestal dedicated to 'Magna Carta symbol of freedom under law'.

**Magna Carta (1297 version with) with seal.**

# Endnotes

[1] Adams, Max, *The King of the North,* p.4.

[2] At its zenith, the Roman Empire's population is estimated at between 50 and 90 million, around 20% of the then world population (see also Chapter 4, note 16). One of its largest cities, Alexandria's 1st century CE population is estimated at between a quarter and half a million people. The proportional relation of books to people is impressive.

[3] Darke, Diana. *Stealing from the Saracens: How Islamic Architecture Shaped Europe,* p.31 *et seq.*

# CHAPTER SEVEN

# POWER SHIFTS

Far away, at the 751 Battle of Talas, which took place on the river at the border between modern Kazakhstan and Kyrgyzstan, forces of the Abbasid Caliphate and their Tibetan Empire allies defeated the army of the Emperor Xuangzong of Tang (685-762). It was the only confrontation ever to take place between the Arabs and the Chinese. Talas marked the end of the Islamic Empire's expansion eastward and the Chinese advance westward: a turning point in the global balance of power. Arab control of the western section of the Silk Road and increased banditry caused the Chinese to look to an increase in sea power to bolster trade.

The Sunni Abbasids had gained Shiite support in displacing the preceding Umayyads, because they were descended from the Prophet's uncle. The Shia believed that ruling authority should descend from Muhammad's family. Such was Abbasid success that they accumulated the world's largest known empire at the time. Spreading quickly from its supplanting of the Roman and Persian empires in Asia Minor, Islam was further introduced to inner and central Asia, where it took root. Islamic rule now extended from the Mediterranean to the Himalayas. A story, possibly mythical, has Chinese prisoners revealing a great secret.

Many of these soldiers were mercenaries, some of whom may have learned the secret they were imparting in previous employ. Their knowledge of a new material caused immense change. Previously, the verses of the Qur'an had been etched upon bark, stone, papyrus, or whatever came to hand, but communication had been via that predominant ancient facility: memory. Now, knowledge of the art of papermaking allowed the holy text to be written as a book for the first time. Whatever the truth of the tale of the technology transfer, before Talas there were no paper mills in the Abbasid empire; afterwards they spread rapidly in the Iraq area. The first Abbasid paper making began in Samarkand, with a mill established in Baghdad in 794. The art then spread throughout the Arab world, transporting the Qur'an and its message. A late arrival, the first paper book known in Christian

Europe came from a mill built by the Islamic rulers of Valencia, Spain in 1151.

In the former Persian empire, while Islamisation was quite quick, Arabisation worked only as far as its script. The Persians kept their language. Trust being essential to currency confidence, the Abbasids had no option other than to continue to use the preceding regime's dirham (coinage). While new coinage now showed Arab governance, it continued also to bear the Zoroastrian symbolism of the Sasanians. To Persian nobility, with their long cultural history, their Arab conquerors were merely parvenus, to be looked down upon. Therefore, the Caliphs would use their derived wealth first to buy knowledge to achieve respectability for their own language, and then explore and deepen it. Thus, they purchased, or otherwise acquired, many ancient classical texts.

The result was a rich mingling of cultures, restricted to the top of society, with a determined popular Persian identity continuing alongside the religious conversion. Ptolemy's 150 BCE *Almagest,* a work of mathematical astronomy, explained in detail how to predict the positions of the planets, sun, and moon on any given date (past, future, or present). Therefore, it became the astronomical accompaniment to Islam because its religious festivals, such as Ramadan, were based on the cycles of the moon. A condition of a peace treaty with the Roman Empire's successor state, Byzantium, in the 9th century was said to have been provision of a copy of the *Almagest.* By such indirect means, many classical works which would otherwise have been lost or unknown were rediscovered and preserved for posterity.

However, an indigenous Arab scientific culture was also to arise. Abu al-Faraj Muhammad ibn Ishaq al-Nadim (d. 995 or 998), also known as al-Warraq ("the Copyist") and erroneously as Ibn al-Nadun, compiled a bibliographic-biographic encyclopedia, known as the *Kitab al-Fihrist (The Book Catalogue)* which attempted to survey the opinions of the "ancient sciences," as they were known in his time. Mixture of legend and anecdote, the thrust was to direct a history of science (astrology and astronomy) to Babylonian and Egyptian roots, updated by the Greeks from the time of Alexander, thereby emphasising the presence of Persian input. In addition to identifying planetary cycles, 8th century Persians were credited as translating Byzantine books of logic and medicine from Greek and Coptic into Persian, and then Arabic. Those works had been protected in temples, their translation predating the Abbasid ascendancy. [1] Thereafter, the translation business provided substantial income for the literate classes.

The strength and longevity of both former imperial bureaucracies was such that the new occupying culture was provided with a sound administrative base. However, the land and tax collections in Iraq used Persian, but in Byzantine Syria, the language of revenues was Greek. The new rulers had to instruct reluctant bureaucrats to learn and employ Arabic throughout their realm. Writers also emerged to produce texts helpful to the replacement ruling class. There were books on ruling and leadership, one of which, *The Mirror for Princes,* refers to trade having laws and being an occupation worthy of respect. Whilst merchants were middle-ranking at best in the hierarchies of West and East, merchants were given esteem and respect in the Arabic empires. The seeking of lawful gain being written in the *Hadith* (the narratives of the teachings and life of the Prophet) as the duty of every Muslim, bolstered by statements favourable to trustworthy merchants, it condoned the pursuit of free trade in open markets.

The enjoyment of profit from the fair, honest conduct of business and trade was encouraged. Operational schemes to avoid the usury ban, such as partnerships and allowing profit from the resale of goods, were complemented by innovative Islamic banking. This allowed the competing religious instructions to be met while facilitating the capital access necessary to compete in trading with Indian, Chinese and Greek merchants. Varieties of partnership thus arose whereby the participants contributed different resources, such as capital, labor, or market access and knowledge. The emphasis on faith-based business alliances shaped medieval commerce, the Islamic practices spreading into Christendom.

Baghdad had grown into one of the world's great cities, with a population of a million within a few decades of its founding. Like a latter-day Alexandria, a great library arose in the city, which attracted scholars, philosophers, and translators from all over the known world. Scholarship even extended debates to reconcile Aristotle's rational philosophy with the divine revelations of the Prophet. His injunction to "seek knowledge everywhere, even if you have to go to China" helped fuel a translations business boom. The relevance of the Prophet's injunction was proved by the acquisition of paper. Without it, there would have been no Golden Age of the Abbasids.

The House of Wisdom was founded by the Caliph Haroun al-Rashid as a private library, but was formally instituted by his son, civil war victor al-

Ma'mun (786-833), the 7th Caliph, who also brought numbers of well-known scholars to study, discuss, and share information there. It was open to Christian and Jewish scholars as well as Muslims, and by the 9th century it had the largest selection of books in the world. Its works in the humanities and sciences included astronomy, alchemy, cartography, chemistry, geography, mathematics, medicine, and zoology. Texts originated from Greek sources, with Syriac, Persian, and Indian contributions, supplemented by the works and research of the scholars. Described in their 830 *Book of Artifices,* the ingenious toys and automata of the Banū Mūsā brothers marked the continuing entertainment function in the popularisation of science and engineering. Serious project managers, although feuding enemies of the mathematician al-Kindi, their generous sponsorship of classical translation brought much further ancient scholarship to revived attention.

Ruling from their rival capital of Cordoba in al-Andalus, the Umayyad Caliphs were determined not to be outdone. They, too, patronised philosophers, doctors, scientists, and mathematicians, as well as transplanting an entire Middle Eastern culture. Introducing crop rotation, irrigation was applied to the multiple new yields of oranges, lemons, apricots, mulberries, watermelon, bananas and, from India, the new staple of rice. Even the English garden was to benefit from acquisitions from the Arab world: carnations, irises, and the rose. The Empire of Mali, the largest in west Africa, controlled trade into the Mediterranean coast and the Middle East for a period of over 400 years. From a trade base of salt for gold, Berber merchants brought gold, slaves, grain, and ivory across the Sahara and, in the opposite direction, a great library grew in Timbuktu. The Berbers exploited rock salt mines in the Sahara and brought with them the manual for fair trading, the Qur'an. The resultant wealth brought monumental religious architecture.

Mansa Musa, (c.1280-c.1337), in the 14th century the controller of the richest known gold deposits which then amounted to half the world's supply, distributed so much gold in Cairo when he undertook his Hajj in 1324 that its value declined by 10%. He brought with him large numbers of slaves and a retinue, remarked upon for its polite, pious, well-behaved demeanour. Part of his mission was to recruit scholars for import to Mali. As an aspect of this mission, he literally put his country on the map. The Berber traders had tried to keep their trade secret. By 1450, Mali had over-expanded, losing territory to its sub-kings, and fell to entropy. The end of empire by the 17th century was to coincide with the new influx to Europe of the gold of the Americas and a redirection west of a portion of the slave trade.

Astrology and astronomy being sound businesses too, translations also spurred scientific advance. The Andalusian astronomers Ibn Bajja (Avempace) (c.1085-1138), Ibn Tufayl (1105-1185), Ibn Rushd (1126 - 1198) and Nur ad-Din al-Bitruji (Alpetragius, d.1204) all disputed the astronomy of Ptolemy (100-170), first because of its incompatibilities with Aristotle; then, by Ibn Rushd particularly, finding serious flaws in that of Aristotle. Far to the east, in Damascus, Ibn al-Shatir (1304-1375) had shown Ptolemaic astronomy unable to cope with observable planetary motion, confronted Aristotelian assumptions of uniform speeds of movement, challenged their failings, and posited a cosmology of his own. In 1375, al-Shatir had produced a theoretical lunar model identical in every respect with that of Copernicus of 1543.[2]

The exchange of goods brought with it the exchange of knowledge; either way, it was good for business. Practical education was enhanced by the mastery of the new tasks, arts, and crafts. A novel, wide-ranging regional language developed. Everyone from Andalusia to Afghanistan learned to speak a form of Arabic. That was supplemented by the new import from China of paper. Cheap, light, thin, available in bulk, paper was vastly preferable to unwieldy parchment. Books could now be made and copied in large numbers. By the 13th century, Baghdad, Bukhara, and other cities had many public libraries and bookshops, numerous publishers, employing multiple copyists.

One such further exchange example was the remarkable transformation of arithmetic, bringing an immense power to the use of numbers written upon paper, which replaced the abacus as a means of calculation.[3] The idea, ruthless in its penetration, had come from India via Baghdad where two scholars, al-Kindi (801-873) and al-Khwarizmi (780-850), had written paper books showing how to replace the convention of the use of written

al-Kindi

words to describe numbers, thus rendering *alpha* and *beta* as 1 and 2, the numerical sequence progressing to 9. Further, they illustrated how these could be arranged to facilitate quick calculation. The most startling innovation was the addition of 0 to symbolise no value. Between these ten digits, any number could be recorded. Through al-Khwarizmi's concept of the balancing of an equation through subtraction and the cancellation of

al-Khwarizmi

terms, he has been dignified as the father of algebra. The Latinised form of his name, Algoritmi, is the stem for the term algorithm, the device via computing which now dominates Internet commerce - and all of our lives.

Muhammad ibn Musa al-Khwarizmi, a Persian or Uzbek mathematician, astronomer, geographer, and cartographer, was a scholar at the Baghdad House of Wisdom. His a*l-jabr* ("transposition"), one of the two balancing operations he used to solve quadratic equations and published in the *Compendious Book on Calculation by Completion and Balancing* of 1202, showed how a process of linear and quadratic equations could determine an unknown value. On translation in Spain, the Arabic word for "thing" (*shay*) was transcribed as "xay" because the letter "x" was pronounced "sh." This word was shortened to "x" over time, so becoming the universal symbol for an unknown value. Latin translation provided the basis from which Western physical sciences developed, algebra being essential to the process.

While it is likely that the Indian numeral form had come into existence and working use before the formalisation of al-Kindi's introduction of Brahmi numerals, al-Khwarizmi had mixed practical legal, religious, and abstract motives behind his adaptation. In his introduction to the book describing algebra, his aim was to work with:

> [...] what is easiest and most useful in mathematics, such as men constantly require in cases of inheritance, legacies, partition, lawsuits, and trade, in all their dealings with one another, or when measuring lands, digging canals, and making geometrical calculations.[4]

Elegant and brilliant in its mathematical summation, al-Khwarizmi's invention presaged a fatal assumption. By completing and balancing, he could reduce every equation to six simple, standard forms and then show a method of solving each. He provided geometrical proofs of each method. Thus, he could use his notation and the rules of *al-jabr* and *al-muqabala* to simplify any kind of problem. Presumably he was thinking only of directly applicable mathematics, anticipating the complexities of the quadratic. Nonetheless, the implication was clear: any problem could be reduced to one of his six categories. Here lies the root of the delusion of the quants and devotees of economism: that all human decision making and life expression itself can be reduced to mathematical formulae. Theoretical physics may continue the search for an equation of no longer than half an inch which explains the operation of the universe, but universal management remains aspirational, at best. Of inestimable benefit to humanity, even algebra can be taken too far.

Unknown in the West until much later, and albeit in a different sense, the comprehensive business guide of the otherwise unknown 11th or 12th century merchant, Abu al-Fadi Ja'far Ibn 'Ali al-Dimashqi, *A Guide to the Merits of Commerce and to Recognition of Both Fine and Defective Merchandise and the Swindles of Those Who Deal Dishonestly*, demonstrates a sophisticated trading environment. He argued that a wealthy person was to be respected, for "he makes good use of his fortune." Al-Dimashqi's work includes an evaluation of commodities, pricing, record keeping, fraud identification, and sales techniques. He has been credited with the early formulation of price theory and demonstrated clear understanding of supply and demand, as well as the need for division of labour. Three types of merchant are described: the traveling trader, wholesaler, and exporter. He also outlines three types of trade: cash sales with a time limit for delivery; purchase on credit with payment by installment; and by *muqarada,* where investors and shippers pool resources and risk. Countertrade is also featured. Al-Kindi and al-Kharizmi's techniques would have been in common, everyday use, with pricing in particular benefiting from algebraic calculation.

The Ismaili sect known as the Fatimids took power in Egypt and Syria in the 10th century, their name deriving from claimed descent from Fatima, the Prophet's daughter. This made them acceptable to the Shiites. Patrons of science, medicine, and engineering, they saw education as a means of spreading the faith. With territory stretching from Morocco to the Red Sea, their distinct ethical trading standards within a legal framework made for a commendable commercial system, greatly enhanced by the arithmetical advances, widening further commercial opportunity.

Al-Khwarizmi's trigonometry and improvements on geographical knowledge included contributions to the refinement of the astrolabe. This instrument had been designed to facilitate the discovery of direction through the computation of the positions of the planets, modified by the Andalucian inventor and scientist al-Zarquali (1028-1087). After his writings had been translated into Latin in the 12th century and the technology introduced, the instrument became a crucial navigational aid to the western explorers of the early 15th century. The first European astrolabe maker, the Jewish astronomer Abraham Zacuto (c.1450-1510), equipped Columbus with instruments and charts for his expeditions. The impetus to invention, however, had been religious; as the Prophet had required that all Muslims should face towards Mecca at prayer time, mosques had to be constructed with their prayer shrines built in the correct direction.

Hussain ibn Sina (980-1037) - known also as Avicenna, philosopher, mathematician, astronomer, poet, geologist, and identifier of force in physics through heat, light and mechanical operation - produced one of the first encyclopedia and the comprehensive, million-word *Canon of Medicine* which revised and updated the medical works of the Roman court physician Galen (129-c.210).

**Miniature of 'Avicenna'**

Once translated into Latin, this became a standard European textbook and medical manual for six centuries. It described 760 drugs, extending to such instruction as how an eye operates and the removal of cataracts.

Newton's work on optics had been anticipated by the physicist, astronomer, and mathematician Hasan Ibn al-Haytham, latinised as Alhazen (c.965-c.1040), whose translated insights into the processes of how reflection and refraction cause light to bounce off objects assisted the development of the telescope in the West.

**al-Haytham 'Alhazen'**

He is also credited for his exposition of principles of visual perception and optics as the father of that study. Al-Haytham provided the first demonstration that vision occurs in the brain rather than the eyes, and the first explanation that vision happens when light reflects from an object, then passing to the observer's eyes.

One of his students, the astronomer, mathematician, and poet Omar Khayyam (1048-1131), was the first to conceive of a general theory of cubic equations and to solve every type. Best known in the West from the 19th century translation of his poetry (although some of the quatrains were attributed only), the *Rubáiyát* contains the timeless verse of permanent relevance to managers, historians, and all who reflect:

> The Moving Finger writes; and, having writ,
> Moves on: nor all thy Piety nor Wit
> Shall lure it back to cancel half a Line,
> Nor all thy Tears wash out a Word of it.
> [Quatrain 51]

Contemporary of al-Haytham, and Iranian correspondent of Avicenna, al-Biruni (973-1050), the greatest polymath of the Islamic Golden Age,) incorporated ancient Greek thought within his philosophical works. Considered one of the greatest of scientists of all time for his work in physics, mathematics, astronomy, and natural sciences, he was also a neutral, unbiased historian of India. His analyses, although unknown in the West, were rediscovered by the British in the 17th century, where his Indology expertise

**al-Biruni**

regarding Hindu society was found useful to their expansionist policies. His scientific approach to geography (through hydrology) led to his prediction of there being land mass in the location in which the Americas were subsequently discovered.

Much further east, and far from al-Biruni's Khwarazm, modern west Uzbekistan, northern Turkmenistan, and the Cairo-based al-Haytham's

Basra origins, humanity had first tried to get closer to the light sources of stars by building observatories. The oldest in Asia (and perhaps the world), was the Cheomseongdae (star gazing tower) in Gyeongju, South Korea, built in the 7th century CE under the Silla dynasty.

**The Cheomseongdae**

Built out of 362 pieces of granite, it is thought to have symbolized the number of days in the lunar year. Its foundation myth featured Queen Seondeok, whose first decree as a princess, before her accession, was the construction of the tower. Her aim was to facilitate the acquisition of astronomical knowledge by all her people, rather than it being the preserve of the elite. Such popular action being unusual and opposed by many conservatives, very few of the nobility attended the opening ceremony.

Management, too, was part of the eastern advance. There is a possibly apocryphal story that Omar Khayyam, Nizam al-Mulk (1018-1092), then an unknown of lowly origin, and another friend, promised to help each other should one achieve prominence. Nizam was first to rise, ultimately serving highly successfully as vizier to two sultans of the Seljuk Empire for over 25 years. He wielded extraordinary influence as vizier with full authority consolidating the pre-eminence of Persian governance, while reconciling differences between Persians and Turks. Written at the Malik-Shah I's (1055-1092) request, his *Book of Government* was accepted by that sultan as the effective national constitution. Using historical examples to discuss effective rule, justice, and the role of government in Islamic society, he followed Sun Tzu in advocating espionage and methods of state surveillance.

The comprehensive, detailed, realistic advice and statesmanship record has been compared in method to that of Machiavelli. His systematic foundation of higher education institutions has been credited with initiation of the trend towards university systems. Knowing of the enmity towards him, just before his assassination, he bluntly advised Malik-Shah that they were equal co-rulers as his statesmanship had secured the throne; were he to be toppled, so would the sultan. Malik-Shah died, presumed poisoned, shortly after the assassination of Nizam. These events had followed a Shia – Sunni scholarly debate, said to have converted both Nizam and Malik-Shah to Shiism.

The full benefits to the West of access to the learning acquired by the scholars of the caliphates and of the East were impeded by religious prejudice. The medieval Andalusian polymath Ahmed ibn Rushd, known also as Averroës, was an encyclopaedic writer, contributing to: logic; Aristotelian and Islamic philosophy; theology; Islamic jurisprudence; political, psychological, and musical theory; geography; mathematics; medicine; astronomy; and physics.

**Ahmed ibn Rushd
'Averroës'**

Although a defender of Aristotelian philosophy against the theology of the Ash'ari School of Sunni Islam, he had a greater influence in the West, earning the sobriquet of "the Commentator" for his detailed revisions of Aristotle, to which he contributed comment on almost all of his works. His stance was brave; since philosophy does not accept the overriding authority of a God and the laws derived from Him, the process of open-ended philosophic reasoning is forbidden to pious Muslims. The Islam of parts of the world today is more extreme than that of the time of Averroës when he revised Aristotle.

This greatly increased Aristotle's popularisation: an advance for the cause of education in that classical thought and knowledge was again available to the educated, an important variant to the otherwise constant theological preoccupations, and an ultimate impediment where Aristotle's errors were converted into indisputable dogma. Where the study of the literature of antiquity had been continued in Greek Byzantium, it was the Latin translations of ibn Rushd's work which spurred the recovery of Aristotle's legacy in the West. The reference of Aquinas to him as "the Commentator" and Aristotle as "the Philosopher" well illustrated the Christian coyness of the times. William of Malmsbury (1080-1143), leading English historian of the previous century, had deplored his colleague Adelard of Bath's (1080-1152) embrace of Arab reason and scientific and mathematics translations as "dangerous Saracen magic."

Aquinas, saint, Dominican friar, Catholic priest, Doctor of Divinity, theologian, jurist, highly influential philosopher, and pillar of the Church regarded Averroës as the greatest commentator on Aristotle but disagreed with his religious and theological arguments.

Aquinas (1225-1274) argued that reason is found in God, which much influenced Western thought, polarising positions arising in political theory, moral philosophy and ethics, natural law, and metaphysics. His attempts to synthesise Aristotle's ideas with the principles of Christianity mirrored ibn Rushd's similar efforts with Islam. Saint to the Catholic Church, he is there regarded as the model teacher for those studying for the priesthood. He occupies the pedestal of the highest expression of both reason and speculative theology, his works essential reading for ordination studies and the "sacred disciplines" of philosophy, church history, liturgy, Catholic theology and canon law.

**Saint Thomas Aquinas**

**FOOTPRINT:**
The 12th Century European Renaissance

- In their missions to proclaim and explain, historians'
  approach to the times in Europe between the fall of Rome
  and rise of modern times has been to identify periods where
  distinctive growth and change occurred: harbingers of the
  Renaissance. Demonstrating that the Dark Ages were dark
  only because we knew little of what happened, the flash of
  Celtic civilisation reaching Scotland's northern isles became
  a notable phenomenon in the short-lived mid-7th to mid-8th
  century Northumbrian Renaissance. A flowering of high art,
  literary achievement, and strong (if homicidal) government
  (marred by a defective defence policy) contributed to an
  expansion of European civilisation.

- Further rebirths have been detected in the political consolidation, centralisation, and promotion of learning by Charlemagne, and the expansion of ecclesiastical power promoted by another Holy Roman Emperor, Otto I, (912-973). A much greater movement gained the historians' title of the 12th Century Renaissance.

- This period of rediscovery and reform has been used by medieval historians to illustrate progress towards the early modern period. It can best be appreciated through three distinct contexts: economic and social; literary and cultural; and the political and legal. The first saw the growth of towns and cities with the management of urbanisation. As population increased across Europe, new areas were brought under cultivation to sustain the growing communities. Culturally, a great flowering followed the rediscovery through Greek and Arab sources of many classical texts, long considered lost. These stimulated the growth of universities and the great cathedral schools, promoting the expansion of Chartres, Bologna, Canterbury, and Oxford. The parallel development of the vernacular brought literary expression in French, German, Italian and English, with an accompanying rebirth of fiction

- Politically, growing stability was promoted by the rise of the nation state and strengthening of the Church and Papacy. Great advances were made legally through the development of legal systems, the Bologna recovery of Roman law and the English institution of the common law with a jury system. Significant though the changes were, with management consequences the young 14th century knight could retire to bed with dreams of redemption, courtly love, and chivalric excellence. By contrast, his 12th century contemporary would be far more likely to harbour fears of hell fire and damnation.

Bede, an earlier luminary, was a graduate of a monastery school who also subsequently taught. Viewed as the leading Christian scholar up to the time of Charlemagne, this "father of English history," also took an ecumenical approach. Nonetheless, the understanding of what constituted knowledge, its transference and acquisition, had undergone a concentrated reduction by medieval times.

Thus, the revival of Aristotle, and discussion and allowance of Islamic thought and business methods, helped the recovery of Europe. Yet the Islamic regions which had done so much to follow the Prophet's bidding and create wealth through innovative trade did not maximise their gains, for different religious reasons. Inheritance law divided up a deceased business partner's estate between family members, thus dispersing resources and limiting businesses to a size which did not require outsider participation. Transference of the benefits of Islamic knowledge acquisition and resuscitation helped Europe, but Islamic society did not benefit from the new, refined European techniques because its own social structures inhibited their development.

Moreover, Abu Hamid al-Ghazali (1058-1111), who had achieved the status of a *Mujaddid,* "renewer of the faith," had contributed two major works. *The Revival of the Religious Sciences* and *Incoherence of the Philosophers* represented a dual assault. He claimed that the spiritual teaching of the founders had been forgotten while Aristotelian science was in error. As one who according to *hadith* tradition manifests every century to restore Islam, al-Ghazali and his works were formidable opponents. An Islamic orthodoxy of sorts, symbolising a victory for religious thought, presented a challenge to scientific endeavour, compounded by the Mongol invasion and the fall of Baghdad.

In the West, the major scientific developments of the 16th and 17th centuries were partially attributable to the discoveries of the New World and the release of the wealth arising. This fuelled the expulsion of Islam from Spain. The courts of Europe through various means, some derived from past Islamic initiative, could fund scientific discoveries of scale and manner beyond that of sultans, caliphs, and wealthy individuals. The Islamic world might still produce scientists of brilliance and genius, but they had to find the right patron, any patron, if they were to progress. Such a state of affairs continued for much of the world until very recently. Meanwhile, the faith, at least, could be renewed.

China was also limited by factors which had been key to its growth. The Chinese had known all about paper and the changes it could facilitate for a very long time. Emperor Wu (156-87 BCE), seventh emperor of the Han Dynasty, had already made the study of the works of Confucius compulsory, enforcing the message that loyalty to the state ranked above all. In 140 BCE, he instituted the imperial examinations, whereby 100 official appointments were to be made, based on performance in an academic test. Most candidates were commoners, unconnected to the aristocracy. For the first time, in both China and the world at large, people from rural districts without money or privilege could, if they demonstrated sufficient intelligence and secured a recommendation, achieve governmental positions.

Those positions brought influence, wealth, and power. The glory of success was reflective: huge honour accrued to the successful candidates' homes, families, and villages. To fully emphasise the point of his meritocratic policy, Wu appointed several scholars from his intake as some of his closest, most trusted advisors. Such were the consequences for effective government that, by the reign of Emperor He (r.88-105 CE), improved writing materials had become essential. Writing was either upon bamboo, which was too heavy; or silk which, although in rough pieces, was still very expensive. In neighbouring Korea, farmer's sons could sit for the very difficult civil service examinations adapted and adopted from China, but success was rare. Although sons of artisans and merchants were allowed entry to examinations in China, this was not the case in Korea.

Lun (48-121 CE) entered the Han court in 75 CE via the, possibly involuntary, eunuch route, which granted access to female royalty. Able and frequently promoted, by 89 he oversaw the manufacture of instruments and weapons. He rose further by participating in court intrigue, becoming an associate of Consort Deng Sui (81-121), an official mistress to the Emperor He of Han (79-105). In 105, he claimed to have invented the composition of paper. Perhaps he did; perhaps he claimed the invention of another as his own; anecdotally, inspiration arrived through the observation of paper wasps making their nests.

While his exact formula has been lost, the written record shows the ingredients to have been: tree bark, usually mulberry; hemp remnants; cloth rags; and fishing nets. The mixture produced felted sheets which were then suspended in water, the water subsequently drained, drying into a thin, matted membrane, which could be peeled. Rewarded financially and with office, the man responsible for the invention died by drinking poison, dressed in finest silk, to evade the imprisonment which awaited him on the accession of Emperor An (94-125), whose mother had been a victim of Consort Deng Sui, in whose machinations he had been involved.

Because of the literacy and literature promoted by paper, China was able to develop much quicker, using the cheap, new material for almost everything conceivable. The early product list includes: wrapping paper; umbrellas; parasols; wallpaper; kites; playing cards; lanterns; and teabags. The Tang Dynasty (618-907 CE), after a period of civil war and unrest, realised that social cement was available through an expanded examination system, the propaganda being that opportunity was now open to all male citizens. Anyone could apply to sit the examinations, not just those recommended by existing government officers. Religion was enlisted: Buddhist monks were paid by local communities to pray for and teach the rural poor.

In the West, the Egyptians had developed material to accommodate writing from the pith of the papyrus plant. Sheets of such material, joined side by side, could be rolled to make a scroll to constitute a book. Thinly cut sheets of wood and wax tablets offered further recording means. Treated animal membrane from goat, sheep, or cattle was used to form the vellum or parchment favoured in the recording of official documents and major texts such as the Bible. Chinese paper was much cheaper, more adaptable, and of multi-use: a vastly superior management device.

Curriculum, pervaded by Confucian ethics, was expanded to include civil law, military strategy, agriculture, and geography. The emphasis upon loyalty and obedience produced cultural homogeneity. Under the Song Dynasty (960-1279), the scholastic imperial bureaucracy expanded further. By 976 there were approximately 30,000 candidates per year; by the end of the 11th century, 80,000; and by the end of the dynasty, some 400,000, creating an intellectual population far outnumbering that of Europe. China's neighbours Korea, Japan, and Vietnam had all acquired the technology by the 7th century.

The necessary mass production was achieved by printing, using the carved wood block method. Laborious but effective, suited to the linear nature of Chinese characters, some 500 classic Confucian texts, history books, and reference works were carved onto wood blocks to provide examination candidates with study materials. There are estimated to have been at least a thousand schools throughout China to assist preparation for the civil service examinations.

By the 12<sup>th</sup> century, China's population had expanded to over 100 million, making traditional currency in the forms of silk bolts or copper coins expensive to manufacture and difficult to carry, resulting in shortages of supply. The wood-block printing of the world's first paper currency had commenced under the emperor Hien Tsung (r.806-821), with the consequent establishment of state money-printing factories, employing thousands of workers. Known as "flying money" as it was so much lighter than coin, these were originally promissory notes, redeemable against copper coin from government banks.

Sober management preserved value but eventually the government issued more notes than it held in cash, causing inflation, and so from the 12<sup>th</sup> century produced the world's first "flat money" whose only value was that declared by law, with no promise of redemption. Inflation led to hyperinflation, particularly where the requirement was to fund military adventures, resulting under the Ming dynasty in the 15<sup>th</sup> century in a reversion to silver coinage. In what may be described as "idea" terms, currency notes had been mismanaged, having to be reinvented by the Swedes and English from the later 17<sup>th</sup> century.

Broad economic policy was accepting of market approaches where monopolies of desirable commodities such as copper, coal, salt, iron, tea, and porcelain could be administered by hereditary bureaucrats and updated, abandoned, or replaced according to circumstance. Grain taxes financed such infrastructure as ports, canals, and roads. This "socialist" economy was supplemented by the tolerance of private trade, albeit heavily influenced by merchant princes and through direct public ownership. Private sector control was a continuing bureaucratic preoccupation. State management required the energy of entrepreneurialism, under control. The Offices of Overseas Trade at each port regulated, supervised, and taxed all maritime commerce.

Meanwhile, the Song Dynasty's inventive progress had been interrupted by an invasion of Manchurian double-dealing horse-breeders, previously allies, leading to the division of China into two parts: the Jirchens, who became the Jin Dynasty in the fertile north, relegating the Song to the mountainous south. The loss of their iron and steel industries denied the Chinese their nascent industrial revolution, forcing an expansion of Indian Ocean trade. What followed was the medieval world's finest example of risk management. It was underpinned by one of the greatest arms races of history and the invention of spread investment.

The Song rulers challenged their finest, best-developed brains to create every possible technological advance: practical education was applied to military need. Inevitably, the result arrived by chance. Around 850 CE, Taoist monks had been challenged by the imperial authorities to find an elixir for everlasting life. During their experiments, a mix of sulphur with saltpetre, other mineral ores, and honey proved to be devastatingly explosive: they had accidentally invented gunpowder. Such transformation of everlasting life into instant death was a reverse of a direct order which would have appealed to Taoists such as Chuang Tzu. An arms industry followed with such devices as grenades, catapult bombs, cannon, and flame throwers.

Trade had flourished in and through ancient Persia. That empire had also to defend itself against the incursions of the nomadic horse-breeders who dwelt on, and north of, the steppe lands. Alexander had travelled as far east as modern-day Tajikistan. Hellenisation had followed, civilisations colliding there and in Afghanistan. The name of the recent and continuing conflict site of Kandahar is a corruption of Alexandria, one of the many such foundations the conqueror named after himself. Memorial to a different conquest, the 4th and 5th century CE Buddhas of Bamiyan, located on the Silk Road, blown up by the Taliban in 2015, were commemorative of the Shiite Hazara peoples' then conversion to Buddhism from India.

The connection between Persia and China had arisen through the latter's continuing, almost insatiable, demand for horses. They were needed for the armies, there being so many potential and actual enemies along China's borders, as well as for internal conflicts and control. The most highly prized horses came from Uighur territory in the north western region of Xinjiang, their sales making great wealth for tribal chiefs. Persian traders expanded their enterprises. As Chinese luxury goods such as silk travelled west, they were joined by expensive and exotic commodities from the south: Red Sea pearls, jade, lapis lazuli, frankincense, myrrh; and consumables such as apricots, coriander, cucumber, pistachios, and pomegranates. Linking the Roman, Persian and Chinese Empires, the Silk Road began the globalisation of trade. The seizure of this trade artery by the Jin was, thus, traumatic for the Song.

In response to the vital requirement to keep river waterways open and to control the sea trade routes now that the Silk Road was closed to them, the

Song developed China's first standing navy. The dangers to trade encouraged merchants to spread their risk, leading to the world's first known portfolio investment schemes. They cooperated in guilds, spreading investment across several expeditions. As goods had to be carried across the Indian Ocean and into the Persian Gulf, seaworthiness was essential. Tung oil secured water-tight bulkheads, as the oil from the pressed seed of the nut of the tung tree hardens on exposure to air. If one part of a junk were damaged, the ship would not sink. Steering was improved, assisted by the mid-11$^{th}$ century discovery of how a magnetised needle might be strung through a thread, so serving as a compass. This further invention was in regular Chinese shipping use by the early 12$^{th}$ century. Tension between the Confucian and Taoist approaches could be seen in the trade partnerships being short-lived, and for particular purposes. Indicative perhaps, Fo Lien, an 80-junk owning wealthy merchant who hired mangers to trade for his partnerships, was a Muslim.

By the 14$^{th}$ century, the imperial bureaucracy had categorised traders into groups: "persons immediately in charge," sole proprietors; managers; financial backers; and partnerships or consortia. The state insisted on reciprocal co-operation. Private ships might be requisitioned to provide space for public grain, but could fill what remained with their own goods. Such convenient intervention could secure a merchant against market failure.

The extended family being the greatest protection against state domination, Chinese enterprises expressed through that means greatly expanded upon the Roman model. The concept became of religious expression in the honouring of ancestral spirits, thus making wealth pursuit and the exclusion of outsiders a duty, practice, and spiritual expression. The Roman patricians had honoured ancestry even to the preservation of generations of death masks. The Chinese again progressed further; the whole of society being engaged in the ancestral sanctity of money-making security.

Yet, for all their great innovative effort, even the expansion of their Indian Ocean trade, the Song could not resist the forces of nature which combined to create dual disasters. Firstly, the climate change which, beginning in the high latitudes of the northeast, cooled global temperatures from the 13$^{th}$ to 19$^{th}$ centuries. Secondly, the rise of Temujin, the brilliant military leader, planner, and manager, who became known as Genghis Khan (1162-1227).

Pastoral, nomadic, tribal steppe dwellers had
no survival options beyond uniting and
conquering new, fertile lands. This second
son of a tribal chief from a Mongol
confederation, by a mix of charisma,
diplomacy and leadership skills, united rival
Mongolian tribes of Uighurs, Merkits,
Keraits and Tatars. Some 200,000 people
were dependent on Genghis Khan's coordination of expansion.

His command demands were ruthlessly
enforced through disciplined organisation.
Like the Roman legions, he operated in
groups of ten, although his units were
magnified and even more tightly controlled.[5]
The levels were ten, one hundred, one
thousand and ten thousand, with unit leaders

**Genghis Khan**

reporting to the next level. The whole army numbered from 100,000 up to
130,000. Cowardice and desertion were not tolerated. If one soldier
deserted, his entire unit was executed; if a unit of ten deserted, the same fate
befell the hundred to which it belonged.

Excellent planning, itself the result of foreknowledge and reconnoitring of
which Prometheus and Sun Tzu would have approved, brought swift
success. Emulating Caesar's approach to the conquest of Gaul, whenever
Genghis encountered an enemy city, he issued a simple ultimatum:
surrender or die, the price of surrender being total loyalty. Advancing as far
as the Great Wall by 1213, the Mongols penetrated further to Beijing,
sacked it, and headed west, reaching the edge of the Islamic world in 1219,
then turned north into Russia where the horde divided to conquer Georgia
and Crimea. On the return journey, they defeated the armies of the ruler of
Kiev and six Russian princes, upon whom they bestowed a bloodless
execution: crushed to death under the weight of a banqueting table at which
the Mongol generals celebrated their victory. At his own death, Genghis's
empire extended from the Caspian Sea to the Chinese east coast, but his
heirs took it even further, extending into Siberia, Russia and more of Central
Asia. In 1241, their victories over the Polish, Hungarian and German forces
of Christendom had left Europe open. The death of Genghis's successor,
Ögedei Khan (1189-1241), occasioned a retreat because tradition required
a Grand Council to confirm the succession of the next Great Khan.

However, Hulagu (1218-1265), Genghis's grandson, returned in 1258 to completely destroy Baghdad, the Abbasid Caliphate, and its cultural heritage – and the then greatest library in the world, the House of Wisdom.

The Mongols had a further disaster to confer. It is commonly held that rat-borne fleas were again responsible for the Black Death which struck Europe between 1347 and 1351, in turn causing societal upheaval comparative to that suffered by Justinian's late version of the Roman Empire. Responsibility must also be borne by humans. Plague originated in the province of Hubei in the early 1330s, spreading to eight further provinces along and across the Silk Road by the 1350s, and is thought to have been carried westwards by Mongol traders. The consequence represents the world's first experience of biological warfare, and the greatest terror attack ever perpetrated.

In 1346, Janni Beg (d. 1357), Khan and commander of the Golden Horde, was laying siege to the Crimean port of Kaffa when plague struck, forcing him to abandon the attack. His army's few survivors piled their dead upon catapults, propelling the disease-ridden corpses over the walls of Kaffa, there infecting the Genoan traders and post defenders who dwelt within. By the time the Genovese had sailed home, most were dead – but enough survived to pass on the deadly disease. As great an unforeseen disaster as ever experienced, over the next three years the trade routes linking the world became conduits for disease. After devastating China and the Muslim world, the inadvertent terrorism of the leader of the Mongol army contributed to the deaths of over 40 million Europeans, more than half of the total population. Life expectancy fell to around the age of 17.

A vivid contemporary account of the siege and subsequent infection of the Black Sea region was written by a Genovese, Gabriela de Mussi. A 2002 academic journal review concluded that biological warfare was practised and provides the best explanation of the entry of plague into the city and region. While stating that Crimea was "pivotal" as the source of the infection of the Mediterranean basin, the study's author adds that the further entry of the plague to Europe from the Crimea, given its prevalence in Asia and as far south as Mecca, was likely to have been independent of this effect. Undoubtedly however, the Kaffa incident was biological terrorism and a contributory factor to the spread of the plague .[6]

Further consequences included economic dislocation, producing peasants' revolts in both France and England; labour shortages which required states to create standing armies or to have to employ mercenaries; and enact sumptuary laws to prevent newly enriched lower classes dressing above their stations, so threatening the established order. Thus, finance bargains had to be struck by rulers in parliaments or other bodies, which led to concessions in power and privilege. Women benefited as an unexpected consequence for the resultant decline in labour availability gave them greater employment opportunities.

Manpower shortage still required armies to acquire new weaponry. It took years of practice from early youth, for example, to train an English longbow archer. The further deadly Chinese export of weaponry employing gunpowder had arrived just in time: in 1342 at the siege of Algeçiras, Islamic defenders used cannon against Christian attackers, to great effect. Within a century, the technology had been improved to the extent that castle fortresses could be destroyed. The great walls of Constantinople finally fell to the concentrated, explosive cannon fire of the Ottoman Turks - with immense consequences. Byzantium had enjoyed a technological defensive lead from around 672 when its "Greek Fire," a napalm mix, defeated an Arab fleet. Fire had been a weapon of warfare from ancient times but the secret recipe, a Byzantine refinement, had been additional to the core naphtha and quicklime ingredients. The liquid incendiary mixture (propelled through pressurized nozzles, igniting on contact with water) twice repelled Arab invasions, various Slav assaults, and was in use up to the 11th century. Perhaps the secret was lost. A vital contributory cause to the fall of Byzantium was poor defence technology management.

Set against the barbarism, slaughter, and loss of life through disease, the overall effects of the Mongol invasions had been largely beneficial. Converted to Islam in 1295, the Mongols immediately realised the benefit of Persian bureaucracy to consolidate their rule. They adopted with it the Greater Iranian national culture, as epitomised in one of the world's longest epics, the Shahnameh (Book of Kings) of poet Ferdowsi (c. 940 -1020), with which they so identified as to refashion it for themselves, producing illustrations to which were added Mongol faces. After the further invasion atrocities of Timur (Tamerlane) (1336-1405), the pattern was repeated by his Timurid successors.

Mongol rule had opened the way for Islamic traders to import westwards such beneficial innovations as paper making and compasses, together with the "sleeper" gunpowder. The explosive recipe had first been published in the West by Roger Bacon (1219-1292). This English friar, natural philosopher, and Oxford lecturer on Aristotle disclosed the information in his 1267 *Opus Majus*. Such practical matters complemented the intellectual advances in algebra, science, and the business application of the spread investment portfolio.

Europe needed these innovations. Indeed, it needed any help it could get. From the fall of Rome, it had descended to the foot of the civilisations' rich list, the least successful developing continent. The population had rapidly declined. Migrations, invasions, and disease had caused chaos; successor states slowly arose but, for all the grandeur with which Charlemagne had been crowned by Pope Leo III in Rome on Christmas Day 800, there was little wealth for society to enjoy. State investment in education as a means to an end was best illustrated by the rump of Rome squatting by the Bosporus. Byzantium, still then the world's greatest city and renowned as such, circled by Islam to the west and south, permanently threatened by barbarian invaders to the north and east, had responded with bribery, Greek fire, and attempts to further civilisation.

In the mid-9th century, followers of the Byzantine philosopher-monks Cyril (826-869) and Methodius (815-885) set out to accomplish major tasks: communication for and with the Slavic languages, initially in the Greater Bulgarian area but with particular onward reference to Russia, and to translate the bible and parts of the liturgy. The brother monks had made both a great contribution and confusion simultaneously. Their mission was to Moravia, the eastern part of what is now the Czech Republic, where they stayed for over three years. There, Cyril invented the new alphabet and phonetic script with which to transcribe Slavonic speech. The language he chose, however, was Macedonian Slavonic. The Moravians did not understand this language; the mission failed. Separately, the Cyrillic alphabet and script survived. The great hope was that the conversion of the leaders of the Slavic world to Orthodox Christianity would stimulate the civilised progress of temporal rule.

Although initially hopeful of Bulgaria, then Kiev as the leader of a new, eastern empire for Christ, attention later focused further into Russia, with the rise of the princes of Muscovy, leaving a trail of assumptions of the title of Tsar, a corruption of Caesar.[7] There, they had to deal with a race of Nordic chameleons: pirates; merchants; conquerors. The Vikings had exploded out of the northlands in all directions. Those who went south travelled down the great rivers, gaining their name from their prime activity: rowing their boats. These rowers, in Old Norse "*rods*", became known as the *Rus*, with their place of settlement, initially Kiev, acquiring the further syllable.

Raiding and then trading from the 7th century, the Rus formed settlements in Russia and Ukraine. They traded commodities including furs and slaves for Islamic silver, progressing so far as to reach Baghdad. Their activities were documented by an Arab scholar, Ahmad ibn Fadlan (879- 960), famed for his accounts of travel with an Abbasid caliph. Originating from the eastern seaboard of Sweden, the tattooed but otherwise near-perfect physical specimens were otherwise described by ibn Fadlan as "the filthiest of God's creatures," who would openly engage in group sex, between trading honey, slaves, silver, and furs. Witness to the sea burial of a Volga Viking chieftain, he observed the mass rape of the slave girl allocated the role of joint immolation with the dead Viking, arranged in a sitting position to maintain his position of command.

The *Rus* settlements developed into principalities and prince republics. Vladimir I of the Rurik dynasty, (c.958-1015), Prince of Novgorod, on the death of his father was forced to flee to Scandinavia when one of his brothers followed the ancient management tradition of accession to power by the fratricide of disposing of the other sibling, proceeding to conquer the *Rus* territory. This was a loose federation of East Slavic, Baltic and Finn peoples living in the areas of contemporary Belarus, Russia, and Ukraine, known as Rus'land or Kievan Rus. Vladimir reconquered the area. By 980, he had consolidated the Rus' realm. His conversion to Christianity in 988 and subsequent ascent to sainthood has been held by the 2022 incumbent of the Russian Federation presidency, in a pale imitation of Charlemagne's Christendom, as justification for his invasion of Ukraine. The Rurik dynasty had continued until the 16$^{th}$ century. Local management uses and expressions of history continue to surprise external observers.

By the start of the 9$^{th}$ century, the Rus were settling in Kiev - by the 10$^{th}$, Novgorod. Bling display was high, with gold bracelets prevalent but trust low: wearers of such ornamentation had bodyguards accompany them to the lavatory. Eventually, a trade agreement was reached with Byzantium, but this was more about the right to trade. Previous Rus raids in pursuit of such privilege had been fought off with Greek fire. There was to be no immediate rescue of the West by the East. Assistance was not to arise until the times of Napoleon, Kaiser Wilhelm II, Hitler, and space station collaboration.

However, the Romanovs were able, from the 17th century, to consolidate and manage their rule by granting land to their nobility, to whom they conferred ownership of the peasantry, the serfs, in combination with the Orthodox Church. This was all enforced through a harsh penal code which imposed the death penalty for 63 crimes. The manner of execution included burying alive; routine punishment was using the knout: a rawhide whip with metal attached which ripped off skin to the bone, ten strokes being sufficient to kill. Management by fear took root.

The compensatory mystical element was the supposed spiritual bond between the Tsar as the "little father" of his people, the greater version being heavenly. Thus, the nobles were the managers, the serfs the workers, and the tsar the chairman, CEO, and celestial representative, all bound together by Orthodoxy and devotion to the motherland. Roman emperor deification after death had transmuted into a refined version of monarchical divinity, not only in Russia. The parallel there was with Caesar who, as a Venus descendant and Pontifex Maximus (chief priest), had also headed the state religion as accompaniment to his Dictatorship for Life. Continuing the position seen in Darius the Great, unity of state and leadership of religious belief enforced the management tool and source of empowerment of the divine right of kings.

Autocracy ruled; the autocrats, however much they subsequently toyed with reform, remained bound by a fixed managerial concept. Even late in the 19th century, as deep an ethical thinker and explorer of human psychology, Fyodor Dostoyevsky (1821-1881), in such novels as *Crime and Punishment* and *The Brothers Karamazov,* saw the tsarist autocracy as "a mystery, a sacrament, an anointment … the primary fact of our history".[8] As the tsars subscribed to this self-interested view, even Piotr Stolypin (1862-1911) (the ablest of the ministers of Nicholas II), struggling to manage between ultra-reactionaries and cold-blooded, murdering, criminal Marxists had to realize that ultimately the greatest obstacle to saving the autocracy, however long-lived, was the autocracy itself. After many centuries, it took warfare and revolution to change the nature of temporal rule in Russia. The direct, if attenuated, line and link of divinity from Venus to Caesar through Rome and Byzantium to Muscovy, Moscow and the family of Nicholas II expired in volleys of bullets and bayoneting in the basement of Ipatiev House, Yekaterinburg, on the orders of Vladimir Ilych Ulyanov, known as Lenin, in the night of 16-17 July 1918.

**FOOTPRINT:**
**Management Opportunities Rise and Fall**

- **Christianity was revived and renewed in Europe. Trade was facilitated via waterways, church events, and monastic development.**

- **Islamic, Persian and Chinese advances were punctuated by Mongol warfare, invasion, and plague.**

- **China retreated.**

- **At last, Constantinople fell. Attempt was made to bring Eastern Europe and Russia into a development orbit.**

# Endnotes

[1]  Saliba, George. *Islamic Science and the Making of the European Renaissance,* pp. 50 -51.

[2] *Ibid,* p.196

[3] The most comprehensive guide to the subject is to be found in Boyer, Carl B. *A History of Mathematics*, 2011 and chapter 11, *The Islamic Hegemony*, pp. 203-223. A footnote's footnote, in 1981, during an education management consultancy in Indore, the largest city in the Indian state of Madhya Pradesh, the author asked the manager of the bank he was visiting why he, his clerks and tellers, were still using the abacus. The answer was that their replacement by adding machines and computers would cause unemployment.

[4] Masood, Ehsan. *Science and Islam A History,* pp. 142 -143.

[5] Both numeric and behavioural control systems appear to have been common throughout history. In medieval England, a crime prevention measure was "tithings." Groups of ten men, to be formed as part of a manor or parish population, entered into a "frankpledge" whereby they were responsible for the punishment of any of their number accused of a crime. Failure to comply resulted in the entire group

being fined. The tithe, in cash or kind, as one tenth of income was a common secular and religious tax base.

[6] Wheelis, Mark. "Biological Warfare at the 1346 Siege of Caffa", *Emerging Infectious Diseases Journal,* Volume 8, Number 9, September 2002, Centres for Disease Control and Protection.

[7] A simple illustration of the aspiration is the number of east European medieval states which adopted Tsar as the official title of its head:

First Bulgarian Empire (913-1018);

Second Bulgarian Empire (1185-1396);

Serbian Empire (1346-1371);

Tsardom of Russia (1547-1721), replaced by *imperator* (emperor) but continuing to be so known outside Russia until 1917; and

Tsardom of Bulgaria (1908-1946).

The first Tsar was Simeon I of Bulgaria (864-927);

The first Russian to use the title of Tsar was Mikhail Yaroslavic, Prince of Tver (1271-1318).

[8] Montefiore, Simon Sebag. *The Romanovs,* p. 442

# CHAPTER EIGHT

# CROSS-FERTILISATION, FINANCIAL SERVICES, REALISM...AND CHILDREN

Scientific, technological, and thought development there may have been in later medieval and early modern Europe, but childhood, apart from at the very apex of society, had largely ceased to exist. Children as young as three worked in the fields and would continue to do so well into the modern era. There was no distinction between child and adult, especially once basic communication ability had been attained. Schools were ungraded, no age distinctions applied; classes of mixed ages from six to thirteen were the norm. Indeed, medieval education was not intended for children. Schools were vocational establishments for the production of clerks and clerics, with knowledge transmitted as received truth and conducted upon an entirely adult basis. Thinking and change were at higher levels.

As questioning the faith might court punishment for heresy, and thus death, inquiry of any kind could be dangerous. Disputing received knowledge was not encouraged. Whatever it was, it was this way for the ancient authorities said it was so. Aristotle and Pliny, for example, for all their virtues and errors, had gone unquestioned for centuries. Discipline was harsh; physical education and expression neglected. To medieval Europe's credit, however, schooling was available for girls via convents and their establishments.

The later medieval period in Europe saw the gradual establishment of universities. Entry age followed the Roman pattern for higher education, beginning at from 13 to 14. By the 13th century, there was an established, two-tiered curriculum: the "trivium" of the familiar grammar, rhetoric, and logic, followed by the more adventurous "quadrivium" of arithmetic, geometry, music, and astronomy. This seeming revival, however, was subject to the requirements of its sponsor, which bent knowledge to its own requirements - or to popular speculation and wishful thinking. Even Isaac Newton, beacon of the early Enlightenment, occupied a significant part of his career with alchemy and astrology (both were still viewed as an aspect of astronomy).

An infamous illustration of medieval European arithmetic quoted divine arithmetical omnipotence: in the beginning, God made 22 works; there are 22 generations from Adam to Jacob; there are 22 Old Testament books (counting up to Esther); and 22 letters of the alphabet out of which the divine law is composed: therefore, there are 22 sextarii in a bushel.[1] Yet, another cost variable was being added to trade - this time by divine calculation.

The other side of the coin, literally, was the Western world's need for precious metal for its currency. The height of Abbasid prosperity from the 8th to 13th centuries grew by a huge expansion of the money supply, released by plunder from Byzantium and Egypt, and West African trade through the Sahara. Whilst money can be made of anything, even the Maldives' cowrie shells, (three millennia ago the Chinese currency, their depiction forming the character for money, which found their way into Indian, African, and Indonesian trade), Europeans required metal of value for their coinage.[2]

From around the Mesopotamian mid-3rd millennium, a measure of silver, the shekel, had replaced edible barley as currency. King Alyattes of Lydia (618-561 BCE), now part of modern Turkey, had issued the first coinage of standard weights of gold and silver. Their marks indicated the amount of precious metal and identification mark of the issuing authority. Money and its value were now expressed in coins, a continuing means of commercial management. By Roman times, this was of three types: the *aureus* (gold), replaced by the *solidus* in the 4th century; the *denarius* (silver), exchanged in the same era for the *argentarius*, and the *sestertius* (bronze) which outlived the empire with base metal substituting for bronze. In the 8th century CE, Western prices were still being quoted in *denarii* but there was a continuing problem: stagnant Europe had to cope with the growing shortage of precious metal.

One method was the ancient stand-by of plunder, to which the Islamic world was vulnerable. Both the Crusades and repossession of Spain had strong economic motives and were part of the business plans of the Voyages of Discovery. The business cultures of its exponents of state managed trade: Portugal, Holland, France, and Britain were all variations on the ancient theme of Phoenician and Carthaginian naval capitalism. The further method of a revival of slavery - to dig and service mines, as tradable commodities in the plantations' businesses, and as exemplified back in the Islamic and African worlds over centuries - juxtaposed the achievements of high culture and the transmission of knowledge through trade. A management innovation born of cross-fertilization brought a further change dimension, with the benefit of relative religious security: financial services.

At the turn of the 13th century, a Pisan merchant namedLeonardo Fibonacci (c.1175-c.1240/50) ventured to Algeria to assist his father's trading post. Traveling in the region, he discovered the remarkable transformation of arithmetic. Impressed by his findings, Fibonacci published the *Liber Abaci* (Book of Calculation) in 1202. This spread the innovation throughout Europe, earning him a visit to Emperor Frederick II (1194-1250) and, in recognition of benefit to public accounting, a salary by decree from the Republic of Pisa. Fibonacci was probably the first, and perhaps for many years the only, person to achieve public honour for services to accountancy. His work included the explanation of fractions and the decimal system, thus simplifying calculations from cumbersome Roman numerals.

The effect of the *Liber Abaci* was enormous. Everything arithmetical related to daily life in Europe and the non-Islamic world changed, most strikingly in book-keeping, the calculation of interest, and money changing. Within two centuries, the new arithmetic was present throughout commerce and banking, leading to the growth of the banking industry. Fibonacci quite literally led by example. Many of the examples were drawn from commodities trade in items such as spices, cheese, oils, and hides, and applied to money making through lending and interest charges. This led to merchants being able to expand trade, because the lender gained incentive. This greatly encouraged the mercantile expansion of the Italian city states, without which the growth of Venice and Genoa could not have occurred. The increasing sophistication and simultaneous revival of ancient practices can be seen in the Genovese systems of shipping risk computations: premiums of 3% were charged for merchant vessels sailing in armed conveys, 7% for unaccompanied vessels on shorter journeys.

Nonetheless, there was a religious obstruction. The lending of money at interest was deemed a sin by the Catholic Church in the 12th century, incurring the penalty of excommunication, with defenders of the practice branded as heretics in the 14th. Usury was not allowed under Judaism either, but there was an escape clause: it was permissible where the borrower was not Jewish. Even then, prejudice added another obstacle: it took most of the 16th century for Venetian Jews to achieve citizenship and permission to participate in the lucrative trade with the East.

The further innovation of double entry book-keeping, allowing the tracking of debits and credits, deposits, and withdrawals, is of unclear ancestry. One account, ignoring Fibonacci, attributes a Franciscan Friar, Luca Pacioli (1447-1517), who began working as a tutor in Venice around 1464 and writing on arithmetic, as "father of accounting and book-keeping." Holding the first European mathematics professorship at Perugia, he continued to teach and write, with his first book published in Venice in 1494. Three years later, he moved to Milan where he lived with Leonardo da Vinci (1452-1519), who illustrated some of his works, in particular the "golden ratio" used in architecture and the first illustration of skeletonic solids.

Pacioli's initial work, applied mathematics, was for merchant need, dealing with such essentials as barter, exchange, profit, and algebra. This was followed by the first printed work in the vernacular to describe the double entry accounting method in 1494. He introduced the terms and practices of journals, ledgers, debit, and credit descriptions. The ledger method had accounts for assets, liabilities, capital, income, and expenses. Assets' definition included receivables and inventories. Proof of a balanced ledger was demonstrated through the year-end closing entries against a trial balance. In addition to this foundation of modern accounting, he progressed to cost accounting and the ethics of the processes.

Belying the latter-day tendency to view accountants as uninteresting, Pacioli also published treatises linking mathematics with practical, magical entertainment: mathematical puzzles, card tricks, juggling, fire eating, methodology of dancing coins; on chess, geometry, mathematical and artistic proportions, and perspective. His shared household with Leonardo, until they were forced to flee by a French invasion, must have been a place of considerable fun. Fun is a developmental and causative factor recognised by some educationalists, but not always fully appreciated in management or history.

Although the attribution of Luca Pacioli's paternity of modern accounting rests on his written evidence, one of his works (on artistic proportionality), has been criticised for plagiarism. In the case of double entry book-keeping, it is more likely that he recorded and possibly improved upon, what was already in practical use: a further example of the "copy and adapt" managerial process. The double entry method is known to have begun to be practiced in Florence by the de Medici bank, (1397-1494), a century earlier. Leonardo, epitome of the "Renaissance Man," spent his youth in Florence. He was close to Botticelli (1455-1510) and other artists under the direct patronage of the Medici. Speculative but persuasive, it is possible that Leonardo knew of Medici banking practices and communicated or confirmed these to Pacioli - whose own mercantile patrons must have experienced Medici banking method.

The Franciscan regularised, codified, and probably improved upon existing best commercial practice. However disseminated, the Medici double entry book-keeping practice greatly boosted trade and so enhanced its own wealth. As a result, the family patronage supported many of the works of the Renaissance. However, while double entry book-keeping had been known in the Islamic and Indian worlds since 1000, maritime traders from Venice, Genoa, and Britain were well versed in risk management, market knowledge and logistics. Trade management was an inevitably reciprocal process.

The Medici, more gangsters than businessmen in the mid-14th century, often represented as having fathered modern banking, were ruthless, efficient money-people. Their like had long been known. A cuneiform clay tablet surviving from the 17th century BCE promises the bearer a quantity of barley on harvest. Functioning from benches – *banca* – in stalls by temples, where deposits might be stored and oaths sworn, Roman bankers were part of society fabric; Mithraic cult strong rooms were housed *inside* military forts' headquarters buildings. The original Medici establishment was a stall near the Florence wool market. Giovanni Medici (1455-1510), who had acted as a currency trader for the family in Rome, returned home enriched by the business, determined to make it respectable as well as lucrative. An immediate manifestation was the use of multiple currencies, with the Vatican having a pressing conversion need.

Such had been the uncertainties of the political times of the 11th and 12th centuries that merchants had to rely on family members as agents in the key trading cities of Europe to conduct their importing and exporting businesses. Rather than send coin, the purchase of a bill of exchange from a banker became a naturally preferred payment method. Double entry book-keeping allowed the recording of a transaction at the agent's location, and the home head office. What was paid at one location was recorded as received at another. This helped to keep the agent and foreign employees honest, giving records providing detail of revenue, interest, capital, and depreciation, as well as an overview of profit and loss. The limited liability known to the Romans now recurred through the Italian *compagnia*, those structures which arose with the expanding firms now trading in scale in, with, or through the application of the newly discovered financial techniques.

Giovanni Medici managed the business on a partner basis, with branches in Rome and Venice, more added subsequently, with the further addition of woollen concerns. This diversification, with the branches being run on a profit-sharing junior partnership basis, added to trade in the bills of exchange increasingly being used to finance transactions. Efficiency ensured through meticulous double entry book-keeping took the family to its dominance of Florentine and European banking, and one of its daughters, Catherine, (1519-1589) to reign as Queen of France (1547-59) and become the mother of three further kings (Francis II [1544-1560], (Charles IX [1550-1574]), and (Henri III [1551-1589]). Although the Dutch, Flemish, Swedish, and English succeeded the Medici banking hegemony, their model of limiting risk through a mix of lending, currency trading, and commodities dealing based on a profit-sharing partnership matrix laid the foundation of modern banking – and it all began from the precise arithmetic embodied in double entry book-keeping.

By the 15$^{th}$ century, business records and partnership agreements had become much more financially specific, itemizing such matters as capital gains, losses, deferrals, reserves, depreciation, labour, and production cost, with difference between fixed and liquid assets. Black Death destruction, the spread of knowledge from other civilisations, and the creativity of consequent invention and adaptation prepared the ground for European capitalism to emerge as the dominant business form - albeit subsequently challenged by other variants.

Growing to a city of around 150,000 in the 15$^{th}$ century, Bruges was situated at the crossroads of the northern and southern trade routes, with a well-developed canal system and access to the sea. Its entrepreneurial merchants developed a financial market in parallel with trade in cloth, woollens and lace, becoming an entrepôt for grains and wines. This generated wealth sufficient, by the 15$^{th}$ century, to be part of the new and rising Flemish art movement, whose new oil painting techniques were to have increasing significance in Renaissance art.

Europe was advancing but, even so, the Islamic world still had major contributions to make. The historian and philosopher Ibn Khaldūn (1332-1406), discussed also in Chapter 13 in the *Muqaddimah,* was summarising real trade requirements, the need for free markets, and advances in management techniques. He addressed the role of the merchant in society, the importance of the profit motive, and the need for rulers to provide security so that their people might supply goods and services - particularly

**The canals of Bruges in West Flanders were key to the medieval
and early modern prosperity of this trade, finance and artistic hub.**
Photograph by the author.

to safeguard against the jealousy of those wealth accumulators who, by their
very activities, generate wealth for others. He was anticipating much of the
thought of Adam Smith four centuries in advance. Offering commercial
advice, he notes that goods might be stored until prices rise, or suggests
buying where cheap and selling where markets are high. Either way, he
expresses the advice of which the Elder Cato would have approved: buying
cheap and selling dear.

Ibn Khaldūn noted types of trade where margins were higher encouraged
merchants to have confidence in using law as a protection and to deter the
unscrupulous, warning against its risk. Thereafter expulsion from Europe,
and wars and invasions in the Islamic world causing it to re-form in three
identities - Ottoman Turkey, Mamluk Egypt and the Safavid Empire of
Persia - there was a continued growth of administrative literature for their
own purposes, which built on, rather than extended, the business
applications already reached.

Even so, Istanbul, Turkey was to surpass European provision of education.
A European education based upon unquestionable received information
with insufficient books, requiring extensive rote learning and memorising,

was not a lively or particularly attractive inducement to study to those whose parents could afford the activity. Chivalric literature enlivened aristocratic study towards the end of the medieval period.[3] Yet, for all its dull drudgery, repression, and dogmatic perversions, progress occurred and learning advanced. Able people progressed the long recovery from the destruction of the ancient, civilised world. Technical advances, particularly the maritime, increased the ability to explore and expand.

The discovery of new worlds was accompanied by a recovery of some of the old. The rediscovery of ancient Greek and Roman works in the libraries of Islamic Andalusia, Africa, and the Near East, coupled with the Indo-Islamic advances in mathematics, combined with the intellectual renewal which began in Italy in the 14th century. Revolt against the stultification of the Church was complemented by a renewal of the values of classical culture. The cannon balls which exploded on impact having at last breached its massive defensive walls, the fall of Constantinople in 1453 closed the old trading routes to the East, fuelling the search for a western route to the Indies. Intrepid adventurers voyaged south and west from Europe, first under royal patronage and then financed by nascent business. The new worlds bred merchant adventurers, opened vast sources of wealth, and commenced the creation of colonies and trading posts. The business of discovery unleashed entrepreneurial enterprise onto a larger stage.

Curiously coincidental with the replacement of Byzantium by the Ottoman Turks in 1453, advances in technology and science coupled with a revival of the classics began to bring wider, major change for Europe. In the field of management, however, it took a political thinker to bring the next advances. His name alone sums up his legacy: Machiavelli.

His view was one of stark reality. He approached the world as he saw it to be. The context is a further state management crisis. Just as the Greek city states of antiquity had fought among themselves and attracted foreign predators, so the risen, prosperous Italian cities faced similar issues. Although trade and business leaders had prospered through the introduction of modern banking, the medieval states of 14th and 15th century Tuscany, particularly Florence, Pisa, and Siena, were fighting each other or further Italian cities, or embroiled in conflict with France, Spain, and the papacy.

Because of the potential catastrophes of large personnel losses to a small state, the citizens preferred to engage mercenaries. Although some of these *condottieri* commanders were able, many were not, and mercenaries also had an aversion to being killed, injured, or discomforted. Thus, interminable warfare with perpetual looting and unreliable armies provided a context of perplexing dimensions into which the imposition of order was no straightforward political task.

A modern parallel may be drawn with management consultants. They are available for hire to competitors, claiming a professionalism which maintains client secrecy - an enviable aspiration where maintained, but ever vulnerable to human nature, as well illustrated when the former managing director of the arch-modern corporate mercenaries, McKinsey, and Co., Rajat Gupta (1948-) was jailed for two years for insider trading in 2012. A fellow senior partner and former director, Anil Kumar (1958-), got two years' probation for his admission of guilt and testimony against his former boss, so continuing the mercenary tradition of turning on each other when fortunes change.

One man, however, thought he had the answers for such behaviour. Niccolò de Bernardo dei Machiavelli (1469-1527) is infamous for his short work, *The Prince*, written in 1513 but published only posthumously in 1532. Still controversial, it is often neglected that the book was, and still is, the most widely discussed apparent job application in history.

### Niccolò Machiavelli

His thesis was that morality was incompatible with politics. By extension, this was to be applied to business management in our own times practically by Rajat Gupta, theoretically by Michael Jensen (1939-), and their myriad acolytes. [4] Unfortunately for Niccolò, the potential patron to whom he addressed his work, the Magnificent Lorenzo Di Piero De' Medici (1452-1514), did not offer employment.[5] Machiavelli had survived a career as a civil servant and diplomat near, but not at, the top of political public Florentine service. He found himself on the wrong side of history when the Medici returned to power. Like Cato the Elder, he retired to his farm to write, his output including drama, novels, poetry, politics, and history. Just as his intended patron's father, Piero the Unfortunate, Machiavelli suffered misfortune in his own career, this because of the fluctuations of fortunes in his political occupation. Unsurprisingly, he took a somewhat jaundiced view of the goddess the Romans called Fortuna, beautiful on approach, hideous from behind, although viewed by their Stoics as character forming:

> "I conclude, therefore, that as fortune is changeable whereas men are obstinate in their ways, men prosper so long as fortune and policy are in accord, and when there is a clash, they fail. I hold strongly to this: that it is better to be impetuous than circumspect; because fortune is a woman and if she is to be submissive it is necessary to beat and coerce her. Experience shows that she is more often subdued by men who do this than by those who act coldly. Always, being a woman, she favours young men, because they are less circumspect and more ardent, and because they command her with greater audacity." [6]

Such sentiments have contributed to the image of Machiavelli as the devil, "Old Nick" (an anachronistic misnomer), an amoral, immoral practitioner and adviser of the darkest of political arts with an adjectival function: Machiavellian, and an extra, added ism. The word extends as easily to studies of corporate management as it does to daily life. As a body of thought, it presented a new way of openly addressing politics, government, and management - and hence how any and all enterprises might be managed, for core to the thinking was that *the end justifies the means*. Plato and Aristotle's ideal republic was replaced by one based on *realpolitik*, how things really were, and the realities of the politics of Machiavelli's time were extremely distasteful indeed.

Cesare Borgia (1475-1507) was given in *The Prince* as an example of a successful ruler - one who started almost from scratch, albeit under the

patronage of a prince of the Roman Church, his father, and by ruthless application carved out a state for himself. Cesare was one of the four illegitimate children of Pope Alexander VI (1431-1503), whose ecclesiastical career had been advanced by his uncle, Pope Callixtus III (1378-1458), with his appointment to the rank of cardinal.

### Pope Alexander VI (Rodrigo Borgia)

The Borgias had turned the papacy into a family business, Alexander giving the same rank of cardinal to his son Cesare on his graduation from university.

While the second Borgia Pope was acknowledged as a highly competent administrator, diplomat, and politician, in addition to the misbehaviour cited above he also had a daughter by his mistress and children by other women. He was criticised for his lavish living, overspending, simony (the sale of church offices), and lascivious behaviour. This included allegations of orgies at the Vatican with persistent accompanying rumours of the disposal of opponents by poison. Cesare's sister, Lucretia (1480-1519), is commonly associated with this recurrent management method of dispatch, but apologists claim either family peer pressure in mitigation or innocence maligned by guilt by association.

Cesare resigned his church office to pursue his goal of attaining a principality in Central Italy, acquiring lands there, finally dying in battle in the attempt to retain them. Italy was a difficult political area. Mercenary armies were almost as unreliable when they had been paid as when they had not, with mercenaries' management organisations acting effectively as prototypes of early trade unions, bargaining on pay and conditions of service. The Spanish had invaded. The dukedoms warred amongst themselves, changed sides, manoeuvred neutralities and alliances as the French intervened, whilst the popes brokered and aggrandized. Machiavelli's achievement alone in staying alive was considerable. This background explains, if not entirely excuses, the philosophy of precept and action which he set forward. He addressed power directly: the intelligence of a ruler might be measured by the quality of the men around him; if an enemy is to be hurt, that should be so hard that vengeance will not follow.

Machiavelli knew that political survival depended on realism without sentiment. That meant conflicts of interest had to be recognised and resolved: by force, trickery, or diplomacy. Even so, there would always be risks and the need to appreciate the nature of the different dangers, accepting the least bad as good. To deal with external dangers, it was necessary to sustain internal loyalty and commitment. As nothing could be achieved without survival, that came first. If power had to be achieved by force and guile, consolidated by cruelty, it still required consent to be secured. Therefore, the best power, once achieved, was that which had to be exercised least. His method was empirical, which has brought the "father of political science" label.

He based his shrewd, unblinking work on the history of Rome and the experiences of his lifetime. His direct challenge to human hypocrisy is hard to refute, for Machiavelli bases his theories on irrefutable fact. He brought political science, and hence management theory, to a new and developing point with the proposition that an action's evil or good can be decided only in the light of what it is meant to achieve and whether it successfully accomplishes that. Consider, compare, and contrast the 20th century Honda mission statement of *"Yamaha wo tsubusu": "*We will crush Yamaha".[7] The Samurai tradition might have been realistically expressed, but ultimately both sides gained from the exchange.

Machiavelli remained trenchant:

On Mercenaries:

> Mercenary commanders are either skilled in warfare or they are not: if they are, you cannot trust them, because they are anxious to advance their own greatness, either by coercing you, their employer, or by coercing others against your own wishes. If, however, the commander is lacking in prowess, in the normal way he brings about your ruin.…Experience has shown that only princes and armed republics achieve solid success, and that mercenaries bring nothing but loss; and a republic which has its own citizen army is far less likely to be subjugated by one of its own citizens than a republic whose forces are not its own. [8]

It would be wrong and unfair to liken management consultants and business school faculty to mercenaries, but managers will note similarities in certain circumstances. Moreover, early industrialists and economists such as Adam Smith were distrustful of managers, where the mercenary parallel might also be drawn. It is not too fanciful to compare the career of Cesare Borgia with the aspirant, acquisitive industrial manager-partners of Robert Owen's day.

On Praise, Blame and Morality:

> So, a prince has of necessity to be so prudent that he knows how to escape the evil reputation attached to those vices which could lose him his state, and how to avoid those vices which are not so dangerous, if he possibly can; but, if he cannot, he need not worry so much about the latter. And then, he must not flinch from being blamed for vices which are necessary for safeguarding the state. This is because, taking everything into account, he will find that some of the things that appear to be virtues will, if he practices them, ruin him, and some of the things that appear to be vices will bring him security and prosperity.[9]

On Cruelty and Compassion, and whether it is better to be loved than feared, or the reverse:

...the answer is that one would like to be both the one and the other; but because it is difficult to combine them, it is far better to be feared than loved if you cannot be both. One can make this generalisation about men: they are ungrateful, fickle, liars, and deceivers, they shun danger and are greedy for profit; while you treat them well, they are yours. They would shed their blood for you, risk their property, their lives, their children, so long, as I said above, as danger is remote; but when you are in danger, they turn against you...

...Among the admirable achievements of Hannibal is included this: that although he led a huge army, made up of countless different races, on foreign campaigns, there was never any dissension, either among the troops themselves or against their leader, whether things were going well or badly. For this, his inhuman cruelty was wholly responsible. It was this, along with his countless other qualities, which made him feared and respected by his soldiers. If it had not been for his cruelty, his other qualities would not have been enough. The historians, having given little thought to this, on the one hand admire what Hannibal achieved, and on the other condemn what made his achievements possible. [10]

Machiavelli was referring back to the *Melian Dialogues*, Sarpedon's remarks on Sulla, and the notorious third Roman Emperor, Gaius [Caligula] (12-41 CE), said to have often quoted a line from the tragedian Accius (170-c.86 BCE): "I scorn their hatred if they do but fear me," rendered by Suetonius as *oderint, dum metuant*: "let them hate so long as they fear." In the 20th century, the distinguished Singaporean statesman Lee Kuan Yew (1923-2015) continued to echo the sentiment:

> Between being loved and being feared, I have always believed Machiavelli was right. If nobody is afraid of me, I'm meaningless.[11]

However, Machiavelli sought balance too. On the need to avoid contempt and hatred, Machiavelli writes of Severus, who won empire by a mixture of trickery and military prowess, and his son, Caracalla:

> he [Severus] who had the qualities of a ferocious lion and a very cunning fox, and that he was feared and respected by everyone, yet not hated by the troops. And it will not be thought anything to marvel at if Severus, an upstart, proved himself able to maintain such great power; because his tremendous prestige always protected him from the hatred which his plundering inspired in people. Now Antoninus Caracalla, his son, was also a man of tremendous qualities which astonished the people and endeared him to the soldiers; he was a military man, capable of any exertion, and he scorned softness of any kind, at the table or elsewhere. This won him the devotion of the troops. None the less his ferocity and cruelty were so great and unparalleled (after countless individual murders, he put to death great numbers of Romans and all the citizens of Alexandria) that he became universally hated. Even those

closest to him started to fear him; and as a result, he was killed by a centurion when he was surrounded by his troops. Here it should be noted that princes cannot escape death if the attempt is made by a fanatic.[12]

Caracalla's mistakes had been to put the centurion's brother to death with disgrace, to threaten the centurion daily – and yet retain him in his bodyguard. Yet, even if Caracalla had behaved sensibly, Machiavelli implies the danger to rulers regarding fanatics is eternal.

Machiavelli's awareness was acute and unblinking. He saw the political, managerial value of dissembling and hypocrisy. Rulers should appear to be compassionate, true to their word, devout and without guile; but not too attached to such virtues, for if the situation required it, the reverse practices would be necessary. Machiavelli's ideal realism was the manager who knew how to use the jargon of the day but not be bound by it, whilst ignoring flattery and eschewing self-delusion. For success and progress, which he saw as the combination of Fortune, or circumstances, and one's own capacity or skill, it remained necessary also to have the stability and protection of a strong state. Machiavelli was the first thinker to write that real life involves conflict; and that conflict can be productive and creative: a profound change which people took very seriously. A free people would always be more successful because they were prepared to fight for that freedom. Such freedom is bound to involve conflict, especially between social classes.

The advent and spread of printing throughout Europe gave Machiavelli's work great currency, his evocation of Roman history, part of the rediscovery of the classics in the Renaissance, and his humanism chiming with the rising resistance of science to theological dogma. Largely condemned by both sides of the Reformation, distorted by the resulting devilish image, his work has yet proved to be lasting.

Driving force of both the Renaissance and Reformation, such humanism, could provoke all sides. Riots followed Desiderius Erasmus' revision of the meaning of "*logos*" to "in the beginning was the conversation" instead of "word" - the Church maintained an undistinguished record of defending the indefensible. Those knowledgeable of Greek would not translate *logos* to "word." The philosophical expression of "rational divine intelligence" may be set aside the more commonplace expressions of thought, principle, word, and speech. Erasmus was certainly correct in attempting to give a more expansive translation of a complex issue.

The ends and means debates continue - from the novels of Dostoevsky (1821-1881), *Crime and Punishment* and *The Brothers Karamazov* in particular, to John Stuart Mill's (1806-1873) philosophic proposition and the application of the utilitarian philosophy of Jeremy Bentham (1748-1832) of *"the greatest good of the greatest number,"* to President Truman's (1884-1972) nuclear action to end the Second World War. As apt and applicable to management as to any form of human expression, Machiavelli's exposition and proposition are essential determinants of the ethics and practice of management and management education, in any form.

It should be noted that Machiavelli was not himself devoid of morality, charity, and humanity. Rather, when he held that a ruler forced to govern in a manner contrary to those principles in order to maintain his power was, it was out of practical necessity. What came later, in the 19$^{th}$ century, to be expressed as *realpolitik* had a different moral tone. Machiavelli knew right from wrong, what was moral and what was not. His was essentially a stance of pragmatism and preservation, not necessarily of expansion and acquisition, where circumstances were such that political survival depended on realism without sentiment. That meant conflicts of interest had to be recognised, hence resolution by force, trickery, or diplomacy was necessary.

Even so, there would always be risks and the need to appreciate the nature of the different dangers, accepting the least bad as good. To deal with external dangers, it was necessary to sustain internal loyalty and commitment. As nothing could be achieved without survival, that came first. If power had to be achieved by force and guile, consolidated by cruelty, it still required consent to be secured. Therefore, the best power was that which had to be exercised least once achieved.

Machiavelli's concern was with the management of an active state; however the reverse was continued in the opposite part of the world. Confucian education underpinned the state bureaucracy, with goals of harmony and balance which, while desirable, are not natural procreators of the economy. Management by containment declined into entropy. Even though China had become advanced in such production of scale as bulk porcelain, the base remained that of state monopolies which succeeded simply because of the domestic market size but increasingly suffered by not being exposed to competition. The royal granaries, the Grand Canal, and the Yellow River dyke systems in China were all in decay by 1800. Europe being concerned with itself and expansion into new worlds to the west, south and southeast of itself, China remained isolated. That is, until re-opened by European violence and forced trade in the 19th century - actions which Niccolò would have understood.

Even then, there was not much for European education to be proud of. Sultan Suleiman I, (1494-1566), known as "the Magnificent" in the West but "the Lawgiver" in the East, whose great-grandfather had conquered and sacked Constantinople with his advances to Belgrade, Buda, and the gates of Vienna, became at his capital the finest provider of education in Europe. His was a very practical realism, seeking to renew the energy of the original, expanding version of Islamic empire. Onto Shari'a law, which he could not change, Suleiman grafted a single, long lasting code covering matters such as taxation, land tenure, and criminal law, the most comprehensive since that first great codification achievement of the Roman Eastern Emperor, Justinian (482-565). Suleiman raised the status of Christian land workers above serfdom, thus causing Christian serf and peasant immigration into Ottoman lands. Religious toleration, particularly of the Jews, meant that while European popes and monarchs talked of a crusade against him, armed resistance to his advances remained; but without retribution.

Ottoman advances into Europe can be interpreted as Suleiman's attempt to make a new Roman Empire, but in the name of the Sunni version of Allah. What was to prove Suleiman's final offensive was halted by the Crusaders' last stand when the Knights of St John led the surprisingly successful resistance in the Great Siege of Malta of 1565. One of Suleiman's commanders disastrously disobeyed orders. The normally highly competent Ottoman forces made crucial strategic mistakes, a split command having to retreat at the end of the campaigning season. Like their Roman predecessor, Suleiman and the Ottomans had also to cope with a difficult eastern neighbour and opponent: Shia Iran. With difficulties on two fronts, the aging Suleiman was required to take the option of discretion.

Suleiman inclined neither to indiscipline nor indecision. In his advances into Europe, any soldier who trampled on sowed fields or failed to respect townspeople was executed on the spot. Conforming to the Ottoman practice of putting all his near male relatives to death on his accession, Suleiman otherwise displayed enlightened governance. However, although further styled "the Perfecter of the Perfect number," he also demonstrated similar superstitious numerology to the Christian medieval attribution of weights' equivalence. Such were Suleiman's achievements and attributes that he was associated with the number ten, that of good fortune, with ten being the number of Commandments; Muhammad's disciples; of the parts and variants of the Qur'an, of the toes, the fingers, and the astronomical heavens of Islam; and so, the 10th ruler of his House, born at the beginning of the 10th century, the year 900 of the Hegira (1493 CE). He must, therefore, be blessed indeed. Medievalism did not depart readily. Yet Suleiman, along with Maria Theresa of Austria (1717-1780), may be seen as one of the first of the early modern enlightened despots.

His overall aim was to make Constantinople – known by that name until the 20th century adaptation and adoption of Istanbul – the centre of Islamic civilisation. Together with ambitious construction projects such as palaces, mosques, and bridges, he reorganised craft education and extended the school system. Schools attached to the mosques provided virtually free primary education, where boys were taught to read and write, as well as basic Islam. Further education became available at the *medreses*, which were colleges where the curriculum included philosophy, grammar, astronomy, astrology, and metaphysics. Higher *medreses* provided university level education, like their western counterparts, for entry to the clergy.

Artistic societies were formed, roughly equivalent to a hybrid of the European guilds and later academic societies, whereby trade skills reached levels at which a distinctly Ottoman cultural identity was established. Even the Sultan contributed directly as a poet incognito. However, although this was a relaxed Sunni Islamic empire continuing for some three hundred years, it outlived its initial achievements, limping its way across the centuries to become the "sick man of Europe" until terminated by Kemal Ataturk's (1881-1938) intervention in 1922. Brilliant early leadership and management fell victim to entropy, decline having begun with Suleiman's three commanders' catastrophic strategic mistakes in the Great Siege of Malta.

**FOOTPRINT:**
**More Management Methods Emerge**

- Quantitative applications and measures accompanied CEO advice, consultants, and the "techies" of their day. This provided means of maximisation and advance within the traditional contexts of autocracy and the expressions of love and fear.

- Through Turkey, Suleiman created a tolerant Islamic empire which was to last for a further three hundred years.

## Endnotes

[1] The *sextarius* was a Roman measure of capacity. One *sextarius* was the equivalent of 35.4 cubic inches or, in liquid form, one pint (0.58 litre). 24 *sextarii* made one *urma* of 849.6 cubic inches (13.92 litres). 48 *sextarii* made one *amphora*. 24 *sextarii* for half an *amphora* would have been an arithmetically correct direct conversion. Bushel capacity at litre equivalent being 35.24 litres under both American and former British weight capacities, simple direct conversion would have been more correct, if not exact. The divine version calculation produces a 0.6% extra profit or loss depending on whether buying or selling.

[2] In the East New Britain province of Papua New Guinea (PNG), the Tolai people continue to use shell money, known as tabu. The tabu provides the basis for barter business in essential goods such as rice, sausage, and cooking oils. Used for feasting and spiritual purposes; initiation, bridal and funeral ceremonies; dispute settlement; fee payments; equipment and goods purchases, local stocks have been exhausted by unsustainable farming methods. The sea slugs whose shells are adapted to make stringed tabu must be imported from neighbouring islands. Always exchangeable against kina, the hard PNG currency, the 2020 Covid lockdown caused a kina shortage and a tabu increase in use and value:
https://www.vice.com/en_au/article/9kp5ye/papua-new-guinea-tolai-tribe-shell-money.

[3] It marked an ethical ideal revival in secular social and moral virtues. Society management had now secular as well as spiritual ideals, with trade exhibiting its own *mores*.

[4] Dealt with at length in a subsequent publication, Jensen with a late partner began the "shareholder value" mythical application to the joint stock company, an unscrupulously amoral system of governance which has fuelled the ever-growing inequality of rewards under capitalism, productive of anomalously disproportionate CEO payments.

[5] Grandson of the original Magnificent Lorenzo De' Medici (1449-1492), ruler of Florence and most powerful patron of the Renaissance, and father of Catherine, (Queen Consort of France to Henry II, Regent to him and to his sons Charles IX and Henry III), himself ruler of Florence from 1516 and created Duke of Urbino by his uncle, Pope Leo X. The descriptive nomenclature of history has provided rulers with appellations as diverse as the Fat, Bald, Mad, Fair, Unready and several Greats, there have been only two *Magnificoes*. Lorenzo gained the accolade as the patron of the Florentine Renaissance, Suleiman for his domestic reforms and foreign adventures, even though a few of the latter ended in defeat: before the gates of Vienna, in Malta, and at his death in 1566 on his last Balkans campaign.

[6] Machiavelli, Niccolò. 1995. *The Prince*, trans. George Bull. XXV, p.80, London: Penguin Classics.

[7] This 1981 clash was roughly translated in the reporting article as: "We will crush, squash, butcher, slaughter, etc., Yamaha!" (Freedman, Lawrence. 2013. *Strategy*, Oxford, p. 568). Honda cut prices, increased advertising, and introduced new product designed as a necessary fashion accessory. At some cost, Honda captured the domestic market. Yamaha recovered by selling its unsold stock overseas while reinventing itself through product innovation. The conflict ultimately produced successful strategies for both companies.

[8] Machiavelli, *op. cit.*, XII, p.39.

[9] *Ibid*, XV, p. 49.

[10] *Ibid*, XVI, pp. 52-3.

[11] "Lee Kuan Yew: his most memorable quotes," *Daily Telegraph*, 23 March 2015.

[12] Machiavelli, *op. cit.*, XIX, pp. 62-63.

# CHAPTER NINE

## REBIRTH AND RENEWAL, ROUGH AND READY

Despite the external stimuli of the Ottoman advance, the progress of the Renaissance was nonetheless slow. In the early 17th century, the eminent scientist Galileo Galilei (1564-1642) found himself in deep trouble for his conclusion from the works of Copernicus and his own observation of helio-centralism: the earth moved around the sun. Nicolaus Copernicus (1473-1543) had formulated a model of the universe which placed the sun at the centre, conveniently for his comfort, publishing just before his death. Copernicus's evidential fact conflicted with Church dogma.

According to biblical writings: "the world is firmly established; it cannot be moved"; "the Lord set the world upon its foundations; it can never be moved"; "And the sun rises and sets and returns to its place".[1] A papal inquisition in 1616 spoke against the scientist: Pope Paul IV ordered Galileo "to abandon completely … the opinion that the sun stands still at the centre of the world and that the earth moves, and henceforth not to hold, teach or defend it in any way whatsoever, either orally or in writing."

Found guilty of holding to Copernican theory at his trial in 1633, Galileo was imprisoned and subsequently held under house arrest until death. Famously, his recantation to save his life was said to have been followed by the muttered denial, "And yet it moves." Such conflict at the apex of education was accompanied by gradual change in the lower reaches, but it still required the massive upheavals of the Reformation and its Counter to consolidate and expand the achievements of the Renaissance.

The period began with the works of Copernicus and concluding with those of Isaac Newton is known as the Scientific Revolution. This was less revolution of knowledge and more so one of ignorance, marking when scholars realised that they did not know the answers to their most important questions. The deficiencies in mathematics as he found them induced

Newton to devise the laws of motion which set the foundation for the Industrial Revolution, a scientific achievement of genius, outside and beyond then conventional thinking.

**Russian postal recognition for Galileo**

The established but pre-modern religions such as Christianity, Islam, and Buddhism, rested on the assertion that everything about the world was already known, revealed either by an Almighty or past sages. The search began for completely new knowledge. That was accompanied by the counter assertion of the value of humanism. The gradual spread of the Renaissance across Europe in the 15th and 16th centuries saw the rise of humanism in revolt against the constrictions of the medieval world view. However, that change promised rather more than it delivered and for the bulk of the population, drudgery, and illiteracy continued as before. The aspirations of the humanists, epitomised by Vittorino da Feltra's (1378-1446) foundation in Mantua in 1453 of the Casa Giocosa called the "Happy House," were a return to the ideals of the ancient Greek philosophers.

The purpose of "liberal education" was to develop intellectual, spiritual, and physical capacities to enhance the enrichment of life. The means were primarily a rediscovery of the classics, but with the study of content replacing that of form. Grammar became a means to understanding rather than an end in itself. What Plato and Cicero said became more important than how they said it. The curriculum still followed the medieval content, with the additions of history, games, and physical education, but the tools of access to classical literature were now employed to enhance and promote further understanding, gaining increasing adherence. Nonetheless, there remained the dangers of the writings of the ancients also being viewed as an alternative form of holy writ: Aristotle's cosmology did not support helio-centralism, and so Galileo must really be in error.

The Casa Giocosa and its companions, still a tiny minority, also gave expression to that occasional but alien notion that learning could be fun. This truly revolutionary ideal was accompanied by an expansion of opportunity: the school was for pupils aged from six to their mid-twenties. However, life continued as it had done for over a thousand years for the bulk of European humanity, untouched by these changes; while the humanist ideal affected secondary education, the reflex of tradition had ensured that the significance of memorisation, form, and discipline continued. The most significant expression of changing attitudes came not in how knowledge might best be acquired and expressed, but how religion might better improve its dominance in the process. Management was still by faith, fear, and instruction. When Martin Luther unleashed his *Ninety-Five Theses* in 1517, he thought that he was merely provoking academic debate. To his astonishment, the greatest educational change agent, printing, had carried his ideas for reform throughout Europe within two months.

As noted above, wood block printing was used to distribute examinations questions. Buddhist, Confucian, and Taoist texts had been produced in China from the 7th century, and by the 11th merchants' workforces could reproduce up to ten thousand pages per day by that method. Even so, it was still cheaper to have books reproduced by hand copy, and so the woodblock method remained dominant in the East until the later 19th century. Although movable metal type was also known earlier in the East, most widespread in Korea, it did not supplant woodblock.

Johannes Gutenberg (c.1400-1468) is usually credited with the European innovation of printing using movable metal type at Mainz (near Frankfurt), but, as happens not infrequently with innovation, there were at least two further collaborators to whom credit should be given. The result was the Gutenberg Bible of 1455. Printing presses sprang up quickly throughout Europe, and then across the world. The explosion of knowledge had truly begun. A single press could now produce 3,600 pages a day, whereas hand copying did not get beyond low double figures per copyist.

The business opportunity was immediately identified by Gutenberg's bookseller neighbours, even before the Gutenberg bible appeared. The first book fair was held in Frankfurt in 1454. Before printed books appeared, Frankfurt was the centre of the manuscripts' sales business. The investor Johan Fust (1400-1466) and printer Peter Schoffer (1425-1503), who had taken over Gutenberg's printing enterprise following a legal dispute, established the fair in a business redevelopment. The model was now a centre for book marketing and the logistics hub for the dissemination of the new products.

The Reformation opened the markets further. Scholars sought new works to study; they also had their own wares to put to market; and booksellers and merchants now had opportunity to gauge market trends, types, probabilities, and possibilities. The Counter Reformation was similarly good for business, as were the schisms of Protestantism, and so the enterprise grew. Frankfurt remained Europe's most important book fair until the 17th century, when Leipzig gained ascendancy due to being better adapted to the needs and nature of the Enlightenment. From the mid-20th century, Frankfurt regained its position as the world's largest trade fair for books, having the greatest numbers of visitors and publishing companies represented.

Although the moving type technical advance, "hot metal" indeed, owed nothing to academic or religious debate, it was immediately dominated by their proponents, with the further consequence of challenging and changing the political establishments. At a succession of strokes, for the next actions were the circulation of the printed translations into the languages of the peoples of Europe, the entire ecclesiastical establishment became open to challenge: the received word of God could now be read, understood, or interpreted by all literate people. The clerical closed shop had been irreversibly opened, despite conservative forces attempting to resist. At last, albeit initially slowly for the indulgence could be dangerous, literate people could now think for themselves, if not necessarily in safety.

One such pioneer was William Tyndale (1494-1536), who produced the first printed English translation of the Bible in 1526, having had to flee his country for European exile to do so. Ten years later, he was betrayed, caught, and imprisoned for heresy in Brussels, subsequently executed by strangulation, after which his body was burnt at the stake. His dying prayer that his king,

Henry VIII (1491-1547), would open his eyes appeared to be effective, for two years later Henry authorised the publication of an English translation of the Bible which was largely that of Tyndale.[2] This conversion is perhaps more attributable to Henry having come across a printed work by chance, Tyndale's 1528 *The Obedience of a Christian Man*, which provided a rationale for his break with Rome. Nonetheless, the means for challenge and change in religion, still the dominant controller of education, were now available.

The issue was their application. The word "humanism" was not known or established until the 19th century, but may be said to describe a large body of thought which can be dated in ancient times from c. 1350 BCE India, thereafter embracing the concepts of Lao Tzu, Buddha, and Confucius. This is in addition to finding expression from 6th century Greece onwards, much amplified from the 1st century BCE through the works of Cicero.

Medieval Islam played an important role in the application of rational thought, contributing significantly to mathematics, architecture, and the preservation, translation, and application of the Greco-Roman classical texts. The Renaissance inspiration was of a return to human, rational values, and approaches in rejection of the domination of dogma, superstitious, or supernatural belief. Rational, empirical, evidential critical thinking characterised the change. Subsequent development of the concept included both secular and religious approaches. At its simplest, humanism looks to evidential based science to understand the world, with the application of improving values the better to inhabit, manage and govern it.

The humanist goals and expression of the early Renaissance had proved to be largely a false dawn for education in general. Although the curriculum had expanded, just as had happened in ancient Rome, form recovered its dominance: grammar and memorising continued to dominate, to the exclusion of physical education and with no concessions to fun. The volcanic effect of the Reformation was to reinforce the emphases on discipline and the expression of the faith. The difficulties created can be seen in the dilemma of the Dutch humanist Catholic priest noted above, Desiderius Erasmus, credited with excellence in his Latin biblical translations and theological writings. Whilst opposing the Church's abuses, he sought reform from within, proposing a middle way, and found himself attacked by both sides.

The spread of printing might be described as the First Internet Age, forming the basis for a social media of its times. Without it, Luther and his ideas would have remained obscure. He would probably have been declared a heretic and subjected to the medievalism of being burnt at the stake, where decency was available only if the executioner first procured exit by strangulation, the act disguised by the rising smoke. As in the social media of our times, the appearance of unity soon shattered, with the trolls here being the extremists of various persuasions who jumped into different aspects of the debate; heretic incendiaries received the real thing in retribution. Both sides burnt each other's champions. In a striking parallel with our own times, the new social media of printing led to an eruption of information which, in turn, had magnifying effects. Secrets and mysteries were much harder to preserve. Once everyone literate could read the Bible and commentaries thereon, the entire basis of society, and consequentially its management, began to change.

Monarchs, especially when in conflict with the Church, speedily exploited the new technology. In England, denying any role for the papacy and placing himself at the head of his newly established State Church, Henry VIII had an urgent need to ensure his subjects' compliance with his novel orthodoxy. His decrees were, therefore, promulgated throughout the country, supported by an endless succession of pamphlets and books. Among the propaganda issued through the agency of Henry's chief minister, Thomas Cromwell (1485-1540), was the seed from which the Brexit plant grew to bedevil the early twenty-first century. Henry's realm became the British Empire. It was a separate, independent part of a European Christendom's geographical expression with an identity all of its own. No matter that its only imperial possession was the beleaguered enclave of Calais, or that its own geographical expression was inaccurate due to Scotland's separate monarchy; as an Emperor, Henry could not be accountable to that suzerain of kings, the Pope. A stand was being made for the independence of royal autocrats and the subordination of state religion to their will, a further step in managerial statecraft.

However, where monarchs found themselves on the same side as ecclesiastical authority - as did Francis I (1494-1547) of France when confronted by a placard campaign employing virulent language against the Church, deeming that to extend to his own position as a Most Christian King - repression followed. Between 1541 and 1544, six Parisian bookseller-publishers were prosecuted, of whom one was tortured and two burnt at the stake. The Sorbonne began in 1542 to compile the first index of forbidden books. While it is ever managerially necessary to maintain a sense of proportion, Francis proceeded further, claiming Protestantism was "high treason against God." The punishments of torture, loss of property, galley slavery and death were justified and inflicted, at the cost of thousands of lives - all to papal approval.

An epitome of the changing times can be found in Alessandro Farnese (1468-1549), beneficiary of a humanist education, pope as Paul III from 1534, usually described as the last pontiff of the Renaissance, and the first of the Counter Reformation. Family connections made him a cardinal at 25, his sister being a mistress of the infamous Borgia pope, Alexander VI. Paul III took a mistress, by whom he fathered five children and one of which he made Duke of Parma. His elevation of two of his grandsons to the rank of cardinal at the ages of 14 and 16 displeased the reform party within the Roman Church, along with the bull fights, horse races, fireworks displays, Vatican balls, banquets and epicurean delights which decorated his papacy. They were only tolerated because of his encouragement of reform and effective administration.

This was a highly important factor, for the Roman Catholic Church can be viewed as the world's first truly multinational business, thus needing sound management. Its command structure followed that of the ancient imperial army. Its advertising budget, from the Lindisfarne Gospels onwards, used high art to produce unforgettable images, ubiquitous marketing triumphs, visible in the stained-glass windows of rural churches, or magnificently in the Sistine Chapel and religious houses of Bruges. The crucifix brand symbol was an overt persuader long before Madison Avenue began trading. The pre-Reformation business of the trading of indulgences, paid pardons to expiate sins, was a solid, lucrative international revenue earner. Religion was inter-continental big business. The ability to pay for masses to be said for their souls and the purchase of indulgences as penance for their sins had been a great income generator, supplemented by dedicated donations, for the monied and aspiring classes. The Catholic enthusiasm for good works and Protestant equation of salvation with meritorious hard work gave new direction to religious expression.

Paul III supported the Council of Trent of 1545 which addressed reform issues such as idolatry while ignoring the most obvious need for reform, the papacy itself, but provided a vehicle of unity to a religion in disarray through the revolt of the Protestants. Blatantly adulterous and corrupt, this pope, excommunicator of England's Henry VIII, nonetheless displayed a moral stance in his administration. The consequences of the Counter Reformation which he instigated were eight civil wars within France, the victims being the Huguenots; a war between France and the Netherlands lasting over 80 years; and the Thirty Years War of 1618-48, which ravaged northern Europe. The beneficial consequences are cited as having been the codification of the liturgy, halting Protestant advance and the reinvigoration and discipline of the Church.

France certainly lost by the emigrations of the Huguenots. Among the countries to gain from the influx of some 200,000 refugees was England with 50,000 and Ireland with 10,000. In addition to the scientists and intellectuals were many skilled craftsmen, who had both the means to move and the resources to contribute to new businesses. Thus, many manufacturing, artistic, and scientific communities were energised. Specialists in such trades as silk weaving, printing, bookbinding, watch making, paper making, with such further crafts as gunsmiths, cabinet makers, and jewellers, revitalised and inspired many industries.

As an example, the further increased persecution of the Protestant Huguenots by Louis XIV (1638-1715) from 1685 having further stimulated their emigration to England, some ten members of the gold and silversmith Harache family arrived in London from France, where their admission to the Goldsmiths Company increased the volume of high-quality produce. Producers and authors of some famous pieces, they dealt in second hand product with banks such as Hoare and Co. (founded in 1672, the UK's oldest bank and the fourth oldest in the world), serving as advisers on metal collateral as well as the realisation of its value. Their family company lasted until the end of the next century; their activities stimulated the expansion of English banking.

The first governor of the Bank of England was Sir John Houblon (1632-1712), the son of Huguenot immigrants, whose community supplied 10% of the Bank's founding capital. At the delicate foundation stage, where Tory landowners were suspicious of Whig initiatives such as the Bank (particularly as to how it might affect property), a reassuring figure was necessary to demonstrate the probity, security, and risk limiting capacities of the new institution. A successful merchant and highly respected in the city, Houblon served also as Lord Mayor, Master of the Grocer's Company, and Lord of the Admiralty during his tenure as Governor. Thus, a model scion of persecuted Protestant dissenters brought solidity and credibility to a new state engine, the financial power of which, in time, would help defeat the country of his family's origin in four successive wars.

Perception of such wider economic and political realities did not deter the Counter Reformation. The Church continued to be concerned with the immediate. Repression was a further favoured tactic, for the Roman Church had found itself to be in considerable difficulties for some time. In 1439-40, Florentine linguist Lorenzo Valla (1407-1457) had proved that the "Donation of Constantine" by which the first Christian Emperor was purported to have bequeathed his western empire to the papacy, thus justifying the temporal power of rule over the Papal States and requirement for the Holy Roman Emperors and monarchs in general to pledge fealty to or obey the popes of the day, was a forgery. Particularly prominent in the 13th century, the scope and influence of the forgery is not to be underestimated. It had given the papacy great power, the effective over-lordship of Christendom, cause of much and great mischief.

In addition, abuses such as the sale of offices, redemption of sins in exchange for currency, and offences as blatant as the papal begetting of children represented a towering monument to abuse and corruption. Most shocking, perhaps, was not that Church and papacy were colossally corrupt, but the widespread acceptance and societal accommodation thereof. What the Church said, went; and if you paid it enough, you usually got what you wanted. That did not apply universally, as Henry VIII of England discovered when other political pressures on the papacy denied him the marriage annulment he sought but, to keep the faithful in order and ensure its revenue streams, the Church had to reform whilst seeking to reinforce discipline. Meanwhile, the printing of the Bible in the vernacular had immense cultural consequences: the dialects of the many German states combined to produce modern German.

In England, the language of Shakespeare and Milton became common parlance through the King James' version, complemented by *The Book of Common Prayer* which, an integral part of the explorers', traders', and colonists' baggage, spread a uniform version of English throughout the world. This was education through the "soft power" route, pervasive, persuasive, and predominant. Singing the same song to the same tune and the integrity of both notes and lyrics was a further consequence of printing to music. Now that exact scores could be printed, there was less memorising, and less need or opportunity for improvisation. Composers now had control, beginning the pathway to the classical and romantic orchestral forms, the popular rather than folk song.

Thus, the Roman Catholic Church, while ridding itself of its worst abuses and indulging in costly purges, inevitably sought to increase its control of the rump of the faith. This meant the advent of the highly disciplinarian methods of organisations such as the Jesuits, the Society of Jesus, yet which embraced the ancient Roman value of oratory. The expression of such oratory, "perfect eloquence," was to be through evangelism for these soldiers of God, but the aims of education were seen also to emphasise uplifting of the whole person, devoted to the common good. Once again, there was clear reversion to the aim of ancient Roman education whilst including the Greek dimension of the whole person. Curriculum was, otherwise, that of the times.

The Jesuits were founded by former soldier Ignatius of Loyola in Spain in 1534, approved by the morally schizophrenic Pope Paul III in 1540, and finally saw a member attain church primacy in 2013 as Francis, the 266th pope. They are the second highest religious order provider of schools, with 324 in 55 countries and 168 tertiary institutions in 40 countries. The largest, the Lassallian educational institutions, have over 560 in over 80 countries, with added elementary schools. Jean-Baptiste de la Salle's (1651-1719) foundation of a school in 1694 included several innovations, teaching in the vernacular and dividing classes according to attainment.[3] Adventurous, they accompanied the spread of Catholicism into the New World.

The first college in Canada was founded in 1635 by Jesuits. On taking possession of the territory, the British forbade the recruitment of members into the order and seized its properties. Invited to return by a pragmatic Canadian government in 1842, the Jesuits focused their efforts on education, founding colleges in several Canadian cities. Determined, perhaps due to being derived from a military background, Loyola's spiritual army was characterised by its unquestioning discipline, loyalty, and perseverance. Vanguard of the Counter Reformation, the Jesuits were firm in their convictions, persevering in actions.

An impression of 17th century boarding Jesuit secondary education in Antwerp for the wealthy is given in John Evelyn's (1620-1706) diary:

> 5th October, 1641. I visited the Jesuits' School, which, for the fame of their method, I greatly desired to see. They were divided into four classes, with several inscriptions over each: as, first, *Ad majorem Dei gloriam;* over the second, *Princeps diligentiae*; the third, *Imperator Byzantiorum;* over the fourth and uppermost, *Imperator Romanum.* Under these, the scholars and pupils and their places, or forms with titles and priority according to their

proficiency. Their dormitory and lodgings above were exceedingly neat. They have a prison for offenders and less diligent; and, in an ample court, to recreate themselves in, is an aviary, and a yard, where eagles, vultures, foxes, monkeys, and other animals are kept, to divert the boys withal at their hours of remission. To this school join the music and mathematical schools, and lastly, a pretty, neat chapel.[4]

Continuing his travel to Italy, Evelyn found Venice University to be flourishing, especially in the study of physics and anatomy, with none of the science lectures "comparable, or so much frequented, as the theatre for anatomy, which is excellently contrived both for the dissector and spectators".[5]

Medical schools were not allowed a dissection license in Britain until 1832, almost two hundred years later, by which time the body snatching trade had reached a peak. Previously, only the corpses of executed criminals had been allowed for dissection. With executions running at around 55 per annum and medical school cadaver demand at ten times that number, supply and demand economics eventually prevailed in licensing. Evelyn was a harbinger of progress; many years before John Locke was to make such practices known and fashionable, Evelyn had characterised his education of his own son with physical and verbal punishments replaced by a system of rewards, emulation, and self-discipline.

The uneven pattern of educational advance among the elite was mirrored, at best, by the general state of elementary and secondary education teaching throughout the 17th and 18th centuries. Incompetent teachers imposed cruel discipline through a pedagogy still based on memory, drill, and rote learning. Meanwhile, as the main sponsors of education, the churches were primarily concerned with their own priorities, leavened by charitable good deeds, rather than the very obvious intellectual and educational needs of their flocks.

Catholicism had preserved its unity and continuity since the Reformation but Protestantism, as is the way of dissent, was of a fissiparous tendency. This produced a triple lurch into emphases on discipline and distinctive provision. As a new form of the Christian religion, Protestantism had to be defended, secured, and established in its rectitude. The sects into which it had split each had their own doctrinal particulars to expound and protect. All the various branches had to demonstrate zeal and resistance to sin. Therefore, the "pagan" content of classical education had to be diluted, with the mechanics of form restored back towards the medieval in a retrograde action. Progress was to be found, however, in Protestantism's insistence on the need for universal education. Commencing in Germany, there was an increasing insistence on vernacular elementary education whereby even the children of the poor – the great majority – could learn to read and write, receiving and understanding religious education and instruction.

By contrast, in the universities and secondary Latin grammar schools by the 17th century, study was becoming increasingly remote from reality. No longer the exclusive tongue of religion, or the language of commerce, nor even the language of communication for academic matters, Latin was declining into niche status, the requirement for its continued study being justified by such supposed virtues as being good for mental exercise.[6] Classical linguistic studies, particularly in schools, continued to hold precedence over the advance of scientific knowledge, method and – crucially – inquiry. Tuition remained similarly retrograde but change, at last, was coming.

We are accustomed to aiding our understanding of the passage of time and the ebb and flow of knowledge by attaching labels of convenience. Thus, this chapter has already travelled from the ancient world to the medieval and past the early modern; we have taken conceptual steps from the Renaissance to the Reformation and are now to embark on the Enlightenment; and while we have noted agricultural husbandry and economics, glimpsed Voyages of Discovery accompanied by commercial and technical innovation, we have yet to encounter the Industrial Revolution. Without being too facetious, it is important to note that these labels and concepts were not relevant or applicable in their times. People did not comment on the loss of their hand-loom weaving living by grumbling, "It's that industrial revolution." People got on with their lives as best they could within the observable conditions of their times. However, they had to manage them.

One such condition was the combination of folk legend, superstition, fear, bigotry, and religious competition in the European witch trials of the 16th and 17th centuries. An indicator of the credulousness of the population and the culture of myth embracing exported to North America, culminated in the Salem trials of 1692-3. Neither formal nor informal education was necessarily accurate or reliable as transmitters of knowledge. Confident of its supremacy, the medieval Church had denied the existence of witchcraft, although the folk myth persisted sufficiently for Pope Alexander IV to have issued a prohibition against prosecutions in 1258. Never a religion nor a competitor to it, this was a collection of superstitions, supernatural lore meant as guidance and protection for everyday living. Yet, the supposed offence was rediscovered, with over 80,000 tried for witchcraft. More than half of those tried were convicted, often resulting in their being burnt alive, commencing from 1550.

Recent research suggests that the phenomenon resulted from the Catholic and Protestant Churches now having to compete for adherents, being thus induced in the religious market to demonstrate their capacities to identify the devil at work, and so to destroy him – or, rather often, her – with as much a display of zeal and vengeance as possible. The religion of choice could be identified by the highest charred body count. The peak witch-burning period coincided with the Counter Reformation, the optimal competition time for adherence collection. Detailed findings showed that 40% of all witchcraft prosecutions occurred in Germanic countries, with the second highest figure being for Scotland, both areas where religious denominations were struggling for supremacy. Contrastingly, the solidly Catholic bases of Italy, Ireland, Spain, and Portugal had only 6% of the collective European total.[7] Free choice in religion was a dangerous matter.

Superstition lingered long in countryside outposts, however. The Baptist "Prince of Preachers" Charles Spurgeon (1834-1892) reported in 1872 that "the public generally were not aware of the extent to which there was a belief in witchcraft, especially in the rural districts." His examples included "a man professing to be a white wizard, and an old woman paying him to cure her bewitched pigs by cutting off their tails," and the credulous "farmer, who had a large number of acres, but a small quantity of brains." These strictures were accompanied by a state education inspector's report which found the condition of education and morals in Norfolk to be "deplorable beyond measure, complete with juvenile depravity".[8]

Such medieval folk practices as "sin eating" had been exported to the American colonies, continuing in some of the English and Welsh rural areas and dying out only in the late 19th century. Sin consumption was probably a pagan-derived form of post-mortem insurance where, through the media of bread and ale consumed at a funerary occasion, an expired person's sins were taken aboard by the sin eater, this being a low person of probably ill repute, so fitted to carry the extra burden of guilt. The pre-Reformation Catholic practice of selling absolution from sins had been translated, at the bottom of the market, into a cheap form of sin garbage disposal. Superstition is as marketable a commodity as warped theology in ill-educated communities.

Yet, the "cunning men" and "wise women" found in many a village might better be viewed as hedge medical practitioners, healers, and therapists. Fortune telling mixed with advice; herbal remedies with incantations, which were effectively instructions for use; recovery of stolen goods' locations or veterinary applications: useful, cheap services. Inherited abilities, real or believed, were employed for centuries as part of the social fabric, performing helpful if unreliable functions. Thus, the lower orders had ways of managing themselves. The Church, however, had always disliked popular magic, for it had people-management purposes of its own.

The circumstances in which educational reformers such as Joseph Lancaster (1778-1838) were born were a combination of many factors and influences. A time of emergent energy and opportunity, whilst still restricted by powerful and historic forces, was also bound with such lasting superstitions. Effect, influence, and futures could not be known. Life could be dealt with only as it appeared. Tyndale had done something obvious, courageous, and world changing - but paid for it with his life. Galileo had saved his life with a recantation worthy of the holder of the keys of the Catholic heaven. Peter had denied Christ under duress. Now, Christ's earthly vicar had compelled Galileo to deny science. It was a dangerous life at the top of society and learning; just as it was at the bottom, where folk medicine practice in the company of a cat could be fatal. Popular education was not yet a significant societal agenda item. The topic alone remained dangerous.

Juan Luis (John Ludovic) Vives (1493-1540) was not the first educator to experience that reality. Appointed by Henry VIII tutor to his daughter Mary (1516-1558) the Catholic Catalan Vives, from a converted Jewish family, is little known today although awarded yet another of those ubiquitous patronymics as the "father of modern psychology." It is not known if Freud knew of or read him; unlikely that the current management psychologists are acquainted with his theory and practice; yet their occupation – and license to gain income – began with Vives in the 16th century. He also wrote a highly regarded Latin textbook and was an advocate of education for all women.

His controversial *De Institutione Feminae Christiane* ("The Instruction of a Christian Woman," 1524; revised, 1538) drew directly from Plato and Aristotle on women's intellectual equality with men and set forward a cautious if restrictive humanist approach to the education of girls.

**Juan Luis Vives**

Vives argued for the education of all women, irrespective of social status or ability. Immediately recognised as a practical guide to universal education - for the work progressed from childhood to adolescence, marriage, and widowhood - his book achieved wide recognition. That width, however, was still confined to a restricted literate sector, to which the teachers of the time did not necessarily belong. Nonetheless, it was a significant step along the education management road: the tutor to the then-heir to the English throne was in print, with a whole book devoted to the cause of universal education for girls.

The book was dedicated to Catherine of Aragon (1485-1535), first wife to Henry VIII. Vives had probably realised the possible career move, like that of Aristotle to the tutorship of Alexander of Macedon, of becoming mentor to a monarch. He was equipped for the task in his diagnosis of social need, for he also wrote of rational teaching and learning systems, and the relief of urban poverty. Thomas More and Erasmus praised his work, the latter confessing his expectation that Vives would surpass him. The first scholar to analyse the psyche directly, attracting the further label "godfather of psychoanalysis," he also connected cleanliness and well-being to health, disapproved of the use of the mentally ill for sport, and instead recommended medication or understanding for their treatment. Vives was one of Comenius's most significant sources in the historical labelling world - perhaps one of the "godfathers of education management." Intellectually gifted he may have been, but he was not politically astute. He inevitably backed the wrong side in Henry's matrimonial dispute, lost office and had to flee to Bruges, where he died.

However humanist his education of Mary I, upon gaining the throne she had her father's body disinterred. The remains were burnt, this being due punishment for Henry VIII's heresy against the Roman Church. An inveterate incendiary, during her five-year reign she had 284 Protestant dissenters burnt at the stake, at a rough average of one per week for every year of her fanatical reign (1553-1558), dedicated to the bloody restoration of Catholicism. A further 34 died in prison, with nine prosecuted posthumously. In mitigation, thousands more were killed in France.

There, the issue was the very personal question: how are you going to be saved? The Protestant answer was by grace, arguing that religion as practised by Catholics was little more than a confidence trick; Luther had shown the extent of its abuses, Calvin the path to salvation. There had been a gradual revulsion against the Jesuits and Catholic authoritarianism. France was held together by its monarchy, now suffering the new minority of Charles IX (1550-1574) under the Regency of his mother, Catherine de Medici. Power and salvation being inextricably linked, Catherine tried unavailingly to reconcile Catholics with Protestants. With the Protestant leadership unable to trust their Catholic counterparts, regal mother and son appear to have approved the subsequent culling of the Protestant leadership and many of their followers.

The St Bartholomew's Day massacre of 23-24 August, extending into October 1572, alone claimed somewhere between 5,000 and 30,000 Protestant lives, killing more Christians in a single incident than throughout the entire period of the Roman Empire. Between two and three thousand were slain in Paris alone, many more in the provincial cities. Such was the bitterness of the dispute that people saw their neighbours as vermin, to whom they could do as they liked. The choices offered were stark: death, exile, or abjuration. There was no return to Protestantism for the abjurers. Although the cost of lost Huguenot (Protestant) talent was high, in strictly religious terms the brutal policy worked.

Major change had been achieved and European society redirected, albeit in a rough and ready management fashion. Policy, opinion, and management in early modern times dealt in certainties. Management by certainties bred oppressors and those willing to be sacrificed. Burning at the stake was meant to give a taste of hellfire, so offering the recalcitrant the opportunity to recant and save their souls. Refusal meant martyrdom in the faith and security in heaven. Monarchs could not tolerate denial of their divine standing, as that removed their right to rule. Such conflicts of absolutes bred new forms of organisation. In England, the rejection of Catholicism became part of nation building, thus burnishing Protestant identity. In France, Catholicism became further entrenched.

## FOOTPRINT:
### Religious Upheaval, Stasis and Pragmatism

- **The dominant monotheism of the West provided its own managerial control unity until entropy produced violent change.**

- **The greatest innovations had come via the competitor religion of Islam, but its restrictive social requirements inhibited full benefit.**

- **Pragmatism was demonstrated at the high levels of Medici banking and Machiavellian political theory by burning dissenters and sin eating at the low.**

# Endnotes

[1] *Psalms 9:1, 96:10* and *Chronicles 16:30; Psalm 104:5;* and *Ecclesiastes 1:5.*

[2] Tyndale's input to the 1611 King James version of the Bible, produced by 54 further scholars, has been estimated at 83% for the New Testament and 76% for the Old Testament.

[3] Known as The Brothers of the Christian Schools, the Lasallians are not to be confused with the Congregation of Christian Brothers, an Irish foundation dating from 1802 and also engaged in education.

[4] Evelyn, John, *The Diary of John Evelyn, Vol. I*, Project Gutenberg e-book #41218, 29 October 2012, pp 35-6. The Latin translations are: to the great glory of God; diligent first citizen (*princeps,* the early legionary designation, distinguishing a premier citizen and thus being the title adopted by Augustus to disguise his *de facto* assumption of imperial status); Byzantine emperor; Roman emperor).

[5] *Ibid,* p.147. Italy had a history of medical progress. Salerno's medical school, begun in the 9th century, reaching the height of its fame in the 11th to 13th, synthesised recovered ancient Greek, Byzantine and Arab learning in medicine, achieving considerable advance. As the University of Naples expanded, Salerno's influence

declined, but its learning and more sophisticated techniques had greatly improved medicine in the peninsular.

[6] It is surprising perhaps that the academic obsession with Latin persisted for so long. It is one of this author's minor achievements to have proposed and gained the unanimous support of a general meeting of the Student Union of the University of Manchester in 1967 for the abolition of the compulsory study of Latin as part of the modern history degree course. The university acquiesced, substituting classical studies, preserving its dignity and the continued employment of the academic staff affected.

[7] Leeson, Peter T and Russ, Jacob W. "Witch Trials," *Economic Journal*, 16 August 2017.

[8] Huitson, John. *A Plan for Education: the British and Foreign School Society and Elementary Education in England and Wales 1814-1870*, p. 40.

John Amos Comenius 1592–1670

# CHAPTER TEN

# ENLIGHTENMENT COMES TO EDUCATION

Vives was undoubtedly a precursor, whatever the foibles of his royal pupil, but truly significant educational advance can be said to have commenced with a Czech from Moravia, John Amos Comenius. Pursuit by the Counter Reformation during the chaos of the Thirty Years' War because of his theology only caused him to become peripatetic, living and working extensively throughout Europe, extending even to Sweden, the Netherlands, and England. This effectively accelerated the spread of his ideas, especially the educational.[1]

A further Tudor tutor, Roger Ascham (1515-1568), of Latin and Greek to the Princess Elizabeth and Latin Secretary, responsible for her correspondence in that language to Mary I, wrote *The Scholemaster* in response to a government colleague's request for advice on how best to have his son educated. Writing within the home tuition and classics context, Ascham advocated gentleness and persuasion in tuition, with translation and explanation of classical authors instead of rote learning as the preferred method. John Brinsley the Elder (1581-1624) adapted Ascham's methods to the grammar school, adding emphasis on the vernacular and the need for teacher training in his *Ludus Literarius* of 1612, anticipating here some of the ideas of the Moravian.

Those ideas were not all his own, however. The thought of John Amos Comenius (1592-1670) derived from a variety of sources but, for convenience and with acknowledgment to the scholars of the Herborn Academy, it is the published ideas of this philosopher, theologian, and pedagogue which will be summarised here, for they commenced the Enlightenment in education. Comenius's contributions were theoretically, practically, and methodologically exceptional. The dawning of rationalism and replacement of superstition and dogma by the intellectual movement known as the Enlightenment was complemented by the advances achieved by Comenius. Drawing upon the investigatory principles and thought processes of Bacon on science, and Descartes on philosophy, he was the first systematically to apply their approaches throughout education. Beyond doubt or dispute, Comenius was the founding father of education management.

A powerful group of intending education reformers invited Comenius to England in 1641. Among their number were one of the founders of parliamentary democracy, John Pym (1584-1643), the Bishop of Lincoln, and Robert Boyle (1627-1691), the "father of modern chemistry" and best known for Boyle's Law concerning the relationship between gas and pressure.[2] The plan was to establish the Pansophic College, probably at the government owned but then vacant Chelsea College, with the mission to be the general headquarters of a campaign against ignorance, effectively a world university. Unfortunately, the ignorance campaign was usurped by those of the English Civil War in 1642, the attempt abandoned, and Comenius left to continue his writings elsewhere. However, the visit did perhaps bear later fruit.

One of those who met Comenius was John Winthrop (1606-1676), younger son of the Governor of Massachusetts. There had been discussion in London about the native inhabitants, for whom Comenius had sketched a whole plan for their education and conversion to Christianity. Winthrop took Comenius's plans and text with him on his return, where the materials were conveyed to the newly founded Harvard College, then built of wood but with a brick hostel for Native Americans. The London talks have been credited with providing a beginning for the Royal Society, which received its charter in 1662. As this was followed by similar foundations in Paris, Berlin, and elsewhere in Europe with the institution of mutual correspondence on matters scientific, irrespective of warfare, some approximation to Comenius's vision was begun on both sides of the Atlantic.[3]

The full title of Comenius's appropriately named *Didactica Magna*, completed c.1631 but not published until 1657 is instructive of itself, an early example of the management mission statement:

> The Great Didactive Setting forth The Whole Art of Teaching All Things to All Men or a certain Inducement to found such Schools in all the Parishes, Towns and Villages of every Christian Kingdom, that the entire Youth of both Sexes, none being excepted, shall Quickly, Pleasantly & Thoroughly Become learned in the Sciences, Pure in Morals, trained to Piety, and in this manner instructed in all things necessary for the present and for the future life, in which, with respect to everything which is suggested, its

> Fundamental Principles are set forth from the essential nature of the matter,
> its Truth is Proved by examples from the several mechanical arts, in order
> clearly set forth in years, months, days and hours, and, finally An Easy and
> Sure Method is shown, by which it can be pleasantly brought into existence.[4]

Comenius was very clear in his aims and objectives, too. He began with a
classical quotation, citing the injunction of Pittacus: *"Know thyself"*, that
advice also set in stone at Apollo's temple at Delphi.[5] This he extended into
ruling oneself, so directing into knowing God through scripture and hence
the expression and renewal of that knowledge through education, itself to
be a universal experience. The *Didactica* formed a general theory of
education, this on the further principle of "education according to nature,"
extending into the organisation and management of a school system. That
arrangement, from the stages of nursery, elementary, and secondary schools
to college and university, remains the standard for much of the world. Its
adjunct of the concept of life-long learning accompanied the structure.

The language, sentiment and purpose were straightforwardly egalitarian,
clear in religious conviction:

> 1. The following reasons will establish that not the children of the rich, but
>    of alike, boys and girls, both noble and ignoble, rich and poor, in all
>    cities and towns, villages and hamlets should be sent to school.
> 2. In the first place, all who have been born to man's estate have been born
>    with the same end in view, namely, that there may be men, that is to say,
>    rational creatures, the lords of other creatures, and the images of their
>    Creator. All, therefore, must be brought to a point at which, being
>    properly imbued with wisdom, virtue and piety they may usefully
>    employ the present life and be worthily prepared for that to come ... for
>    love is in direct ratio to our knowledge.[6]

He was similarly direct regarding women and social equality:

> They are endowed with equal sharpness of mind and capacity for knowledge
> (often with more than the opposite sex), and they are able to attain the
> highest positions. ... If any ask, 'What will be the result if artisans, rustics,
> porters and even women become lettered?' I answer, If this universal
> instruction of youth be brought about by the proper means, none of these
> will lack the material for thinking, choosing, following and doing good
> things.[7]

Equally blunt was his criticism of schooling:

the method used in instructing the young has generally been so severe that schools have been looked on as terrors for boys and shambles for their intellects and the greater number of the students, having contracted a dislike for learning and for books, have hastened away … those who remained at school … did not receive a serious or comprehensive education, but a preposterous and wretched one.[8]

Adamant that teaching, like everything else, should follow natural order, he fulminated that "the natural order, that the matter comes first and the form follows, is not observed. Everywhere the exact opposite is to be found".[9] He then identified the errors, such as the primacy of grammar over experience of language, and provided both general guidance and subsequent example texts.

Taking the natural approach, from his own understanding of children, he set about providing that which would secure their interest and even enjoyment. However, he still emphasised the very obvious need "That nothing should be taught to the young, unless it is not only permitted but actually demanded by their age and mental strength".[10]

His complementary work in further publications, particularly in textbooks, expanded upon curriculum and pedagogic method. His approach was entirely novel, embracing such concepts as education might be interesting and fun, with his *Orbis Pictus* of 1658 being the first illustrated textbook for children. All his texts followed the same fundamental ideas. As befitted his peripatetic experience, foreign languages were to be learnt through the vernacular. Following the natural behaviour of children, objects were used both to introduce a child to new language and the worlds to which they, in turn, related. Thus, the child was afforded access to social and physical environments, and this was complemented by instruction in religion, morality, and the classics. The manner of the acquisition of knowledge was to be pleasurable, the right and experience of education to be universal.

Comenius further addressed himself to the issue which, a century and a half later, Joseph Lancaster was to take into practical effect:

I maintain that it is not only possible for one teacher to teach several hundred scholars at once, but that it is also essential.[11]

Large classes were one answer, but he had another idea:

If matters be arranged in the following manner, one teacher will easily be able to cope with a very large number of children. That is to say… If he

divide the whole body into classes, groups of ten, for example, each of which
should be controlled by a scholar, who is, in his turn, controlled by one of
higher rank, and so on.... It is not necessary for the teacher to hear the
lessons or inspect the books of each individual scholar; since he has the
leaders of divisions to assist him, and each of these can inspect the scholars
in his own division. The teacher, as chief inspector, should give his attention
first to one scholar, then to another.[12]

To Comenius, proper teaching meant "ease, thoroughness, and rapidity." It
focused upon objects to generate interest and imagination, from which
language could be drawn and the memory stimulated, thus leading to the
retention of knowledge. Practical learning meant learning by doing: learning
to paint was by painting, writing by writing, dance by dancing. Here was
the practical wisdom advocated by Aristotle. Teachers should not, he warns,
"leave any subject until it is thoroughly understood." That was balanced,
however, by further practical advice. If learning a language, a complete
vocabulary was not necessary. Even a linguistic master such as Cicero had
confessed to not knowing many of the words common to artisans although
he had said that he could not teach anyone oratory who had not first learned
to talk.

Morality was to be learned from the wisdom of the past but practised in the
present by constantly doing the right thing, family and close associates
having the duty to be exemplars. Not all was progressive religious
liberalism: contrary to his attachment to the classics, "pagan books,"
lascivious works such as the poetry of Ovid, were to be removed from
schools. Punishment, however, was not to be an act of retribution, for
whatever was done could not be undone, but administered as a deterrent to
discourage the error from being repeated.[13] He progresses through further
pedagogic methods, some easily characterised as "tips for teachers," others
on the dialectic model with students in divisions correcting each other's
work on an adversarial basis, but the whole comprising a quite formidable
body of managerial work.

It remains a monument to education theory and practice, the commencement
of education as a subject and discipline in its own right. He extends to the
four-tiered system of schooling concluding with university and travel, and a
final religious peroration.[14] Within that very forest of practical wisdom, an
essential seed had been sown. It was to take the entrepreneurial street-wisdom,
skill, and sheer nerve of a youth from the depths of Southwark to realise the
advice of Comenius's own mentor, Pittacus: "Know thine opportunity."

This was a complete revolution from the medieval system and methodology, helping to secure the crucial Protestant commitment to universal education and indicating release from the drudgery of the school experience endured by children for centuries, as exemplified as late as 1599 in Jacques's sad speech in Shakespeare's *As You Like It:*

> And then the whining schoolboy, with his satchel
> And shining morning face, creeping like snail
> Unwillingly to school.

It is, however, one thing to produce a clearly, largely correct, well thought through, creative, and universally beneficial process; it is quite another for it to be noticed, recognised, or acted upon. Initially, the work was ridiculed. It was not until much later, after isolated examples, that illustrated books for children became common, together with the use of objects in teaching. Until then, *aides memoire* such as the hornbook continued as primers for children's study. This originated in England around 1450. It consisted of texts such as the alphabet, Roman numerals, prayers, or other religious material pasted upon both sides of a short-handled wooden board, covered with a transparent sheet of horn or mica.

In another context of numerals' and civilisations' clash, to Joseph Stalin the question was attributed, "How many divisions has the Pope?" Pursued by them and their consequences rather than in control thereof, Comenius lacked the power, presence, or patrons to emphasise and enforce the sense of his message. It was not until the mid-19$^{th}$ century, long after his death, that the full importance of his approach was recognised and many of his ideas widely accepted and adopted. This circumstance complicates and illustrates the fallibility of attaching labels to historical events and persons. Comenius preceded Joseph Lancaster, a main object of the second book of this management study, but his work was less known. In practical terms, Lancaster takes precedence, leading to the *reductio ad absurdum* of "who's the father" of education management? For if it is further observed that as Lancaster's contribution has been similarly neglected, like that of Vives, Machiavelli, and Cato, the exploratory term of "pioneer" becomes possibly appropriate; bearing in mind the business dictum attributed to John D. Rockefeller: "never pioneer."

Meanwhile, attitudes to curriculum, manners, and behaviour at England's oldest universities continued in the traditional manner. The antiquarian, natural philosopher, early archaeologist, and incomparable gossip John Aubrey (1626-1697) includes memoirs of academic life in his *Brief Lives.*[15]

Of Thomas Batchcroft (1572-1662), Master of Gonville and Caius College, Cambridge, he wrote:

> Memorandum: In Sir Charles Scarborough's time (he was of Caius College) Dr… (the head of that house) would visit the boyes' chambers, and see what they were studying; and Charles Scarborough's genius led him to mathematics, and he was wont to be reading of Clavius upon Euclid. The old Dr. Had found in the title "…e Societate Jesu" and was much scandalized at it. Sayd he, "By all means leave-off this author, and read Protestant mathematical books.[16]

The method of inculcating knowledge by violence continued, even in higher education, entry to which began in the early teenage years. Aubrey records:

> At Oxford (and I do believe the like at Cambridge) the rod was frequently used by the tutors and deans on his pupils, till bachelaurs of Arts; even gentlemen-commoners. The one Dr. I knew (Dr Hannibal Potter, Trin. Coll. Oxon) right well that whipt his scholar with his sword by his side when he came to take leave of him to goe to the Innes of Court.[17]

Although Aubrey was an opponent of corporal punishment, wholly ahead of his times in believing that a school should be "the house of play and pleasure," as a last resort allowed the use of "finger stocks" (thumbscrews).

**'Finger Stocks'**

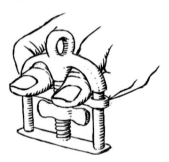

Heavily influenced in his writings on education by Comenian ideas and those of Samuel Hartlib (1600-1662) and John Hall of Durham (1627-1656), Aubrey opposed the dominance of the classics, favoured the primacy of mathematics and science, and demonstrated humanity in his insight:

> I very well remember that excessive whipping when I was a little child did make a convulsive pain in my tender brain which doubtless did me a great deal of hurt. 'Tis a very ill thing to cross children; it makes them ill natured.[18]

It did little for adults either. Alexander Gill (1565-1635), high master of St Paul's, attempted also to impose authority beyond the school gates. He was sued for whipping a colonel for urinating in the street. Another aggrieved person would not pass the school without an armed guard. Ralph Kettell (1563-1643), President of Trinity College at Oxford, was practical in his management of his college, always carrying scissors in his muff so that he might cut over-long hair of scholars, of which he much disapproved, and ensuring that his college had the finest supply of beer. He had observed that scholar drunkenness was greatest when they went out into the town to drink. His higher quality alcohol ensured that they preferred to drink at Trinity, which enjoyed the lowest university drunkenness rate in consequence.[19] Dionysus management is a continuing theme.

Richard Allestree (d.1682), royalist soldier and divine, wrote or contributed to *The Whole Duty of Man* in 1658, which contained the admonition: "The new borne babe is full of the stains and pollutions of sin which it inherits from our first parents through our loins." Original sin must thus be punished. Ferocity justified, parental and household violence was common, as were punishments such as the forced drinking of urine for bed-wetting, confinement in a cellar and flogging just "for nothing." Of some two hundred counsels on advice for child rearing before 1700, only three omitted the recommendation that fathers should beat their children.[20] The children of the aristocracy might have only a brief time at home, barely knowing their parents. Out-sourced to wet nurses from birth, after an eighteen-month weaning period, a child could be dispatched to school as a boarder at six. Parental attention was limited.

Productive in the parental creation of abstracts, the dominant early Enlightenment philosopher John Locke (1632-1704), "father of Liberalism," contributed to the burgeoning theoretical debate with his *Some Thoughts Concerning Education* of 1693.[21]

### John Locke

Locke's *Thoughts* was a best-seller of its times, running to 53 editions in the 18th century alone and serving as the standard philosophical text for almost a century. A core message was the desirability of the exposure of a child to ideas and experience; another, the rejection of corporal punishment except in the case of obstinacy. The intended reach was limited, however: this was how the aristocracy and gentry, subsequently broadened to the

middle classes, might best educate their offspring.

His proposition was that the mind of a child was a *tabula rasa,* a blank slate, without innate ideas. Thus, opposing the Catholic-originated but Protestant-emphasised doctrine of original sin, Locke's objective was the education of that mind, for which he put forward three methods: development of a healthy body, a virtuous character, and an appropriate curriculum. Drawing from Aristotle and Juvenal's *Satire X,* Locke sought *"mens sana in corpore sano"*: a healthy mind in a healthy body; balanced personal management development.[22]

Expression was to be enjoyable and useful, with curriculum including science, geography, astronomy, and anatomy, and the learning of modern languages were to gain presence; choices of types of education were, moreover, to be useful, suited to aptitudes. Children's aptitudes could be discovered through parental observation and their activities and interests. His concern for the impressions which could be made from the association of ideas extended to admonishment of domestic servants who might peddle tales of sprites and goblins, so misdirecting a child into the ways of darkness. The child was to be encouraged to seek knowledge. While recognising the reality of the condition of childhood, Locke still desired children to become adult as soon as possible. Virtue, in his construct, being a combination of rationality and self-denial, Locke's goal was swift escape from the irrational. Girls were to have the same opportunity for education as boys - although treated differently, with the expectation that their education would be by tutor, taking place at home.

Locke's exploration of the mind and mental state produced the idea of its being composed of "faculties," these having a relation to aptitude. Although the theory was subsequently disproved, the word interestingly survives in the organisational structures of institutions of higher education. Locke's conception of faculties included perception, discrimination, comparison, thought, and memory. Knowledge arose, Locke believed, when these faculties were exercised. A function of schooling was to train the faculties, with subjects such as mathematics or Latin thought to be particularly suitable as mental exercises. Not all of Locke's thought was progressive, for this error could serve as a justification for the prolongation of medieval method. The empirical and experiential aspects of his work, with the insistence upon learning from objects, reinforced the advocacy of Comenius and emphasised the trend towards object-lessons: to pictures, models, relics and to the nature observation and field trips which slowly began to balance traditional learning from books.

Part of the popularity of Locke's educational philosophy probably derived from the eminence in progressive ideas of its author. His empiricism, classical republicanism, and liberal theory are mirrored clearly in the United States' Declaration of Independence. The famous phrase "life, liberty, and the pursuit of happiness", arising from his consideration of rights in his two treatises on government, complemented his thought on governance as expressed in the doctrine of the separation of powers. Thomas Jefferson nominated him, with Bacon and Newton, as one of the three greatest men who ever lived.

A very different great man to Locke, the Francophone Genevan Jean-Jacques Rousseau (1712-1778), turbulent philosopher, novelist, composer, and hero of the Jacobins of the French Revolution, had predictably very different ideas on education.

**Jean-Jacques Rousseau**

He believed that a child grew and developed in all aspects, much like a plant. Holding that the child has innate goodness, it followed that all social institutions distort children to fit their requirements and therefore interfere with natural growth; so, education's aim should instead be the promotion of that natural growth.

This completely opposite approach to established practice began what we now term "child centred learning", but the extremity of Rousseau's views meant that the teacher's function became almost observational. He advocated development of the senses and the physical until between the ages of 12 and 15. This is when he thought the intellect began to develop, at which time study of particular subjects became appropriate.

That learning, however, was to be via the child's exploration of his environment, driven by whatever interested him; he was not to be instructed, rather he had to discover information for himself. Only from 15 was learning from books applicable. The manner of any instruction was also reviewed. As all children were different and developed at different rates, the faculties' theory was rejected as it stunted natural growth. Schools should, therefore, provide a controlled environment in which natural growth could occur. The teacher's function was to provide guidance into society. The exaggerated freedoms and primacy of individuality were matched at the opposite pole by the lack of recognition for social integration and need.

Expressed in his novel *Emile* in 1762, Rousseau's utopian treatise on education, while holding that a child could educate itself to be good under supervision, conceded this to be unrealisable because the evil of the world, as symbolised by Paris, was unavoidable, thus being bound to fail. *The Social Contract* of the same year opened with his most famous slogan: "man is born free but is everywhere in chains," by which he meant that modern states repress the birth right of freedom and humanity's natural goodness. While this made him the darling of the revolutionary Jacobins of France, it opposed the phrase originator Hobbes's insistence on the human tendency to conflict.

That the Jacobins lionised the wrong hero was first anonymously exposed by Voltaire with the revelation that Rousseau had fathered five illegitimate children, all of whom he had abandoned on the steps of a hostel for foundlings. Such hypocrisy as embracing then abandoning both his native Calvinism and its antidote of Catholicism, in a context of conflict between money and morality, made an increasingly erratic Rousseau a difficult hero, at best.

Rousseau's revolutionary tastes were indulged considerably, and outposts of his ideas did find expression, but their prime service was the rejection of the old, stultifying systems and the further opening of consideration of the state, the nature of childhood, the educative processes best suited to need, personal, and societal. Nonetheless, the educational debate was widening, and business responded to opportunity.

Trade remained dominated among the modernising societies of the 16th to 18th centuries by mercantilism, the theory which measured a country's strength by a favourable balance of trade, supported by stores of gold, tariffs and protectionism. While Adam Smith's market revelations were to come, the new and growing education business illustrated the strength of markets.

# Endnotes

[1] Comenius was the last bishop of the Unity of the Brethren Church, an evangelical descendant belief of the followers of Jan Hus (1372-1415) - an early reformer, now mainly known as the Moravian Church.

[2] John Williams (1582-1650), Bishop of Lincoln 1621-1641, Archbishop of York from 1642-1650, was an active parliamentarian, imprisoned in the Tower of London from 1636-1640, for subornation of perjury. As civil war loomed, Pym favoured the Puritan side while Williams attempted a middle course. The young Robert Boyle, son of the richest man in England (the Earl of Cork), was in London learning Italian, preparatory to a visit (during which in 1642 he was in Florence when Galileo died there, an event which much concentrated his mind on science). Talent, and financial and political skills were all briefly assembled for a major education management initiative but almost immediately dispersed by events.

[3] Paton, John Lewis. *The Tercentenary of Comenius's Visit to England, 1592-1671*, http://www.eschol- ar.manchester.ac.uk/api/datastream?publicationPid=uk-ac.

[4] Comenius, Johann Amos. trans. M W Keatinge, *Didactica Magna*, London, Adam and Charles Black, 1907; pdf Cornell University Library: http://www.archive.org/details/cu31924031053709.

[5] Comenius, *op. cit.,* p. 25.

[6] *Ibid*, p.66

[7] *Ibid,* pp.68-9.

[8] *Ibid,* p.77.

[9] *Ibid,* pp. 115-116.

[10] *Ibid,* p.138.

[11] *Ibid,* p.164.

[12] *Ibid,* p. 166.

[13] *Ibid,* p. 192, 204-5, 249.169.

[14] *Ibid,* pp. 183

[15] Ed. Clarke, Andrew. *'Brief Lives', chiefly of Contemporaries, set down by John Aubrey, between the Years 1669 & 1696,* Clarendon Press, Oxford, 1898.

[16] *Ibid,* Vol. I, p.94. Sir Charles Scarborough (1615-1694) was physician to Charles II, James II, William III and Mary II.

[17] *Ibid,* Vol. II, p.171. Hannibal Potter (1592-1664) was successively student, fellow, and president of Trinity College, Oxford; installed in 1643, removed by a Parliamentary Visitation in 1647, restored in 1660. During the Cromwellian ascendancy, he lost his then last clerical living, a curacy, as retribution for reading the *Book of Common Prayer*.

[18] Ed. Stephens, J E. 1972. *Aubrey on Education*, Vol. 1. London and Boston, Mass.: Routledge and Kegan Paul, p.8.

[19]*Ibid*, Vol.II, p.20

[20] Plumb, J H. 1975. "The New World of Children in Eighteenth-Century England," *Past and Present,* Part 67, Cambridge University Press, p.65.

[21] Locke, John. 1693. *Some Thoughts Concerning Education,* London: A and J Churchill at the Black Swan at Paternoster-row. Retrieved 28 July 2016 via Google Books.

[22] *You should pray for a healthy mind in a healthy body.*
*Ask for a stout heart which has no fear of death,*
*and deems length of days the least of Nature's gifts that can endure any toil,*
*that knows neither wrath nor desire and thinks*
*the woes and hard labours of Hercules better than*
*the loves and banquets and downy cushions of Sardanapalus*
*\* What I commend to you, you can give to yourself;*
*For assuredly, the only road to a life of peace is virtue.*
* Represented as Ashurbanipal (r. 669-631 BCE), the last king of Assyria but probably confused with his brother, Shamush-shum-ukin, notoriously characterised as a figure of decadent self-indulgence who died in circumstances of orgiastic destruction. The 1827-8 Delacroix painting of *The Death of Sardanapalus* is in the Philadelphia Museum of Art.

# CHAPTER ELEVEN

# APPLIED RELIGIOUS AND SECULAR THEORY

René Descartes (1596-1650), often known as the father of modern philosophy, is accredited as one of the key figures of the Scientific Revolution, a series of events which marked the emergence of modern science.

Developments in mathematics, physics, astronomy, biology, human anatomy, and chemistry transformed the views of society about nature. A most determined rationalist, Descartes together with Leibniz and Spinosa, although they differed, were crucial in the bestowal of the Age of Reason title upon their times.

**René Descartes**

Known also for his development of algebraic geometry, Descartes' rationalism was opposed by the empiricists Hobbes, Locke, and Hume. Empiricism holds that all knowledge is acquired through experience. Descartes' most famous existential philosophical statement of "cogito ergo sum," "I think therefore I am," reflected his deep interest in epistemology, the study of the nature and applications of knowledge. In his own construction of a system of knowledge, Descartes discarded perception as unreliable, concentrating instead on deduction as the sole method, reasoning from one or more premises to reach a conclusion.

Employing such method as theology and physics, Descartes investigated the connection between mind and body, and how they interact. Mind and body, he concluded, were distinct but closely joined. According to Descartes, two substances are really distinct when each of them can exist apart from the other. He reasoned that God is distinct from humans, and the body and mind of a human are also distinct from one another. The mind or soul was a thinking entity, the body, unthinking. His interpretation of dualism broke from the Aristotelian teleological concept whereby phenomena were explicable by the end of their expression, thus admitting the new science of Galileo and Copernicus, but leaving open religious belief and the immortal soul through the power of the mind. The mind could exist without the body, although they were closely joined, but the body could not exist without the mind. His contention that the mind held innate knowledge was opposed by Locke.

Descartes' dualism coincided with his accession to celebrity. Baruch Spinoza (1632-1677) held a diametrically opposite view.

In Spinoza's perspective, the emergence of the universe must have been from a single, ultimate cause. The acceptance of such an eventuality meant that humans, their souls, and nature are merely aspects of a single reality, some single substance, governed by the same forces. By extension of the thought, it means that God and creation are part of the same substance. This means that humans with nature participate therein too, and that mind and soul are the same substance as matter. Thus, all is matter, all is mind, and everything is God. Such ideas were not only heretical within the theologies of the time (including Spinoza's own Jewish context), the deeper their consideration, the more society itself was threatened.

**Benedictus (Baruch) Spinoza**

Over fifty biblical verses, from both testaments, give humankind dominion over all the earth and our fellow animal, plant, and mineral inhabitants. If nature was ultimately the same substance as God, then people's claim to dominion was impossible to sustain. Deprived of its authority to do as it wished to its environment and fellow beings, humanity's behaviour required radical review and revision. That was several steps too far. The convenient Cartesian fudge gained an acceptance, whereas Spinoza suffered an assassination attempt and expulsion from two religions: Judaism and Christianity.

Science itself was to prove Spinoza right on several determining issues. Mind being resultant from material behaviour makes it a part of matter, humans share evolutionary origins expressed through (yet to be discovered) DNA with plants and animals, and all inhabitants of the universe are subject to its physical provisions. The cognitive and behavioural shifts necessary to embrace Spinoza's view were much too large and challenging, even for a movement as powerful as the Enlightenment to embrace. Descartes' dualism came to define the Enlightenment, despite its own premise proceeding in an entirely opposite direction.

In contrast to Machiavelli, Thomas Hobbes (1588-1679) founded a philosophy which has functioned as the respectable root for most subsequent western political thought.

Hobbes' response to Machiavelli's discussion of a ruler's love or fear policy preference was that, expressed in Part I of his *Leviathan*, fear of another's power provided a counterbalance to the appetite for power, thereby preventing people from struggling constantly for its attainment. Humans sought peace only because of fear of death and bodily harm. To Hobbes, mediation between fear and power was termed "manners," the forms and expression of management.

**Thomas Hobbes**

Influenced by study of Thucydides, Hobbes saw Pericles as a supreme leader, a ruler who prevented mob rule but managed the society sensibly. Particularly in *Leviathan*, by which biblical reference he meant the state, Hobbes set forward his social contract theory. While applied to the relationship between people and the state, the theory could be naturally expanded to relationships between the managers and the managed. The further contrasts, however, included his view of human life, particularly in war, and not education but its reverse, ignorance, which he characterised in Part IV of *Leviathan* as the Kingdom of Darkness. His view on people in times of warfare is one of the most frequently quoted descriptions of human existence:

> And the life of man, solitary, poore, nasty, brutish and short.[1]

A hundred years after his death, during yet another war, the human condition had not much changed for those at the base of the social pyramid, who had sought alleviation by turning to crime. The majority of those convicted were likely to have taken that route because of need, or the habit of their poor environments; and there was much law of which to fall foul. By 1800, in England there were 200 capital offences, including the pickpocketing of goods valued at more than one shilling, and shop lifting articles greater in value than five shillings.[2]

Hobbes was not an easy man, although he worked well with Galileo and Francis Bacon, also tutoring Charles II. Such were the controversies that his work provoked that a committee was set up in an echo of Socrates to demand that he stop publishing, for he was widely read. Monarchists were angered by his assertion that power was granted by the people, parliamentarians by his agreement that the monarch ruled by divine will; he disagreed with his friend René Descartes, the man who had instigated much of the Enlightenment philosophical debate with his famous existentialist declaration of initial truth. By having antagonised the Church in arguing that the king oversaw scripture and a long-running dispute with a bishop, Hobbes upset atheists by taking the sacrament when he mistakenly thought he was dying; the aggrieved superstitious attributed the Great Plague and Fire of London to his God-bothering. Any university lecturer association during his lifetime with what was termed "Hobbism," as a euphemism for atheism, was subject to dismissal. Nonetheless, he began modern political philosophy and social theory.

He identified three laws of nature: desirability and search for peace; in that process we must be prepared to give up some of our natural rights, such as a degree of liberty; and that people must adhere to the undertaking - hence, the social contract. Rousseau's 1762 version, *The Social Contract,* required that individuals set aside their personal and sectional interests, acting only for the common good, with government acting in line with the general will of the people. The issue here is what might constitute the common good. Notions of freedom and the prices for compromise had, however, fully entered mainstream political thought.

The prolific French writer Francois-Marie Arouet, better known by his *nom de plume* of Voltaire (1694-1778), was an even greater populariser of the Enlightenment. A two-and-a-half-year exile in London assisted his understanding of English culture, resulting in the publicising of the works of Shakespeare and Newton in Europe. Rather than an original philosophical mind, Voltaire's talent lay in stimulating essay writing, drama, satire, and a novel. He gave wide credence to the ideas and ideal of the rational and scientific approaches, becoming most famous for his debunking of his character Dr Pangloss's belief that everything was for the best and in the best possible of worlds in his novel *Candide*, a parody of the philosophy of Leibniz. Opponent of sectarian wrangling, his approaches were direct: superstition was to religion as was astrology to astronomy. Able writer and journalist, he is best remembered perhaps for the pithiness of his sayings, the most famous of which are ubiquitous:

> I disapprove of what you say, but will defend to the death your right to say it.
> If there were no God, it would be necessary to invent him.
> Man is free at the moment he wishes to be.

Voltaire made a very substantial income from his writing and, like many of the philosophers of the Enlightenment, was a rich man.

Such fortune did not attend Thomas Paine (1737-1809). The son of a Quaker corset-maker who struggled to pay for his grammar school education, he failed at teaching, tobacco selling, tax collection, running away to sea, and at marriage. This continued experience of hardship informed his career, strengthened by the Quakerism which emphasised that all human beings are born fundamentally equal, and the necessity for moral courage to represent truly held beliefs. Tom Paine was well equipped to pursue the pathways of reform and freedom.

A chance meeting with the polymath inventor of the lightning rod and bifocals, Benjamin Franklin (1706-1790), gained Paine a letter of recommendation. Franklin's stature as a prominent scientist, political theorist, diplomat, and author opened all doors. This time, Paine's attempt to sail succeeded, Franklin's letter helping him to a writing appointment with *Pennsylvania Magazine,* of which he soon became editor.

His first notable article was a call for the abolition of slavery, followed by the 1776 essay which made him famous: *Common Sense.* This argued the moral duty and practical necessity for America to seek independence from Britain. Adding an attack on hereditary monarchy, he further argued that a republican government founded on the principle of the equality of its citizens was the optimum means of preventing civil conflict.

Such was the power and popularity of the writing that it sold in large numbers - 120,000 in the first three months of publication - and was persuasive in helping to make up the minds of many of the major figures of the American revolt as to the desirability of independence.

**Thomas Paine**

Thetford's most famous son, standing outside King's House (Norfolk, England) holding a copy of the Rights of Man.

Paine continued his campaign throughout the conflict, so effectively that George Washington rallied his troops' flagging morale before the battle of Trenton on Boxing Day, December 1776, by having Paine read aloud to them in groups. The scale of Paine's achievement is immeasurable, and stands as one of the greatest feats of informal education history.

Returning to England, Paine turned his attention to the revolution in France, which the writings of the *philosophes* and the American example had done so much to assist, addressing the criticisms of Edmund Burke (1729–1797) in his *Reflections.* In Paine's best-known work, *The Rights of Man*, published in February 1791, the thesis was that government was legitimate only when it is established by the people as a whole: it had to be of the people, for all the people. Therefore, the only legitimate government was democratic republicanism, for that best represented the totality of the human rights to which people are unable to individually attend, and so give up to government in order that all rights be secured. He went even further, addressing the issue of poverty and proposing a welfare system: lower taxes and subsidised education for the poor; a progressive income tax for the monied.

Why was it, he wondered, were the poor those who suffered mainly from the punishment of execution? These were people bred without morals, cast out upon the world without prospect, exposed to sacrifice by vice or legal barbarism. This was altogether too much for government, parliament, and the British establishment. In May 1792, a royal proclamation was issued against seditious writing. Charged with treason, Paine fled his land of birth forever.

From the British frying pan, he leapt into the French fire. Welcomed at first, even gaining a seat in the National Assembly, he had been too radical for the British but was now found not radical enough by the Jacobins of France. His inability to speak French could not have helped. Denounced by Robespierre (1758-1794) for his association with the moderate Girondins and imprisoned, his life was saved only by the intervention of the future American president, James Monroe (1758-1831). If Hobbes was able thoroughly to annoy a lot of people, Paine had the ability wholly to infuriate. In *The Age of Reason,* completed just before his arrest in 1794, he argued for deism against both atheism and Christianity, with an assault upon the vengeful, smiting God of the Old Testament.

*Agrarian Justice* of 1797 again addressed social justice and basic rights, proposing that a civilised state should leave no individual worse off than they would have been before civilisation. In fact, he observed, the poor of every country in Europe were worse off than the Native Americans of North America. Land and property tax to accumulate capital for redistribution was the remedy put forward. He found on his return to the United States of 1802, which he had done so much to help create, that his popularity was much dimmed. *The Age of Reason* had offended and alienated. His life ended in illness and obscurity.

Paine's fate is mirrored in the way he has been treated by history. More a propagandist than a philosopher, yet one who did help change the world, he is not usually cited among the great stimulating thinkers of the Enlightenment. Of those, the rationalist ethics of Baruch Spinoza (1632-

1677), opponent of Descartes, inverted medieval thought through biblical criticism, laying the groundwork for the Enlightenment. His interpretation of God as Nature prepared the ground for James Lovelock's (1919-2022) Gaia hypothesis and associated belief systems.

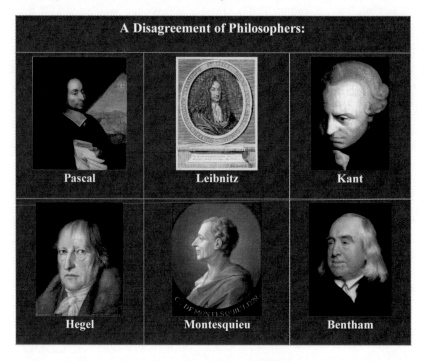

**A Disagreement of Philosophers:**

Pascal — Leibnitz — Kant

Hegel — Montesquieu — Bentham

Blaise Pascal (1623-62) argued against nature abhorring a vacuum, Jesuits for their rationality of a belief in God, designed the first calculating machine, and began the investigation of probability, discussed further below.

Gottfried Wilhelm Leibniz (1646-1716), polymath, inventor and philosopher developed calculus independently of Newton, the binary numerical system with machines anticipating the computer and, although not an empiricist, was a proponent of rational thought.

Immanuel Kant (1724-1804), further discussed below, whose claim that the mind plays an active role in constituting the objects of knowledge, formulation of moral law, and consideration of aesthetics, stimulated generations of philosophical inquiry.

Georg Wilhelm Friedrich Hegel (1770-1831) introduced the dialectical method in terms of the concepts of thesis, antithesis, and synthesis, with application to the unfolding of Being, as absolute across history. He defined history as the progress and development of freedom, finding deep patterns of reason within its underlying structures. Central to philosophy, Hegel took history very seriously, describing it as the progress in the consciousness of freedom.

Spinoza's rational, scientific approach was held in tandem with a definition of freedom as learning to love the world and its perfection of reality, whereby God and Nature become the same, and true enlightenment derived from reason, which required that toleration be extended to beliefs. Commentators have noted similarities with the Vedanta tradition of Hindu philosophy, but other comparisons made further east than India, to Taoism, appear to have been neglected.

At a very practical level, Blaise Pascal had most important contributions to make to the insurance industry, for he observed that fear of harm ought to be proportional not merely to its gravity but also to its probability. The first formal analysis of probability emerged from an exchange of letters between Pascal and Pierre de Fermat (1607-1665). Again, a game was the stimulus. An inveterate gambler was seeking means to compensate lost chances of winning when a gaming session suffered interruption. The Pascal and Fermat solution to the division of the "pot" of an interrupted game rested on three mathematical concepts: the probability of winning any particular game; the compound probability of winning successive games; and the expected value of total winnings had the gaming period been completed. Pascal's was the first calculation to bring together different probabilities with a subjective evaluation of possible outcomes. Thus began the quantification of the risk business. He had a further tip for managers:

Pascal observed:

> When we wish to correct with advantage, and to show another that he errs, we must notice from what side he views the matter, for on that side it is usually true, and admit that truth to him, but reveal to him the side on which it is false. He is satisfied with that, for he sees that he was not mistaken, and that he only failed to see all sides. Now, no one is offended at not seeing everything; but one does not like to be mistaken, and that perhaps arises from the fact that man naturally cannot see everything, and that naturally he cannot err in the side he looks at, since the perceptions of our senses are always true. People are generally better persuaded by the reasons which they have themselves discovered than by those which have come into the mind of others.[3]

In an argument, therefore, the first step to resolution is to indicate the ways in which the others are correct, employing empathy, so to allow them to discover the counter argument for themselves. Thus, the opponents convince themselves to capitulate. Empathy, in effect, gives opponents permission to lower defences, preventing them from maintaining and hardening their stance. If they are, instead, immediately told all the ways in which they are in error, there is no incentive for cooperation. Yet, if concession is apparently first offered by allowing that the others' strong points are appreciated, then the door is open for your own strengths to be heard and appreciated.

By contrast, the stern Hegel had several observations of relevance to this study. Depressingly, he considered that our learning from history is that we do not learn from history. Further, it was his opinion that governments have never learned anything from history or acted upon principles deducted from it. Nevertheless, he was determined upon one matter in particular: that education is the art of making man ethical. However, Enlightenment thought was not always progressive, and vulnerable to uses beyond the originating concept. Thus, Hegel's dialectic came to be intertwined both with Marxism and conspiracy theory.

Despite Kant's considerable and highly influential output concerning duty-based ethics, his observation that science and ethics were separate has been used as an excuse by "scientific" managerialism, as discussed extensively in a later volume. All the philosophers cited above made outstanding contributions, some of surpassing brilliance. All remain, like those sketched earlier, immense contributors to education and, from the applications of their thought, eventually came to assist the determination of the mental processes of successor humanity, and so the terms and forms of following education and management.

Yet Tom Paine, an early reviver of the inspiration of Pericles in 1776, not only produced ideas and plans which have become an accepted part of progressive politics, but within his own lifetime demonstrably helped to achieve enormous change. His mistake was that in challenging everything, he managed to offend almost everyone. As the force of his arguments, ethical and moral stances were as uncomfortable as they were largely irresistible - the only recourse was to ignore them, and him. Others were more amenable, even Voltaire, the satirist of Leibniz. Ultimately however, in the history of education, it is the great popularisers like Voltaire, Paine and, as we shall see, the publisher Newbery who, in their differing, distinctive ways brought popular, applied education to the masses. This was another kind of renewed, significant management: the broadcasting of new ideas to create change.

Another would-be populariser by other means, and with immense power to implement desired change, came from another world entirely. Peter I the Great of Russia (1672-1725; r.1682-1725) considerably expanded his realm, brought the Enlightenment and many institutions deriving from it to his country - and was to travel and behave, for a monarch, in a most unusual manner in order to do so. Peter had undergone a desultory, eccentric, and thoroughly dangerous personal education within an Orthodox religious context, even more stultifying than the unreformed Catholic version. Unusually tall, eventually reaching six feet eight inches (wholly exceptional for his times), tireless, restless, exceptionally strong, epileptic, probably autistic, brilliant, and an imposing presence, he was uninterested in formal education, refused to read books or learn languages - although he did acquire some German.

Peter enjoyed Greek mythology, Roman history, and alcohol. Grammar and philosophy went unattended; an acquiescent tutor allowed him to indulge his interests in military manoeuvres, cannon fire and, in the sort of reversal which became a feature of his life, his version of the Aquinas vision of trade within society, involving carpentry, a life-long hobby and recreation. At the age of eleven, proud to be a bombardier, he was firing cannon and parading troops from his improvised personal army of some 300 attendants. The present of a French sextant, a navigational tool then unknown in Russia, so fascinated Peter he determined to find out about ships. With his friends he rebuilt an old boat, so beginning his involvement with matters naval, concerning which he went on to establish Russia's first naval base at Taganrog, and its first fleet.

The teenaged Peter attracted and acquired a band of friends of varying ages which essentially became his court, known as the Jolly Company, prime qualification for which being the ability to drink long, hard, and to excess over lengthy periods, with occupations such as mocking the processes of religion. In order not to offend the Orthodox, the target was Catholicism. His former tutor presided as the prince-pope, sitting on a beer barrel, with Peter as his "proto-deacon." The Drunken Synod would proceed to formal Dionysus/Bacchus worship, all the officials of which as cardinals or archdeacons bore obscene, penile related titles, except for Archdeacon Fuck-Off. Club rules included the instructions of finishing each drink, getting drunk daily, and never going to bed sober. Several of his ministers died of alcoholism. The advice of mythical Silenus was followed, involuntarily or not.

This lifestyle continued until Peter's death from a grotesquely painful bladder ailment. His court was a mixture of military and civil administration in a permanent state of carousal. Senior generals and secretaries also held positions such as Archdeacon Thrust-the-Prick. Yet Peter believed in God, if only as justification for his own holy monarchy. The exceptional scale of debaucheries ultimately served only to enhance his equally exceptional, energetic, wide-ranging authority. He had acquired the license, in every sense, to rule as he saw fit. Peter's vision was to modernise Russia, strengthen its armed forces, and expand its territory, and thus required identification and application of gifted retainers to execute his enormous visions. His Roman Saturnalia imitation inversion games, where he enjoyed being a bombardier and mixing with ordinary sailors and shipwrights, enhanced his mystique, helped his understanding of his subjects, even enforcing his holy autocracy.

Supposedly *incognito*, as "Peter Mikhailov," although everyone knew who he was, in 1697 he embarked on a European tour. Probably the most diplomatic incident-packed royal tour ever, he was accompanied by an entourage of some 250, including such Jolly Company adjuncts as trumpeters, dwarves, and cooks, achieving the memorial of the wife of the Elector of Hanover, mother of England's George I (1660-1727): "a very extraordinary man ... at once very good and very bad."[4]

At the Zaandam shipyard at Amsterdam, he joined as a shipwright to learn naval architecture. Quickly realising the need for bulk technology transfer, he ordered each of his nobility companions to fund the purchase of a ship for his new navy, subsequently dispatching 50 further aristocrats to train in the shipyards of Holland, and recruited experts of every type and class to go to Russia, there to implant the knowledge and skill bases necessary. An educational, technological, and industrial exchange of a formidable, breath-taking scale was achieved in an exceptionally short time, worthy of a highlighted mention in any history of education management. Peter, being Peter, could not have achieved what he did without the other side of the Hanoverian observation gaining notice. "Power tends to corrupt," Lord Acton (1834-1902) observed, "and absolute power corrupts absolutely. Great men are almost always bad men..."

In London, Peter and his troupe lodged at the immaculate residence of John Evelyn in Deptford. Like rock stars of the 1970s, they trashed the place. Furniture was used as firewood, curtains as lavatory paper, bedding destroyed, and paintings used for target practice. Peter discovered an implement which he had never seen before among the garden equipment: a wheelbarrow, which delighted him. So enamoured was he that he organised wheelbarrow races which severely damaged Evelyn's topiary. Perhaps diverted by an English actress mistress, he continued his practical explorations of human anatomy by avid attendance at post-mortems and the pulling of the teeth of any of his party who complained of toothache.[5] Back in Russia, ever the micro-managing autocrat's autocrat, Peter's control-freakery extended to all conceivable detail.

In his decree creating the Admiralty building, he specified that no one was allowed to defecate except in the appointed places, disobedience punished by whipping and having to clear the excretion. Not being one to duck his perceived responsibilities, Peter supervised the torture by the knouting of his treacherous son and heir, Alexei (1690-1718). A skilled executioner could kill a man by knouting with a few blows. Alexei had received forty-nine lashes, which would have cut his back to the bone, before Peter again visited his son in the torture chamber for a further session, lasting three hours, after which the young man died.

His personal monument, in the example of Alexander the Great, was the founding and creation of a capital city in his own name, at the head of the Neva River on the Gulf of Finland, entrance to the Baltic Sea. St Petersburg served as Russia's capital from 1713 to 1728, again from 1732 to 1918, and remains Russia's cultural capital and second city. The city on the Baltic arose through the labour of Swedish prisoners and conscripted peasants, effectively slave labour, to the designs of a Swiss Italian, and French architects. The death rates, as upon his rowed galleys in the Baltic, were high. The early city featured a palace, museum, and university, colleges, and an Academy of Sciences.

The modern ideas, designs and learning were thrust upon Russia, whether liked or not. Where the aristocracy (the boyars) sought to cling to the old ways and their symbols, Peter made them cut off their signature beards, a sacrifice they detested but with which they had to comply. Here was absolute monarchy at its rawest, enacting the practice of the Enlightenment in a severely autocratic manner and with a practical vigour far beyond the studies of the *philosophes.* He had to face the dilemma of all autocrats. They hold all and ultimate power but protest at the behaviour of their assistants for not thinking for themselves:

> "They imitate the crab in the course of their work," wrote Peter, "so I'll deal with them not with words but with my fists."

Peter warned that if they did not get to work "It will be the worse for you!" Only fear worked. He frequently punched or beat his grandees with his cane. Many understandably resented his menacing hyperactivity.[6] Machiavelli, however, would have understood.

Catherine the Great (1729-1796, r. 1762-96), a much more civilised, if similarly sexually liberated, enlightened despot took Russia further along the roads of expansion through diplomacy and conquest, to reformed administration and the foundation of new towns. However, in her efforts to achieve consensus from her reactionary aristocracy and gentry, she left serfdom untouched, casually compensating successions of former lovers with gifts of thousands of "souls," while allowing reform proposals slowly to sink into inaction through prolonged bureaucratic discussion (a result of her search for accord).

Economic progress began with her introduction of a paper currency which held its value throughout her reign, an impressive indicator of confidence. She encouraged the immigration of entrepreneurs and craftsmen by the attractions of loans and concessions. A development of small industries began, but Russia remained a largely rural undeveloped economy. Yet, she took many bold cultural steps such as corresponding with Voltaire, offering him, Diderot, and their companions a refuge when they were threatened with reprisals because of their irreligious radicalism. Like Peter, she also recruited foreign experts, particularly leading scientists, and economists. As patron of the arts, she presided over the Russian intellectual enlightenment, venturing so far as to establish the first state-financed educational institution for women in Europe, the Smolny Institute, in 1764. Her private art collection formed the foundation of the great Hermitage art museum.

Key to her personal success was her realism regarding the limits of autocracy:

> One must do things in such a way that people think they themselves want it to be done this way.... My orders would not be carried out unless they were the kind of orders that could be carried out.... I take advice, I consult and when I am convinced of general approval, I issue my orders and have the pleasure of

observing what you call blind obedience. And that is the foundation of unlimited power.[7]

Catherine is illustrative of the crucial power of leaders not being that of command, but positioned central to a network. Theirs, in matters of policy, is the power to persuade. In organisations, this can set the culture, its morality and behaviour.

Frederick II of Prussia (1712-1786, r.1740-86), another Great, was more interested in the arts and culture before ascending to the throne, adopting Pericles as the model of patronage. He marked his opposition to Machiavelli's *Prince* as the then textbook for rulers (and, by extension, senior managers everywhere) with his own *Anti-Machiavel,* an idealistic French language refutation, published anonymously in 1740. Distributed in Amsterdam by Voltaire, it proved to be highly popular. Frederick's vision of himself was as a philosopher-king akin to the models of Plato, Aristotle, and Marcus Aurelius. On accession, as a Freemason who preferred French to German culture, he was the darling of the *philosophes.* A life-long, albeit interrupted, correspondence followed with Voltaire.

Threatened with execution by his father, at the age of 28 the young monarch had outwitted his powerful neighbours to seize the rich Austrian province of Silesia. He fought a broad alliance for over twenty years with only Britain giving occasional support, eventual victory turning Prussia from a small state into a leading European power. A gifted flute player, Frederick considered himself as a philosopher and was seen as the most enlightened ruler of his age. A supporter of atheists who, for reasons of state, chose not to come out regarding his sexuality or absence of religion, Frederick saw culture and the arts as a substitute for the latter (and probably an expression of the former). The relationship with Voltaire began as something of a flirtation but floundered on the writer's quarrelsome nature and unprincipled, rascally behaviour, recovering in an intellectual reconciliation. Balance exhibited by Frederick illustrates formidable managerial skill, from his expression of rule to suppressive control of his personal preferences.

Warfare and the expansion of Prussia, at both of which he was highly successful, occupied much of Frederick's time - but he did make practical interventions in the economy and education. Swamp draining and land reclamation was encouraged to improve the food supply, a thousand new villages being created to accommodate an influx of some 300,000 immigrants, a canal network constructed to bring the crops of turnip and potato to market. He founded the first veterinary school in Germany and brought the Prussian Academy of Sciences up to a full international standard. According to the view taken of his military successes and undoubted administrative excellence, Frederick deserves his title. Yet, for such a hero of the *philosophes,* the social and educational gains were slim. As the Romanovs were beginning to learn, there was only so much that an autocrat, no matter how efficient, enlightened, or energetic, could do.

This lesson was experienced most painfully by the third of the contemporary Enlightenment supporting monarchs, Joseph II, Holy Roman Emperor, (1741-1790, r.1765-90). His inheritance was that of Charlemagne, consolidated by his Hapsburg family's habit and talent for dynastic marriage. Theirs was the ultimate family regnant business. His mother, Maria Theresa, had established a busy, reforming regime marred by incomplete management, giving a meddling character to its administration; a trait Joseph was to inherit and exacerbate. The title dated from 800, suffered a period of interregnum, was recreated in the $10^{th}$ century, and took a final form in the $13^{th}$. Its rule was elective, prone to dynastic control, sprawling over central Europe in an agglomeration of units: kingdoms, principalities, duchies, counties, Free Cities. After Napoleon's creation of the Confederation of the Rhine in 1806, the title was abolished by Francis II (1786-1835), who then ruled as Emperor of Austria and King of Hungary. Joseph's education was a mixture of the writings of Voltaire and the encyclopaedists, with the advice of specialist officials in the running of a multi-national, multi-cultural state.

Joseph attempted construction of a rational, uniform, centralised government for his diverse territory, led by himself as the supreme autocrat, another philosopher-king. His aim was to make his people happy, but that happiness was in accord with his vision of what that ought to be rather than the peoples' actual desires. His prodigious efforts were attempted to be enacted through the issuing of some 6,000 edicts and 11,000 new laws, all designed to reorganise and reorder the empire. Further to achieve this, officials were recruited and appointed by merit only, irrespective of race or class, and expected to share the enlightened despot's passion for reform and dedication to service. The list of reforms, at first sight, is deeply impressive: full legal system reform included abolition of brutal punishments, equal treatment for all offenders; abolition of the death penalty; the ending of press and theatre censorship; full freedom extended to serfs, with serfdom abolished; rents regulated; land income taxed; new factory privileges effectively ended guilds; customs law promoted economic unity.

Elementary education was made compulsory for all boys and girls; practical higher education for the elite was supplemented by scholarships for the able poor; religious minorities allowed their own schools; and the language of instruction changed from Latin to German. The power of the Catholic Church was reduced and attempt made to separate it from Rome, subordinate to the state. Bishops had to swear loyalty to the state; clerics deprived of the tithe; seminaries were subject to government inspection. The sector expanded, financed by the forced sale of monastic lands and closure of some 700 monasteries, the lost income compensated from the proceeds of sales; church courts abolished; holy days cut; the Mass simplified; many religious orders banned, including the Jesuits; and marriage made a civil ceremony.[8]

Certainly, one of the greatest examples of a regal entrepreneur who never knew when to stop, an engine without a brake, Joseph interwove upsetting his subjects with annoying his neighbours. His foreign policies were all aimed at aggrandisement; they all failed. The aristocracy opposed his land and taxation reforms, and both landlords and peasants opposed his cash payments insistence as there was insufficient money supply to replace their barter system. Where the nobility disliked his despotism, they were equally offended by his egalitarianism. The general population disliked the widespread interference with their daily lives. It appeared that, rather than for his people's good, Joseph was reforming his state according to his own beliefs. Resistance to the reforms led to the reaction of enforcement, the authority of choice being the secret police.

The achievement of egalitarian freedom through repression was not a workable concept. Hungary naturally opposed the imposition of the German language, one result of which was that whilst Austria gained a civil code in 1786, Hungary did not achieve the same provision until 1959. Faced with rebellions in Belgium and Hungary, and a further distracting war with Turkey - such widespread resistance to his reforms that many had to be suspended or modified - a deeply depressed Joseph died young, aged 49, having requested that his epitaph read: "Here lies Joseph II, who failed in all he undertook."[9] He was succeeded by his sensible brother Leopold II (1747-92), who in his short reign shrewdly extended an effective moderate enlightened despotism.

An understanding of the limitations and central dilemma of autocracy remains essential for all managers, especially the leaders of organisations. The leading enlightened despots were all great systems devisers and exponents, who avoided any reform which would impact upon their own power. Reform was for other people, subjects who would remain subject. Historians have been divided in their view of Joseph II. As a management study, there are the very obvious lessons of not trying to do too much, too quickly; of the desirability of planning major change, consulting the representatives of those most likely to be affected and proceeding with caution; the entrepreneurial *caveat* already instanced; not being distracted by external agenda and maintaining focus. There is also the further perspective upon the actions of all four of these enlightened despots of the ideas of the Enlightenment themselves.

Here, the ideas might see Peter and Catherine as not having done enough to establish a modernised Russia; Frederick as either a militaristic harbinger or builder of German unity; and Joseph as the arts patron of Mozart and Beethoven, many of whose abandoned policies were subsequently implemented.

Six Despots with aspirations to Enlightenment:

Suleiman I of Turkey — Peter I of Russia — Catherine II of Russia

Maria Theresa Holy Roman Empress and ruler of the Habsburg dominions — Joseph II Holy Roman Emperor — Frederick II of Prussia

A lot of ideas had been let loose, which no individual or government could hope to manage; it was more a matter of managing within their contexts.

Beyond such excitements, however, causation remains a topic of permanent debate in the philosophical, scientific and historical communities. From the concatenation of events following the Reformation, Counter Reformation, Enlightenment and technological advance, further themes of great consequence emerge: the Protestant embrace of the Pauline biblical instruction to work out their own salvation, the British agricultural and industrial revolutions, and the growth of what became known as capitalism.

There remains, however, a bizarre but stubbornly continuing footnote to the Enlightenment. In the Electorate of Bavaria, now a southern province of Germany, a secret society was founded on Mayday, 1776: the Illuminati. The goals were opposition of superstition, obscurantism, the influence of religion over public life, and what were seen as other abuses of state power. Bavaria being then, as now, of a broadly conservative nature, the Illuminati leadership sought to attain its ends through manipulation, covert if necessary, in order to end the machinations of the powerful in their exercise of injustice by the means of control, rather than domination. Lumping the Illuminati with Freemasonry and other societies deemed secretive, Elector of Bavaria Charles Theodore (1724-1799), encouraged by the Catholic Church, issued outlawry edicts repetitively: in 1784, 1785, 1787 and 1790.

The movement had attracted persons of note, such as the writers Goethe (1749-1832) and Herder (1744-1803); Ferdinand, Prince of Brunswick– Lüneburg (1721–1792); and the Hungarian deputy leader, astronomer Franz Xaver von Zach (1754–1832). The founder, Adam Weishaupt (1748–1830), as a professor of civil and then canon law, was an unlikely dangerous revolutionary. Patron of the arts but sharing a mutual dislike and distrust with his subjects, notoriously controlled by his courtiers, Charles took the line of least resistance when the Illuminati's conservative and clerical opponents claimed their continuing presence underground, instituting campaigns of vilification that they were causative of such evils as the French Revolution.

Such is the way of suspicions of societies which have declared their activities to be clandestine, the reputation of the Illuminati, and invocation of its name as the alleged motivator behind countless unsubstantiated conspiracy claims and theories, has attained mythic status. That pursuers of the ideals of the Enlightenment should have needed to have recourse to indirect tactics to avoid persecution, then have that visited upon them as vile; then be condemned to immortal obloquy seems, as one of the *philosophes* might have said, a little harsh.

# Endnotes

[1] Hobbes, Thomas. *Leviathan*, Vol X111. 9.

[2] Of mixed ancestry, the shilling derived as a twelfth of the Roman *solidus*, successor to the *aureus,* known in the 7th century as a small gold coin. Of the same size and weight, a silver version under a Germanic title was designated by Charlemagne as one twelfth of a silver pound, at 20.3 grams of silver. By Hobbes's time, the "sterling silver" shilling contained 92.5% silver.

[3] *Pascal's Pensées.* 1958. New York: E P Dutton & Co. 1. "Thoughts on Mind and Style," 9-10, p.4.

[4] Montefiore, Simon Sebag, *op. cit.* p. 86. Sophia, Electress of Hanover (1630-1714) was heiress presumptive to the British throne under the 1701 Act of Settlement, dying less than two months before she would have become queen. An Enlightenment supporter, she was a patron of Leibnitz.

[5] *Ibid,* p. 87.

[6] *Ibid,* p. 111.

[7] *Ibid,* p.208.

[8] The banned orders, whose funds were diverted into the state Religious Fund, were: Jesuits; Camaldolese; Friars Minor Capuchin; Carmelites; Carthusians; Poor Clares; Benedictines; Cistercians; Dominicans; Franciscans; Pauline Fathers; and Premonstratensians.

[9] Davies, Norman. *Europe: A History*, p. 672.

# CHAPTER TWELVE

## RELIGION, THE RISE OF CAPITALISM, AND EMIGRATION

While productive of spiritual and behavioural renewal, revival and reform, the century of the Counter Reformation, from the start of the Council of Trent in 1545 to the close of the Thirty Years' War in 1648, had been marked by frequent warfare. Attempted reconversions by armed force, plus conflict with Turkey, were paid for by Spain - in particular by huge borrowing and heavy taxation, curbing enterprise, and aborting growth. France, too, paid a heavy price for its wars and Protestant repression: the great Catholic powers pursued their version of religious duty to their economic disadvantage. By contrast, Calvinist Holland, already favourably placed for economic take off by the inheritance of the medieval trade fairs routes, was pushed by a mixed farming and trading oligarchy, the practical, work-ethic based religion of which was conducive to enterprise:

> So, then my beloved, just as you have always obeyed, not as in my presence only but now much more in my absence, work out your salvation with fear and trembling.[1]

Fear and trembling were more the lot of the victims of Dutch early physical trade warfare and colonialism, the Catholic Portuguese in particular. However, the assiduous following of the instruction to labour six days of the week was ideal for the expression of a religion dedicated to the working out of salvation, particularly where the charging of interest was seen as socially and morally good. Moreover, the religiously tolerant Dutch provided sanctuary to refugees of other persuasions with capital, and the ability successfully to deploy it.

The Protestant, Calvinist, or Puritan work ethic, expressed through the attributes beloved of Cato of frugality, discipline, and hard work, were seen as part of the expression of the Protestant faith.[2] Derived from Luther's thinking, the Catholic notion of good works was transmuted into a disciplined way of life whereby the Protestant believers, individually and as a society, had an obligation to achieve a state of grace through their daily work. The result, nonetheless, was that while charity might relieve some poverty, there remained a considerable issue with the provision and nature of labour. Although the Protestant work ethic is much represented in western literature and practice, it should be noted that the Shia form of Islam also practices a significant work ethic.

Such ethics must be balanced, however, by the critique of the socialist economic historian R. H. Tawney (1880-1962), known for his seminal work *Religion and the Rise of Capitalism* (1932). Economic development in the 16$^{th}$ and 17$^{th}$ centuries led, he argued, to a division between business and social morality: Christian teaching was subordinated to the pursuit of material wealth. He memorably summarised his argument in an interpretation of Adam Smith: "If preachers have not yet overtly identified themselves with the view of the natural man expressed by an eighteenth-century writer in the words, trade is one thing and religion another they imply a not very different conclusion by their silence as to the possibilities of collision between them." The characteristic doctrine was one which left little room for religious teaching as to economic morality, because it anticipated the theory, later epitomised by Adam Smith in his famous reference to the invisible hand, which saw in economic self-interest the operation of a providential plan. The existing order, except in so far as the short-sighted enactments of Governments interfered with it, was the natural order, and the order established by nature was the order established by God. Most educated men in the middle of the century would have found their philosophy expressed in the lines of Pope:

> Thus, God and Nature formed the general frame,
> And bade self-love and social be the same.[3]

Naturally, again, such an attitude precluded a critical examination of institutions, and has left only those parts of life which could be reserved for philanthropy as the sphere of Christian charity - precisely because they fell outside that larger area of normal relations in which the promptings of self-interest provided an all-sufficient motive and rule of conduct.[4]

Whatever the religious and ethical persuasions, agriculture had long dominated the economy in England, as elsewhere, occupying most of the labour force, much of the capital, and required the use of most of the managerial talent available. Around five per cent of the population controlled the land in the medieval period. Those landowners had increased production, able to sustain a growing population until the Great European

Famine of 1315-21, when between a quarter and half a million people died of starvation. Meanwhile, landlords with large holdings, farmed efficiently, were able to sell surplus product at high prices. Consequently, more land had been brought into cultivation, efficiency improved through crop rotation; whilst the pastoral sector, source of the export earning wool trade, increased profitability. This peak of demand fell rapidly in 1348- 49 as the Black Death reduced the population by between 30 and 40 per cent.

Successive plague waves continued the diminution. Management became an immediate issue, with honest and competent reeves – land supervisors – being difficult to recruit, giving impetus to landlords turning instead to renting out their properties. Distrust of managers, subsequently so common in early industrial businesses, had medieval antecedents. Although government acted to restrict the movement of labour, its scarcity resulted in labour becoming dearer, capital and land cheaper, rebalancing the economy.

Arable land was now less profitable than pastoral. As the population expanded again in the 16$^{th}$ century, two routes emerged to the achievement of agrarian capitalism. There were landlords who increased pasture and converted freeholds into leaseholds, where they had more control; and aspiring peasant tenants who increased their tenancy holdings and were more likely to effect improvements. This left a rump of poor cottagers who laboured for a living. The archetypal feudal system, never uniform, had changed, with serfdom (being unfree) replaced by villeinage (tenancy of unfree land). This progressed into the 16$^{th}$ century where free tenants paid cash rents, producing the yeoman farmer, and labourers gained annual contracts. That workforce was drawn from the surplus family labour of small holders, whose assets probably included animals with common land grazing access.

The labour shortage had caused landowners to hire people whilst also seeking to decrease costs and diversify production. There were by-products, such as the improved employment opportunities for women. The next great change in England came with the 1536-41 dissolution of the monasteries, ending the strongest proponents of feudalism and releasing large amounts of land for sale and rent. Even then, agrarian change had always proceeded slowly and unevenly, dependent upon change occurring elsewhere in the economy, requiring new technology and practice to be suited to specific environments, with tenure reform being subject to varying paces of gestation.

Feudalism enjoyed varying life spans, lasting in France until the French Revolution of 1789, and in Russia until its revolt of 1917. If the key to

England's eventual economic rise was its early transition from feudalism to capitalism, then that had begun as early as the 12$^{th}$ century, with the later Black Death as a catalyst rather than a prime cause. Nonetheless, labour scarcity had led to agricultural expansion through tenure reform, increased innovation, and technological advance. Cato had known of the suitability of different soils to varying plants, but the increased sophistication of crop rotation from the 17$^{th}$ century greatly increased yields. Also assisting this increase was the adjustable depth plough, more commonly used from around 1730, which reduced pulling requirement by three quarters.

Landowners from the 15$^{th}$ to 17$^{th}$ centuries progressively enclosed previously open land or sold to yeomen farmers. Landless labourers also lost grazing rights through the enclosures, resulting in the expansion of vagrancy into the creation of the begging bands which induced Elizabeth I (1533-1603) to introduce the Poor Law Act in 1601, as noted below. Migration from the countryside to the towns produced the increasing labour force required by the industrial revolution whilst the improved agricultural production fed a rising population. The pressure upon the land and the population, however, fed emigration to the new colonies, as did dissent and persecution of the religious minorities produced through the upheavals of the Reformation. The economics were simple:

> In the early nineteenth century, labour and capital were more abundant in the Old World than in the New World; therefore, wages and interest rates were low in the former and high in the latter. By contrast, land was far more abundant in the New World, so rents were lower there.[5]

Transatlantic emigration inducement was high. The shortage of labour resultant from the Black Death had a positive effect for the common people. The period from 1350 to 1500 has been described as "the golden age of the European proletariat", in stark contrast to the next two centuries.[6] Average life expectancy at birth fell from 43 in the 1500s to the low thirties in the 1700s.[7] It was not only religion which drove the impetus to emigration.

Forces shaping societal management were complex. While the *philosophes* and the enlightened despots sought to influence and change the institutions of society from the top, the religious increased their pressure on personal conduct. All the while, the reality to the mass of people was a decline in their standards of living and well-being. As the technology of navigation and seafaring improved, so too did the demand for transport to environments hoped to be an improvement on that currently endured.

# Endnotes

[1] *Philippians* 2: 12-13.

[2] First expressed by Weber, Max. 1905. *The Protestant Ethic and the Spirit of Capitalism.* New York: Dover, republished 2003.

[3] Tawney, R H. 1926. *Religion and the Rise of Capitalism.* London: republished Mentor (1953) and Peter Smith (1962), pp. 191-192.

[4] This is Tawney's version of Pope. The original reads
   "That reason, passion, answer one great aim;
   That true self-love and social are the same;
   That virtue only makes our bliss below;
   And all our knowledge is, ourselves to know".
   Alexander Pope, *An Essay on Man*, IV, 395-8

[5] Bernstein, William J. 2008. *A Splendid Exchange How Trade Shaped the World.* New York: Grove Press, pp.340-41.

[6] Braudel, Fernand. 1974. *Capitalism and Material Life 1400-1800,* pp. 128 ff, Glasgow: Fontana.

[7] Wrigley, Edward and Schofield, Roger. 1989. *The Population History of England 1541-1871*, Cambridge: Cambridge University Press.

## The little k Play.

### BASE-BALL.

THE *Ball* once ſtruck off,
    Away flies the *Boy*
To the next deſtin'd Poſt,
    And then Home with Joy.

### MORAL.
Thus *Britons* for Lucre
    Fly over the Main ;
But, with Pleaſure tranſported,
    Return back again.

T R A P -

# CHAPTER THIRTEEN

# BUSINESS, EDUCATION, AND THE POOR

Commonly throughout Europe in the 16th and 17th centuries, the growing complexity of the print industry led to a functional split. As the Church lost its battle to control printing, the master printer now concentrated on direct production. A combination of roles ensued: the bookseller-publisher. [1] These hybrids negotiated at trade fairs, print shops, and with authors, some also writing and publishing their own material. To raise the capital necessary for the production, advertisement and distribution of a book, the French method was by cooperative syndicates. The English preferred the subscription approach.

Publishers issued a prospectus to potential buyers, soliciting signatures in confirmation of copy purchase. If there were insufficient subscriptions, the book was not published. If necessary, capital was raised, the subscribers' names were used as endorsements; the more subscribers, the greater the likelihood of a reprint. In an intriguingly contemporary echo, some authors used the subscription method either to further bypass the publisher or increase their fees.

Copyright in the primitive form of prohibition or the granting of a license to print arose shortly after the introduction and spread of the printing technology. In England, from the 16th century, all books had to be registered with the Stationers' Company. This monopoly was not renewed in 1693. Instead, the Copyright Act of 1710 gave publishers protection for a limited period after publication, initially 14 years. [2] It was the world's first full, statutory protection. In France and the United States, copyright was not fully established until after their respective revolutions, and internationally not until the adoption of the Berne Convention at the end of the 19th century. Although English and Scottish publishers disputed provisions, copyright stimulated literary production.

John Newbery (1713-1767), the "father of children's literature," was a printer who married well. He began a publishing business in Reading, moving on swiftly to London. He published adult books at first but spotted the opportunity of a new market, *A Pretty Little Pocket-Book* appearing in 1744.

**John Newbery**

The price was six pence, but for an extra two pence the buyer received a red and black pincushion, this to be used by the child to record their behaviour: red for good, black for bad, with the promise that the novelty would "infallibly make Tommy a good boy and Polly a good girl."[3]

The child-sized book came with a brightly covered cover, its contents including proverbs, poems, and an alphabet song; the illustration here a slightly later (1787) American edition. Not one to fail to capitalise on an opportunity, Newbery advertised his other products within the books and the stories themselves. His patented medicine quoted to cure distemper in cattle and scrofula, gout, scurvy, rheumatism, and leprosy in humans, "Dr Robert James's Fever Powder," featured in his most popular production, *The History of Little Goody Two Shoes.* The heroine's sick father is unable to obtain the powder in time, dying as a result.

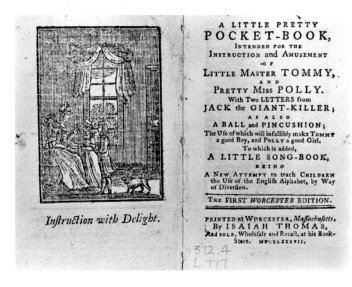

*Inſtruction with Delight.*

A LITTLE PRETTY
POCKET-BOOK,
INTENDED FOR THE
INSTRUCTION and AMUSEMENT
OF
LITTLE MASTER TOMMY,
AND
PRETTY MISS POLLY.
With Two LETTERS from
JACK the GIANT-KILLER;
AS ALSO
A BALL and PINCUSHION;
The Uſe of which will infallibly make TOMMY
a good Boy, and POLLY a good Girl.
To which is added,
A LITTLE SONG-BOOK,
BEING
A NEW ATTEMPT to teach CHILDREN
the Uſe of the Engliſh Alphabet, by Way
of Diverſion.

THE FIRST *WORCESTER* EDITION.

PRINTED at WORCESTER, Maſſachuſetts,
By ISAIAH THOMAS,
And SOLD, Wholeſale and Retail, at his Book-
Store. MDCCLXXXVII.

Indeed, here were Comenius and Locke in action, their ideas expressed by an astute man of business. Naturally, he extended further to the popularising of the newly discovered sciences. A series of books by purported schoolboy Tom Telescope, but actually by Newbery and the Irish novelist, poet and playwright Oliver Goldsmith (1728-1774), presented a succession of popular lectures. The multiple editions, highest seller of these being *The Newtonian System of Philosophy Adopted to the Capacities of Young Gentlemen and Ladies,* helped Newbery to achieve substantial prosperity.

Having discovered a winning formula, Newbery milked it. The message of *A Pretty Little Pocket-Book,* among the riddles, dietary advice, games, and information, was that prosperity would follow as a consequence of properly learning lessons. Thus, in successive tales, industrious work is inevitably followed by success; altruism is rewarded; and in this ideal meritocracy, the benefits of prosperity are attained. Often the tales follow the life of an orphan who receives punishment for bad behaviour and reward for good, culminating in virtue triumphant, garlanded with benefit.

Certainly, the Berkshire farmer's son turned printer's apprentice who started his publishing business aged 27, moved it to London aged 30, and had produced the national best-selling *Pocket-Book* sensation four years later, might claim with justification that industriousness brings reward. So popular and influential were the Newbery publications that, in 1922, the American Library Association created the John Newbery Medal in his honour.

### The John Newbery Medal

This medal is awarded annually for the "most distinguished contribution to American literature for children".

However, dependent factors, such as the condition of the market, were also relevant to success. Parents, it must be remembered, are the ones who initially buy children's books. As the market developed, pulp fiction for the young grew as a parallel genre. Fairy tales and fantasies might be deplored by subsequent earnest reformers, but the aspiring scribblers, low publishers and hack writers of Grub Street had a living to earn, too.

The market for such parental expenditure, whether of the uplifting or escapist, had been slowly growing for a very long time indeed. In England, the medieval Church had continued to educate those joining their communities through monastic establishments, with schools being established to teach Latin grammar to sons of the aristocracy and those designated to enter the clerical profession.[4] As the prime source of literacy throughout Europe, Latin dominated. Training and education for the practical occupations was provided by the apprenticeship system. The higher education of the two oldest universities of the English-speaking world, Oxford from 1096 and Cambridge 1209, were dominated by training to enter the clergy from their beginnings.

There were some independent establishments in England, however, from the late 6th century onwards, usually charity schools. From these, "public schools" emerged. The term originally meant that access was not restricted by parental location, occupation, or religion. [5] In short, control and management was by public means, whereas private schools were businesses operated for their proprietors' profit. The foundation of the first independent schools, like Winchester (1382), Oswestry (1407) and Eton (1440) was linked closely to the universities. It was not until the early 17th century that borough corporations unconnected with either church or university provided a grammar school, the earliest of which was at Bridgnorth in 1603. Meanwhile, for those who could afford it, home tutorial continued.

Although he had broken with Rome, Henry VIII had not embraced Protestantism. Profligacy and the cost of his French wars were recompensed by his nationalisation of the monasteries, the disposal of which greatly enriched the gentry while requiring the Crown to compensate for the loss of their social support functions by the introduction of the punitive Vagrancy Act of 1547. The new form of poverty relief provided that any able-bodied person not working could be branded with a V, sold into two-year slavery, or whipped and returned to their birthplace. Child vagabonds were forced into service. Consistency in religion, however, was maintained by the continuation of the Latin mass. Henry bequeathed the further religious issues to his young son, Edward VI (1537-1553), and on his deathbed appointed, or had foisted upon him, a Protestant-packed Regency Council.

As the first English monarch to be raised as a Protestant, Edward allowed his government to proceed with a series of changes so deep that all the reforms of his six-year reign could not be undone by the five-year tenure of his half-sister Mary, or be successfully integrated within the *via media* of his other sibling, Elizabeth I. Among those surviving reforms was the reorganisation of the grammar schools.

His father's dissolution of the monasteries provided the funding which his personal foundation of new schools required. Redeployment was available for those of clerical background who embraced the reformed religion. The grammar schools themselves, new and old, were made free. In theory, universal education had arrived. Anyone could now attend, even if they could not afford school fees. There was only one problem: very few children went to school, for their parents required their continued services. Child labour, at home or hired out, was vital to maintain the family budget. Communities relied upon a fully committed workforce.

> Hark, hark the dogs do bark,
> The beggars are coming to town…

This nursery rhyme dating from the 13th century echoed need: the need of communities fearful of what the vagrants might do and the costs which must necessarily be incurred; the management need of local and national authorities to control disturbance, suppress sedition, and halt the spread of disease; and for those forced into vagrancy by poverty. Philanthropy in various forms could only achieve so much. Vagrants had helped spread the plague, the songs of wandering minstrels were sometimes a way of conveying coded or allusive information, and the land enclosures coupled with the beginnings of industrialisation had greatly increased the numbers of landless rural poor and urban unemployed.

Elizabeth I sought to address the problem in the 1601 Act for the Relief of the Poor. This was a further step in the emergence of the formation of the early modern English state. In 1563, the Statute of Artificers had sought to fix prices, cap wages, restrict workers' freedom of movement and protect the apprenticeship system by the imposition of training rules. No one could practise a craft or trade without having first served a seven-year apprenticeship to a master.

Guilds had arisen from parish groupings where conditions had fostered the growth of a particular trade. By the end of the medieval period, they had long regulated urban trades' wages, with apprenticeships as an entry control - although Guild members could benefit from shorter training periods and other advantages. Guilds continued to look after their own. Before the Reformation, ranked hierarchically and with their own often prestigious meeting halls, they had been strong Church supporters, endowing many causes. This includes some still surviving, such as the Merchant Taylors' public school, founded in 1551.

London's Livery Companies, the term deriving from the specific form of dress worn by a nobleman's retainers and then extended to that denoting a specific trade, evolved as trade associations from the guilds. They became corporations under Royal Charter, responsible for training and regulation in their respective trades, extending to labour conditions, industry standards and wage control. Significant in charitable activities and networking, the livery companies continue with further civic responsibilities. They retained voting rights for such senior offices as London's Lord Mayor, the City of London retaining wide powers of local government. The Merchant Taylors (seventh in Livery Company precedence) founded a number of schools throughout the country. After the Carmen (vehicle drivers) achieved their status of becoming a Livery Company, seventy seventh in precedence in 1740, there were no new creations until 1926, after which the post-modern world re-entered that of the pre-modern, with numbers at the time of writing having escalated to 110.[6]

Trade and craft education thus remained within the practical, working trade system. Local magistrates controlled rural wages. Labourers required permission to transfer employment. As a particular discouragement to collective bargaining, imprisonment could follow if workers and employers agreed wages above the set rates. Progressive in that the powers and actions of the medieval guilds were now curtailed and controlled, the resulting economic restrictions were gradually eroded, leading to the abolition of the Act in 1813, after which time a person practicing a trade without having completed a seven-year apprenticeship could no longer be prosecuted.

For those without work, the 1601 Poor Law measure was a consolidation of earlier legislation, with four main provisions. Those unable to work through age or disability were to be cared for in alms houses. The able-bodied poor were to be set to work in a House of Industry, equipped with materials. The workhouse with accommodation and hard labour was a later, gradual development from 1723, reinforced by the New Poor Law Act of 1834. Vagrants and the "idle poor" were to be consigned to "houses of correction," which in practice became prisons for minor offenses such as drunkenness or prostitution but included punishment by hard labour. Pauper children were to be given into apprenticeships. Since cost was a significant factor in providing houses of correction or workhouses, "outdoor relief," which allowed the provision of food, clothes and even money, became a favoured action. This was particularly true of southern England, though there were several regional variations. The country was being managed, on a continuing *ad hoc* but controlling basis.

The significance of the legislation to popular education was that the system was tied to localities, the administrative unit being the parish, under the jurisdiction of a justice of the peace. The around 1,500 parishes differed in wealth, capacity, and attitude. The Overseers of the Poor, paid for from the parish rates charges and who determined poverty types and treatments, were a further cause of variation. Co-operation and joint venturing between parishes attempted to cut costs, but each parish remained responsible for its own poor. It had the power to evict arrivals and return those who did not find work after 40 days to their home parishes. The poor were thus encased within a jurisdiction, impelled to gain work, receive hand-outs if "deserving," or were subject to punitive measures. Under the Poor Law, from 1692 "Parish apprenticeships" came to be a way of providing for orphaned, foundlings, and illegitimate children but, to avoid dilution of the apprenticeship system which catered for the more established sector, the magistrate administrators directed the children into lower status occupations, such as domestic service for girls and labouring for boys. Effectively, this was a market requiring the means to uplift.

Such means were begun at the intellectual level. Francis Bacon (1561-1626), Viscount St Alban, rose to become Lord High Chancellor but fell in disgrace on corruption and debt charges in 1621. He is also known as yet another of the founding fathers, here that of empiricism in scientific method. Bacon had stated that he had three goals: to uncover truth, serve his country and serve his church. Well connected, related to Lord Burghley, Elizabeth I's Secretary of State and spymaster, Bacon advanced under James I (1566-1625), who subsequently paid his fine and saved him from prison. He devoted his retirement to writing. The inheritance of Plato survived in his utopian tale of *New Atlantis* (1626) where a Council of Wise Elders mandates all key decisions. In his 1620 publication, *The New Instrument,* Bacon argued that knowledge is power. The test was not truth, for science always admits the possibility of error, but whether it empowered; did it have a use? Bacon's connection of science with technology was new, but only came to be appreciated slowly. The learning phase can be marked between governments' sponsorship of scientific societies in the 18th century to the state support of research in the 20th.

Bacon argued for scientific knowledge to be gained by inductive reasoning and the close observation of nature, with a sceptical approach designed to prevent scientists from misleading themselves. We arrive at truth by asking questions and assessing evidence. Still the basis for scientific investigation today, this marked a new departure in the theoretical and methodological approaches to science. While this was a major inspiration to the stratosphere of European intellectualism, market reality close to earth still approximated too much to that of ancient times.

A broad definition of the nature of this market by the late 18th century may be commenced with the estimate that between £30 and £40 per year [c. £1,680 to £2,240 in 2015] would be required to support a family, with around £1 per week necessary to avoid debt. With the lowest wages being around a shilling a day, both parents in such circumstances needed to work. Around two thirds of working family incomes would be spent on food and drink. A common labourer's family diet, at least in stable times, would be wheat bread, potatoes, cheese, tea, small beer, with some meat (pork or bacon) and vegetables on Sunday. Wheat flour prices fluctuated, so oats and barley substituted. While common in Scotland, this was resisted in England because loaves quickly became stale. Bread prices in London rose from around six pence per loaf in 1779 to almost double in 1800. As the poorer or casual labourer made about £10 per year, such increase could amount to a day's pay and more. A woman was paid around two thirds of male earnings for the same work. By contrast, a land-owning peer made around £10,000, a year while a successful farming knight would gather around £800 - more than his labourers could make in a lifetime.

In hard times, the diet declined further, such as bread or potatoes, water, and onions only. Coastal areas and ports had access to cheaper fish products, especially when nature was bountiful as during the 19th century herring glut, the fish expertly preserved by the Dutch salting technique, later refined on the British North Sea coasts by kippering. The poor condition of the roads, however, inhibited distribution, keeping transport costs high. As improvement began to be affected through the increase in turnpike roads in the 18th century, although such installation could also be the cause of active discontent, greater food variety increased. However, the diet would have been like that of a Roman legionary - grain based, depending on his location within the empire, except that the Roman would have had more meat (from game to sausages), wine, and more access to vegetables. The British armed services in the 18th century preferred rural to urban youth recruits; the former was usually stronger and of better build.

Designed for an agrarian population, the Elizabethan Act required successive amendment to attempt to cope with growing industrialisation, the effects of repeated bad harvests, and by the end of the 18th century the disruption caused by the wars with France.[7]

The Peasants' Revolt of 1381 had been followed by occasional outbreaks of rioting in successive centuries for a variety of causes: food shortages, industrial issues, and religious conflict being the most usual. Parallel disturbances had occurred in Italy and France. The English revolt, supported by the rural population and a wide spectrum of opinion in the southeast, had been initially defeated by the monarchical duplicity of the boy-king Richard II, (1367-1400), but left salutary lessons. There were to be no more poll taxes. The rural community had established itself as a group of people whose interests had to be considered. The fear that there might be a repeat experience acted as an important corrective in the evolution of policy, royal and parliamentary, that the interests of those who lived in and worked on the land had to be taken into account. Learning that extortionate taxes for foreign wars were unacceptable, Richard lost his throne for refusal so to indulge. Religious incitement having been a key element of the revolt, increased religious repression remained a continuing feature of English politics until the 19th century.

Participants in such civil disturbances were primarily urban artisans and industrial workers, often apprentices, although rural disturbances had a political impact, in particular during the early 19th century. The lowest ranks of the rural and urban poor were not much involved. Repression by government and the local authorities maintained control and, while trade unions remained illegal, the growth of the friendly society movement provided a rudimentary form of social security. For example, in Essex in 1801, there were 205 friendly societies with membership by 1815 of over 20,000, amounting a decade later to around 7% of the county population.[8] A weekly payment ensured sickness and old age benefit. The further emolument was charity.

It has been argued that by the mid-17th century, philanthropy had become a major source of funding for education, particularly in England. However, as this coincided with a period of further religious controversy, when almost all university graduates entering teaching were clerics, the question followed of what brand of philanthropy was being extended by the funding from the landed gentry, professional, and mercantile classes Charity schools, known also as blue coat schools, began in London in the mid-16th century and spread throughout most of the English and Welsh towns and cities. By 1710, in the London area alone there were 88 charity schools; by the end of the century, this had become the predominant form of elementary education, where schoolmistresses taught reading, writing and arithmetic: the three Rs.

*Educo,* the Latin root of the word "educate" means to lead or draw out, yet throughout the history of education there has been concentration upon what to put in. That was the nub of Rousseau's argument. The dominance of the Church in Europe after the fall of Rome entailed education becoming for and part of religious purposes. When that Church shed its Protestant dissenters, they too, in turn, split amongst themselves. The fracturing of Christendom being for political as well as doctrinal issues, it was inevitable that a Protestant state, once established with a Church of its own and State and Church being coterminous once more, that the more radical branches should go off in their own directions.

All very well within Christian toleration this might be; but not when the dissenters challenge or are perceived as challenging the orthodoxy, and hence legitimacy, of the newly Established Church itself. Coping with the lure of the old Catholicism was one thing; having to cope with Protestant priests dissenting from the state religion was quite another altogether. Charles II (1630-1685), restored to the throne after the Puritan Cromwellian interlude, was not having, in his and the view of his Lord Chancellor, the Earl of Clarendon (1609-1674), any more nonsense.

The Clarendon Code was composed of four separate Acts, supplemented by the further legislation of the Test Act of 1673, the uncompromising title of which demonstrated a certain conviction by the Crown to maintain what it saw as a continuation of the Elizabethan *via media*: "An act for preventing dangers which may happen from popish recusants".[9] Egalitarian freedom in the priesthood was abruptly curtailed. Bishops were re-empowered to ordain subordinate clergy, reversing the Puritans' levelling policy under Cromwell's Commonwealth. The Code prescribed the form of rites of the Book of Common Prayer as those of the Established Church, requiring any government or church office holder to comply thereto, and making it compulsory in religious service. Over 2,000 clerics refused to take the oath and were expelled in the "Great Ejection" of 1662, losing their livings as a result. Another consequence, although perhaps more due to popular English pragmatism, was a tendency to more moderate forms of religion, and less of it. Church services, and attendance to those remaining, declined throughout the 18th century.

To inhibit the disobedient clergy from further insurgency, however, meetings for unauthorised worship of more than five people who were not members of the same household were forbidden. The Protestant victims of the Code and Great Ejection became known as "nonconformists", the ministers of which persuasion were forbidden from coming within five miles of their former livings and were not allowed to teach in schools.[10] This latter provision was not repealed until 1812 with the 1690 Toleration Act, which allowed dissenters places and freedom to worship if they subscribed to a loyalty oath. Persons of all faiths being able easily to trade with each other on the London stock exchange was good for business. The 1673 Test Act enforced compulsory oath swearing for any military or civil office, the oaths being those of supremacy, allegiance, and a declaration against transubstantiation. Repeal here was affected by the Catholic Relief Act of 1829. Oxford and Cambridge Universities required students to submit to the Church of England's 39 Articles.

The response was the creation in England of dissenting academies, and the export of intending dissenting clergy to Scotland or to Calvinist-based higher education abroad.[11] The Common Fund Board, begun in 1689, and its successor Presbyterian Fund Board, initially gave scholarships to Presbyterian and Congregational ministry candidates. However, doctrinal differences soon emerged, leading to a board for the Congregationalists to be established in 1695. This existed to help poor ministers and induct those already in possession of a classical education into the particularities of the doctrine of their nonconformist sect. Some academies had curriculum wider than the universities, providing modern history and the practical sciences; some provided modern languages such as French and German or High Dutch; also provided were the studies of philosophy, literature, and theology. Some of Locke's works, attacked by traditional authorities, became standard discussion texts. Academies, which also supplied board and lodging, were funded by fees and philanthropy. The educational reach extended to several dissenting grammar schools, but re-integration within the mainstream followed in the 19th century with the establishment of London University, Durham University and, later, further provincial universities and the reform of Oxford and Cambridge.

However, this was not before the academies had made some significant achievements. One of the most influential was at Newington Green, then to the north of London, run by Charles Morton (1626-1698), an empiricist follower of Hume whose career concluded with the vice presidency of Harvard College. The language of instruction was English, the curriculum advanced and varied, and tuition of a competence sufficient to have attracted the praise of one of its most famous pupils: the novelist, journalist, merchant, and spy, Daniel Defoe (1660-1731). The Daventry academy was attended by Joseph Priestley; the Tewkesbury Academy by Joseph Butler. The academies' main contribution was the sheer quality of the education they provided, so much so that they even attracted Anglican students. Within their own confines they also bred theological debate, intellectual inquiry being such as to undermine Dissent itself: free thought became precisely that.

Being run by the schoolmasters themselves without boards and bureaucracies to rule and control, strict Calvinism was leavened by different, doctrinal, and more liberal approaches.[12] Business noticed, and so private enterprise commercial schools followed, catering to the same income group but without the religious commitment. These were cheap, often short-lived pops-up of varied quality. Their practical curriculum additions for boys had the purpose of preparing students for apprenticeship or employment: spelling, mathematics, handwriting, business letter writing, preparing accounts; technical drawing, with additions according to the teachers' origins, such as navigation. Girls' provision remained perfunctory.

The Georgian period began with the overhang of the previous two centuries' religious controversies and ended with the population at large being nominally Christian, in a form of deism more akin to that of the ancients. Fears of eternal damnation persisted, alongside that of offending the Almighty. Church attendance, no longer compulsory, declined. While their zealotry occupied much of the pulpits and prints, the contention was now noisily within religion, between the varieties of Anglicanism and the sects of nonconformism, each proclaiming that theirs was the way.[13] As literacy spread as much through home, family and peer instruction as formal means, so the religious movements seeking to involve the masses in their beliefs had to face the continuing conundrum of once people had learned to read, there was little control of what they might read, or think, believe, or decide as a result.

What was certain, however, was that those in control of the religious business possessed impressive acumen. The Anglican bishopric maintained a solid administration, sustaining the Established Church as the UK's largest and wealthiest institution, a distinct management success deserving of study.[14] The nonconformists produced impressive business networks, the Quakers in particular. Despite the evangelical vigour of the Church's

Clapham sect, led by such luminaries as the opponent of slavery William Wilberforce (1759-1833), by 1812 there were 186 Anglican churches in London and 256 dissenting.

Education is usually reactive to a context. The French events of 1789 were no exception, with all those dissenters earnestly talking to each other. The young William Wordsworth (1770-1850) best expressed the euphoria of his generation in Book 10 of *The Prelude*:

> Bliss it was in that dawn to be alive
> But to be young was very heaven.

The radically inclined Charles James Fox, (1749-1806) opposed his former mentor Burke's prophesy of the release of an uncontrollable force for violence, the scrapping of all versions of social control, fatally leading to a central, controlling state. This prevailing view dominated British politics until the end of the 1820s. The French revolutionaries' great mistake had been the execution of Marie Antoinette (1755-1793). One's own regicide, as with Charles I, might be accommodated; but decapitation of foreign royalty was distinctly bad form. Limitless tyranny could only follow; as it did with Napoleon.

The counter argument that Napoleon was little different in his French hegemony aspirations to Louis XIV and XV was undermined by his sponsoring of German nationalism. The Revolution had recognised the dignity of the citizen as such, stimulating politics to treat people as upholders of rights. Napoleon had reverted, however, to monarchical behaviour, making a brother a king and elevating generals to princes. The traditional British attitude of stopping the French, whatever they were up to, prevailed. Here, they failed in the matter of the American Revolution, where French military support and the intervention of Tom Paine had crucial legacy impacts. Coinciding, exporting dissent exerted a major management change beyond the contemplation of the chattering dissenters of 1789.

**FOOTPRINT**
**Age Of Reason: A Universe Running On**
**Natural And Naturally Recurring Laws**

- The Enlightenment philosophers, in declaring him a genius, took the Newtonian concept of nature and natural law as justification for their departure from outdated dogma.

- The Age of Reason, personified in Newton, could be extended. A universe run under natural and naturally occurring laws might be applied to political and other systems, such as self-interest, as Adam Smith (1723-1790) posited in economics. Natural order might be managed.

- Before approaching Smith's demonstration, which was to have major and lasting impact, it is necessary to understand the economic and intellectual context in which he functioned and sought to manage.

# Endnotes

[1] As an example of the presentation, John Aubrey records the name of Richard Billingsley, whose book was entitled: "*An Idea of Arithmetic, at first designed for the use of the free-school at Thurlow in Suffolk, by R.B., schoolmaster there, 1665: sold by W. Morden, bookseller in Cambridge,*" *op. cit.* p.103.

[2] Statute of Anne 1710: *An Act for the Encouragement of Learning by vesting the Copies of Printed Books in the Authors or purchasers of such Copies, during the Times herein mentioned.*

[3] The penny is among the first known English coins, silver minted initially in the 8th century CE. Derived from the Roman *denarius,* known subsequently in Europe as the denier and later around the Mediterranean and onward as the dinar, it's abbreviation until the currency reform of the later 20th century remained d. The first copper penny coin was struck at the Soho Mint, Birmingham, by Matthew Boulton in 1797.

[4] The oldest known school in England is the cathedral established King's School, Canterbury, founded by St Augustine.

[5] The Public Schools Act 1868 gave seven schools independence from either the Crown or the established Church: Charterhouse, Eton, Harrow, Rugby, Shrewsbury, Westminster, and Winchester, each managed by a board of governors. In 1869, Uppingham School convened what became known as the Headmasters' and Headmistresses' Conference (HMC). The resulting grouping, now numbering over 200, although private, is known as "public schools." It is a key component of "the establishment," that agglomeration seen to comprise the British ruling class. Fees now compare with those charged for MBA courses.

[6] The top ten Livery Companies:
1.  Mercers
2.  Grocers (spice merchants)
3.  Drapers
4.  Fishmongers
5.  Goldsmiths (bullion dealers)
6.  Skinners (fur trade)
7.  Merchant Taylors (tailors)
8.  Haberdashers (clothiers in fine material, such as silk or velvet)
9.  Salters (salts and chemicals)
10. Iron mongers

The ten most recently chartered:
Information technologists
World traders
World conservators
Fire-fighters
Hackney carriage drivers (licensed taxicab drivers: those who have "the knowledge")
Management consultants
International bankers
Tax advisers
Security professionals
Educators
Arts scholars

Those in waiting at the time of writing: public relations practitioners, entrepreneurs, human resource professionals, nurses, investment managers. [The later listings might be more reflective of desires for recognised personal and professional status in public perception but could also be held as a random reflection of needs for societal acceptance, nursing, firefighting and Hackney carriage driving excepted.]

[7] The wars with France extended sporadically over two decades: 1792-97; 1798-1801; 1805-1807; 1813-14; and 1815, with Napoleon's "continental system" blockades greatly disrupting trade. The first and second periods of conflict were accompanied by food riots at home. In 1809 the combination of a French glut and scarcity in England enabled a delighted Napoleon to profit hugely from trading with the enemy. During Napoleon's exile in Elba, the price of wheat in England fell from c.120 shillings to 70 shillings* per quarter ton. Wishing to continue their enormous

profits, import duties ensuring English producers a minimum of 63 shillings per quarter ton, the landowning aristocracy lobbied for "corn law" legislation to extend their bounty. The poor, refusing advice to eat bread adulterated with barley, marched in the streets, protesting before Parliament.

*There were 12 pence to the shilling and 20 shillings to the pound. Inevitably a rough guide only but, according to the National Archives currency converter, one pound in 1790 would have been worth £56 in 2005.

[8] Amos, S W. 1971. "Social discontent and Agrarian disturbances in Essex 1795-1850," Durham University Theses On Line, http://etheses.dur.ac.uk/10399/.

[9] The Corporation Act, 1661; The Act of Uniformity, 1662; The Conventicle Act,1664; The Five Mile Act,1665. Further legislation, the 1662 Quaker Act, required the swearing of an oath of allegiance to the king, this being contrary to Quaker religious belief.

[10] The term first included Presbyterians, Congregationalists, Baptists, Calvinists and other "re- formed" groups, subsequently including further sects: Methodists, Unitarians, English Moravians, Plymouth Brethren and Quakers. By the mid-19th century, some 50% of church attendance was nonconformist. Their presence was notable in Wales, coastal areas, and communities close to danger, like pit villages, and among the rising urban middle classes.

[11] John Calvin (1509-1564) was a French humanist lawyer whose prominence in Protestantism caused his exile to Geneva, where he linked with compatriots of the same persuasion, and further to Strasbourg, then returned to Geneva. His sermons, theology and their summary in his *Institutes of the Christian Religion* became prominent forces in the Reformation. Although initially close to Luther, their doctrinal split gave Calvinism a specific influence. Further refugees, now from the religious fire of Mary I in England, John Knox and companions, imported Calvinism on their return. The Congregational, Reformed, and Presbyterian sects embrace his theology. This is characterised by predestination and the absolute power of God in the afterlife to determine salvation or damnation. The religious disputes of the time were of a reciprocal incendiary nature. Calvin's denunciation of an opponent, Servetus (1509 or 1511-1553), in 1553 led to his advancement to the leadership of the Protestant cause and the latter being burnt alive as a heretic. Within the confines of his faith, Calvin was presumably one of the "Elect" predestined by the Almighty to triumph in such a conflict.

[12] Joseph Priestley (1733-1804) was a chemist, natural philosopher, grammarian, educationalist, dissenting minister and political theorist, probably best known as a contender for the discovery of oxygen, for his contributions to utilitarianism and the founding of Unitarianism. His sympathy for the ideals of the French Revolution led to the mob burning down his house and his emigration to the more congenial dissenting climate of Pennsylvania. Joseph Butler (1692-1752) was an Anglican bishop, moralist, theologian, and philosopher whose critiques of Hobbes and Locke are held to have influenced David Hume, Adam Smith, and John Henry Newman (1801-1890). His Bible fundamentalist views provoked particular controversy.

[13] The early 18th century dissent count is estimated at: "about 179,000 Presbyterians, 59,000 Congregationalists, 58,000 Baptists and 38,000 Quakers, with the numbers declining by up to 40% by 1740" (Porter, Roy. *English Society in the 18th Century,*

p. 179). John Wesley's movement, originally within Anglicanism, with its evangelism and ability to communicate with the poor and the common man, had only 24,000 adherents in 1767, rising to 77,000 by 1796. Nonconformism was strongest in the towns. The main forces of the impetus to self-help and self-respect among the workforce were Methodism, the New Dissent of Baptism and Congregationalism, and the example of the practices of Quaker business.

[14] This injunction was proved prescient in January 2023 at the time of proof reading when a report for the Church Commissioners, the body charged with management of the Church of England's over £9 billion endowment fund, traced its origins to a financial scheme known as Queen Anne's Bounty, an investment vehicle established for the South Seas Company's engagement in transatlantic chattel slavery. In an attempt to "address past wrongs", the Church Commissioners' board is to set up a £100m fund to deliver over the next nine years a programme of investment, research and engagement: see Harriet Sherwood, "C of E setting up £100m fund to 'address past wrongs' of slave trade links", *Guardian*, 10 January 2023, https://www.theguardian.com/world/2023/jan/10/church-of-england-100m-fund-past . The Church is avoiding use of the term "reparations" on the grounds that the scheme will not compensate individuals but instead will support projects "focussed on improving opportunities for communities adversely impacted by historic slavery". In an attempt to ensure that the Church's response is carried out "sensitively and with accountability", an oversight group is to be formed "with significant membership from communities impacted by historic slavery". The Church Commissioners' chairman, Archbishop of Canterbury Justin Welby, said that the report "lays bare the links of the Church Commissioners' predecessor fund with transatlantic chattel slavery. I am deeply sorry for these links. It is now time to take action to address our shameful past". It was only in 2019, the report discloses, that the Church Commissioners "became more conscious" that "the transatlantic slave economy played a significant role in shaping the economy, society and church we have today." While it might reasonably be asked what, precisely, does the weasel expression "became more conscious" actually mean (that some Commissioners were semi-conscious, even unconscious perhaps?), David Walker (1957- ), Bishop of Manchester and the Commissioners' deputy chair, conceded that the Commissioners "recognised that it was important to know its past better in order to understand its present". Gratifying though it is for there to be distinguished ecclesiastical agreement with a basic management thesis of this and its companion books, it must be recorded that the South Sea Company's main commercial activity between 1714 and 1739 was transatlantic slavery, expressed through purchase and transportation. The Queen Anne's Bounty fund invested significantly in the South Sea Company and received many benefactions from persons linked to, or who profited from the transatlantic chattel slavery and plantation economy. Bounty funds were used either to pay a cash stipend to poor clergy or the purchase of land from which clergy received an income. Slavery issues are further addressed in the companion volume to this study: *Managing Mass Education, and the Rise of Modern and Financial Management,* particularly in its Case Study 1, *Going for a Zong.*

# CHAPTER FOURTEEN

## REASON AND ENLIGHTENMENT

Had his personal brand of Christianity been known, Sir Isaac Newton (1648-1727), a rare Cambridge scholar who remained Christian but refused to take holy orders, and was so allowed by Charles II, would have been condemned as a heretic.

**Sir Isaac Newton**

Among many great scientific achievements, Newton finally fully proved helio-centralism: that obedient to the laws of motion and gravity, the sun and its planets constituted the solar system, with the former at the centre. Galileo was at last undoubtedly proved to have been correct.

An awkward individualist, Newton illustrated in this own career an apparent transition from superstition and the occult to the purely rational. Seemingly, he had later concentrated only upon scientific exploration.

In an earlier generation, Dr John Dee (1527-1608), mathematician and adviser to Elizabeth I who coined the term "British Empire," had progressed in the opposite direction. A geometrician whose navigation tuition assisted Elizabeth's leading seamen, he also delved deeply into alchemy and the occult. Dee straddled the worlds of science and magic; Newton journeyed from superstition to become one of the brightest leading lights of mathematics, physics, astronomy, and the Enlightenment itself, acknowledged among the greatest scientists of all time. Yet he also continued with biblical prophetic interpretation pursuits and other occult explorations albeit, and fittingly, in seclusion.

In his *Philosophiae Naturalis Principia Mathematica* of 1687, Newton determined the laws of motion and universal gravitation. These became the foundation of physics and its derivatives until the late 20th century and the development of the theories of quantum mechanics. Newton's classical mechanics illustrated the determination of the paths of comets, the equinoxes and tidal motion. Coincidentally with Leibniz, he developed infinitesimal calculus. His investigations of optics produced the first practical reflecting telescope, the proof of the colours of the spectrum by the passage of white light through a prism. Further achievements included an empirical law of cooling, theoretical calculation of the speed of sound and the making of great advances in mathematics. Sensitive to criticism, a dispute with fellow Royal Society member, Robert Hooke (1635-1703), caused him to withdraw to concentrate further on his work, this leading to the production of the *Principia.*

Although internationally recognised and given the customarily sinecure post of Master of the Mint, the inveterate practical investigator Newton took the job seriously; sometimes disguised, even pursuing detection in taverns during his thirty-year tenure, reforming the currency and combating clipping and forgery. The great re-coinage of 1696 revealed counterfeit currency to have amounted to 20%. In a major act of monetary management, to last for 200 years, he established the gold standard in 1717, defining the pound in terms of gold weight (£4.25 per troy ounce). This dogged, inspiring man wore his accolades lightly, writing to Robert Hooke in 1676, but it should also be observed that Hooke was a small man, sensitive of his lack of height and notably irascible:

> If I have seen further,
> it is by standing on the shoulders of giants.

If there was to be natural process, what then of the Enlightenment and its philosophers? What, indeed, a cleric and Prussian government official had asked in 1783, is Enlightenment? An answer was supplied a year later by Immanuel Kant (1724-1804) in an essay employing that question as its title:

> Enlightenment is man's emergence from his
> self-incurred immaturity.

That immaturity, Kant maintained, is not due to a lack of understanding but arises from a lack of courage. Reason, intellect, and wisdom were present;

the failure was not to use them. "Lazy and cowardly" submission to the "dogmas and formulas" of political or religious authority is caused by our being uncomfortable in thinking for ourselves. Even where the dogma is discarded, stagnation would follow for minds have not been cultivated. Graduation from such mental immaturity can be achieved through reason, applied by and with courage. Famously, quoting Horace, he enjoined: "*Sapere aude*" – translated as "Dare to be wise!" or "Dare to understand." One of the most important injunctions of history, this is the original, foundational demand for freedom of thought and speech.

Practically minded, Kant was cautious of revolutions, such as that in America, for he feared that the "great unthinking masses" would become subject to new dogma. His hope was that there would always be a few who could think for themselves, so helping the rest. Even office holders, such as priests and government officials, could think and speak for themselves in their private capacities. Religious institutions and their dogma could be changed by successive generations, for the former could not bind the latter. It was in man's interest to overcome the barriers which prevented the use of reason.

Aligning himself with the enlightened despot Frederick II the Great of Prussia, Kant saw fewer obstacles to "universal enlightenment" because of Frederick's rule but made an important distinction. At his time of writing in 1784, people were not living in an "enlightened age", but they did dwell in an "age of enlightenment." That age is conventionally placed in the latter two thirds of the 18$^{th}$ century, spilling out from the previous century's Scientific Revolution and Age of Reason, and flowing into the mid-19$^{th}$ century period of classic liberalism.

However, the cross current of Romanticism in art, music and literature which can be dated from the end of the 18$^{th}$ century up to a peak in the mid-19$^{th}$, with its emphases on emotion, individualism and the glorification of all things past (particularly preferring the medieval to the classical), was a reaction both to industrialisation and the rigours of Enlightenment thought.[1] Replaced by realism and nationalism from the later 19$^{th}$ century onwards, Romanticism had a significant influence on politics, and on ordinary life, where the elevation of nature, folk art, and the heroic gave mental relief from the realities of urban industrialisation. The increasing emphasis on individualism did, however, harmonise with the individual courage of thought espoused by the Enlightenment. The term "Middle Ages" to identify the period between the end of the Western Roman Empire and the onset of the Reformation had first appeared in English in 1783. Enlightenment was thus a further cutting edge of modernity.

Of the Enlightenment itself, four themes are clear: reason, science, humanism, and progress. The common denominator was reason. Provided that argument, opinion, or judgment could be argued as reasonable, it could be held accountable to objective standards. The test was reason. This was not to claim that humans were or could be perfectly rational; rather, it was because many of the thinkers recognised that people were not particularly reasonable in their habits of thought and behaviour that emphasis upon a rational approach was necessary. Reason could be further refined to understand the world, which included an understanding of humankind. The many thinkers below disagreed about much, but all believed that there was a universal human behaviour, and pursued their inquiries through many routes such as: anthropology, social and evolutionary psychology, and cognitive neuroscience. Replacing the view that morality came from God, duty was seen to come from membership of society.

Humanism was pursued with vigour; a secure secular morality was required as an antidote to the constant cycle since the Crusades of religious warfare, carnage, and the civil terrors of Inquisition and witch-hunting. Moral concern was focused upon the individual, even though particular activity might concern the greatest good of the greatest number. Empathy with individual suffering brought concern and pressure for the reform of such social injustices as harsh sentences for trivial offences, sadistic punishments, and slavery. Enlightened applications brought an end to barbaric excesses which had been commonplace for centuries. However, the Enlightenment thinkers did not wish to change human nature, nor engage in social engineering or behavioural influence. Their idea of progress was to concentrate upon and to improve social institutions, thereby promoting the human condition. The retreat from, or reaction to, the Enlightenment of some of contemporary society might be compared to the cultural institutionalisation of individual and group mobile phone communication cultures today.

The Enlightenment philosophers targeted government, educational establishments, laws, and markets for attention as establishments whose activities impacted greatly upon people. Human inventions, within the social contract, were to be designed or improved to enhance citizen benefit. Selfish acts which might benefit individuals but impoverish society were to be discouraged. The greatest enactment of Enlightenment thinking, the US

Declaration of Independence, famously sought to secure its citizens' right to life, liberty, and the pursuit of happiness. Here was the epitome of the Hobbesian social contract. The torch bearers of the Enlightenment were people of their times, unaccountable now for what they did not know then, imperfect, as they would acknowledge and confused in various of their attitudes – as illustrated by the US Founding Fathers. However, they have also not been fully understood in another sense. The person now to be studied is of famous repute in economics. Yet he was also a moral philosopher whose economic theory rested upon the Enlightenment concept, echoing Aristotle, of prosperity following correct moral action.

To understand the economics propounded by the moral philosopher Adam Smith, which was to have major and lasting impact, it is necessary first to recall the economic and intellectual context in which he functioned. The Physiocrats in 18th century France believed that land was the ultimate source of all wealth, and markets should not be constrained by governments, seen by Smith as "perhaps the nearest approximation to the truth that has yet been published upon the subject of political economy." This was the first real school of economic thought, the first to argue against mercantilism.

**Adam Smith**

Smith saw the discovery of America and the passage to the East Indies as "the greatest events recorded in the history of mankind."

Yet this would not have assisted Europe's mushroom growth from the mid-18th century without the pillaged silver from the New World with which to purchase Chinese and Indian goods, and slaves from Africa with which to furnish the Caribbean and American plantations.

While the benefit of "armed trading" opened markets, in 1775 Asia still accounted for 80% of the world's economy, with the Chinese and Indian economies combined amounting to two thirds of global production.

There was particular point in Smith's approval of Quesnay's work on China (see Chapter 5). A Eurocentric view of global modern economic history cannot be sustained until the late 19$^{th}$ century, when steamships substantially undercut Arab, Indian and Chinese shipping. Chinese and Persians could not catch up quickly with the emerging, industrialising military version of trade because they thought, organised, and managed their societies differently. Thought was now being expressed in new forms in the West, applied with vigorous, organised management.

Edinburgh and Glasgow were, at the time, the greatest universities of Europe. Despite Scottish primacy in education, its history before and by Smith's birth was desperate. There was religious and civil war; political turmoil; battles between Presbyterians and Episcopalians; marauding armies; Highlander problems; antagonism between different governments of Scotland; and vital questions of economic development. In his *Civil Liberty* essay, Hume famously remarked: "something changed at the end of the 17$^{th}$ century when commerce became a reason of state," for all states had to become commercial if they meant to maintain themselves.

How they had to do that was to develop commerce, a deep and real problem for small states such as Scotland. The consequences of the disastrously unsuccessful Darien scheme on the Panama isthmus of the 1690s had helped precipitate the 1707 Act of Union between England and Scotland.[2] The question dangled of how successful the creation of this novel free trade area would be. The result, Smith later observed, was so successful as to be beyond dispute. Even so, the stability associated with successful commercial development did not apply by Smith's time. The Highlanders had invaded as part of the Jacobite Rebellion of 1745; the political scene was one of wild republicans, radical Christians, and worries of renewed war and invasions. It was the desire for real stability which inspired Smith's investigation of how the actions of individuals affected entire societies and his passionate argument against the regulation of markets.

Adam Smith's formal education began at what was reputed to be the best burgh school in Scotland, transferring to Glasgow University at 14, progressing to Balliol College, Oxford in 1740, where he considered the teaching much poorer. He found that the staff taught little, possibly a result of their all having clerical livings. Shortly after leaving, he began public lecturing in Edinburgh, which earned him a professorship teaching logic at Glasgow in 1751. He later took a tutoring position which allowed travel to London and Europe, where he was able to meet contemporary intellectuals including Voltaire, Benjamin Franklin, Francois Quesnay and d'Alembert (1717-1783). His two major publications, *The Theory of Moral Sentiments* (1759) and *An Inquiry into the Nature and Causes of the Wealth of Nations* (1776) made his reputation, whereby another paternity has been derived: "father of modern economics." His advocacy of empathy in human relations, mutual understanding, and sympathy contained in *Moral Sentiments* led naturally to his view of the important social role of labour and self-interest in the *Wealth of Nations.* It is vital to stress that Smith was a moralist before he was an economist, that he was influenced by Taoist thought, and that both of his books are built on the common idea of the mutual benefit to be derived from exchange. *Moral Sentiments* concerned obligations and duties; *Wealth,* benefits with altruism and self-interest balanced.

The combination of Smith's arguments and progress of the industrial revolution led Britain to abandon the restrictions of mercantilism and monopolies, turning instead towards free trade, a preoccupation from the mid-19th century onwards. Based on his exemplar study of pin manufacture, Smith contended that productivity creates wealth, with productivity increased by the division of labour. Smith's further argument was that competition and rational self-interest could lead to economic prosperity. As the Roman Empire had been a free trade area, so the expanding British Empire exported this broadly liberal economic model around much of the world. Competition was held to ensure that the owners of resources, from land to labour, would use them efficiently and economically. Such use would be balanced by rates of return in equilibrium, adjusted for particular factors such as unemployment, hardship and training. Behind all of this has been held to be the workings of an "invisible hand." This can be seen as a goad to unthinking entrepreneurs following self-absorbed, unconscious pathways. If the hand was invisible, the armed might behind burgeoning international trade was all too apparent.

Economists notoriously disagree. There is no ultimate consensus, much as the moralising Smith might have wished, on what that "invisible hand" is, should be, or might be. Eschewing the facetious, it remains difficult to comprehend the invisible without the appropriate instruments; and here there is no final consensus on what those might be. The obvious religious or superstitious identities aside, the simplicities of supply and demand, and market forces, armed or otherwise, remain the clearest candidates, with Taoist characteristics. Such was the devotion of Margaret Thatcher (1925-2013) to the notion of the free market that she has been said to have carried a copy of Smith's work in her copious handbag, although this assertion seems more likely to have been an illustrative urban myth. However, while there was no novelty in perceiving people to be grasping go-getters, seeing greed as natural and even admirable rather than one of the deadly sins, Smith's notion of an unseen but providential force which would turn such activity to the benefit of all was, and remains, a pervasive, persuasive, ultimately highly convenient idea of quasi-religious stature.

Either you have faith in Smith's version of a free market or you don't. It may even be the way of the Tao, or it may not. It is tempting, in stressing Smith's embrace of the eastern thought of the Tao, to note Khayyam's possible Iranian linkage, the Moving Finger being a digit of an Invisible Hand. The duality, and inherent contradiction between a moral, quasi-religious faith and a secular belief, begs the further question of whether the free market is an end in and of itself, and whether that is of universal benefit, for the nature of competition is that someone inevitably loses. The controversy regarding contemporary amoral economism stems from a reversal of Smith's premise where morality came first.

The Enlightenment can be seen as a battle of where we go next. Smith's contribution was unfinished, for he did not complete and destroyed all the notes for a third volume which would have unified his work. The final subject was meant to be the triumph of law over patronage, where wise legislation would rule society for the good. The commercial society he sought required justification. He maintained that to be an economist you must also be a historian, appreciative of the breadth and nature of human experience. Commercial societies in the past had fallen victim to agricultural interests, as typified by Rome's defeat of Carthage.

To Smith, a commercial society was one in which every person, in some measure, becomes a merchant, using markets to meet needs. As the division of labour showed, markets were more efficient in that specialisms allowed for greater productivity. Although self-interested, capital generated wealth for others and promoted civil liberty. People put something aside from their wealth to provide for the future, bringing benefit to themselves and others. Justice applied in that where money was made, it would make more for everyone else. In the "natural progress of opulence," the market worked if left alone. Realist Smith retained a low view of business persons and special interests for he noted how the "spirit of corporation" could influence parliament and public policy. He warned against special interest interventions but remained canny and cool when it came to his own. He delayed three years before publishing *Wealth of Nations* while awaiting the outcome of what he termed "the present disturbances" in North America. The eventual 1776 publication was able to demonstrate by highly significant example that mercantile empire was a failed economic model.

David Ricardo (1772-1823) had studied *Smith's* book carefully, over 150 notations having been found after his death in his copy. These formed the basis of his 1817 *Principles of Political Economy and Taxation,* where it has been said that if Adam Smith had explained what the capitalist system was, Ricardo explained how it works.

### David Ricardo

He developed a model of economic rent. This was the amount received by the supplier of an input in excess of the amount necessary to secure its supply. His chapter on foreign trade began with a statement overturning mercantilism, the 16th to 18th century gold and silver bullion-based national economic policy which promoted government regulation at the expense of foreign powers:

> We should have no greater value if, by the discovery of new markets, we obtained double the quantity of foreign goods in exchange for a given quantity of ours.[3]

Ricardo's law of comparative advantage showed how it was economically better for international trade partnerships and reciprocity to function, although that was not fully comprehended at the time. The principle was that it was best to trade goods the production of which were a strength - hence English wool and French wine made for compatible, mutually beneficial trade. From such a base, further trade could flow freely. Although such a staple was not beneficial to the wine producing Portugal, Ricardo's place of family origin, this comparative advantage principle underpinned the consequent principle of free trade. The eclectic Ricardo further pursued a philosophical radicalism which appealed to all sides of the progressive movement.

A social libertarian, he supported Catholic emancipation, abolition and mass education for the poor. A landlord himself, he opposed the vested interests of landowners, particularly as enacted through the Corn Laws. Viewing himself as lacking in education, he sought guiding principles, across a broad spectrum. A productive, manufacturing Great Britain could mitigate those landed interests which friendly associates such as James Mill (1717-1783) and Jeremy Bentham viewed as pernicious. Ricardo sought natural causes of economic benefit. With free speech limited by the conditions of his times, Ricardo's radicalism was tempered by discretion. Much of his economics were concerned with distribution, not redistribution.

Adam Smith's motivations had included the avoidance of injustice emerging through such conflict as arising through religious wars. Part of the re-balancing of society was people being able to attain and retain moderate wealth. Such aspiration, endeavour and realisation were to come through societal movement, naturally guided.

It must also be appreciated that Smith used the invisible hand notion in his writings thrice only. The first was a scornful remark c. 1758 in his *History of Astronomy* regarding explainable phenomena being attributed to the invisible hand of Jupiter (Zeus). The *Theory of Moral Sentiments* of 1759 cites the rich being led by an invisible hand inadvertently to divide with the poor the fruits of their improvements: the origin of "trickle down" theory. *The Wealth of Nations*, 1776, at Book IV, Chapter II, Paragraph IX, refers to an individual intending only his own gain concerning investment in domestic or foreign markets who "is led by an invisible hand to promote an end which was in no part of his intention." Nowhere does he use the definite article. It is always "an invisible hand." The phrase was employed in economics only from the 20th century and has been used since as a foundation for diverse thought and argument, with Smith's name in consequence used to dignify much with which he might not have agreed. Neither he, nor the other British philosophers cited below, believed in absolutely free markets.

Since it involves practitioners and students of the notoriously gloomy and ultimately inexact subject, there is unlikely ever to be conclusive proof of all of Smith's thinking, or that attributed to him, on what was then termed political economy. Neo-classicism holds that value is dependent on what the buyer is prepared to pay. Smith was controversial in his own day and remains so still, particularly where his name is attached to policies and institutions which conflict with his moral stance, where value may have differing meanings. A contemporary management theorist has posited the ambitious alternative that a "visible hand," in the form of highly competent, well-organised management can defeat the invisible forces; a remarkable stance when opposing forces are invisible and hence unknown in scope, capacity, and power, and discredited by the evidence.[4]

One simple truth, however, is the observable and provable: to repeat, in free trade, someone always loses. Smith had the wisdom to recognize that, pointing out also that civil government is necessary to protect the rich against the poor from seizing its assets. Echoing Aristotle, he further observed:

> What improves the circumstances of the greater part can never be regarded as an inconveniency to the whole. No society can surely be flourishing and happy, of which the greater part are poor and miserable.[5]

Smith had followed ideas such as the division of labour of the Dutch immigrant political economist and satirist Bernard de Mandeville (1670-1733), whose poem *Fable of the Bees* (1705, 1714 and 1723) had scandalised society. One of the first to recognise the role of the consumer in society rather than the state, he argued that private vices were essential to a healthy economy. Those who strove to make the world virtuous would make it poor. Gambling diverts money from those who do not know how to value it to those who do and can invest it wisely. Dishonesty supports lawyers who use the proceeds to support their cooks and tailors. The public benefits from private vice.

Many of our virtues are disguised vices. An unlicensed medic practising as a form of psychiatrist, de Mandeville warned that as success could breed evil, people had to be careful what they wished for. Self-interest came from pride, a contention which Smith opposed. In the management context, de Mandeville can be seen as the first social scientist, considering society and what holds it together, all social virtues deriving from self-preservation.

Smith's compatriot and close friend David Hume (1711-1776), highly influential in the Anglo-Scottish Enlightenment and subsequently, warned of the problem of inductive reasoning: we are not justified in believing that the sun will rise tomorrow on the basis that it has always done so in the past. In any venture, especially the commercial, absence of observed volatility should never be confused with an absence of risk.  In considering the workings of the mind, Hume identified the principles of association as three: resemblance, contiguity in time and place, and causality.

Although modern study has much advanced and we no longer think of the mind going through a sequence of ideas, one at a time, but instead through a great deal of simultaneous processing, at the time of the Enlightenment, one of its leading minds was considering how the ideas themselves were coming into being, forming, and communicating.

The great goal of the Enlightenment was the enhanced happiness of the people, its consummation being seen throughout the succeeding centuries in the inspiration of social reforms which bettered their lot. Hume posed the great question of how to approach human nature, and hence its happiness.

### David Hume

Hume's empirical investigation into human nature aimed to discover the extent and force of human understanding. Opposing the rationalists, he argued that the passions (emotions) govern human behaviour in a work recognised as the founding document of cognitive science. His precocious publication of *A Treatise of Human Nature* at the age of twenty-three, dry but brilliant, was not well received, his career stalling as a result. His suspected atheism barred him from university teaching. Rescue came through tutoring and then librarianship at Edinburgh University, which gave him the time and scope for research and writing.

He produced a *History of England*, which became a best seller and the standard work of its day. For the first time, the subject was broadened to science and the arts, beyond the usual march of monarchs, politicians, and conflict. His intention in philosophy was to construct a science of man by which to appraise the psychological basis of human nature, arguing that moderation came through passion rather than reason. His sentimentalist causation approach was that sympathy was the chief source of moral distinctions.

Before Hume, as with Descartes, philosophy began with a religious premise. Hume took God out of the picture. Morality had to mean something independent of God. Effectively, the management of human affairs had to be through a morality informed by empirical evidence. Such a human relations philosophy for management application was one of empiricism, scepticism, and naturalism.

The Enlightenment replaced the belief that morality comes from God with the idea that duty comes from our membership of society. There is a continuing issue with the further derived philosophy, however, in that ideas or nuances particular to the philosopher's times may be re-interpreted later for newly present purposes. In the case of the starkly asocial Jeremy Bentham, whose utilitarianism did detach morality from values of instinct and the constituents of good to form a single principle of reason, the test being "the greatest happiness of the greatest number," its entry into a distinct if misguided form of economic thought is understandable. However, such adaptation would not necessarily have met with Bentham's approval. Locke and even Hume have also been invoked as roots for such movements as the "radical individualism" of Milton Friedman (1912-2006) and the Chicago school. These have led to an emphasis in managerial capitalism economics, and hence education, for such items as morals being matters for individuals; self-interest as a behavioural assumption; and a focus upon human imperfections – none of the present extremes of which the Enlightenment philosophers are likely to have approved.

Despite such later misapplications of his thought, Hume stood as a monument, one of the greatest intellects of the age, exemplar of the vitality of 17th and 18th century cultural life north of the border. Such vitality flourished as the restrictions to the English universities did not apply to those in Scotland, established during the 16th and 17th centuries. [6] Previously, Scots had to travel to England and beyond to receive higher education, and for the purposes of a second degree continued to do so. The later 17th century English religious restrictions meant the development of two-way traffic: English dissenter students going north; dissenter Scots in pursuit of higher learning going to Europe. The international contact and exchange helped the integration of Scotland within European intellectual life, so importing the developing humanist ideas.

Scotland's administrative structure was a mixture of 33 counties and hundreds of "burghs," or towns, which had separate legal and administrative status, with the largest becoming designated as cities. In 1560, an attempt to provide a school for every parish failed. Existing burgh schools were maintained, some reformed into grammar schools; "song schools" continued to provide specific musical and liturgical education for choristers;

and new foundations conforming to either the parish or grammar school mode.[7] They were funded by a mixture of kirk (church), local "heritors" or parish proprietors or landholders, burgh councils, and parents able to pay. Kirk inspection checked teaching quality and doctrinal rectitude. Unregulated "adventure schools" essentially competed according to local needs. Many teachers were part-time, generally low-ranking clergy.

Curriculum in the better establishments extended as far as French, classical literature, Latin, catechism, and sports. Acting on an earlier Privy Council command that every parish establish a school, the Parliament of Scotland through the 1633 Education Act imposed a tax on local landowners to provide the necessary endowment, the measure made effective by further legislation in 1646. The heritors had to provide a school and pay the teacher; the kirk oversaw its quality. By the late 17th century, lowland Scotland had a complete system of parish schools, but many areas continued to be without provision in the highlands. Boys enjoyed a much fuller curriculum than that afforded to girls, whose study was frequently confined to reading but not writing, knitting, and sewing. Illiteracy rates in Scotland in the later 18th century have been estimated at around 85% for women and 35% for men.[8]

Andrew Melville (1545-1622) graduated from St Andrews University at the age of 19 with the reputation of being the best young scholar in the land, progressed to study and achieve academic posts in France before being appointed, at the age of 27, to the chair of humanities at the Academy of Geneva. There, he encountered Protestant refugees from the St Bartholomew's Massacre of 1572, including the leading thinkers of the day on political science, civil law and ecclesiastical liberty. Immediately on his return to Scotland in 1574, he was appointed Principal of the University of Glasgow and began its reform. He enlarged the curriculum, establishing chairs in divinity, science, philosophy and languages, improved delivery and so enhanced the university's reputation that student numbers greatly increased. He was so successful that he was asked to participate in the reconstruction of Aberdeen University the next year. In 1580, he was requested to reprise the achievement at St Andrews University, where he was appointed Principal of St. Mary's College. His duties included the teaching of theology, Hebrew, Chaldee, Syriac, and Rabbinical languages.

He created a fashion for the study of Greek literature, but his anti-Aristotle stance and religious fervour brought him into conflict with colleagues; his resistance to the imposition of episcopy caused him to flee to England to escape a treason charge. Resuming his lectures on return, he eventually succeeded to the Rectorship of the university in 1590, only to be returned to the chair of theology because of his outspoken behaviour, particularly concerning "God's sillie vassal" King James VI (1566-1625), and continued to defend the Kirk against the invasion of state power. His incautious expressions caused him to be summoned by the King, now James I of England, to London as part of the royal bid to establish religious peace. Once more, outspoken behaviour cost him dearly: a sarcastic Latin epigram critical of the monarch was notified to James, who retaliated by imprisoning Melville in the Tower of London for four years. Free speech had a price. On release, he left for Europe once more, accepting a Chair at the University of Sedan.

Melville is a fine example of the awkward, outspoken academic, as difficult in his way towards James I as the Younger Cato was to Caesar but without the grislier consequences, or Galileo to Popes Paul V and Urban VIII. Nonetheless, it was through such turbulent speakers to power that the foundations to great progress could be laid. It took over 1,500 years for an approximation to the Catos' ideas of a republic to come to a new reality, and in another continent; Galileo and Melville's intellectual legatees had swifter rewards. Academic freedom had to be fought for.

The quality of Scottish education and poverty of its homeland encouraged emigration. The British colonial expansion provided opportunity and financial incentives, particularly for doctors and engineers. Presbyterian Scot John Witherspoon (1723-1794) went further, bringing ideas from the Scottish Enlightenment to the College of New Jersey, which became Princeton University, as its long-serving formative president in 1768. He was an adherent of the Scottish school of common-sense realism propounded by such thinkers as Thomas Reid (1710-1796), the sociologist Adam Ferguson (1723-1816), poet James Beattie (1735-1803) and mathematician Dugald Stewart (1753-1828). Critics of Hume, Locke, and Descartes, they envisaged humans as social beings able to perceive common ideas, in which process judgment was inherent and interdependent. Common sense, therefore, was the foundation of philosophical inquiry. The politically active Witherspoon, a signatory of the Declaration of Independence, became a formative influence in the development of the U.S. national character. Congressman, convening moderator of the first General Assembly of the Presbyterian Church of the USA, and highly influential educator, Witherspoon embodied a unity of church and state in the formation of the new republic, realising Enlightenment ideals in a practical, common-sense manner of pragmatic management.

Meanwhile, the ideas and ideal of the Enlightenment were being disseminated across Europe and further in North America. Unsurprisingly, having been repressed for so long by the Roman Church and confined by the restrictions of Aristotelian thought on what was termed "natural philosophy," many of the emboldened Enlightenment writers and thinkers had a scientific background. Simultaneously, aided by the application of the discoveries and method of the Islamic world, the restriction of Galen's dogma on medicine was broken.[9] Thus, alchemy and astrology also lost scientific credibility, and religious authority began to be replaced by that of science.

Similarly, while the growth of scientific method and overthrow of religious dogma influenced the practices of free thought and speech, the political and social consequences were not always acceptable to the leading *philosophes* themselves. The French Revolution and American Independence caused fissures in Enlightenment support among monarchies and the bourgeoisie. Rousseau criticised science as diminishing happiness, distancing humanity from nature. Still dominated by religion, the universities were slow to change. Newtonian physics did not become commonly taught until the mid-18th century, almost a century after the publication of the *Principia*. European university student numbers remained constant throughout the 18th century, although they did increase in Britain. Under that "natural philosophy" umbrella, science was divided into physics and a combination of chemistry and natural history. This was further divided into sub-categories such as anatomy, biology, geology, mineralogy, and geography.

Usually, change in science teaching came slowly. Physical principles' demonstrations, for example, only gained lecture room presence from the 1720s. Yet, change could also be rapid and immediate. All French colleges and universities were abolished in 1808 and reformed as the single *Université Impériale,* which made the further innovation of dividing the arts and sciences into different faculties. Other change was uneven: Britain was divided with much greater advance, as noted above, in Scotland; in Germany, monarchy promoted science and the universities taught in the vernacular; in Sweden, university professors were given license to choose their own course textbooks and plan the curriculum themselves; and the Dutch universities had been quick to adopt the Newtonian approach.

Even then, advances in knowledge could be culture-bound and slow. Parts of the Arab world remained centuries ahead. The Tunisian-born of Yemeni descent, who served the Egyptian state as a jurist but was also a literary figure of high standing and brilliant historian of the Arab world, Ibn

Khaldūn became known in the West only from the end of the 17th century, receiving major attention only in the mid-19th. He is seen as a forerunner of historiography, sociology, economics, and demography. His philosophy and theory of history received exceptional scholarly praise; his political economy, where he described an economy as being composed of value-added processes, is argued to be the first in its field. His sociology has been seen as an identifier of the business cycle. The intellectually curious, all-conquering Timur summoned him to meet and dispute towards the end of both their lives, such was the scope of the achievement of his *Muqaddimah.* Yet, it took half a millennium for the West to begin to comprehend the scope of immense Islamic world achievement.

In 1375, Ibn Khaldūn retreated into the Sahara, emerging four years later after having written one of the most important studies of history ever. Drawing on regional history and a personal experience which had included the loss of many of his family to the Black Death, losing in several court intrigues, and imprisonment, he set out a cool analysis of the rise and fall of dynasties. He felt that Timur's triumphs bore out his theories. His management argument was that group solidarity was vital to success in power. However, this always decayed within five generations. Urban dynasties grow tired, inevitably becoming vulnerable to overthrow by rural insurgents. It was not until some three centuries later that he was rediscovered in the West as a profoundly prescient political scientist, philosopher of history and, as one of the great thinkers of the Muslim world, a forerunner of both sociology and management thought.

So staid, archaic, and insular was the English higher education system, certainly impervious to the likes of Tunisian polymaths, inevitably advance was greater outside it than within it. New institutions, public and private, were created to meet demand, and the professions themselves provided means for study. Many of these institutions and innovations sought to meet the needs of business and its security, emphasising mathematics, this being increasingly necessary for the practice of such trades and professions as the merchant, engineer, or military officer. Such was the proliferation of learned societies and academies during the late 17th and early 18th centuries that a new network for scientific information exchange and stimulation to further discovery was created. With the appearance of some 70 new institutions, means for hugely increased dissemination of knowledge at the highest levels had been achieved.

London led the way with its Royal Society in 1662, followed by Paris in 1666 and Berlin in 1700. As the formal movement spread, country by country, royally chartered, it was accompanied by unchartered societies, nationally, regionally, spreading to provinces. The role of the national societies included direct contact between scientific bodies and government. State sponsorship brought prestige and finance with the benefit of management freedom for the societies; the state gained state-of-the-art knowledge and the benefits and by-products of scientific investigation. The knowledge business was under way.

Joint projects between societies increased intellectual exchange, but the formal communications achieved through published scientific journals became the most important form of contact between scientists. Society members thus enjoyed access to ideas and colleagues, with the opportunity to publish themselves. However, while the Royal Society published quarterly from the early 18th century, other formal societies had longer publication periods. Such delay, plus mistaken rejections, stimulated a growth in the private market, which also benefited from translations being required as vernacular publication became common. As the volume of publications increased, so did the range of the subject matter, which, in turn, stimulated the market for niche, specialist periodicals, such as *Botanical Magazine*, first appearing in 1789.

Such knowledge was further expanded by the growth of encyclopaedia and dictionaries, the prime examples of which were the works of Denis Diderot (1713-1784), and Samuel Johnson (1709-1784). The increasingly literate were hungry for more knowledge, and more prosperous societies, such as Britain and North America, could afford to pay for works of increasing length. Paradoxically, the mobs in support of the Jacobins of the French Revolution who had been inspired by the works of Rousseau, Diderot, and his fellows, could certainly neither have read nor afforded Diderot and Jean le Rond d'Alembert's *Encyclopédie, ou dictionnaire raisonné des sciences, des arts et des métiers* first published in 1751.

To deter the French authorities from interfering, publication was fictitiously announced to be from Neuchatel in Switzerland. Actual publication came subsequently from Geneva, which also enabled a lowering of price to subscribers.

**Denis Diderot**
Co-founder, Chief Editor, and
contributor to the Encyclopédie,
assisted by Jean le Rond d'Alembert.

This part-work of over thirty-five volumes was composed of some 71,000 entries. It was formally suppressed in 1759, causing the withdrawal of d'Alembert and other powerful figures, but Diderot kept writing – although it was secretly sabotaged by his printer who defaced or destroyed some latter entries. It was not until 1772 that subscribers received the final volumes. Issued in quarto and octavo editions from 1777, its simple yet ambitious aim was: "to set forth as well as possible the order and connection of the parts of human knowledge".[10]

This was expressed through a framework conceived as a tree of knowledge. The tree showed division between the arts and sciences, a reflection of the growth of empiricism, but their unity as spreading from philosophy-tree-trunk, the centre of knowledge and learning. Antithesis to religion was shown plainly: theology was merely a minor branch of the tree, close to that of black magic. In contrast, the *Encyclopaedia Britannica*, begun in 1771, followed earlier German models of 1712 and the *Hand-lungs-Lexicon* of 1721 which concentrated on practical reference concerning trade, scientific, technical, commercial, and education topics.

Memorialised in one of the finest of biographies, James Boswell's (1740-1795) *The Life of Samuel Johnson,* the subject is one of the greatest of English writers. An editor, critic, biographer, poet, moralist, and essayist, he is most famous for linguistic management. *A Dictionary of the English Language,* published in 1755, became the definitive English dictionary until the 20th century. It was compiled in eight years. The French Academy equivalent was produced by 40 people in 40 years, allowing Johnson to make an amusing if unflattering comparison. A tall, thick book of over 40,000 entries, and a selling price equivalent today to around £350 ($485), it was not the easiest to acquire or use, nor did it make a profit until years later.

### Samuel Johnson

Johnson's particular innovation was the use of literary quotation to illustrate derivation and meaning, thus unifying and defining the English language. The benefit to literature, education, national identity, and global growth is immeasurable.

His social activities also had a unifying and broadcasting effect. In 1763 he formed "The Club," an informal grouping of his friends meeting in Soho every Monday evening: the painter Joshua Reynolds, political philosopher Edmund Burke, the actor David Garrick (1717-1779) and poet-playwright Oliver Goldsmith, later joined by Adam Smith and Edward Gibbon (1797–1794). The cross fertilisation which such informal institutions facilitated mirrored those of the coffee houses. Popularising of the new learning had begun.

The ideals of the Enlightenment, reason, humanism, and progress are timeless, quoted by the recent celebrant of its journey as never having been so relevant than at the present time.[11] A caveat must be entered, in that by the later 19th century humanism exhibited indications of becoming too complacent and individualistic, spawning the racial and nationalistic characteristics leading to Nazism. Ideas are ever vulnerable to perversion. Marx's doctorate was in Greek philosophy. As this book's introductory banner declares, ideas are ruthless. They are also what makes any of us a person.

# Endnotes

[1] Samuel Taylor Coleridge (1772-1834), poet, critic, and philosopher, is illustrative of the cross currents of his times. With his friend William Wordsworth, he founded the Romantic Movement in England, while introducing the German idealist philosophy school of Kant and Hegel, advancing Shakespearean literary criticism, and contributing poetry of variable quality but including such masterpieces as *The Rime of the Ancient Mariner, Christabel,* and *Kublai Khan.* His fellow poet and friend Robert Southey was the biographer of Joseph Lancaster's rival Andrew Bell. Coleridge managed recurrent ill health by resort to laudanum, to which he became addicted, finally consuming opium dissolved in brandy in the amount of two quarts per day.

[2] The Darien scheme of the late 1690s was an attempt by the Company of Scotland, at the cost of 20% of all money circulating in that country, to establish a New Caledonia colony on the Isthmus of Panama, planned to accommodate an overland route connecting the Atlantic and Pacific oceans. More than 80% of attempting settlers died within a year, the settlement was abandoned twice, finally succumbing to a siege and blockade by Spanish forces. Poor planning, divided leadership, tropical disease epidemics and an English trade blockade made failure inevitable, resulting in the financial ruin of the entire lowlands of Scotland and providing the spur to the completion of the Act of Union with England of 1707.

[3] Bernstein, William J, *A Splendid Exchange*, p. 305.

[4] Chandler, Alfred D Jr. 1977. *The Visible Hand The Managerial Revolution in American Business*, Harvard, 1977. A summary appears in Wilson, John F. *British business history, 1720-1994*, pp. 3-8.

[5] Smith, Adam. *The Wealth of Nations*, Book 1, Ch.8, p.96, Para.36.

[6] St Andrews, 1413; Glasgow, 1451; Aberdeen (King's College), 1495; Edinburgh, 1582; Aberdeen (Marischal College), 1593. The two Aberdeen universities amalgamated in 1858.

[7] Confusingly, the term "song school" was also applied to elementary education establishments up to the 14th century in England. Medieval schools' primary function being education for religion, young male choristers were trained to sing before their voices broke, with further initial education as an adjunct. The military counterpart was the use, begun by the Chinese and introduced to Europe by the Ottomans, of young boys as drummers to provide battle signals. By the 18th century western armies marched and manoeuvred to the sounds of fife and drum. Drummers received a basic education from the age of seven and were treated as mascots by their regiments. Military management made use of all available resources, originating the marching military band.

[8] Houston, R A. *Scottish Literacy and Scottish Identity: Illiteracy and Society in Scotland and Northern England, 1600-1800*, pp. 63-8.

[9] Aelius Galenus, Galen of Pergamon (129-210), was the most highly regarded medical authority of the Roman Empire. He made significant contributions to anatomy, physiology, pharmacology, and neurology. His belief that medicine and philosophy were linked influenced his own contributions to logic while helping to

confer the term "natural philosophy" to embrace the various branches of science. Although his dissection of monkeys and pigs provided for some medical advances, he did not examine human cadavers. While considerably improved and corrected by the Islamic scholar Avicenna from the 11th century, consolidated by the Scola Medico of Salerno, the remaining errors continued to confuse medicine for well over a thousand years. He misattributed the circulation of the blood and was responsible for the myth of the influence of the "humours" of black bile, yellow bile, blood, and phlegm.

[10] d'Alembert, Jean le Rond. *Preliminary Discourse to the Encyclopedia of Diderot*, p. 4.

[11] Pinker, Steven. *Enlightenment Now,* p. xvii.

**Lloyd's Coffee House, Lombard St, London**.
[Drawing by unknown 19<sup>th</sup> century artist.]

# CHAPTER FIFTEEN

# ENLIGHTENING THE PEOPLE

The spread and growth of coffee houses, which also sold tea and chocolate, from Oxford in the mid-16th century first allowed academic society to meet and engage in unregulated conversation. The absence of alcohol allowed for sober discussion. Such access to free speech and unrestricted reading was invaluable, as the misfortune of Hannibal Potter (see Chapter 10, note 17) amply demonstrates. Regulated through licensing, women were not allowed. Charles II briefly attempted suppression in 1675, but had to retreat in face of public outcry. Scholars could discuss theories and experiments outside the formal disciplines; the latest academic developments could be speculated upon, ideas exchanged; and great virtuosi, as they were called, seen, and heard in full voice. All this for the cost of a dish of coffee, with free newspaper access, at an admission price of one penny. One such of the virtuosi was Sir Christopher Wren (1632-1723), Britain's finest architect, rebuilder of some 52 churches after the great fire of London, and whose masterpiece is St Paul's Cathedral.

These "penny universities" became extremely popular. The conversational joining fee being so slight, access was easy. Interested members of the public unable to afford academe could gain knowledge and participate in discussion of the very latest findings and speculations. Thus, education became a central coffee house activity, with informal lessons and lectures being available on occasion. The fashion spread to London in 1652, where coffee house lectures on popular scientific subjects such as mathematics, chemistry, and astronomy were enthusiastically received.

One such noted contributor was Robert Boyle, another the irascible, polymath scientist Robert Hooke, Curator of Experiments at the Royal Society, whose work on gravitation prefigured Newton, identified elasticity, and made significant contributions to geometry, horology, microscopy, palaeontology, astrology, and architecture. His inventions included the watch coils and springs developed through his practical horology. As Surveyor of London, he acted as assistant to Christopher Wren.

The appeal of coffee houses to the likes of Samuel Pepys, John Aubrey, and George Frideric Handel's (1685-1759) patron the Duke of Chandos was considerable and, despite the interruptions of fire and plague, became established public house venues.[1] While open to all, such venues grew into, or contained, clubs of particular persuasions. At the upper end of society, from the end of the 18th century, they were replaced by gentlemen's clubs. The oldest of these, Mrs White's Chocolate House, mainly devoted to gaming, began in 1693; Boodles followed in 1762 and the Marylebone Cricket Club (MCC) in 1787. Their companions of today were founded progressively in the years following 1815, the year of the Waterloo victory, the date at which historians commonly begin to approach the 19th century.

Coffee house style was for relaxed, polite, civilised debate. Theoretically democratic, club rules were designed to deter riffraff. Individual character inevitably emerged. Philosophy, science, and politics were supplemented by sectional interests such as banking and insurance, and non-formal tuition became available with the teaching of languages, dancing, mathematics, and the sciences.[2] Down-market coffee houses attracted low life and were associated with prostitution. Professional groups such as clergy and doctors gathered at particular venues, with some of the latter using the facilities as their consulting rooms.

At the end of the 18th century, London was estimated to have over 3,000 coffee houses. Businesses operated from several of them. The restoration of the monarchy after the sober morality of the Puritan Commonwealth had loosened behaviour. An increase in gambling was attended by concern to manage risk. Coffee shops became ideal venues for such new ventures. The insurance market had begun at Tom's Coffee House. Securities were traded at Jonathan's. From such concerns came some great enterprises and institutions, a prime example being that which grew from Edward Lloyd's Coffee House in 1686 on what is now Lombard Street.

Information exchange concerning maritime insurance, especially during the period between the 1730s and 1760s, became formalised into a Society of Lloyd's at the Royal Exchange, containing 79 life members and founding Lloyds of London. The insurance industry, detailed further in a subsequent publication, formally commenced. Barred from that exchange because of their rude manners, numbers of stockbrokers plied their trade from Jonathan's Coffee House nearby. Beginning in 1744 at the Virginia and Baltic Coffee House in Threadneedle Street, the Baltic Exchange began operations. Its 650 members' companies today engage in the trading and settlement of maritime industry derivative contracts. They are responsible for a large proportion of all dry cargo and tanker fixtures and, as well as the sale and purchase of merchant vessels, provide shipping information. Significantly, all members subscribe to a code of conduct.

The symbiotic relationship created between coffee houses and the press was emphasised by two publications in particular: *The Spectator* and *The Tatler*. Purveyors of news and gossip in a reciprocal manner with the readership, both journals were able to encourage civilised behaviour and provide social education. Thus, they contributed greatly to the improvement in public behaviour by the turn of the century observed by such an acute commentator as Francis Place (1771-1854). The gossip, however, was not always reliable. Over a century later, Benjamin Disraeli (1804-1881) was dismissing reports of massacres in Bosnia-Herzegovina as "mere coffee house babble." Politically, the Puritans favoured coffee houses because of the absence of alcohol. Royalists disapproved of free-speaking subjects engaging with such dangerous ideas as republicanism. The houses undoubtedly assisted the growth of what by the end of the century had clearly become a distinct intellectual class.

The coffee house decline has been attributed to several factors. The axis with the press became an over-reach when the houses attempted to form a news monopoly, provoking ridicule and stimulating replacement by political and literary clubs and societies. Government policy in favour of the East India Company encouraged the substitution of the cheaper tea as a staple beverage. Women, barred from coffee houses except where they ran or served in them, were able to enter these new rival tea houses. The penny universities had served their purpose. Their hundred years of informal education and facilitation had given rise to an immense improvement in common knowledge and manners; encouraged magnificent literary, scientific, financial, and business skills; and assisted the formation of institutions which changed Britain and the world. Of some 350 years' standing, Lloyds of London is still the world's leading market for specialist insurance.

Coffee houses had not been the sole great inspirers of the change resultant upon the realisation of some of the ideas and processes of the Enlightenment. Inspiration could also be drawn from learned expositions, or by popularisers, to the general public. Curiosity was great; there were livings and reputations to be made. Some lecturers gained academic status and posts. In experimental physics demonstrations and lectures alone, between the 1730s and 1790s, some 70 different providers of classes gained hundreds of attendees to courses which varied in length from a week to a year. Many of the courses were held in the evening to allow attendance after work. Denied university entrance, women attended in considerable numbers. The lecturers produced books and pamphlets, with the science performers adding instruments and patent medicines. All were available to provide private tuition. Course content was generally a mix of theories with spectacular, theatrical demonstrations. Comenius's educative principles were finally being realised: the public was enthralled by the object lessons so entertainingly put before them.

Pressed into the loan of their finger rings, which the demonstrator placed in a glass jar through which was then passed an electrical charge, the audience next witnessed their property dancing about. In France, the inventive Jean-Antoine Nollet (1700-1770) performed the "electrified boy" demonstration, a popular stunt much copied by lecturers elsewhere. A young boy would be suspended from the ceiling horizontally by silk cords and an electrical machine then used to magnetise him, thus causing the various objects placed near him by the lecturer to be attracted to him. The saying employed to justify such demonstrations as science was derived from an often-employed Enlightenment expression: it was no more possible to explain the magnetic sense to one who had never felt it than it was to explain colour to a blind man. The most spectacular such public demonstration was made in Paris in 1783 by Jacques-Alexandre-Cesar Charles (1746/7-1823), a lecturer whose classes were attended by such luminaries as Benjamin Franklin and Alessandro Volta (1745-1827), when he became the first man to ascend in a balloon.

The demonstration dissemination method continued into the 19$^{th}$ century, led by distinguished scientists like Humphry Davy (1778-1829), Michael Faraday (1791-1867), and James Clerk Maxwell (1831-1879). Davy's experiments with laughing gas (nitrous oxide) had caught public attention before his move to London. From his new base at the London Institution, he thrilled his audiences with lectures on "Galvanism," which might disclose the secret of life itself. This prompted the nephew of the eponymous Luigi Galvani (1737-1798), a Bologna physics professor, to lecture at the Royal College of Physicians. He applied electricity to the corpse of a hanged murderer, rushed directly from the gallows to the anatomy theatre. Muscles quivered; an eye opened. Authority intervened and such demonstrations were stopped, but popular interest in the physical and metaphysical increased, for linkages to and speculation upon the workings of mind and body inevitably followed.

Galvanism was one of the inspirations for Mary Shelley's (1797-1851) creation of *Frankenstein,* published in 1818, a topic she is known to have discussed with traveling companions Percy Shelley (1792-1822) and Lord Byron (1788-1824). Galvanism was the confusingly named but competing use of chemical generated electricity as ascribed to Volta, inventor of the chemical electric battery, but derived from the "animal electricity" generation of electrified current within biological organisms as observed by Galvani. Shelley was in the habit of producing a bottle containing chemicals, brown paper, and a wire at family gatherings, where the members were made to sit in a circle holding hands for the poet then to electrocute them. The management of popular science included family entertainment.

It also gave opportunity to quacks. The most infamous of these was "Dr" James Graham (1745-1794), a pioneer sex therapist, showman, and peddler of electrical cures. His electro-magnetic musical Grand State Celestial Bed was exhibited at London's Pall Mall and in Edinburgh between 1781 and 1785. This featured a canopy within which musical automata, fresh flowers, doves, fragrances, and gaseous emissions provided the setting for a 3.7 x 2.7-metre bed which tilted to positions designed to give the best prospect of conception. Meanwhile, the electrified mattress activated organ pipes and a clockwork display, crackling with electricity, dedicated to Hymen, the god of marriage, illuminated the bedhead, reading: *Be fruitful, multiply and replenish the earth.*

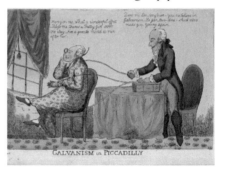

GALVANISM in PICCADILLY

**An Affluent Man receiving galvanic electric therapy from a French quack doctor in London's Piccadilly:**

"Dere mi L'or Angloise", says the doctor "– you no believe in Galvanism. Regarde – two – dree shock more make you young again." "Mercy on me", replies the rich man., "what a wonderful effect. Blefs me, there's a Pretty Girl over the way. I've a great mind to run after her."

The introduction to France of Newton's *Principia* had been made by Voltaire in 1738, but only achieved a full French translation in 1756.

Newbery's opening of the popular publishing market for scientific texts in Britain encouraged further accessible publications for adult markets which were literate but not inclined to pore over original, learned works. The subject attracted literary attention, even praise by poetry; but not all approved. William Blake (1757-1827) objected to what he saw as science's simplicities detracting from God's mysteries.

The opening up of society was further notable for the advances made by women. Aphra Behn (1640-1689), a spy like her fellow writer, Daniel Defoe, had been the first woman to earn her living by writing. Mary Astell (1666-1731) from Newcastle pioneered feminism, teaching while supported by a group of aristocratic women in London. A century later, Jane Austen (1775-1817), was providing some of the English language's finest fiction. Female education, however, remained restricted. Excluded from formal higher education and the professions, except by family connection, they were not immediately welcome to all the Enlightenment luminaries, Rousseau especially, where the lamp of gender equality burned dim, if at all.

Nonetheless, ideas will have their way; and especially where the ideas are about freedom and science. Aided immensely, perhaps, by the gender of her patron, Catherine the Great, Princess Yekaterina Dashkova (1743-1810) achieved the directorship of the Russian Imperial Academy of Sciences of St. Petersburg in 1783, the first woman to lead a scientific academy. In Britain, the career of Caroline Herschel (1750-1848) in astronomy began with assistance to her brother, William (1738-1832). Her discovery of an octet of comets, these being the first by a woman, and writings concerning the fixed stars brought her to considerable prominence. Other women advanced elsewhere by similar means, and through contributions of illustrations and translations. The unconventional, combative writer and philosopher Mary Wollstonecraft (1759-1797), Mary Shelley's mother, who taught for a period at a noted school in London's Newington Green (dissenter stronghold, nearby the home of Daniel Defoe), took matters rather further. Her 1792 *A Vindication of the Rights of Woman* argued that men and women should be treated as equal rational beings; the social order founded on reason; and that woman appeared to be inferior to men only because of their lack of education. Even so, her teaching performance had been ordinary, instructing girls in needlework.

Wollstonecraft was seeking to build on the work of others, such as Mary Astell, the first English feminist and strong proponent of female education.

Otherwise, a staunch Tory supporter of the episcopacy, Astell had begun philosophical discourse in opposition to Aristotle, Locke, and Descartes. Rather than accept women being ruled by men, she had taken Descartes' theory of dualism, a separate mind and body, to promote the idea that they, as well as men, had the ability to reason. Therefore, they should not be treated so badly. Astell posed the radical question that if all men are born free, why are all women born slaves?[3] The explicit and implicit issues of societal management further raised, but not resolved, by Enlightenment aspirational declarations, such as that of 1776 of American independence, continue to resound.

Indeed, Wollstonecraft's *Vindication* of 1792 followed the French playwright and pamphleteer Olympe de Gouge's (1748-1793) *Declaration of the Rights of Woman and of the Female Citizen* of 1791, itself based on the *Declaration of the Rights of Man and of the Citizen*, the human rights foundation document set by France's revolutionary National Constituent Assembly of 1789. Although just five copies of de Gouge's pamphlet were printed, the work only gaining wide presence later as both women were active in moderate Girondist circles, they were likely to have been familiar with each other's work. De Gouge's continuing belief in a constitutional monarchy on the English model caused her to dedicate her *Declaration*, confusingly, to Queen Marie Antoinette. Obsessively headstrong, knowing that she was making her way to the guillotine as her ideas would have undone the French Revolution if adopted, she was executed in the session which also dispatched Marie Antoinette. Her defiant remodelling of the causes of others had been seen before in her *Contrat Social*, named after Rousseau's *Social Contract*, in which she proposed marriage based upon gender equality. The slogan by which she is most remembered is that which best expressed her fierceness of egalitarian belief:

> A woman has the right to mount the scaffold.
> She must possess equally the right to mount the speaker's platform.

Women managing Death, Fame and Achievement
in the 18th Century

Caroline Herschel          Mary Shelley

Mary Wollstonecraft

Marie Antoinette      Marie Olympe de        Maria Edgeworth
                          Gouges

Each of the women pictured had exceptional careers. They all had to manage
the prejudice against their sex which made their lives difficult, each to
encounter life challenges which could bring unimaginable conjunctions.
Caroline Herschel surpassed her brother in achievement and longevity. The
Wollstonecrafts, mother and daughter, had both to encounter and overcome
extreme danger and express literary talent in difficult circumstances.
Perhaps the strangest of conjunctions was Marie Antoinette and Olympe de
Gouges, both accustomed to appearing in public, who went to their final
stage together: the guillotine. Only Maria Edgeworth appears to have had it
all: landed wealth, a literary career, part of an ever-expanding family, with

successful, if strict, estate management. What management lessons might we draw from their experiences?

In contrast to de Gouges and Mary Wollstonecraft, English Tory Edmund Burke (member of parliament, philosopher, political theorist, and author) was a staunch advocate of the upholding of moral virtues and the importance of religion as an adhesive to bind both into society. A supporter of the American Revolution and Catholic emancipation but a vehement opponent of the French Revolution, he is yet another to whom paternity of the abstract has been ascribed: father of modern British conservatism. His essential contentions were that chaos would result from natural rights being applied through the tearing down of the structures of established government; the proper attitude of those who aspired to power were humility, modesty, and a sense of public duty.

Like Burke in supporting American independence but opposing revolution, one of the harbingers of liberalism, Charles-Louis de Secondat, Baron de La Brede et de Montesquieu (1689-1755), known simply as Montesquieu, popularised despotism as the term to qualify autocracy, and introduced the profoundly influential political theory of the separation of powers in the management of a state. His celebration of Britain's newly established constitutional monarchy and union with Scotland was contrasted with the French perpetuation of autocracy in *The Spirit of the Laws* (1748) – and hence despotism, thus achieving the distinction of his books being banned in France, while achieving recognition in much of Europe, praise in Britain, and considerable influence in its North American colonies. His doctrine of the separation of the powers of the executive, legislature, and judiciary became the widespread constitutional model. Principled government establishment with checks and balances, whereby no person need fear another, found favour with James Madison (1731-1798) and his colleagues.

The further accolade of being banned by the Catholic Church and placement on the Index of Prohibited Books was gained in 1751. However, Montesquieu is at least as celebrated for the idea stated in Chapter 2 of Book XX of *Spirit*:

> The natural effect of commerce is to bring peace. Two nations that negotiate between themselves become reciprocally dependent, if one has an interest in buying and the other in selling. And all unions are based on mutual needs.

If Montesquieu is correct, and similarly Sun Tzu for his observations on the lack of benefit from prolonged warfare, then a distinction must be made between the universal and general, between groups and individuals. As we shall see in a subsequent volume, times were better for many during the Franco-British wars. Peace brought hardship. One of the most prominent figures in this study, Ambrose Crowley III, like fellow Quaker arms manufacturers, did very well out of the Napoleonic conflict. 20th century warfare contributed to greater equality.

Wollstonecraft, feminist icon, had another corner to fight. She unleashed a ferocious critique of Burke's opposition to the French Revolution, following that in 1792 with *A Vindication*. Pursuing her aims by meeting with the new French ambassador to London, the notoriously crafty, cynical, corrupt Talleyrand (1784-1838), she asked for French girls to be given the same rights to education as men. In her own plan for national education, Wollstonecraft was egalitarian only up to a point: the provision was to be co-educational but, after the age of nine, the rich and the poor schooled separately. Stranded in Paris during the continued revolution in which she lost her Girondin friends to the guillotine as the Jacobins instituted their Reign of Terror, she survived only by a fake marriage to her American, blockade-running, adventurer lover. On return to England, she married another, the writer and philosopher William Godwin (1756-1836), only to die giving birth to Mary, she who was later to marry poet Percy Shelley. Godwin's unsparing memoir of Wollstonecraft's unconventional life destroyed her public reputation for generations, so detracting from her causes and assisting those opposed to female equality.

Other less flamboyant female reformers persisted, however. Maria Edgeworth (1768-1849) and her father, the prolific landowner and inventor (of the precursor to the caterpillar track) Richard (1744-1817), father of twenty-two children by four wives, in 1798 published *Practical Education*. Dominated by an insistence on attending to the child, this combined the ideas of Locke, Rousseau, Joseph Priestley, and others, based on the premise that early experiences and associations are formative and long lasting, emphasising hands-on learning and the entertainment to be derived from experimentation. Clearly, Enlightenment ideas and their modes of expression had become mainstream, although the Edgeworths' objection to religion and fairy tales as fit topics for discussion with children was something of an impediment to wide acceptance.

Maria Edgeworth spent much of her life in Ireland, writing and managing family estates, where such High Tory attitudes as might be suggested by association with Sir Walter Scott (1771-1832) and illustrated by her refusal of relief during famine to her tenants unless they were up to date with their rents did not suggest any tenderness or departure from societal norms. However, her writings were predominantly liberal and secular, exposing negligent Anglo-Irish landlords and addressing such issues as slavery. Reformers were not necessarily radical, nor *vice versa*. Maria Edgeworth and the Elder Cato would probably have had much in common regarding farm management. She also illustrates the tensions inherent between the apparent progressiveness of Enlightenment thought and action and the practical needs of ordinary humanity.

The Reverend Thomas Malthus (1766-1834), for example, in his *Essay on the Principle of Population* of 1798 held that although an increase in national food production improved the well-being of the people, this could only be temporary because it would lead to population growth which, in turn, would reduce that production to below that of the commencement of the cycle. Abundance would cause population growth instead of the desired stability of a higher standard of living. Therefore, populations would grow until those at the bottom of society suffered from their greater susceptibility to disease, shortages, and famine. He therefore criticised the Poor Law for a propensity to lead to inflation, rather than improving the condition of the poor. Grain import tax, the Corn Laws, which kept wheat prices high, was therefore preferable because food security was more important than popular well-being or increased wealth. Such conditions, he proclaimed, were attributable to God's power to compel virtuous behaviour. In business terms, that meant self-dependence through divine inspiration as the means to social and economic improvement, at a mortality rate cost.

Malthus was disproved by the food industry being able to meet demand. At the time, he was largely opposed by his associate David Ricardo, born a Jew but a convert to Unitarianism, whose family then ostracised him, a banker who earned the right to pronounce on economics by first making himself a fortune. Ricardo's proposals to parliament in 1811 had been rejected but, as a loan contractor, he was part of a syndicate which raised successive loans of £12 million, £22 million, and £49 million between 1810 and 1813. He was, thus, impressively rich when he shorted British securities by stoking rumour that the British had lost the battle of Waterloo and thus buying them at a heavy discount, and selling at immense profit when the true outcome of the defeat of Napoleon was known. Such shorting exploits were contradictory to Smith's moral stance while illustrative of capital market forces, demonstrative of the duality of political economy. It was long-term economy, however, which won the argument. Continued agricultural improvement maintained and increased the food supply.

Ricardo is generally ranked as one of the most important of the classical
political economists after Adam Smith. To his contemporaries, including
Wollstonecraft's husband William Godwin, he was viewed as the victor in
a debate against Malthus, his advocacy of free trade and theory of the value
of labour seen as preferable routes to understanding and progress. Self-
dependence was common to both, but it is important to bear in mind the
harshness of the thinking of some of the Enlightenment leaders, and the
continuing presence either of a deity amidst apparent rationality or,
alternatively, the assumption of divine rationality. Zeus would not have
agreed with either proposition.

The intellectual stimulus of all this activity helped promote widespread
curiosity. Innovativeness, invention, and the exploration of the natural
world became highly popular: there was an impetus to improvement. In
industry, it was not that England was ahead of the international field, more
that it was able to transform ideas and prototypes into serviceable industrial
applications - if not the ideas themselves but the idea to implement them
drove the changes. This was partly because of the absence of state control.
Where centralised bureaucracies dominated in Europe, in England the
inventive had either to find capital to back their ideas or provide it
themselves. This inevitably made for freer expression but also explains the
dominance of early Quaker finance: those with money helped their Friends
with good business ideas to bring them into expression, the innovator,
manufacturers, and financiers learning from each other in mutual
collaboration. This was practical, applied education, eventually to reach
such industrial scales as the financing of Abraham Darby's iron works and
the world's first freight and passenger railway.

From 1700, there had been a slow growing but wide change to social
attitudes. One reason advanced for this was the growth in literacy and
increase in the size of the reading public. Although estimates put the total
English readers at between 60,000 and 80,000 at the end of the 18th century,
out of a population of around 6 million, that readership was influential.
Reading provided an outlet for women; the circulating libraries decreased
costs for all; and the armies of domestic servants were likely to read what
was available within the house. Newspapers and magazines carried
serialised fiction; scientific and philosophic discoveries and insights fed
curiosity: journalism had arrived.

Fed by Enlightenment ideals, the belief had grown that nature was inherently good but, if not, certainly not evil: the evil derived from man and his institutions. While restricted to the elite, the changes embraced attitudes to women, slaves, and animals, as well as to children. Combined with social aspiration, the greatest inspiration of all to expenditure, this fed ambition with encouraging results for children: the rising middle-class child for which had to be bought the latest Newbery publication, just as the dame school needed more books to maintain and attract parent patronage. As children for the monied classes became counters on the social climbing ladder, the reputation of their school reflecting on parental status, so children's literature portrayed images of an ideal parent's ideal child: unreal perhaps but the vending of hope, illusion, and the symbols with which to keep up with the neighbours are sales opportunities long known to commerce.

So they were too in the fine art family portraiture business - from the 1730s, paintings of ideal family groups in idyllic surroundings began to become the wall hangings of choice for the elite. Thomas Gainsborough (1727-88) painted *The Artist with his Wife and Daughter* in mid-century (pictured left).

Child portraits became popular, a genre for which Joshua Reynolds (1723-1792) could charge £150 (c.US$11,222 -£8,400 today). New models of childhood began to emerge where nurture took precedence over nature, and the psychology of parental relations was considered. Treating children as pets, friends and objects of pride became fashionable and, to European neighbours, unusual:

> They have an extraordinary Regard in England for young children, always flattering, always caressing, always applauding what they do; at least it seems so to us French Folks, who Correct our children as soon as they are capable of reasoning, being of the Opinion, that to keep them in Awe is the best Way to give them a good Turn in their Youth.[4]

Centuries of education dominated by the classics finally gave recognition to children when Aesop's fables were widely translated in 1692. The entrepreneurial publisher John Newbery had competition from Thomas Boreman (d. 1743), who published for children *Three Hundred Animals* in

1730 and *Gigantic Animals* in 1740, and Mary Cooper (d.1761), a copyright acquirer and publisher whose *Tommy Thumb's Pretty Song Book* of 1742 is the first known collection of fairy tales in English. Edward Augustus Kendall (1776-1842), an early writer of travel in America, boosted the Newbery catalogue with his anthropomorphising of birds. A variety of birds – swallow, wren, canary – talk to each other, illustrating human failings, such as the theft of birds' eggs. The talking animal tradition, from Kipling to Grahame and Disney, had begun. By a century after Roger L'Estrange (1616-1704) had published his translation of Aesop, every common subject had been made available to children; there were books for younger and older children, novels, even music instruction; and the circulating libraries had all acquired juvenile sections. The industrious working class had full access. The scientific lecture demonstrations had child accessible counterparts: museums, zoos, puppet shows, automata, curiosities, and monstrosities.

Translations of Aesop into various European languages had begun in the 12th century, gradually expanding into a new flowering in the Renaissance. The fables were aimed at children, initially as a very gentle way of introducing classical culture. Such is the powerful simplicity of the tales, many of the summary morals have stuck into common parlance: "look before you leap"; "pride comes before a fall" and "slow and steady wins the race." Indeed, an author cited in a subsequent publication entitled one of his recent publications, "The hare and the tortoise." Nothing is known for certain of Aesop himself, but he is reputed to have been a slave, possibly black, and very ugly. His stories tell truth to power, the underdog often wins, and witness is borne to the everyday life of the common people of ancient Greece and Rome. This legendary figure often shows the wisdom of the slave in contrast to the foolishness of his master. Educators saw the work as a way of promoting awareness of right and wrong. As a popular form of literature for children, it carried vital moral questions which could remain with their hearers thereafter, such as, "What is a moral life?" Naturally subversive, the fables made frequent and important use of animals as significant symbols. It is no accident that George Orwell's (1903-1950) probably best loved masterpiece is entitled *Animal Farm*. That type of fabulous satire is precisely the sort of offence which caused Apollo reputedly to hurl Aesop off a cliff.

The same trickle-down phenomenon applied to indoor entertainments, such as cards. Of 7th century Indian invention, refined in China during the 9th century Tang dynasty and progressing through Europe by the 15th, these adult gaming diversions, playing cards, now became educational instruments. Simple designs extended into rudimentary lessons in music. The cartographer John Spilsbury (1739-1769) employed the technique of cutting up maps to teach geography, so inventing the jig-saw puzzle. Before his early death, he had thirty different jig-saw maps for sale. Although luminaries like Maria Edgeworth denounced such toys as useless, the market for educational games had been opened. Old games such as hoops, tops, marbles, pitch and toss were superseded.

Many novelties emerged, from board and card games to working and demonstration models of many types, from animal farms to dolls' houses, to working mills and looms over which inflatable globes might preside. There were no specialised toy shops in 1730, but by 1780 they were ubiquitous; by 1820 the trade in children's toys and literature had become "very large indeed".[5] The jig-saw was part of the further phenomenon. Paved roads, the new canal system, and improved conveyances allowed people to travel more. Horizons had expanded for the middle and lower-middle classes, new worlds beckoned, and they wanted their children with them.

Despite the passing of the ancient world - blocked by one form of religion but aided by another, across boundaries set by geography and politics, through the agency of human activity - ideas and innovation had won through, even reaching the education of children. It should also be noted that although research has shown the early modern family to have been as affectionate as its 18th century successor, the difference was the resources, access to their disposal, and management of the opportunity arising: all of which supported the arguments of Locke, Rousseau, and Comenius.[6] Late, perhaps, but children had arrived on the social agenda, with the elite and middle classes attending more to their needs and management.

## Endnotes

[1] James Brydges, 1st Duke of Chandos (1673-1744), described by Jonathan Swift as "a great compiler with every court," was very wealthy through exploitation of public office. He also supported the poet Alexander Pope (1688-1744), caricatured in retribution by another coffee house habitué, William Hogarth (1697-1764), for servility. Pope first visited a coffee house at the age of 12. His *Rape of the Lock* arose from coffee house gossip. Noted attendees included John Dryden (1631-1700), Henry Fielding (1707-1754), and Oliver Goldsmith.

[2] Among famous coffee houses other than cited above were: *The Grecian* (lawyers); *Turk's Head* (housing); *Buttons* aka *Letter Box*, as writings were left there for newspaper use.

[3] Astell, Mary. *Some Reflections upon Marriage,* London, Printed for John Nutt, 1700.

[4] Porter, *op. cit.,* p.267, quoting Henri Misson (1650-1722), whose observations related only to the elite. A quite different contrast could be made. Chimney cleaning with brushes was usual in Europe; England preferred the use of climbing boys; factory accidents produced multiple child mutilations.

[5] Plumb, *op. cit.*, p.90.

[6] Bailey, Joanne "Reassessing parenting in eighteenth-century England" in ed. Berry, Helen and Foyster, Elizabeth. 2007. *The Family in Early Modern England.* Cambridge: Cambridge University Press. p. 209, note 2, supplies five supporting texts.

# CHAPTER SIXTEEN

# EXPLORING APPLICATIONS TO CHILDREN

The benefits of Andrew Melville's interventions had been to lay the foundations for the uniquely practical form of humanism which was to characterise the Scottish Enlightenment. Francis Hutcheson (1694-1746), Professor of Philosophy at Glasgow from 1729, contributed significantly to the development of utilitarianism, while his students David Hume and Adam Smith were to enjoy a permanent pre-eminence in their respective fields. Further Scottish Enlightenment figures of note include the agronomist James Anderson (1739-1808), held by some to be the root of Marx's critique of agriculture, inventor of an animal-drawn heavy plough, publisher, friend and co-operator with Jeremy Bentham, and correspondent with George Washington; William Cullen (1710-1790), chemist, agriculturalist, friend and physician to David Hume whilst professor at the Edinburgh Medical School, noted for systemising and promoting medical knowledge when it was the foremost education establishment of its type in the English-speaking world; and physician and chemist Joseph Black (1728-1799), holder of chairs successively at Glasgow and Edinburgh, known for discoveries of magnesium, carbon dioxide, latent heat, and specific heat.

James Hutton (1726-1797) is another awarded posthumous paternity, apt in that he had no children of his own. The "father of geology" was a physician, chemical manufacturer, naturalist, experimental agriculturalist and geologist who originated a fundamental principle of geology: the theory of uniformitarianism. This posits that the features of the earth's crust are formed by natural forces over geologic time. Extensions of his argument and observations concerning processes such as sedimentation and erosion have been advanced to the Gaia "living earth" hypothesis. By the end of the 18th century therefore, an international and domestic intellectual framework was securely in place to support an advancement of its humanity at least in proportion to the rising population: estimated for England at 5,200,000 in 1700; 7,754,875 at the 1801 census.[1] It now remained to transfer at least some of the educational advance to more children.

If life for the children of the aristocracy and lower middle classes had greatly improved, it was still characterised by adult assumptions, repressions, and obsessions, rather than by what children were, needed, and cared for. The sexual openness of the 17th and earlier 18th century gave way to what could be brutally enforced abstinence. The prohibitive publication *Onania* had reached twelve editions by 1727 and remained a best-seller throughout the century. Advertised extensively, the anti-masturbation tract told a tale of sinners, consequences and redemption for those achieving the salvation of continence. Gradually, folk tales and quack doctors attributed most known illnesses to the supposedly sinful practice. The market responded with restrictive machines, "curative" medicines, and extremes of such cruelty as the circumcision of young boys without anaesthetic. The enforcement of chastity in both sexes was by violence, in one form or another. While the Evangelical revival brought forward powerful images of dark forces and actions, repression was the answer to inconvenient realities. Moreover, as the implacable, restrictive moralities of the blinkered Sarah Trimmer, discussed below, came heavily to influence education and religious publishing, children were left in a position of permanent, stressful dilemma:

> Children, in fact, had become objects: violence and noise, natural to children, were deplored, so was greed for food as well as lust. Obedience, honesty, self-control were the qualities desired and inculcated. They were to stay firmly in Eden with their hands off the apples and deaf to the serpents.[2]

Basic British elementary provisions occurred in dame schools from the 17th to 19th centuries. Many of these were day care facilities where the children learned little, as the female overseers were often illiterate. As in Scotland, girls might learn knitting and sewing. They frequented dame schools more than boys, for whom there was a wider provision. As late as 1838, it was established that half of the attending children were taught only spelling, with minor provision for basic grammar and mathematics. In North America, however, education at dame schools could be of a high standard. There, law in New England states, such as Massachusetts, required children to be able to read the Bible. The female teachers were paid in coin or kind and taught a curriculum with an additional R: reading, writing, arithmetic and religion. These superior dame schools offered languages, music and dancing. The Puritans were impelled by the notion that Satan would seek to prevent understanding of the Bible, and so literacy was paramount.

The impetus to Bible and Christian literature study, however, was expressed in Britain by the Society for Promoting Christian Knowledge (SPCK), founded in 1698 by Anglican priest Thomas Bray (1656 or 58-1730). In

1696, Bray was appointed by the Church of England to organise its parishes in the colony of Maryland. Already a successful author of popular theology, Bray drew on his foreknowledge of the task facing him to demand a budget for the provision of books, their being in short local supply, beyond the resources of parish priests. Two years later, the initiative was applied to England and Wales as an Anglican mission, establishing SPCK as the prime publisher of Christian books in the United Kingdom, with a related society for Scotland forming in 1709. Its list included pamphlets for specific communities, such as prisoners, soldiers, and seamen; liturgical literature; and more general works on religious topics. The texts provided an instructional tool. SPCK progressively founded Anglican charity schools for the 7 to 11 age group, and inspired further provision. Charity school uniforms, provided for free, became a badge of poverty. Such schools were often financed by subscriptions, or derived from bequests. SPCK followed the 19$^{th}$ century expansion of the British Empire, supplying books and supporting missions. Evangelism was a continuing part of the entertainment industry, for thousands would flock to hear missionary sermons. The lurid tales and illustrations of "primitive" societies, as portrayed in many religious magazines, had their own further attractions.

As children had largely been unable to benefit from Edward VI's education reform because of the requirement to supplement the family budget, there was but one day in the week upon which popular education might be made widely available. Credit for the innovation of the Sunday school is spread among a number of persons and locations. From the ideas of Luther and John Knox, attribution is sometimes given to the Wesleyan mystic Hannah Ball (1734-1792) of High Wycombe, although there are candidates from 1763, 1770, and 1778, and the paternity title generally bestowed upon Robert Raikes (1736-1811), who began such a school, and publicised the idea through the family business. Once more, a publisher's business sense came to the aid of education.

Raikes had succeeded his father as proprietor of the *Gloucester Journal* in 1757. He had rendered philanthropic assistance to those detained under the Poor Law, the house of correction being part of Gloucester jail. His approach to the poor boys thus housed was to emphasise the path of virtue as being preferable to that of the parental or individual waywardness which had resulted in incarceration, and that intervention and example should begin early. Thus, the education market day was to be Sunday: children would not be required to work, nor would their lay teachers. The curriculum began with the children being taught to read and write; thence to read the catechism of Lord's Prayer, Apostles' Creed, basic sacramental knowledge, and the set book, the Bible. Attendance was from 10 a.m. until midday; then from 1 p.m. for a lesson, followed by church attendance, then catechism repetition until after 5 p.m., at which time the pupils were enjoined to go home without noise.

### Robert Raikes

Raikes's education management experiment began in 1780 in the Gloucester home of one Mrs. Meredith, for boys only with the older assisting the younger, provision for girls following subsequently. More schools opened in due course, emboldening Raikes to fund the experiment and use his *Gloucester Journal* to publicise the initiative. Despite the approved praise of the enlightened Adam Smith, progress was not smooth, for reactionaries, as ever, found grounds for opposition. Objections during the 1790s ranged from the dangers of indoctrination for political propaganda purposes; the undesirability of the desecration of the Sabbath; and the weakening of parental authority in religious instruction at home. Nonetheless, an estimated 250,000 children attended Sunday schools in 1787, rising to 1.2 million by 1831, the number of schools being around 1,700.

Raikes might best be understood, like the evangelical anti-slavery advocate William Wilberforce (1759-1853), as a man conscious of the advantages of his position, moderately wealthy and born into said wealth, whose religiously-guided conscience informed him that everything was at stake, including society itself. This was not merely a pious exercise or doing good where that was necessary; the ulterior motive was to achieve a position of power, not elective or within government, but that of an overriding stature: moral authority. Such authority would be impressive to fellow citizens, causing them and his social superiors thus to follow the bidding of that authority whilst impressing God at the same time. Meanwhile, good was undoubtedly done, albeit sometimes with violence. Raikes was known to make errant children walk to school with weights or logs tied to their legs, took them home to be birched, and punished liars by holding their fingers against a stove or fireplace until they blistered.[3]

Motivation for such determination has been ascribed to the monied middle class, then denied a voice in parliament, for whom everything was at stake. They had to succeed:

> Their aim was to establish a personal ascendancy above the herd as right-minded, responsible and successful citizens, and at the same time to impress their worth upon their social betters, including God.[4]

Their objectives included a collective voice, a cohesive identity, establishing a parallel power to the legislature. The aristocracy could be challenged, confronted and influenced by their own moral authority, intimidating inferiors and impressing their superiors in the process.

One such bastion of enthroned moral superiority was Sarah Trimmer (1741-1810). A boarding school graduate, she had helped her family's fortunes through ingratiating herself with Samuel Johnson by producing a copy of Milton's *Paradise Lost* to help settle a literary disagreement between him and her father. The connection assisted subsequent royal employment for her father, removal to west London, and a consequent marriage with twelve children.

In 1786, she was inspired by Raikes's example to establish the first Sunday school in her new home parish of Old Brentford, then combined with two local clergymen to organise the funding for more. Demand far exceeding supply, Trimmer restricted entry. Attendance was for five-year-olds and upwards, one child per family, under single sex provision. Cleanliness was encouraged through combs and brushes being provided to all who needed them. With the predominant aim of their being able to comprehend the Bible, the children were taught to read.

Impressed, Raikes recommended Mrs. Trimmer's organisation to all those seeking to establish Sunday schools, bringing another important connection, Queen Charlotte (1744-1818); urging Mrs. Trimmer to solicit her advice on starting a Sunday school at Windsor.

**Sarah Trimmer**

Her call on the wife of George III
(1738-1820) was a catalyst to her
entry to public debate. She had
already published two books: a
religious introduction for children,
and a religious history. *The
Oeconomy of Charity*, 1786, was
intended to counter the opposition to
Sunday schools. In doing that, it
instead moved onto the grounds of
increasing middle class power. She
argued that responsibility for the
education of the poor rested with the
middle class, and that its moral
expression through Bible study
would ensure that the poor absorbed and drew the appropriate theological
and political lessons. Those who showed ability at Sunday school were
directed to the charity schools which functioned on more days of the week.

Progress from the Sunday school, however, was uneven. A scheme to teach
girls spinning and weaving failed. Trimmer was critical of the SPCK funded
charity schools, which relied upon rote learning. There is academic debate
concerning Trimmer's interventions. She is criticised for her rigid
distinctions between what she understood to be the deserving and
undeserving poor, and the imposition of middle-class morality and values.
Children fed by charity, Trimmer wrote, ought to be humbly grateful. The
objective was that poor children should be virtuous and pious, rather than
gain equality of opportunity or economic advance. Hers was a High Church
mission to control the masses. Yet, while being wholly reflective of her
times, whatever her motivations, she was providing education where it was
most urgently needed. No doubt many of the students absorbed the morality;
yet the newly acquired literacy could encourage students to think for
themselves, or to discard that which they did not consider appropriate.

Her literary career burgeoned. She wrote for adults, she wrote for children,
even for their servants: *The Servant's Friend* of 1786-7 was intended for all
ages. Together with her contemporary, the dissenter poet and essayist Anna
Laetitia Barbould (1743-1825), she revolutionised children's literature.
Barbould has the greater claim to literary merit but fell out of favour because
of her support for the French Revolution. Her *Lessons for Children* of 1778-

9, consisting of four age related reading primers, in large type with wide margins, progress in difficulty and are based on Locke's precepts: learning is through the senses and in dialogue between parent and child. Highly popular and formative in the English-speaking world, reprinted many times, the texts took the reader through the interconnectedness of human experience, linking animals, people, nature, and the divine. Although Mrs. Trimmer claimed that the *Treatise on Education* of Isaac Watts (1674-1748) was her inspiration, the remarkable coincidence of a mother on a nature-walk with her two children in her *An Easy Introduction to The Knowledge of Nature and Reading the Holy Scriptures Adapted To The Capacities For Children* of 1780, argues otherwise. After collaboration with her brother John Aikin (1747-1822), the unfortunate Barbould, who had given up sugar in protest against slavery and whose mad husband had tried to kill her, betrayed by former friends in the joint cause of reform in France, ceased to publish. Barbould had also taught with distinction at the noted Palgrave Academy, whose curriculum featured the sciences and modern languages, the numbers of pupils at which grew from four to 40 during her eleven-year tenure.

The dissenting moralist Barbould's reflective rationalism was replaced by the authoritarian High Anglicanism of Trimmer. Her view of nature was as a reflection of the greatness and goodness of God, although she did make progress toward a greater position for women. Newbery's company still did good business, holding the catalogue which sold most literature for children. By 1800, Mrs. Trimmer's output was the largest contributor to the Newbery list. She further commissioned Bible illustrations for which she wrote commentaries, the printed pictures being separately available as wall hangings, or bound in sets into books. Success bred success: she followed with the same technique applied to ancient Roman and British history, then the New and Old Testaments. The publishing stable also ran a monthly periodical for eighteen months, *The Family Magazine,* containing "religious tales for Sunday evenings" and "moral tales for weekdays," the venture seemingly abandoned because of unsurprising exhaustion.

Nonetheless, she continued, with a succession of publishers, to produce books for the poor children attending charity schools and was enough of a businesswoman to realize that the enterprise required extensive funding. Sarah joined the SPCK and made a proposal. Twelve copies of her 1792 treatise *Reflections upon the Education in Charity Schools* were sent to the SPCK sub-committee which chose the books for funding. The treatise argued that the by-now century-old curriculum required updating, for the facilitation of which she suggested a further seven books which she would write to order. All but one, a commentary on the Book of Common Prayer, was accepted.

The most popular of these were her *Charity School Spelling Book* (1799), one the first books for the poor which had large print and wide margins, an anthology of Old Testament stories, and a pedagogical aid, *The Teacher's Assistant* (1800). Her most popular work, *Fabulous Histories* (1786), in print for a century, concerned a human and an avian family which learn to live together, following virtue and rejecting vice. The tale reflected stable hierarchies and the maintenance of order, with the poor being compliant and rejection for those failing to conform. Mrs. Trimmer was concerned to maintain the rational, insisting to her readers that her stories were not real. She subscribed to the common fear of fiction, especially fairy stories, for their supposed capacity to frighten, mislead and pervert young minds. The paradox that she was herself peddling fiction, gaining income and seeking to advance religion meanwhile, required most earnest protestations.

Finally, through *The Guardian of Education,* a periodical published 1802-6, she mixed instructional ideas, textual extracts, evaluations of educational theory, and reviews of children's literature, thus extending the latter as a genre. If Newbery was the father of children's literature, then a trinity of women could advance maternity claims. If Edgeworth and Barbould were ahead of her intellectually, the output of the redoubtable Trimmer, with her addition of critical review, certainly placed her as a mother superior. In her opinion-forming intent, Sarah's deep conservatism stressed the primacy of religion, followed by hierarchical social stability, disapproval of the dangerous notions of revolutionary France, and condemnation of fantasy and the irrational. This was tempered, however, by her agreement with Rousseau and the Edgeworths that children should be allowed to enjoy their childhood, rather than being forced into adulthood too early.

Even so, she was firmly convinced that God was the only refuge in troubled times while indulging in the conspiracy theory that the French *philosophes* and their educational theories aimed at revolution and the overturning of Christian society. In reality, the rationality to which Sarah Trimmer subscribed told a different story. For all its intellectual prowess and advance, at the time of Joseph Lancaster's birth, England ranked at the foot of Europe's educational standings, needing whatever foreign input at grass-roots level which it could get. England also ranked as the suicide capital of the world, with its citizens paying more in tax than did the French under the *ancien régime.* Most learning remained informal, learning for living, or to make a living.

Whilst the classics provided a veneer of civilisation for the upper classes (with the subject matter's inaccessibility providing a sense of superiority within itself), most people's learning originated with folk lore, nursery rhymes, and songs, with numeracy acquired through card games, dominoes in Europe from the 12th century, darts in the 20th, and the necessities of daily life such as measurement or budgeting. Sewing samplers provided girls with improving or cautionary mnemonics. Auto-didacticism was prevalent, children and adults acquiring their book learning by themselves. Newbery's inspiration flourished at many levels. Inexpensive, improving, self-teaching aids abounded by the end of the century.

Within the formal system, some grammar school curriculum was improving. However, social conditions, especially in the boarding sector, were forming into that type cited in the next century in *Tom Brown's School Days* (1857): the terrorising of younger boys by their elders. Violence, bullying, and drinking were common, and rebellion occasional. Even Eton had to call out the militia on one occasion; the Riot Act had to be read at Winchester School in 1770 following a pupil rebellion. As university attendance declined, so the public school became distrusted by the liberal classes for the same reason: their "diet of birch, boorishness, buggery and the bottle". They, therefore, opted for employing private tutors instead.[5]

Writing of his family's experience around 1780, Francis Place reported that he and his brother were sent to the school run by "savage Jones," so nicknamed because of the frequent punishments inflicted - and the delight he took in the task. The curriculum was learning to read, write, and cipher, with a single spelling book, arithmetic text, and a Bible. School hours were from nine to twelve and two to five. A column and a half of spelling had to be learnt by heart and copied every morning. In the afternoon, there was arithmetic and Bible reading, with catechism or examination in the tenets of the Church of England twice a week. Six boys were called daily, in rotation, to show their work. Any failures were punished with two to 12 strokes of a stout cane, in extreme cases 14, on both hands, according to whether Jones was in a good or bad mood:

> A few strokes would swell the hands considerably and when ended would bruise the hands sadly. If a boy endeavoured to evade a blow or shrunk from it, he was sure to have a rap on the underside to make him hold his hand fair, and such was the dexterity of the master that he could spread the blows all

over the hand, and when he meant to be more severe than usual, he would make the end of the cane reach to the wrist…. There was constant emulation among the boys to shew how they could bear punishment.

Spartan management lived on. Place reports that he was never behind in his work and should never have been beaten at all, had he not chosen to provoke Jones: "I was frequently beaten".[6]

He had a better experience under "my good master Mr. Bowis" at his next school, "for the confidence he taught me to repose in myself and especially in whatever I believed to be true; for the notions of perseverance he caused me to imbibe … and a reliance on honest industry … I regard his instructions as laying the foundation of much of the happiness and prosperity I have enjoyed." These had made Place "*comparatively* chaste amidst scenes of excessive debauchery and among remarkably dissolute associates," kept him honest, prevented violence, "and under the most pressing of circumstances and the lowest state of poverty saved me from either recklessness or despair".[7] Francis Place must have been a joy to teach, and his later teachers effective in their calling.

Towards the close of the century, education had become a free market where the education children received was determined by parental preferences and income, resulting in the perpetuation of existing societal norms rather than changing them. Meritocracy applied to the exceptional such as, in their very different ways, to James Cook and the engineer George Stephenson (1781-1848), "father of the railways." The variegated educational system tended to reinforce cultural and gender distinctions. Ironically, this stability factor aided the argument of those in favour of the education of the poor, there being significant demand in that sector. English society was highly differentiated and contradictory. Its boisterous patriotism loved its monarchy but revelled in the lampooning of the royal family. It sang of roast beef but largely subsisted on bread and cheese. Life was characterised by huge divisions between the ruling class and the ruled, between the rich and poor, starkly illustrated during the century by the increasing development and elegance of the capital city north of the river, at its centre and westwards, whereas to the east and south of the Thames "there was only stinking industry – distilleries, rope-works, tanneries, shambles and shipyards … bawdy houses, hogs and fogs".[8]

New charities were founded in London as pauperism increased: ten in 1771-1780; eighteen in 1781-1790; and thirty in 1791-1800. Sunday school graduate Thomas Cranfield (1758-1838), another successful tailor, this time born in the parish of Southwark and baptized like John Harvard at St Saviour's Church, established 19 free Sunday schools in the poorer areas of London, beginning with one on Kent Street in 1798. In its earliest days, Cranfield had to struggle for financial support, reportedly exclaiming after yet another rebuff:

> "Alas, poor Kent street" he involuntarily said to himself as he retired; "is there none to take thee by the hand?"[9]

He was speaking of the place where Joseph Lancaster, future mass education manager, was born, on 25 November 1778.

**FOOTPRINT:**
**The Ideas Of Enlightenment Deeply Affected Management On Many Levels**

- The ideas of Enlightenment deeply affected management at many levels.

- An intellectual class extended thought into revolt, revolution, and institutional reform.

- Business people developed and exploited markets, with the children of the better off a prime target.

- Education of the poor began to be an issue.

# Endnotes

[1] Scotland's population is estimated at 1,000,000 for 1707, and stood at 1,608,420 by the 1801 census. Wales's population in 1620 is estimated at 360,000, and quoted at 587,000 in the 1801 census. Ireland's population doubled from c. 4 million in 1790 to 8 million in 1840, from which peak a steady decline began, not halted until after the Second World War.

[2] Plumb, *op. cit.,* p.93.
[3] Kendall, Guy. *Robert Raikes*, pp. 70-72.
[4] Porter, *op. cit.,* p.291.
[5] *Ibid,* p.163.
[6] Ed. Thale, Mary. *The Autobiography of Francis Place,* pp. 41-2.
[7] *Ibid,* p. 61.
[8] Porter, *op. cit.,* pp. 45-46.
[9] Cranfield, Richard. 1844. *Memoir of Thomas Cranfield of London.* Boston: Massachusetts Sabbath, p. 85.

**Crowley House and Crowley Wharf at Greenwich,**
looking westward towards the Royal Naval Hospital.
[Image from M W Flinn, *Men of Iron, p.53.*]

The Warehouse (at the end of the path) adjoining the River Thames was constructed for ironmaster Ambrose Crowley III in c.1704-5 to facilitate his growing trade in the iron business. On three floors, with the goods doors facing the river on the upper floors, and a large family home close by, had obvious business and social advantages. Crowley House, immediately to its left (east), hidden from view behind the large riverfront warehouse building, was purchased a year or so earlier.

[The warehouse was subsequently demolished in 1853, and Crowley House cleared away in 1855 after failing to find a new buyer. The site then remained generally open, with later use as a horse-drawn tram depot and stables, until Greenwich Power Station was built there from 1906.]

# CASE STUDY (1):
# THE FIRST MAN OF MODERN INDUSTRY:
# THE CROWLEY INDUSTRIAL SYSTEM

**Sir Ambrose Crowley III (1658-1713)**

Ambrose Crowley I (d.1680, exact birth date unknown) lived in the county of Worcestershire in the industrial Midlands of England, where he had an agricultural small holding and metal-bashing business as a maker of nails. His eldest son, Ambrose II (1635-1720), was bequeathed his start in life by his father, by the transference of metal skills but little capital. He was left a shilling, with a third of a pound to be shared with his wife and children, in Ambrose I's will. The descriptions "nailer," "blacksmith" and "ironmonger" were applied during his career, suggesting a steady rise from humble origins. By the 1670s he was trading in Stourbridge, at the heart of the Midlands metals business as an ironmonger, that then being not retail but a wholesale, middleman occupation buying from ironmasters and forge masters, the producers of pig or bar iron, the raw material which iron manufacturers processed to make objects. He then sold on to the metal craftsmen – slitters, blacksmiths, nailers – and to merchants, and engaged in some of the manufacturing processes.

Pig and bar iron required further process as it was brittle, thus unsuitable for untreated manufacture. The economics favoured the manufacturers. Production required capital for plant and fuel, the availability of coppice wood for charcoal also limiting location. Only coal was required for further processing and small objects had high value proportionate to their weight, with transport costs to market also being low. Thus, business could be begun at low capital cost, with good profit prospects.

Ambrose II expanded his business quickly, soon progressing beyond iron and steel trading. Between 1680 and 1700, he acquired forges, mills, and mill ponds, processing pig iron and putting out bar iron to local slitters for it to be further refined into rod iron for nail making. He had begun as a nail maker, now he was selling the nailer's raw material; and his scope had widened for he also imported bar iron from Sweden, this being of higher quality and suitable for steel making. Steel was then a niche product, sold normally only in small quantities. Ambrose II expanded this area of his business, selling some in bar form, some made into anvils and hammers.

His contemporary, adjoining county neighbour and fellow Quaker Abraham Darby I, equipped his Coalbrookdale works with hammers and bellow-boards from Ambrose II's Stourbridge base. The Darby's Coalbrookdale enterprise is usually cited as the commencement of the industrial revolution, for its new patented process of using local "coking coal" to produce cheaper cast iron goods. From building the Stourbridge industry, Ambrose II expanded into Wales with a blast furnace to the north of Cardiff, diversifying further into water supply in Devon.

During the course of the Civil War (1642-51), George Fox (1624-1691) had begun to preach his version and vision of Christianity. The name for this derived from the magistrate before whom Fox appeared in 1650 on a charge of blasphemy: Quakers, because, said Fox's version, "I bade them tremble at the word of the Lord." Quakers are considered in more depth in a subsequent publication. These members of the Christian movement, the Religious Society of Friends, are characterised by their belief that each human being has the ability to access experientially "that of God in every person," avoiding creeds and hierarchical structures. A period of persecution in 17<sup>th</sup> century England, later rescinded, promoted their emigration to North America where, unsurprisingly, they met persecution again, this time from Protestant Puritans in Massachusetts. They found refuge in West Jersey, Rhode Island and the Quaker-established Pennsylvania, a commonwealth run under Quaker principles, but progressed ever onwards to the west coast, where they founded the first Christian college in Oregon.

In Britain particularly, and the United States, Quakers were very successful in business. Excluded from public office because of their beliefs, Quaker energies were channelled by those beliefs into productive occupations, prime among which were financial services, manufacturing, and fulfilment of the duty to assist fellows, all cemented by kinship and trust.

The Quaker network financed widespread industrial projects. Some of their original companies trade still as large and important businesses, such as the finance houses Lloyds (1884), Barclays (1896), Friends' Provident (1832), and the accountants Price Waterhouse (1849). The Quaker confectioners Fry, Cadbury, Rowntree, biscuit makers Huntley and Palmer; and the merchant Pease family, one of the founders of Barclays, financiers of the world's first commercial freight and passenger railway venture, the Stockton to Darlington line; Clarks Shoes; and shipbuilders Swan Hunter (now a design company only) were all distinguished by their care for their workers and large philanthropic activities, reflecting their belief that their faith had to be active in good works.

Fox's movement, founded in 1654, first became organised in Worcestershire the following year, with Ambrose II as an early, keen adherent. This had the advantage of access on virtual foundation to what became the remarkably effective Quaker business network. Abraham Darby I (1678-1717), a significant beneficiary and participant, had the subsequent disadvantage of becoming a victim of the high standards of service to others required by the sect. The network was powerful. Ambrose II suffered from his own generosity, his profligacy in perceived service, and forgetfulness in old age. He became the softest of soft touches, exploited by many, despite the continued efforts of his exasperated eldest son to remedy the situation. On his death, his much-diminished fortune was unable to meet all the bequests from the £3,000 which Ambrose II believed he had left. Ambrose II's business passed to his three younger sons but did not survive them. His eldest son, Ambrose III, who predeceased him, in contrast left the legacy of a thriving business which lasted for a further century and a half.

Ambrose III's upwardly mobile father had determined that his conspicuously able eldest son should follow the family trajectory. Ambrose III had been sent to London, apprenticed to a Draper and son of a Quaker, Francis Plumstead, who died in 1710, still owing money to Ambrose II. The apprenticeship was to an ironmonger. The Drapers was an important Livery Company, at inception ranking third in precedence concerning the wool and cloth trades. This apparent incongruity arose because the freedom of one of the livery companies was a pre-requisite of entry to City government, wherein merchants formed a powerful pressure group. By the time of Ambrose III's apprenticeship, being part of the system was what mattered, not the actual craft itself. By 1684, he had completed his service, setting up his own warehouse and office in Thames Street, from which he directed his business for some twenty years, and close to which was the Merchant Taylors' school, which educated his children. His initial career was in the selling of small items of ironmongery, such as frying pans, nails, and brads, but this acute man of business already seems to have outsourced his supply.

The commencement date is uncertain but in the year of the completion of Ambrose III's apprenticeship he had written a remarkable business plan in the form of a very direct letter to his father and the ironmasters of the Midlands, telling them of what he was about to do, and not to interfere with it: "soe silence is yor interest as well as mine".[1] Crowley's initiative might be seen as a late example of what some historians have termed "the age of the projectors," usually ascribed to the late 16th and early 17th centuries. The projects were grand schemes, based loosely on reality.

An important near-contemporary but significantly coincidental 1709 peace proposal by William Penn (of Pennsylvania) that the War of Spanish Succession (1701-1714) should be settled by the French having the American territory north of the Great Lakes and Hudson River, and the British the Mississippi valley and the lands to the west, has been cited as an example:

> Whitehall lacked significant imperial goods goals of its own during the war. Those it supported – and frequently abandoned – were the initiatives of the projectors.[2]

Such projector access was to have considerable importance later.

The perceptive Ambrose had seen the opportunity which conflict would bring, for he began his north-eastern enterprise in 1688 at the latest, when

James II (1633-1701) had begun to expand his navy in anticipation of war against the Dutch. The ousting of James and ascension to the English throne of the Dutch William III (1650-1702) made warfare inevitable; but against the French. That began with an alliance against France, the Nine Years' War of 1688-1697. The comprehensive French victory at the 1690 battle of Beachy Head meant that a huge fleet rebuilding operation would follow if Britain was to regain dominant sea power.[3]

If he was envisioning a lengthy conflict with either the Dutch or French, in which the main English contribution would be at sea with new naval construction, hence causing heavy and increasing demand for nails in particular; then Ambrose III's contemporaneous establishment of works in northeast England was a piece of considered, brilliant foresight – or, foreknowledge gained through his London connections. A risk-taking entrepreneur who invested heavily on one outcome, only to benefit from another, with conflict as a constant, Ambrose can certainly be viewed as a projector. To others, his scheme might have appeared deranged. Yet, it had the clear-headed logic, business knowledge and acumen with daring courage, which characterised his career. There was an enormous demand to come, which would commence industrialisation to satisfy. Government's need to finance the process led to the creation of the Bank of England. Demand and finance could make industrialisation happen, at last. Ambrose Crowley III set about managing it.

Ambrose, from his London base, had a factory built on the north-east coast at Sunderland, the building partially constructed with stone from a ruined chapel built in the time of Bede, whose monastery was nearby. The north-east of England had no experience of the metals industry, so training of the workforce was necessary. He supplied it by bringing workers from Stourbridge and, most importantly, Belgians from Liège, with state-of-the-art skills in the processes he sought to establish. Such was the local discontent at the presence of so many unaccustomed foreigners, with strange habits and Catholic faith, that he had to intervene, petitioning the king to prevent their molestation "on account of the religion or otherwise."

The sympathetic James II granted the petition, instructing the Bishop of Durham to "take speedy and effectual care that the Petitioner's workmen be protected and quieted in their carrying on the manufacture".[4] The choice of Sunderland allowed easy import of high quality Swedish and Russian bar and pig iron and, after processing and manufacture, the cheap and efficient export by sea of product along the eastern and southern coast, the locations of many prime customers, the navy in particular. Crowley's metal ware followed the sea-coal shipping routes. For both construction and repair, the latter essential as British ships at that time were of inferior quality to their Spanish and French rivals, quality nails and, especially anchors, were of great value.

Swiftly becoming a main ironwork contractor to the navy, in 1691-3 Crowley greatly expanded his north-eastern business. Victory at the battle of La Hogue and destruction of a French fleet at Cherbourg in 1692 had left England as the dominant sea power but with a constant need to maintain and improve its fleet: a ready market beckoned, with high demand. Ambrose left Sunderland, possibly seeking cheaper or more amenable labour circumstances. He took a ninety-nine-year lease over a corn and fulling mill at Winlaton, adding further premises at Swalwell, both being settlements near Gateshead, between the rivers Tyne and Derwent. He adapted and expanded it into a major integrated ironworks, ultimately creating what became Europe's biggest industrial site. This included a finery/chafery forge, plating forge, slitting mill, cementation steel furnace, blade grinding mills, anvil shop, hardening shop, and nailmakers' and filemakers' workshops, together with warehouses, offices, and housing. At the Winlaton site, the ironworks buildings were constructed in squares as a mix of domestic and industrial units. His total workforce numbered over 1,000. Ambrose III's creation became the wonder of the early industrial world.

It was not until 1770 that Matthew Boulton (1728-1809), Boswell's "iron chieftain," was employing half that number. Producing the steam engines of his partner James Watt (1736-1819), his output made the mechanisation of factories and mills possible.

The initiating driving force of the industrial revolution had been anticipated by Ambrose III by over half a century. Moreover, Ambrose Crowley had further anticipated F.W.Taylor by two hundred years. His factory enterprise, being an agglomeration of multiple work units where each manufacturing master retained his freedom within Crowley's prescriptive management *Laws* and materials supplies, anticipated the then "advanced" methods of the regional management centre (at which in 1980 this author began his academic Management Studies career) whereby each lecturer was, as described at an industrial tribunal, "a semi-autonomous work unit" and can be seen reflected in the management freedom theory expounded in the current century.

Even more remarkably, Ambrose III remained a successful manufacturer and trader, but no more than that until the final fifteen years of his business career. The additional waterpower derived from the Derwent flowing down from the high Pennines allowed the capitalist management, construction and

operation of his own slitting and rolling mill, thus cutting out and undercutting many of his former suppliers, the "cheates" of the Midlands. Mining along and above the Derwent valley, and that of the Tyne, brought access to the transport system for mined deposits of iron, lead and coal, conveyed speedily by wagon. Further conveyance by keel, a shallow or flat-bottomed river cargo boat, gave access to the port at Newcastle.

(above) **Winlaton Mill steel warehouse in 1893, with the rolling mill visible at the far (north) end of the millpond of the 'Great Pool' used to power the mills.**

### Crowley's Iron Nails

Ambrose III had begun his nail manufacture when the new technology had allowed the growth of that industry. Nail makers had previously worked by hand using imported iron  rods, the reason for the concentration of the industry in London; the only alternative being the expensive and laborious method of hand-chiselling. The invention of the slitting-mill greatly reduced the cost of nail rods, the nail now being within the price range at which there was high demand. Such was that demand, by the end of the 18th century, up to half of the English iron market was for nails. However, it was not until further process improvements in the 19th century allowing nails to be made from wire permitted the manufacturing process to be more mechanised. Until then, the manufacture had to be by hand, each nail cut and individually shaped from the nail rod. Thus, to service the mass market, large numbers of workers had to be employed.

However, the initial business of nail-making being a craft then new to the region, and for following product, required Crowley to devise a management system. His Gateshead business was complex, employing over 1,000 workers and, right from the start, he ran it from London. His London presence was imperative. He had to be close to his customers, particularly the Admiralty, operations sites such as the naval dockyard headquarters at nearby Chatham, the financial centre of the City, and the associated powers both there and in parliament. Yet, as master, he had also to direct the productive source of the business. For this he devised techniques of shop floor organisation, discipline, and welfare. There was no doubt as to who was boss. All instructions in the *Law Book of the Crowley Ironworks*, the collected management manual of Ambrose and his son, John, began "I DO ORDER."

Employees were housed on company property, provided with a doctor and poor relief where applicable, although all recipients had to wear a badge inscribed "Crowley's Poor." There was an elected works committee, sickness payments, and overseer requirement to treat the workers with respect. The technologies and skills developed at the Crowley works led to the foundation of the Sheffield steel industry. His core business extended to the mercantile marine and then into the domestic market. Among the reasons for this exceptional early provision of an industrial management system, and an enlightened one at that, was that only the military contracting business was of a scale sufficient to require such provision. The sole contemporary comparison was to the Chatham naval dockyards where Defoe had observed "tho' you see the whole place as it were in the utmost hurry, yet you see no confusion, every man knows his own business".[5]

A multi-phase dam on the river Derwent and use of the mill ponds allowed the water to be drawn off to wherever it was needed. This then advanced engineering lasted with only limited development until eventual closure in 1863. As well as being an important early example of the factory production system, Crowley's works included a remarkable form of worker welfare provision, possibly because he had to attract workers to a sparsely populated area, bear the training cost, and retain his investment. The site was chosen because of its proximity to local coal, and the Derwent, Wear and Tyne rivers for water supply and goods' transport. The unique product need in metal manufacture at this period of small masters was for quality control, which was then viable only in bulk orders.

For the armed services, standard Crowley product such as anchors and sheathing nails had to be reliable. Thus, exceptionally and virtually anachronistically, a large industrial complex far ahead of its time was created to supply the demand. Ambrose III called his concentrated industrial units "factories." The term "factory", distinct from a workshop, had previously often applied to an establishment for traders carrying on business in a foreign country, as exemplified by the Genovese trading post at Kaffa when the city was subjected to biological warfare by the Khan, Janni Beg, in 1346. Crowley appears to have been an early user of the modern industrial use of the word.

There had been one earlier attempt at the establishment of an industrial factory in England, which had failed. To rescue the enterprise, another factory was built nearby after John Lombe (1699-1722) had travelled to Piedmont in the exercise of the valuable art of warfare recommended by Sun Tzu - economic espionage - to discover the secrets of *throwing* in silk spinning; one early design of a machine for which appears to have been by Leonardo da Vinci. Italy had been the most advanced Western practitioner of the silk industry since the 13$^{th}$ century. By the 17$^{th}$ it had developed a mechanised spinning process to produce thread ready for different types of weaving. Lombe's spying was successful. He even returned with skilled Italians able to use such equipment and acquired a fourteen-year patent for the machinery, to be installed at the purpose-built new factory in Derby. Learning of this, the King of Sardinia Victor Amadeus II (1685-1759) imposed an export ban on raw silk, and was rumoured even to have commissioned a female assassin to dispatch Lombe. He died suddenly and mysteriously before processes could be begun. Although the Derby factory continued, the silk weaving business on patent lapse was subject to competition from factories in Cheshire. 19$^{th}$ century visitors complained of the conditions and treatment of child labour. Only the mill building survived; as the Derby Industrial Museum,[6] subsequently renamed Derby Silk Mill. Ambrose Crowley III, who was in charge of a much larger and longer-lasting operation, can thus be confirmed as the founder of large-scale British factory manufacturing; in addition his welfare provision for factory workers making a double 'father figure 'first.

Ambrose's bulk business most probably came from naval supplies. The British navy was the world's largest and busiest, if not fighting then protecting, sea trade routes. It required constant maintenance, especially to its wooden hulls. It had been discovered that copper sheeting was an excellent protective, but this was expensive. The common substitute was wooden sheaths, the fixing in place of which required vast quantities of nails. These could be supplied in considerable bulk from Winlaton, which could also supply the most common iron ware articles. There were six naval dockyards, four in the Thames estuary at Deptford, Woolwich, Chatham and Sheerness, with two more at Portsmouth and Plymouth. The London yards could be supplied by sea from Winlaton, with Ambrose's London warehousing allowing storage, and transhipment to the south coast.

His London operation was expanded to accommodate the growing trade and his social advance. A large new house, warehouse, and wharf were constructed at Greenwich, for the building of which he typically imported cheaper labourers from the country. He had established clear superiority over his competitors - the long-established iron traders of the Midlands - by three well thought out and implemented business innovations. He could get his goods cheaper and more efficiently to market; his bulk outsourcing over distance was unique for its times; and he was adaptable, able to respond quickly to change and opportunity. Possessed of quite outstanding ability, he brilliantly integrated and managed the many components of a diverse business, introducing industrial supply chain factory management. This was the world's first of its type, prototype of the ultimate business models of the industrial revolution as typified by north-east neighbours, the Vane-Tempest family, the Lords Londonderry. Quarried goods from their lands were conveyed to their port of Seaham Harbour, loaded upon their ships, transported to London where their agent made disposal; control of the means of production, distribution, and sales was, by then, the ultimate capitalist model. Ambrose III was the harbinger.

Typical naval contracts for the period were for items such as: axes, bolts, chisels, files, shovels, tongs, forks, hatchets, fifteen different varieties of hinges, pitch ladles, latches, seven varieties of locks, pots for pitch, saws, scrapers, screws, staples, thimbles, curtain rods, hoops, anchors, and over a hundred different types of nails. To supply the demand, in addition to a domestic market which included such household items as pots and frying pans, Ambrose III had built three factories comprising two slitting-mills, two forges, four steel furnaces, many warehouses, and multiple smiths' workshops for the production of a formidable range of goods. A further large warehouse was added at nearby Blaydon. The complex was under a Newcastle based manager, whose instructions were specified in the *Law Book* in Order 29: customs duties were calculated to the nearest farthing; full quantities checking and such strict shipment instructions as:[7]

> Be sure to take great deal of care it [the iron] is not mixed with landing, and when you send it up in keels be sure you see the same so loaded in the keeles that two sorts not easily distinguished may not be mixed together. Be sure

to send up to Blaydon a note of the contents of each keel and what claim [incoming shipment] or claims the iron belongs to with the marks of the iron and the number of barrs counting a barr broke in 2 or more pieces but one barr and also mention what the keel-men is to have. You are not to lend, sell or exchange any iron upon any notion or consideration without a special order from me and then always to see weighed what you lend or sell. You are expressly to charge the keel-men not to throw out any iron till the manager at Blaydon hath come or send to take accot. thereof. [8]

In the Midlands, four warehouses at Ware, Wolverhampton, Walsall, and Stourbridge held stock for distribution, thus utilising the long-established trade base and network to Crowley purposes, a form of reverse takeover. The Stourbridge distribution hub served also as a purchasing centre for local bar and rod iron. Ambrose III could buy according to price and need: from local production to Midland's sourcing, to Russian and Swedish import, even exploring import from Massachusetts. As early as 1702, Ambrose III had been consulted by William Penn concerning the establishment of ironworks in Pennsylvania.[9] The Greenwich head office, wharf, and warehouse were supplemented by five warehouses in the city around the original Thames Street location. Stocks were held at all six naval dockyards. He employed agents abroad. His biographer observed:

> Thus, sixteen years had sufficed for one man, unaided, to create what was probably the greatest industrial organisation of his age.[10]

## Crowley's Management Control

As much an autocrat as the monarchs discussed above, Ambrose III took no partners and doubted the integrity and wisdom of individual managers. In his preamble to *Law 83*, he stated:

> It hath by experience been found that where government or people leave the management of their business to any single person, that their interest suffereth for want of advice, their estate wasteth for want of checks upon their managers, their business upon any change or death hath been put in any great disorder, which occasioned all wise governments and people to leave the management of their business to more than one, believing Solomon to be equal with his character in saying, "In the multitude of counsellers is safety."[11]

Control was therefore established through and by committees, these being composed of officials with departmental responsibilities, although Ambrose III attempted to legislate in *Law 57* against the evasion of responsibility by managers "saying they are not one and cannot act alone" whilst combating negligence, procrastination, possible dishonesty, and inappropriate initiatives: all the problems of autocracy, in short. The committees were instruments of managerial control, he being the sole arbiter, able to change terms of reference and operation as he saw fit. There were no models to guide him. He followed the rational logic of process needs, the earliest example of industrial scientific management. This was the origin of codified industrial management and practice. "Management," as a discrete object of industrial study and application, starts here: autocracy, supported by bureaucracy, under a systematic process, including welfare provision.

Above the committees was the Council, the members of which Ambrose III stipulated, "must be named by me." On accession, the Counsellors had to swear an oath of individual responsibility to promote the proprietor's best interests, keep proceedings secret, "and in all things discharge a good conscience and faithfully discharge the trust we have taken upon us."[12] Council assembled at 5.00a.m. on Monday mornings to read Crowley's letters, termed "Council Instructions." The letters were to be opened in the presence of two or more Counsellors, with the Treasurer forbidden from ever being the first to open a letter. On Tuesdays, at 7.00am in summer or 8.00am in winter, a more general Grand Council was to convene. There were other meetings, such as those to regulate worker debt repayments to the firm. The Counsellors, where reported by two or more others, were liable to pay fines for lateness or other misdemeanours, the fines being equally divided annually among the Council.

Crowley looked for personal integrity as the prime Council membership qualification, rather than managerial experience. This was a possible reason for his addition of a third tier of management control, a "Comptrol or Committee of Council," to consist of three persons nominated by him to expedite matters, meeting three times per week and reporting weekly to the Council. That body had then to reply to the Council Instructions and transmit its own orders and decisions to the factories, recording the detail as minutes in its journal, a copy of which was sent weekly to Ambrose III in London. Councillors had many routine tasks, closely detailed in the *Laws*, and were also expected to take an interest in organisation and suggest improvements.

As well as various subcommittees, there were four further committees for different aspects of administration: metals' carriage; treasury; mill affairs; and survey (quality control). This was a particularly important function, for each item continued to be made individually but had to conform to specifications. Since workmen could attempt to cheat by, for example, making nails from lead rather than iron, so increasing the weight by which they were paid, each product had to be diligently examined before market release. Survey Committee work was wide ranging across the factory, including: unloading and checking; tools' issue; determination of which products each workman should make; and iron slitting requirements. Committee membership was usually drawn from senior clerks and officials but contained a number of master-workmen who were chosen, presumably, on integrity grounds. Status appears to have been as equals. Each department had a small clerical staff and clear function, each defined in the *Law Book*, with cross-checking backed up by a fining system.

Payment was for a standard six-day week of eighty hours. However, the nature of some officials' work was necessarily irregular. To maintain a careful check on this time-keepers, called Monitors or Warden, were appointed to keep "time papers" for each official, recording times of arrival and departure, ring bells at the start, meal times and end of the working day, and make spot checks unpredictably, twice daily. Absence or signing out neglect was then to be inquired into. Even so, Ambrose III found himself "horably cheated by the Monitor" in 1701 when two officials were allowed their wages without their work having been inspected.[13] Smoking was prohibited but moderate drinking could be allowed, although payment for consumption time required London's permission, a circumstance bound to put severe pressure by thirsty men upon their Monitor.

It is natural to wonder how many of his instructions were more honoured in the breach than their observance. Ambrose III was certainly aware of where admirable theory could fall victim to practicalities as when, for example, the "vile practices of some fooles" misclassified assorted ironware as "sundry," making it "impossible to know what's made or coming." Such regular error required the warehouses always to be well-stocked, creating further cost, since much of his product being sold on a bespoke basis, required an exact supply. Crowley's observations in the *Law Book* of the breaking of his code include the demand "that I may immediately know where the blame ought to be laid for that capitall crime of making that which is not wanted."[14]

The workforce reflected the transitional nature of the times. In addition to the clerks and officials were the heavy equipment operators usually paid weekly wages, except where work or materials were short; those in casual employment, such as masons and carpenters, which was steady during the expansion years, paid by piece rates, or on hourly or daily bases; and then the nail and other iron ware makers, who functioned on the master-journeyman-apprentice basis. A 1702 listing gives 132 masters employing 36 hammermen and 29 "boys," the majority of which worked in stalls in the factories. There was further outsourcing to the surrounding villages when demand was sudden or high, provided that, to maintain quality control, the rod iron was bought from Crowley.

## The Division of Labour, and Control Issues

Early in *The Wealth of Nations* (Book 1, Chapter 1), Adam Smith makes his famous remarks concerning the division of labour and productivity, from which some have drawn the conclusion that he invented the term, or perhaps derived it from his pin factory exposition. Smith published *Wealth* in 1776. In 1766, the Earl of Shelburne (1737-1805), great grandson of William Petty (1623-1687), the surveyor who began national accounting in Britain, had attributed the success of the Birmingham hardware trades to three factors: the division of labour; simplifying tasks so that even a child could participate in manufacturing; and the workers' making of small individual improvements. Earlier, William Petty in his *Political Arithmetick* of 1690 had studied its function and use in Dutch shipyards. Matthew Boulton had explained to the Earl of Warwick (1746-1816) in 1773 that it was the separation of processes which allowed British manufacturers to compete with Europe.[15]

The Crowley works continued to flourish in the mid-18th century and it is inconceivable that the rising industrialists of the Midlands were unaware of the working practices of the greatest manufacturing concern of the age, either copying it or following long established practice - most probably both. Smith was merely observing common industrial practice. He deserves credit for observation and recording. If anyone deserves credit for instituting the practice of large-scale division of labour in manufacturing, it is Crowley and his subsequent, imitative colleagues. A case might also be made for the silver workings of 5th and 4th century BCE Athens, where metal working from ore separation to finished jewellery could be accomplished on one site.

The old and new systems inevitably collided. Labour division disputes and dysfunction between the nominally independent masters and the hammermen caused Ambrose III to insist that the local schoolmaster be charged with drawing up contracts between the two, including factory dismissal in the event of disturbance. At first issued with tools by the factory, Crowley found that they were subject to abuse and lost value. He therefore made a supply charge, with repair and maintenance the workman's responsibility. He greatly minimised the opportunities for theft, wastage, and fraud by issuing the masters with a weekly upper limit of raw material, which further incentivised the workmen, for their earnings depended upon the production of the maximum quantity of finished product. This was inspected at weekly reckonings, the finished product delivered to the Nail or Ware Keeper. After deductions such as insurance contributions or loans repayments, the Cashier then paid the workman.

Crowley was conspicuously considerate in making payment. The factory bell was rung to warn of reckoning times and the officials under strict instructions to be quick and cheerful, "allways considering that their time is their bread and how grievous it is to them to be unnecessarily delayed."[16] Loans were made to assist relocation costs for workers moving to the factory, and to assist in instances of unexpected hardship. Coal was supplied for household use at workman's rates, and rent instalments for accommodation in factory houses would also be deducted. Rents for local landlords could be collected by this method too. Employees were allowed grazing at the company farm for moderate rents. An assessment method ensured that the debts never became large, again enshrined in company law, with publication to ensure transparency and an appeals process.

The most intractable labour problem was that of "running out of stock," for which the master could have many excuses but which in reality were attributable to theft, mismanagement, or poor workmanship. The *Law Book* made many provisions, including spreading the loss charge across the whole work force through deduction to the company's insurance scheme, in the hope of peer pressure creating good practice, but is unlikely ever to have solved the problem entirely. The administrative issue was communications. Ambrose III and his successors were constantly engaged in writing letters; an army of clerks laboured to service the linkages between the north-east, Midlands, London, suppliers, and agents abroad. Post between Newcastle and London took three days, a factor which could be accommodated within the Crowley system, which divided its accounting time into predictable seventy-day intervals, but the difficulty lay in the dilatoriness of some officials, requiring the provisions of Law 57, which prescribed detailed instructions for correspondence with head office.

These were underpinned by moral authority: there was no greater rudeness than not to answer a letter, nor any greater impudence than a servant could make to a master. By insisting that if one Counsellor did not answer, then all others must, Crowley appears to have won. The method of postal control worked, less urgent communications transported by ships constantly plying between Newcastle and London. The management disciplinary principle goes back to the Roman practice of decimation, the execution of a tenth of a unit in the event of mutiny; or desertion and failure, as in the case of the Golden Horde of Genghis Khan; and medieval community discipline through the imposition of tithing.

Long practical experience had given Ambrose III a less than glowing opinion of human nature. The language and approach of a number of the *Laws* is couched in terms of biblical severity. Pilfering, wastage of time and materials, and evasion of duty were all Satan's work, devilishness to be eradicated. This stringency, however, was all part of his practical planning, for he was engaged in building a community, described as "this society" or "my people." Workers were given numbers as an aid to their being monitored. He insisted on workers' complaints being heard and taken seriously, even to the extent, if not resolved at local committee level, of their being put in writing as a label attached to the originating goods so that it might be read by Ambrose himself when the shipment reached London.

## The Welfare of "Crowley's Crew"

Convinced that good industrial relations, and therefore untroubled production, could only be established by plain justice, in 1690 he established his Court of Arbitrators, some eight years before parliament legislated to give arbitration, that process known to the Elder Cato, a legal basis. The Crowley private court had five arbitrators, the first of which was the company chaplain, two were Crowley nominees, and two elected by the nailers and odd ware makers. A distinction seems to have been made between the unrepresented wage earners and the piece workers, since the latter sold only the product of their labour rather than their labour itself.

The arbitrators were paid at the rate of nine pence per hour for their services, but all had to behave themselves. Among the twenty-three possible grounds for dismissal was being found in a public house during working time. The purposes and practices of the Court changed over time, with a shift in emphasis to the distribution of the Poor fund, the insurance system, and to the prosecution of offenders. This court aspect continued well into the 19th century, records surviving of such matters as the theft of turnips from company fields, the borrowing and lending of iron, and unauthorised product sale.

The *Laws* would have been read to groups of workers, some passages regularly, with messages reinforced. Sir Ambrose used his control vehicle also to supply secular homilies and social restrictions. "Extravagances Discouraged" was the subject of Order 85:

> Whereas Mr. Crowley hath made it his observation that morning drinking hath been of fatal consequence to all that have made a practice of it:
>
> 1) It is of all things the most destructive to business;
> 2) It destroyeth health, memory and understanding;
> 3) It produceth nothing but folly and madness;
> 4) It wastes the only time to do business … it is therefore declared that Mr Crowley will take effectual care to discharge all such as shall for the future practice the drinking of any strong liquor before they go to dinner.

Various employees, whom Sir Ambrose named, had "all rendered themselves unfit for any business, and reduced themselves to extreme poverty," by misconduct in gambling, drinking, and sprees in nearby Newcastle, "which hath been the ruin of several." Further examples of extracts of the *Laws* are to be found in **Appendix 2**, together with photographic copies of some of the original documents, now housed in the British Museum.

The Crowley Laws have been criticised for being more about prevention than cure. It was, however, entirely reasonable for the times for Ambrose III to have believed that department to have been the responsibility of organised religion, in the cause of which he built a chapel and installed a chaplain at Winlaton. Order 105 established the chaplain's duties. These included the provision of Anglican Sunday services, to hear workmen's reasonable complaints, plead the cause and help the oppressed, assist the injured, visit the sick and "rebuke vice and promote virtue." The chaplain was to "forbear frequenting alehouses … or at least not to make any considerable stay there."[17] Although raised at the very heart of Quakerism and benefiting from the Quaker metals business network, from his arrival in London Ambrose III appears to have become apostate and embraced Anglicanism. As many of his workers appear to have been nonconformists, the form of religion within his chapel must have been from conviction, allied to practical London business needs.

His son, John, added a company doctor, whose role was specified in a further *Law Book* Order. He was to attend all those who worked direct for

Crowley and paid their insurance fee "to the Poor's box." Their children received care without charge, while care could be refused for misconduct. The doctor was required to attend daily. Further skilled consultation was available in case of patient need. There were fines for abuse of the service. From a general fund to which the factory and its employees contributed, a schoolmaster was appointed to work an eight-to-nine-hour day, teaching the workmen's children. His duties included setting a good example, teaching respect to elders, correcting such misbehaviour as swearing and lying, treating all children equally and encouraging ingenuity and virtue. Not only was education for workers' children highly unusual in the 18th century, it became a local landmark. Winlaton became known as Knowledge Hill, with a street in the village bearing that name. Each worker was required to subscribe to a fund for the school master, whose further function appears to have been as Clerk for the Poor, this being the clerical work for the operation of the insurance scheme.

The operational funds realised were kept for security in Crowley's cash account, limiting the clerk to the keeping of accounts. Employee contributions were at a fixed weekly rate, originally at one farthing in the shilling, varied according to demand. The fund combined a number of separate contributions, such as to secure stock as a safeguard against workmen "running out of stock," a widow's allowance, church fees and funeral expenses (towards the costs of which the firm maintained its own hearse which it lent out free of charge). The regular 17th and 18th century small coin shortage was supplemented by Ambrose supplying his own leather equivalents, the currency good in the locality; further augmented by his own paper currency notes, acceptable in all local shops, markets, and houses where food and drink were sold.

An example of varied rates shows that when a rate of two and a halfpence in the pound was declared, the employer paid eight shillings and nine pence a week; at a five pence rate, the employer paid twelve shillings and six pence weekly. The system flourished for a century but was progressively discontinued thereafter, particularly when the business fell out of Crowley hands, and the end of the French wars brought a decline in contracts with consequent unemployment. As late as August 1788 the Crowley welfare provisions were moving a visitor to write in *Universal Magazine:* "What eulogy can be equal to the benevolence and virtue thus displayed?"[18]

Ambrose III had required skilled labour at both clerical and industrial levels. He took on 46 apprentices himself, enrolled at the Drapers and so presumably clerical. These came from a wide social range, evidence of Crowley's emphases on integrity and talent. Skilled industrial workers were sought for in the Midlands, Yorkshire, and Derbyshire, with Crowley even seeking women nailers, for such employment was known in the Midlands, although without apparent great success. Arrivals were meticulously catalogued, one purpose being identification in the case of a subsequent absconder who had accumulated large debt. Whereas pursuit and recompense were unlikely, the person would be recognised if re-employment was attempted. Recipients of the relocation allowance were contracted to give six months' notice and not to work within a 50-mile radius of Newcastle.

Although there was some accommodation for workers allowing barrack style occupation, the newly built stone houses constructed around squares (in which no swearing was allowed) lasted for over 200 years. With rent provision built into his system, Crowley's employment must have been attractive in the unstable labour environment of the times. Periods of lay-off occurred through such eventualities as interruptions to the water power supply and suspensions of warfare. There could have been no continuity of employment for piece workers during peace time. While Ambrose III's exacting standards meant that no employment was secure, ships' masters in particular being prone to dismissal for negligence, the very security which his system provided may have resulted in subsequent abuse. Some former senior employees who had risen to responsible positions were subsequently dismissed for such offences as drinking, poor time keeping and lying.

That the Crowley system was a form of social control designed to maximise efficiency and profit may be a charge to its demerit, it must also be considered that rioting labour due to poor conditions and treatment was not uncommon elsewhere. The rules were stringent, mainly falling on the clerical workers, but the forbidding of dangerous practices such as smoking, which could and did cause fires, bore down on all. The penalties for inveterately misbehaving skilled metal workers, whom Crowley did not wish to lose, were graduated, slowly moving from increased small fines to loss of privileges, and ultimate outlawry where the sinner kept employment but lost status, such as being reduced to hammerman. There was the appeals process for the punished aggrieved, but the ultimate and sole arbiter remained Ambrose III (or his successor) himself.

To keep informed, he made use of informers, an important management information systems' component when the then largest factory in the world was being run at a distance of some 250 miles. The thinking was also in accord with Sun Tzu's perceptions on the value of espionage. Crowley was using a local workforce to meet a national product demand in turbulent international circumstances. He had no precedents upon which to rely. The tightness of the organisation kept the outside world at bay. This enforced the authority of the managers. It is not stretching language too far to begin considering them as "professional" managers. They had titles and could have final authority for their work area, subject to appeals and arbitration: Ironkeeper; Warekeeper; Surveyor; Toolkeeper; Husbandman; Treasurer; Cashier; Clerk of the Mill; Governors of the Poor; and they met in, attended, or could be called before the Council. The blunt use of the terminology 'Poor' is instructive. While the welfare policy allowed for a Poor House to be set up for workers fallen upon hard times, the 'Poor' category applied also to those persons unable to afford to acquire stock unaided; they did not have capital reserves; and nor were they destitute or paupers: they were as described but able to do a job. While Crowley might complain against some of the behaviour which arose from their condition, he was balanced in his judgments, as demonstrated in *Order 103* (see **Appendix 2** extracts). He was decisive where he had to be:

> And whereas some workmen, out of a pettish fantasticall humor and without any reasonable cause, have made it a practice to be bringing in their stocks and threaten to be gone, it is ordered that when any workman, let it be who will, shall in such a frantic humor throw up his stock or iron or tools, shall be judged a disturber of the peace of the work and shall be entered 'outlaw': (Law 64).

His workers largely followed the Ambrose III lead. "Crowley's Crew" were to be found on the side of law and order during times and at a location where disorder and violence were common. Where workers elsewhere participated in the bread riots of 1767, the Winlaton workers petitioned the Gateshead magistrates. Vigorous their other political demonstrations might have been, including battling with the keelmen of the opposite persuasion, "Crowley's Crew" were staunchly Tory, supporters of the government, law, and order. An effigy of Tom Paine was hung in January 1793 at Swalwell and Winlaton.

The district had its own annual Hoppings, an entertainment featuring competitive dancing, foot and donkey races, grinning [gurning] for tobacco, and such exhibitions as a man eating a cock alive. Common sports included bear-baiting, cock-fighting and poaching. It was said that as Crowley's Crew were unmatched, national champions poachers, causing Crowley to have to promise a neighbour he would try to preserve his game from the raiding workmen. Generations of muscular smiths excelled in boxing and physical sports. The Winlaton Vulcans Rugby Club, founded in 1896 and still flourishing, carries on a long tradition. In the 19th century, the locality joined the side of reform, but from the foundation of the Crowley works until 1815, the "Crowley Crew" was firmly on the side of that economic self-interest identified by Adam Smith.

## The Ambrose Legacy

Ambrose III rose quickly in the City, and needed to. Such were the government's debts to him that an apparent attempt at compensation was made by his inclusion in the public-private partnership (The South Sea Company) created in 1711 to engage in monopoly trade in South America. He acquired a fine house in Greenwich on the River Thames to accommodate his large family of nine children, four sons and five daughters, and for entertaining his widening circle of social and business contacts. The house was expensively furnished, with an Inigo Jones (1573–1652) wooden staircase, great gallery, and panelled walls. He adapted the wharf opposite later known as Crowley Wharf, building a warehouse next to it, enabling him to carry on his business from home, often using sea-post to send his instructions to Newcastle direct. All this came at a cost.

His local government career which began as a parish officer in 1690, progressed inexorably upwards: to City Councillor, Sheriff, Alderman, then a knighthood, and election to parliament in 1713. The election was disputed but Sir Ambrose died before he could take his seat, or the case be heard.

**Sir Ambrose and Lady Mary Crowley**
From the tombstone at Mitcham Parish Church

There is no known record of the cause of death, but overwork may have been a factor. In addition to single-handedly managing his country's largest industrial organisation, performing considerable City duties, standing for election to parliament, executing family commitments which included wedding and dowry matters for one of his daughters (the marrying off of whom would have cost him around £50,000 in dowries, roughly £3 million today, by 1724), and the persistent benefaction delinquencies of his father, he was also deputy chairman – effectively chairman because of the actual chairman's frequent absences – of the South Sea Company. In reality, he had had no choice other than to accept this position as eradication of a substantial government debt in what became a notorious business venture. In addition, he had further subscribed over £36,000 for shares - a third of his wealth. It is tempting to speculate that if such an acute man of business as Sir Ambrose had lived, the subsequent South Sea Bubble collapse of 1720 or direct slave trade involvement from 1714 might have been prevented; but it is equally reasonable to consider that from the insider trading from which directors were able amply to profit that, as a businessman, he may have recognised an opportunity.

At death, Sir Ambrose's personal estate was worth £70,000. His son John, the only one of his four sons to outlive him, inherited a business with capital assets well in excess of £100,000 - roughly £6 million today ($8.3 million US). John Crowley (1689-1728), who succeeded his father ably in business, continued the company on the same lines, expanding the *Laws* with the assistance of John Hanmer who had been Ambrose III's general manager, whilst based at and living in the great house at Greenwich. That rendezvous became the seat of all the company's senior managers as the Crowley family control gradually declined.

John Crowley took the business into a further dimension with the addition of colonial trade, facilitated by Quaker connections and relatives through marriage. Here, the market was for tools such as hoes, spades and edging tools to equip the plantations, as well as the implements necessary to maintain the slave trade. Enlightened though their treatment was at home, the blacksmiths of Winlaton made indirect necessities for slaving, such as manacles, ankle irons, collars and padlocks. They neither invented that business nor participated at first hand but, like so many of their contemporaries, they colluded in an evil of the times.

John died young, as did his two sons whilst succeeding heiresses fell prey to aristocratic fortune hunters. John's widow, Theodosia, effectively ran the firm through the company managers for the next half century, outliving her daughters. Two of their widower husbands later inherited, but their interest in the business was financial only, allowing a manager to buy into the company. The eventual sale of the Crowley company over a century later in 1863 was preceded by a manager making a bonfire of the company papers, requiring the diligent Crowley biographer to construct his account largely from outgoing written records.[19] Sir Ambrose III's Quaker ethic of plain, fair dealing was reflected in the "unblemished probity" quoted in his epitaph but it is unlikely that he was popular, for his biographer observes:

> To a fiery determination to get his own way in everything he tackled, he added a ruthless disregard of the unpopularity that usually rewards this kind of persistence. His opponents, worn down by the batteries of his invective, gave way ultimately rather than submit to more.

> Whether it was the Navy Board making excuses for the delays in payment, officials in his factories temporising to excuse inefficiencies, or his young half-brothers in Stourbridge grasping for more of their share of their father's dwindling assets, all were met by the same tireless domination. "The orders I have made," he roared at his officials in Winlaton, "are built upon such a rock that while I have my understanding it shall be out of the power of Satan and all his disciples to destroy them." Nor was this firmness of manner reserved exclusively for his servants: it was visited alike on his family, the Navy Board and even his fellow parishioners in the City.… Sir Ambrose's success was the fruit of his integrity: his customers, particularly the navy, learnt that, within the limits imposed by the industrial conditions of their day, Crowley's word was his bond, that Crowley's goods were good, and that Crowley delivered the goods. [20]

Good profit, indeed. Here was the product of enlightened autocratic management upon the principles of the economics of Adam Smith, with the expression, connections, and practice of Quaker ideas and ideals. The management road may have been long, hard, tortuous, and winding, but in the Crowleys it reached an apogee. As with some other great changes and examples in the course of history, it was marvelled at during its time, but the example was not much followed. To his biographer, Ambrose III was "a giant among pygmies … more than merely an astute businessman … he was one of the formative characters in the evolution of modern industrial society … the real significance of Crowley's experiment lies not so much in his contribution to the evolution of large-scale organisation, as in his belief – amply translated into practice – that it was possible to combine successful capitalist enterprise with a concern for the well-being of his employees."[21]

Crowley had a work force of 1,000, over three main sites. As late as 1860, a "large" factory was being defined as one "employing upwards of 150 persons and making an extensive use of power machinery."[22] As power for all the early mills and factories of the industrial revolution came from water engineering rather than the steam engine, Crowley's enterprise qualifies as being somewhat more than "large." The viable employee limit in textile mills and mining at that time was from 150 to 200. The Crowley example of the size of what industrial production *could* be managed is outstanding. He paid his senior managers well, overcoming Adam Smith's scepticism of the value and competence of salaried managers. From the 1690s there had been growth in the promotion of business projects. Many failed; many were aimed more at promoter enrichment than the production of goods, a continuing phenomenon; and opportunities for fraud found unscrupulous takers.[23]

That the outstanding Crowley model was not fully followed has been attributed to the early industrialists being their own men, entrepreneurs following their own lights, training their managers, successors, and associates practically, on the job.[24] The widening need for the management of large-scale industry had begun in the first half of the 18th century. The Derby silk-throwing mill, copied from an Italian model, employed 500 workers but was not very successful. Organic development continued without wide recognition of the model and standards set by the Crowleys. However, the Cowen family, owners of a gas retorts and fire clay bricks works at Blaydon, adjacent to the Crowley's Winlaton and Swalwell plants, were certainly influenced by Sir Ambrose's neighbouring innovations and provide a fascinating case study in how industrial processes diversified.

The Winlaton Blacksmiths' Friendly Society "for the mutual relief of each other when in distress and for other good works" was formed by twelve men meeting at the New Inn, Winlaton, owned by a former Crowley smith who now possessed his own forge, John Cowen.[25] Joseph Cowen the elder (1800-1873) had begun working life as a blacksmith. He became the Friendly Society's first secretary. His forebears and relatives had been employed at the Crowley works.

Joseph Cowen Snr. developed and patented a type of fire clay brick, the best of its kind, so successful that it became known throughout Britain and most of Europe as the "Blaydon brick." Raw materials acquisition and product export took him into the mining and shipping businesses. The needs of the latter brought him into public service as chairman of the Tyne Improvement Commission, 1853-1873, during which the river was widened, deepened, and had obstacles removed, so becoming suitable for the heavy engineering and shipbuilding businesses expanding along its banks. His rewards were great local popularity, building upon his reputation as one of the leading protestors against the Manchester "Peterloo Massacre" of 1819, and a seat in parliament. Joseph junior, his eldest son (1829-1900), while commercially acute and successful, was most interested in politics.

However, Cowen's attitudes and actions have been cited as owing much to the values inculcated into his family by the Crowley practices.[26] Speaking of his home village at a Blaydon Burn Lodge meeting of the Durham Miners Union on 7 October 1883, Joseph Cowen Jnr. reminisced of the Crowley ironworks:

> When many busy centres of industry in Durham were moorland and forest, Winlaton was the seat of vigorous industry. The semi-socialist experiment of Crowley was interesting both politically and industrially; it got together a body of workmen who gave a distinctive character to the village; who afterwards acted as pioneers in the special trades in other districts. They lived in a community; they adjusted their differences at voluntary courts; they had a church and a school; a cock pit and a bull ring. They were stout church and king's men, rough and loyal.[27]

Some of those men are pictured here:

**Chain-Makers: Part of "Crowley's Crew" (above)**

**Standing Blacksmith (on left)**
**Richard Hurst, Blacksmith at Winlaton Forge (on right)**

**Winlaton Old Forge**
Apart from the Old Forge, only the foundations of the former Crowley Ironworks factory premises remain. The Winlaton site is now a public park.

The Cowen belief was that the duty of the middle class was to aid the working class to self-improvement. Joseph Jnr. opposed what he considered to be the self-interest of both Whigs and Tories, and the radicals of the Manchester school. His assistance was to sanitary reform, temperance, and education, particularly Mechanics Institutes. Influenced also by George Jacob Holyoake (1817-1906), radical newspaper editor, definer of the Liberal, coiner of "secularism" and "jingoism," he saw the cooperative movement as the means to the prosperity and progress of the working class.[28] Thus, he aided the establishment of the Blaydon cooperative store, the success of which he promoted, assisting the initiative's rapid spread throughout the region. He presided over the 1873 Cooperative Congress. Crowley values, if not systems, were perpetuated by a near neighbour.

[For a full photographic detail of the remains of the Crowley and successor works, including external archive, library and record material, see the Endnotes.][29]

## Case Study Reflections

The Crowley story offers important perspectives on the early organisation of industrialisation case study method, and on academic tunnel vision:

1. The Crowley attention to welfare as an integral component of early industrialisation, perhaps influenced by Quaker roots, was remarkable. Large though the enterprise was, its start-up nature allowed for a distinctive culture in what was for many years the largest commercial management manufacturing exercise of its times.

2. The tale is complete, apart from that lost through the destruction of company papers. A measured view can be taken over time of the lessons to be learned.

3. What aspects of Crowley's management technique and practice might be held to be of continuing value?

4. As a reflection on the tendency to narrowness of academic research, thought, and writing, with the ideological bent of what might still be better termed political economy, it is surely remarkable that Adam Smith's reputation has been inflated in countless texts by the attributions concerning the concept of the division of labour. The truth is that he recorded what was common knowledge and practice

among metal-bashing manufacturers, instituted on a large scale by Ambrose Crowley III, then others, over half a century before Smith wrote about it. Arguably, division of labour had been in operation since Egyptian pyramid construction, shield production and Phoenician fleet deployment.

5.  Sir Ambrose III's early death meant that he had no involvement in the direct slave trade business of the South Sea Company from 1714 to 1739. Crowley products however did support slavery and its enforcement in transport and the plantations. However viewed in retrospect, such business, abhorrent now, was normal for its times and, when set beside the "semi-socialist" nature of the Crowley welfare system is illustrative of how human value judgments and perspectives vary and change over time. Future generations, for example, are unlikely to look kindly on the conduct of present day climate change deniers.

## Endnotes

[1] Flinn, M W. *Men of Iron*, p. 38.

[2] Alsop, J D. "The Age of the Projectors: British Imperial Strategy in the North Atlantic in the War of Spanish Succession," p.50:
https://journals.lib.unb.ca/index.php/Acadiensis/article/down- load/11899/12743 .

[3] The product of the Crowley iron works enabled the British navy to contain the USA and defeat the French. Admiral Yi of the Royal Korean Navy won all 16 battles against Japanese fleets in the wars of 1592-98, his principal weapon being the "turtle ship." This employed the raw material differently. The *kobukson* was the world's first iron clad ship, used in the ancient manner to ram the enemy, with forward fire through a dragon prow. That design remained in use into the 19th century; Western marine technology employed iron cladding only then. Although combat methods were different, it might be noted that the eastern advance was not replicated for over 250 years, while Western seagoing technology developed independently to allow sale to the Japanese of the vessels and armament with which to defeat Russia in 1905, so facilitating Japanese annexation of Korea in 1910. Materials' uses remain central to combat management.

[4] Flinn, *op. cit.,* p.41.

[5] Porter, *op. cit.,* p. 195.

[6] The renamed Derby Silk Mill museum on the original site opened in 1721, claims to be the world's first factory, the contention based on supply by a single power source, fully mechanised. The Crowley concern was not fully mechanised, but had a work force of over 1,000, operating in units and using water as both a power and transport supply. Publicity semantics cannot deny the pioneering primacy of the Crowley concern.

[7] A quarter of a penny. Minted in silver, then tin, the first copper farthings were issued in the early 17th century under James I. By building on his experience of the usefulness of small denomination coinage in Scotland, James instituted a successful intervention in monetary management, also licensing private production to the exclusion of the Royal Mint.

[8] Flinn, *op. cit,* p.121.

[9] William Penn (1644-1718), an early Quaker, benefited from the bestowal of a large piece of Charles II's American lands as payment for debts owed to his father. The territory included modern Delaware and Pennsylvania. Delaware seceded to form its own state. Penn founded Philadelphia, enjoyed good relations with Native Americans and was an early advocate for both United States and European unions.

[10] Flinn, *op. cit.,* p. 55.

[11] *Ibid,* p.194

[12] *Ibid,* p.195.

[13] *Ibid,* p.202.

[14] *Ibid,* pp. 204-5.

[15] Uglow, Jenny. *The Lunar Men,* p. 212.

[16] Flinn, *op. cit.,* p.211.

[17] *Ibid,* p.255.

[18] *Ibid* p.232.

[19] In his 1962 Preface, M W Flinn at p. vii quotes the regret of Manchester University's Professor T S Ashton in 1924 that the Crowley business had "not received from economic historians the attention which the range of its experiments in welfare methods would appear to merit." Flinn added that Dr W H Chaloner, also of Manchester University, had suggested, assisted, and encouraged his work. This author is also a Manchester graduate, coincidentally taught by Chaloner, who now has the honour of recommending the Crowleys' history and record to Management Studies, a continuity which the Manchester Business School might care to note.

[20] Flinn, *op. cit.,* pp.64-6.

[21] *Ibid,* pp.252-255.

[22] Pollard, Sidney. *The Genesis of Modern Management*, p.21.

[23] *Ibid,* p. 33.

[24] *Ibid,* p. 35.

[25] Hodgson, T R. 1826. *Winlaton Blacksmiths' Friendly Society.* (Gateshead Libraries 2000). p.1.

[26] Waitt, E I. *John Morley, Joseph Cowen and Robert Spence Watson: Liberal Divisions in Newcastle Politics, 1873-1895,* pp. 3-4. Cowen sat in parliament as a radical Liberal from 1874 to 1886, leaving to devote his energies to his *Newcastle Chronicle* newspaper and manufacturing interests. It was said of him that he not only knew all the conspirator revolutionaries of Europe but maintained half of them. Frustrated at his inability to gain reform suitable to his requirements, he supported the rising labour movement to bring forward candidates to unseat his town's two Liberal MPs. The vote was split, thus giving the Tories control. The nearest inheritor of the Crowley values legacy reverted, in effect, to the same political stance of Sir Ambrose, a direct Tory supporter.

[27] Hodgson, *op. cit.* p. iv.

[28] "A Liberal is one who seeks to secure for everyone the same rights, political, social or religious which he claims for himself or his party," George Jacob Holyoake, *Holyoake MSS*, 3011, British Library.

[29] Bowman, John Frederick. April 2018. *The Iron and Steel Industries of the Derwent Valley. A Historical Archaeology,* pp 161-188. Ph.D. Thesis. Newcastle University School of History, Classics and Archaeology. url: http://theses.ncl.ac.uk/jspui/handle/10443/4427.

# CASE STUDY (2):
## JAMES COOK'S VOYAGES OF DISCOVERY

**Captain James Cook**

Navigator, cartographer, and explorer who, through his Pacific Ocean and antipodean voyages, successfully eliminated the sailors' disease of scurvy, facilitated the collection of much new botanical, fauna, and floral evidence, while also beginning the political, social and economic processes of globalisation.

In an expanding world, James Cook (1728-1779) travelled more and further than most. His career, exceptional though it was, illustrates more important facets of Britain's practical educational development during the Enlightenment period, as well as its expansion. He was the second child of a farm labourer whose employer paid for him to attend the local school. After five years, aged sixteen, he was apprenticed to a grocer and haberdasher, found the work not to his taste, and was introduced by the grocer to Quaker ship-owners in the coal trade at the port town of Whitby. He entered a further three-year apprenticeship on colliers and coasters plying the sea-coal trade between Newcastle and London. That apprenticeship required the study of algebra, geometry, trigonometry, navigation, and astronomy. On its completion, he progressed to work on trading ships in the Baltic Sea, gaining promotion within a year to mate on a brig. Offered command of the small, two-masted warship soon after, Cook volunteered instead for service in the Royal Navy.

The British navy, unlike its army, could then tolerate meritocracy. That of France could not, where social status took precedence over competence in seamanship. This was an important reason for the defeats of the French navies of the time, despite initial technical superiority in ship design. That advantage was soon lost through the frequent capture of French vessels, and their consequent reuse and design appropriations. Superior human management here defeated technological primacy. Cook's first posting in 1755 featured the capture of one French ship and the sinking of another, shortly afterwards gaining his first command as temporary master of a cutter, a single mast vessel, lowest in official naval classification. He became qualified to navigate and handle a Royal Navy ship by passing the Trinity House master's examinations in 1757.[1]

Originally given a Royal Charter by Henry VIII to control pilotage on the Thames, Trinity House was a corporation further empowered by Elizabeth I in 1566 to provide warning beacons and markers to dangerous waters, progressing to light house provision and seamen's welfare charity. It served for some time as a guild-equivalent examining body, thus ensuring the professionalism of British maritime officers. As a master (navigator) during the Seven Years' War, he displayed his skills in cartography and navigation of much of the entrance to the St Lawrence River, thus greatly assisting General Wolfe's (1727-1759) celebrated surprise attack on Québec in 1759. So accurate as to be used for the next 200 years, Cook's subsequent large-scale maps of the coasts of Newfoundland and hydrographic surveys caused the Admiralty to engage him to command a scientific voyage to the Pacific Ocean.

Cook made three exploratory journeys. They were to transform people's knowledge of almost half the world and its inhabitants, from the Antarctic to the Bering Straits, producing an extraordinarily dramatic change in what one part of the world knew of the other.

The declared purpose of the first voyage was to observe and record the transit of Venus across the sun, this for the benefit of a Royal Society inquiry. Trigonometry arising would enable the calculation of the exact distance from earth of the sun. Such restricted single purpose was supplemented by a team of scientists and artists led by the naturalist and botanist Joseph Banks (1743-1820) and Daniel Solander (1743-1782), pupil of Carl Linnaeus (1707-1778), the "father of taxonomy" who formalised binomial nomenclature.

The Admiralty granted Cook the necessary authority of promotion to lieutenant to legitimise his command; the Royal Society guaranteed a gratuity of 100 guineas to add to his naval pay. The transition was observed, although not fully satisfactorily, from Tahiti in 1769, causing Cook to open his sealed orders: to search for Australia. He found and mapped New Zealand and the Australian east coast, where the first European contact was made with the indigenous peoples. His import of an example, Omai, a Tahitian, helped create the image of the "noble savage." He claimed the entire coastlines he had explored for Britain.

Changes initiated by Cook were permanent. He had shown the viability of long voyages, his first extending from 1768 to 1771. The wealthy landowner Banks was able to trump his contemporaries by making his Grand Tour extend around the world. On return, Banks was able to claim most of the credit for the discovery of new and exotic species, such as bougainvillea and the kangaroo, representing the voyage as having been under his leadership, with Cook serving as the ship's captain. Banks's design of a ship for a second voyage was viewed by the Admiralty as unwieldy, likely to sink, causing Sir Joseph to withdraw and leaving Cook with full command. He furthered navigation through trials of the longitude timepieces of John Harrison (1693-1796) and others, and demonstrated extraordinary skill in his navigation of Antarctica. Cook had made use of the skills and knowledge of the master navigators of Polynesia, jointly producing a map with one of Polynesia and Melanesia. This time, Cook won full credit for his achievements, becoming globally famous.

Progress was rapid. The first settlers arrived in Australia in 1778. Quaker origins were reinforced for between 1818 and 1843 the prison reformer and Quaker Elizabeth Fry (1780-1845) visited 106 convict ships bound for that destination. The Romans had exiled malefactors and awkward citizens such as Ovid. The British now entered a period of managing crime by mass deportation.[2]

Unable to resist exploration, Cook refused to be retired, making further voyages of discovery before his death in 1779. During the War of

Independence, Benjamin Franklin (1706-1790) had written to captains of
American vessels instructing them, if they encountered Cook, not to engage
in hostile action but to treat him as a benefactor. First treated in a god-like
manner in Hawaii, on return there for repairs, he had attempted to secure
the return of the theft of a cutter by taking a local king hostage. He was
killed in the ensuing scuffle, but his remains were treated with honour.

The farm boy from north-east England, sponsored by his father's employer
and aided by Quakers and the apprenticeship system, rose by means of his
abilities, with the further assistance of professional examinations and a
meritocratic naval system, to be further sponsored by a Royal Society, map
vast previously unknown territory, and lay a further formidable foundation
stone in the creation of the British Empire. For all its manifold formal
educational demerits, the informal and vocational elements of British
national provision had much to recommend them. Cook's leadership of his
men in adverse conditions alone fully qualifies him for any study of that
area of management.

Yet, this last great terrestrial voyage of discovery brought wider mixed
results, with many unintended consequences. Product of the Scottish
Enlightenment, the physician James Lind (1716-1794), proved in a
controlled 1747 experiment that the sailors' common disease of scurvy
could be prevented, and cured, by eating citrus fruit. Scurvy caused sores,
haemorrhages, gum disease, teeth loss, jaundice, depression, and death.
Although the beneficial effect of lime juice had been well known for many
years, the Admiralty did not implement Lind's findings. Cook loaded his
ship, *Endeavour*, with sauerkraut, ordering his crew to eat fruit and
vegetables whenever the vessel landed. No sailors died. Men were punished
if they did not eat the sauerkraut, the officers instructed to sing the dish's
praises at table. The achievement of scurvy-free long-distance sailing was a
huge triumph of ship management.

Cook's diet was soon adopted by all navies, saving many lives. His
expedition brought back much data: anthropological, astronomical,
botanical, geographical, meteorological, and zoological; yet much of the
data had military application. Britain's naval power and empire were greatly
increased and the colonised lands were soon overrun by settlers, to the cost
of the local inhabitants: human, flora, and fauna. Local populations declined
by as much as 90%. The Māori of Zealand suffered discrimination; the
Aborigines of Australia much more so; and the Tasmanians were effectively
exterminated. Introduction of the rabbit and cane toad to Australia has

caused immense agricultural damage, as has that of the rat to the region's low nesting bird life. The management lesson is that great change in knowledge, data, and their applications will have wide consequences, making contingency planning and provision essential against the unforeseen and unintended.

Cook was fortunate that the Royal Society could afford to pay him the rough equivalent of £6,500 today as his bonus, but its dependence on member subscriptions meant that it was too expensive for the artisan class. Still an elite diversion, societies sponsored research and experimentation, offering prize contests. Sometimes, the scale of the scientific task was beyond the purse of even the Royal Society. The inventor of the marine chronometer, the amateur clock maker John Harrison, had the inducement of a Parliamentary prize of the equivalent of £2.8 million for a device to calculate longitude, his fourth chronometer version being used by Cook during his latter voyages. 5,000 miles of previously unknown coasts were surveyed on the final voyage by using longitude. Practical education had led to practical intervention and gain. Interventions and inducements compensated, to some extent, for the lack of formal higher education participation in research and discovery.

In making scientific work a tradition for the Royal Navy, a practice adopted by other nations, Cook was an inspiration. While the ill effects of his voyages were typified by the spread of disease among the local populations; he may be credited nonetheless with the commencement of globalisation.[3]

## Case Study Reflections

Cook's career is illustrative of three major aspects of practical management:

1. Societal structure provided a farm boy with peculiar advantages for his times. Quaker sponsorship and Royal Navy meritocracy gave opportunity unlikely to have been attained in any competitor country at the time, with results of major and enduring international consequence.

2. Important national investment in scientific investigation and applications was accompanied by Cook's own initiative in the dietary care of his crews, again with far reaching results.

3. While the unforeseen consequences of the discoveries were again extensive, and despite the misadventure of his own death, a heavy price for a tactical mistake by a man of friendly intent towards newly encountered peoples, Cook epitomises a key dimension of the nature of management. Management is leadership, and *vice versa*, at any level, and it is not possible to divide the two. The entire burden of a complex enterprise into the unknown, deploying new technology, carried out far from base and without communications, was executed by a well-trained, highly competent leader and inspirational manager – who made a fatal mistake.

4. James Cook can be seen, like Ambrose Crowley III, as one of the first of modern technocrats but subject to an ancient condition. They both died at the peak of their powers. Cook, a marine and career manager of surpassing expertise, was also ultimately unlucky.

5. Students of management are invited to consider the attention due to the Catos, Cook, and Crowley in Management Studies.

# Endnotes

[1] The beginning of a senior officer Royal Navy career is well illustrated, albeit a little later in time, in Patrick O'Brian's magnificent naval novel series, commencing with *Master and Commander*.

[2] A mixture of deportation and mass movement had spurred the group emigration of large numbers of the reiver "riding families" from the Scottish borders to Ulster, particularly the Fermanagh area from the accession of James I in 1603. The lawless reivers, hard families of an ungovernable nature whose way of life extended over four centuries, accepted their relocation as an escape, in their view, from persecution; in the eyes of authority, endemic banditry. Some reivers compromised by joining the Dutch in their fight with Spain. However viewed, a precedent for the removal of misbehaving citizenry had been set.

[3] Different perspectives on Cook's life, career, and influence can be found in: Hough, Richard. 1994. *Captain James Cook*. London: Hodder and Stoughton; Collingridge, Vanessa. 2003. *Captain Cook: The Life, Death and Legacy of History's Greatest Explorer*. London: Ebury Press; and McLynn, Frank. 2011. *Captain Cook: Master of the Seas*. New Haven and London: Yale University Press.

# CHAPTER SEVENTEEN

# INDUSTRY, INNOVATION AND EDUCATION

Contemporary with the Cowens but a century from Crowley, another co-operative movement supporter, Robert Owen (1771-1858), had become wealthy, first as an investor and then as manager of a large textile mill at New Lanark, south of Glasgow. In a combination of trades typical of the times, Owen's father was a saddler, ironmonger, and local postmaster. One of seven children, Robert had little education but, again typically, read widely. First apprenticed to a Lincolnshire draper, he worked in London drapery shops, moving on to Manchester where, as Pittacus would have approved, he found his opportunity. He first borrowed £100 from a brother, went into a partnership to make spinning mules (an invention for spinning cotton thread), then became a mill manager, subsequently partnering with others to establish a further Manchester mill.

Owen then married and, with his partners, in 1799 bought his father-in-law's mill in New Lanark. This was a substantial concern, employing or contracting with a work force of around 2,000, some 500 of which were children, brought to the mill from the poor houses of Glasgow and Edinburgh. A common feature of factories before legislative correction in the mid and later 19th century was the "truck system" whereby employees received pay tokens which could be used only in the company shop. It made economic sense for employers to purchase in bulk, as the Crowleys did for their factory shop, while paying cash to their workers. The unscrupulous exploited truck; Owen did not, instead pioneering co-operative distribution. He instituted the eight-hour day in his factory and campaigned for it outside. He provided benefits for his workers, and education with care for their children. Free education was extended from adult to nursery schooling. Quality goods' manufacture and efficiency were incentivised. The results were good behaviour and increased production.

Partner disagreements resulted in Owen selling his shares, making his fortune, and devoting himself to philanthropy. A deist convinced that physical, moral, and social influences formed character, his construct for social reform embraced Enlightenment thought. His establishment of a model community in America under socialist principles gained him a hearing from the serving British prime minister and US president, and a number of former and future presidents. The ideas found attention but the ideal communities' model failed, costing Owen most of his fortune. He continued to campaign.

Reform was progressively achieved in factory management during the 19$^{th}$ century but it was not until the 20$^{th}$, across the Atlantic, that theories and derived practices began to be heard and accepted. Management was finally to become a topic in its own right, even if industrial prime methodology had been available for consideration for over two hundred years. This idea had taken a long time to achieve realisation. The reason for the lengthy pause and for the century delay following the next great management innovation probably lies within the slow understanding of three factors:

- realisation of the need to maximise efficient industrial output;

- capital recognition of the rewards such improvement could bring;

- application by the educational community to industrial and commercial need and opportunity, not least that of its own self-interest in supplying the necessary service.

Until the end of the 18$^{th}$ century, the predominant opinion was that management was a function of direct involvement by the owners. If it had to be delegated, then the business was endangered. That alone was a powerful incentive to limit the size of the business. However, improvements in marketing, technology, and communications from 1750 required that, if businesses were to succeed, they should grow beyond the size which a sole owner, or small group of partners, could supervise. Thus, within a competitive environment, they had to learn to cope. Managers had to be acquired. Some emerged; some were already in place, awaiting promotion; some had to be trained. In the earlier originating search, Ambrose Crowley III had made promotions from his artisan shop floor foremen, based first upon character. In this, he had anticipated Adam Smith's objections to managers, for in Smith's view they would be unreliable, untrustworthy, and so destructive of a business. Crowley wanted men he could trust; the niceties of skills' acquisition could follow.

As with the Elder Cato, the first business for management recourse was agriculture. The principles of agricultural management did not change significantly between the 16th and 18th centuries, and nor had the basic instructions: buy in the cheapest market but sell in the dearest. The managerial instrument was the agent, the equivalent of Cato's *opera* and *vilicus*. His duties included tenancy agreements, rent collections, supervising the home farm, keeping accounts, paying staff, tithes and taxes, whilst deterring poachers and, if the landlord was absent, supervising the household. The novel feature was that the estate agents communicated with each other - competitively at market, cooperatively in land tenancies and sales. Experience was gained and shared which also had transferable value.

Mining being a further feature of land holding, experienced practical managers with knowledge of such essentials as accounts and the legal procedure might be allocated to, or apply for, positions in such new industries as the increasing mining of coal to fuel industrial production. Management education was by the cascading method of shared experience. Crowley's detractors have argued that his workers' housing was no more than agricultural economics, the rural-tied cottage practice applied to industry. This forgets the basis of the Crowley business: the proximity of water power, ease of transport, and the closeness to both coal and metal ores. He had to import his workers and so supply housing, but that was a consequence of the application of a rational business model, not a determinant. That he made his system hard but fair, operated with humanity, is to his credit and sincerity of intent. Sometimes, landowners were faced with inescapable industrial consequences.[1]

The textile industry also grew organically. The putting-out system grew from mercantile capital. Merchants gained markets, out-sourced production, and coordinated distribution. The management of many small, domestic workshops being a task impossible to closely supervise, it was quite natural for them to seek machine-made factory product. The scale of domestic enterprise embezzlement and the numbers of people involved, some clothier merchants employing hundreds and thousands of workers, prevented any comprehensive accountancy, and led to the demand for more efficiency. Thus, mechanised product production began first as part of the putting-out system, growing into the factory mode.

The finished model was the introduction of the steam loom between 1815 and 1835. Ever in the vanguard, the Quaker Pease family of Darlington had introduced 300 power looms to their worsted mills by the early 19th century.[2] In such industries as file making, the merchant-domestic system had increasing presence. It was the progression of that into the factories which marked the onset of the industrial revolution. Management came first from that process, then into it, with managed production on one site. However, such growth was accompanied by the alternative: subcontracting, a practice compatible with the various stages of the transition process, within, through and across which various interlocking devices might apply, often in co-operation with other businesses. In this transitional period, management was according to need and design, rather than functions.

Nor was provision uniform. Collective groups of miners might be working small pits in the Midlands on contract whilst mines in the more advanced north-east were being let out by landowners, with pit owners investing in deeper shafts, using more complex equipment, such as steam engines. Collective bargaining in the long-established Cornish tin mining industry had led to the growth of group leading "captains," whose skills were such that they were sought to apply their expertise to new mines throughout the country. In the cotton industry, by the 1830s, half of the child labour force of 20,000 was employed by subcontractors. As late as 1815, most weaving was by contract, within factory or without. Crowley had used this method, with his factory. Sometimes, the coordinators of such activity, the "managers," bought out the original owners.

Of the employees of Josiah Wedgwood (1730-1795), the potter and entrepreneur credited with the modern industrialisation of pottery (the Romans and Chinese having achieved mass production first), over 10% were paid by subcontracting men, many of whom employed their children. Railway and canal construction were the largest subcontracting businesses, naturally leading to the emergence of distinct, career management. The out-putting, domestic, and subcontracting methods were not distinct "stages" of industrial development, whereby they were superseded by the factory system; rather, in varying ways, they merged into it. One consequence was the comparative freeing and distancing of the owner-entrepreneur from the actual work processes, allowing evasion of the different and larger management problems entailed in substantial scale factory production. Since European industry followed the same traditional pattern, there was nothing to learn from Europe and, as the British began their industrialisation, there were no continental models to follow; merely a large market to exploit.

Not all industries developed at the same time, or at the same pace. Coal mining had shown size problems well before 1750; handloom weaving, archetypal impetus to Luddism, dragged on pitiably long into the 19th century.[3] Locations changed: mining and early metallurgy were largely rural industries, but as villages grew around them and towns extended, they became urban. Labour relations changed. Neighbourly synergies and co-operation where the new industries were proximate encouraged management development; remaining isolation did not. Some of the technology was completely novel, requiring new work and supervisory practices; some was an extension of existing provision, requiring operational adaptations. The necessities of narrative can make the industrialising process appear more orderly than it was. This was a time of a concatenation of influences, desires, and technological advance - the will and need to create wealth; maximise opportunity; explore and exploit technological advance, the availability and mobility of labour; and multiple advances from individual inspiration to networked capital to inventions of scale - out of all of which came industrial manufacture and the transformation of trade and society. Appreciation and learning from that experience may have relevance to the creation of skills and processes needed now to encounter the needs and opportunities of the information technology and artificial intelligence revolutions.

Key management issues then were the factory layout, division and organisation of labour, and timing of activity. As illustrated in a subsequent volume, unification of mass production and the measurable start of modern management came first in education. Within industry, uni- and multi-product firms had different issues; employees might be skilled, however defined, semi-skilled, or of specialised or general manual application; full or part-time, children, or subcontractor gang masters. The uneven, evolving task was the management of this unpredictable, variable, sporadic growth in singularly uncertain times. As businesses enlarged, a tier between the owner and later, his board, and supervisor or foremen – neither then a common term – became necessary. The uneven development was characterised by necessities, and these became most evident in the new businesses created by, or contributing to, the industrial evolution. These were most obvious in the construction sector, in such resulting concerns as canals and railways, and the consequent operation of the new services and utilities created. Thus are encountered the origins of the modern industrial manager, explored further subsequently.

This narrative division also marks education parallels, for there are three separate but interlinked strands to consider:

- Education for management;
- Education in management;
- Management education.

Whereas curriculum, method, and reach for the bulk of young society, the poor, remained dire, at the levels upwards there had been improvement. The academies in particular had produced vocationally relevant subjects and appropriate skills. These were matched by the better grammar schools. Quality provision was patchy. There were particular strengths in the north of England, where proximity to the more advanced and relevant schooling of Scotland combined with many particular local factors to stimulate vocational applications. In Stoke Newington in London, Nottingham, and Bristol, there were outstanding schools. Their product was relevant to more businesses directly than industry alone. An observer reported that by 1796 "the north of England had 'become quite a manufactory for Bankers' and Merchants' clerks".[4] Denied political power, the nonconformists, Quakers, and Calvinists particularly invested in their material benefit which entailed education for practical application, and that meant to the application and services of the new science.

Even the old universities found a place for the sciences, whilst the new ones and the colleges to which they became eventually linked looked to the needs of their localities. The John Owens College, which began with a commercial school, in mid-century grew into Manchester University. The 1834 School of Medicine and Surgery in Newcastle was complemented by the 1871 establishment of Armstrong College for study of the physical sciences. Both became part of the federal Durham University. The College was one of the many benefactions of the inventor and industrialist William George Armstrong (1810-1900), the first engineer to gain a seat in the House of Lords. Patterns elsewhere were similar: industrialists of lowly origins made from their success donations to create and improve the education necessary to pursue the growth to which they had contributed. Philanthropic and self-interested, for their industries needed the constant refreshment of employees suited to maintenance and expansion requirements, higher education had increasingly to play the tunes paid for by the great pipers. It was a financially fortunate divine who had supported the foundation which became Harvard College, chartered in 1636 and America's oldest corporation; now it was wealthy industrialists, merchants and bankers who originated.

All these new creations, in their different ways, required managers. The combination of village schooling and apprenticeship had, in places, been effective in formal education, many of the most outstanding leaders of the industrial revolution having risen through that route.[5] That effectiveness, however, was patchy. In some areas, for managerial requirements, all that was available was men trained in their craft but without even the most elementary education. Industry owners had many reasons to turn first to their families for managerial assistance. Products of good grammar schools could be trained into the business, thus opening up junior partner routes, with skills passed on among a trusted, closed circle.

Otherwise, there were friends and relations networks to tap into (reciprocally). Learning was on the job, in house, but informed through the interlinked networks. Results could be amazing where these networks were strong, as demonstrated by the Quakers. Private schools also contributed to, and benefited from, the nascent industrialisation. The Napoleonic wars had provided the cheap by-product of language tuition from French prisoners, and so traveling salesmen became enabled. As the upper levels of society became wealthier, so the best education was required for its children, and private tuition became a mark not only of quality, but social desirability. There were practical considerations here, too.

Within what was an uneven tempo of development, where backwardness and owner narrow-mindedness inhibited, and where nepotism was not always appropriate or efficient, education for management was the best of what was available. Not available in all areas, stronger in some than in others, and at a time when much less was known, therefore more encompassable, the broad advertised vocational curricula were:

> For commercial subjects: modern languages, often described as commercial; book-keeping; shorthand; commercial law and customs of the main trading countries, including taxation; economics; commercial calculations; geography and navigation.

> For science and technology: mathematics, pure and applied, physics, and chemistry; anatomy, botany and zoology; engineering, surveying and astronomy.

> For special interests: subject groups, such as naval and military studies; literature and history; fencing and dancing.[6]

Apprenticeship to a successful merchant, although potentially providing direct access to a lucrative career, could be more expensive; the lower private school fees, therefore, gave clear market choice. As management opportunity grew, systems to support and profit from that growth rose. There was education for and in management, but management was not yet a recognised entity or study in or of itself; management education and Management Studies were yet to be developed. However, the onset of the industrial revolution had been accompanied by the application of managerial systems. Boulton and Watt, at their Soho works, had followed Crowley, wittingly or not, in introducing standard operating procedures; specifications; work methods; production planning; standard times and data; audits; incentive wages; mutual insurance; with parties and a bonus at

Christmas. In Massachusetts, Eli Whitney (1765-1825), invented the cotton gin which made upland short cotton into a profitable crop. The 1818 milling machine applied further techniques of scientific method, as well as quality control, interchangeable parts and the span of management control.

**Cotton Gin**
– meaning "cotton engine" – is a mechanical machine that quickly and easily separates cotton fibres from their seeds, enabling far greater productivity than manual cotton separation. Its introduction revolutionised the cotton industry.

Charles Babbage (1791–1871), the polymath, "father of the computer", and factory management expert, was the inventor of the first programmable computer. In his Difference Engine, data and programme memory were separated. Operation was according to instruction. Conditional jumps were enabled by a control unit, with a separate input/output (I/O) device.

Personality clashes with assistants and collaborators, and government loss of confidence resulting in the cessation of support grants, caused the projects to remain at the design and partial prototype stages, although some success towards the mechanising of calculations was achieved using steam power.

PORTION OF BABBAGE'S DIFFERENCE ENGINE.

**A portion of Babbage's Difference Engine design:**

**Charles Babbage**

The Difference Engine (previous page) led to more complex electronic designs, and his further Analytical Engine included all the essential ideas of modern computers.

Although his original engines were never completed, with only parts of his prototypes surviving. a century after his death the Science Museum, London, proved the validity of his initial computer design by building his Difference Engine to its original specifications. With the final construction of Babbage's updated (1847–1849) Difference Engine No.2, using his plans and 19th century tolerances, 1889–1891, Babbage's theoretical accuracy was proved correct. The Babbage designed printer for the machine was completed in 2000. The UK's Science Museum made two models. One is privately owned, displayed in the Computer History Museum in Mountain View, California. The other can be seen in the Science Museum, London.

**The Difference Engine being utilised (right, below).**
**The Output End Crank (left, below).**

Building on French research, Babbage had realised that the concept of mass production could replace human division of labour by direct application to arithmetic. Mathematical tables of the time being fallible, prone to error, Babbage sought means to calculate series of values automatically. Multiplication and division could be avoided by using the method of finite differences. His later Analytical Engine was programmable by using punched cards, thus making the transition from mechanised arithmetic to general, all purpose, computation applications.

The further step in Babbage's invention of computing was the contribution of his correspondent, Ada Lovelace (1815–1852), the poet Lord Byron's only legitimate daughter, described in a subsequent volume as the first computer programmer. The trio completed by Alan Turing (1912-1954) may fairly be represented as the greatest of the management foundations of the digital age.

In 1832, Babbage had published *On the Economy of Machinery and Manufactures.* Revised and running to four editions, the book classified machinery, rational factory design, profit sharing, piece rates, and the commercial advantages to be gained through division of labour. He observed that skilled workers spent time performing below their skill levels. Therefore, costs could be cut by lower-skilled workers performing the menial tasks, with the higher-skilled being restricted to their areas of expertise. While apprenticeship and training were fixed costs, Babbage argued, they could be recovered through his advocated form of factory system. His observations extended to the effect of various colours on employee efficiency; and were said to have influenced the design of the 1851 Great Exhibition.[7]

The division of labour concept was a facet of Karl Marx's (1818-83) work and influenced contemporary French and German economic thought. In 1860, the editor of the *American Railroad Journal,* Henry V. Poor (1812-1905), from whom the research and analysis agency Standard and Poor's traces its origins, had begun the practice of organisational analysis with his compilation of the financial, communications and operational details of the rail and canal systems.

Deviser of the first modern organisation chart, the Scottish born Daniel McCallum (1815-1878), an American railway engineer and general manager, in 1856 set forward six principles of management, the culminating binding of which was the requirement for a system of personal accountability throughout the organisation. Emile Oscar Garke (1856-1930), a German immigrant electrical engineer who had risen to managing directorships in that industry had published *Factory Accounts, their principles and practice* in 1887 with his company accountant John Manger Fells (1858-1925), which was the first application of cost accounting to manufacturing.

J. Slater Lewis (1852-1901), a land agent and surveyor turned engineer, inventor, and business manager, published *Commercial Organization of Factories* in 1896, which had significant impact in Britain. His further expanded and detailed manufacturing cost accounting, with organisation and operational application, was intended as a practical guide. Lewis also set forward clear and stringent managerial duties. He mentored the British born son of American parents, Alexander Hamilton Church (1866-1936), known for his five books on cost accounting and management between 1908 and 1923. Beginning as a manager in electrical engineering and telephony, Church progressed to factory management and then to journalism as European manager for *Engineering Magazine,* for which he began writing on management. He relocated as a consulting engineer to the US, through which he was able further to study manufacturing efficiency and factory organisation. There he collaborated with Leon P. Alford (1877-1942) a mechanical engineer, American Society of Mechanical Engineers (ASME) administrator and organisational theorist. Based on Babbage's ideas, Alford and Church produced systems of industrial management, emphasising industrial relations and "human engineering." The significance, as expressed by two historians of modern business management is that:

> …both Lewis and Church used the word "organization" in the same sense as management, that is, a process not an entity. By 1900, there was therefore a concept of management as a separate function in the operation of a firm, including the distinctiveness of the work of the manager.[8]

There was thus a wholly discrete, independent and earlier "scientific management" process, known and in operation, before a further contributor to that operative concept made his intervention.

**FOOTPRINT:**
**Industrialisation Required Management**

- Process, production, markets, labour, and welfare required close attention in pragmatic circumstances, where management derived from immediate needs in what then appeared as a rapidly expanding environment, full of exotic wonders and wide opportunities.

- Practical men of business began to study how matters might best be managed.

# Endnotes

[1]The most striking is the story of the James family of Gateshead. Landowners, they had made their fortunes from coal. Walter Charles James (1816-1893), a successor Hull MP to William Wilberforce, was raised to the peerage by his friend Mr. Gladstone in 1884, as the first Baron Northbourne of Betteshanger, a pleasant, rural retreat in Kent, near Deal. His son, Walter Henry James (1846-1923), Liberal MP for Gateshead from 1874-93, succeeded to the peerage and left the House of Commons towards the end of Gladstone's final premiership. Wishing to escape from coal and industrial grime, the second Lord Northbourne retired to the family estate at Betteshanger. Coal was discovered on their lands once more, mining beginning in 1920, on the largest of the Kent coalfields.

[2] Edward Pease (1767-1858), a Quaker Darlington woollens manufacturer, was the main promoter of the Stockton to Darlington railway, opened in 1825, which became the North Eastern Railway. Along with the engineer George Stephenson, he shares the "father of the railways" title. His dynasty produced nine members of parliament. Causes included abolition, foundation of the Peace Society, legislation against cruelty to animals prohibiting bear-baiting and cock fighting, and a personal appeal in 1854 to Tsar Nicholas I to prevent the Crimean War. Business interests included the purchase and development of Middlesbrough, the establishment of the great engineering enterprise Robert Stephenson and Company, and foundation of the *Northern Echo* newspaper. His remarkable dynasty is chronicled in: Kirby, M W. 1984. *Men of Business and Politics.* London: George Allen and Unwin.

[3] Invoking the name of the mythical "King" Ned Ludd, said to live in Sherwood Forest, habitat of the more believable but still very largely mythical Robin Hood, weavers in Lancashire and Yorkshire mounted attacks of destruction upon the machines which were putting them out of work. The machines themselves were subcontract out-putted, being for stocking and cropping fames for the textile industry, housed in village homes. There was no national organisation behind this spontaneous movement but as it coincided with rural disturbances under the further mythical "Captain Swing," the authorities were much disturbed, reacting repressively.

[4] Pollard, *op. cit.,* p. 129.

[5] Examples include: Richard Arkwright, spinning/water frame inventor, factory system developer (1732-1792); Joseph Bramah, locksmith, machine tool maker, and hydraulic press inventor (1748- 1814); William Edwards, bridge builder (1719-1789); Samuel Garbett, industrialist (1717-1803); John Gilbert, land agent and canal engineer to the Duke of Bridgewater, (1724-1795); Timothy Hackworth, first superintendent of the Stockton to Darlington Railway, locomotive engineer and exporter (1786-1850); John Heathcoat, lace manufacturer (1783-1861); John Kennedy, cotton manufacturer (1769-1855); Matthew Murray, engineer (1765-1826); John Beaumont Neilson, hot blast iron smelting inventor and industrialist (1793-1865); John U Rastrick, iron founder and engine builder (1780-1856); Richard Roberts, machine tool design and manufacture (1789-1864); George Stephenson, inventor, civil and mechanical engineer, "father of the railways"; Jedediah Strutt, cotton industrialist (1726-1797); Richard Trevithick, mining engineer and producer of the first pressure steam engine (1771-1833); and Josiah Wedgwood, potter and entrepreneur.

[6] Pollard, *op. cit.,* p. 131.

[7] Wilson, John F and Thomson, Andrew. *The Making of Modern Management,* p.7.

[8] *Ibid,* p.9.

Frederick Winslow Taylor

# CHAPTER EIGHTEEN

# F.W. TAYLOR AND THE ORIGINS OF MODERN MANAGEMENT STUDIES

It was shown in Chapter 16 that there was a wholly discrete, independent, and earlier "scientific management" process, known and in operation before a further contributor to that operative concept made his intervention. In the historical context, from the antecedents of Babbage, Poor, McCallum, Garke, Fells, Lewis and Church, it can be seen why Leon Alford might at the American Society of Mechanical Engineers (ASME) have opposed Frederick Winslow Taylor. Similarly, the ASME was also responsible for stimulating interest among engineers and industrial manufacturers. Taylor, however, was an important catalyst in the expansion of Management Studies.

The earlier Taylor family having followed the economic logic and religious social convenience of emigration from England, it was in one of its former colonies, a nation then 63 years old and nine years away from the conclusion of its civil war, Frederick Winslow Taylor (1856-1915) was born in Germantown, Philadelphia, Pennsylvania.

His working life spanned almost exactly the rapid initial industrialisation and phenomenal economic growth of the United States of America. As the following motor industry was to turn blacksmiths' forges and stables into garages and vehicle show rooms, Taylor began employment at a further time of transition where the management and working practices of the new industries required adaptation, improvement, and redefinition. It was also a period where "management" was open to a variety of approaches: the requirements of production; ends versus means concepts of labour and production; Hobbesian social contracts or Machiavellian management driven by fear; Protestant work ethics; and the consequences and demands of dramatic growth increases. Taylor's family was of Quaker stock.

While not a notably practising Quaker himself, Taylor's ethical inheritance was suited to what he attempted to accomplish. The epitaph on Taylor's

gravestone bears the legend: "Father of Scientific Management." He has
been routinely cited thereafter as the father of modern Management Studies,
the point of departure for those engaging in that activity. The relevance and
linkage of his work to such study and application has been summarised by
no less an authority than Peter Drucker (1909-2005), himself similarly
celebrated as "the father of modern management." Drucker's verdict was:

> The need today is neither to bury Taylor nor to praise him. It is to learn from
> him. The need is to do for knowledge work and knowledge worker what
> Taylor, beginning almost a century ago, did for manual work and manual
> worker.[1]

Drucker was a management consultant, writer, and educationalist whose
work is seen as a significant contribution to the practical and philosophical
foundations of the business corporations of the pre-Internet age. The
proponent of the concept of management by objectives, Drucker was a
leader in the development of management education. Direct lineage from
Taylor to the MBA industry of today is clear. Taylor and Drucker are
commonly regarded as the first of the modern management gurus, a
phenomenon investigated subsequently in a case study in a later volume.
However, there was opposition to Taylor from inception. With history,
antecedents, and status within industry on his side, Alford disputed Taylor's
methodology and his approach, his counter being sufficiently powerful to
persuade the ASME not to publish Taylor's book.

Taylor's family wealth derived from land and property ownership. An able
student, he had passed the entry examinations to Harvard University,
intending to become a lawyer before failing eyesight caused him to abandon
study. As he recovered sufficiently later in life to gain a degree by
correspondence in mechanical engineering, to be able to write extensively
and execute an increasing number of demanding management roles,
presumably the damage was not permanent, perhaps caused by excessive
reading under kerosene lamp illumination. Instead of a place among the
gilded youth of Harvard, Taylor began his working life as a labourer in a
steel mill. He undertook an apprenticeship as a pattern maker and machinist,
rising to become gang boss, assistant foreman, and foreman of the machine
shop. Progress continued to include installation, maintenance, and repair of
new machinery; chief of draughtsmanship, in charge of new machinery and
building design; concluding with becoming the chief engineer until 1890.

During this first phase of his career, Taylor's improving drive was
concerned with the various methods and processes of steel-making, its

casting into many different types of form and size, and the design and performance of the various tools required. The devotion to minutiae which would have served him so well in the legal profession now had another means of highly practical expression. His employer, the Midvale Steel Company, was not as efficient, prosperous, or competitive as might have been desired, and also had an important new contract to service: steel making for the Brooklyn Bridge. There was an obvious need for improvement, an opportunity which Taylor grasped. As a gang boss, he began a campaign to eliminate "soldiering," the process of workers deliberately restricting output. The economic background is important to a full understanding of Taylor's motivations. In 1870, pig iron was 85% more expensive in the United States than in England, and by 1913 this gap had narrowed to 19%.[2] There was continuing incentive throughout Taylor's period of activity to reduce production costs, as well as an historical justification. Adam Smith had begun with a study of pin production. Taylor commenced with pig iron.

There was no incentive for the workers to produce beyond a set standard; if they did so, they were still paid the daily rate. At first, after simple encouragement failed, Taylor tried to teach how to improve lathe performance for "a fair day's work" but, as soon as he did so and gained some success, others would mitigate that by "soldiering" and then, as a last resort, induce a machine breakage as demonstration that the increased production was damaging. In pursuit of "a fair day's work," Taylor had to conclude that no one knew exactly what that was. Building on Babbage's factory visits study, wittingly or not, he began his "fair day's work" definition with the concept of a differential piece rate, presenting a paper thereon to the ASME in 1893. He was also concerned with technical improvements, filing some hundred patent applications of which he emerged as holder or co-holder of 45. One such joint patent regarding tungsten steel tooling made him a considerable fortune. This pattern of practical innovation consolidated by papers or applications was repeated throughout his career.

While Taylor's contribution to development is clear, annoyingly to historians and students of his output, there are many areas lacking in clarity. These are partly due to Taylor himself. He was not scientific in his methodology - imprecise and contradictory on dates and timing, where ideas and adaptations were his own, the result of collaboration, or culled from elsewhere is not always clear. Some sources aver that he spoke the language of the shop floor with ease and frequency. His first biographer was subject to many pressures to amend the text and succumbed. His widow insisted on many excisions, especially the profanities, and destroyed some of his papers. His adopted sons had a bonfire of many more. We know that he bent his recount of events to suit his purpose, most clearly in his record of his most famous of experiments, that of the handling of pig iron. However, the sum of his writings, effectively edited and collected occasional papers, are published under the title *Scientific Management*, comprising *Shop Management* [1903], *The Principles of Scientific Management* [1911], and *Testimony Before the Special House Committee* [1912], the republication in 1947 being aimed at the post-war reconstruction market.[3] Taylor's engineering career gave him experience of a number of industries. His emphasis was on improving productivity, for which his point of departure was the study of what constituted a particular job or task.

According to his testimony to Congress, he began his time studies at Midvale in 1881. Two years later, he devised "functional foremanship," dividing up and specifying "subforemen" within a work gang, each having specific tasks such as instruction card man, time man, inspector, gang boss, and shop disciplinarian. "Functional foremanship" was refined to embrace such roles as "speed boss," "repair boss" and "cost clerk," the whole subsequently being refined into a planning department. That particular insight, on the grounds that planning is essential to the improvement of production, is held to have been one of Taylor's most significant innovations.

As general manager at the Manufacturing Investment Company (MIC) commencing in 1890, he refined the book-keeping system. Six years later, now at the Johnson Company of Pennsylvania, installing these book-keeping methods, he remedied the lack of any organised system for the storage of production materials by devising and installing a complete systematic storekeeping system, meanwhile applying his differential piece-work system to the electric motor plant.

In 1895, he had the idea of publishing hand-books on the time of building trade tasks, hiring an observer covertly to record stop watch timing of: excavation, masonry (including sewer work and paving), carpentry, concrete and cement work, lathing and plastering, slating and roofing, and rock quarrying. The watch was concealed within a "watch book," itself containing time-study forms to record the data.

**Taylor's 'Watch Book'**

Increasing production at his next company, Taylor progressed onwards to the Quaker founded Bethlehem Iron Company, the site of what became his most well-known exercises. His famous time study foray there concerned an analysis of the process of handling pig iron: picking up, carrying, and depositing. The timing and method of the activity was measured by piece-rate reward. The results and account of the process have been disputed, with good cause. Similarly, subsequent experiments with shovelling also attracted criticism. The ultimate issue, however, is not that these experiments had failures, even fabrications, rather that they were attempted at all.

Analytical devices for their processes were conceived. The commencement and application of the results of work analysis was the start of focus on productivity. He applied his work study methodology, slide rule measuring and technical improvements, cumulated in the construction of the concept first known as the "Taylor system" but which he termed "scientific management." That appellation itself was coined by a Supreme Court judge. The complementary motion studies of Frank (1868-1924) and Lilian (1878-1972) Gilbreth gave rise to the "time and motion" terminology. In search of curriculum, Harvard embraced Taylorism, using him as a lecturer between 1908 and 1914. A mathematical and accounting system rather than science, a misattribution which has continued to haunt Management Studies, it might also be viewed as a tool in the management consultant's box.

The Taylor management system was installed fully in only two plants. In both instances there was a personal relationship between Taylor and the company president, one of whom was a local fellow Unitarian. One company, Link Belt, saw success: by 1910 Taylor's system had doubled output per employee, with costs reduced by 20%. The other, the Tabor Company, was used by Taylor, who took a financial interest, as a training and systems introduction vehicle. His command and control "scientific" methodology has been seen as deskilling labour and his results dubious, over-emphasising quantitative analysis at the cost of supplying faulty foundations to the new area of academic application: Management Studies.

After a nervous breakdown, he ceased company employment to become a full-time consultant. The spread of adaptations of parts of his ideas and processes were sufficient to spur Congress to investigate. Since the American Society of Mechanical Engineers' acceptance of his first technical paper on belting in 1893, and first published management paper on a piece-rate system and partial solution to the labour problems of 1895 (assisted by the lobbying of Henry Towne (1844-1924), an early systematiser whose Yale Lock Manufacturing Company was to be cited in his publications), he had progressed in 1906 to the presidency of the ASME, the pinnacle of his profession. Before Congress, in January 1912, Taylor vehemently attacked the negative views of his system with a succession of negatives of his own:

> Scientific management is not any efficiency device, not a device of any kind for securing efficiency; nor is it a bunch or group of efficiency devices. It is not a new system of figuring costs; it is not a new scheme of paying men; it is not a piecework system; it is not a bonus system; it is not a premium system; it is no scheme for paying men; it is not holding a stopwatch on a man and holding things down about him; it is not time study; it is not motion study nor an analysis of the movements of men; it is not the printing and ruling and unloading of a ton or two of blanks on a set of men and saying, "Here's your system; go use it." It is not divided foremanship; it is not any of the devices which the average man calls to mind when scientific management is spoken of. The average man thinks of one or more of these things when he hears the words "scientific management" mentioned, but scientific management is not any of these devices. I am not sneering at cost-keeping systems, at time study, at functional foremanship, nor at any new and improved scheme of paying men, or at any efficiency devices, if they are really devices that make for efficiency. I believe in them; but what I am emphasising is that these devices in whole or in part are not scientific management; they are useful adjuncts to scientific management, so are they useful adjuncts to other systems of management.
>
> Now, in its essence, scientific management involves a complete mental revolution on the part of the workingman engaged in any particular establishment or industry – a complete mental revolution on the part of these men as to their duties toward their work, toward their fellow men, and toward their employers. And it involves the equally complete mental revolution on the part of those on the management's side – the foreman, the superintendent, the owner of the business, the board of directors – a complete mental revolution on their part as to their duties toward their fellow workers in the management, toward their workmen, and toward all of their daily problems. And without this complete mental revolution on both sides scientific management does not exist.[4]

Essentially, Taylor was arguing that all the cited practicalities were relevant but that unless employers and labour were of the same fair mindedness in pursuit of the "first class," in production, process, output, investment and remuneration, his attempt at a synthesis would not apply. Underpinning that synthesis was the frank assertion of his first major publication:

> This book is written mainly with the object of advocating high wages and low labour cost as the foundation of the best management.[5]

Dealing with minutiae as well as drawing the big picture, a sense of Taylor's methods and results can be drawn from his exhaustive work on shovelling. Although he was ultimately unable to prescribe the ideal shovel or shovelling precisely, by the organisation of work gangs, time study, instruction, appropriate tool supply, and maintenance and movement planning, the co-operative management and labour force at the Bethlehem Steel Company produced startling results. The number of labourers was reduced from c. 400 and 600 to 140. The average tonnage moved per man per day increased from 16 to 59. Average earnings per man per day increased from \$1.15 to \$1.88 while the average cost of handling a ton declined from \$0.072 to \$0.033.[6]

Taylor's abrupt manner, presentation of his findings and recommendations in mechanistic terms, and such methodology as covert stopwatch time-keeping provoked hostility in work environments where change was threatening, especially to the less educated. Hence his genuine search for "first class" performance and insistence on the need for a cooperative mental revolution could ring hollow to those faced with changes to their method and manner of work. Like many an agent of major change, his difficult attitude can be seen as his own worst enemy. Yet, like Cato the Elder, another difficult man, he wrote of the importance of equitable business: fair dealing; a fair day's wage for a fair day's work. He made frequent mention too of "the first class man," and that concept derived from the classics, those inspirational works and writings which so informed the foundation and constitution of the United States of America.

Little attention has been paid to Taylor's sporting prowess. He played golf and tennis to high standards, winning the doubles title of the latter in the forerunner national competition to the US Open. He also played cricket. That sport is unique in its mixture of individual and team performance, strategic and tactical dimensions according to changing conditions, and social egalitarianism on the pitch, if not in organisation and status off it. He used the game as an example in *The Principles of Scientific Management*: "Whenever an American workman plays baseball, or an English workman plays cricket, it is safe to say that he trains every nerve to secure victory for his side", which, by contrast, was not the case in his workplace.[7] Taylor was seeking to import the ethos, commitment, and spirit of games such as cricket into daily labour, a worthy if somewhat overenthusiastic aim.

Nonetheless, he was also a practical engineer, in contrast to his testimony to Congress, producing a succinct positive analysis of his system in *The Principles of Scientific Management:*

> It is no single element, but rather this whole combination, that constitutes scientific management, which may be summarized as:
>
> Science, not rule of thumb.
> Harmony, not discord.
> Co-operation, not individualism.
> Maximum output, in place of restricted output.
> The development of each man to his greatest efficiency and prosperity.[8]

Taylor can be seen as the rationalising agent to the conclusion of the second phase of the Industrial Revolution, patron of the manual labourer. Promotion of co-operation and rejection of individualism competed with other American values. He might also be viewed as a fusion of the ancient management authorities Cato the Elder and Confucius by enlightened, empirical, scientific method. Whilst the educational improvements begun early in the 19th century accompanied the technological advances of heavy engineering, the bringing of focus to the industrial results produced the dynamism in the economy which, fuelled by two world wars, for a subsequent half a century brought results in the United States approximate to the harmony of the mental revolution which Taylor had envisaged. His incentivised, standardised tasks appeared to function well for organisations with routine processes and applications.

The impetus for improved output was the competitive economic requirements to reduce costs, increase production and quality. However, Taylor, the Gilbreths, and their adherents had neglected human nature. Scientific management was exploited by some employers and managers as a way to gain more power, and hence remuneration, generally at the expense of lower paid workers, setting targets beyond the reasonable. In Britain, the latter characteristic was attributed to the likes of the autocratic Arnold Weinstock (1924-2002), who built the UK's General Electric Company (GEC) and its famous cash mountain, only for its wealth to be squandered by his successors. Expressions of Taylorism could become excessively analytic, judging a company by single measures, leading to value neutral "scientific" quantitative method, and opening the way to the polar reaction of the human relations management thinkers, reactive and sensitive to "slave labour" criticisms.

In Stalin's Soviet Union, which implemented a version of Taylorism, the miner Alexei Stakhanov (1906-1977) gained fame in 1935 by extracting 102 tonnes of coal in five hours and 40 minutes, 14 times his quota. The achievement was surpassed later that year by the reported mining of 227 tonnes in a single shift. This Hero of Socialist Labour then rose in management, ending as a deputy of the Supreme Soviet. He gave rise to the Stakhanovite movement, aimed at raising production. The veracity of the figures was disputed, but the distortion of Taylorism led to the setting of near impossible tasks for workers, with punishment when those targets were not met.

**Alexei Stakhanov**
supposedly explaining his system
to a fellow USSR miner.

It was subsequently revealed that while Stakhanov had indeed mined the coal, using the then latest technology of a heavy power drill, he had been assisted by four helpers, who cut and erected the pit props, gathered and loaded the coal and led the donkey pulling the carts.[9]

The "research" element of Taylorism made the new area of Management Studies more acceptable to universities now hosting business schools. The research product made for a teachable curriculum. The process took power from labour and capital, so empowering management and its advisers, of whom Taylor was an early example. While entrepreneurially he sold organisational methodology as science, such was the paradox with his written belief of what actually constituted scientific management, to a man of conscience the contradiction was perhaps at the root of his nervous breakdowns.

Academe further sold organisational method as science, and consultant entrepreneurs sold the adaptations on. Managerialism can be said to have begun, if not with Taylor, but with those who capitalised on his experiments and results, however they might have been obtained or devised. As

Christianity has attracted criticism for elements of its composition having journeyed far from the inspiration of Christ, so some expressions of Taylorism were distant from his intent. Peter Drucker, however, was convinced that Taylor was the agent of change to the realisation of the American Dream:

**Peter Drucker**

Frederick W. Taylor did what no one had even thought of before: he treated manual work as something deserving study and analysis. Taylor showed that the real potential for increased output was to "work smarter."

According to Drucker, it was Taylor who defeated Marx and Marxism. Taylor's Principles of Scientific Management not only tremendously increased output, it made possible increasing workers' wages while at the same time cutting the product's prices and thereby increasing the demand for it....

Without Taylor, the number of industrial workers would still have grown fast, but they would have been Marx's exploited proletarians. Instead, the larger the number of blue-collar workers who went into the plants, the more they became "middle class" and "bourgeois" in their incomes and their standard of living. And the more they turned conservative in their lifestyles and their values rather than becoming Marx's revolutionaries.[10]

Karl Marx had considered the worker to be a self-motivated actor in the work place, a context in which capital and labour would always be antagonistic. His solution was that the workers would revolt and seize control, becoming the owners of capital. This was precisely the issue which Taylor's concept of scientific management had set out to confront. Yet Taylor and his companion, subsequently critic and competitor Frank Gilbreth, were attacked later for the alleged dehumanizing nature of their time and motion studies, as satirized in Charlie Chaplin's (1889-1977) *Modern Times* of 1936. [11] Ironically, it was the Stalinist adoption of a debased version of Taylor's idea which most justified the criticism. In the growing management and management education industries, the contrasting human relations approach had gained increasing prominence. Drucker's rediscovery and re-emphasis of Taylor was thus highly significant.

Taylor had also stimulated domestic life. In the *Principles* he had suggested their relevance to home management. As women came to believe that Taylorism and the growing availability of household machinery could relieve of time-consuming domestic chores, so high schools and colleges began offering home economics courses. An American Home Economics Association was founded in 1909. *The Ladies Home Journal* and similar magazines published articles on scientific management. A prominent advocate, teacher and writer Christine Frederick (1883-1970), made a career of teaching women how to apply Taylorism to their housework. In her 1912 *New Housekeeping* she related how she determined to discover from such "experts" as Gilbreth and Henry Ford (1863-1947) how they operated, then sought to apply the knowledge.[12] Comparing the family home with business and factory as places of production, she sought a parallel whereby the home's output was measured, improved and subject to "the science of efficiency." Taylorism entered domestic life progressively in the company of the vacuum cleaner, washing machine, telephone, refrigerator and motor car.

## Endnotes

[1] Drucker, Peter F. "The Coming Rediscovery of Scientific Management," *Conference Board Record*, June 1976, p.27.

[2] Bernstein, *op. cit.*, p. 340.

[3] Taylor, Frederick Winslow. 1947. *Scientific Management*. New York: Harper & Brothers.

[4] *Ibid, Testimony*, pp. 26-7.

[5] *Ibid, Shop Management*, p.22.

[6] *Principles of Scientific Management*, p. 71.

[7] *Ibid*, p. 13. For an understanding of the managerial aspects of cricket, see Brearley, Mike. 1985. *The Art of Captaincy*. London: Hodder and Stoughton.

[8] *Ibid*, p.140.

[9] Newman, Dina. "Alexei Stakhanov: The USSR's superstar miner," *BBC World Service Magazine*, 30 December 2015.

[10] Drucker, Peter F. 1989. *The New Realities.* New York: Harper and Row, pp. 188-9.

[11] Gilbreth, Frank B. 1911. *Motion Study: A Method for Increasing the Efficiency of the Workman*. New York: D. Van Nostrand Co. Gilbreth began his published studies with an examination of bricklaying systems in 1909.

[12] Frederick, Christine. 1913. *New Housekeeping: Efficiency Studies in Home Management*, Garden City New York: Doubleday Page and Company.

CHAPTER NINETEEN

THE GROWTH OF MANAGEMENT THEORY

Taylor's system had gained an academic presence as early as 1909, when an associate helped to initiate a course on organisation and business management at the University of Pennsylvania using a book for which Taylor provided comment and material, although this was overtaken by publication in 1911 of his own *Principles of Scientific Management.* In the same year, a number of Taylor's peers and associates sought to formalise their group, following the formula begun in the 17<sup>th</sup> century, into a Taylor Society, eventually settling on the "Society to Promote the Science of Management," after Taylor's death renamed in 1915 as the "Taylor Society: A Society to Promote the Science of Management." It merged subsequently with the American Management Association (AMA).

Henry S. Dennison (1877-1952), president of an eponymous manufacturing company, economic analyst, and organisational theorist, became influential in the movement's growth, active in both the Taylor Society and the AMA, lecturing at Harvard Business School, and serving as industrial adviser to Presidents Woodrow Wilson (1856-1924) and Franklin D. Roosevelt (1882-1945). His implementation of scientific management principles at the Dennison Manufacturing Company was balanced by attention to wider labour issues: an unemployment fund, reduction in working hours, non-managerial profit sharing and the establishment of health and personnel services.

Such provision can be seen as part of the human relations movement in Management Studies, heir to the welfare provisions of the pioneering industrialists Robert Owen and Ambrose Crowley III of the early 19<sup>th</sup> and 18<sup>th</sup> centuries, commenced in the late 1920s. It was derived from the series of studies at Western Electric's plant at Hawthorne, a suburb of Chicago, mainly by an Australian sociologist, Elton Mayo (1880-1949), appointed professor of industrial research at Harvard Business School in 1926. Unfortunately, he was found subsequently to have behaved fraudulently, including using the title of doctor without being so qualified, distorting others' research evidence to make it fit his theories, and relating those to forms agreeable to employers, the better to extract consultancy fees.

Thus, low pay and poor working practices were not to blame for trade unionism and industrial conflict. The issue was rather one of worker psychological weakness, which needed understanding and support. Mayo's selective findings from puzzling evidence noted the effect that working in groups had on the individual: production increased when workers knew they were part of a project; even in tedious work, group and peer pressure were important; that it was group conception which produced consensus on what amounted to a fair day's work rather than that of the efficiency engineers; informal grouping within organisations influenced corporate integration; and that conflict between management and workers was inevitable unless each party appreciated the position of the other. Workers were not machines. They were human beings and needed to be treated as such with an understanding of their social and emotional needs.

**Elton Mayo**

Mayo stressed the necessity of high-quality leadership. A clear, organised leadership style was considered important to communicate goals, promote cohesiveness, and ensure decision-making that was coherent and efficient.[1]

Whereas Taylorism was as undoubtedly an engineering approach as Mayo's was sociologically driven, academic conflict between the two maybe owed more to the imperative of the latter practitioner's institutional employment need to produce papers and publications to secure and extend tenure than to real differences in goals. Both approaches used partial, even extreme, perspectives based on dubious research. However, they both sought a fair day's work for a fair day's pay, harmony between employers and employees, a congenial place of work, with consequent increases in the quality and quantity of production. They were complimentary rather than contradictory. Yet as pillars of the temple of the business science of academe, neither was secure.

Elton Mayo and Mary Parker Follett (1868-1933), an earlier management theorist who lectured at Harvard in the 1920s, led the human relations counter to the perceived mechanistic approach of Taylorism. The indirect emphases of her Quaker influenced approach contrasted sharply with the dubious assertions of the brash Australian Mayo.

### Mary Parker Follett

Mary Parker Follett had introduced the ideas of networked "soft power" from a much more reliable evidential base. "Mother of modern management" and inspiration for the study of organisational development, this Quaker sociologist defined the management importance of informal processes in hierarchical organisations. She saw conflict as a diversity mechanism creating the opportunity to develop integrated solutions, coining the "win-win" philosophical approach in the process.

She thought it a mistake to believe that social progress would result from people acquiring more material goods and education, or capitalists becoming less selfish. Her equitable approach to labour relations was reflected in her view of the labour movement: neither working for a person nor paying a person's wages ought to confer power over them.

What became known as the human relations school extended the influence of organisational development research, industrial and organisational psychology, behavioural and management theories, consequences and techniques. This gave more attention to individuals, emphasising that if workers prospered, so would the business: the needs of both would be reconciled. Appealing to employers because of their potential benefits, these became staples of the burgeoning management education industry. This spawned training programmes, concentrating on the cultivation and improvement of supervisory, development and organisational skills. Topics typically embraced career development, delegation, motivation, mentoring, and monitoring, cumulating in action planning for skills integration with employment on return to the work place. Ideally, the theory then informs practice with the results in turn feeding back into the training process, generating refined knowledge and theory.

A further complementary management bureaucracy theory was propounded by Max Weber (1864-1920), erroneously often cited as "father of sociology".[2] He and others argued that leadership required divisions of labour and so divided organisations into rational hierarchies with lines of authority and control, rules and regulations. This posited that organisations develop comprehensive and detailed standard operational procedures for all routinized tasks, as Ambrose Crowley had demonstrated two centuries

earlier. Weber's attitude was ambivalent. He saw the advantages of the bureaucratic mechanism in its precision, lines of control, and unified process but appreciated its dehumanising nature, particularly regarding the operative cogs in the machine.

**Henri Fayol**

Roughly contemporaneous with Taylor but nonetheless independently, the French engineer Henri Fayol (1841-1925) was a pioneering advocate of management being an acquired skill. He identified management functions in his *General and Industrial Management,* published in 1916, representing all the things that management needs, as:

1. division of labour, whereby tasking is divided but all combine for the good of the whole;

2. authority: selfishly or benignly, the use is to achieve the ultimate good of all members and society as a whole;

3. discipline, in behaviour, ethics, efficiency and effectiveness;

4. unity of command, or clarity of purpose, whereby employees know exactly what to do;

5. unity of direction, which might be provided by an individual, a group, or a set of values;

6. subordination of individual interest to a common goal, whereby individualism or identities are not lost but contribute to the success of the whole company;

7. remuneration for effort: a fair day's work for a fair day's pay, via direct reward, profit sharing, or other motivations according to need;

8. centralisation: a person, group or set of principles by and where the buck stops;

9. chain of command: employees need to know their place and duties;

10. order and purpose, the maintenance of which is seen as key;

11. equity and fairness between management and staff;

12. stability of tenure: allowing for change but managing people whereby the right people fulfil the right jobs;

13. initiative encouragement: the encouragement of subordinates to improve their management, using delegated power effectively; and

14. *esprit de corps* (team spirit): the consolidation of purpose through confident, forward movement dedicated to overcoming obstacles.

In addition to which, all managers perform five functions: plan, organise, command, coordinate, control. Subsequent theoreticians added: staffing, directing, reporting and budgeting; with a further subdivision into three types of roles. The interpersonal are defined as figurehead, leader and liaison; the informational as monitor, disseminator and spokesperson; and decisional: entrepreneur, disturbance handler, resource allocator, negotiator.[3] Definitions and enumerations are here reminiscent of the Elder Cato's cataloguing in his *De Agri Cultura* of farm tasks, administration, and activities. Nothing much had changed in the management administration world over three millennia. Fayol's framework is generally accepted, and although a variety of further theoretical approaches derived from these roots, his is not the only standpoint from which to view management.

The behavioural approach has followed the human relations track, looking to stimulate performance through emphasis upon group dynamics, motivation, leadership, communication and job satisfaction. It has expressed through such methodology as quality circles, consensus management and team building emphasised by best practice. Management, here, is an art based on a premise of essential human good, to which not all may subscribe. Management as a science is considered through operational research, mathematical and statistical methodology in problem solving, computer simulations, and modeling. Technophobia, unfamiliarity, or lack of operational expertise can limit the use or appreciation of these tools. Significantly, however, Fayol had stressed the importance of judgment and wisdom in the making of management decisions.

The development of behavioural economics (see also below) has brought an emphasis on bias. The negative aspect is how such a phenomenon can exercise unconscious behaviour to the extents of denial, disruption and dysfunction. Positive approaches tend towards nudge theory and behaviour: how beneficial outcomes can be produced by such external influences as gentle, melodic jazz promoting healthy eating. There are four further current theories abroad in the management studies field: contingency; systems; chaos; and freedom.

**Contingency theory** derives from the notion that "it all depends," the situation requiring the type or mix of approaches necessary. Thus, the autocratic mode is best suited to "hard end" activities such as many military operations, and some start-up businesses where the leader is the only person with knowledge of all the processes necessary for the concern to progress: the Ambrose Crowley III approach. "Soft end" concerns such as public sector organisations like education or medicine might better benefit from a more collegial, facilitative style. In either case, Catherine the Great's remark on the nature of her unlimited power sounds a cautionary note, while Joseph II is a monument to attempting too much.

**Systems theory** relies on the consideration that as parts constitute a whole, the removal, adaptation, or improvement of a part will affect that whole. The first step then becomes to analyse the parts which comprise that whole, thus identifying inputs, processes, outputs, and outcomes, all of which share feedback. An organisation could be seen as a system with inputs of raw materials, technologies, money, and people. Those inputs are then processed to form the outputs of goods or services, which then form the outcomes, such as improved quality or productivity. Each may be assessed. Feedback occurs at each stage, from employee and customer perspectives, and from the external environment. The overall system contains such sub-systems as departments or production lines, each of which may be analysed in the above way, and provide feedback.

These approaches have gained considerable credence in management training and have become important in widening the perspective of organisational study. The approach can identify how inefficiencies are occurring where, for example, individual areas of a business might be working well but deficiencies in some areas are reducing overall effectiveness, individually or through defective coordination or inter-relation. Systems theory was not quickly embraced but has enjoyed an increasingly standard acceptance. John Boyd (1927-1997) used the second law of thermodynamics to argue that closed systems led to internal confusion and disorder, known as entropy. Like all theoretical approaches to human behaviour however, it can be prone to misunderstanding, over-elaboration or abuse. A university vice-chancellor once informed the author in 1982 of why he was unable to act on institutional reform: the system was but a sub-system of the ministry of education, and that was a sub-system of government, which was a mere subset of the world order; and he couldn't do anything much about that.

The greatest criticism of systems theory is that any system can be affected, altered, or rendered nugatory by external matters beyond its control. Another is that the modification of one or more parts on reassembly do not improve the performance of those left unattended. As with all tools, care in use is necessary.

**Chaos theory**, a sub-system of systems theory, holds that the commonly understood perception of the second rule of thermodynamics, all systems tend to chaos, applies to organisation and management, hence the condition known as entropy. Here, whereas managers are always seeking control and often add structures to support such control, some events are uncontrollable and unforeseeable, and amendments themselves can be cause of implosion. Such theory conflicts with that of a leading contemporary management thinker identified below, regarding unintended consequences and the perspective of the siege of Kaffa.

Chaos theoreticians are said to be prone to taking their exemplars from biology, but a better source is probably physics. The first law of thermodynamics states that the quantity of energy in the universe remains the same. The second law, however, is that as energy is transferred or transformed, wastage occurs and so quality is diminished, leading to a natural tendency in any isolated system to degenerate into a more disordered state: thus, all systems lead to chaos. Curiously however, this modern debate directs straight back to the philosophy of the ancients, Lao Tzu, Chuang Tzu, and Confucius in particular.

**Management Freedom theory**, a 21st century development, claims significant successes. The central thesis is that "there is no basic reason why employees cannot function with full freedom".[4] Research indicates that a number of major corporations replaced hierarchical control with systems and cultures, within which "employees are self-motivated to develop and fully utilise their potentials while functioning with full responsibility, full authority, and full accountability – i.e. with full freedom".[5] Results have shown major companies achieving considerable performance improvement, but not all of them continued the experiment; incoming CEOs brought their own systems with them. There is linkage to the **market-based management system** based on free-market principles which, while essentially and successfully argues against the failed communistic models, does not necessarily prove its continuing independent validity. It does demonstrate an attempted ethical market approach discussed further in a later publication.

**Behavioural Economics** began as a distinct area of study in the early 20th century with the observation that while economics might ignore psychology, it could not disregard human nature. Some economists such as Vilfredo Pareto (1848-1923), discussed below, subsequently included the psychological dimension in their work. However, it was not until the dramatic advances made by Daniel Kahneman (1934 -) and Amos Tversky (1937-1996) that the subject gained wide recognition, Kahneman winning a Nobel Prize in 2002. Their approach, developed as Prospect Theory, was to compare cognitive models of decision-making under conditions of risk and uncertainty to economic models of rational behaviour. They proved that emotions such as fear of loss, or greed, can alter decisions, indicating an irrational component in the decision-making process, such as greater preference being given to loss avoidance than to gains reward. The approach has been taken further by others, such as Richard Thaler (1945-) and Cass Sunstein (1954-), whose development of Nudge Theory to influence mass behaviour found practical political expression through such leaders as UK prime minister David Cameron (1966-).[6] Practical consequences for management decision making are examined in depth in a subsequent publication.

Within Management Studies, there have long been diverse subject, study areas and disciplines. While these may be complementary with healthy competition, supremacy struggles and imperialist tendencies also scar the groves of academe. Unqualified quantitative method has created pathways, decorated with Nobel Prizes, leading towards disaster. A version of economics known in this work as economism has inflicted amorality and dysfunction of catastrophic proportions, blighting government and corporate governance. Another as adumbrated above has provided behavioural insights of brilliance mixed with subliminal methods raising critical issues of control. All are investigated later. This book has been concerned with foundations and eternal issues: basics necessary to understand the management phenomenon. It is further supplemented by a successor volume which takes those stories onward, together with the progress of practical management. Such foundations have been necessary to bring forth contexts through which a summary work devoted to **Improvements** can have effect.

However, all theory and suggested practical action, however brilliant and incisive, will be wholly irrelevant where management behaves badly, inappropriately, or improperly, at whatever determining level. It is that further consideration which contributes substantially to the **Improvements** which this work seeks to establish. The end of this first story of management through history is, thus, the overture to what happened next, when mass education unleashed the power of mass production, marketing, consumption, communication, and conflict. It is therefore most apt for an **Improvement** to feature as a Case Study in the successor publication *Managing Mass Education, and the Rise of Modern and Financial Management*, concerned with managing communications between children in situations arising from conflict.

## Endnotes

[1] Mayo, Elton. 1933. *The Human Problems of an Industrial Civilization*. London: Macmillan. Mayo, Elton. 1945. *The Social Problems of an Industrial Civilization,* Harvard University Press.
[2] Weber, Max. 1947. *The Theory of Social & Economic Organization,* Oxford: Oxford University Press. The parental claim, however, is an overstatement. Even if the strong 18/19th century founding claim of Adam Ferguson is discounted, Ibn Khaldūn had clearly marked the territory in the 14th.
[3] Mintzberg, Henry. 1973. *The Nature of Managerial Work*. New York: Harper and Row. Mintzberg's argument was that management was not about Fayol's functions' concerns, but with what managers actually do.

[4] See Carney, Brian W and Getz, Isaac. 2009, (revised 2015). *Freedom Inc*. New York: Crown Business.

[5] Nobles, Bill and Staley, Paul. *Freedom-Based Management*, www.42projects.org/docs/Freedom-BasedManagement.

[6] See: Kahneman, Daniel. 2012. *Thinking Fast and Slow*. London: Penguin; Kahneman, Daniel, Sibony, Olivier, Sunstein, Cass R. 2021. *Noise*. London: William Collins; and Thaler, Richard H and Sunstein, Cass R. 2012. *Nudge*. London: Penguin.

# CASE STUDY (3):
## MANAGEMENT MATTERS

The prolific management, business, and leadership writer Morgen Witzel (1960-) has identified a number of apparent universal laws applicable to management, the breach of which fundamentals and constraints may be unwise.[1] Aristotle's advice of *phronesis* should be recalled throughout. What follows is for consideration, adaptation, and implementation by prudent managers. Those not already identified above are summarised below as Witzel's Rules of Management, with only minor interpolated comment. Historians are ever wary of "answers" and unequivocal generalisations, and scholars of ethics prefer principles to rules because life can be too complicated for the application of the latter, but with those *caveats* only, the fruits of Witzel's scholarship are presented:

## Witzel's Rules of Management

### Entropy

As all matter and systems decay and decline, so inevitably do organisations, but they may be revived by the injection of new resources: capital, technology, intelligence. As the decay process is inevitable, the sole recourse is to fresh thinking. This may involve hiring and firing, disposals and acquisitions.

### Adaptation to Circumstance

While belief in the evolutionary theory of Charles Darwin (1809- 1888) may be contested, his finding that organisms change and adapt is incontestable. They respond to the pressures of each other and the environment.

Herbert Spencer (1820-1903) expanded the concept into "social Darwinism," whereby some people could be perceived as better adapted, and so more likely to succeed. This thinking was applied to business: the fittest would survive and the weak would fail. This, however, was a mistake, for what Darwin discovered and recorded was that those best able to evolve and adapt would succeed. Moreover, humans may also empathise, support, and co-operate with their fellows. Competition is not the only operational mode but the necessities to recognise the need to change and to adapt are essential.

## Yin, Yang, and Paradox

These rules have been identified in detailed presentation concerning oriental philosophy, discussed above. The behaviourist management theorist Charles Handy (1932-) has adapted the paradox paradigm to modern conditions, noting that:

- in the performance of work, brain has replaced brawn, but the human mind is unpredictable and harder to control;

- pay rates rise steadily at the top while they stagnate or decline in real terms at the bottom;

- fewer people are responsible for increasing global productivity;

- people are working longer hours without having any real rise in living standard;

- the world appears to be richer but no happier;

- businesses increasingly have to focus on mass markets and niches, having to be global and local simultaneously;

- values change as people age, with young and old in frequent disagreement;

- we are all individuals but need to be part of a group;

- whereas the concept of justice depends on equity and fairness for all, global inequalities and injustices are readily apparent.

These paradoxes are mirrored in many organisations, where further examples abound. Managing in and within paradox is a constant state of being (as the Taoist writers asserted).

## Unintended Consequences

Whereas chaos theory argues that all actions always have unintended consequences, a further explanatory approach asked by the sociologist Robert K. Merton (1910-2003) why such results often occur, produced these reasons:

- **ignorance:** erroneous or insufficient information, or lack of awareness of other factors;

- **error:** wrong decisions made for wrong reasons, perhaps due to ignorance;

- **interest immediacy**, whereby the perpetrator calculates that the burden of the unintended consequences will be borne by others;

- **basic values**: people act according to pre-conceived notions of how they should act, regardless of consequences, thus governments of the left or right increase or cut taxation, without regard to the risks of capital flight and borrowing costs or possible effects on revenue generation or employment;

- **self-defeating prophecies**: the agronomics intended to resist the Malthus predictions of the consequences of population growth by increasing the food supply did unforeseen damage decades later through pollution, pesticide over- and misuse, ground-water resource loss and other depredations.

The listings are disputable in some areas. The calculation of the cost of a deal to any responsible businessperson would include an unintended consequence factor, otherwise known as contingency. Sometimes, the unintended can be as explosive as the accidental, suitably Taoist - discovery of gunpowder; the discovery of a further use for the angina treatment Viagra; the multiple beneficial uses of the derivative of willow tree bark; aspirin. The yin to the yang of these benefits may be found in the 1922-1933 USA Prohibition experiment, which saw some decrease in alcohol consumption and a massive increase in organised crime. Since unintended consequences will always occur, it is advisable always to have insurance, and a contingency plan, with a budget.

## The Hierarchy of Needs

Influenced by Indian concepts, the American psychologist Abraham Maslow (1908-1970) argued taxonomy of human needs can be made in five categories:

- **physiological**: that necessary to maintain life: food, water, sleep and other basics;

- **safety**: security for individuals and family, with property safe from harm or damage;

- **belonging**: to another or groups, with the respect and esteem of others;

- **self-esteem and self-respect**;

- **self-actualisation:** the fulfilling of potential, perceived destiny or vocational calling.

People may move up or down the levels, the last of which may not be attained or desired. Applied to management, the hierarchy is most important regarding groups, where motivation can be key to productivity. Witzel cites complementary research which has segmented the Indian market into the resigned, strivers, mainstreamers, aspirers, and the successful. Here, what people think they need dominates their behaviour, not necessarily what they already have. People are not necessarily permanently fixed on the scales. Levels of fulfilment can be dependent on activity: a board room hero might be a golf course dunce, and *vice versa*. Those at the top might be all too ready to tread upon the fingers of those attempting to scale the same ladder behind them, and indeed to kick away the ladder altogether.

A counter argument is that people may have well-connected, happy lives but little money. A flourishing social life and robust health, mental and physical, are important to rich and poor, irrespective of hierarchy.

Douglas McGregor (1906-64) elaborated further with his influential 1960 concepts of Theories X and Y. The former assumes that workers lack ambition and must be coerced; the latter posits that as work is a natural human function, people will aspire and rise to positions wherein they might express their creativity, thus finding personal freedom. Attractive but simplistic, this contrast between low-level and high-level needs may also have dual operation: people might be both, or either, at different times, according to circumstance. The behaviourists' permanent paradox is that humanity is inconsistent and may be contradictory. Therefore, it is possible only to adhere to the very basics: people work because they need to, so producing goods and service. Customers need, or think they need, these. The common factor of needs, the balance, is the producer of growth, the discovery and realisation of profit or service from which becomes the managerial task.

## Kautilya's Rule

In his *Arthashastra,* discussed in Chapter 5, Kautilya stated that: "The king shall be ever active and discharge his duties; the root of wealth is activity, and evil its reverse." That action primarily was to uphold dharma, meaning "righteous duty." This goes beyond "doing the right thing" to the upholding of natural law, so that all may live in harmony. While Platonic and Confucian states would be subject to entropy, and so decay, dharma allows for fluctuation and change, requiring only the maintenance of a just balance. To that, all, meaning workers and employers, have a duty to cooperate, thus facilitating activity which, in turn, creates wealth.

## Buffett's Rule

The celebrated American billionaire investor Warren Buffett (1930-) stated "never invest in anything you don't understand." Witzel makes the distinction between knowledge and understanding: knowing about something is not enough, as events like the dot com bubble and disastrous acquisitions such as Friends Reunited prove. We knew in my consultancy business as early as 1993 that the 2008 crash was coming because one of our associates was making a continuing, booming living from banks, very many of whose employees did not understand derivatives. Even expert tuition does not guarantee whole class comprehension, as was the Confucius experience.

## Grove's Rule

Detailed in a subsequent publication, Intel's Andrew Grove (1936-) observed that, in business, "only the paranoid survive." His management concern is performance, in a real world where no plan ever survives intact. Therefore, with constant attention to strategic problems, managers must constantly question, debate, share information, challenge data, adapt, and so deny entropy.

## Moore's Rule

Intel co-founder Gordon Moore (1929-2023) stated that the transistor density (number of components) of integrated circuits would double every two years, although this has slowed latterly. As well as being an indicator of when to invest in new computer technology, the consequence is that the skill levels, knowledge, and adaptability of those using the computers must increase at the same pace if entropy, dysfunction, and competitive loss are to be avoided. Now that compound semiconductors are being predicted to have replaced silicon by 2040, Moore's Law is probably itself vulnerable to entropy. Yet the compound versions may conform to Moore's pattern. Historical analysis over time will offer answers.

## The Pareto Principle: The 80/20 Rule

The Italian engineer, economist, and philosopher Vilifredo Pareto (1848-1923) had discovered that 80% of Italian wealth was concentrated in the possession of 20% of the population. Joseph Juran (1904-2008), an American engineer and management consultant specializing in quality, found that about 80% of quality defects were found in some 20% of the production process. He named this finding the Pareto Principle in Vilifredo's honour, thus confusing two discrete issues. Quantitative interference in qualitative matters having been found to be unworkable, the accommodation recommended is while accepting the reality that there will never be complete efficiency, to concentrate instead on effectiveness: the sum total of the value of customers' service, for example.

The principle was reinterpreted and expanded from business to careers and personal life by Richard Koch (1950-) to posit that most worthwhile results come from a small amount of effort. Thus 80% of outputs will result from 20% of inputs; 80% of results come from 20% of efforts; 20% of products, and customers, usually account for 80% of sales.

## Rule of the Span of Control

Vytautas Andrius Graicunas (1898-1952), engineer and management consultant, studied mathematically the power relationships between a manager and subordinates, concluding that the optimal number was between four and five. Modifications have been achieved through reducing hierarchies and increasing or decreasing reporting requirements but the rule of the span of control, to some degree, continues to exist. Since how power and control are distributed determines organisations' functioning, the only way to cope with the rule is through improved communications: people have to talk to each other.

## Parkinson's Law

Naval historian and public services' management commentator Cyril Northcote Parkinson (1909-1993) famously observed in the book which bears his name:

> work expands to fill the time available for its completion.

It has been further contended that the consumption of resources expands to meet their supply, and that the more efficient their production, the greater their consumption. Thus, budgets are rarely underspent; cars are more fuel efficient but fossil fuel consumption continues to rise. Witzel concludes that this Law is ever-present. All that can be done is to combat entropy by the encouragement of change.

## The Iron Law of Oligarchy

The term arose in ancient Greece to describe the rule of powerful persons who combined to run government, creating institutions to protect and perpetuate their rule. Thus, Republican Rome was presented under the legions' banner of SPQR - *Senatus Populusque Romanus:* The Senate and People of Rome. The senators were the oligarchs. The danger to oligarchs was always one or more of their number breaking ranks to seize power, as did Sulla, Caesar and Augustus, the Napoleons, and Hitler subsequently.

Therefore, oligarchs have always been careful to institutionalise. It was observed in his 1911 book *Political Parties* by the sociologist pupil of Max Weber, Robert Michels (1876-1936), that in elite theory there was "an iron law of oligarchy". The law dictates that, as organisations grow, they become more conservative, less democratic, transforming into oligarchies whereby control devolves upon a small clique who have gathered and gained power. This self-evident phenomenon is visible wherever we care to look. Those oligarchies may be entirely selfish, may believe that they act in the organisation's best interests, may even have some disinterestedness. They act not only to maintain or increase their own power, but to deny that to others. Oligarchies are particularly keen on excluding those they perceive as threats or have different beliefs or approaches. While there may be "good" or "bad" oligarchies within any organisation, especially where there is bureaucracy, Witzel argues that such is the strength of the iron rule that efforts at making organisations more egalitarian and democratic may be wasted, suggesting instead that energy is better put into encouraging the oligarchies to increase responsiveness and positive change.

## The Peter Principle

The Canadian educationalist given to the study of hierarchies, Laurence J. Peter (1919-1990), propounded the eponymous theory that "in a hierarchy, every person rises to the level of their own incompetence," a proposition particularly justified by studies of the military. Circumvention of the principle may be achieved by continuous management training and education, placing organisational needs above such factors as personal loyalty, achievement rewards, and inflexible ladders of promotion.

A former senior practitioner has observed:

> I always felt this was not a comment on the individual; rather it is a comment on the weakness of those who enable him to rise.… In my experience one of the worst types of manager is the person who has progressed to the top level of their skill, is deemed worthy of retention/more reward, and is thus progressed into supervisory/junior management as the only next step, there to find that they have neither the skill, aptitude nor eventually the wish to be there. They can't go back to their "skill job" because that looks like demotion, so they are left stranded in management.[2]

Achievement of a managerial position may also inhibit. The observer of managers in   action, Henry Mintzberg (1939-) noted:

> …the day someone becomes a manager for the first time, everything changes. Yesterday you were doing it; today you are managing it. That can be quite a shock.[3]

## Gresham's Law

Attributed to Sir Thomas Gresham (1519-1579), discussed in a subsequent publication, the principle that "bad money drives out good" was deduced either from observation in his work concerning exchange rates, or in advising Elizabeth I to restore fuller metal value to the coinage debased by her father, and attributed to him in 1857 by the Scottish economist Henry Dunning Macleod (1821-1902). Others such as Copernicus had also identified the principle. In coinage, people hoard the fuller metal versions, thus maintaining the circulation of the debased. It has subsequently been employed as a metaphor for bad service, product, or performance. As recovery here is difficult, quality assurance and careful personnel selection and training are the recommended preventatives.

## Martin's Rules

Witzel has summarised the thirteen rules for banking recorded under the name of Sir Thomas Martin (1669-1765), who had joined the family business successor to the Grasshopper, Martin's Bank, in 1699, becoming a partner in 1703. They were written under the name of another whose partnership dated from 1745 and so must have expressed the banking practise wisdom gained over considerable time. The main rules, condensed, are:

- Banks should not lend beyond their limits;

- loans should not be made unless the borrower can offer genuine collateral and can reasonably be expected to repay;

- banks should be prudent and encourage prudence, for this will attract and maintain prudent customers, so ensuring good, stable business;

- not be involved in complex or difficult business from which little profit can be expected, or in speculation.[4]

Witzel comments that the larger the loan, and the larger the repayment and interest demanded, the higher the likelihood of default. Worse can actually occur: so great is the loan that default would endanger the bank, resulting in the borrower becoming "too big to fail," a known and corrupting phenomenon extremely dangerous in that, as the 2008-10 crash demonstrated, the entire financial system can be at risk of collapse. Negative reaction to Martin's Rules has included wonderment that profit was made under them - and yet it was, in abundance.

Greater regulation since the crash appears to have stabilised the system. Even so, old-fashioned perhaps, but respect for Martin's Rules with banker and borrower education and training still appear to be the only safe financial means by which to proceed.

## Deming's 14 Points

Witzel included Fayol's 14 Points, discussed in Chapter 19, in his essentials list and added those of the statistician, engineer, and management consultant W. Edwards Deming (1900-1993). Whereas Fayol considered the need of the whole organisation and put it first, Deming came from the opposite direction, focusing on the individual. They share the same ground, however, in the prominence given to purpose. Deming was writing within the further context of advising American business on response to the competitive threat from Japan, a circumstance his own consultancy had helped to create. The points are:

1. Create constancy of purpose.

2. Adopt a new philosophy for leadership and purpose, creating added value for the customer.

3. Cease dependency on inspection to achieve quality but integrate quality within the product.

4. Instead of awarding business on price, consider total costs of good and bad quality.

5. Continuous improvement of production and service.

6. On the job training: to improve, people need to learn from and through their work.

7. Institute leadership, motivating, enthusing and inspiring others.

8. Replacement of fear by favour as a motivator.

9. Break down barriers between departments, making the whole company responsive.

10. Replace slogans, exhortations, and targets with reasons to achieve, with space for that.

11. Replace mechanistic box-ticking such as quotas, management by objectives and numbers with motivational leadership.

12. Remove barriers depriving employees of the right to be involved with the quality of their work.

13. Institute a rigorous programme of education and self-improvement: better people work better.

14. Everyone within the company is to be involved in the transformation: quality being everyone's concern therein, all are to be involved in its achievement.

Deming's point 5 is replaced by a stronger version advanced by Charles Koch in a subsequent publication. Witzel argues that both Fayol and Deming are correct within their terms, even though their propositions are paradoxical. Therefore, the task of the manager becomes one of balance. How that is to be achieved, he suggests, is in:

## Drucker's Rule

Peter Drucker (1909-2005), management guru, offered one rule, that which binds all:

> The only valid purpose of a business is to create a customer... If a business does not serve its customers, there is no value for its shareholders, employees, or itself. Businesses therefore must create, or find, customers, building and perpetuating a relationship, which evolves according to needs and demands. Drucker's belief was that entrepreneurs created value beyond themselves, for society, which generated prosperity, one way for people to achieve freedom: "Founding, owning, and managing a business was therefore a righteous act, one that benefitted the whole of society.[5]

The idea has long antecedents - from Thucydides, the impartial "father of scientific history," to Aquinas in the 13th century, and Ibn Khaldūn in the 14th. The 12th century merchant al-Dimashqi's condition was that the trade should be conducted in an ethical and honourable fashion, with merchants redistributing their earnings rather than hoarding. If the purpose of business is to provide goods and services which people need, and the purpose of services, such as universities and business schools, is also to meet that need, then the creation of customers is an ethical matter, aimed at the benefit of society as a whole. As businesses exist to serve society, the goal arises of goods and services which can be made available at prices which poor people can afford.

Because of their lesser mobility, lack of access or skill in using the Internet, the poor tend to have less purchasing choice, resulting in their paying more for the same commodity. Witzel quotes Japanese and Indian companies as recognising the problem and successfully making affordable goods for the poor widely available. He warns against the spurning of Drucker's rule, arguing that selfish businesses will be found out by their customers, who will go elsewhere. He leaves the final choice to his readers. Witzel's invaluable distillation of wisdom, neatly tied by Drucker's rule, offers a comprehensive and comprehensible route to thought and action.

## Perceptions of Management

Such activity, however, must encounter the consequences and challenges for management brought by the continuing advances of information technology and artificial intelligence. With such managers as the rogue bankers, reckless institutions, and myopic politicians responsible for the 2008 credit crunch and its consequences, Machiavelli is more the man for that territory, the other side of the human relations coin, the one more attuned to the expressions of social media:

> The first opinion that is formed of a ruler's Intelligence is based on the quality of the men he has around him. When they are competent and loyal, he can always be considered wise, because he has been able to recognize their competence and keep them loyal. But when they are otherwise, the prince is always open to adverse criticism; because his first mistake has been in his choice of ministers.... But as for how a prince can assess his minister, here is an infallible guide: when you see a minister thinking more of himself than of you, and seeking his own profit in everything that he does, such a one will never be a good minister, you will never be able to trust him.[6]

However reliable the minister or manager, among the dangling questions cogently posed in his sixteen books (to date) by the writer and professor, Henry Mintzberg, is what is "managing"? Among the answers he offers are:

> It is controlling and doing and dealing and thinking and leading and deciding and more, not added up but blended together. Take away any one of these, and you do not have the full job of managing.... The overriding purpose of managing is to ensure that the unit serves its basic purpose ... the job of managing is significantly one of information processing, especially through a great deal of listening, seeing, and feeling, besides just talking.[7]

Managing, moreover, is rooted in context, just as its study is context and history dependent. Top, middle, and lower tier managers may share hierarchical ranking but what they do, and how and when they do it, will vary according to multiple factors. It is also a facilitative role, ultimately impossible of quantification:

> Management ... means getting things done through other people, whether that be on the people plane (leading and linking) or the information plane, (controlling and communicating). Even on the action plane, managers do and deal largely to enable others to get things done...[8]

> Managing is about achieving a dynamic balance across the information, people, and action planes, while reconciling the concurrent needs for art, craft, and science, all the while juggling many issues.[9]

How this may be assisted is explored in the **Improvements**, coming soon.

# Management Competence

Even so, among the juggled issues is an unavoidable essential. Can the person do the job? Is she or he competent? In 1922, arguing that managerial competence could not be achieved without training, the pioneering management accountant, organisation and method academic, and author L R Dicksee summarised his 1906 and 1910 major works[10] where he defined the basic qualities of a manager as being:

- Organising ability
- Accurate and painstaking attitude
- Firm and decisive will-power
- Adaptability in manner
- Originality and imagination
- A cool and quiet demeanour
- Self-control
- Sound health

These contributed to Right Thinking, which Dicksee saw as resulting from character and vision, expressed in Right Doing.

A century later, based on his career-long observation of managers at work, Henry Mintzberg defined four categories of management competence:[11]

### A. Personal Competencies
1. Managing self, internally (reflecting, strategic thinking).
2. Managing self, externally (time, information, stress, career).
3. Scheduling (chunking, prioritising, agenda-setting, juggling, timing).

**B. Interpersonal Competencies**
1. Leading individuals (selecting, teaching/mentoring, coaching, inspiring, dealing with experts).
2. Leading groups (team building, resolving conflicts/mediating, facilitating processes, running meetings).
3. Leading the organisation/unit (building culture).
4. Administering (organising, resource allocating, delegating, authorising, systematising, goal setting, performance appraisal).
5. Linking the organisation/unit (networking, representing, collaborating, promoting/lobbying, protecting/buffering).

**C. Informational Competencies**
1. Communicating verbally (listening, interviewing, speaking-presenting-briefing, writing, information gathering, information disseminating).
2. Communicating nonverbally (seeing - visual literacy, sensing - visceral literacy).
3. Analysing (data processing, modelling, measuring, evaluating).

**D. Actional Competencies**
1. Designing (planning, crafting, visioning).
2. Mobilising (fire-fighting, project managing, negotiating, dealing, politicking, managing change).

# Management of Consumption

There remains also an unending question, addressed in various forms throughout history: the management of society through control of display and consumption through sumptuary law. Regulation and management of consumption is notoriously difficult. The first written Greek law code in the 7th century BCE restricted female movement and dress, forms of male display, and the drinking of undiluted wine. The Roman Republic had series of laws regulating luxury. The successor Empire reserved a cape of the expensive, uniquely colour-fast Tyrian purple for the emperor alone even at the height of its extravagance, with senators allowed a gold-edged purple stripe on their togas. In China, sumptuary laws existed in one form or another from the 3rd century BCE Qin dynasty until reform under the Ming in the 16th CE. Japanese provision was most extreme, where from the 17th century the clothing of people of every class was strictly regulated. By the 19th century, this was a matter of social dysfunction where the merchant class had the resources to dress more expensively than their samurai superiors. Gold jewellery, silk and long robes for men were forbidden under Islam.

Between the 13$^{th}$ and 17$^{th}$ centuries in Europe, sumptuary laws were addressed to the entire population but primarily intended to demark people according to their station. Social rank and hierarchy were enforced by limits on consumption and display - particularly fabrics, furs, trims and colours. The main targets were the middle classes, the poor having little choice in dress or diet. The social objective was control, with defence of the position and power of the nobility. The gentlemen classes were, themselves, divided into a "society of orders," with social divisions between gentlemen, knights, and the various levels of aristocracy, all enforced by sumptuary laws defining what each group could wear. Gentlemanly status was also meant to be about behaviour, in theory at least. A frequent illustration was made of the social ranks in the terms of the human body: the king was the head; the gentle classes as the hands and arms, and the poor as the feet, all presided over by God, the Creator. Within that creation, there could be exceptions, but they had to be clearly marked, such as the compulsory striped hoods, arm badges or tassels for prostitutes.

Sumptuary laws were also an attempt to regulate trade by restraining expenditure on luxuries, preventing foreign suppliers from draining capital reserves. A Montaigne essay railed against only princes being allowed in France to eat turbot, wear velvet and gold lace. A 1571 English statute compelled all English males aged over six and not of gentlemanly class or upward to wear woollen caps, emphasising social distinctions while encouraging the wool trade, the price for disobedience being three farthings per day. Despite such penalties, the laws were widely disregarded. Introduced briefly to the Massachusetts Colony, they were abandoned within two decades.

To control populations by either repression or the creation of national identity, both sumptuary law discouragement and encouragement have been used. An English governor prohibited the Irish in the 16$^{th}$ century from wearing national dress; Scottish highland dress was prohibited by the monarchy in the 18$^{th}$ century, encouraged in the 19$^{th}$ and subsequently managed into a tourism revenue stream. State consumption management has a chequered record. Although the English eighteenth century "gin craze" was ended after five Acts of Parliament had been passed against it, with only a property tax on the places of sale proving effective, alcohol prohibition failed in Maine and other US "dry states" in the mid nineteenth century, and nationally in the USA in the next. Smoking bans in public places appear to be effective, for example, rather than prohibition of consumption. Sumptuary control remains largely a matter of personal management. Alcohol is prohibited, with variations, in nineteen countries; recreational cannabis is decriminalised in 30 countries, illegal but unenforced in some 15, and legal in three.

Monument to the difficulty of state consumption management is the position of the United States, where at the time of writing recreational cannabis was legal in ten states, two US territories and the District of Columbia; but illegal as a Schedule 1 drug at federal level, prohibiting even medical use, although the federal government has not intervened. US Indian reservations may legalise either medical or recreational cannabis use. Comenius and Winthrop might have been amused.

In management matters, theories may be reduced to proven rules but in the matter of the management of consumption, as with so much else, it is a matter of circumstance, knowledge, and judgment, at the time.

## Case Study Reflections

1. The most effective and far-reaching examples of mass management of consumption have been seen in the restrictions imposed by authorities in the combat of the COVID-19 pandemic.

2. Equally, the effectiveness of the management of the controlling of the disease - the failures and successes - are self-evident matters of record, where that has been preserved and presented with accuracy and integrity.

3. The study makes a presentation of empirical evidence, drawn from contrasting sources interpreting evidential records. An impressive breadth of scholarship has drawn forth a list of findings in the expression of management which appear to offer sound reliance. The tireless research of an indefatigable scholar illustrates the enormity of the management concept.

4. Understanding and experience of our subject remains a journey. At least, a start has been made. More discoveries await. Reader advice, quest suggestions and observations are most welcome.

5. The hardest immediate question to ask is perhaps the simplest: would it have been better management to allow COVID-19 to rage unhindered

except for basic precautions which did not inhibit the economy, so allowing business to proceed as normally as possible, while allowing vaccines to be sought and produced, thus preventing the enormous damage and costs arising to the world's economy and future generations? What would Machiavelli and Aquinas have advised, and Apollo's oracle at Delphi perhaps pronounced?

# Endnotes

[1] *Management from the Masters*, Bloomsbury, London, 2014.

[2] Brian Murphy (1950- ), 2018 email to the author, reconfirmed "I still believe the words to be true", 2 August 2022.

[3] Mintzberg, Henry. *Simply Managing*, p. 98.

[4] These are: *"Proper Considerations for Persons Involved in the Banking Business:*
1) Some Judgment ought to be made of what sum is proper to be out at a constant interest.
2) A proportion of Bonds, Land tax tallies, and silver to be ready on sudden demand.
3) A proportion of Government Securities, as navy Bills.
4) Not to lend any money without application from the borrower and upon alienable security that may easily be disposed of, and a probability of punctual payment without being reckoned hard by the borrower.
5) All loans to be repaid when due, and ye rotation not exceed six months.
6) Not to boast of great surplus or plenty of money.
7) When loans do not offer, to lend on Stocks or other Securities, buy for ready money or sell for time.
8) When credit increases by accident upon an uncertain circulation the money may be lent to Goldsmiths, or discount bills of exchange.
9) 'Tis prudence and advantage of a Goldsmith that depend upon credit, to endeavour as near as possible upon the yearly settling Accounts to have the investiture of that money in Effects that are easy to be converted into money.
10) To appear cautious and timorous contributes very much to give persons in credit an esteem among mankind.
11) Avoid unprofitable business, especially when-attended with trouble and expense.
12) 'Tis certainly better to employ a little money at a good advantage, if lent safely, in order to have a greater cash by you, tho' possibly you may extend your credit greatly.
13) When it shall be thought proper to call in old loans the demanding of them ought to be in the names of all the Partners."
Quoted in Bisschop, W.R *The Rise of the London Money Market 1640 – 1826,* pp. 128-129.

[5] Witzel, Morgen. *Management from the Masters,* p.134.

[6] Machiavelli, *op. cit.,* XXII, p 7.

[7] Mintzberg, *op. cit.,* pp. 36, 38, 43.

[8] *Ibid,* p. 117.
[9] *Ibid ,*p.180.
[10] Dicksee, Lawrence Robert. 2018. *The True Basis of Efficiency,* reprinted London: Forgotten Books.
[11] Mintzberg, *Simply Managing,* p. 68.

# CONCLUSION

As end also marks a beginning. Three narratives have intertwined. While management followed practical requirements, hierarchically expressed, family, tribally and nationally based, societies developed according to location, religion, custom and usage. Myth and empirical evidential inquiry, along with analytical and creative thought, has characterised human development. The rehearsal of ideas of improvement, education development, principles, and purposes ended with a continuing question by the end of the 18$^{th}$ century: essentially, what was there for the great majority of people, whatever the nature of control? Demand was present, supply scarce and of variable quality. After millennia, how was mass education to be achieved?

The penetration of ideas into society, meanwhile, might be gauged by the businesses inspired. If myth and the tales and heroes of Homer inspired Caesar's and Alexander's imperial adventures, thinkers like Comenius, Luther and Locke; Galileo, Bacon and Newton, in time, made a lot of money for publishers, games and toy manufacturers, just as computer gaming designers and companies do today. Great ideas do descend to trivia, and may so arise therefrom. The management of ideas is a business function, their implementation a practical matter, all within a managerial political framework. The foundations of management can be seen in the institutions which those practical adaptations produce.

The communication of ideas, now instant for much of the world, took time. The losses of ancient civilisation were only slowly, partially recovered, and worsened by ethnocentricity, eastern isolation, and western arrogance. It took centuries for Europe to discover Indo-Arab mathematics and accountancy, over a millennium to gain the secret of silk making, and it is doubtful in the extreme whether the acknowledgment by Adam Smith of the importance to his moral and economic thinking of Taoism and Confucianism has even yet been appreciated or fully understood in the West.

Graber and Wengrow may be correct in their thesis that received understandings of the broad sweep of human history are mostly wrong. How sense is made of the human past, including the origins of farming, property, cities, democracy, slavery and civilisation itself through such records of the earliest indigenous thinkers as may be intuited or discovered, still leaves us with the Thucydides' record of the Athenian reply to the citizens of Melos concerning the demands for payment, liberty, or death, as their league alliance condition:

> You know as well as we do how the world goes.
> Justice is only in question between equals in power.
> Otherwise the strong do what they can and
> the weak suffer what they must.

Whatever the outcomes, for either side, they had to be managed. Winning the war and losing the peace is not unusual. The scale of loss may be catastrophic, triumph merely transitory, which circumstances possibly explain why management decision theory is influenced more by the fear of loss than the appreciation of gain. Indeed, in hard times of conflict, what was there, wondered Thomas Hobbes:

> No arts; no letters; no society; and which is worst of all, continual fear,
> and danger of violent death: and the life of man, solitary, poor, nasty,
> brutish and short.

Religion might offer an alternative existence, and philosophy another way to cope with, even manage, the present. The management narrative has produced exemplars, again questioning application to future need, and rehearsed the managerial heritage. Socrates asked pertinent questions; Plato justified the elite; Aristotle sought freedom through a prudent good life. Rome had provided all the basics, from management education texts to essential organisational structures surviving its fall and supplying a continuing framework through the Church: the attempted translation of ideas into reality, and autocratic method. The Song dynasty was unable to sustain its business and management innovation and progress. The erratic and sporadic nature of the management process has reflected a variety of leadership practices styles. The ancient world saw commercial development from temple capitalism to public-private partnerships, armed trade and the convoy system to entrepreneurial enterprise. Pantheism was replaced in the West by monotheism, the variety being a source of conflict.

The concern of the East was more the way of life than its next expression. A Taoist might live the paradox of high ability, choosing happiness in poverty over the luxurious jeopardy of courtly service. In business, innovation came through accident (gunpowder), cross-fertilisation (algebra and accounting), and the revolutions in communication (printing). Progress was hindered (by the Church and Islamic restrictions), with losses of consequence (Greek fire; the Ming international retreat; Athenian democracy) from multiple causes. Foundations may crumble, requiring archaeological rediscovery.

There are many candidates, highlighted through the use of the case study method, which deserve special emphasis - from the Catos to Machiavelli and the enlightened despots, but the two individuals and abstract examples selected are illustrative of larger scale change than even that sparked by Luther. Crowley's micro-management of the world's first industrial and welfare integrated complex demonstrated that industrialised manufacture was possible, where demand so required, so truly commencing the modern "industrial revolution." That the further industrialisation process took so long was a feature of dysfunctional development. Key ingredients were absent, moving at different paces: mass education; a shift of emphasis away from theological dispute; technological applications.

The Islamic world, from a dramatic foundation, produced a synthesis in religion and trade at the conjunction of fair dealing but was inhibited by the absence of primogeniture, primacy given to religious thought, invasion, and the redirection of wealth. Division of inheritance mitigated inequality but deterred entrepreneurial growth. The Chinese forsook the opportunity of major economic and strategic advance for the comfort zone of a vast but isolated domestic market. In the West, the periods spanning the Age of Reason and the Enlightenment produced new knowledge and ideas, introducing rationalism as an aid to thought and a management tool which, with dissemination aided by developing technology, brought greater attention to bear on how business and society might best be managed. The desire to increase production efficiency led to applied educative techniques in industry, particularly in the US, and the creation of business schools.

From the theory and practice stimulated came multiple approaches, writing, and teaching, and the creation of a new industry: Management Studies. These multiple causative and conflicting factor reviews now have expression in the state of and prospects for growth towards mid-21st century management: the conclusion of which will be what we make it. That this is not a straightforward matter is foreshadowed by the first, abstract case study of **Management Matters**, and even where we can be certain regarding facets of management as revealed through theory, research, practice, resulting policy, and implementation, there is no uniform certainty, especially where consumption by humans is concerned.

This third case study is addressed to a simple, practical question. What is it, after three millennia of human aspiration, endeavour, and application, that might be reliably known to work in Management Studies? The foregoing study of significant events, discoveries, and thought will bring us to a first staging post of an apparently reliable guide to basic management truths. Here, indeed, are some very clear Management Foundations, tangible proofs, and demonstrations of certainties upon which further to construct. At this stage, however, such study is not even a footprint. We're not there yet. The great management crises of our times have yet to be encountered. There are further journeys to undertake before they are reached.

Yet to be considered in this digital age are the next phases of management development and its context: mass education, the power of voluntary associations, mass population movement, industrialisation, global reach and the rise of the manager. The first of the **Improvements** in a successor volume brings opportunity for reader interaction and practical implementation.

There is later consideration to come of managerial capitalism, the advance and demerits of neo-liberalism, the fate of the joint stock company and its managerial failures, the growth of big tech, and the presence of the business school. Corporate, international, and particular aspects of management await investigation as the big beasts of contemporary Management Studies are encountered: managing economics, growth and inequality, decision making, strategy, well-being, the advance of technology, and the conundrum entitled the Athena Issue. Dominating all is the spectre of climate change, the greatest management challenge humanity has yet to face, perhaps the determinant of its very future. The test of the Management Foundations is yet to come.

It is hoped that the promised **Improvements** will make a positive contribution. There is a chance to reform management and Management Studies in order for them to better serve society, with safeguards against past errors. To aspire to such achievement, it is necessary to have gained some understanding of where we are, and how we got there, so more prepared to encounter what comes next. This book has sought to provide a commencement survey of early management footsteps and foundations. Next, with focused studies, comes the progression to practical new beginnings.

**FOOTPRINT:**
**Marking and Managing the Passage of Time**

- Humanity began with star gazing, sun dials and such timers as the hour glass sand-timer and water clock.

- Public, church, and civic clocks spawned personal devices.

- On our electronic devices, we may mark the formation of the time of the universe itself through the images recorded by the James Webb space telescope, named after the second NASA Administrator James E Webb - a very senior manager indeed.

- This book has journeyed from cave art to cuneiform to algebra and the computer.

- Recording and broadcasting resulting information may be routine management activities, but understanding the journey is a step-by-step process too.

# APPENDIX (1):
## GUIDE TO EGYPTIAN BASIC ALPHABET SCRIPT

| | | | | | | | | | |
|---|---|---|---|---|---|---|---|---|---|
| | A | vulture | | L | lion | | W | chick | |
| | B | leg | | M | owl | | X | cloth | |
| | C | cup | | N | water | | Y | feathers | |
| | D | hand | | O | chick | | Z | bolt | |
| | E | feather | | P | stool | | CH | tether | |
| | F | viper | | Q | hill | | KH | sieve | |
| | G | pot | | R | mouth | | SH | basin | |
| | H | wick | | S | cloth | | MAN | | |
| | I | feather | | T | loaf | | WOMAN | | |
| | J | cobra | | U | chick | | ANKH | | |
| | K | cup | | V | viper | | | | |

# APPENDIX (2):
## EXTRACTS FROM
## *THE LAW BOOK OF THE CROWLEY IRONWORKS*

### Introduction

**Begun in the late 17th century and added to in the early 18th, this** *Law Book* **is the first modern industrial management manual.** Although long known to economic historians, it is largely, undeservedly, unknown to Management Studies. The *Law Book* codifies the house rules made by Sir Ambrose Crowley III and his son, John (1689–1728), for the governance of their ironworks complex at Winlaton, County Durham, England. Revised and updated through the experience and growth of a business of remarkable size for its time, the regulation of the then largest manufacturing enterprise in Europe provides a remarkable and unique insight into the leading industrial and social community of its day. The factory accommodated over 1,000 employees. Those progressively more automated of the next century housed numbers in the low hundreds. This *Law Book* is the primary, major source for the birth of industrial management.

Reasons for its neglect by Management Studies include the obsession with novelty, comparative neglect of history, and the sheer bulk of the manuscript, some sense of which can be gained from the photographs in this Appendix. The Surtees Society at the University Durham has published a valuable abridged version of the Crowley Laws which conveys a portrait of the world's first comprehensive industrial society. The Society is correct in its observation that piecemeal quotation has detracted from the *Laws'* historical value. In introducing this remarkable management source to scholars and exponents of Management Studies here, I have tried to remain true to the value of the source in this further abridgement by providing extensive extracts, while choosing passages of particular relevance to the understanding of early industrial processes and organisation, directly exemplifying continuing management issues, insights and practice.

The drive, dominance and competence of the Crowleys shines through their creation. The labour problems they had to resolve will be familiar. They have experience of being "horably cheeted" by "villans," of inefficient employees, and those ruined by drink. Yet they emphasise, time and again, to their clerks of the need to take care of "my people," to ensure they are paid on time, and have their grievances fairly addressed. Paternalists who made use of informers, they were assiduous in ensuring their people's welfare. School, chaplain, doctor, and farm access were all provided long before Robert Owen sought to provide social benefits to his workforce. The company's hearse maintained the dignity in death of Crowley's Poor. That blunt but accurate description applied to those workers without the resources to buy tools and stock. The inarticulate might resort to the Chaplain to plead their case against "the cruelty of my clerks to my workmen." Apostate Quaker he might have been, but Church of England Ambrose remained close to religion, the paragraphs and clauses of the *Laws* being always referred to as "verses", for this was a serious business, where being caught making a joke cost a fine of a penny.

To manage the world's largest industrial complex at a distance of two hundred and fifty miles required written laws for every eventuality. The clerks were kept busy, even if they were inconsistent in such spellings as "aggrieved" or "agrieved." Spellings have been reproduced as written. Variations will have arisen through the usage of the times and the clerks' mistakes. The *Laws* were made to be read, heard and obeyed; recorded for reference; "horably" colourful on "villans," for rhetorical emphasis. As *Law 97,* paragraph 24, stipulates, large numbers of laws were to be read on specified days. Requirements on memory would have been little changed since the times of Herodotus.

Regular shipping to and from the rivers Thames and Tyne ensured communications' delivery and receipt. In a striking example of co-determinism long before German industry had reached such a stage, the Crowleys' Grand Council of section heads were compelled by the *Laws* to make their regular, timed contributions, with severe penalties for non-performance. At shop floor level, the attention to the minutiae of factory tasks prefigured that given much later by F W Taylor. There is an irony in Crowley's main product being a larger version of that upon which Adam Smith was to base his trade observations. If Smith's pins showed the business way to wealth, it is no exaggeration to write that, in every sense, Crowley nailed it. Much of the evidence for the origins of modern industrial management, and hence, Management Studies, now lies in the reader's hands.

The Crowley *Law Book,* containing some hundred or more laws, was indexed, as shown in the photograph towards the end of this Appendix; though not directly relevant for current purposes as is not possible to show all the laws here.

The further abridged selection presented next is grouped into three main sections:

> Crowley, and the Council Committees;
> Workers, Overseers and Managers; and
> The Welfare Services.

While no substitute for the historical integrity of the complete bound manuscript, and listed to impart meaning rather than in any numerical order, it is hoped this sample makes for a management-focussed understanding of the types of work, jobs, and administration involved in the operation of the Crowley Ironworks.

The *Laws'* English is that of the times, when the language was still evolving, and the punctuation limited. As instanced before, there are various alternative spellings of common words in certain places of the text, but with the same meaning. For example the word 'accountant' may occasionally be spelled 'accomptant'; the word run appear variously as 'run', 'runn' or 'runne', and so on. The copperplate writing is of Clerks' many hands. The language was meant to be heard by the workmen, read by the Clerks, and enforced by Crowley's managers. Footnotes are included at the bottom of some pages to assist comprehension. Enjoy![1]

---

[1] Sources: British Museum, Add.MS. 34,555 (in 307 folios of approx. 115,000 words); ed. MW Flinn, *The Law Book of the Crowley Ironworks*, Publication of the Surtees Society, Vol. CLXVII for the year M.CM.LII, Andrews and Co, Durham and Bernard Quaritch, London 1957. The generous waiving of copyright and granting of reproduction permission in the interests of scholarship by the Surtees Society is gratefully acknowledged.

# CROWLEY AND THE COUNCIL COMMITTEES

## ORDER NUMBER 80

### Putting Orders in Practice

**I HAD better any order had never been made provided it be not put into practice,** and the not inflicting the penalties upon the offenders doth not only destroy the intent of the order, but weakens all other orders. So I do declare: -

1. That if any penalty be due to any person by vertue of any order made, and the person it is so due to shall neglect to do his utmost to recover the same, shall pay the value of the penalty due to him to he that shall inform of such his neglect.

2. And whereas sundry orders have not yet penalties put to them and others have thought adviseable to leave the punishment and rewarding the informer discressionally which must be determined by me or the Councill at London where always compassion will be shewed to mistakes and ignorance if the party own the same; but the fraudulent, negligent partys and he that driveth at others' interest more than mine, the lyar and prevaricator, must expect but little favour.

3. Whereas I have observed that severall people have solicited me to grant matters expressly against orders and my apparent interest, and some when I have answered I will consider of it, others, when I have made no answer at all but gave them to be convinced in their own thoughts of the evil of their request, have affirmed that I have granted their desires; I, considering that if this vice should be allowed, there would be a gap for the making all orders useless and a ruinous factory must soon follow, for remedy of which I do declare that no orders shall at any time be suspended, no prudent and saving management suppressed, but by me in writing and upon the same form mentioned or by a Councill order which must be always entered into the Councill journall and a coppy sent to me. But all such suspensions of orders shall never be in force above three months without the same come confirmed by a Councill Instruction.

4.  When any officer shall be divided, as the Ironkeeper's being in two parts, that is one to deliver, the other to pay the cash; in such cases the respective persons are to take notice of all directions given in any matter relating to their part as if the same was particularly ordered for their parts. Whereas it hath been practised by some vitious clerks and officers who are governed by neither reason nor justice to see and to their knowledge suffer another clerk or officer ignorantly to act or do things not to the best advantage; and, having opportunity, does not nor will not better inform them. A servant of this principle, his aim must be to disquiet the work and destroy me, and such vicious persons ought to be discharged; and to the end I may better know them, I do hereby promise a reward of five shillings to those that shall convict any of my clerks or officers that shall knowingly suffer any other clerks or officers to act or do in any sort of manner or station not to the best advantage and not modestly inform them better, which said sum of five shillings shall be paid to him or her upon conviction of the party. But if it shall appear that the clerk or officers did inform or instruct the other clerk or officer at the same time of his seeing them act any matter not for the good of the service or to the best advantage, and the said clerk or officer would persist in his own way and not receive instructions, then the clerk or officer that admonished is cleared of the information, and he may put the obstinate person in the court and my damage shall be paid to the knowing advisor.

5.  When a new order is made, it repealeth all that hath been wrote and ordered upon that head, and nothing but the new order and what is or shall be wrote after the said order shall be made shall be observed.

6.  Whereas I have been informed that some disaffected clerks and other designing villans to be left at large whereby they may unjustly attack my interest, have insinuated to others that some of my orders are not necessary and that it would be foolish to comply with them, others have scoffed and derided them, and others have raised false constructions of them; I do therefore desire all persons whatever to give me information of any person that shall make games at any order or that shall be guilty of any action whereby any of my orders may be broken.

# NEW LAW NUMBER 83

## Council

**It hath by experience been found** that where government or people leave the management of their business to any single person, that their interest suffereth for want of advice, their estate wasted for want of checks upon their managers, their business upon any change or death hath been put in great disorder, which hath occasioned all wise governments and people to leave the management of their business to more than one, believing Solomon to be equal with his character in saying 'In the multitude of counsellers is safety'. I do therefore order: -

1. They must be named by me and then they are to sign in the Council journal this declaration, to be attested by three present: - 'We whose names are hereunto subscribe do most solemnly protest and declare, every one for himself, and not one for another, that we will be faithfull and just to John Crowley Esqr., and his successors, his and their secrets keep, and promote his and their interest to the utmost of our skill and industry, and do our best endeavours to prevent any design or contrivance whereby his or their interest may be injured. We do also most seriously promise that we will be conformable to his orders and keep the debate in Council secret, and in all things discharge a good conscience and faithfully discharge the trust we have taken upon us.

2. I have moreover considered that it may be necessary, not only for the mature and speedy accomplishing the affairs brought before my Council, but for the ease of my workmen living remote from their assemblys and a deliberate determination of all causes and concerns, that out of these numbers be chose three or more to be named by me of the Comptrol, and such others as I shall judge meet to be of the Committee of the Council whose offices I appoint as under.

$1^{st}$ As soon as my letters come to hand, the persons to whom directed immediately call two of the Comptrol to his assistance, in their absence two of the Council, who are hereby ordered to fix to the proper persons for answering each verse by minute entered in their book for that purpose.

*2nd.* They are hereby further commanded that all the same session, before they adjourn, to appoint per minute a proper person or persons to transcribe the verses for the Counsellers at Winlaton and Mill

No.1, which persons so appointed, upon failure within three hours after the adjournment of said Comptrol, shall be lyable to a fine of one penny to the informer for each verse omitted to be copied and forwarded to the respective persons at their proper places as appointed.

*3rd.* I do likewise charge that they, at their sessions which must be three times a week at least, set forth per minute in a plain and intelligible manner the omission or commission of the breach of any one or more of the laws and orders in Councill verse 13296.

*4th.* Be it moreover ordered that all remarks made per minute be brought before the Grand Council at their assemblys once a week, to be their ratifyed or disapproved as they shall see necessary.

*5th.* Those of my Committee of Council I do hereby oblige to attend precisely att seven a clock every Wednesday evening to hear and determine all requests, complaints or appeals of workmen with true regard to my orders, favouring the just and carefull and in no respect to encourage the persons who are guilty of the breach of Law 48, particularly verse 2, and Order 57.

*6th.* But to prevent the hearing of the workmen's addresses or agrievances, and that part of the members may not wait of others to the detriment of my workmen in loosing their time, I command that whoever shall not attend at the prefixt hour to be reckoned by the watch, shall pay 6d. to the members attending.

*7th.* All minutes made by the Committee I do hereby order to be brought before the Grand Council as in sub-division 4 of this verse the very same week the same is laid before the Committee.

3. For the confirmation of contents of verse 2 of this Law, and a thoughtfull settlement of my affairs, I hereby order that the several members of Council except Ironkeeper at Winlaton, whether of Comptrol Committee or otherwise, attend at a Grand Session every Tuesday morning exactly at 7 a clock from the 25th. of March till 28th. September, and from the 29th. September to 24th. March, 8 o'clock. Each person herein neglecting, unless by unforeseen accidents in certificate and lawfully tested by two of Committee, shall forfeit and pay 6d. to the Council, 5d. of which to be paid into their box and 1d. to the informer, and moreover he who shall, during Council is assembled, be guilty of any of the following crimes, shall pay the

several summs annexed to them, to be instantly paid, to be equally divided amongst the Council once a year: -

| | | |
|---|---|---|
| 1.To swear | 6d. |
| 2.Curse | 6d |
| 3.To assault or strike any person | 5s. |
| 4.To give anyone the lye | 6d. |
| 5.To challenge any person | 1s |
| 6.To give reflecting and provoking language, | |
| To pay as Council shall order, not exceeding | 6d |
| 7.To talk of anything forreign to the business | 4d |
| 8.To interrupt another till hath heard the other's | |
| offer | 2d |
| 9.Every jest or joque | 1d |

If any of our Society shall after conviction wilfully or obstinately refuse to pay the fine, the Treasurer is hereby impowered to stop it out of the first wages, and the Council per minute in that assembly to fully mention the obstinacy of such member whereby I may characterize him as an enemy to our constitution.

4. If any person whatever belonging the Council after assembly shall presume to absent upon any pretence whatever above five minutes from the first convention to the close of the session unless by minute entered in the proceedings signifying the true reason thereof, or upon debate at the request of Council, shall for each default pay 6d. to the Council box.

### Council Directions EN (Verse 115, 26th. December, 1704)

**And** I do appoint to chuse six new Committee men and do order that you see they be chosed in a fair way and not such that by their evil practices are not quallified; and that the oddware men choose three and the nailers three, and recommend to them to choose men of good principle of a quiet and sober temper.[2] To such I shall always give a due regard to what they write, and my workmen will find all matters of agrievance redressed; but if they chuse men of turbulent spirits that will set forth agrievances and there is none, it's but reasonable to think that it will much lessen their complaints of real agrievances and quite overthrow my good designe to have all my people's agrievances laid before me, and then I will never be wanting to do them

---

[2] For the Committee of Aggrievances.

justice. When the six committee men are chose, pray let this be read to them. I would have you consider the trust you have taken upon you. It's no less than to hear all my people's agrievances, and duly dispatch every reckoner and chearfully in their due course. You are to lay them before me without favour or affection, ill-will or hatred. You must not be afraid to write against any of my clerks,   if they in anything abuse my people or do not in all lawfull hours give their attendance and also to have a due regard to the quality of the iron in all respects, whether good or bad. Your not commending good iron may occasion me to forbear buying that I ought to buy.

Never make a hasty complaint but do it with thought and consideration, and let nothing prevail with you to make any fault or neglect worse than it is, for that made me give so little credit to the former committees. And assure yourselves, while you are unbiased in your complaints and lay the plain truth before me without threats or ill-becoming language, I will with patience hear you and redress what I think in conscience is my duty. I also recommend to you to use your best indeavours to keep my people quiet and peacable, and show them a good example and shun the pernicious advice of that base and wicked fellow, Za. Goodwin, who always was the promoter of villany, vice and the overthrow of all that was good. I also recommend to you where you see any of my people agrieved, that you complain first to the Council. If they do not relieve you, then write to me.

# WORKERS, OVERSEERS AND MANAGERS

## LAW NUMBER 18

### Ironkeeper's Charge

**Book-keeping procedure for the entry of claims of iron** as they arrive at the factory.[3] The iron, when received at the factory, is to be stored in bins in the warehouse and careful records kept by the lronkeeper of the stocks held.

## OLD LAW NUMBER 96

### Frauds in the Ironkeeper

**Every Unit 5 the Accountant is to examine the lronkeeper's books** and report on any instances of the Ironkeeper issuing more iron than the stock list permits, or allowing a workman to have a stock of iron for more than ten weeks without making a reckoning. Many other offences of Ironkeepers are listed for the detection of which informers may receive up to twenty shillings.

## LAW NUMBER 104

### Stock List

**Every Unit I the Governors are to draw up a list** showing the stock of iron to be allowed to each workman. Workmen not satisfied with their allotment may lodge an appeal. A copy of the stock list must be sent to London for approval every second week. Those workmen who have offended seriously against certain laws may not be allowed stocks.[4] Only those who have never run out of their stocks may be allowed more than one week's stock at a time.

---

[3] For an analysis of these entries, see P. W. Kingsford, "Sir Ambrose Crowley: Pioneer of Modern Management," *The Manager*, July, 1954.

[4] They would therefore lose their status as master workmen, and be obliged to seek employment as hammermen or journeymen.

# LAW NUMBER 7

## Toolmaker

**When any workman owes the toolmaker more than sixpence** for tools supplied, the Cashier may collect the debt for the toolmaker by deductions from the workman's wage. The toolmaker may then come every Saturday to receive what the Cashier has collected on his behalf. Complaints by workmen against the toolmaker's charge may be dealt with by two members of the Committee of Aggrievances.

# LAW NUMBER 63

## Toolkeeper

**All tools belonging to the firm are to be charged to the Toolkeeper** who is to keep an account of the tools in his charge. Newly arrived workmen are to pay for their initial issue of tools at the rate of 4d. per week, but all subsequent issues of tools are to be paid for at the first reckoning after the issue. Every Cypher Week, the Toolkeeper is to inspect tools held by workmen, and if necessary order them to pay for any damage sustained.[5]

# LAW NUMBER 54

## Tooles

**Formerly it was the practice to lend tools to workmen free of charge,** but losses were incurred through damage to tools and carelessness in their use. Accordingly, when workmen require tools of less than eight shillings in value, they are in future to be sold to them by the Warekeeper. Anvils are to be maintained at the workmen's cost, but re-steeled at the firm's cost. Similarly, bellows are to be maintained normally at the workmen's cost, but re-leathered at the firm's cost. Carelessness in the use of tools or anvils is punishable by fines. Every Unit 9, the Council are to appoint a suitable person other than the Toolkeeper to inspect all tools (particularly bellows and anvils) and report any damage to the Committee of Aggrievances, who are to charge the workman responsible accordingly.

---

[5] A period of audit and account for materials.

# LAW NUMBER 45

## Surveyors

**Whereas I have received great damages by reason of unskilfull, negligent and corrupt Surveyors**, who (without regard to the great trust reposed in them) have not taken that due care to prevent errors in making of goods as they ought but have carelessly passed them by when made, without considering that goods ought to be made saleable, serviceable and in every respect fit for their intended use; and that there is not anything can do me so much prejudice as ware made not to answer that design and end it's made for. Ware bought that is not in all respects fit for the service intended exposes the ignorance, knavery or great carelessness of the Surveyor; and, therefore, for remedy, I will here sett forth his duty, which I do strictly require him to observe and perform.

1.  That he ought to be ready in the knowledge of all terms belonging to ware, one that thoroughly understands his order, knows good workmanship, the use goods are designed for, and how they are applyed, so that he may the better give true directions to the workmen and demonstrate the same to their understandings. And if any person shall be so vile as to undertake the surveying of goods and pass the same before he be qualified as aforesaid he may expect I shall require satisfaction for what damage I shall receive through his ignorance and presumption; but where any Surveyor has workmen under his charge that are ordered to make goods he is not utterly capable of surveying, in such cases he is to crave the assistance of such as can survey them, who is hereby required to give the needfull directions to the workmen for the well making, and when made to survey the same and certifie thereunto; but in case there is none that will allow capable of surveying as aforesaid, that then all the Surveyors are to look back, and see what directions hath been given at each respective place for that specie, and to enquire amongst the workmen who is most knowing therein and advise with them, and then the Committee of Survey are to appoint who shall survey the same.

2.  That the Surveyor or Surveyors do all they can to make every workman rightly understand what he is to make before he begins any sort of ware, and that he or they takes effectual care to direct him according to this order in force, and if they have a pattern that they are sure [it] is in all respects according to the said order in force. They may let the workman take his own measures from the pattern, or if he leaveth a pledge for the

value as valued or for want of a valuation double the real value, then the Surveyor or Surveyors must carefully give the workman measures upon sticks or other ways as shall be most advisable; and not only so, but to prevent any error that may be committed or direction in writing or otherways or any misunderstanding or deficiency of the workmen's in any respect whatever, I do positively order that all and every workman, as soon as he has made the first specie of any ware that is new to him or he is turned to after he hath been long on other sorts of ware, that he bring the same with the directions he had to the Surveyor who is to examine it first by the directions the workmen had and then by the order, pattern or directions in force, and if neither directions or patterns, then by the best of the Surveyor's skill. And in case the work is defective in any respect, the Surveyor is to assign the fault and give further directions how the same may be remedied, and then send the said workman again to make another and bring the same to him, which he is to survey as afforesaid and to continue till the workman brings one that is right, which the Surveyor is to mark. And in case the workman shall vary from the pattern so marked, to be mulcted the full damage. But in case the pattern (confirmed as afforesaid) shall be wrong and the workman make accordingly, the workman must not be mulcted for the Surveyor's mistake, but the Surveyor must answer the damage to me as in verse 1 is expressed.

3.  You must allways carefully observe that the last order, pattern, generall directions or instructions is and must be accounted the order in force, and all other former orders, patterns, directions or instructions must be null and void.

4.  And for all new Surveyor's orders, patterns, directions or instructions whatever that shall be hereafter sent, the Surveyor is to take all opportunities to compare them with the old orders, patterns, directions or instructions, and advise with the most knowing work men, and then seriously consider the use of the goods and reason for the new variation; and in case he believes (or can learn) that anything may be added or altered to make the orders more usefull, he is to draw the same upon writing according to the best of his skill, and lay before the Committee of Survey who are to consider of the same and give their opinion at large to come to me with all convenient speed.

5.  And the better to prevent the great evils of not having goods made in all respects as they ought, it is hereby ordered whenever you receive any

complaints of any ware whatever, that the Surveyor takes the first opportunity to acquaint the workmen of the faults complained of, and make them sensible of the same, and that he is very carefull to see the next amended particularly of the faults complained of, and in all respects made as they ought to be.

6. The Surveyor is (as oft as the ordinary business will admitt) to go amongst the workmen in the work and see that they work well and workmanlike and in all respects as they ought. If otherways, to mildly reprove, and better inform them, and when his directions in the working part can be of service, he may stand by them a short time till he has made them sensible of their error and directed them how to amend, and seen them perform accordingly.

7. The Surveyor in performance of his office must be very prudent and cautious and allways have a great regard to what the workmen say, and especially in hearing their allegations and reasons where they are rationall; and where he is not very certain, rather let three faults pass without a rebuke than find one where there is none, for that renders his judgment weak in the workmen's sight, and lessens the authority his words ought to have over them.

8. The Surveyor has all in charge relating to the well making and buying of ware, from the iron till compleated and delivered to the Warekeeper; and that erroneous plea is hereby utterly barred (except as per verses I and 13) which Mr. John Pemble in a notorious and impudent manner endeavoured to usher in, such as measuring, steeling, hardning, grinding, blacking, shape, weight, prices, contrary to order, more than demanded, or anything else that might render them dear or for performance of this or that particular part; but the Surveyor has charge of all as aforesaid, and is carefully to inspect all ware bought and pass a nice survey on the same, both with respect to quality and quantity and price, in all which respects the Surveyor is to be just and use a good conscience to me, and never pass any goods that are unsaleable or unserviceable but utterly destroy all such as shall be offered, or deface them in such a manner as may prevent their being put upon him in the greatest hurry, and then return them to the maker.[6]

---

[6] John Pemble was Surveyor at Winlaton Mill until dismissed for dishonesty (Law 26, verse 13; Law 39, verse 10).

9.  And for all ware of any kind whatsoever that shall be made faulty for want of materialls, or deficient in workmanship, or anything else that may render it not so saleable and serviceable, or not so valuable to deserve the currant price as ware of that sort and size (and made in all respects as it ought to be) is worth, yet not so bad as deserve to be utterly destroyed, the Surveyor is to fix an equivalent great trust abatement in view of the workman's short performance; and herein it is highly necessary that the Surveyor should duly consider the reposed in him, that he is made an absolute judge between me and my workmen, [and] is hereby positively forbid to spare the workmen upon account of any favour, affection, gratefull relation or commiseration, by laying or pretending the work is bad, the iron was unfit, the workman wanted materials, is poor [and] would have been chargeable to the Box, or any other pretence whatever (except as in verse 15); and as well knowing that his sparingness to them is a robbing of me, so also on the other hand he is hereby positively forbid laying his abatements the heavier on any upon the account of any private peak, ill-will or hatred. And as a spurr to his duty he must allways consider that if once he be prevailed with to pass goods without an equivalent abatement, he must allways do the like to that workman and to as many more as he shall divulge it to or shall by any means be sensible of it; and that either through good will to me or ill-will to him he may have good reason to believe I shall be informed of it. However, he may assuredly know, when the goods comes to be surveyed here, his integrity and the uprightness of his judgment past between me and workmen will then be certainly discovered and be called in question to answer for his partiality if he hath been guilty of any.

10. The Surveyor is allways to be ready to do all the good offices he can for the workmen in seeing that suitable and proper iron, steel or any other materialls be provided for them, and do all that in him lyes to prevent the workmen's running into any errors whereby to deserve abatements; and when he cannot by any means prevent it, he must do it with regret and pity and never reflect or glory in their misfortunes.

11. He must do all that in him lyes to give the workmen a ready and chearfull dispatch, allways considering that their time is their bread and how grievous it is to them to be unnecessarily delayed. There- fore, he must be as expeditious as he can in his surveys without causing the workmen to wait longer than they need, and must use no partiality in giving anyone undue preference, but must survey that person's goods first who first

legally demands a survey, and to everyone in their due course without giving anyone just reason to complain.

12. In case any workman shall bring in ware that he knows to be unserviceable or any way defective and endeavour to hide the fault by stopping it with pitch or grease or any other thing or matter, or use any means whatever whereby to deceive the Surveyor and pass off such faulty ware, he must in a more exemplary manner be mulcted and pay 2s. 6d. to the informer; and if the Surveyor be the first discoverer he is to inform the Committee of Survey and lay the unserviceable goods, with the circumstances, before them, who are to hear both sides and judge of the matter and if it appears to be the Surveyor's due, they must allow it him, but the Surveyor is never to receive any such information money otherways than by order of the Councill or Committee of Survey.

13. Notwithstanding anything contained in verse 8, it is here provided that when goods are ordered to be weighed or measured by any other than the Surveyor, they must test on the reckoning note and also on the label what they by order performed; and in such cases as these and as per verse I is sett forth the Surveyors shall not be accountable for what is tested to be so performed by another.

14. In case any workman shall go on in making of ware without first making a sample approved of as in verse 2 and their ware be found faulty, they shall be abated to the full value of their damage and no plea to be allowed in their or their hammermen's favour; and if the wages due to them and their hammermen will not make reparation their collectable account of debt must be debted for what the wages falls deficient, it being very unreasonable that I should suffer through the negligence of workmen, especially where the workmen may easily prevent their working amiss by observing of order.

15. It is here further provided that in case of an order from me at London to put workmen upon ware they never made before or at least were never perfect at, in such cases the Surveyor may be sparing in his mulcting of them for faults committed really for want of skill, notwithstanding anything contained in this order to the contrary, but not where the errors are for want of following orders as to weight, measure, size or distance of holes, or any other fault which they by care might prevent.

16. I have found it of absolute necessity to order, and do order all people that survey to see whether the goods they survey are demanded and not supplied; if more than in the general demand, then to see what was entered upon their reckoning notes or any order given them in writing, and in case they are upon the reckoning note or they prove any order given for the making such ware, then the workman are not to be blamed but the person that so demanded the goods must be rebuked and the same entered upon the label. But in case they are not upon the reckoning notes, nor the workman can produce no order for making the said goods, he must be abated for making contrary to order in such an exemplary manner as may not only deter him and others from being guilty of the like crime for the future, but may also pay my damage for such goods lying dead upon my hands and disappointment of the ware they ought to have made. And whether there be abatements or not abatements, the Surveyor is to say on the reckoning notes and on the label, 'Surveyed by A.B.', putting his name, and is upon the reckoning notes to demand what sort and quantity the workman is to make next, which quantity must never be more than they and their men can make in eight days, Sundays and holydays exclusive; and in case the workmen shall make more than shall be demanded as aforesaid, to be subject in all respects to be abated as for ware made contrary order, although it doth not exceed the General Demand.

17. And whereas John Pemble did in a most felonious manner turn one man from working on my stock to his own, and from twelve shillings per week to above twelve shillings per day by the valuation, and when told of it, said 'twas not his business to fix the price; therefore to prevent such wicked pretences for the future I do positively order and declare that the Surveyor shall [only] have power to turn. a man from working on my stock and waste to his own without an order from me on his first shewing the Council this verse and have their directions therein.[7]

18. The Surveyor, whenever he receives a valuation of goods either by demand or otherwise before he exposes the same (for fear there should be any mistake), he is to consider the price fixed; and if he thinks it more than [it] ought to be or that he can have them made cheaper, he is to keep the matter secret, and by the first post advise me thereof and must divert the reckoning of such goods till he has received further directions from me or the workmen are brought to accept the lower terms he thinks they

[7] For Pemble, see footnote 6

can be brought for. And in all doubtful matters he must be sure never to allow more than the lower rates, and be cautious of giving too much wages, being   it will be much more easier to return the workmen what they have too little than it will be to take from them if they have too much. And he must be always mindfull to observe where either ancient or new rates are too much  that he take all prudent  method in reducing the same to an equality by offering the work to such as are willing to make it at the cheapest price with due regard to the well performance.

19. And whereas that notorious fellow Pemble ushered in that evil practice to prevent just equivalents with the workmen in view of short performance by often paying their whole demands as is sufficient, referring the abatements to me although as often as so done was condemned because (1) it was so long before the goods came to my hands that the evils was repeated before the offenders could be made accountable [and the offenders] were thereby encouraged to make their ware with short performance-till they were not able to make reparations or run away to avoid it. (2) It was throwing the Surveyor's work upon me. (3) It was seldom proposed but with a design to defraud me. (4) It was no manner of reparation of satisfaction to me, I having reserved power within myself to mulct them where the Surveyor has not discharged a good conscience.[8] (5) While this is encouraged it is not reasonable to think the workmen will do otherwise than be deficient in the making of their ware.  Therefore I do order that if any Surveyor shall be so base  as to pass a reckoning without making just and full abatements he shall be accomptable for the damage himself.

20. Whereas I have sustained damage by having unserviceable patten rings taken in, as doth appear by the great quantities returned, I do therefore order that the Surveyor against every Unit 6 seeth that all returned patten rings be sorted and what the workmen are by Order 65 obliged to make good, that every workman's make of such rings are laid by themselves and the respective makers sent for, and if they can make appear that Surveyor hath not done them justice as mentioned in the aforesaid number 65, that the Surveyor doth them right and also to let them know the time their rings will be put up to be sold by auction that they may have the liberty to bid; and what loss shall appear to be that their account

---

[8] The remainder of this law is a separate 'continuation' that follows Law 74 in the manuscript. Another continuation, following Law 89 in the manuscript, is simply a repetition of verses 20-29; this 'continuation' is followed by yet another repeating verses 13-19.

of debt be debted for the same in the same Unit 6, and in case the Surveyor shall neglect or refuse putting up what shall be in hand every Unit 6, for what damage shall be thereby the Surveyor shall pay.[9]

21. In case any workman shall think himself aggrieved by your abatements or otherwise you are to permit them to write what they have to say and send the same with the label, as is more fully ex- pressed in Order No. 26, verse 12, and in Order No.25.

22. Whenever you allow money by way of grace, that is for extra workmanship, be sure [you] see you have the extra workmanship before you allow the grace, and when you see the workmen perform well let them have a lawfull grace cheerfully allowed.

23. Whereas it hath frequently happened that when any new sorts of ware has been made or sorts not frequently made before by the maker, there has been gross errors committed by the reason of the Surveyor's or workmen's ignorance or carelessness, and hath been practiceable with several Surveyors when such faulty ware has been made and who to add to their prejudice have hindered my early correcting the faults by either delivering such ware to the Storekeeper or neglecting to pack and send forward the same till they have been in an extraordinary manner prest to it. Through such means I have been an unspeakable sufferer. Therefore to prevent this mad and repeated vice I do order that never any new sorts or faulty goods be delivered to the Storekeeper for the country sale more than may probably be sold in two months, but that all Surveyors in their stations and all concerned do what in them lies to pack and cause to be packed and send forward per the very first all new sorts of goods or such as are not frequently made or are any ways faulty, and to mark such casks, bags or parcels with '+' to denote they must be sent forward with the very first; and whoever shall inform of any Surveyor or other person concerned that shall not at all times show true obedience hereunto shall receive five shillings from the aggressor.

24. And whereas it may sometimes happen that a person may survey goods that doth not abide on the spot or cannot be present at the packing, in such cases those that surveyed must write upon a piece of paper their opinion of what they have to say or would say relating to the goods if they were present at the packing, which paper must always be annexed

---

[9] Order 65 is no longer extant.

to the label or the label wrote put upon the same paper and carefully packed up and sent with the goods.

25.  For the better improvement of our orders, you are to acquaint all knowing workmen that whoever shall lay before me or discover to you any order, pattern, directions or instructions to be any respect defective and how the same may be amended and made more effectual to answer the end goods are designed for, they may expect a suitable reward for their pains.

26. Whoever Surveyor, clerk or assistant shall take out any rates, prices or dimensions of any sort of nails or other goods whatever out of my books unless for those employed as constant workmen, except by a particular direction from me or the Committee of Survey, shall be any ways instrumental in the assisting others, or shall knowingly be found to countenance others forging, shall pay 10s. to Esquire Crowley and 10s. to the informer.

27. Whoever shall deliver any person or persons the prices, rates or dimensions of any sort of goods or shall be privy to the delivery thereof except as excepted in verse 26, and upon good proof be found guilty, shall pay 30s. to the informer.

28. If any hardner of tools shall strike his mark or suffer the same to be done by any others on any tools before hardened or be proved to be carelessly hardened, shall for each offence pay five shillings to the informer and be obnoxious to such further damages as I may justly lay to his charge.

29. If any workman whatever shall make more goods than he has order for from the Surveyor, he shall for all such goods so made contrary orders be abated one penny in the shilling over and above all other abatements which is customary for ware contrary to order; and if any officer shall reckon off any goods so made contrary to  orders without abating one penny in the shilling, the same shall be stopt out of his wages; and if the value of them exceed 20s. they shall not be reckoned off without orders from London on forfeiting 2s. 6d.

# LAW NUMBER 70

## Warekeeper

1. **No person whatever but the Warekeeper shall sell or deliver any ware** except shipped off by my order and by the proper officer, and in case the Ironkeeper, Nailkeeper or any other person shall in contempt of this order sell any goods and receive money for the same, shall pay the value of the money so received to the informer.

2. If any customer cometh for any goods which the Nailkeeper hath and the Warekeeper hath not, in such cases the goods must [not] be charged by the Nailkeeper to any customer but first to the Warekeeper and by him only delivered to the customer.

3. The Warekeeper is not to trust any person except such as shall be entered in the Prime Stock Leiger (under the title of 'Trust'), and none shall be entred in there but by my order or by the order of the Counsell and they assign their reasons in the Councill journal; nor no person to be trusted more than is there limited but what the...............you may trust any sum they shall desire.[10]

4. No person is under any circumstances to be trusted if they owe more money than all the goods they have had in the last 26 weeks, till such time as they have paid for all the goods that have been delivered three months or longer.

5. In every Unit 3 and 8, under the account of sales, the Councill are to subscribe, 'We did permit the credit above to be given which doth not exceed the limitation given us in Order 70, verse 3'; and if any large credit given the Councill are never to omit assigning their reasons for the same.

6. In case the Warekeeper should trust beyond the directions here given or shall neglect to collect from the workmen what shall be trusted to them by the limitations in verses 30, 31, 32 and 33, if any loss arise, it shall be the Warekeeper's loss, and he shall likewise be in danger of losing his place.

7. The Warekeeper is hereby obliged not only to deliver anything to the Nailkeeper, Accomptant, Surveyor, Cooper or any other of Mr.

---

[10] A space has been left here in the manuscript.

Crowley's servants without a receipt for the same in a book for that purpose; and when the said goods are brought to account in the Unit 3 and 8, to cross the said receipt, but to remain intelligeable.

8.  Every Account the Unit is 3 and 8, the Ware Sales Book must be cast up and ware credited at the prime cost for what hath been sold for the last five weeks inclusive, and proofs made to see whether the profit and the cost just ballanceth the sale, a coppy of which must be sent to London every Unit 3 and 8; and the Ware Book must have no other posting Units but 3 and 8, and under those figures all postings out of the Ware Book must be observed. To these postings the day of the month must be entred in the leiger.

9.  You must always when you charge any person with goods mention his christian and surname and the place of his abode, and underneath who the goods are sent by, and so fully that a full and satisfactory proof may be made.

10. The Warekeeper is not upon any terms to receive, meddle or take any ready money but is to enter the same in the Book of Ware Sold under the title of 'Ready Money', and the Warekeeper…[the script ends here.].

# ORDER NUMBER 103

## Monitor [11]

**Whereas it hath been found by sundry I have imployed** by the day have made no conscience in doing a day's work for a day's wages, nor have not had a due regard in doing their duty by labouring to do their utmost in the lawfull propagating my interest and answer the end of their being paid. Some have pretended a sort of right to loyter, thinking by their readiness and ability to do sufficient in less time than others. Others have been so foolish to think that bare attendance without being imployed in business is sufficient, and at last thought themselves single judges what they ought to

---

[11] In Council Instruction 8, 17 December, 1700, verse 35, Crowley wrote: 'I have employed my thoughts much upon this order and doe designe in a few dayes to throw myself out of all other business for two or three days to compleat it so far as to put it in practice.… However, nine months later the law was still not completed, for Crowley wrote, 'In verse 35 I was last upon this, but cannot yet compleat the order, but have found myself horably cheated by the Monitor ' (Council Instruction 38, 25 September, 1701, verse 146).

do, and came to that imaginary justice that they have thought that if they do as much as those that do least intitleth them to their wages, for getting the parable in the gospell that it is entirely in the master's pleasure to pay him as much that cometh in the eleventh hour as he that came the sixth hour, and no injury to he that came first; and by their oft thinking of their own side only have broke through their agreement, the eye of justice and the trust imposed in them, not considering that if they think their agreement grievous they ought to give warning and thereby legally intitled to demand an advance or a discharge, and not think because they have sold the pound too cheap will therefore deliver but three quarters. Others so impudent as to glory in their villany and upbrade others for their diligence thinking that their sloath and negligence with a little eye service intitleth them to the same wages as those that discharge a good conscience.

On the other hand, some have a due regard to justice and will put forth themselves to answer their agreement and the trust imposed in them and will exceed their hours rather than the service shall suffer. I have in a most serious manner taken into consideration the numberless number of persons that have been ruined by the extravagancy and negligence of their servants, and my charges in wages being so great and without there be a due care taken that I have service answerable to the wages I pay, it is plaine I had better knock off trade and make use of my stock otherwise.

To the end that sloath and villany in one should be detected and the just and diligent rewarded, I have thought meet to create an account of time by a Monitor, and do order and it is hereby ordered and declared from 5 to 8 and from 7 to 10 is fifteen hours, out of which take 1½ for breakfast, dinner, etc. There will be then thirteen hours· and a half neat service, which being multiplied by six is 81 hours, which odde hour is taken off. Also to the end there may be no disputes in the Monitor's giving me the turne of the scale and the parties that charge their own time have no pretence to over charge me, it is hereby declared that the intent and meaning of eighty hours must be in neat service after all deductions for being at taverns, alehouses, coffee houses, breakfast, dinner, playing, sleeping, smoaking, singing, reading of news history, quarrelling, contention, disputes or anything else forreign to my business, any way loytering or imploying themselves in any business that doth not altogether belong to me.

1. That the Monitor is to lye every night over the Ironkeeper's office, the Nailkeeper's or Surveyor's office, and be every morning in his office before 5 of the clock, and that he always entreth down the minute of his

first comeing into his office; and for the greater certainty of his integrity, the first person he seeth that is in the Monitor's List, he is to desire them upon their time paper to mention the day, hour and minute, in words at length, of his being in his office, which is where the minute diall is fixed and at no other place to be entred or commenced from.

2. No persons whatever are to be entred upon the Monitor's time till the hour and minute they shall shew themselves at the Monitor's office to the Monitor ready for business, and desire their time to be entred 'Come'; and in case the Monitor shall knowingly enter any person earlier than the minute hand of his clock or watch is when he first seeth them, although the alligations be ever so plausible, shall pay tenn shillings to the informer.

3. And for the better making known the office hours, the Monitor is to cause the bell to be rung and tolled, and no other person whatever, as is directed in Order 16, verses 1 and 2. As soon as the bell beginneth to toll, he is to instantly enter himself and all others that go to meales 'Run,' and then he to go to the sundry offices and if any be there he is to tell them he is going to breakfast or dinner and if their business doth not permit them to go, then he is to let them remain upon the book 'Come', and upon his returning he is to instantly go into the sundry offices and finding any absent that he left 'Come', he is to enter their 'Run' the hour and minute he entred those 'Run' that went to meales.

4. When the Monitor leaveth off at night, he is to go into the offices, and if he misseth any that are under 'Come', and allow them no time for that spell. All that he seeth in business he is to tell them the hour and minute and enter them all 'Run ', which they are to note in their respective papers of time, and enter the time they shall afterwards spend in business in their papers of time. And to the end that clerks may be justly paid for such further time as they shall spend in my business and not in the Monitor's account of time, it is ordered that they severally keep an absent paper, which they are to title thus: -

Wm. Wright's time paper for [Account] 892:[12]

---

[12] William Wright appears to have been Nailkeeper at Winlaton between at least the years 1700 and 1709, in spite of having been accused of being 'horably remiss in what relateth to [his] office' in November, 1700. In 1708, on a recruiting tour, he secured the services of ten smiths, and accompanied them from London by sea to Newcastle. In 1712, he married Elizabeth Merriman, of Winlaton, in Ryton parish

| Wm Wright: | Hrs. | Mins. |
|---|---|---|
| Saturday, begun at 4, entred not till 5, and went to Bladen to ship a keel of goods for Ralph Jackson at 7, so employed till 11.[13] | 5 | 0 |
| Monday, entred 'Run' at 7 at night, continued at work till 9. | 2 | 0 |
| Tuesday, went at 8 to trye Thomas Meanley's stock and came [back] at ½ hour past 8. | 0 | 30 |
| Wednesday, begun at 4, entred 'Come' not till 6. | 2 | 0 |
| Thursday, the Monitor absent, 'Come' at 5, 'Run' at 8, 'Come' at 9, 'Run' 12, 'Come' at 1, 'Run' 4. | 9 | 0 |
| Friday, entred 'Run'at 7 at night, 'Come' continued till 10. | 3 | 0 |
| | 21 | 30 |

In this week I imployed myself the twenty-one hours and thirty minutes more than I believe my time being upon the Monitor's book.

4. (cont'd). Every Saturday morning the Monitor is to carry the book of time to the Accountant, first subscribing to it these words: 'This account of time is to the best of my knowledge true and in all respects conformable to the Monitor's Order No.[103]; and I have not taken any person's word for 'Come' but have personally seen them in their offices and have allowed no time to any that in the spell I did not see them go or tell them I had entred them 'Run', and am ready to make oath I know nothing of your injury in your time except what is sent to you wrote on the backside of this.

church (Council Instruction 4, 5 November, 1700; 6, 5 December, 1700; Law 6, preamble; P.R.O. Adm. 106/627; The Registers of Ryton, Marriages 1581-1812, ed J. Baily, Sunderland, 1902, p. 47).

[13] Ralph Jackson was employed by Crowley as master of the *Anne* for many years. Before that, in 1696, he was serving as mate of the *Mary and Sarah*, a vessel employed by Crowley on the Newcastle-London route. In that year, Jackson was described as being 'aged about thirty and two years, of a midle stature, his owne haire, a black brown complection' (P.R.O. Adm. 1-06/483).

5. That no person shall have any time allowed them upon the Monitor's book or their extra paper of time but what shall be spent in the office they belong to and the Accountant's office in setting forth their accounts, or in going to any other office provided the same be within the Square, and in no dwelling house or room other than offices and warehouses, the Monitor is to keep an account of all persons whatever coming in the offices and goeing although paid by the year, my son, or my meniall apprentices.

6. In case the Monitor be ill or otherwise or negligent, he is not to take any person's word by hearsay, but to leave the same for the parties themselves to enter in their absent paper.

7. When the Monitor shall make a call or in going to meales or from business or otherwise, he shall find any person absent, he is to draw a line through their last 'Come' and allow them no time.

8. In case the Monitor shall after his entry of 'Comes' or 'Runs' alter the hour or minute soe as the party's time of attendance is enlarged, shall pay tenn shillings to the informer.

9. In case the Monitor shall find that he hath injured any person of their entrings of 'Comes' or 'Runs' to any person by the foregoing verse, the Monitor is not to alter the same but to keep his account paper unaltered, and is to certifie the circumstances of the mistake at large and enter the same under the party's own account of extra time, to which he is to subscribe his name.

10. The Monitor is twice or oftner at uncertain times in every day besides when he cometh from or goeth to meals to make a call, that is to see all in his books 'Come' be in their severall respective stations or otherwise in my service in the Square, if not to runn a line through the houre and minute of their 'Come' and reckon no time for the same and to enter the same at the latter end of his account of time in words at length, and so fully that if the partie charge the absent time it may be enquired into.

11. In case the Monitor shall enter any person 'Come' one minute or more before he actually seeth they are 'Come' to their respective office, shall pay tenn shillings to the informer.

12. And if the Monitor shall allow any person time upon any spell and doth not actually see them 'Run' or tell them the minute he entreth them

'Run', shall pay tenn shillings to the informer.

13. And in case the Monitor shall neglect to go to every office and enter all present 'Come' that is in the Accountant's, the Nail keeper's, the Surveyor's, the Cooper's, the Yardkeeper's, upon his first coming to the Monitor's office in the morning and from his meals or otherwise absenting before entreth upon any other business whatever, shall pay 2s.6d. to the informer.

14. Whereas I have been most horribly abused by the coopers not doing a day's work as they ought, but have imagined that when they have done what coopers do in piece work that cometh to their wages they have done sufficient, forgetting the hours that is spent in running backward and forward to do such business they toyl in carrying their tools and hoops backwards and forward, the many days nothing at all to do, their being paid but once a year and oft never paid and there is not one man in England that payeth a cooper weekly [...][14] And to the said end I may have an honest day's work as I honestly pay them their wages, I do order that upon the cooper's particular absent time paper, he entreth thus:-

| | |
|---|---|
| Saturday | Made 5 half barrells. |
| Monday | Sawed and splitt clap boards sufficient to make 10 dozen half barrells stowed. |
| Tuesday | Put on 100 hoops in trimming old casks |
| Wednesday | Made six kilderkins.[15] |
| Thursday | Headed up 10 half barrells, 2 hogsheads, 4 barrells, and made 5 half barrells |
| Friday | Took in 2000 hoops as per Claime 2348, stowed them, the weigher being sicke, helped in the warehouse 11 hours. |

15. To prevent any cooper's service being twice mentioned, some time in every day the Monitor is to see what is charged to be done the day before, and upon all casks made or any ways repaired he is to put R on the bottom head. If an old R, to run the pencil over again, so as he may not mark one cask twice. The Monitor is under the cooper's absent paper to say, 'I have made enquiry of the Surveyor and Nailkeeper and have marked all the casks made new and repaired and do believe the charge

---

[14] One line of the text illegible due to fading.
[15] A kilderkin was a cask of the size of a quarter of a tun, or half a barrel (O.E.D.).

is right'.

16. The Monitor is to keep an account of all wallers', carpenters', joiners', day labourers' time imployed in and near Winlaton, and the account is to be entred with the clerks and sent to me every Saturday night. And in case any person whatsoever shall employ any person and not see their names put in the Monitor's book or agree with the workmen that if they do not come to enter their 'Comes' and 'Runns' they will not be paid, the person so neglecting shall pay the wages, the Treasurer being hereby forbid to pay any person wages except those who are in the Monitor's book.

17. The Monitor is not to enter his own time 'Come' till he hath entred all other present after his entring into the office.

18. The Monitor is by no means whatever to faile of his duty every morning from 5 to going to dinner, and if he taketh any liberty it must be after dinner or rather in the evening.

19. If any person absenteth himself after the fifth spell, the Monitor is not to enter their time but to leave it to the party to enter themselves in their own extra paper; but in such cases the parties so oft absenting must the next morning shew the Monitor their extra paper of time.

20. No person is to be absent from the Square upon any pretence whatsoever before he hath acquainted the Monitor and he hath entred him 'Runn', and those that shall refuse or neglect to come to the Monitor and order their 'Runn' entred, the Monitor is upon the first missing of them to runn a line through the hour and minute of their last 'Come' and allow them no time for that spell.

21. And all clerks are to carry their respective time notes to the Accountant who is to cast up all their neatt spell of time in the Monitor's book and take out the loitering hours and the remainder is to be called the Monitor's Neat Time; and then he is to cast up his extra account of time that each party giveth of themselves. Then he is to take in each person's absent paper and see that the same time be not entred in the Monitor's account of time. If so, the Accomptant must subtract such time from their own paper of time and the remainder is to be the Corrected Extra Time, and when the Accountant hath done this he is upon the cheque sheet that comes that Saturday night to enter the totall of every person's

Monitor's Neat Time, that is what the Monitor maketh, and then what their own time paper maketh, in the following manner: -

|  | Hrs. | Mins. | Hrs. | Mins. |
|---|---|---|---|---|
| William Wright, Monitor's Neat |  |  | 48 | 06 |
| Extra Corrected | 10 | 0 | 58 | 06 |
| John Humpatch, Monitor's Neat | 70 | 0 | 70 | 0 |
| Robert Collins, Monitor's Neat | 80 | 0 | 80 | 0 |

under which the Accountant is to subscribe, 'I have truly given you the sundry heads of the paper delivered to me without any alteration or letting any person know how their account of time being incoherent with the Monitor's account of time. Robert Collins', a coppy of which he is to keep. And when the week's account for that service is compleated and sent to London, the Accountant is to draw up the account of time upon the State of Cash sheets that shall then be sent next to London, thus:

An account of time for 892 adjusted. The Monitor's and the extra account is put up in Cask 3742.

| William Wright's whole time | 70 | 07 at the hour |
|---|---|---|
| John Humpatch's whole time | 73 | 03 at the hour |
| Robert Collins' whole time | 60 | 00 at the hour |

'We do each respectively for ourselves acknowledge that we have received the sundry sums to our name and is in full of all charges and demands whatever to Friday night week 892, and declare we do not know of any time here charged by ourselves other but what is according to the true intent and meaning of your Monitor's Order No. 103, except what we have under our respective hands mentioned by indorsement on the backside this account of time and declaration'.

22. And when the perfect account of time is entred upon the State of Cash sheet, the Accountant is to carefully bundle up the Monitor's account, the Extra accounts, as they were originally made without coppying and see the same be packed with the next casks packed for London with such goods as shall be shipped by the next ship, to which papers the Accountant is to subscribe, 'I have kept these papers all in my custody since I had them and am sure no alteration hath been made'.

23. It is here ordered that no person shall have any time allowed them for being in company, in drinking with any person, although at that time they are doing my business.

24. It is further ordered that no person shall have any time allowed them for smoaking, although they are in my business at the same time.

25.That no person shall have any absent time allowed him without before that absent time he goeth to the Monitor's office and desire to be entred 'Runn '.

26.That no person upon time shall desire or demand or use any means to come to the knowledge of that time the Monitor have born them upon his account of time, except so farr back as the last 24 hours and no longer, till after the State of Cash where the first account is sent away by the Accountant.

27. If any person shall be employed in the service before 5 of the clock in the morning and after 9 at night, which ought not to be but upon case of necessity, they are in their absent papers to set forth in particulars the service they shall be doing in these unseasonable hours.

28. Whereas being informed that it hath been a common practice for clerks to charge me with time spent in drinking with persons, pretending the same was for proper [forwarding of] my interest, and have thereby most unjustly taken that for an excuse to extort from me moneys for [what] they have spent in unnecessary drinking even to the great neglect of my business. It is therefore by this order ordered that no time shall be allowed or charged that shall be spent in drinking. But it is possible at some time moderate drinking may be of use to the service and there may be a reason to consider such time, which shall never be otherwise than by a speciall direction from London grounded upon the allegation that shall be made upon the party's respective paper of absent time.

29. Whereas some people, under pretence that the Monitor hath done them injury, have in a most impudent manner threatened the Monitor with revenge or have used such discourse that the Monitor has been afraid to do his duty, and those threatening villains have thought thereby to cheat me of their time without controwle; for remedy whereof I do forbid any person or persons prying into how they are born upon the Monitor's book except they desiring to be answered to any for the last 24 hours, but if any

person hath just reason to believe the Monitor hath done them injury they are to get a voucher to take notice of their entring their coming and running, and when they shall find the Monitor do anything to their prejudice, to lay the matter before me or the Councill. And if any person in contempt of this order and justice shall threaten the Monitor or otherways upbraid him for justly executing his office, shall [pay] 2s. 6d. to the informer.

30. If any person shall think himself agrieved by having less time allowed him that he really hath performed, in such cases he is to make out his allegation to the Councill, who are to examine into the matter, and, finding his allegation to be true, are to order the same to be paid and charged to the next perfect account of time with the coppy of the alligation.

31. And whereas I have been informed that sundry clerks have been so unjust as to reckon by clocks going the fastest and the bell ringing before the hour for their going from business, and clocks going too slow and the bell ringing after the hour for their coming to business, and those two black traitors Fowell and Skellerne have knowingly allowed the same; it is therefore ordered that no person upon the account doth reckon by any other clock, bell, watch or dyall but the Monitor's, which clock is never to be altered but by the dock-keeper and then when all people are entred 'Runn', and absent time is ceaced.[16] Any superior officer, if he seeth an inferior to him be negligent or loytering or otherwise foolishly spending the time he standeth 'Come' in the Monitor's book, may and is required to go to the Monitor's account of time and enter or cause the Monitor to enter so long time loytering as the neglect shall in justice deserve.

32. To the end all clerks may have justice in what service they shall do unknown to the Monitor, absent papers are ordered to enter such service in, and the same is in a great measure left to the integrity of the clerk himself, and the same justice ought to be showed me. When the Monitor shall enter any person upon his book 'Come', and the person shall in any wise expend that time in any service foreign to my business and the true intent and meaning of this order, they are required on their extra paper to mention what time they so spent during their going upon their own

---

[16] Fowell was discharged in 1701. "Black traitor" and "rogue" iron keeper Francis Skellerne was dismissed after two months in 1701 for neglect of duty, a hardened villain whose treachery "had almost ruined the work." (Council Instruction 37, 19 September, 1701; Law 96, verse 3; Law 103, verse 31.).

business or account, and subtract the same from their own charge and bring to account only the remainder.

33. If any person whatsoever shall see any clerk or the cooper out of the Square, and hath reason to believe they are born upon the Monitor's book, they may demand of the Monitor his book, and in case they do not stand 'Runn', the informer shall have one shilling instantly by the Treasurer, and the person not entred 'Runn' debted for the same, without he maketh appear he did inform the Monitor of his going or was at the Monitor's office and he not present, then the Monitor to be debted for that one shilling.

34. Whereas the Monitor cannot by the direction of this order allow any person time while he is at meales or otherwise absent, without he seeth them in their respective offices at his return, yet where the said clerk cannot without prejudice to the service go to meals with the rest, may enter such time in his extra paper.

35. Whoever shall informe of any clerke or others upon the Monitor's book of time that shall enter extra time in his time book or paper when there is not a visible occasion or shall pretend services when it shall appear the same are not performed or if performed not in the time there mentioned, shall receive tenn shillings reward.

36. Notwithstanding any clause contained in this order or elsewhere, the Monitor may and it is hereby ordered that he allow all officers who have any business to perform one houre for their coming and going from or to Mill No. I or Swalwell, that is half an hour backward to the time they [leave] and half an hour forward to the time they go away.

37. If the Warekeeper or whoever else is Monitor at Winlaton, Manager at Bladen, Warden at Mill No. 1, Porter or Watchman at Swalwell, shall neglect every Monday to send or give the Accomptant at Swalwell a true coppy of all the goods each hath received for the foregoing weeks lawfully tested by two of the Councill, shall for each offence pay sixpence to the informer.

# LAW NUMBER 16

## Reckoning

**Whereas I have had great and grievous complaints of my workmen loseing much time for want of a regular method** and certain time of reckoning and the legall demanding the same; and having taken the same into my most serious consideration, and considering that the workmen's time is their livelihood and that they ought in justice to be speedily and cheerfully dispatcht, I do order: -

1.  That the Surveyor, Nailkeeper, Ironkeeper, Cashier, Warekeeper, and Accomptant shall give their constant attendance in their respective offices and not upon any pretence absent themselves the hours undermentioned, and till such longer time as they have dispatched all reckoners that hath before the expiration of the time here mentioned in an afternoon legally demanded a reckoning, viz., every Tuesday, Wednesday and Thursday from eight to twelve, from one to four; every Friday from eight to twelve and from one to seven; every Saturday from eight to twelve and from one to four. Upon no pretence whatever the officers above mentioned are to absent themselves from their offices except as is hereafter mentioned and not otherways.

2.  To the end the workmen may be att a certainty when to come and demand a reckoning, I do order that the bell is rung at the times before mentioned to begin to reckon, and att the expiration of the times of demanding of reckonings as aforesaid the bell be tolled, all which times to be reckoned by the Monitor's watch and not otherways.

3.  Att bell tolling att 12 all the officers may lock up (being they must come att one), although in the middle of a reckoning.

4.  The Nailkeeper may every Christmas Day and the two following days, Easter and Whitsun Mondays and Tuesdays, and every Court Day in the forenoon refuse to reckon, provided he be an Arbitrator, else not.

5.  The Nailkeeper may refuse to reckon from one man above three bundles of iron after six o'clock on a Friday and three o'clock on a Saturday.

6.  No workman is to reckon for himself or any under him above once in twenty-four hours.

7.  No oddware man may demand a reckoning on a Saturday.

8.  He that cometh with all his ware first in office hours and demands a survey, his ware is to be first surveyed.

9.  After any workman's ware is surveyed as aforesaid, he hath power within the hours mentioned to demand a reckoning, and he that demands a reckoning first is the first to be reckoned with, and so in course, never letting any have an undue preference in their reckoning by favour or prejudice.

10. Upon all reckoning notes where any ground ware is, the Surveyor is upon the reckoning notes to say 'grinder'.

11. If the Surveyor, Nailkeeper, Ironkeeper, Cashier, Warekeeper, or Accomptant shall be out of their respective offices in any of the hours before mentioned ordered for attendance (and not sick or ill at home), or shall wilfully or obstinately refuse or delay any workmen in their reckonings, the Arbitrators are to judge what such workmen might have reasonably gott in that time, which the person or persons so offending are presently to pay to the aggrieved persons or pay double cost.

12. Whereas I have found severall Surveyors, Nailkeepers, Iron keepers, Cashiers, Warekeepers and Accomptants have frequented alehouses and other houses from their offices in office hours pretending they would come when called, which hath proved the ruine of those sotts which practised the same, created many unnecessary quarrels and been of great prejudice to the work and workmen in generall; I do therefore, for preventing the said evils for the future, declare that if any of the before mentioned officers or their assistants shall be absent from their respective offices in attending hours otherways than as this law allows or by apparent sickness to be fully proved by the aggressor, shall pay five shillings to the informer which shall be deducted out of his next sallary.

13. Upon a shipping of nailes the nailkeeper may absent in attending or reckoning hours for so long as he is shipping and not longer, providing he doth not stay above four office houres for any one keell; and he is first to put up on the nail warehouse door in writing the hours of his going and the probability of his returning.

14. When the Nailkeeper shall make a proof he may then put a stop to reckoning hours Tuesday and Wednesday morning only, and no more.

15. The Ironkeeper upon his proof may put a stop to reckoning houres Tuesday and Wednesday and no longer, he having first directions from the Councell and giving four days' notice upon his office door.

16. Upon no sham or pretence the reckoning or attending hours are to be broken other than is here directed.

17. Any workman living out of the Parish of Ryton must reckon on a Friday or Saturday, but of all other reckoning houres they are to be dispatched in their reckonings before any that are not begun to be reckoned within the Parish of Ryton.[17]

18. Whereas every Saturday in the Cypher Week is an extraordinary busy day in setting the ten weeks' Collections; and preparing for the new demand, so it is here ordered that no workman shall demand a reckoning after twelve of the clock on a Saturday that shall be in the Cypher Week; and to the end that no workman may be disappointed in not reckoning in the afternoon, the Nailkeeper is every Monday of the Cypher Week to put up a paper in the nail warehouse with these words, 'This being the Cypher Week, none can demand a reckoning after 12 o'clock on Saturday next'.

19. When any Ironkeeper or Warekeeper surrendereth up their place and are not ordered by me to be done upon surprize, notice must be given by the new Ironkeeper or new Warekeeper att least four days before to signifye in writing the Monday it will begin, to the end workmen may be supplied for Monday, Tuesday and Wednesday which is to be the longest time the reckonings are to be stopt.

20. The Ironkeeper may refuse any workmen from coming into his iron warehouse till he hath dispatched those that have a right to reckon first.

21. When any officer shall absent by the authority of this law or otherways it shall not be allowed an excuse for any others to absent.

22. In case the Ironkeeper shall stop reckoning with any workman or

---

[17] See Law No. 86, "outworkmen".

workmen above twenty minutes for the taking, receiving in and stowing each fother of iron after the same shall come into the Square, such longer time shall be given to the workman for damage as in verse 11.

23. Whereas in verse I in this law it is ordered that the attending hours on. a Saturday shall terminate att 4 a clock, yet it hath been found that notwithstanding the time after four a clock was purely allowed to dispatch what other business was to be done to come away on Saturday night, the same hath been sundry times mispent and what business might have been done in due time hath been driven off till a very unseasonable time of the night and sometimes till 4 or 5 a clock on a Sunday morning. To prevent which it is ordered that if any of the attending officers mentioned in this law shall absent themselves from their respective offices after the reckoning houres on a Saturday above 40 minutes to be reckoned by the Monitor's account of time and not otherways till the full business shall be compleated that is to come away that post, or that two of the Councill then present shall certifie their attendance is not required, which said liberty is not to be taken [ until?] after 40 minutes past seven on the said Saturday night; and whoever shall offend in this shall pay half a week's sallary to the officers that doth attend, provided they do inform on or before Tuesday morning next following.

24. That either the Surveyor, his Assistant or the Nailkeeper write 'Surveyed', to which they must put their names to denote they have surveyed them.

25. That they enter what the workmen must make next upon the reckoning note, both for sort, size and quantity, together with the quality of iron he must take, as in Law 14, verse 15.[18] In case any Surveyor, Nailkeeper, Ironkeeper, Cashier, Storekeeper, Ware keeper, Accountant or their assistant, or any other officer or their assistant shall be at an alehouse or absent from their respective business or offices in attending hours otherwise than is allowed by Law 16, or shall at any time either in or out of office hours accept of any treat at the alehouse or anywhere else, or any other gratuity, fee or reward from a workman, or shall suffer a workman to pay more than their club, on information being made and the fact proved, shall pay 5s. to be deducted out of his next salary, one half of which shall go to the informer and the other half shall be brought to account in favour of Winlaton Poor. And for the more effectual

---

[18] There only remain ten verses in Law 14.

preventing the evils complained of, it is likewise ordered that if any one inform against a workman treating or bribing any officer or assistant in any manner whatsoever contrary to the intent and meaning of this order, the said workman so offending shall forfeit the sum of 2s. 6d., one half of which shall go to the informer and the other as above to Winlaton Poor. N.B. if any workman treat an officer, the said officer is at liberty to inform against the workman or the workman may inform against the officer, and is intitled to the reward as any other informer.

26. That the Ironkeeper never letteth them have more iron than will make the said ware, except when even barrs and bundles are too much, with a regard [not] to exceed a stock to last eight days, as in Law 14, verse 15.

27. In case the Ironkeeper shall reckon with any workman, that the note shall not be subscribed 'surveyed' as aforesaid, and the quantity and sort of ware they are to make next incerted, shall pay sixpence to the informer.

28. Notwithstanding anything contained in Law 14, verse 15, Law 23, verses 5 and 9, Law 45, verse 17, or anything contained before in this law where provision is made against the pernicious practice yet upon consideration that I have been so prodigious a sufferer by long reckonings, the product whereof has always been perpetual plagues either by ware contrary order, keeping faulty ware from my timely inspection, or the keeping of ware so long that oppertunities of shipping and sale of the goods has been lost, my customers disappointed and disobliged and the goods laid long dead on my hands to my great prejudice; therefore [that] I may the more effectually prevent this great evil for the future, I do order:-

29. That if any workmen be out above eight days before he bring in his ware to make a reckoning, that he be severely rebuked; but if above ten days before he brings in his ware to make a reckoning that his stock be reduced one third part; if he be out above fourteen days that he be abated over and above all other abatements one sixteenth part of his wages; if sixteen days then one twelfth of his wages; if above eighteen days, one eighth; if above twenty days one second; above 27 days three fourths; if above 31 days then all his wages.

30. But that no hardship may by this order be put upon my workmen when accidents do happen to prevent and put the due complyance herewith out of their power, such as sickness, lameness or the like, it is here provided that if any such accident happen, the workmen may send to and acquaint

the Surveyor with his present circumstances as soon as ever he finds himself disabled to reckon within the short time appointed, so that the Surveyor may take proper measures either by having what part is finished brought in, or what is begun finished by another, or by setting any other workman upon the work, or otherways as he sees necessary to answer his demand, with regard to his limited time and oppertunity of shipping. And the workman to be acquitted from any damages that afterwards happen by virtue of this order. But if the ten days are expired before he informs the Surveyor or cause him to be informed, for as many days as the time is ellapsed after the said ten days the penaltys to be good against the aggressors, and so farr be paid but no farther.[19]

31. But on consideration that the Governors are very oft called off from their work upon the Poor's concern, and those that work upon anchors and grapwells may sometimes be retarded in their reckonings, for which reason you are to allow them three days more in each particular than is allowed as aforesaid. (Sent in verse 12278 April 7th,1713).

32. The frequent complaints from the workmen of the Surveyors and other officers has caused an enquiry into the reason of it, which we find to be chiefly owing to their frequenting the alehouse and accepting of licar from the workmen, and is the cause of so much partiality and why one man has all the best of the work, and another the worst and is beyond expression injurious to the executors by their having a great deal of bad work made, and a great many goods contrary to order, the Surveyors for a pott of beer being so base as to skreen all things of that kind, or at least to lett them pass with little or no abatement.[20] And notwithstanding Law 16, verse 12, the executors are very credibly informed that a great many officers spend the greatest part of their time at the alehouse, come often drunk to the office, are ill-natured and abusive to the workmen, and evade the fine of five shillings by getting one of their own confederates to inform against them; we, therefore, with the approbation and direction of the executors, to prevent the like evils for the future, do order the undermentioned to be immediately put in force.[21]

---

[19] The remaining verses in this law are from a continuation inserted after Law 27 in the original, and may therefore be a later addition.
[20] The executors of John Crowley, suggesting that this verse was written or rewritten after his death in 1728.
[21] There follows a word-for-word repetition of verse 25 of this law, excluding the first and last sentences.

# LAW NUMBER 10

## Lending Forbid

**Whereas it hath been found by experience that the lending money** hath much distracted all proofs, been the occasion of much loss, made endless disputes, and created a great deal of trouble and disquiett to me and my business; I do therefore order: -

That no person whatever do lend at pay beforehand any of my money upon any account or pretence whatever, except as in verses 3, 4, and 6, or an order from me only. And where money so lent is charged, to mention the number of my letter where such leave is given or the number of the law where the same is allowed.

# THE WELFARE SERVICES

## LAW NUMBER 97

### Clerk for the Poor

**The raising and continual supporting of a stock to relieve such of my workmen and their families** as may be by sickness or other means reduced to that poverty as not to be able to support themselves without some assistance, the teaching of youth, and other matters of so great concerns are so incumbent upon us that there is no avoiding of a general contribution for the same. And considering there cannot be too safe a guard upon the money so charitably given by me and my workmen to secure it from the attempts of base designing persons, I have therefore for sundry reasons with the advice of the Arbitrators thought fitt to have the money so collected for the Poor to remain in my cash, to the end I may the better see how the same is applyed, as by Law 107 doth more fully appear, by which the Clerk for the Poor is prohibited from meddling with any cash, but the person that is to receive any moneys is to receive it directly from my Cashier and not otherwise. Notwithstanding which it is absolutely needfull that they have a clerk, and that he be qualified to perform the sundry following offices: -

1. He is to officiate in the duty of a clerk to the chappell and be obedient to the Chaplain in all matters thereunto relating, provided nothing be done or commanded contrary to the cannons of the Church of England and the laws and orders of the factory.

2. He is carefully to teach and instruct the workmen's children and to be governed by the following directions: - from the 29th. of September to the 25th. of March, from 8 in the morning till 12, and from I to 4 in the afternoon; and from the 25th. of March till the 29th. of September, from 6 till 11, and from 1 to 5, to be constantly in his school except Sundays and other days appointed by the Church be kept holy or by proclamation and the 12 days of Christmas, all Court days and what other day or days the Governors and Councill shall permit under their hands in writing.[22]

---

[22] This verse suggests that the Clerk for the Poor was the sole schoolmaster, however

3.  He shall not upon any account of races, cock-fightings, rope-dancers or stage players dismiss his scholars or any of them or absent himself, but shall constantly attend his school as aforesaid.

4.  He shall not without the consent of the Governors and two of the Councell give his scholars leave to play or absent himself above half an hour in any one day in school hours, except sickness or by permission as afforesaid.

5.  He shall carefully teach all his scholars that are capable of learning the Catechism of the Church of England as contained in the Book of Common Prayer.

6.  Every Court Day when the Unite is 8, he shall upon demand bring two or three lines of the writing of such of the workmen's children as are under his care and lay the same before the Governors that his conduct may the better be judged of.

7.  Upon notice of the Chaplain, he is to bring such of his scholars to be examined in publick about the catechism as are capable to say the same.

8.  He is to take care to make his scholars shew due respects to their superiors and especially aged persons, and to correct such as he finds guilty of lying, swearing or such like horrid crimes, but above all things set a good example before the children himself, example availing more than precept.

9.  He is at proper seasons to come to the office and endeavour to make himself master of the Poor's Account, to know our civil laws and orders, and not to think much for his information to ask any questions, for the wisest may learn, and there is not a rock upon which more have split than that of conceitedness to think he is too old to learn or too wise to be taught.

10. He is to carry it with an even hand to all his scholars, and not despise any for their poverty, but to encourage ingenuity and virtue in all of them and not discourage any by shewing more than ordinary favour or care to

---

Law 53, verse 35, mentions schoolmasters at Swalwell and Mill No. 1. The later law is probably a revised version drawn up during John Crowley's management (1713-28), indicating some expansion in the educational service.

such children whose parents may be able to be gratefull.

11. Every Monday in the evening after the account of the Poor's cash for the precedent week is made up in my books, the Poor Clerk is to come to the Cashier and demand the Collection Book for the awards, and carefully cast up what the Cashier hath made 'Received ' of any workmen or others in the Award Book, and compare the totall with what the Cashier makes himself debter for in 'Cash'; and finding the same agreeable to his addition, to put the two letters of his name in the Cash Book where 'Awards' hath the credit.

12. He is to see that the nailers' wages and clerks' and other salaries liable to pay the Poor be right, and to inspect into the Time Book and see that no deductions is made of any person that ought to pay. And when the neat money that is to pay to the Poor is made appear, he is to value the same at 9d. per pound or as the assessment at that time shall be, and see the Cashier hath carefully charged himself and credited the Poor with what he ought to do for that and all other money coming to the Poor, to which he is to put the two letters of his name as for the awards.

13. The Clerk is chearfully to enter all landlords their rents for houses and shops and see the same charged and collected according to the landlord and tennant's agreement.

14. He is carefully to observe Law 8, and see that rents have the preference of all awards.

15. He is not by any directions, cause or means whatever to make any preference in entering the payment of the court awards for debts, but is to let the same be paid in its proper course, as is directed in Law 61.

16. The Clerk is carefully to observe how the Cashier collecteth for the Poor, and if he find he hath not done his duty but paid the reckoner money without taking his due collections, he is instantly to acquaint the Governors who are hereby required to assemble and have the same inspected into; and [if they] find the Clerk in the right, the Cashier is to be debted for so much as the reckoner ought to have paid and the said reckoner creditted for the same as is directed in Law 24.

17. He is hereby authorized and required, as often as may be, to inspect into the Ironkeeper's delivering more iron to any workman that what is

allowed by the Stock List; and where he finds the Iron keeper hath been
guilty herein, he is presently to inform the Governors who are to see that
the Poor have justice and the Ironkeeper charged as is hereafter ordered.
And for the Clerk's encouragement to be carefull herein, the Ironkeeper
shall be obliged to pay 2d. for every 56 lbs. he shall so discover the
Ironkeeper hath delivered beyond the Stock List or what he hath
authentick notes for from the Committee of Survey as per Law 33, verse
5.

18.The Poor's interest wholly depending upon the preserving the
workmen's stocks from being run out and imbeazled, and considering
that those that are elected Arbitrators for the workmen ought to be
persons of such honesty and integrity to be examples to others in
industry, contrary to which in the late administration no less than three
of the five Governors were found guilty themselves of running out their
stocks and other high misdemeanors, which villainous contrivances was
carried on almost to the ruin of the publick stock and credit. The Clerk
is therefore, as often as possibly he can, to observe what workmen the
Governors or any of them are most inclined to favour, or if any of them
use any means to hide or evade to coming to light any person's faults
whatever, either by running out of stock, borrowing and lending, selling
of iron or iron wares in breach of law, or any other clandestine way or
means what- ever, or if he finds or believeth there is more friendship
between the Governors or any of them and any of the workmen, he is
not to fail but communicate the same to one of my Councill who is to
inspect into the matter and fairly and fully lay the same before me.

19. The Poor's Box having per the greatest of villainies and base practices
of those appointed Governors suffered to that degree that no less than
the whole factory, my workmen and their families' utter ruin lay at stake,
and the Ironkeeper less at liberty to debt the Poor for what iron was so
felloniously conveyed away amongst them, the Ironkeeper by trusting
them more stock than allowed, the Governors and workmen
confederating together and imbezling the same, and a great assessment
upon me and my well disposed workmen to repay the same. To prevent
which for the future, the Clerk is carefully and stedfastly to observe Law
51, and not suffer the Poor to be charged with any iron or stock run out
but what is certified by the certificates as is there mentioned.

20. To the end the Clerk may more strictly observe his duty in seeing the
Poor hath justice done in what's charged upon that account, it is ordered

that as soon as any workmen's stock is tryed and found wanting, he is to inspect into the Iron Book and see that the party found out of stock hath not more iron than allowed by the Stock list. If not, he is to draw certificates for the iron wanting for the Governors to sign, and when signed, to deliver the same to one of the Councill (other than the Ironkeeper or a Governor), who is to inspect into the Governors' management in that certificate. But if the Ironkeeper have broke the laws by delivering more iron than the Stock List, or after the 8th. day, without the Surveyor's note as Law 33 directs, and that no loss is sustained thereby, the Clerk is then to draw up the same in the following manner, and lay it before the Governors: -

Account 1220, April 1st, 1709

Danll. Luckcock's stock was tryed and found in hand 42 lbs.

| His allowance in the Stock List | 56 lbs. |
|---|---|
| Found in hand as before | 42 lbs |
| | |
| Poor to be debted with | 14 lbs. |
| The Ironkeeper's stock is | 112 lbs. |
| Allowed by the Stock List but | 56 lbs. |
| | |
| The Ironkeeper debtor to | 56 lbs. |
| The Poor debtor as before to | 14 lbs. |
| | |
| For which iron in the Ironkeeper's hands is credited | 70 lbs. |

21. And whereas the late Governors were notoriously wicked in running out their stocks and having a power to discharge the Clerk and by that means might keep him in subjection and oblige him to stifle their evil actions; for remedy I do order that no person shall discharge the Clerk during his not being guilty of the breach of these laws and what other laws shall be made with my approbation.

22. And whereas in verse II of this law it is ordered that the Clerk every Monday in the evening shall examine the Collection Book for the Poor and awards for the precedent week to the end the same may be complyed with, it is ordered that every Monday (when no shipping or Ironkeeper's proof is begun that day), in case the Cashier shall not have his accounts adjusted by 7 of the clock that night, he shall pay the Clerk 2d. But if the

Cashier shall make it appear under the hand of two of the Councill other than himself within 24 hours that it was the Nailkeeper's fault and that he had done his part, in such cases the Nailkeeper is to repay the Cashier what he shall have paid to the Clerk as aforesaid.

23. The Clerk on the days hereafter mentioned is to read the respective laws, in order to which he is obliged to ring or cause to be rung at 8 of the clock in the forenoon the bell for one quarter of an hour to give notice of the same, and then in the Poor's Room to command silence and in an audible manner to read the laws appointed to be read that day.

24. To the end no workmen may be corrupted or ensnared by ill designed persons and afterwards plead ignorance in the laws, and that all people may be the better enabled to be knowing and skillfull therein and be sensible of the many advantages that attend all orderly and sober persons in the work, it is ordered that every Court Day, the 26th December, and on Whitsun Monday, the Clerk of the Poor in the Poor's Room as afforesaid read the following laws;- on the 26th. of December, if not on a Sunday, and if on a Sunday then on the 27th., and also on Whitsun Monday: Law No. 35, 37, 38, 42, 43, 44, 46, 47, 53, 56, 57, 59, 62, 63, 69, 71, 73, 74, 76, 90, 94, 97, 99, 101,105.[23] On Court Day next before the 29th. of May, the narrative is to be read.[24] When the Court Day is in the Unit 3, shall be read the following Laws, viz:- Law No. 6, 7, 8, 9, IO, II, 13, 15, ID, 17, 19, 23, 24, 27, 32, 33, 34, 36, 40, 45, 48, 49, 50, 51, 52, 53, 54, 55, 61, 62, 64, 72, 74, 80, 81, 92 verse 19, 96, 97, 99, 108, 69, 70 verses u, 16, 17, 21, 22, 23, 24, 25 to 36, 37, 42.[25] When the Court Day is in the Unit 8, shall be read the following laws, viz:- Law No. 8, 9, 10, 12, 23, 28, 34, 39, 44, 45, 61, 62, 63, 64, 74, 99, 102, io4, 15, 16, 17, 19, 22, 23, 24, 48, 49, 50, 51, 52, 53, 55, 78, Bo, 85, 90, 96, 97, 98.[26]

25. And in case the Clerk of the Poor shall willfully neglect or re- fuse to read the said laws at the place: and on the days and times before mentioned, or shall wilfully leave out or otherwise alter the true intent and meaning of the said laws or any part of them, shall for each offence

---

[23] Of these laws, Nos. 76, 90 and 94 are no longer extant. The remaining laws, however, include well over 40,000 words, so that the reading of these laws can hardly have taken less than four or five hours!

[24] Nothing is known of the narrative mentioned here.

[25] Of these laws, Nos. 92 and 108 are no longer extant.

[26] Of these laws, Nos. 78, 90, 98 and 102 are no longer extant.

pay five shillings to the informer.

26. And whereas I have found many times that honest informers, by making their informations to the Governors or some of my officers, have oftentimes not only been slighted and disappointed instead, of cruelties put upon them as the malice of the said officers could invent though their information was apparently true; I do therefore order that for the future all information be made to the Clerk of the Poor, who is cheerfully to receive and encourage, dispatch and stand by the said honest informers. In order to which I do order the Clerk of the Poor to have a book for that purpose, wherein he is to enter the name of the informer, the name of the offender and the day and hour with the crime, without aggravating or mitigating the same or any part thereof, and the first entered must be accounted the informer; and if the Clerk shall neglect or refuse entring the said informations above half an hour, shall forfeit and pay to the said informer 5s. for such his neglect.

27. The Clerk is not to receive any reward, treat or gratuity for entring down any information.

28. The Clerk is not permitted to have any action or award in the court upon his own account against any person, unless by the con- sent and permission of the five Governors, and then he is to charge himself with usual fees for the use of the Poor.

29. Every Monday morning when the Unit is 3 and 8, the Clerk is to put up in the nail warehouse in the most visible place a declaration in these words: 'On Wednesday next at a quarter past 8 in the forenoon, the laws will he publickly read in the Poor's Room, and being Court Day the undermentioned causes will be heard and determined by the Arbitrators: -
    A.B. Plaintiff;  C.D. Defendant
    E. F. Plaintiff;  G.H. Defendant
And so mention all the names of the plaintiffs and defendants of all the causes that are to be heard that day.

30. And whereas it hath been a practice by former Clerks to enter sundry persons' debts into the Poor's Book that hath no right to the same and thereby let the workmen take up goods at any rate to bring them into debt, the persons that trust them think if it be but entered in the Poor's books the publick stock is obliged to pay the same, which hath much disturbed the Poor's account and brought a scandall upon the publick by being

ingaged in a debt which does not belong to them; it is therefore ordered that the Clerk shall not enter into his or the Poor's Book any money due from any workman to any person whatever (except for rent and what is awarded in court by the Arbitrators, or where I may have occasion to give some particular directions).

31. Upon the same sheet where the particulars of the Poor's account is entered to be sent to me, the Clerk is not to fail entring the proceeding where I am plaintiff.

32. And to the end I may be fully satisfied that the Clerk hath done his duty in reading the sundry laws and verses of laws in the said respective days afore-mentioned, he is upon the said sheet of the Poor's account to enter the number of the law and part of the law he did read on the Court Day last past on the following manner:- 'On Wednesday being Unit 8, November 12th., 1708, at 8 of the clock in the forenoon in the Poor's Room were publickly by me read Law 16, 24, 33, 34 (from verses I to 18), etc.,' 'till all the laws he did read be enumerated and then to subscribe his name.

33. The afore-mentioned Clerk's salary to be 5s. 6d. per week, and upon his diligence and care in the Poor's concerns the Governors may award him as a gratuity any sum not exceeding 10s. in any one ten weeks, setting forth their reason at the same time what moved them to allow the said gratuity notwithstanding Law 49, verse 15, or any other law to the contrary.

34. Whereas some Clerks have entred accounts in the Court against Sir Ambrose Crowley's Surveyors, officers and other clerks at the suit of workmen relating to their reckonings upon the account of Sir Ambrose Crowley, when the workmen in such cases can have no other relief than by appealing to the Councill or to Sir Ambrose Crowley in setting forth their case in writing upon or with the labells sent with the said goods it is therefore ordered that if the Clerk shall enter or suffer any account to be brought against any Surveyor or officers for observing their laws, orders, instructions, directions or remarks, shall forfeit and pay to the defendant his whole charge and 12d. for his trouble.[27] But it is here provided that nothing by this is intended to put a stop to any action that shall be brought by any workman against any Surveyor, officer or clerk for being absent in office hours, or for giving any reckoner an undue preference, or for any

---

[27] This procedure is set out in Law 26.

personall abuse, or for the breach of any law, order, instruction or direction whatever whereby the workman is prejudiced.

35. In case the Clerk should absent himself from his duty contrary to verse 4 in this law, or at any other time without the licence of three of the Councill first had and obtained, shall for each offence pay 5s., one half of which is to be paid into the Poor's account and the other to the informer.

## CHAPLAIN'S ORDER NUMBER 105

**Whereas I have considered the cruelty of my clerks to my workmen** in not giving that attendance and dispatch they ought and govern them with that rigor that few of them durst complain of their aggrievances; to prevent such evils for the future, the minister being or ought to be a person that will boldly plead the oppressed's cause and see that his flock neither wanteth spirituall nor temporal assistants, and the better to enable the minister to perform so good a work, I do determine that the minister for the time being till attainted with unjust practices or breach of Arbitrators' [Law] No. 49, verses 1-20, to be Chief Governour and Arbitrator. And to the end he may be no ways byassed as some clerks moved for their paying separate would attempt, it's therefore ordered: -

1. That the minister shall not receive any benefit in any fine whatsoever from any clerck or officer belonging to me.

2. The minister shall every Wednesday in the year be in the Court Room or some other fixed place by 10 of the clock and on Court Days to tarry till the Court is over, and on all other Wednesdays to hear all reasonable complaints of the workmen, and do all that in him lyeth to help the injured and oppressed; and if the aggressors be obstinate and fair means will not prevail, to order the Clerk [of the Poor] to put them in the Court, and if anything extraordinary to lay the same before me.

3. That the minister doth at spare times read all the civill orders and to well consider them and lay before me what alterations he thinketh may make them more useful to maintain justice, keep the peace, and to relieve the injured and to punish vice and disorders, and communicate the same to the Councill and the Governours, and take their opinions and then lay the same before me.

4. For the reasons mentioned in Councill Letter OZ, it is ordered that the Chaplain shall pay the same pound rate as the clerks and workmen shall from time to time to pay.

5. For the reasons mentioned in Councell Letter OZ, it 1s ordered and declared that the Chaplain for the time being shall not receive any present or gratuity of any kind whatever from any person that in consideration of their hearing him in the chappell or their having a seat of any kind whatever in the chappell, but shall do his best to provoke them to give to the publick. And in consideration of the Chaplain being debarred of the countrey's assistance, he is to have four shillings a week, which is to be comprized in his agreement.

6. The Chaplain, as oft as desired by Sir Ambrose Crowley or his successors or his or their Councell, is to goe and negotiate his or their affairs to the best of his skill and judgement, he or they allowing him reasonable charges, but noe allowance for time.

7. It is ordered and agreed that the Chaplain is to have sixpence every time it is his turn and he doth audit the Poor's account as is in Order No. 107, verse 15, directed. Alsoe it is agreed that the Chaplain is to have twopence per hour while in Court on a Court Day, as in Order 49, verse 21, and without breach of his order and agreement.

8. It is ordered that the Chaplain shall reside in Winlaton and not ingage himself to do the office of a minister in any other place, except by now and then serving neighbouring ministers as they may [request].

9. It is for the reasons mentioned in Councell Letter PA, dated 11th. December, 1707, ordered and declared, that if the minister shall appoint any General Assembly or shall by himself or any other person gett any paper signed relateing to himself or his successors, the Chaplain shall be discharged, and such papers of subscription is declared void and of noe effect.

10. The Chaplain is to read prayers as is directed by the Church of England established by law every Sunday in the fore and afternoon, every Wednesday and Friday, and such holy days as shall be agreed upon between the Chaplain and Governors; to preach every Sunday twice, except in the forenoon when the Governors or Councell shall permite of the youth being chatechized, and a homily to be read; to preach [a]

sermon the Wednesday before a sacrament day; to preach on such holy days as shall be agreed upon between the Chaplain and Governors; to visitt the sick, and rebuke vice and promote vertue, and other occasionall offices of his duty.

[End.]

.

# MSS photographs

Law Number 3: Expenses and Extravigant

Law Number 4: Articles to be Valued Distinct

Index for the Laws

Law Number 1: Proof of spy

The author is pleased to record his gratitude to the staff of the Manuscript Room of the British Library, St Pancras, London for permission to photograph and reproduce here the images presented on the next four pages.

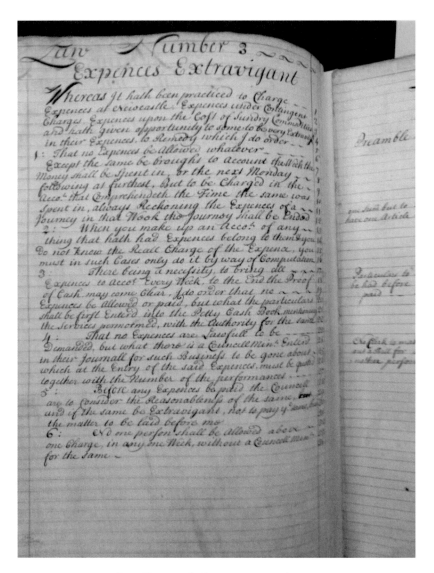

**Law Number 3: Expenses Extravigant**
[Photographed by the author.]

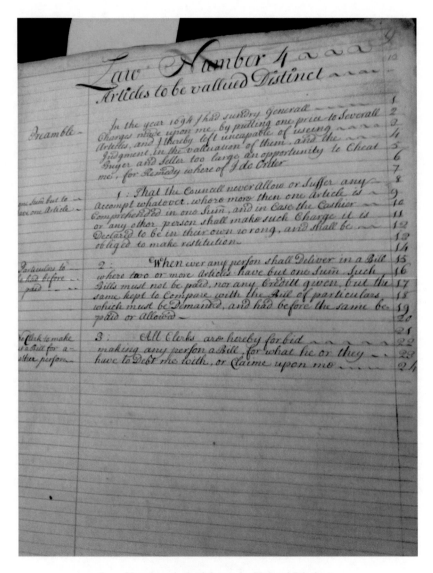

**Law Number 4: Articles to be Valued Distinct**
[Photographed by the author.]

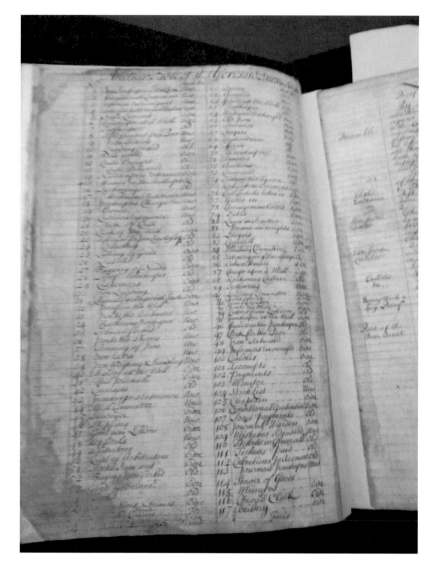

**Index for The Law Book of the Crowley Ironworks**
[Photographed by the author.]

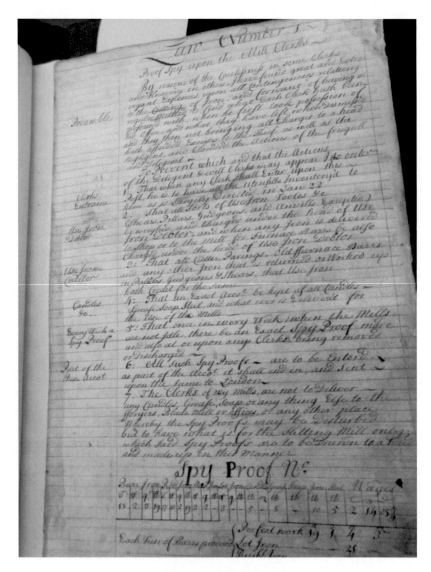

**Law Number 1: Proof of Spy**
[Photographed by the author.]

**Espionage Note:**

The Crowleys were correct to be concerned about espionage, and take precautions; spy-proofing taking first place in their domestic legislation indicative.

The image of the 1893 Winlaton Mill Great Pool in the Ambrose Crowley Case Study (1) is taken from *Crowley's,* a publication from the Land of Oak and Iron Trust, which carries extracts from an 18th century diary written by a Swedish ironmaster. *Illustrated Travel Diary, 1753-1755: Industry in England and Wales from a Swedish perspective*, was written by Angerstein, R, trans. Berg, Torsten and Peter, reproduced by the Science Museum London in 2001.

The state institutions regulating the Swedish iron industry at the time had become concerned with perceived threats to their supremacy as the main exporter of bar-iron to Britain, and Angerstein consequently conducted a detailed investigation into the iron industry of England and Wales - and notably the Crowley enterprise -  producing figures on such matters as worker payments, manufacture process, and the weights of various goods; the whole report providing a forensic dissection of the Crowley  business. For example:

"In the anchor forges, of which there are three at Swalwell, all work is done by hand, and there are generally six to seven sturdy men in each forge, who are either paid by the day, when they earn 9 to 12, 12 to 14 shillings a week, or by the cwt or £3 per ton, when the anchors are smaller. Anchors of every size are made, from 1 cwt to 74 cwt in weight. The three anchor forges together use 6 to 7 tons of Swedish iron per week from Gothenburg. I was told that anchors weighing 5 tons are only made for naval ships in wartime…

Iron rolled into strip is used for hinges, both large and small, and sold to the smiths at 22 shillings a cwt or £22 a ton. The finished hinges are sold back to the factory for 7 pence a pound…

The bar-iron forge can produce 250 tons a year, using English and American pig iron, but the slitting mill has a capacity of 500 tons of iron per year, provided there is no shortage of water…

At Winlaton there are two workshops for axes. A smith is paid 4 pence a dozen for forging file blanks of 1lb in weight or thereabouts."

The "Spy Proof" notation at the foot of the manuscript *Law Number 1*, above, was a clearly justified defence, based on an accounting code and cypher system, presumably of Crowley invention. Espionage regarding internal discipline and the external extraction of private data was a growing feature of industrial management.

# BIBLIOGRAPHY

Adams, Douglas. 2004. *The Restaurant at the End of the Universe*. London: Pan.

Adams, Max. 2014. *The King of the North The Life and Times of Oswald of Northumbria*. London: Head of Zeus.

Adkins, Lesley, and Adkins, Roy A, 1994. *Handbook to Life in Ancient Rome*. Oxford and New York: Oxford University Press.

d'Alembert, Jean le Rond, trans. Schwab, Richard N. 1995. *Preliminary Discourse to the Encyclopedia of Diderot*. Chicago and London: University of Chicago Press.

Alsop, J D. "The Age of the Projectors: British Imperial Strategy in the North Atlantic in the War of Spanish Succession." (Autumn 1991): 30-53: https://journals.lib.unb.ca/index.php/Acadiensis/article/download/11899/12743 .

Amann, Wolfgang and Goh, Jenson, eds. 2017. *Phronesis in Business Schools: Reflections on Teaching and Learning,* Greenwich, United States: Information Age Publishing.

Amos, S W. 1971. "Social discontent and Agrarian disturbances in Essex 1795-1850." Durham University Theses Online: http://etheses.dur.ac.uk/10399/.

Aquinas, St Thomas. 1269–72. *Summa Theologica, Prudence:* https://www.newadvent.org/summa/3047.htm

Aristophanes, trans. Sommerstein, Alan H. 2003. *Lysistrata and Other Plays.* London: Penguin.

Aristophanes, trans. Barrett, David. 2007. *Frogs and Other Plays.* London: Penguin.

Aristotle, trans. Sinclair, T A and Saunders, Trevor J . 1981. *The Politics*: London: Penguin.

Aristotle, trans. Ross, David and Brown, Lesley. 2009 . *The Nichomachean Ethics*. Oxford and New York: Oxford University Press.

Astell, Mary, 1700, *Some Reflections Upon Marriage, Occasioned by the Duke and Duchess of Mazarine's Case; Which is Also Considered,* London: Printed for John Nutt, near Stationers-Hall: http://digital.library.upenn.edu/women/astell/marriage/marriage.html.

Aurelius, Marcus. 1997. *Meditations*. London: Penguin Classics.

Bailey, Joanne. 2007."Reassessing parenting in eighteenth-century England" in ed. Helen Berry and Elizabeth Foyster, *The Family in Early Modern England.* Cambridge and New York: Cambridge University Press.

Barber, Richard. 2014. *Edward III and the Triumph of England.* London: Penguin.

Baumard, Nicolas *et al.* "Increased Affluence Explains the Emergence of Ascetic Wisdoms and Moralising Religions." *Current Biology,* Volume 25,(January 2015), 10-15. https://dx.doi.org/10.1016/j.cub.2014.10.063.

Beard, Mary. 2015. *SPQR A History of Ancient Rome.* London: Profile Books.

Bernstein, William J. 2008. *A Splendid Exchange How Trade Shaped the World.* New York: Grove Press.

Bible: *Chronicles, Ecclesiastes, Esther, Psalms, Philippians.*

Bisschop, W R. 2018. *The Rise of the London Money Market 1640 – 1826.* London: Forgotten Books Classic Reprint.

Boesche, Roger. 2003. *The First Great Political Realist: Kautilya and His Arthashastra,* New York: Lexington Books.

Booker, Christopher. 2006. *The Seven Basic Plots: Why We Tell Stories.* London: Continuum.

Boorn, GPF van den. 2013. *Duties of the Vizier.* London and New York: Routledge.

Bowman, John Frederick. April 2018. *The Iron and Steel Industries of the Derwent Valley. A Historical Archaeology.* Ph.D. Thesis. Newcastle University School of History, Classics and Archaeology. url: http://theses.ncl.ac.uk/jspui/handle/10443/4427.

Boyer, Carl B. 2011, *A History of Mathematics.* Hoboken, New Jersey: John Wiley & Son.

Braudel, Fernand. 1975. *Capitalism and Material Life 1400-1800.* Glasgow: Fontana.

Brearley, Mike. 1985. *The Art of Captaincy.* London: Hodder and Stoughton.

Brech, E.F.L. 2002. *The Evolution of Modern Management,* Bristol: Thoemmes Press.

Byron, Lord. 2011. *Ode to Napoleon Buonaparte*, Fourth Edition. London: British Library, Historical Print Editions.

Carney, Brian W and Getz, Isaac. 2009 (revised 2015). *Freedom Inc.* New York: Crown Business.

Casson, Lionel. 1998. *Everyday Life in Ancient Rome.* Baltimore and London: Johns Hopkins University Press.

Cato, trans. Dalby, Andrew. 2010. "On Farming", *De Agricultura.* Totnes, Devon, UK: Prospect Books.

Chandler A D Jr. 1977. *The Visible Hand: The Managerial Revolution in American Business.* Cambridge, Mass.: Harvard University Press.

Chien, Ssu-ma. 2000. "An Introduction to Economics" from "Biographies of Merchants and Industrialists," cited in Moore, Karl & Lewis, David, *Foundations of Corporate Empire.* London: Financial Times/Prentice Hall.

Cicero, trans. May, James M, Wise, Jakob. 2001. *On the Ideal Orator (De Oratore)*, New York: Oxford University USA.

Clarke, Andrew, ed. 1898 *'Brief Lives', chiefly of Contemporaries, set down by John Aubrey, between the Years 1669 & 1696.* Oxford: Clarendon Press.

Colbert, Elizabeth. 2022. *Under a White Sky*, London: Vintage.

Collingridge, Vanessa. 2003. *Captain Cook: The Life, Death and Legacy of History's Greatest Explorer.* London: Ebury Press.

Comenius, Johann Amos, trans. Keatinge, M W. 1907. *Didactica Magna.* London: Adam and Charles Black. pdf accessed Cornell University Library: http://www.archive.org/details/cu31924031053709.

*Confucius,* trans. Chin, Annping. 2014. *The Analects.* New York: Penguin.

Cranfield, Richard. 1844. *Memoir of Thomas Cranfield of London.* Boston: Massachusetts Sabbath Society.

Darke, Diana. 2020. *Stealing from the Saracens: How Islamic Architecture Shaped Europe.* London: Hurst.

Davidson, James, 2016. *Courtesans and Fishcakes: The Consuming Passions of Classical Athens.* London: Fontana.

Davies, Norman. 1996. *Europe: A History.* London: The Bodley Head.

Defoe, Daniel 1887, *An Essay Upon Projects*, Project Gutenberg eBook, transcribed from the Cassell& Company 1887 version: www.gutenberg.org/files/4087/4087h-/4087-h.htm.

Dicksee, Lawrence Robert, *The True Basis of Efficiency.* 1922, reprinted London: Forgotten Books 2018.

Drucker, Peter F. 1976. "The Coming Rediscovery of Scientific Management." [New York] *Conference Board Record*, June 1976, reprinted in Drucker, Peter F, *Toward the Next Economics and other essays*, pp 97- 108. 2010. Boston, Mass.: Harvard Business Press.

Drucker, Peter F. 1989. *The New Realities*, New York: Harper and Row.

Eliot T S, 1973. *Murder in the Cathedral*, London: Faber & Faber.

Encyclopedia Iranica, *Education In the Achaemenid Period*, Vol. VIII, Fasc.2, pp 178-179 quoting Posener, G *La premiere domination Perse en Egypte.* 1936. Cairo: Honoré Champion.

Evelyn, John. 2012. *The Diary of John Evelyn, Vol. I*. Project Gutenberg e-book #41218, 29 October 2012: https://www.gutenberg.org/files/41218/41218-h/41218-h.htm.

Finley, M I. 1999. *The Ancient Economy*. Oakland CA: UC Press.

Fisher, H A L. 1960. *A History of Europe*. London: Fontana Library.

Fitzgerald, Edward, trans. 1938. *The Rubáiyát of Omar Khayyám*. London and Glasgow: Collins Library of Classics.

Flinn, M W ed. 1957. *The Law Book of the Crowley Ironworks,* Publication of the Surtees Society, Vol. CLXVII for the year M.CM.LII. Durham: Andrews and Co, and London: Bernard Quaritch.

Flinn, M W. 1962. *Men of Iron*. Edinburgh: University of Edinburgh.

Follett, Mary Parker. 2013. *Dynamic Administration: The Collected Papers of Mary Parker Follett*. Eastford, CT USA: Martino Fine Books.

Fox, Robin Lane. 2006. *The Classical World.* London: Penguin.

Frankopan, Peter. 2016. *The Silk Roads*. London and New York: Bloomsbury.

Fraser, Sir James George. 1890. *The Golden Bough.* www.digireads.com.

Frederick, Christine.1913. *New Housekeeping: Efficiency Studies in Home Management*. Garden City New York: Doubleday Page and Company.

Frye, Richard N. 1996. *The Golden Age of Persia*. New York: Barnes & Noble.

Fung, Yu Lan. 1931, reprinted 1989. *Chuang Tzu A Taoist Classic*. Beijing: Foreign Language Press.

Galassi, G. (1996) "Pacioli, Luca c.1445-1517", in eds. Chatfield, M. and Vangermeersch, R., *History of Accounting: An International Encyclopedia,* New York: Garland Science, Norton 2012.

Gilbreth, Frank B. 1911. *Motion Study: A Method for Increasing the Efficiency of the Workman*. New York: D. Van Nostrand Co.

Goodman, Martin. 2008. *Rome and Jerusalem*, Penguin: London.

Graves, Robert. 1955. *The Greek Myths*. Penguin: London.

Guisepi, Robert, ed. 2014. *The History of Education*, International World History Project, history-world.org/history_of_education.htm.

Guisepi, Robert. ed. *The History of Education*, World History Encyclopedia: https://www.worldhistory.org/edu.

Guy, John. 2019. *Gresham's Law: The Life and World of Queen Elizabeth I's Banker*, London: Profile Books.

Halacy, Daniel Stephen. 1970. *Charles Babbage, Father of the Computer*. New York: Crowell-Collier Press.

Handy, Charles B. 2020. *Gods of Management, The Four Cultures of Leadership*. London: Profile Books

Harari, Yuval Noah. 2015. *Sapiens: A Brief History of Humankind*. London: Vintage.

Harris, Edward M *et al*. ed., 2015. *The Ancient Greek Economy: Markets, Households and City-States*. Cambridge: Cambridge University Press.

Heather, Peter. 2014. *The Restoration of Rome*. London: Pan Books.

Herodotus, trans. Rawlinson, George. *The Histories*. London: Everyman.

Hobbes, Thomas, Malcolm, Noel ed. 2012. *Leviathan*, Vol X111. Oxford: Oxford University Press.

Holland, Tom. 2005. *Persian Fire*. London: Abacus.

Holland, Tom. 2009. *Millennium,* London: Abacus, 2009.

Holland, Tom. 2010. *The Forge of Christendom,* London: Anchor Books.

Holland, Tom 2013. *In the Shadow of the Sword.* London: Abacus.

Homer, trans. Hammond, Martin. 1987. *The Iliad*. London: Penguin.

Homer, trans. Rieu, E V, Rieu, D C H. 2003. *The Odyssey.* London: Penguin.

Hoopes, James. 2008. *Hail to the CEO: The Failure of George W Bush and the Cult of Moral Leadership*. Westport, CT: Praeger.

Horne, Charles F, ed. 1917. *The Sacred Books and Early Literature of the East, Volume XII: Medieval China*. New York: Parke.

Hough, Richard. 1994. *Captain James Cook*. London: Hodder and Stoughton.

Houston, R A. 2002. *Scottish Literacy and Scottish Identity: Illiteracy and Society in Scotland and Northern England, 1600-1800*, Cambridge: Cambridge University Press.

Houston, Stephen D, ed. 2004. *The First Writing: Script Invention as History and Process,* Cambridge: Cambridge University Press.

Huitson, John. 1985. *A Plan For Education: the British and Foreign School Society and Elementary Education in England and Wales 1814-1870*, unpublished MS, Bath, 1985, copies held at Brunel University Archives and at IBDEA, Low Fell, Gateshead.

Juvenal, ed. and trans. Green, Peter. 1998. *The Sixteen Satires: Revised edition*, London: Penguin.

Kahneman, Daniel. 2012. *Thinking Fast and Slow.* London: Penguin.

Kahneman, Daniel, Sibony, Olivier, Sunstein, Cass R. 2021. *Noise*. London: William Collins.

Kautilya, ed. and trans. Rangarajan L N. 2016. *The Ashastrata*. Gurgaon, Haryana: Penguin India.

Kendall, Guy. 1939. *Robert Raikes*. London: Nicholson and Watson.

Khaldûn, Ibn, trans. Rosenthal, Franz. 2015. *The Muqaddimah*. Princeton NJ and Woodstock, Oxfordshire, UK: Princeton University Press.

Kirby, M W. 1984. *Men of Business and Politics*. London: George Allen and Unwin.

Koch, Richard. 1997. *The 80/20 Principle*. London and Boston MA: Nicholas Brealy.

Kyle, Bruce. "Henry S Dennison, Elton Mayo and Human Relations Historiography", *Management & Organisational History*, 2006, 1: 177–199.

Kynaston, David. 2002. *City of London 1815–2000*. London: Chatto and Windus.

Landels, J G. 1978. *Engineering in the Ancient World*, Berkeley, CA: University of California Press.

Leeson Peter T and Russ, Jacob W . "Witch Trials," *Economic Journal*, Volume 128, Issue 613, (2018): 2066–2105. https://doi.org/10.1111/ecoj.12498.

Locke, John. 2016. *Some Thoughts Concerning Education*. Cambridge University Press 1980.  Retrieved 28 July 2016 via Google Books. London: A and J Churchill at the Black Swan at Paternoster-row. https://books.google.co.uk/books/about/Some_Thoughts_Concerning_Education.html?id=sXw7pa7Fd_QC&redir_esc=y.

Lynn, Michael R. 2016. *Experimental Physics in Enlightenment Paris: The Practice of Popularization in Urban Culture,* Ch. 4, in eds. Bensaude-Vincent, Bernadette and Blondel, Christine. *Science and Spectacle in the European Enlightenment*. Oxford and New York: Routledge.

MacGregor, Neil. *Living with the Gods*. 2019. London: Penguin.

Machiavelli, Niccolò, trans. George Bull. 1995. *The Prince*. London: Penguin.

Mair, Victor H. 1994. *Wandering on the Way: Early Taoist Tales and Parables of Chuang-Tsu.* New York: Bantam Books.

Man, John. 2005. *Genghis Khan,* London: Bantam.

Martial, trans. Wills, Gary. 2007 *Epigrams*. London: Viking Penguin.

Masood, Ehsan. 2017. *Science and Islam A History*. London: Icon Books.

Mayo, Elton. 1933. *The Human Problems of an Industrial Civilization*. London: Macmillan.

Mayo, Elton. 1945. *The Social Problems of an Industrial Civilization*. Boston: Harvard University Press.

McKeon, Richard, ed. 2001 *The Basic Works of Aristotle.* New York: Modern Library.

McLynn, Frank. 2012. *Captain Cook: Master of the Seas*. New Haven CT and London: Yale University Press.

Merriman, Roger Bigelow. 1944. *Suleiman the Magnificent, 1520-1566.* Cambridge, Massachusetts: Harvard University Press.

Mintzberg, Henry. 1973. *The Nature of Managerial Work*. New York: Harper and Row.

Mintzberg, Henry. 2013. *Simply Managing*. Oakland CA USA: Berrett-Kohler.

Mintzberg, Henry, Ahlstrand, Bruce, Lampel, Joseph. 2009. *Strategy Safari Your Complete Guide Through The Wilds Of Strategic Management,* Second edition. Harlow, UK: Pearson Education.

Montefiore, Simon Sebag. 2017. *The Romanovs,1613-1918*. London: Weidenfeld & Nicholson.

Moore, Karl and Lewis, David. 2000. *Foundations of Corporate Empire*. Edinburgh and London: Financial Times/Prentice Hall/Pearson Education.

Morrison, J S, Coates, J F, Rankov, N B. 2000 *The Athenian Trireme*. Cambridge: Cambridge University Press.

Newman, Dina "Alexei Stakhanov: The USSR's superstar miner," *BBC World Service Magazine*, 30 December 2015. https://www.bbc.co.uk/news/magazine-35161610.

Nobles, Bill and Staley, Paul. *Freedom-Based Management*, www.42projects.org/docs/Freedom-BasedManagement.

Nobles, Bill and Staley, Paul. 2017. *Questioning Corporate Hierarchy*. Freedom Press.

Nonaka, Ikujiro and Takeuchi, Hirotaka. "The Big Idea: The Wise Leader," *Harvard Business Review,* May 2011 Issue.

Norwich, John Julius.1998. *A Short History of Byzantium*. London: Penguin.

Norwich, John Julius. 2016. *Sicily*. London: John Murray.

Norwich, John Julius. 2017. *Four Princes*. London: John Murray.

O'Brian, Patrick. 1970. *Master and Commander*. Glasgow: Collins

Osborne, Robin. 2008. *The World of Athens, An Introduction to Classical Athenian Culture*. Cambridge: Cambridge University Press.

Ovid, trans. Raeburn, David. 2004.*Metamorphoses.* London: Penguin.

Pagden, Anthony. 2013. *The Enlightenment and Why It Still Matters.* Oxford: OUP.

Pascal, Blaise. 1958. *Pascal's Pensée.,* New York: E P Dutton & Co.

Paton, John Lewis Alexander. 1941. "The Tercentenary of Comenius's Visit to England, 1592-1671". *Bulletin of the John Rylands Library*, 26.1(1941) 149-157, Manchester, UK. http://www.eschol-ar.manchester.ac.uk/api/datastream?publicationPid=uk-ac.

Peters, Scott. www.egyptabout.com,

Phillips, Margaret Mann, *Erasmus and the Northern Renaissance*. 1949. London: The English Universities Press.

Pinker, Steven. 2011. *The Better Angels of Our Nature*. London: Penguin.

Pinker, Steven. 2019. *Enlightenment Now*. London: Penguin.

Plato, trans. Lee H D P. 2007. *The Republic*. London: Penguin.

Plumb, J H. 1975. "The New World of Children in Eighteenth-Century England," *Past and Present,* Vol. 67 1(1 May1975), 64 – 95.

Plutarch, *The Parallel Lives,* Vol. III, Loeb Classical Library Edition. (1919). www.loebclassics.com.

Pollard, Sidney. 1968. *The Genesis of Modern Management*. London: Penguin.

Pope, Alexander. *An Essay on Man*, IV, https://www.poetryfoundation.org/poems/44899/an-essay-on-man-epistle-i.

Porter, Roy. 1991. *English Society in the 18ᵗʰ Century*. London: Penguin.

Potter, D S and Mattingley, D J. 1999. *Life, Death and Entertainment in the Roman* Empire. Ann Arbor, Michigan: University of Michigan Press.

Qian, Sima. 1959. *Records of the Grand Historian*. Beijing: Zhong-hua Book Company.

Rosen, William. 2008. *Justinian's Flea Plague, Empire and the Birth of Europe*. London: Pimlico.

Saliba, George. 2011. *Islamic Science and the Making of the European Renaissance*. Cambridge, MA and London: The MIT Press.

Scheidel, Walter. Morris, Ian. Saller, Richard P eds. 2007, *The Cambridge Economic History of the Greco-Roman World*. Cambridge: Cambridge University Press.

Schiedel, Walter. 2012. *The Cambridge Companion to the Roman Economy*. Cambridge: Cambridge University Press.

Ed. Scully, Val. 2021. *Crowley's*. Dunston, Gateshead: Land of Oak and Iron Trust.

Shakespeare, William. (1595) 2015. *Julius Caesar*. London: Penguin.

Smith, Adam. 2007, *Theory of Moral Sentiments*. Open Library: FQ Classics.

Smith, Adam. 1982. *The Wealth of Nations*. Penguin, London.

Stephens, J E, ed. 1972. *Aubrey on Education*, Vol. 1. London and Boston, Mass.: Routledge and Kegan Paul.

Subramanian, V K. 2003. *Maxims of Chanakya*. Abhinav Publications: New Delhi.

Suetonius. 2007. *The Twelve Caesars*. London: Penguin.

Swade, Doron. 2002. *The Difference Engine: Charles Babbage and the Quest to build the First Computer*. London, Penguin.

Tawney, R H. 1926. *Religion and the Rise of Capitalism,* London 1926: Routledge; republished Mentor (1953) and Peter Smith (1962).

Taylor, Frederick Winslow. 1947. *Scientific Management*. New York: Harper & Brothers.

Temin, Peter. 2017. *The Roman Market Economy*. Princeton University Press: Princeton and Oxford.

Thale, Mary, ed. 1972. *The Autobiography of Francis Place*. London and New York: Cambridge University Press.

Thaler, Richard H and Sunstein, Cass R. 2012. *Nudge.* London: Penguin.

"Theoi Greek Mythology", www.theoi.com.

Thucydides, trans. Warner, Rex. 1954. *History of the Peloponnesian War*. London, Penguin.

Tolai (people of Papua New Guinea): https://www.vice.com/en_au/article/9kp5ye/papua-new-guinea-tolai-tribe-shell-money .

Tzu, Sun trans. Lionel Giles. 1910. *The Art of War.* 5th century BCE, Republished 2009 through Wheelers, Glenfield, Auckland, New Zealand; Pax Librorum Publishing House.

Uglow, Jenny. 2002. *The Lunar Men.* London: Faber & Faber.

United Nations, Department of Social and Economic Affairs, Population Division. 2017. *World Population Prospects*.

Urwick, Lyndall F. 1957. *The Life and Work of Frederick Winslow Taylor.* London: Urwick, Orr and Partners.

Virgil, trans. West, David. 1987. *The Aeneid*. London: Penguin.

Vives, Juan Luis, trans. C Fantazzi. 1996. *De Institutione Feminae Christiane*. Leiden, New York, Cologne: E J Brill, republished 2007. Chicago: University of Chicago Press.

Waitt, E I. 1972. *John Morley, Joseph Cowen and Robert Spence Watson: Liberal Divisions in Newcastle Politics, 1873-1895* PhD thesis, Manchester University. Copies are available also at Newcastle upon Tyne and Gateshead public libraries.

Wallace–Hadrill, J M. 1952. *The Barbarian West 400 – 1000*. London: Hutchinson University Library.

Watson, Burton. 1968. *Chuang Tzu The Complete Works.* New York: Columbia University Press.

Watts, Michael R. Vol 1 1978, Vol 2 1995, Vol III 2015. *The Dissenters.* Oxford: Clarendon Press.

Weber, Max. 1905, republished 2003. *The Protestant Ethic and the Spirit of Capitalism*. New York: Dover.

Weber, Max. 1947. *The Theory of Social & Economic Organization.* Oxford: Oxford University Press.

Wheelis, Mark. "Biological Warfare at the 1346 Siege of Caffa", *Emerging Infectious Diseases Journal,* Volume 8, Number 9, September 2002, Centres for Disease Control and Protection.

White, K D. 1984. *Greek and Roman Technology.* Ithaca, New York: Cornell University Press.

Wickham, Chris. 2005. *Farming the Early Middle Ages: Europe and the Mediterranean, 400-800.* Oxford: Oxford University Press.

Wilde, Oscar. 1893. *Lady Windermere's Fan.* London: Methuen & Co. [1977-2021]. https://www.gutenberg.org/files/790-h/790/-h.htm

Wills, Deborah. "Sarah Trimmer's Oeconomy of Charity [1787]: Politics and Morality in the Sunday School State". *Lumen.* 12 (1993): 157-66.

Wills, Deborah. "Sarah Trimmer", *Dictionary of Literary Biography,* 158. (2006): 340-348.

Wilson, John F and Thomson, Andrew. 2006. *The Making of Modern Management.* Oxford: Oxford University Press.

Wilson, John F. 1995. *British business history, 1720-1994.* Manchester and London: Manchester University Press.

Wing, R L, ed. 1986. *The Tao of Power.* Wellingborough, Northamptonshire, UK: The Aquarian Press.

Witzel, Morgen. 2012. *A History of Management Thought.* London and New York: Routledge.

Witzel, Morgen. 2014. *Management from the Masters.* London: Bloomsbury.

Witzel, Morgen and Warner, Malcolm, ed. 2013. *The Oxford Handbook of Management Theorists.* Oxford: Oxford University Press.

Witzel, Morgen. 2018. *The Ethical Leader.* London: Bloomsbury Business.

Wrege, Charles D., Greenwood, Ronald G. 1991. *Frederick W. Taylor, The Father of Scientific Management: Myth and Reality.* Irwin, Illinois: Business One.

Wren, Daniel A and Greenwood, Ronald G. 1998. *Management Innovators: The people and ideas that have shaped modern business.* New York: Oxford University Press.

Wrigley, Edward and Schofield, Roger. 1989. *The Population History of England 1541-1871.* Cambridge: Cambridge University Press.

Xenophon, trans. Henry Dakyns. 2019. *Ways and Means:* independently published.

# AUTHOR PROFILE

Dr Ian Waitt is a businessman with over three decades' experience. During 17 years in education, he taught at secondary school, undergraduate, and postgraduate levels. Both as an international consultant and in business, he has worked in UK, Canada, USA, Russia, Korea, and many European, African, and Asian countries. His management experience embraces all sectors: private, public, and voluntary. His business portfolio includes import-export trade, conference and event devising and organising, education management, and politico-economic consultancy. Writer of a major business biography, he has co-edited and contributed to a book on simulation in management education, written on technical education, published learned and press articles, and has even co-authored a history book for children. Award winning writer, editor, and main author of *College Administration*, described by *The Guardian* in 1980 as "the college bible," the definitive guide to UK public sector further and higher education of its day; it was commended by the UK Library Association as a reference book of the year, tying with the *Oxford Companion to Law*. He now chairs a grain company, a consultancy, and a business development institute. Distilling a lifetime's experience, his new definitive, activist, text and reference work is also the first ever history of management, education management, and management education.

**Dr Ian Waitt**
[Photograph by Susan Diamond.]

# SEQUEL SYNOPSIS

The management journey continues with the next volume, ***Managing Mass Education, and the Rise of Modern and Financial Management: Footsteps and Foundations.*** Here, against a vivid picture of late 18th–19th century life, and through the profile of a charismatic teacher and wayward genius, the reader is given insight into the process of education management which enabled the production of a workforce capable of seeing through the commencement, implementation and development of the first and second industrial revolutions and beyond. As Western society underwent profound major societal change, the interdependent growth of modern management and practical implementation of new financial systems can be seen as driven and shaped by conflicting pressures. Warfare, armed trade, emigration and exploration brought unprecedented business opportunities. In an ever expanding world of new ideas, discoveries, scientific and technological inventions, in the addressing of famine, disease, and all the challenges of expansion, demand for education for all became a dominant issue.

As society changed, old, out-dated systems and ways of working needed continually to be modified or replaced. "If we want things to stay as they are," di Lampedusa famously remarked in his novel *The Leopard,* "things will have to change". The *Footsteps and Foundations* journey is intended to indicate and stimulate management approaches and responses which are capable of change and applicable to current needs. So, how best to build a solid management foundation, one adaptable enough to stand the test of time?

As a summation of expression, thought and opportunity, a graphic image drawn from ancient history for a foundation already shown capable of endurance through time is presented on the front cover. The image is of proven provenance, still of practical use and relevance. Labyrinth was the name given by the ancient Greeks to a structure, sometimes underground, containing a number of chambers and corridors that made passage in or out difficult. In legend, the Minotaur was housed in a labyrinth built for King Minos of Crete at Knossos. This classical 7-course 'Cretan Labyrinth', as depicted at the beginning of this book, became a popular design. It often featured on coins from as early as the 5th century BCE. By the 12th to 14th centuries CE grand pavement labyrinths appear on cathedral floors in Northern France, notably Chartres, Reims and Amiens.

Although these may have inspired the passion for turf mazes and hedge mazes in Britain, a maze, with which a labyrinth is often confused, has multiple entry and exit points with many dead ends and false routes to negotiate. It is quite easy to get lost in a maze. A labyrinth has only one entry and exit point and a continuous path to the centre, albeit a winding one. The twists and turns symbolically represent the ebbs and flows, the ups and downs of life, possibly allowing time for reflection. In a labyrinth there is no likelihood of encountering a blind alley. As long as the path is followed, with forward motion maintained, the centre will eventually be reached, with the way to the exit attainable.

The format of the next book is much the same as this one, except with different aspects of management to explore with staples to remember. The use of footprints and case studies continue to guide the reader on this ongoing management journey, though now covering different terrain and passing through a further set of problems, opportunities and obligations. Whether facing the 18th century squalor of London urban deprivation, the opportunities presented by an expanding USA economy, the development of the railways, the campaigns against slavery and its subsequent abolition, or humanity coming to grips with the latest technologies, all topics contain management lessons to be learned and dwelt upon.

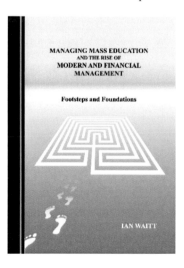

# INDEX